SINGAPORE
THE PREGNABLE
FORTRESS

A Study in Deception,
Discord and Desertion

Peter Elphick

Hodder & Stoughton

British Library Cataloguing in Publication Data

Elphick, Peter
Singapore: Pregnable Fortress – A Study in Deception,
Discord and Desertion
I. Title
940.5425
ISBN 0-340-61316-5

Typeset by Hewer Text Composition Services, Edinburgh
Printed and bound in Great Britain by
Mackays of Chatham Plc, Chatham, Kent

Hodder and Stoughton
A division of Hodder Headline PLC
338 Euston Road
London NW1 3BH

0340-613-165-1571

This book is dedicated to all the servicemen and women, and to all the civilians, who suffered three-and-a-half years of harsh imprisonment under the Japanese.

Dedicated to the Whitehall Warriors

A mighty island fortress
The Guardian of the East
An up-to-date Gibraltar
A thousand planes at least,
It simply can't be taken
T'will stand a siege for years
We can hold the place for ever
And bring our foes to tears.
Our men are there in millions
The defences are unique,

But the Japs did not believe you
SO THEY TOOK IT IN A WEEK.

This piece of doggerel (kindly supplied by Harry Blackham)
went the rounds of some of the Far Eastern prisoner of war
camps.

CONTENTS

LIST OF PHOTOGRAPHS

Photographs

Section One

1. Colonel B.W. Key and Royal Battalion, 11th Sikh Regiment; A.H. Dickinson, Inspector-General of Police

2. Singapore: the Inner Harbour, c. 1940; Sir Josiah Crosby; Colonel Francis Hayley Bell

3. Maj.-Gen. W. Dobbie; Rear Admiral and Mrs E.J. Spooner; Lt-Gen. L.V. Bond; Air Vice Marshal J.T. Babington

4. Sir Shenton Thomas and Duff Cooper; C.A. Vlieland; the Defence Committee of the British Cabinet

5. Lt-Gen. Sir Lewis Heath; Maj.-Gen. D.M. Murray-Lyon; Colonel Phillip Parker

6. Air Chief Marshal Sir Robert Brooke-Popham; Admiral Sir Tom Phillips; Air Vice Marshal C.W. Pulford receives Averell Harriman

7. The two faces of espionage: Captain Patrick Heenan, Captain John Becker and Dorothy Crisp; one of the Singapore 'big guns'

8. General Sir Archibald Wavell; Lt-Gen. A.E. Percival; Vice Admiral Sir Geoffrey Layton

Section Two

9. Maj.-Gen. Gordon Bennett; Australian troops arriving in Singapore

Acknowledgements for the use of the individual pictures are included in the captions.

LIST OF MAPS

AUTHOR'S ACKNOWLEDGEMENTS

Thanks are due to the following persons for giving generous and always friendly help during the research for this book. The names are listed alphabetically. Some names have been omitted because the persons concerned wish to remain anonymous. If anyone else has been left out, the omission is inadvertant and I tender my apologies.

Despite this exceedingly large range of indebtedness, I remain solely responsible for any errors and shortcomings in this book, and for how the information supplied has been interpreted.

Richard Aldrich; Major P.J. Arber (Royal Artillery Association); Jeremy Atkinson; Pauline Asbury; William Barber; Terry Barringer (Librarian, Royal Commonwealth Society); Hugh Becker; Harry Blackham; 'Freddie' Bloom; E. Bott; Dr Peter Boyden (National Army Museum, London); William Bowden; Clare Brown (Rhodes Library, Oxford); T.D. Brown; A.K. Butterworth (India); Squadron Leader G. 'Paddy' Calder (New Zealand); Major P.E. Campbell; Dr Elizabeth Carmichael (South Africa); R.A. Carr (Blue Star Line); Dr T.C. Carter; F.A.H. Champkin; Major A.R.E. Clarke; J. Norman Clarke; Mamie Colley; Vi Courtenay-Smith; J.J. Corfield (Australia); Major V.L.F. Davin; Gawain Douglas; Peter G. Dunstan; Carole Edwards (Foreign & Commonwealth Office Library); Dr O. Elliot Fisher; Lieutenant-Colonel Patric Emerson (Indian Army Association); Ninean Evans; Stan Fielding (62 Squadron Association); D. 'Fergie' Ferguson; Madge Fitch; Mark Fletcher; Major J.A. Forsythe; Pauline Foster (Assistant Librarian, Royal Commonwealth Society); Dr A.W. Frankland; John Furness; David Gibson; Basil A. Gotto; Richard Gough; Edward Green; J.F. Griffiths; C.J.A. Haines; John Haines; Kit Hair (née Scarf); Lieutenant-Colonel A.A. Halliley; R.W.E. Harper; Major Robert Henderson; J.H. Hindmarsh; Lieutenant-Colonel C.E.N. Hopkins-Husson; Arthur Howard; Peter James; Lieutenant-Colonel H.M.J. Jensen (Singapore); Alf Johnson; R.B. Johnston (New Zealand); Gordon Keith; Peter M. Kenward; Tony Kirk-Greene; Arthur Lane; Bill Lawson; Sheila Lea; James Leasor; David Lee (Verger, St. Luke's, Chelsea, the

'Piffer' Church); Elizabeth Leetham; Eric Linsell; Elizabeth Loft-Simson; Clive Lyon; R.W.L. McCall; Alistair Macpherson (Haileybury Archivist); Audrey Holmes McCormick; Lieutenant-Colonel C.H.T. MacFetridge; Rena McRobbie (Regimental HQ, Argyll & Sutherland Highlanders); Guy C. Madoc; Patrick R.H. Mahoney; the late J.B. Masefield; Peter Melliar-Smith; Tom Mellows; Lieutenant-General S.L. Menezes (India); Harry and Doreen Miller (Spain); Mary Hayley Bell (Lady Mills); Mike Minns (Australia); W.J. Mondahl; Arthur Monk; Captain R.B. Monteath; Hilary Morton; Nigel G. Morris; Dr Iain M. Murray-Lyon; George Musk (C.P.R. Lines); Group-Captain J. Nancarrow; Major the Reverend Robert Nesham; Alan R. Neville; Lettice Nichols; Kate O'Brien (Liddell Hart Centre for Military Archives); Major Campbell Parker; Major Sir Michael Parsons; Dr Stanley Pavillard; E. Pearlman (Israel); Squadron-Leader R.D. 'Fiery' Phillips; Pitt Kuan Wah (National Archives of Singapore); Philip Reed (Imperial War Museum, London); Rosemary Reford; Captain Robert Reid; Doreen Riley; Anthony Richards; Captain P.J. Rivers (Malaysia); Mike Rogers (Foreign & Commonwealth Office, Records Branch); Nicholas Roskill; J.F.M. Roualle; Emile M. Ryan (Singapore); Lieutenant-Colonel E.L. Sawyer; Jack Scarr; J.B. Scott (Zimbabwe); Lieutenant S.H. Shrives; Professor Stewart Simmonds; G.S. Smith; Sir James Spooner; Squadron Leader J.A. Stephen; H.W. Straithairn; R.W.A. Suddaby (Keeper, Department of Documents, Imperial War Museum, London); Sydney Tavender; Robert E. Taylor; Michael Thistleton-Dyer; Phyllis Thom; Squadron Leader D.A. Thomas; Pamela Thomson (Haileybury Society); Lieutenant-Colonel Charles J. Verdon R.M.; Paul Vickers (Prince Consort Army Library, Aldershot); Bill Wallace; Squadron Leader R.E. Wardrop; Douglas Weir; H.J. Woolnough; Lieutenant-Colonel C.G. Wylie.

My special thanks must go to one of the anonymous helpers. He is an ex-senior officer of the Straits Settlements Police Force. The gentleman concerned is blessed with a highly retentive memory, and has been a mine of information and a source of sound advice.

Thanks are also due to the staff of the following organisations: Oriental and India Office Collections, and the Newspaper Library (both of the British Library); Kensington Central Library, London; Chelsea Library; Australian War Memorial, Canberra; Public Records Office, Kew; Overseas Development Administration, Glasgow; Guildhall Library, London; Library of the School of Oriental & African Studies, London; Imperial War Museum, London; National Army Museum, London; Royal Commonwealth Society Library, formerly London, now Cambridge; Rhodes Library, part of Bodlean Library, Oxford; Feminist Library, London; Liddell Hart Centre for Military Studies, King's College, London; Foreign & Commonwealth Library, London; Registrar-General of Ships and Seamen, Cardiff; Blue Star Lines, London; Canadian Pacific Railway Company, London and Montreal.

Thanks are due to the archival authorities and to the trustees of the various collections of private papers quoted from as listed in the notes and/or bibliography.

Quotations from documents under Crown Copyright in the Public Records Office, and in the Oriental and India Office Collections of the British Library, appear by permission of HMSO. Quotations from the Australian Official History, *The Japanese Thrust*, appear by permission of the Australian War Memorial, Canberra. Quotations from documents in the Royal Commonwealth Society collections appear by permission of the Syndics of Cambridge University Library. Quotations from documents in the Liddell Hart Centre appear by permission of King's College, London.

Special acknowledgements for permission to quote from private documents or tape recordings (further details are given in the text and notes) are due to Mrs J.H.S. Wild; Lieutenant-Colonel E.L. Sawyer: Miss Susan Harrison; Lieutenant-Colonel C.G. Wylie; Basil Gotto; Mrs Elizabeth Leetham; Edward Green; Mrs Lettice Nichols; Major Campbell Parker; Nicholas Roskill; Dr T.C. Carter; Mrs Vi Courtenay-Smith.

Once again John Bright-Holmes, the publisher's editor, has been a source of expert advice and sound criticism. This work would not have been completed in its present form without his professionalism.

Lastly, I must thank my wife. The Far East is her favourite part of the world, but even so, she has shown remarkable forbearance over the past three years as I have immersed myself in the war history of the area.

AUTHOR'S NOTE

Except where the old form 'Siam' is used in papers or diaries quoted from in this book, the title Thailand is used. The change of name was officially made by the Thai government in the late 1930s.

Chinese place names are shown with the anglicised spellings in use at the time.

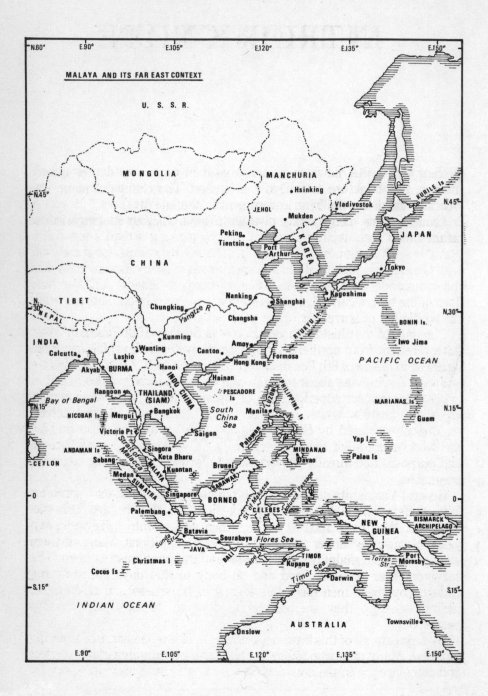

MALAYA AND ITS FAR EAST CONTEXT

INTRODUCTION

In February 1942 newspapers around the world featured on their front pages a picture which was probably the most emotive one to emanate from the Malayan campaign of World War Two.* It was a radioed Japanese propaganda photograph, which showed four British officers with their Japanese escorts marching along a road a few miles north-west of Singapore City. The Britons were heading for a meeting with General Yamashita of the Imperial Japanese Army. One of them was the commander of the British forces, Lieutenant-General A.E. Percival. Two of the others carried shouldered flags; one the Union Flag, the other the white flag of surrender.

The date of that historic procession was Sunday 15th February 1942. After a retreat from northern Malaya lasting seventy days, following the Japanese invasion of 8th December an army of British, Australian, Indian and local forces, was about to capitulate to a numerically inferior, but in every other respect superior force of Japanese. They were to surrender an island fortress which over the years had gained the reputation, assiduously fostered by British politicians and military leaders and by the world's press, of being impregnable. The Japanese, to all intents and purposes had already proved that the fortress was, on the contrary, pregnable.

General Yamashita demanded an ignominious unconditional surrender to take effect from 2030 hours that same night of 15th February. This was conceded. Well over 100,000 soldiers then passed into three-and-a-half years of captivity under the most atrocious conditions. Many of them were to die from malnutrition, sickness and inhuman mistreatment. The survivors bear scars in mind and on body to this day. The suffering endured by these men has left a legacy of bitterness and resentment, feelings so deep they are unlikely to die until the last survivor has passed on.

By no means all of this bitterness, however, is levelled at the conquering Japanese. Many men who fought in the Malayan campaign blame neglect and complacency in the corridors of power in Britain and Singapore for

* see plate 166

getting them into the predicament in the first place. 'This country really dropped us in the shit,' said Geoffrey Adams, a young British subaltern at the time.[1] Captain Reginald Burton of the Royal Norfolks, on hearing the news of the surrender, said it was one of the blackest moments of his life, and his strongest feeling was that all which had gone before had been a terrible waste, for which he blamed the 'powers-that-be'.[2] Harry Blackham, a Royal Artillery sergeant, has attacked the local commanders who were responsible for, 'the barmy, lying and deceitful communiqués emanating from Fort Canning [the British Headquarters in Singapore]. We got fed up to the teeth with reading in the press and hearing on the radio how we "were clearing small pockets of resistance or were successfully counter-attacking", particularly when they named places we had been kicked out of a day or even two days before.'[3] He ends with the comment that perhaps Whitehall had deliberately saddled the Malayan theatre of war with expendable leaders.

A few weeks after the surrender, a long, anonymous, and bitterly worded doggerel poem appeared on the 'wall-newspaper' of Changi Prison where the Japanese had interned civilian Europeans. It included the following lines of outrage at the outcome of the campaign, lines which mock the expertise of leaders in London and Singapore, and the low standard of some of the troop reinforcements which arrived late in the day. Extravagantly phrased it might be, but it encapsulates the feelings of many who were involved in the disaster:

> What plan, if any, they'd evolved,
> May possibly one day be solved.
> Meanwhile, I hold that arrogance,
> Brute force and bloody ignorance,
> Indifference and clumsy bluff,
> Are unmistakably the stuff
> On which these gentlemen relied,
> To mask the rotten core inside.
>
> When placed in charge of nincompoops,
> Even the very best of troops,
> Will rapidly deteriorate,
> To something worse than second-rate,
> Whilst men without experience,
> Develop into an offence.[4]

However, the story of the fall of Singapore is much more than a story of bitterness and human suffering. It will be more lastingly remembered for its effect on world history. It is not overstating the case to say that the battle for Malaya and Singapore from December 1941 to February 1942 changed the world. In the grand scheme of things the loss of Singapore was the outstanding one amongst a series of events which caused a sea-change in Eastern opinion. When the Japanese took control of Indo-China from the French in July 1941, captured Malaya and Singapore from the British, and drove the Dutch from Indonesia in February and March 1942, they shattered the myth of white superiority. Their victories were the death-knell of the European empires in the East. They removed from the Asian mind for ever the notions of white supremacy and European hegemony. Even when disillusionment with the new conqueror set in, which it soon did, the thoughts of Eastern nationalists did not turn to the West, except as a means to get them out of their present predicament. Instead it nourished in them a determination to obtain their independence at the earliest possible moment.

Military disasters occur when a whole series of mistakes, misjudgements and mischances happen to come together in a deadly combination. When they come together in the face of an aggressive, ruthless, well-trained enemy, filled with an offensive spirit fostered in them over many years, then the disaster will be of catastrophic proportions. The fall of Singapore was just such a disaster.

In view of its importance, one can ask why there was never a Court of Inquiry into the loss of Singapore. In a speech made in a Secret Session of the House of Commons on 23rd April 1942, the Prime Minister, Winston Churchill, said:

> I do not at all wonder that requests should be made for an inquiry by a Royal Commission, not only into what took place upon the spot in the agony of Singapore but into all the arrangements which had been made beforehand. I am convinced, however, that this would not be good for our country, and that it would hamper the prosecution of the war. Australian accounts reflect upon the Indian troops. Other credible witnesses disparage the Australians ... There is an endless field for recrimination ... We ... have enough trouble on our hands to cope with the present and the future, and I could not in any circumstances consent to adding such a burden, for a heavy burden it would be, to those which we have to bear. I must ask the House to support the Government in this decision, which is not taken in any ignoble desire to shield individuals or safeguard the administration but solely in the interests of the State and for the successful prosecution of the war.[5]

During a conversation on 2nd May 1942 Churchill took the matter a stage further. He told the American Admiral, Harold R. Stock, that there would be an Inquiry but only after the war was won. Stock reported this to Franklyn Knox, the US Secretary of the Navy. (The bombing of Pearl Harbor, America's own worst disaster, was to have its inquiry in 1945.)

In *The Hinge of Fate*, Volume Four of his *The Second World War*, Churchill wrote:

> I judged it impossible to hold an inquiry by Royal Commission into the circumstances of the fall of Singapore while the war was raging. We could not spare the men, the time, or the energy. Parliament accepted this view; but I certainly thought that in justice to the officers and men concerned there should be an inquiry into all the circumstances as soon as the fighting stopped. This however has not been instituted by the government of the day. Years have passed and many of the witnesses are dead. It may well be that we shall never have a formal pronouncement by a competent court upon the worst disaster and largest capitulation in British history.

That was published in the very year, 1951, in which Churchill regained the Premiership, and although he was to hold that position until April 1955, still no Inquiry was set up. If he had been determined on one 'in justice to the officers and men concerned', he could have ordered it then. Of course by that date many of the witnesses were indeed dead, but not many of the most important ones. By 1951 only one of the top commanders concerned had died: Field Marshal Earl Wavell in 1950. Furthermore, Churchill omitted to explain why he did not push for one during the six years he was out of office. Had he done so, there can be little doubt, with his prestige, that one would have been held.

Churchill's attitude over the matter of a Singapore Inquiry contrasts sharply with that over the fall of Crete which had occurred in May 1941, just nine months previously. Crete was finally abandoned on 31st May, and Churchill insisted that a Court of Inquiry be held immediately. Instructions went out to that effect in early June, and the committee's report was ready in July; but its findings were suppressed.[7]

That Churchill had several good reasons for never pushing for a Singapore Inquiry, will be shown in this book. His finger was well and truly in the pie at every stage. As the historian Raymond Callahan pointed out in his book *The Worst Disaster*, there were 'really two strategies in the Far East. The official one was contained in the Chiefs of Staff paper: Churchill's personal policy consisted of relying on America and hoping for the best.'[8]

The very least that can be said about Churchill in this context is that he failed to recognize in time the danger posed by Japan. It may well be that his conscience pricked him later, for he was far easier in his judgements of the senior commanders in Singapore than he was on those whom he held responsible for the losses in the Middle East in 1941, yet Singapore was by far the greater disaster. One historian, John Keegan, commenting on Churchill's description of the Far Eastern campaign in his *The Second*

World War, wrote, 'by not one immoderate word does the author convey in his narrative how deeply he felt ... [and was] wounded by the humiliating and disastrous episode'.[9] This was probably because Churchill knew he was at least partly responsible for the disaster. Raymond Callahan has pointed out that Churchill's general defence of his role is implicit throughout his account of the Malayan campaign.[10]

During the period of Churchill's return to power from 1951, official historians in both Britain and Australia were busy compiling their respective histories of the Malayan campaign. Cabinet Office files at the British Public Records Office contain many letters and internal memoranda regarding the British undertaking, and a study of them leaves the reader with the impression that the two sets of historians were as much interested in coming to a consensus on the 'facts' to be presented in both histories, as they were in documenting exactly what had happened.

The chief British historian concerned with the Malayan campaign, Major-General S. Woodburn Kirby, paid a long visit to Australia in early 1953 for the express purpose of reaching such a consensus. While in the country he and his Australian counterpart, Lionel Wigmore, interviewed many Australian officers and one British brigadier who was then residing there and who had taken part in the campaign. As a result of that visit not only was much new information obtained, but agreement was reached about a consensus of presentation.

Kirby returned to Britain with a document which cast light on one factor which played a significant part in the unexpectedly short length of the siege of Singapore Island itself, the incidence of deserters. In the event, both the British and Australian Official Histories glossed over this matter. This 'missing' subject-matter is discussed at length in this book. Much material in earlier British files already existed about it, but either Kirby and his team were not given access to the files (they were only made public in 1993) or they had instructions not to make use of the material. Either way, it was one of the many cover-ups that surround the fall of the so-called impregnable fortress.

In 1956, the Australian Chief of Staff in Malaya, Colonel J.H. Thyer, wrote to General Percival commenting on the imminent publication of both the British and Australian Official Histories. He said, 'I'm sure that public interest will be confined to the participants and to students of military history so the watering-down and other modifications do not worry me. The discerning person will read between the lines.'

Brigadier Ivan Simson, who was Chief Engineer, Singapore, wrote the following in September 1970 to H.P. Bryson, a one-time senior Malayan Civil Servant:

> I understood from Kirby verbally that his Terms of Reference from the Cabinet for the Official History was that he was not to

throw aspersions on the leaders. How can one write 'History' on
such terms?

Simson went on:

> Why do we officially suppress Truth? It is nearly always
> unpleasant and we just will not face up to it – even Churchill
> never had his Court of Inquiry ... It is a horrible story as you
> know and it shows how the standard of Integrity is dropping (in
> my opinion) in all leaders.

Some correspondence appeared in London's *Daily Telegraph* in August
1970 regarding the accuracy of some of the 'facts' presented in the
Official War Histories. One of the historians, Brigadier M.R. Roberts,
wrote that it was quite wrong to think that he and his colleagues were
in some way muzzled. However, Brigadier Roberts was not a member of
the team engaged on the particular volume about the Far East. General
Kirby, who died in 1968, was most definitely under some constraints.

The story of the loss of Singapore is indeed, as Brigadier Simson
said, a horrible story. During the campaign itself there were some heroic
deeds, to be sure, and many gallant actions were fought. Some of these are
mentioned in this book. But the loss of Singapore was a disaster caused by
mistakes and misjudgments both at local and Whitehall levels, a situation
made worse by special local factors such as the discord which existed
between some of the senior commanders both before and during the
campaign, the quality of some of the late reinforcements sent there, and
the stories of desertions which could almost make a separate book.

This book is largely thermatic in its presentation. The battles for
Malaya and Singapore are described from Chapter Ten onwards although
references are made to them, and to participants in them, in the earlier
chapters. The chronology of events on pages 427–429 will, I hope, assist
the reader.

In order to place the story in proper perspective, however, it is
necessary to study the rise of Japanese power which made it possible
in the first place, and the steps taken by Britain in her efforts to
counteract it.

Chapter One

The Rise of Modern Japan and its Effect on British Policy

During the second quarter of the nineteenth century various attempts were made by Russia, the United States, and Britain to break down the two-hundred-year-old 'closure' of Japan. This virtual isolation from all contact with foreign influences – the only permitted breach in this screen was the operation of the small Dutch trading settlement on Deshima Island near Nagasaki – had been ordered early in the seventeenth century by one of the Tokugawa dynasty of shoguns. His aim was to prevent dissatisfied elements in Japanese society from using foreign contacts and technology to undermine the shogunate – the Shoguns being the hereditary commanders-in-chief of the Japanese army and the virtual rulers of the country.

Russian interest in Japan had grown during the nineteenth century as its gradual colonization of Siberia took place. It was far easier for Russia to obtain supplies for its fledgling eastern outposts from Japan than from Russia proper. Britain's renewed interest in Japan began after its successes in China in the first Opium War and its acquisition of Hong Kong in 1842. (In 1613 the English East India Company had set up a short-lived and not very successful trading operation near Yedo – today's Tokyo – with the aid of Will Adams, the 'Shogun's Englishman'.[1])

America's interest in Japan increased as she herself became a Pacific Power with the opening up of California after the Mexican War of 1846–47 and the Gold Rush of 1848–49. America had already been trading with China, and began developing whaling interests in the Pacific. In consequence many American ships voyaged close to the forbidden coasts of Japan, and sometimes shipwrecked American seamen received less than friendly treatment from Japanese authorities before being repatriated through the good offices of the Dutch.

An American fleet under Commodore Matthew Perry arrived off Japan in 1853, 'requesting' the opening up of trade relations under the threat of coming back for an answer the following year with a much larger fleet. The future good treatment of any shipwrecked Americans was demanded, which made a convenient excuse for this blatant act of naval pressure. In reality, of much more importance to the United States government was that Japan was an ideally located source for coal bunkers for their steamers.

Within days of the Perry expedition a Russian fleet also sailed into Japanese waters. Under these separate threats the Japanese government had no recourse but to open a door in the bamboo screen. In March 1854 the Treaty of Kanagawa was signed which gave the Americans rights to trade with certain ports in Japan such as Shimoda. A clause in the treaty permitted the Americans to set up a consulate at Shimoda. Although the Japanese attempted to delay this provision, the American diplomatic representative, Townsend Harris, arrived to take up his post in 1856.

A British naval expedition under Admiral Stirling which had arrived in Japanese waters in October 1854 ostensibly in search of the Russian fleet – the Crimean War had started – pushed the door open further. Stirling obtained agreement for British vessels to call for supplies at Nagasaki; but perhaps the real end of Japanese isolation was marked in December 1857 when Townsend Harris at last managed to obtain an audience with the Shogun, Tokugawa Iesada.

During the next ten years this forcible breaching of the screen added to the considerable internal pressures within Japan that emanated from the rising power of a merchant class to which the ruling *diamyo* class had become financially indebted. Finally, after a decade of dissension and political in-fighting, an army fighting in the name of the Emperor Meiji overthrew the Tokugawa shogunate in 1868 after a battle near Kyoto. Although the forces which overthrew the shogunate had been associated in the minds of ordinary Japanese with the desire to expel the 'barbarians' to whom the Tokugawas had opened the door, the new leaders of Japan were pragmatists. They knew there was no way back to the old days of Japanese feudalism. If Japan was to take its place as a force of consequence in the East, then their country needed to modernize rapidly, and modernization could only be achieved with the aid and advice of the industrial nations of the West. The future of Japan had been sealed.

Japan now looked abroad for the supply of raw materials and for markets for her products. She looked especially at Korea both as a market and as a source of iron ore and coal of which there were rich deposits in the north of the Korean peninsula. Politically she saw danger in China's claim to suzerainty over Korea, which was separated from Japan by a strait only one hundred miles across.

In 1894 a rebellion took place in Korea, and China sent in troops in support of the Korean king. This gave Japan an excuse for armed intervention. She soundly defeated the Chinese sea and land forces and drove them out of Korea. She also seized the Liaotung peninsula in south Manchuria, thus protecting Korea's western flank. China sued for an armistice and, under the Treaty of Shimonoseki of April 1895, yielded to the Japanese the island of Formosa in addition to the Liaotung peninsula. China also recognised the full independence of Korea, which meant in essence that the country came under Japanese domination.

However, within days of signing the treaty, Japan was forced by the intervention of Russia, France and Germany to give up the Liaotung peninsula on the grounds that her presence there would disturb 'the peace of the Far East'. Japan, with no allies, was forced to submit to what she called this 'Triple Intervention', but from that day on she viewed the actions of Russia, her giant neighbour to the west, with suspicion and not a little perturbation. These suspicions were confirmed in 1898 when Russia herself leased those parts of the Liaotung peninsula which she had forced Japan to vacate three years before. When Russia also used the Boxer Rising in China in 1900 as a pretext for moving a considerable armed force southwards into China through Manchuria it seemed to the Japanese that Korea, their 'special interest' area, was under threat from nearly every direction.

During the penultimate decade of the nineteenth century, the Triple Alliance between Germany, Italy and Austria-Hungary caused France and Russia to draw closer together. Warning bells began to ring in London. Britain, mindful of its self-imposed and ancient role in holding the balance of power in Europe, was also conscious that she had a large empire to protect.

Since the Napoleonic wars Britain had permitted her navy to decline, not only in numbers of men and craft, but in the quality of her ships. Over the years the Royal Navy had become conservative in outlook and was no longer in the van of marine technological development. When the Crimean War began in 1854, the navy was still largely manned, equipped, and administered as it had been in the eighteenth century. In the course of that war, the Admiralty set about remedying the worst of the navy's inefficiencies, but a parsimonious government had not permitted it full rein. However, the regrouping of the European powers after the signing of the Triple Alliance in 1882, caused a rethink by the British government. The Naval Defence Act of 1889 and its commitment to the so-called 'Two Power Standard' – by which the government accepted the principle that the Navy must be strong enough to meet the combined power of the next two strongest navies – marked the foundation of the modern Royal Navy.

At diplomatic level too, Britain was protecting her interests. The fear of Russian encroachment on her Far Eastern preserves caused Great Britain to sign a Treaty of Alliance with Japan in 1902. (Britain had been training Japanese naval cadets at Greenwich since the late 1870s.) Both countries gained from this treaty, but the Japanese gained more, not least in the implied acceptance that Japan had entered the top league of powerful nations. It went a long way towards wiping out the loss of face that the climb-down over the Triple Intervention had caused the Japanese.

The Anglo-Japanese treaty marked a new phase in Japan's aspirations.

Her self-confidence grew. She was now a nation to be reckoned with. She had learned from the conflict with China that aggression could bring good dividends. Now Russia was demanding exclusive rights to control the resources of southern Manchuria, and was also insisting on the establishment of a neutral zone in Korea, which would have had the effect of dividing that country into two with Russia controlling the northern, and richer half. So, in 1904, after failing to negotiate a peaceful settlement with Russia, Japan embarked on an extraordinary gamble.

The Russian fleet, although it was divided into Far Eastern and Baltic segments, outnumbered the Japanese by 14 to 6 in battleships. Despite this, in February 1904 Japanese destroyers attacked the Russian fleet at Port Arthur, severely damaging three of the seven Russian battleships there. Later, after a costly five-month siege, they captured Port Arthur while their land forces defeated the Russians in Manchuria at the Battle of Mukden. Then, on 27th May 1905, the Japanese under Admiral Togo fought and won the famous battle of Tsushima against the newly arrived Russian Baltic fleet. In contrast to their behaviour later in the century, the Japanese conducted themselves honourably throughout.

Japan had gone into this war safe in the knowledge that she had the moral support of Britain who had herself been worried by the build-up of Russian forces in the Far East. The United States had been sympathetic for much the same reason. This time there was to be no 'Triple Intervention'.

But her victories had been gained at a considerable price and the Japanese, almost at the end of their economic tether, were as pleased as the Russians to sign a peace treaty in September 1905. Under its terms Japan regained the Liaotung peninsula and the Russians acknowledged Japan's special interest in Korea. But the Japanese did not hold on to their captured territories in Manchuria, much to the anger of some of the more militant Japanese back home.

The treaty with Britain was revised in 1905, each country now binding itself to go to the aid of the other if either's interests in the Far East were attacked by other powers. By this treaty Britain was able to concentrate her naval strength in Home and Mediterranean waters at a time when German aggressiveness was increasing. The treaty was renewed afresh in 1911.

When World War One began in 1914, Japan, in accordance with the terms of the treaty, came to Britain's aid; but it was no altruistic move. For in the process Japan began to build on her own spheres of influence. She occupied the German possessions in the Mariana, Caroline and Marshall Islands in the Pacific. More importantly, she took control of the German treaty ports in China, including the naval base at Tsingtao. Britain granted Japan port facilities at Penang in Malaya whence her ships patrolled the Indian Ocean against German submarines and surface raiders. In 1915, the Japanese navy sent ships and marines to Singapore to help put down the Indian Army mutiny there.[2]

Within months of taking over the German concessions in China, Japan issued its so-called 'Twenty-One Demands' on the Chinese Government. The European War had distracted the attention of Great Britain and most of the other countries with vested interests on the Chinese mainland, and Japan coveted the vast natural resources of China for the markets it would give to her own industries. The Japanese demands included: the transfer of German treaty ports to Japan; the employment by the Chinese government of Japanese military and financial advisors; the extension of Japanese rights in south Manchuria; and China was in future to obtain most of her war material from Japan.

But Japan had overplayed her hand. By signalling to the world that she had aspirations to control China, she had offended the strong pro-Chinese element in American society. From that time onwards, the United States looked upon the Japanese with jaundiced eyes. Both the United States and Britain protested at the Japanese demands, but the British protest merely resulted in a fall in British popularity in Japan.

When World War One ended in 1918 Japan was given a League of Nations mandate over some of the former German islands in the Pacific. Thus her influence now extended over Korea and Formosa, over parts of the Chinese mainland (including Manchuria where the Japanese had based an army), and over a chain of Pacific islands that reached almost to the equator. She had gained in power and influence, but she had lost her friendly relationship with Britain and had created hostility towards herself in the United States. Japan still, however, set great store by the treaty with Britain.

By 1918 the balance of world naval power had altered irrevocably. Germany's navy no longer existed, and the second and third positions in the naval pecking order had been taken up by the United States and Japan. Indeed, by virtue of the huge shipbuilding potential it had developed during the war, the United States was poised to take the number one position, for Britain was financially exhausted after four years of war. The centre of gravity of naval power had shifted from the Atlantic to the Pacific.

Ideally Britain would have liked to base a fleet in the Far East – in line with the recommendations made by Admiral Jellicoe in 1920 – to protect British interests in the Far East. Since she was in no financial position to do this, another way had to be found, and this involved the construction of a naval base at Singapore, to which the British Main Fleet could be sent in the event of, or even the threat of, war.

At the Imperial Conference held in London in 1921, special attention was paid to Japan's manifest intention to expand its influence in China. The question of the defence of Australia and New Zealand was also discussed. So was Britain's alliance with Japan. Britain took the view that the existence of the treaty and the ostensible friendship it created could be a possible moral check on Japan's expansionist policies. Australia and New Zealand held the same view. Aware that the United States government was under pressure from pro-Chinese groups in that country who viewed the treaty with considerable hostility, Canada took an opposite stance. No decision therefore was reached on the future of the treaty.

Later in 1921 the Washington Conference was convened, in which the US, Britain, Japan, France and Italy all took part. One of the agreements concluded was contained in the Naval Treaty of 1922 which fixed the ratio of capital ship tonnage at 5:5:3:1.75:1.75 as between Britain, the United States, Japan, France, and Italy. It was also agreed that the status quo of naval bases in the Far East be maintained, but Singapore and Pearl Harbor were specifically excluded from the terms.

The Washington Conference also signalled the end of the Anglo-Japanese Treaty. It was replaced by what was known as the 'Four-Power Treaty', between the British Empire, the United States, France, and Japan. It was not a mutual security pact, but a diplomatic device for winding up the Anglo-Japanese Treaty; for Britain had been persuaded by the USA and Canada not to renew the treaty, and it was considered that replacing it by the 'Four-Power Treaty' would save Japanese 'face'. The Japanese were much less naïve than the western powers thought, nor were they deceived. The ending of the alliance with Britain was remembered in Japan with great anger.

Britain had gained from the Washington Conference. She had developed a special relationship with her major ally, the United States. Under the naval treaty she had avoided getting involved in a naval shipbuilding race, and had retained the right to build a 'defensive' naval base at Singapore. But the disappearance of the Anglo-Japanese Treaty had removed the possibility of any friendly British persuasion being exerted on Japanese expansion policies. This elimination of British influence on Japanese policy, as Professor Richard Storry has pointed out, did 'nothing to strengthen the security of the United States; and of course it greatly weakened the whole strategic position of Australia and New Zealand, to say nothing of Hong Kong and other British possessions east of the Bay of Bengal.'[3]

One of the effects of the banking crisis in Japan in 1927, caused by the existence of many unsound businesses left over from the war boom years, was the rise of a cadre of young officers in the Japanese army with extreme chauvinistic and economic views. These views received extra impetus when the world depression hit Japan in 1930. Japanese eyes were now even more firmly fixed on the rich resources and markets of China. Conquest of that country would, it was felt in military and some political circles, be the way out of the motherland's troubles. In September 1931, the army concocted the so-called 'Manchurian Incident' and began taking control of that country. The League of Nations condemned the Japanese action in 1933 and the Japanese forthwith left the League. In 1934 Japan abrogated the disarmament treaties, and in 1935 withdrew from the London Naval Conference. There were now no external fetters on Japanese naval and military expansion.

In 1936 Japan signed the Anti-Comintern Pact with Germany, a move which she believed would protect her from attack from Russia. With her northern flank thus protected, she launched in 1937 what was to develop into an invasion of China. In December of that year, after the capture of Nanking, the Japanese army embarked on a series of atrocities that would not have been permitted by Japanese leaders of the generation before, and which were to be the forerunners of others in the years to come.

In that same year the Japanese military machine brought the United States to the brink of war by sinking the USS *Panay* on the Yangtze River. They also fired on HMS *Ladybird*. Only a rapid apology to the United States from the government of Japan, which was fast losing control of its military arm, and promises to punish the officers concerned and pay compensation, defused the situation.

The Japanese continued to gain more military successes in China, and in 1938 General Tojo became Vice-Minister of War. When war came to Europe in September 1939 the immediate reaction of Japan was one of non-involvement. Although Japan had drawn close to Germany since signing the Anti-Comintern Pact, the signing of the German-Soviet Pact in the month before the outbreak of war in Europe had come as a slap in the face. To Japan, Russia was still the old enemy.

By the mid-summer of 1940, with Germany having overrun Denmark, Norway, the Netherlands and Belgium, and with the collapse of France, the Japanese considered that Britain could not possibly win the war. So in September she signed the Tripartite Axis Pact with Hitler and Mussolini. In that same month she forced Britain to close the Burma Road, the main route of supply for China's beleaguered forces, and herself invaded French Indo-China.

Japan was casting her eyes southward towards rubber- and tin-rich British Malaya, and the oil-rich Netherlands East Indies, all parts of the Japanese dream of an Asian Co-prosperity Sphere to be led by her. Only the United States Navy, it seemed to the Japanese leaders, was in a position to foil the seizure of the rich European eastern possessions. The stage was set for the Pacific war.

Chapter Two

The Singapore Naval Base

At the end of World War One the British government concluded that the only possible aggressor against the eastern outposts of the Empire was Japan. To counter this threat there was a need for a British fleet to be permanently based in the Pacific. However, at this point Britain was looking not to increase but to reduce the size of her armed Services. Also, her Treaty of Alliance with Japan was still in existence.

In August 1919 the British Cabinet set out the basic principles under which the three armed Services were to formulate their plans and estimates of expenditure over the coming years. Some of these principles were specific to an individual Service, but the single most important one applied to all Services: it was to be assumed that the British Empire would not be engaged in any great war during the next ten years.[1] This rule, known as the 'Ten Year Rule', was in one form or another to be the guiding principle of British defence policy until it was cancelled in 1932. One of the members of the government, though not of the cabinet, which brought in the rule, was Winston Churchill and he supported its adoption.

In view of the rule's central position in British defence policy over the thirteen years of its life, it is interesting that N.H. Gibbs should note, in his volume of the Official History of the Second World War, that 'the process by which a decision on it was reached, appears to some degree casual'.[2] It is difficult, however, to see how this could have been otherwise. In 1919 the world was not yet back on a peacetime footing. The Versailles Treaty was still in the process of ratification, and other treaties were being negotiated. Generally political conditions were in a state of flux, and there was no firm frame of reference on which a government could base a forecast of future events. So it was that the motives behind the imposition of the rule were largely financial, not political or military. Furthermore, as year followed year, successive administrations were to use the rule as a contrivance to delay expenditure on defence projects.

The alternative to basing a fleet permanently in the Pacific was to send one out from Home Waters if and when it was needed. Whichever alternative was used, however, a base somewhere in the Pacific was needed to service the fleet, and in 1921 the Prime Minister, David Lloyd George, asked the Committee of Imperial Defence (CID) to investigate where such a base should be sited. If a fleet was not to be based permanently in the East, then the base had to be capable of being defended by ground and air defences until the arrival of a fleet from home.

The CID examined in depth the rival claims of Sydney and Singapore, having earlier disposed of the other two possibilities, Hong Kong, and Trincomalee on the north-east coast of Ceylon. They recommended Singapore, the case for which had first been advanced by Admiral of the Fleet Lord Jellicoe, because strategically it was in the better position to control sea communications both in the Indian Ocean and in the South Pacific. On 16th June 1921 the British Cabinet approved in principle the Committee's recommendation.

In view of what happened to Singapore in 1942 it can be argued that Sydney should have been chosen instead. But although Sydney was well out of the way of any conceivable major attack from Japan (a Japanese midget submarine raid was made on Sydney in May 1942), it was too far away from Malaya to protect that country's vital rubber and tin production, and too far away also from the Netherlands East Indies and its oil.

During its deliberations the CID coined a phrase to describe the time lapse between the moment a situation arose that necessitated the sending of the fleet to the Far East, and the fleet's actual arrival there. It was called the 'period before relief'. This period was estimated as being 70 days. The actual voyaging time from Home Waters to Singapore was taken as 28 days via Suez (and 45 days via the Cape of Good Hope) in 1937, and these voyage times would have been similar in the early 1920s.[3] The balance of the period before relief was required to mobilise the fleet, including refitting and replenishing stores, and, very important in peace time, to bringing the complements of the ships up to war-manning levels.

In 1922 the site for the base was selected by the Admiralty. It was to be constructed on the north side of Singapore Island on the Johore Strait, a little to the east of the causeway which joins the island to the Malayan mainland. In February 1923, this recommendation was also given Cabinet approval and the planning of the base was ordered to go ahead.

The decision to site the base on the north side of the island meant, in effect, that the southern Malay State of Johore – or at least the part from where the naval base would be within artillery range – would have to be protected as part of the defences of the base if there was to be any likelihood of an aggressor attacking successfully through the Malay jungle. But in 1923 this possibility was discounted. No attacking force could pass through the 'impenetrable' jungle, the military planners said. Only two years later, however, General Sir Theodore Fraser, the new General Officer Commanding (GOC), Singapore, came to a different conclusion. He was convinced that, if an attack on Singapore came, it would be made from Thailand and down the excellent road that ran south along the western side of the Malay peninsula to the Singapore causeway. Fraser reached this opinion in 1925 – pre-dating the similar views put forward by General William Dobbie by a dozen years – and it would not have been too late to change the site of the naval base as little work had been done by then. However Fraser's opinion was never put before the Committee of Imperial Defence, probably because of the entrenched views of those military planners who believed the jungle to be 'impenetrable'.

With the benefit of hindsight, and in the knowledge that Fraser was proven right, it can be said that there was at least one other and much more suitable site on the island for the naval base. It existed on the south-west corner of the island at Jurong. Since gaining Independence the Singapore government has built a vast new industrial complex there, with associated port facilities. Unlike the site on the Johore Strait, to reach which it was necessary to negotiate over twenty miles of difficult water, Jurong lies within five miles of the main Singapore Strait and has natural deep water approaches. In fact ships had to use the eastern entrance of the Johore Strait to reach the base. (The western entrance was too shallow and, anyway, the causeway effectively blocked that approach.) The Jurong site would have been well protected by Singapore's big guns. If, in addition to building the base in the south, the northern side of the island had been fortified, then Singapore would have been much closer to being an 'impregnable fortress'. It would still, of course, have been open to air attack.

In early 1924, when the first, short-lived Labour government gained power in Britain, the Singapore naval base project was subjected to the first of what became a long series of political and military see-saw policies that bedevilled the project over the years. The new Prime Minister, Ramsay MacDonald, decided the project should be abandoned. Ten months later, on the return of the Conservatives to power, it was reinstated.

In November 1924, Winston Churchill, now Chancellor of the Exchequer, requested guidance from the Cabinet in his attempt to reduce expenditure in general, and defence expenditure in particular. Churchill suggested that the naval plans for Singapore (as well as, for example, the cruiser-building project) should be subject to an enquiry 'as to the rate at which these projects could be undertaken consistently with our financial position and the desirability from a political point of view of avoiding any increase in expenditure on armaments in the forthcoming financial year'.[4] He also suggested that the CID should be asked to review the defence situation of the Empire as a whole, and to investigate whether to renew the Ten Year Rule.

Despite the overall need for economies the Naval Staff had continued to hope, and to some extent assumed in their forward plans, that a battle-fleet would regularly be stationed at Singapore as soon as the base could handle it; but they were now jolted by Churchill's wish for more flexible fleet dispositions. Churchill believed there was no danger of any sudden crisis, and that all expenditure on defence projects should reflect that. Following from that he thought, too, there was no urgency about the Singapore development although he agreed it should be developed in time. Furthermore, he saw no good reason for tying up a fleet at Singapore. The Cabinet accepted these views in principle, in spite of the desperate fight put up in particular by Admiral of the Fleet Lord Beatty, Chief of the Naval Staff.

Churchill then went even further. He proposed there should be a comprehensive review of the defence situation every three years and that, if at the end of each triennial period there had been no worsening of the international situation, the 'no major war for ten years period should start afresh'.[5]

While the subject of whether to base a fleet at Singapore occupied the CID itself, a sub-committee under Lord Curzon was asked to consider what the rate of construction of the base and its defences should be, given the current world situation. It was also asked to consider the use of aircraft as a possible alternative to the fixed heavy coastal defence batteries that were planned. It is in the deliberations of Curzon's sub-committee that the seeds of much of the future controversy over the method of protecting the base can be seen.

The Curzon committee accepted the premiss then in vogue that any attack on Singapore would be made from the sea as the Malayan jungle was in no way conducive to a land-based attack. But a decision had to be made on what form the defences against a sea attack should take. The army, supported by the navy, advocated fixed heavy, medium, and close defence gun batteries. The Air Ministry, on the other hand, advocated the use of torpedo-bombers in place of the heavy guns, saying that this combination would be a cheaper and more efficient deterrent against an assaulting force protected by an enemy fleet. This controversy not only delayed the completion of the base, it also caused dissension between the Services; indeed it was not entirely resolved until World War Two provided the acid test for the differing theoretical views.

After months of indecision the army and navy view prevailed. In 1926 the CID recommended that, as torpedo-bombers at that date had not proved themselves reliable against naval forces, and as four years were needed to develop the air forces which would be necessary anyway, the first stage of the Singapore defences should consist of close defence and medium-range guns, plus three 15-inch heavy guns. The question whether aircraft should be substituted for the remainder of the planned heavy guns at a later date was left open. In the meantime, the CID recommended that the Empire Air Reinforcement route, which then terminated at Calcutta, should be extended to Singapore.

The Ten Year Rule underwent a new twist in 1928. On Winston Churchill's prompting, the instruction was given to the Chiefs of Staff that the freedom from war for ten years concept began automatically each morning, and that they were to plan accordingly. Such an ambulatory date meant in essence that, as each day passed, the date for full-war preparation did not come a day nearer, but receded one day further into the future! Perhaps this modification was justified by the economic situation at the time. However, it was to cause rearmament to be dangerously postponed. In particular it was the reason for the near-fatal twenty-month gap between the government's realisation of international danger in March 1932 and the commencement of rearmament in November 1933.

In view of his role in the 1930s as an out-of-office critic of the government's dilatoriness over rearmament, the influence of Winston Churchill in the earlier decisions cannot be ignored for it seriously affected the development of the Singapore base and the general preparedness of the Royal Navy, not least through the rolling date mechanism of 1928 which Lord Trenchard was to describe in a House of Lords debate on 7th March 1945 as 'disastrous'.

As Chancellor of the Exchequer in difficult times it was Churchill's duty to cut expenditure wherever he could. However, were his actions in any way coloured by extraneous, personal factors?

It is generally believed that the man who sometimes liked to refer to himself as 'Former Naval Person' and about whom the famous message 'Winston is back' was flashed around the fleet when he became First Lord of the Admiralty for the second time in September 1939, had a good relationship with the navy. He certainly did much good for the Senior Service during his two tenures at the Admiralty, but his overall relationship with it was not a good one. Being no tolerator of arrogance (except his own), of opposition or of inefficiency, he walked roughshod over many admirals and other senior naval officers during and in the run-up to World War One; and during World War Two, as Prime Minister and Minister of Defence, his relations with the new generation of admirals was often strained; he did not get on with about half of them.

In 1912 he sacked the First Sea Lord and replaced him with Admiral Sir Francis Bridgeman. Bridgeman took exception to certain Churchillian practices such as his habit of sending messages to ships and naval officers without consultation. After only one year Bridgeman went the way of his predecessor. That affair left a stench in the noses of other admirals, not so much over the fact that Bridgeman had been sacked – he had the reputation of being rather colourless – but over the ruthlessness exhibited by Churchill in the manner of the sacking. In an attempt to absolve himself from any criticism after having sacked two First Sea Lords in one year, Churchill read out portions of some of Bridgeman's private letters in the House of Commons, purporting to prove that he had got rid of Bridgeman on health grounds.

Churchill carried on with his habit of interfering in operational matters that were, strictly speaking, the business of the First Sea Lord even after his appointment of the extremely able, experienced, and redoubtable septuagenarian, Admiral Lord John Fisher, to that position in 1914.

It was the resignation of Fisher that became the catalyst for Churchill's own removal from the post of First Lord of the Admiralty in 1915 over the Dardanelles débâcle. Fisher, a man brought out of unwanted retirement by Churchill, had been dragged, grumbling, into giving reluctant support to the Dardanelles plan. But when he saw the first signs of the botched operation that the plan became, he resigned. Although Churchill was chief amongst those behind the campaign, much of 'the contemporary obloquy heaped on his head now seems to have been very harsh and excessive', wrote the maritime historian Stephen Roskill, in his book *Churchill and the Admirals* which carries a full discussion of Churchill's relationship with the navy.[6] Churchill did not seem to hold his loss of office against Fisher, but his wife did. 'There are good grounds for believing that, perhaps as a result of his wife's clearer understanding of Fisher's faults, the association between them did in the end greatly influence Churchill's attitude towards the admirals of a later generation.'[7]

There is also evidence that Lord Beatty, another admiral who had enjoyed some of the fruits of Churchill's patronage, at times held no high opinion of his patron's character. It is unlikely that a bluff seaman like Beatty would have gone to much length to hide his views. Beatty's letters to his wife contain a series of denigrations of Churchill's character. In one early letter, written in 1902, he wrote, 'You are quite right, Winston Churchill is not nice, in fact he is what is generally described as a fraud, and to use a naval expression, all gas and gaiters.' Over the passage of years, Beatty's distrust of Churchill grew instead of abating, despite an outward friendliness. On 3rd July 1917, he wrote,

I find that Winston Churchill has been indulging the world with an article in the Sunday Pictorial ... In it, apparently having forgotten the article he wrote some months ago in which he pronounced the absolutely opposite opinion, he stated that the Navy was doing nothing and must become more aggressive. It is disgusting that a man who has been a Cabinet Minister and First Lord of the Admiralty should be allowed to write articles in a rag of a paper, belittling the officers and the great Service of which he was once head. It is of course useless to expect a man such as he to do anything but intrigue and he has evidently made use of, or is attempting to make use of, a certain feeling that has been put about by some, that the Navy ought to be doing more, to make capital for himself and assist his intrigues to try and push himself into an office.

The letter continued, 'However ... history is only repeating itself and it has always been the same, and there will always be dirty dogs in the world who endeavour to make capital of the difficulties of others.' Seven months later Beatty told his wife, 'our politicians only do things to retain popularity and votes. A man like Winston Churchill seems devoid of real patriotism.'[8]

If Beatty's views trickled back to Churchill, this would have added to his disillusionment over senior naval leaders and the navy in general. Churchill was a great man, but he was human, with human attributes and vices. 'He never took kindly to servicemen who opposed him on any score', wrote Roskill.[9] He could also be petty-minded and vengeful when crossed. So when, during a cycle of government economies, there came an opportunity for him to get his way over opposition from the admirals, it would be understandable if he sometimes permitted old grievances against that Service to colour his views and actions.

It is perhaps in its imposition on the development of the Singapore Naval Base that the effect of the Ten Year Rule – and especially the later rolling-date change to it – can best be seen. Although preliminary work on docking facilities and fuel installations were to go ahead after 1924, they proceeded very slowly indeed. Churchill said in 1925 that there was no need to make preparations involving additional expenditure for placing at Singapore a British battle-fleet at least equal to the seagoing navy of Japan.[10] Japan was Churchill's blind spot, a fact that was to become ever more clear as war approached.

The Royal Navy and the other Services kept up a guerrilla campaign over their estimates despite the fact that Churchill always had the last word. The minutes of a CID meeting held in 1926 state that Churchill said:

> When agreeing after the war in principle to the establishment of a base at Singapore, he had never imagined that the decision would be used as a peg on which to hang far-reaching schemes of alarmist policy and consequential armament. He did not believe that there was any danger to be apprehended from Japan, and he was convinced that the picture of Japan going mad and attacking us had no sure foundation whatsoever. He could not conceive that any Power like Japan would put herself in the position of being exposed to prolonged hostilities with the strongest Power in the world, nor could he imagine what incentive could possibly move Japan to incur the lasting hostility of England and to run the risk of being regarded as a pariah by the League of Nations. If he had foreseen that the decision to develop a base at Singapore would be used as a gigantic excuse for building up armaments and that this country would then be invited to pour out money with a view to conducting war at the other end of the world, he would never have agreed to the development of the base.[11]

This speech must have horrified the admirals.

Right to the end of this part of his career in 1928 – after which, out of office again, he adopted the role of main critic of the government's dilatoriness over rearmament – Churchill as Chancellor of the Exchequer criticised the scope and principles of the current Naval Estimates. For example, it was during that year that he recommended to his Cabinet colleagues, 'that it should now be laid down as a standing assumption that at any given date there will be no major war for ten years from that date; and that this should rule, unless or until, on the initiative of the Foreign Office or one of the Fighting Services or otherwise, it was decided to alter it'.[12]

In considering this change two points need to be emphasised. First of all, there is no doubt that in 1928, and on several occasions before that, the Cabinet decided to extend the application of the Ten Year Rule under pressure from the Treasury. Churchill, as Chancellor of the Exchequer, was therefore primarily responsible for those changes. Secondly, after the rule was rescinded in 1932 there was a two-year time-lag in implementing rearmament because the rule had left behind it not only a legacy of uncertainty, but also an inertia in the government departments concerned with defence.

In a series of letters to The Times in November 1948, a controversy boiled up over Churchill's involvement in these matters. The contenders were Lord Hankey and Lord Ismay. Both men had been actively involved in many of the relevant decision-making processes.

In one of his letters to The Times, Lord Hankey, who had been Secretary to the Cabinet and to the CID at various times from 1912 to 1938, attacked Churchill for his involvement in the modifications to the original Ten Year Rule, and especially the last one of 1928. He contrasted the delaying effect which this modification had on rearmament with Churchill's attitude six years later when, on 7th February 1934, he reminded Parliament of what had happened in 1914 and warned that 'wars come very suddenly'. Hankey strongly criticised the 1928 modification, saying that even at that time there were already signs of re-emergent German militancy, in addition to the possibility of Japanese aggression in the East. Hankey wrote:

> In 1928–29 the pale light of Locarno ... was already fading;
> in Germany [where] the peace treaty was resented, a national
> war organization was being secretly planned and the Allied
> Control Commission had been withdrawn; the coming Japanese
> aggression ... had already been spotted by the Admiralty; at
> home the three fighting services had seriously degenerated under
> the earlier Ten Year Rule; the arms industry had been neglected;
> and our defences had been allowed to fall below the safety level

– a danger against which the Government had been repeatedly warned.'13*

Lord Ismay, who was Churchill's Chief of Staff at the Ministry of Defence during World War Two – Churchill being Minister of Defence as well as Prime Minister – waded in to support his old revered chief. In one of his letters to *The Times*, Ismay acknowledged that it was upon Churchill's advice to the cabinet in 1928 that the basis of the Ten Year Rule be henceforth advanced from day to day, but emphasised 'that he [Churchill] did not visualize that the rule would be observed for a single day longer than was justified by conditions'. He described the extreme case, that the rule might have been cancelled by the British Cabinet 'within twenty-four hours of it having come into force', the implication being that the revolving date now made it easier to cancel the rule whenever conditions warranted it. Furthermore, said Ismay, the fact that Ramsay MacDonald in the early 1930s found it embarrassing to reverse the rule and therefore delayed doing so, could not be laid at Churchill's door.

Hankey did not accept any of this. 'The claim ... that the addition of the revolving date in the Ten Year Rule of 1928 was made to facilitate its eventual cancellation, did not bear examination', he wrote. 'Cabinet decisions could always be changed at short notice and often were,' but, he added, 'to change a Treasury rule sponsored by a powerful Chancellor of the Exchequer is always hard, and sometimes impossible.' The revolving date, he said, 'made it no easier. For its object was to strengthen the Treasury control and perhaps enable the Government to spend our money in a more popular way.'

Hankey went on: 'the lack of foresight shown by the renewal of the Ten Year Rule in an aggravated form sticks out a mile. To the Governments of the 30's the legacy of the rule was extremely embarrassing.' And, he added, throwing in a few phrases from Churchill's own speeches for good measure, 'To the handicap of rearmament was added Mr Churchill's remorseless campaign pursued, "even at the cost of world alarm". Sometimes he "painted the picture even darker than it was", and he stressed "the two-year lag", not realizing that it was at least partly due to his own rule.'

Hankey's criticism of Churchill's modification to the Ten Year Rule has been echoed by several commentators. Russell Grenfell said that 'Service chiefs [were] condemned to endeavour to build their plans on a moving staircase', until the rule was cancelled in 1932.14

N.H. Gibbs wrote in his *History of the Second World War* that, as a direct consequence of the new form of the rule in 1928, the Imperial Conference of 1930 adopted the following resolution – although it was

---

*In one respect was Hankey using the benefit of hindsight? That a national war organization was being *secretly* planned in Germany at that date is not likely to have been known outside the group of Germans concerned.

agreed to by the Prime Ministers of Australia and New Zealand only with reluctance:

> That the present policy of the ultimate establishment of a defended naval base at Singapore should be maintained; and that the Jackson contract [for constructing wharves] should be continued. It was, however, also recommended that, apart from the latter expenditure and such as will be required for the completion of the air base on the scale at present contemplated, the remaining expenditure, i.e. that required for completing the equipment of the docks and for defence works, should be postponed for the next five years, when the matter could be again revised in the light of relevant conditions then prevailing.[15]

The delay in completing the Singapore Naval Base did not, of course, have any direct bearing on the fall of Singapore. However, the delays were symptomatic of British Government dilatoriness over defence matters in general, some of which certainly did play a part in the fall of the fortress; and Churchill himself played a crucial part in creating that situation.

In formulating their early plans for the defence of Singapore it was fortunate for the planners that the Japanese were the only possible aggressor they had to consider. Since 1904 Japanese forces had twice laid siege to well-fortified ports. In that year it had taken them five months to capture Port Arthur from the Russians. In 1914 it had taken them sixty-six days to capture Tsingtao from the German garrison – a fact of which the British were well aware because a small British army contingent had fought alongside the Japanese. On the basis of historical information, therefore, it seemed that the seventy-day period before relief was reasonable from the defence point of view, always providing that a defence force of suitable size and strength was available in the meanwhile.

The planners had to decide on a number of matters: the size of the garrison required; what that garrison needed in the way of armaments and equipment; what guns were required for the seaward defence of the island, for it was from the sea, of course, that any attack was expected; and what air support was needed. These basic problems exercised the minds of successive GOCs at Singapore, and the Imperial General Staff and the Committee for Imperial Defence in London, for twenty years.

The earliest plans were based on unrealistic perceptions, the main one being that the 'impenetrable' Malayan jungle protected the backdoor of Singapore. The jungle which covered the eastern half of Malaya might conceivably have been described as impenetrable, but even that would have been contested by long-time inhabitants of the country. The description certainly did not apply, however, to the more cultivated and more populated western side of the country where a fine road ran down the west coast from the Thai border to the Singapore causeway. By the time the Japanese attacked in 1941, Malaya possessed the finest road network in South-East Asia, as befitted her position as the most advanced country in the area.

Throughout the 1920s and 1930s a string of messages passed between Singapore and London regarding matters of defence. But as fast as the military leaders on the spot asked for additional men and equipment, London would think of good reasons for not supplying them.

The military authorities in Singapore had another, more local and more vocal, adversary contesting some of their plans. This was the Singapore government led by the Governor of the Straits Settlements. In 1927, after the War Office had finally obtained Cabinet sanction for some strengthening of the garrison and for increasing the fixed defences, the then Governor put a temporary halt to the plans. Sir Laurence Guillemard demanded assurances that no part of the cost of the naval base and the associated defences would fall upon the Colony and he held up the necessary land transfers until he received these assurances. Here can be seen the genesis of the lack of co-operation that existed between the civilian and military authorities and which was to plague them right up to 1941. As the danger from Japan grew, this lack of co-operation tended to get worse. Plans to form a branch of the Royal Navy Volunteer Reserve and other matters dealing with reserve forces in Malaya, for example, led to a sustained quarrel between successive governors and the relevant defence departments in London and military officers in Singapore.[16] The governors wanted to know how the costs of the voluntary forces were to be apportioned between *local* defence, for which they were responsible, and *Empire* defence which resulted from the development of the naval base.[17]

Despite all the disputes and changes of policy, however, and the delays, slowly the base and the island's defences took shape. In the end there were twenty-nine large guns covering the sea approaches to Singapore. There were four airfields on the island, two of them in the vicinity of the naval base, one in the south at Kallang, and one in the west at Tengah. And scattered liberally over the island were army camps, stores, ammunition dumps, and other military facilities.

Due to the piecemeal character of the building programmes not all the decisions on what should be constructed proved to be good ones. Perhaps the worst example of lack of foresight was the decision to site the main ammunition depot on Singapore Island dangerously close to other structures, including a military hospital and civilian residential areas.

One other feature of the defence of Singapore needs special mention because from it has developed a saying which has gained almost proverbial status: 'They face the wrong way like the guns of Singapore.' This is one of several myths that have arisen about the campaign. The large Singapore guns were, of course, deliberately sited to cover the sea approaches; but when it came to the crunch many of them were soon made capable of swivelling and firing to landward.

Despite all these problems, when the Second World War broke out in Europe in September 1939, Singapore had become one of the twin-pillars of Britain's world defence policy, the other being, of course, Britain herself. In the eyes of the press, Singapore had become an impregnable fortress, a belief accepted by many people, including some in high places who should have known better.

Chapter Three

The Defence of Malaya, Singapore, and Australia

Because the view was prevalent in military circles in the early 1930s that the Malayan jungle constituted an 'impenetrable' barrier to an attack on Singapore from the rear, it was generally accepted in Britain and Malaya that any assault by Japan on the fortress would be made from the sea and that the Singapore guns would take care of the attackers once they came within range.[1]*

As a result of this misconception little military cognizance was taken of the need to defend the mainland of Malaya in addition to Singapore itself. This view prevailed until 1936, when General William Dobbie became GOC Malaya, and still at times after that.

Even accepting the military view of the impenetrability of the jungle, the policy refusal to do little planning towards defending mainland Malaya seems quite extraordinary. Malaya was the source of about one-half of the world's rubber and one-third of its tin, two commodities of high strategic value. The country was also a valuable source of iron ore, which Japanese mining companies had been exploiting for years. One commentator who was in a position to be well-informed held the opinion that these factors made mainland Malaya, and not Singapore, the more desirable target from the Japanese point of view. Singapore might make (and did make) a prestigious capital for Japan's South-East Asian conquests, but Malaya's riches had much greater significance to Japan's war effort.

It was obviously desirable, however, that any invading force be spotted and attacked by aircraft well before it came in range of the Singapore guns. In 1936 the only airfields on the Malay peninsula were those on the west coast at Alor Star and Port Swettenham, both of which had been built to service the commercial air route from Calcutta to Singapore. Given the comparatively short range of aircraft of the time, these western airfields were of little use for reconnaissance against enemy forces approaching from the north down the South China Sea. There was a need, therefore,

* This assumption that the Japanese would launch a sea attack from the south and not a land attack from the north was in fact at variance with the results of war games exercises conducted over many years by student officers in military academies in both Britain and India.

for airfields on the east coast of Malaya which would extend the effective range of aircraft for both reconnaissance and attacking purposes.

The air force commander in Singapore, backed by the Air Ministry in London, consequently produced plans for the construction of several airfields on Malaya's east coast. It was strategically desirable to place these as far forward as possible from the naval base they were intended to help and protect, so three sites were selected near the town of Kota Bharu adjacent to the Thai border, and another about halfway down the Malayan east coast at Kuantan. The notable, one could say astonishing, aspect of these plans was that they were pushed ahead without any consultation with the army whose job it would be to defend the airfields. (Other airfields were developed elsewhere on the peninsula.)

This lack of consultation between the Services arose from professional rivalry. The two older Services tended to treat the RAF as an upstart, a 'new boy' of unproven ability, and the rivalry was aggravated by each Service's annual battle to increase its own share of the scarce and finite financial resources available for defence. It permeated to the very top of the defence structure in London, but its most severe effects were felt in local theatres of operation. This was especially so in Singapore. The unilateral decision over the siting of the Malayan airfields was the most serious sign of this lack of inter-Service co-operation.

The new airfields were located close to the coast in positions that were impossible to defend against a determined enemy who had successfully managed to land his troops. Lieutenant-General Sir Lewis Heath, who was in command of 3rd Indian Corps during the Malayan campaign, pointed out, when he was giving a lecture in 1942 in Changi Jail as a prisoner of war, that the RAF's programme of airfield construction was detrimental to the interests of the army, for it forced upon the military a ridiculous degree of dispersion:

> In Malaya there was a marked lack of attention paid to proper concealment [of aerodromes] and to the proper dispersion of establishments and aircraft with results which, one thought, were avoidable and lamentable.
>
> This is not a case of being wise after events, for the invitation to attack, which aerodromes on Singapore island offered to an enemy was practically the first adverse comment made when I arrived ... The same comment was applicable to the aerodromes elsewhere in Malaya ... The excuse offered [was that they were] hewn out of jungle and rubber plantations. One doubts whether this was necessary and there was still ... a great lack of imagination employed in obtaining the best possible amount of dispersion and concealment.[2]

In August 1936, while the air force planners were busily engaged in planning and constructing these airfields, Major-General William Dobbie was appointed GOC Malaya.[3] He soon injected an air of realism into current thinking on Singapore defence matters, although he arrived too late to influence the siting of the new airfields.

Until Dobbie's arrival it was considered that, during the north-east monsoon, which blows on the east coast of Malaya from October to March bringing with it relatively high seas and bad visibility, it would be impossible for an aggressor to land troops.[4] This idea was, of course, a prop to the theory that there would be no attack through Singapore's back door. But during the 1936–37 monsoon season Dobbie ordered a series of exercise landings which proved that such landings were possible. Furthermore, he concluded that an enemy would *choose* to attack during this time because reduced visibility would cover the landings both from air reconnaissance and attack. He added that, in his view, mainland Malaya would be the route by which any attack would be made. He wrote:

> It is an attack from the northward that I regard as the greatest potential danger to the fortress. Such attack could be carried out during the period of the north-east monsoon. The jungle is not in most places impassable for infantry.

General Dobbie's Chief of Staff at this period was Colonel A. E. Percival, who was to be GOC Malaya during the Malayan campaign of 1941–42. It is of interest, despite Dobbie's report, and according to General Heath in his lecture, that 'the naval authorities just prior to the Japanese attack in December 1941, still thought that no landings could be made at Kota Bharu during the north-east monsoon'.

General Dobbie was soon made aware that a large Japanese espionage organisation existed in Malaya. He took steps to counter it, and also to increase the military intelligence gathering capability within his own command. He was responsible for having a military officer appointed as Defence Security Officer (DSO), a MI5 appointment, in place of Commander E. H. Hopkinson, RN, who had been doing the job since 1935. The officer, who arrived in Malaya in 1936, was Lieutenant-Colonel Francis Hayley Bell. Unfortunately Hayley Bell's intelligence operation was severely undermined by a complete lack of co-operation from the Head of the Japanese Section of Singapore Special Branch, Major K.S. Morgan. Hayley Bell and Morgan had known each other earlier in China and, for some unknown reason, a mutual antipathy existed between them. As a result Morgan prevented Hayley Bell from having access to Special Branch files.

Nevertheless, Hayley Bell's organization made some significant intelligence coups. One Japanese-speaking agent of his managed to obtain information about provisional Japanese plans for an attack on Thailand

and Malaya. An assessment of this intelligence report together with the results of the landing exercises on the east coast of Malaya, and a re-examination of the topography of the country, all played their part in Dobbie's appreciation of what the Japanese would do if they attacked Malaya. The appreciation was sent to the War Office in November 1937. It accurately predicted, among other matters, that the Japanese, after first securing airfields in Indo-China or Thailand, would land troops at Singora and Patani in the latter country and at Kota Bharu in Malaya, and then advance southward down the highways and railway on the western side of Malaya. The appreciation stated that to hold the naval base at Singapore successfully during the period before relief, the holding of northern Malaya and Johore would be necessary. This could only be done if there was a substantial strengthening of the garrison.

In a letter to Dobbie dated 11th March 1938 Major-General H.R. Pownall, Director of Military Operations and Intelligence at the War Office, commented on the points raised in the appreciation.[5] 'While therefore I admit the weakness of your defences in certain particulars,' wrote Pownall discouragingly, 'I do not regard the remedying of this state of affairs as requiring priority over similar deficiencies in certain other areas.' He went on, 'the existing policy is that our main fleet must sail for Singapore in the event of war whatever the circumstances may be in European waters.'

General Dobbie obviously had doubts about this last statement. (Perhaps he had read what General Smuts wrote as long ago as 1924 when he correctly forecast that tensions in the Far East would arise only after troubles in Europe would make it impossible for the British to send a fleet to Singapore?) In October 1938 Dobbie produced another document which contained new proposals for the defence of Malaya.[6] He said, despite the existence of the official 'period before relief' of seventy days, and despite Pownall's assurance that the fleet would sail, that he 'estimated under existing defence arrangements four months must elapse after declaration of emergency before fortress can be made reasonably secure against attack'. He went on to point out the dangers of an enemy landing on the east coast of Johore. 'I consider it imperative that such essential defences *as can be created in peace must be done now*. For this purpose I estimate £250,000 is required for immediate expenditure on work which will take at least 12 months to complete and which *must be put in hand without delay*.' (Author's italics.)

The funds which Dobbie requested were for a line of permanent defence works in the general area of Kota Tinggi in Johore, and on the north coast of Singapore Island. In the event he received less than a quarter of the sum he asked for and, furthermore, the reduced sum was meant to cover the construction of defences on the island of Penang as well. Despite this response, Dobbie made a start on building the Kota Tinggi line. In retrospect it seems almost tragic that this far-sighted and active general officer reached the army compulsory retirement age in 1939. His successor was not of the same calibre and allowed even this limited defence construction work to lapse.

The new GOC was Major-General Lionel V. Bond.[7] Like Dobbie before him, he was an engineer officer, so he should have had a keen interest in static defences. The circumstances behind his decision not to proceed with the building of landward defences are not known, but what is known is that only £23,000 of the allocated £60,000 was spent despite the fact that the Army's Chief Engineer (CRE) in Malaya, Brigadier J.A.C. Pennycuick, tried to persuade Bond to proceed with the defences. As a result of their disagreeing on this subject, considerable bad feeling developed between the two men, to such a degree that news of it got back to London. Bond's well-known propensity to command from behind his desk rather than go out to see the situation for himself, may well have affected his attitude.

Until August 1938, exactly a year before Dobbie's replacement by Bond, the defence of Singapore and Malaya had been a jealously guarded preserve of the Army, except, of course, when the Air Force took its unilateral decision over the siting of the northern airfields. The Governor of Singapore, Sir Shenton Thomas, despite being titularly Commander-in-Chief, was in the early years only too pleased to be relieved of the work and responsibility over defence. So were many of the senior officers of his administration. Because of this the Defence Committee (later renamed War Committee, then War Council), made up of Service officers and representatives of the civilian government, was dominated by the Army. An army staff officer, with the title of Defence Secretary, was secretary to the main committee and had a seat on most of the subcommittees. Army officers held the majority of the other positions, while for reasons best known to themselves, the naval representatives showed little interest in the proceedings. The RAF representatives did not care for the dominance of the Army but were in no position to do much about it apart from being occasionally obstructive. The civilians on the committee – a mixture of administrators, engineers and policemen – apparently regarded the defence meetings as a bore; a chore to be avoided if possible. This mixture of indifference, placid complacency, and inter-Service rivalry was enough to produce inefficiency. On top of that the Defence Committee had no executive powers, nor any funds of its own.

The Air Officer Commanding (AOC) Singapore in 1938 was Air Vice-Marshal A.W. Tedder (later Marshal of the RAF Lord Tedder). In that year he wrote to Sir Shenton Thomas proposing that a civilian be appointed Defence Secretary. This, he said, would provide much needed continuity in the post, by avoiding the frequent changes caused by the comparatively short tours of duty of army staff officers. This was a constructive suggestion, though one suspects there might have been an edge of self-interest in it; better a civilian in the position than an army officer! Sir Shenton accepted the suggestion and, with General Dobbie offering no objection, C.A. Vlieland was appointed to the position in August 1938.

Charles Archibald Vlieland was then forty-eight years old.[8] He was a very senior officer who had served in the Malayan Civil Service in many different capacities for twenty-four years. Like the Governor himself, he had no military experience, but unlike the Governor, he had made an extensive study of military matters. He was strong-minded, inclined to arrogance, with a stiff and unbending character which accounted for the name people called him behind his back – 'Starchy'.

During Vlieland's first year in the office, everything proceeded reasonably well. In December 1938 he produced a well-received plan for providing food for the civilian population in the event of war. But after General Bond became GOC in August 1939 matters became strained. Bond took exception to a civilian being so closely involved in military matters. On his side Vlieland did not hide his firm belief in Clemenceau's axiom that war was far too serious a matter to be left to the military.*

More basically, the two men looked at the defence of Malaya from very different viewpoints. 'The Governor, AOC, and I,' wrote Vlieland in 1965, 'acted on the very natural assumption that it was our duty to spare no effort to prepare for the extended defence of Malaya, while the GOC considered himself bound by his orders to confine his affairs strictly to the close defence of Singapore.'[9]

During Vlieland's very first interview with Bond in late 1939 the General told him that his own orders were to defend Singapore, and that they did not permit him to concern himself with the peninsula. This is an important statement, since there is no mention in the British Official History of the Japanese war of Bond being given any such directive. However, there is no reason to believe that Vlieland was not telling the truth; no one who knew him ever doubted his veracity; what many people took exception to was his arrogant attitude.

Apart from Sir Shenton Thomas, who at that time fully supported his Defence Secretary's views that the whole of Malaya should be defended, Vlieland had another ally on the Defence Committee. Not surprisingly perhaps, in view of the inter-service rivalry that existed, and that some of his airfields were in Malaya and needed defending, that ally was the new AOC, Air Vice-Marshal J.T. Babington.[10]

Vlieland also held the view, and made it known in committee, that Singapore on its own was of small strategic value, because, he correctly forecasted, Britain would never have sufficient naval resources to send a

---

* In his later writings he pointed out that, in Britain, final defence decisions were made by a civilian in the person of the Minister of Defence, whereas the mother country seemed content to leave the defence decisions in the colonies to the generals.

large enough fleet out to defend it. He also thought there was no likelihood that the £60 million 'fortress' would be attacked from the sea as Singapore was not a principal strategic objective of the Japanese war planners. They would be more interested in the rich Malayan peninsula.

He went even further. He believed that, provided the British held the Malay peninsula, it really made little difference *strategically* if they held Singapore or not. If they held the mainland then, even if the Japanese did manage to take Singapore, they would not be able to use it as a naval base. This view tended to undermine the entire fortress concept which had been so assiduously built up over the years. Such views, of course, coming from an 'amateur', offended Bond.

Despite the clash of personalities 'we were on the way to making the best of the slender resources available,' wrote Vlieland. 'All we lacked was an army commander with orders to defend the peninsula and the requisite tools in the way of air and land forces and modern weapons to do the job.' He continued, 'the tools were never provided and it would appear that His Majesty's Government never intended that they should be once the European war had begun'.

In mid-1939, because of the deteriorating situation in Europe, the Chiefs of Staff in London raised the 'period before relief' from seventy to ninety days, and decided to reinforce the army garrison and the RAF in Singapore. By the time the war in Europe broke out in September that year, the garrison consisted of nine battalions, together with eight RAF squadrons. The RAF had ninety first-line aircraft, but there were no fighters amongst them. The two torpedo-bomber squadrons consisted of obsolescent Vildebeeste planes. This force was entirely inadequate to confront the Japanese, and the situation was made even more precarious when, on the outbreak of the German war, the 'period before relief' was raised again, this time to six months.

Despite the doubling of the 'period before relief', and many doubts in certain quarters as to the practicality of the entire concept, it seemed that Britain intended to maintain Singapore as the eastern bastion of her global defence strategy, with Britain herself being its twin bastion in the west. That, at least, was the view she tried to show to the world, and especially to Australia who looked upon the Singapore fortress as her front line of defence.

One of the bitterest clashes between Bond and Vlieland occurred over the mobilization of the Volunteer Force. This was the local equivalent of Britain's Territorial Army, although it was neither equipped nor trained to the high standard of the force at home. The Volunteers came from all races and included a substantial number of the comparatively few Europeans in the colony. The census of 1931 gave a population of 4.4 million people. Malays and other Malaysians formed 45% of the total, but this percentage was declining. The Chinese formed 39% and this was increasing. The Indians amounted to 14%; and of Europeans there were some 30,000. Most of the Europeans held important positions in the rubber and tin industries or in associated businesses such as shipping and banking. The British government's directive to the Governor was that there was to be no interference in the production of rubber and tin, commodities needed not only for the war effort but for earning American dollars. On the other hand General Bond, with his shortage of regular troops, needed the Volunteers to be trained in case of war. There was a clear conflict of interest.

The clash between Bond and Vlieland came when, at Bond's request, the Governor ordered the mobilization of the Volunteers on the outbreak of the European war in September 1939. 'Starchy' Vlieland's reaction was probably aggravated by the fact that he had not been consulted in advance. Anyway, he objected strongly, saying that the move would adversely effect rubber and tin production. Sir Shenton Thomas, who at this late stage in his career was rather inclined to accept the views of the last person he had met, changed his mind and cancelled the order. It was now Bond's turn to object. The upshot was that the Governor refered the matter back to the Colonial Office in London.

The Governor took the opportunity to point out to London his views on the defence of Singapore and Malaya. These largely tallied with Vlieland's, and were in fact a watered-down version of the rather extreme views held by the AOC, Babington. Babington thought that, in the absence of a fleet, defence should be the responsibility of the RAF, the army's task being limited to the defence of his airfields and the manning of the Singapore guns. These views had not gone down well with Bond at meetings of the War Committee (the new name for the Defence Committee from September 1939), so, as well as the antagonism between Vlieland and Bond, there was now friction between Babington and Bond.

Some personal jealousy seems to have coloured Babington's dealings with the General. As GOC Malaya, Bond was a member of the Straits Settlement's Legislative Assembly, with the privileges that entailed, such as the right to use the prefix 'Hon.', to draw attendance fees and be part of the government processes. Babington was AOC, Far East, with far wider geographical responsibilities, but without those perquisites. (Apparently Shenton Thomas did not see fit to rectify this.) Whatever the cause, a genuine hostility existed between Babington and Bond, and this was known throughout Singapore. Hostesses, even, had to bear it in mind when organizing luncheons and dinner parties; and at social functions to which both men were invited, the way the army faction around Bond kept well away from the RAF faction protecting Babington, was a sight that caused much mirth and gossip.

If Sir Shenton could do nothing about the Bond-Babington affair, he certainly possessed the power to restrain Vlieland, had he bothered to use it. Vlieland was an able, far-sighted man, but because he had the

Governor's ear he was inclined to interfere in matters that were not strictly within his responsibilities. As a result, the War Committee, divided into two hostile camps, accomplished little of value. Most of the strength lay in Vlieland's camp, and Bond found that there was opposition to just about every proposal he made.

When, eventually, the British government's answer to the Volunteer question arrived in Singapore, it was not particularly helpful. It basically left the problem in local hands. The Colonial Office pointed out that, though Malayan manpower could be most usefully employed at that time on the economic front, it was also important that the Volunteers be properly trained. The Colonial Office 'assumed that steps compatible with maintenance of essential industries are being taken to effect this training'.[11] It was also suggested that some form of conscription – which made mockery of the 'Volunteer' title – be considered, providing it did not affect the production of rubber and tin.

In March 1940 Air Vice-Marshal Babington submitted a report to the Air Ministry. He pointed out that, as the 'period before relief' was now 180 days and there was no possibility of even small naval reinforcements in the meantime, the defence of the naval base had fallen on the RAF. In his opinion, once the Japanese had gained a foothold on the Malayan mainland, then nothing would stop them taking the naval base. Therefore, the whole of Malaya must be defended. He demanded air reinforcements.

By 1940 General Bond had changed his mind about the defence of Malaya. In his own report to the War Office he stated that the increase in the 'period before relief' had completely altered the situation. So had the fact that the Japanese now controlled South China, from where they could easily establish air bases in Indo-China and then Thailand from which an attack on Malaya could be covered. He demanded army reinforcements.

While these different reports were being considered in London, the Foreign Office concluded that Japan, after three years of war in China, was in no position to attack the British Empire. This view contrasted with a more realistic one held by the War Office, which considered that Britain's pre-occupation with the German war was likely to encourage Japan to foray southwards, and that the likelihood of this would increase if the British and French forces confronting Germany met with any reverses.

The Foreign Office view prevailed. It conveniently fitted in with the supply situation. Britain was in no position to send reinforcements to an area where danger was not imminent. For the time being Malaya must make do with what it had.

At this juncture Sir Shenton Thomas was about to go home on leave, and it was decided by the War Committee that, while he was there, he should have direct discussions about defence matters with the authorities. The Governor was to be away for eight months. In retrospect his absence from Singapore at this critical period and for that length of time was clearly a mistake, but one that cannot be attributed to him. He had less than three months at home. The remainder of the time was taken up by the difficulties of wartime travel.

During Thomas's absence in London, Singapore's Colonial Secretary, Stanley Jones, took over the Governor's responsibilities, including the chairmanship of the War Committee. If 'Starchy' Vlieland was a difficult man to get on with, then the Hon. Stanley W. Jones was even more so. He 'was too shy to be a good mixer, and anyway was never openly interested in other people's opinions', said the Malayan newspaper managing editor Edwin Glover, in what is possibly the kindest summing up of Jones's character in print.[12]

Duff Cooper, who was to arrive in Singapore in September 1941, sent by Churchill to take up the position of Resident Minister, went much further. He records that Sir Shenton Thomas was, 'much influenced by his Colonial Secretary, a sinister figure called Stanley Jones, who is universally detested in the Colony, where he is accused of having been a defeatist since the beginning of the war'. A picture of Jones published in 1941 in the *Straits Times*, seems to justify Duff Cooper's use of the word 'sinister'. The man had a saturnine aspect, with dark piercing eyes.

One senior member of the civil administration, who knew Stanley Jones better than either Glover or Duff Cooper, was A. H. Dickinson, who had taken over the position of Inspector-General, Straits Settlements Police, in 1939. In a private critique of Noel Barber's book on Singapore, *Sinister Twilight*, he wrote of Jones, 'It would have been better had he never been appointed to Singapore. It is a sad thing to say but he, I think, is responsible for the exaggerated impression of apathy and incompetence which pervades the book so far as the Civil Government is concerned.' Again, when commenting on Jones's lack of co-operation after the Japanese war had begun with a man named Bisseker who had been appointed Deputy Director of Civil Defence, Dickinson wrote, 'It is a sad fact that Jones' appalling refusal to help Bisseker was typical of that attitude (even well before our war) which so antagonized those who could have helped build up the Government image.'[13]

Unlike Vlieland, Jones felt that military matters were best left to military men. Under his chairmanship the balance of power on the War Committee changed. Jones more often than not sided with General Bond. On top of that the Navy, in the person of Admiral Sir Percy Noble, C-in-C China Fleet, began to take more interest in the committee's affairs. He also tended to side with Bond. Now Vlieland, and his ally Babington, often found themselves in the minority. This led to strained relations between Vlieland and Jones, his superior.

This relationship soon worsened. After one disagreement over defence policy between the GOC and the AOC it was agreed by all concerned that the matter be referred to London. Bond and Babington were to state their views in writing and Jones would transmit them to London as they stood.

It was Vlieland's task to draft the telegram incorporating the differing views. To it he added the comments which he 'considered Mr Jones should append,' which mainly concerned the lack of defences on the north coast of Singapore Island. Jones refused to accept the draft even after several hours of argument, saying that he proposed to express no views on the matter at all. Eventually a compromise was reached with which Vlieland said he was 'tolerably content'. The telegram was redrafted and both men initialled it. In the event, the telegram which Jones ordered to be sent bore no resemblance to the agreed draft.

'I do not suppose,' wrote Vlieland, 'that if Jones had kept his promise to me, Churchill's determination to sacrifice Malaya would have been shaken, for even the expressed views of the Chiefs of Staff do not seem to have had that effect. But if the agreed telegram had been sent, at least it would have been impossible for anyone who read it to say he had not been told.* Even the emasculated version of my original draft made it clear that Singapore was defenceless against an overland attack, and unless the peninsula was held, the naval base would be unusable even if it was not occupied by the enemy as it was only reasonable to expect it would be.'

As a result of this incident Vlieland decided to write a defence appreciation of his own. This was never transmitted to London as Jones refused to accept it. In that document Vlieland stated that the Naval Base had long lost its *raison d'être*. There was not, he said, the faintest chance of the arrival of a British Fleet capable of dealing with the Japanese. The base would be useless to each side if the other occupied the peninsula. He pointed out that the basic factor which had caused the break-out by Japan over the past three decades was over-population and the rice problem; that they needed raw materials for industry and a market for their manufactures; but above all they needed rice. He forecast that Japan's initial targets would be Indo-China and Thailand for their rice, and in the case of the former, as a springboard to the south. Anyone who knew anything about the current scramble for rice in the Far Eastern markets and especially Bangkok, he maintained, would know that it would not be all that long before Japan struck.

Vlieland went on to say that the main British military effort must be concentrated on the defence of the north-western plains of Malaya. Alor Star, he said, was the key to the whole defence. If we lost that, complete disaster would follow inevitably.

Vlieland's prediction, it turned out, was broadly correct. It is sad to think that, had he been a man of different character, a man with greater diplomatic skills, his views may have reached London, and that they just may have had an effect on government thinking there.

---

* Vlieland was commenting on Churchill's remarks made in January 1942 that he did not know that Singapore had no northern defences.

In the Governor's absence, as Vlieland bemoaned in his memoirs, 'Jones had it all his own way, not only to the exasperation of the AOC and myself, but to the bewilderment and perturbation of the general public in Malaya.' He went on, 'Most people thought I was responsible for, or at least party to, many of the strange things which were happening.' He was referring especially to the signs of defence activity going on on the southern coast of Singapore compared to the complete absence of any evidence of preparedness in the Malay States.

Jones was soon to annoy Vlieland even more when, at Bond's request, he mobilized the Volunteer Force without consulting him. Jones was probably protecting himself against possible future recriminations when he had the decision ratified by the Singapore Executive Council, which was not usually consulted on defence matters.

Admiral Noble was appalled at the lack of co-operation and co-ordination on the War Committee. Especially was he concerned at the bad relations between Bond and Babington. When, in July 1940, he was recalled to Britain to take up the post of Commander, Western Approaches, he made it his business to report on the unsatisfactory state of affairs in Malaya to Lord Lloyd, the Secretary of State for the Colonies. Unfortunately Lloyd died shortly afterwards and nothing immediately was done about it.

Noble's place as C-in-C China Station was taken by Vice-Admiral Sir Geoffrey Layton. Layton soon took cognizance of the situation on the War Committee, and, as appalled as his predecessor had been, cabled the Admiralty with a report. Now at last the Chiefs of Staff in London were aware of the situation, they took steps to rectify it. In late October they appointed a Commander-in-Chief, Far East, in the person of Air Chief-Marshal Sir Robert Brooke-Popham.[14] By this appointment the Chiefs of Staff recognized that, until the relieving fleet arrived, it was the RAF that held the main responsibility for the defence of Singapore.

In the meantime relations on the War Committee were going from bad to worse. The Colonial Office had earlier asked for information about the strategic storage of rice stocks. This matter had been answered by Jones on the advice of Vlieland but without consultation with Bond whose forces were responsible for the defence of the locations where the stocks were held, most of which were in the north. The crux of this matter was the old problem of how much of the Malayan mainland was to be defended by the limited forces available. Bond complained, and Jones received a roasting from the Colonial Office for this lack of consultation. Subsequently, after due consultation, some rice stocks were transferred from the north to the south, but Vlieland saw in this a sinister threat that Bond was returning to the idea of protecting only Singapore and the south of the peninsula.

In the late summer of 1940 the Chiefs of Staff in London had reviewed the problem of the defence of Malaya *as a whole*, and concluded that, in the absence of a fleet, a total of 336 first-line aircraft was required. They added the proviso that this target could not be reached until the end of 1941. In the meantime, they said, the army should be strengthened, and they recommended that the Australian 7th Division, then under training in Australia, should be sent to Malaya together with two Indian Infantry Brigades.

In the light of the Chiefs of Staff's appreciation, a defence conference was held at Singapore in October 1940. It was chaired by Admiral Layton (Brooke-Popham had not yet arrived in the colony). General Bond, Air Vice-Marshal Babington and Charles Vlieland took part. Also in attendance were observers from Australia, New Zealand, India and Burma. The American naval attaché in Bangkok, Commander A.C. Thomas, was also present. He attended in plain clothes and was ostensibly in Singapore to visit his medical advisor. Britain was determined not to do anything that might offend Tokyo, although equally determined on US involvement.

The principal conclusion of the conference – sent to London over the signatures of Layton, Bond and Babington – was that the Chiefs of Staff had underestimated the number of aircraft required. The required figure was 556, not 336.

In December 1940 Churchill categorically turned down the idea of sending the Australian 7th Division to Malaya. He decided that it must go to the Middle East as originally planned. He maintained that the principal defence of Singapore must be the fleet, and that the idea of attempting to defend the whole of the Malayan peninsula had no merit. Churchill, convinced that Singapore was a fortress, still did not rate the Japanese threat highly. Writing to the First Lord of the Admiralty, A. V. Alexander, on 15th September three months previously, he had said, 'The NID [Naval Intelligence Division] are very much inclined to exaggerate Japanese strength and efficiency.'

Churchill held his Japanese blind spot and his illusions over the Singapore citadel until the end. Both are illustrated in a letter he sent to President Roosevelt on 15th February 1941. After admitting that British naval reserves were insufficient to stand up to the Japanese navy, he added, 'I do not myself think that the Japanese would be likely to send the large military expedition necessary to lay siege to Singapore'.[15]

Sir Shenton Thomas arrived back from leave on 5th December 1940, and it soon became evident to Charles Vlieland that the Governor's attitude towards him had changed. He waited in vain to be summoned to give an account of his stewardship of defence matters in Thomas's absence. On several occasions he tried to contact the Governor by phone, only to be told by an intermediary that he was not available. The crunch soon came. At a meeting of the War Committee on 13th December, Thomas made no move to greet Vlieland whom he had not seen for over eight months; he did not even look at him. Almost immediately the recently arrived Air Chief-Marshal Brooke-Popham launched into a tirade against Vlieland, accusing him of non-co-operation. 'It stank,' said

Vlieland, 'of midnight oil and careful briefing by Bond and Layton, since it referred to matters before Brooke-Popham's arrival in Singapore. I was accused of persistent refusal to take the Army line.' He had no ally now as Babington could not oppose his own service superior, Brooke-Popham.

As Vlieland had always carried out what he thought were the Governor's wishes, he waited for the Governor 'to speak in his own defence, if not in mine'. But Thomas remained silent. Vlieland then spoke himself, pointing out that he was not answerable to any military authority. He added that he had never changed his ground and had no reason to suppose that his chief had. Still Thomas said nothing, and Vlieland then knew beyond any doubt that he had lost the backing of the Governor. He resigned the next day, and left Singapore in February 1941. He was to write later that Shenton Thomas had probably 'bought' an extension of his term in the Governor's office by agreeing to much that he had previously been opposed to, in particular being prepared, as Vlieland claimed, 'to toe the military line'.

In the years leading up to World War Two, Australia looked in confidence towards Britain for all matters dealing with her security; she preferred to concentrate her national income on developing her domestic economy rather than spending more on defence. (In the year 1936–37 Australia's defence expenditure amounted to only one per cent of her national income; the per capita expenditure was only forty per cent of that in Britain.) So she clung tightly to the rather loose legal fetters that bound her to the mother country – which would have been even looser had the Australian government bothered to ratify the Statute of Westminster of 1931 which formally acknowledged her status as an independent country. Together with the common heritage factor, this was an attitude that made it difficult for Australians to take objective decisions on matters which were in their own national interest.

This attitude suited Britain however. With Australia's defence linked indistinguishably to her own, if war was to come to Europe she could rely on the support of an Australian Imperial Force (AIF), as had happened in World War One.

The Australians saw Singapore and a British fleet based there as the foundation stone for the defence of their country. In January 1942 the then Australian Prime Minister, John Curtin, was to tell Winston Churchill in a cabled message that Singapore was a 'central fortress in the system of Empire and local defence'. Throughout the years when the base was being built the feasibility of Britain being able to provide the necessary fleet in the event of having to fight wars in both the east and the west was repeatedly questioned by the Australians. Just as repeatedly they were given assurances. These varied in degree and were sometimes hesitant and devious, and nearly always they were less than specific; yet they were always accepted by the Australians. It suited most Australian politicians, embroiled in their own domestic policies, not to subject such assurances to close scrutiny. As the Australian historian, David Day, has written, 'No one seemed to have asked why they [Britain] were so confident of dispatching a fleet [to Singapore] in war when it had never proved possible in peace.'[16]

Within hours of Britain declaring war on Germany on 3rd September 1939, Robert Menzies, the Australian Prime Minister (until August 1941), hastened to follow suit. Unlike some of the other Dominions he did not even bother to consult his parliament before declaring war on Germany, so confident was he that, on this issue, he had the majority of his countrymen behind him despite the fact that his was a minority government.

Two months after the war in Europe began the British government was still issuing assurances about Australian defence. British ministers were gambling on her hand never being called by Japan entering the war. The stakes were high, not only the safety of Australia, but possibly the future of the British Empire itself. The hole card was the United States fleet based on Japan's eastern flank at Pearl Harbor; and the cards in hand looked strong. There were the navies of France and the Netherlands, both countries with important Far Eastern empires of their own to protect, and the shadow of Russia lying on Japan's western flank, perhaps waiting to avenge herself for the defeats she had suffered in earlier years. In all it seemed a reasonable hand to bet on, especially considering that British Ministers had seriously underestimated both Japan's desire to make war and her capabilities for doing so.

Australia did not immediately jump in with a promise of sending an AIF. Robert Menzies' government was under considerable harassment from the opposition parties. (This had nothing to do with his declaration of war which they supported.) He considered that any attempt to push through the idea of an expeditionary force at that time would be highly unpopular in view of the threat from Japan, although he did not rule out the possibility of sending troops to Singapore and perhaps to the Middle East at a future date.

This 'dilatory' attitude over rushing to the defence of the mother country resulted in some strong words from Winston Churchill, now back as First Lord of the Admiralty. He complained that the one Australian Division being formed was apparently staying at home. He urged that pressure be brought to bear to ensure that Australian troops were in France before the spring of 1940.[17]

Menzies sent Richard Casey, his Minister of Supply, to London to attend a meeting of Dominion ministers. After meeting Casey, the then Secretary for the Dominions, Anthony Eden, reported to the Prime Minister, Neville Chamberlain, on 3rd November 1939:

If we can give Casey a measure of comfort in respect of Japan's political attitude, combined with an indication of our willingness and ability to send capital ships to Singapore should the need arise, the Commonwealth Government will then at once decide that the division which they are now training can proceed overseas.

Lord Halifax urged caution before Britain gave any such assurances based on 'guesstimates' on what the future would bring, and Eden stated that Britain was in rather an invidious position. Churchill would have none of this. Australian fears of Japan were unfounded, he said, and the most they had to fear was tip-and-run raids which would not need an army to repel.[18]

As the man in charge of the Admiralty it fell to Churchill to try to convince Richard Casey that Britain would indeed send a fleet to the Far East were it ever needed, without putting it in so many words. Convinced as he was that there was no serious threat from Japan, especially against Australia, Churchill found no difficulty in providing the framework of the sort of assurance Casey was seeking, without being too specific. He even said that Britain would abandon the Mediterranean if it became necessary to save Australia. This did not much please Chamberlain when Churchill told him about it, making the point that Britain had always before got away with vague promises and avoided giving specific commitments, and anyway, no one could make decisions in advance of the event to quit the Mediterranean. Stanley Bruce, a former Australian Prime Minister and now High Commissioner in London, was a firm anglophile, and probably encouraged Casey to accept the British assurances. There is much evidence that Bruce and that other anglophile, Robert Menzies (who even considered a political future in Britain), played their parts in convincing Australians that Britain rated Australia's security more highly than was in fact the case. It sounded mighty like an apologia for Bruce's ultra pro-British stance, and perhaps indirectly for his own, when Menzies wrote of Bruce in his memoirs: 'In London, he had one country to serve, his own. He never permitted himself to forget it.'[19]

In consequence of these British assurances the partly trained 6th Australian Division sailed for the Middle East in January 1940. In May 1940 (the month of Dunkirk) the Australians sent a squadron of Hudsons to Singapore which released a British squadron for duty elsewhere.

During that month the Chiefs of Staff reported to the British government that the imminent collapse of the French made it improbable that any British naval force could be sent to the Far East. This did not stop the British from advising Menzies a few days later that Britain had 'every intention of maintaining the security of our vital interests in the Near East and of course the Far East'. On 13th June, however, three days after the entry of Italy into the war, Menzies received from Lord Caldecote, Secretary of State for the Dominions, a most secret message that revealed for the first time that Singapore was no longer the number two bastion in Britain's global defence policy; its place had been taken by the Middle East. The message informed Menzies that Britain intended to retain a fleet of capital ships in the eastern Mediterranean to hold Egypt and to restrain the possibility of Turkey entering the war on the Axis side. 'It would be most unlikely that we could send adequate reinforcements to the Far East,' and would 'therefore have to rely on the USA to safeguard our interests there.' The only grain of comfort Menzies might have received from this was that the danger in the East was still largely hypothetical. Two weeks later Britain made the declaration of intent formal by informing the Australian government that, whereas before the fall of France Britain had relied on the French Navy to contain the Italian fleet, now the Royal Navy had that task on top of containing the German Fleet. 'We cannot do this and send a fleet to the Far East.'

This should have been taken by Australia as a warning to take upon herself more of the responsibility for her own defence, or to seek defence guarantees from the United States. But the vestiges of the colonial mentality in Australia were strong (before the war Australia's only representative in a foreign land was a man based at the British Embassy in Washington), and on top of that Canberra had no wish to antagonise Japan by seeming to draw closer to Washington. So she did neither. Furthermore, she now agreed to send a division of troops and more aircraft to Malaya (and later more troops to the Middle East). In the background was the belief, still held by many Australians, that when it came to the crunch the mother country would come good and, somehow or other, a fleet of His Majesty's ships would appear on the horizon.

When in January 1942, during the second month of the Japanese war, Churchill contemplated sending the British 18th Division whose original destination had been the Middle East, not to Singapore but instead to Burma, Prime Minister Curtin told Churchill this would be an 'inexcusable betrayal'. The 18th Division landed in Singapore and within two weeks were prisoners of war.

After 1942 the old relationship between Australia and Britain was never the same. The following factors fed on each other: the pre-war assurances on defence which had been given by Britain, and which circumstances and a change in priorities had caused Britain largely to renege on (as many of the persons involved in giving the assurances, including Winston Churchill, knew would be likely under certain circumstances); the relegation of Singapore – considered by the Australians to be so important to their defence – to a lower position than the Middle East in Britain's table of defence priorities in 1940; lack of pre-consultation with Australia when Britain decided to change the Commander-in-Chief, Far East (Brooke-Popham) in late 1941; the fall of Singapore itself in February 1942, not to mention two other lamentable strategic decisions (for which Churchill was also largely responsible), the campaigns in

Greece and Crete which, like Singapore, resulted in the loss of many Australian lives; the belated ratification of the Statute of Westminster later in 1942; the close relationship that Australia developed with the Americans during the remainder of the war. All these developments undermined the old Imperial relationships and together ensured that the relationship between the island continent and the mother country would never return to its former closeness.

Chapter Four

Espionage, Subversion, and the Indian Independence League

Most of the extensive espionage network in pre-war Malaya was controlled by the Japanese, although they had some peripheral help from the countries, Germany and Italy, which were to become their Axis partners. Most subversion was nationalist inspired, and was mainly confined to the Indians in Malaya, although there were similar activities among sections of the Malay community. Most of these movements were funded or otherwise actively encouraged by the Japanese.

The espionage and subversion situation can only be fully understood within the context of the geopolitical sub-divisions that existed in the country and the political characteristics of the various ethnic groups in the population.

The peninsula was divided, by the British, into three political entities. These were:–

1. *The Crown Colony of the Straits Settlements (SS)*. This consisted of Singapore, Penang, the Province of Wellesley, and Malacca. (The Straits Settlements also controlled two dependent territories, Labuan and Christmas Island.) The Straits Settlements were administered by a British Governor (Sir Shenton Thomas from 1936) who was also the High Commissioner for the Malay States. This dual role meant that the Governor ruled over what was probably the most complicated constitution in the British Empire. Eleven separate governments had to be dealt with before any agreement affecting Malaya as a whole could be reached.

   The Colony was policed by the Straits Settlements Police, under an Inspector-General of Police (IGP).

2. *The Federated Malay States (FMS)*. Made up of the states of Perak, Selangor, Pahang, and Negri Sembilan. The Rulers of these states each had a British Resident. These states were policed as one entity by the FMS Police, also under an Inspector-General.

3. *The Unfederated Malay States (UMS)*. These were the states of Johore, Kedah, Kelantan, Trengganu, and Perlis. The Rulers of

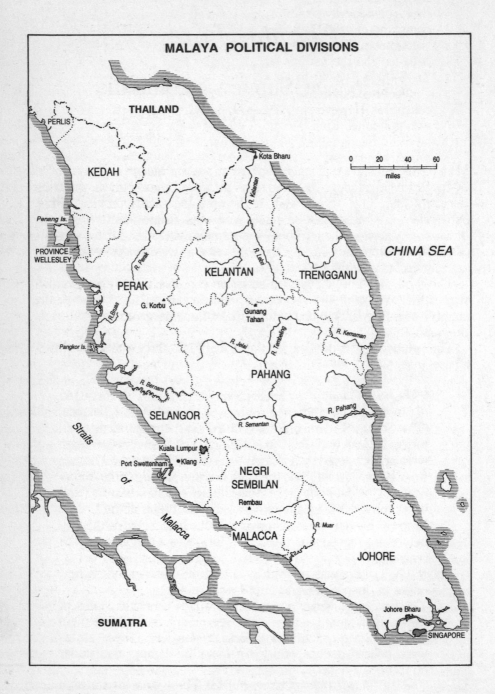

MALAYA POLITICAL DIVISIONS

each of these states had a British Advisor. Each was policed by its own locally recruited and trained police force under the command of officers seconded from either the FMS or Straits Settlements Police. (There was a regular interchange of officers between the the various police forces.) Prior to 1939 neither the SS nor FMS Inspector-Generals of Police could enter an Unfederated State except at the express invitation of the Sultan concerned. However, in 1939, when the IGP, Straits Settlements, was appointed Civil Security Officer for the entire peninsula, he could then go uninvited to any part of the land while about security business.

The population of Malaya (including the Straits Settlements) was divided into the following ethnic groups:

1. *Chinese*. By 1941 this was the largest group overall. Some had been born in Malaya of immigrant families, while others were direct immigrants from China. The Chinese were scattered in every township and village but were concentrated in greatest numbers in the Straits Settlements, especially in Singapore.
2. *Malays*. This was the largest ethnic group on mainland Malaya.
3. *Indians*. A large proportion of these were Tamils who worked on the rubber plantations. (Tamils who were Malay-born were known as *Klings*.) There was an active proportion of Sikhs in the Indian population.
4. *Eurasians*. A substantial number of Eurasians lived in the larger conurbations, but most were in Singapore.
5. *Arabs*. A small but highly influential community found mostly in Singapore, with a few in Malacca and Penang.
6. *Europeans*. The Europeans in the country, estimated to be about 30,000 strong, were mostly engaged in government or in managerial posts in commerce, shipping and industry.

On the basis of political sympathies, the Chinese in Malaya could be divided into four groups. First, there were the adherents of Chiang Kai-Shek, whose Kuomintang movement governed most of China that was not controlled by the Japanese. At the centre of this faction were the so-called Hung League. Second, there were the Communists, who tended to make up for their smaller numbers by being more politically active and vociferous than the others. For a long time the police had been concerned about the activities of this group, and some had been imprisoned for sedition. The league at the centre of this faction was called the Han. Third, the smallest group was the pro-Wang Ching-wei faction which supported the Japanese puppet ruler of Manchuria. Fourth, and numerically the largest group, were those Chinese of pro-British leanings or who were politically independent. The main interest of this group was the pursuit of trade and money. Its members were prone to being dragooned by the other three groups, each of which had its own underground network of agents. Apart from the adherents of Wang Ching-wei, the Chinese were anti-Japanese.

A substantial anti-Japanese fighting force could have been raised from among the Chinese, but the Governor of Singapore refused to countenance this – until it was too late – mainly because he feared the communist element who were likely to make up the greater part of such a force, because they were the most militant. A small force called Dalforce, named after its leader Colonel John Dalley, was mustered towards the end. Although badly armed, it fought well in the battle for Singapore. One of the difficulties Dalley was confronted with, while forming this force, was that the Hung and Han League people would not fight together. They had to be placed in separate companies.

The average Malay peasant, or *ryot*, was not politically minded. The same could be said for those on the next rung up the social ladder, the artisan and clerical class. Between them and the ruling class of Malay sultans and nobles, came the 'intelligentsia', a large proportion of whom were school teachers. It was in this class that signs of nationalism had arisen, to some extent activated by similar influences in the Dutch East Indies. These nationalist views were supported by sections of the Malay Press.

Many of the Indians living in the country were influenced by the views of the Indian Independence League (IIL) which sought the end of British rule in India. The general mass of Indians, normally peaceful and interested in the quiet pursuit of its livelihood, was becoming easy prey to IIL agitators during the year or two before the Japanese war began. In that period the IIL made a bid for complete political control of the Indian population in Malaya. As A.H. Dickinson, Inspector-General, Straits Settlements Police from 1939, was to record, 'the movement was becoming dangerous'.

The Sikh community was strongly organised within itself, but became susceptible to anti-British propaganda emanating from the Punjab and from Sikh exiles in America. Dickinson described the Sikh community as one 'which contributed nothing to the welfare of Malaya, and which could only be regarded as parasitic, stupid and likely to be openly anti-British in the event of disaster overtaking British arms'.[1] (Some members of the Sikh community did act badly during the Japanese occupation. Though some Sikhs displayed great loyalty and bravery, others participated in the more brutal aspects of the Japanese treatment of prisoners. Dickinson's views on this community may have been coloured by hindsight, for he was a prisoner himself during the Japanese occupation, and was writing in the 1960s.)

This, then, was the political and racial background against which Japan set up its espionage system in Malaya; a process that had begun, on any appreciable scale, during the First World War when Britain granted Japan, then an ally, naval facilities in the port of Penang. By then the Japanese Secret Service had had nearly twenty years of successful operations behind it. First set up in 1898, the year Russia occupied Port Arthur, it was said by Colonel Picard of the French Army, writing in 1905, to be 'wonderfully organised'. It used both Japanese and foreign agents, and they played a significant role in the Japanese victories in the Russo-Japanese War of 1904–05. But the Japanese Secret Service did not concern itself only with matters in the northern part of the China Seas. Its agents spread quickly southward, so that by 1905 French Indo-China and Thailand were 'swarming with Japanese agents'.[2] So when the Japanese began infiltrating into Malaya in the First World War they were able to link up with agents in Thailand to the north, and later with espionage networks in Burma and in the Dutch East Indies.

Many of their agents received training at the Nakano Intelligence School outside Tokyo. There, agents were trained not only in intelligence, but also in counter-intelligence and subversion techniques.

The Japanese espionage system in Malaya – if it can be called 'a system' for it was a loose-knit, very complex affair – was mainly engaged in collecting commercial intelligence, but certain cells and individuals were active in acquiring military information. Most of the agents concerned were Japanese residing temporarily in the country and working for ostensibly legitimate commercial undertakings. Most were not full-time agents, but men who merely collected intelligence information in the course of their legitimate work. However, a considerable number were undercover agents whose spying activities were the main purpose of their being in the country.

The Japanese owned many undertakings in Malaya. There were Japanese-owned mines at Dungun in the eastern state of Trengganu, and at Endau further south in Johore. They owned rubber estates, some situated alongside major highways from where troop movements and exercises could be observed. An extensive fleet of Japanese fishing vessels was based at Singapore. These craft regularly called at ports up and down the peninsula, and Special Branch in Singapore was convinced that all were engaged in intelligence gathering. Many of the skippers were naval men, and they certainly had wonderful opportunities for surveying the seas around Malaya and adjacent countries. 'They were operating all the way back to Japan – in reality a permanent standing patrol', wrote René Onraet who was Singapore Police Chief up to 1939. He went on to describe these fishermen as 'South Seas *Ronin*' or 'wave men'.[3]

In every Malay township of any size there was a Japanese photographer, storekeeper, masseur or barber. The infiltration of such 'professionals' seems to have been a favourite ploy of Japanese Intelligence for they worked the same way in India, where they also added dentists to the list of occupations. Japanese dental surgeons set up their practices adjacent to many of the garrison towns in India. One man, later identified as Colonel Nakajima of Japanese Intelligence, was even appointed to be the official photographer to the Singapore Naval Base! Many old residents of Singapore and members of the armed services who served there still possess photographs with Nakajima's 'chop' on them, indicating the range of this man's photographic interests.

In Singapore and some of the larger Malayan towns there were Japanese-run brothels, where *mama-sans* and their girls happily collected information from British military clients along with the fee for services rendered, or perhaps as the fee itself. Some Europeans and Asiatics in Singapore had Japanese mistresses, and these 'were not a negligible source of information', reported Onraet.

Middle Road in Singapore was a centre for Japanese shops, the largest of which, K. Baba & Company, rivalled in size the British-owned department stores in Raffles Place. Baba's management team were known by Singapore Special Branch to be a collecting agency for intelligence. There were several Japanese banks, and shipping lines, some of them with subsidiary warehousing companies ideally placed within the docks complex, and news agencies.

In 1940 the Singapore government estimated that there were close to 6,000 Japanese nationals in Malaya, two-thirds of them men, and that most of the men and many of the women were engaged in espionage activities of one form or another. There can be little doubt that this view was correct. A British Army Intelligence file of the time stated that, in Japan, 'patriotism and the state religion of Shintoism were intimately entwined. The divine origin of the Japanese race and the divinity of the Emperor who was descended directly from the Sun Goddess, was an article of faith and not to be questioned.' (The same report quoted the Japanese poet who had written, 'Japan is not a land where men need pray, for 'tis itself divine'.) Because of this extreme form of patriotism, any instruction from Japanese authorities to collect information would have been dutifully, not to say gratefully, obeyed by overseas Japanese.

In addition to the Japanese residents in Malaya, and the large group of semi-residents in the form of fishermen, Malaya was regularly visited by Japanese 'tourists'. Many of these were military men and scientists, and all were busy acquiring information of strategic value. As the 1930s drew to an end, this espionage activity grew in strength and scope. It is of small wonder that in February 1938 a Foreign Office official in London endorsed a file on this subject with the words, 'Singapore was becoming more of a hotbed for Japanese spies.'[4]

Perhaps the best summing-up of Japanese espionage activities in Malaya prior to the war was that made by René Onraet. As the Inspector-General of Police, Straits Settlements until 1939, he was in the best position to know about it apart from the Japanese themselves. 'For twenty years after the Great War,' he recorded, 'the Japanese expanded their trade in and increased their knowledge of Malaya. They were ubiquitous. Europeans in the East who witnessed the activities of travellers, photographers, prospectors and orchid collectors from close quarters, considered them all to be spies – and, of course, as men who travelled about, they were a menace, but the real villains were the directors of firms and banks, of the semi-official commercial museum, and members of the official consulate.'

Onraet, who was writing about 1945, went on, 'I look back at Japanese activities in Malaya with the conviction of having witnessed a patient and confident preparation for ultimate occupation, all the more easy to organise as no-one thought a military success, on which such an occupation depended, was possible.'[5] In 1938 Onraet became so concerned about the extent of espionage being conducted by employees of Japanese enterprises in Malaya, that he attempted to persuade the Governor to introduce legislation that would compel Japanese firms to employ not less than fifty per cent non-Japanese personnel on their staffs. The proposal was not accepted.

Singapore Special Branch (SB) considered that the office of the Japanese Consulate-General in Singapore was the main conduit for passing on to Tokyo intelligence collected in the south. Proof that this was indeed so was discovered in the Consulate building after the Pacific War began. A cable from the Governor to the Colonial Secretary, of 14th December 1941, states that, 'we have unimpeachable evidence that Jap Consulate including newly arrived Consul-General are members of organisation set up to direct fifth-column'. The Consul-General referred to was Suemasa Okamoto who had only arrived a few days before the war began. For his own safety against 'infuriated Chinese' he was kept in jail until being sent to India on 23rd December aboard the s.s. *King Yuan*. He was later included in the 'exchange' of diplomatic personnel which took place at Lourenço Marques.

The collected intelligence went by diplomatic bag, or was smuggled out on Japanese ships, or was radioed – perhaps from ships in the harbour. In the north, information was passed over the Thai border where it reached the desk of the military attaché at the Japanese Legation in Bangkok. That, too, was then remitted to Tokyo. There all intelligence was sifted and processed by the *Toa Keizai Chosa Kyoku*, the East Asiatic Economic Investigation Bureau, a sort of intelligence clearing house. That office passed on anything of military interest to Japanese Military Intelligence, to the Imperial High Command, and other interested departments.

It was during the radio relaying process from Singapore that some messages were intercepted by American and British Intelligence. One such message, giving the deployment of British and Indian troops and their equipment in northern Malaya, was intercepted on 16th February 1941.[6]

Singapore Special Branch agents had discovered that, from 1934 onwards, Japan's chief intelligence agent in Singapore was Dr Tsune

Ouchi, working in Singapore as chief of the League of Nations Health Bureau. In that position Tsune had diplomatic immunity.

On the military side, Japanese intelligence interests were many and varied. It was known that in 1932 their agents sought information about the Naval Base then under construction, and of certain RAF facilities. They obtained the RAF information from a leading aircraftsman with the name of Graham. In 1933 they bought drawings of the Naval Base from a man called Roberts for the sum of Straits $1300 (over £5000 at today's values).[7] Then, in 1934, a Japanese businessman called Nishimura was arrested, caught in the act of buying plans of the RAF airbase at Seletar. While being interviewed in the SB headquarters in Singapore, Nishimura killed himself 'by taking enough cyanide to kill an elephant'.[8] Later, another alleged Japanese spy committed suicide by defenestration at the Singapore CID headquarters in Robinson Road.

The catalogue of Japanese spy interests is large. Special Branch knew that Japanese agents had obtained drawings of the important Guillemard Railway Bridge over the Sungei Kelantan twenty miles south of Kota Bharu. They had also purchased drawings of the Causeway which linked Singapore to the mainland, together with its associated lock, which worked as a sluice-gate. They had acquired plans of the important Woodlands Railway switch on Singapore Island. In 1937 they obtained information about the guns on Blakang Mati Island (now called Sentosa), about submarine defences, and the gun emplacements at Changi. They set up a fifth-column network, with plans to blow up some of the Singapore defences. One undercover British agent produced a list of potential fifth-columnists who were available to carry out this kind of sabotage.

One official in the Japanese Consulate-General's office had the authority to pay up to Straits $12,000 for any particular item of information. At nearly £50,000 in today's values this indicates just how important the Japanese valued good information from this area. The police also knew that the head of a Japanese silk firm in Singapore acted as the paymaster for agents in and around the island.

It seems that Singapore Special Branch had a mole among the Japanese living in the city. This informant told the police on 29th September 1940 that the Japanese Government had ordered young resident Japanese, presumably the children of officials and others, to organise themselves into a 'Red Blood Patriotic Youth Corps'. The informant stated that 'overseas Japanese youths who have previously received training will form the principal members and will be supplemented by ambitious members of the Japanese Buddhist Youth Association and the Japanese Christian Youth Association'. The plan was that, in the event of war, these youths should harass the rear of British defences and take possession of strategic points.[9] What is interesting about this report is the indication that some of these youths had received training in such matters. Whether or not any of them were ever used, it is obvious that the Japanese were preparing for every eventuality with an awesome sense of dedication.

Despite the weight of evidence about the scale of Japanese espionage activities the British were in a quandary. They were very careful, most of the time, to do nothing to offend the Japanese government which was always looking for excuses to provoke diplomatic incidents. With trouble brewing in Europe the last thing Britain wanted was unrest in the East. Non-provocation was the name of the policy, but at the same time it was necessary for the British to curb as much of this espionage activity as they could. So, in most cases where firm evidence was found, the people concerned were deported with the minimum of fuss; but the policy was considered so important that all such deportations had to be sanctioned by the Foreign Office, through the Colonial Office, in London.

This non-provocation policy often led to inter-ministerial wrangles in London. One catches a glimpse of this when reading some of the cipher messages that passed to and fro between London and the Far East on espionage matters. One of these shows the concern felt by the War Office that the British embassy in Tokyo was issuing transit visas to men who were obviously spies. One such cipher was sent from the War Office to the C-in-C, Far East on 19th November 1940:

No.89520. MOST SECRET.

We are alarmed at the apparent ease with which Japanese Agents are able to work in British possessions in the Far East. GOC, Malaya Command will be able to give you full details of a tour recently made by Taniguchi in North Borneo during which he was able to obtain and telegraph to Japan all the military, political, and economic intelligence of that area that the Japanese could reasonably require. This happened in spite of the fact that we had previous knowledge of his intended tour.

We now hear that Major Kuriya intends making a comprehensive tour which is to include Singapore and North Borneo. A transit visa to Singapore has been granted to him in Tokyo and the Foreign Office are enquiring into the circumstances in which this was given.[10]

Occasionally, however, even the softly-softly Foreign Office approach resulted in diplomatic rows. One of these occurred in early 1938 when five Japanese agents were arrested. Tokyo kicked up a row based on the alleged mistreatment of these men while they were under detention. It is much more likely however, that Tokyo's anger was caused by the importance of one of the members of this group to their espionage network. This man was called Shohei Goma, which was an alias. He was a member of the important Nakajima family, and his elder brother a member of the

Japanese government. Shohei Goma ran an important network of Tamil and Malay agents who monitored the movements of British troops in Malaya. He and his colleagues were deported.

The names of the four agents deported along with Goma were Masaji Hosaka, Tamizo Tsujimori, Ippei Kai and Sakahiko Shirai. It was alleged that Hosaka had been engaged in spying since 1934, and that Kai, the owner of the Central Hotel in Singapore, was engaged in opium smuggling in league with Chinese triad elements, and that the proceeds of the smuggling was spent on spying activities. Tsujimori had links with a well-known Sumatran communist named Joseph Hassan who had visited Japan and there made contact with Rash Behari Ghose, the Indian independence movement militant. Shirai was an expert in explosives. These five men illustrate the range of Japanese spy interests and associated subversion, and reveal that there were links with criminal groups.

A further example of the kid glove approach by the British can be seen in the matter of Dr Tsune of the League of Nations. Special Branch had long suspected him of spying. He had been involved in the Nishimura affair, and in another incident in which two officers of the Japanese Navy were concerned.[11] Special Branch obtained evidence in 1937 that Tsune actually headed the spy network in Singapore. At the instigation of the Governor of Singapore the British government tried to have him removed, but played their hand very carefully indeed. Their representations to the League of Nations in Geneva were long and drawn out. The Secretary-General of the League said, on 10th February 1938, that he could not remove Tsune on his own responsibility without 'fairly detailed evidence of misconduct'.[12] The fact that Japan had quit the international body in 1933 should, perhaps, have made the matter easier, but there is no record of Britain using that ploy to get rid of the man.

Occasionally, keen police officers tended to rock the official British approach. In November 1938 Assistant Superintendent J.S.H. Brett of Singapore Special Branch searched the baggage of Akiyama Motoichu, travelling on a diplomatic passport aboard a Japanese vessel. This led to official apologies being made by the British minister in Tokyo.

Once in a while a case of such importance came along that the British decided on stronger action. In September 1940 Shinozaki Mamoru, the press attaché at the Japanese Consulate-General in Singapore, was arrested. He had been building up contacts with British servicemen since 1938 and a gunner of the Royal Artillery, Frank Gardner, was often seen in his company. Just a few days before his arrest, Shinozaki guided two visiting Japanese army officers around certain military areas in Singapore and Johore. In November Shinozaki was found guilty at the Singapore Assizes of obtaining military information from Gardner and others, and was sentenced to three-and-a-half years rigorous imprisonment in Changi jail.[13] The information Shinozaki obtained from Gardner concerned British troop movements, the presence of the liner/troopship *Queen Mary* in

Singapore, minefields, ammunition stores, the calibre and range of coastal defence guns, the whereabouts of the aircraft carrier *Eagle*, the types of aircraft in Malaya, and much more. For once the British acted strongly.[14]

The arrest and conviction of Shinozaki did not noticeably reduce the scale of Japanese espionage, but neither did it signal anything but a temporary halt in Britain's policy of non-provocation. On 11th March 1941, the Governor of Singapore reported to the Colonial Secretary in London that a known Japanese agent, Takasuki

> spent 21 days in Malaya during which he made four trips from north to the south by rail, motor car, and air. After one week in Singapore he left on a so-called sight-seeing motor tour visiting Johore, Malacca, Kuala Lumpur and Kedah thence Bangkok. He was under unobtrusive surveillance throughout and we know he visited many places where troops are stationed and defence measures have been taken.[15]

However, two months before the Japanese attack on Malaya, in September 1941, the Governor of Singapore reported that two members of the staff of the Japanese Club in Singapore had been arrested for possession and distribution of 30,000 copies of a highly seditious leaflet. One of these men, Hatsuro Hidaka, was sentenced to twelve months rigorous imprisonment, while the other was issued with a banishment order.

Japanese intelligence gathering activities sometimes resulted in reports that still astonish when read today. The effrontery of the Japanese and the do-nothing-most-of-the-time attitude of the Singapore authorities, both stemmed from the British non-provocation policy. In August 1941, for example, two Japanese submarines were reported seen berthed alongside the wharf owned by the Japanese iron-ore mining company at Endau. They left several men and some boxes of equipment behind. Both on arrival and on sailing they evaded detection by the Royal Navy which had ships patrolling the coast.

But even that incident fades into the shade when compared to the one witnessed by Captain C.E. 'Bob' Collinge of the Straits Settlements Volunteer Force (SSVF). Writing from his post-war home in Capetown in 1966 to the committee of the British European Association of Malaya (BEAM) who were compiling an archive of war reminiscences, he recalled:

> One incident remains firmly engraved in my mind, and this relates to my sudden encounter with a Jap officer in full uniform, when I was mobilised as OC Volunteer Armoured Car Company several months before Pearl Harbor, and when carrying out manoeuvres at Endau on the east coast of Johore.[16]

Collinge had drawn up his fleet of armoured cars in a line across the *padang* (the Malay word describing an open plain or area in the centre of a town or village) at Endau, when up drove a motor car with curtained windows. Collinge expected it to contain a Malay bridal pair, by whom such vehicles were used. It was impossible to see into the vehicle, and no-one in the rear of it could see out.

Let Captain Collinge himself take up the rest of the story:

The car pulled up within 20 yards of where I was sitting in my HQ vehicle and out stepped an officer in uniform. I do not know his rank, indeed I never really understood the Jap insignia, but that he was a son of Nippon I had no doubt. In the light of subsequent experience, I should know! He wore a peaked cap with a red hat band. I do not know who was more surprised, myself or the Jap; but he must have been a little startled upon finding himself confronted with a company of armoured cars drawn up in line! He did not glance right or left but put his head down and walked very quickly through the only gap in the line of vehicles, which was between myself and the next car, so that he almost brushed me. I told my CSM [Company Sergeant-Major] who was sitting with me to follow the officer and report his movements but unfortunately I failed to note the number of the car in which he arrived which immediately made off in the direction of Mersing. My CSM reported that the officer had descended the steps of a small attap-roofed jetty and boarded a sampan fitted with outboard motor in charge of a Malay, which made for the open sea. Apart from my CSM and myself, all ranks were resting or eating their lunch under some coconut palms about 100 yards distant, so that only a few actually witnessed the incident. I decided to make a report to Fort Canning [HQ Malaya Command, Singapore] where I sent two despatch riders on motor cycles, with a fairly detailed message. The reply indicated the importance of the officer being treated as secret and further instructions that it must not be discussed with anyone. At the conclusion of this period of mobilisation I received a visit at SSVF HQ in Beach Road from a British Staff Officer, who told me that the policy of the government at that time against Japan was appeasement and that any act which might give rise to an 'incident' was to be carefully avoided. The sequel to all this occurred after the war, when I was informed by some senior British Officers that it was well known that Jap officers were being landed on the Johore coast from submarines and that these generally changed from and into uniform while being conveyed by motor car to and from the area of their activities!

This story seemed so incredible to the BEAM archivists that they decided to run a check on Collinge's veracity, despite his having given his

CSM's name, Elsworth, in support of his statement, plus that of his second in command, Lieutenant Lance Walford, who also saw the incident. BEAM received reports that Collinge 'was highly responsible' and 'an impressive sort of bloke' who had conducted himself extremely well while a prisoner of the Japanese, acting as 'leader' of a camp hut, a highly dangerous position as it was the leader that the Japanese usually picked out for punishment.

Indirect support of Collinge's story came from Colonel J.D. Wyatt, who had been a Staff Officer in Singapore:

> The incident does not surprise me in the least. Nor the suggestion of 'appeasement'. I myself had left Singapore in September 1940 but we had even by that date information of Japanese intrusion and intrigue.

The policeman who had been in charge of the police at Johore before the war, I.S. Wylie, was not surprised at the report either and seemed to accept it as a run-of-the-mill event. He wrote that the Japanese officer at the centre of the story 'may have been an undercover military man who thought his cover had been blown and wanted to get out'.[17]

In addition to their own nationals the Japanese intelligence organisation in Malaya made use of local inhabitants, including followers of Wang Ching-wei, their puppet ruler in Manchuria. They also had contacts with Chinese triads in Singapore with regard to opium smuggling. The expert on such matters in the Singapore Police was Mervyn Llewelyn Wynne who, in 1941, held the third most senior police office in the country. He spent so much of his time producing reports on subversion and the links between Japanese agents and the triads that many persons at high level in the Malayan Civil Service dismissed them as signs of paranoia. H.P. Bryson wrote in 1972: 'I can still see Wynne creeping silently into my room with some blood-curdling information that the authorities wouldn't listen to.'[18] Wynne was a brilliant police officer, and his book *Triad and Tabut*, is still considered a standard work on Chinese triad and Muslim secret society activity.[19] It was no doubt because he considered insufficient notice was being taken locally of his reports that Wynne began writing directly and frequently to Sir Vernon Kell, head of MI5 in London. These reports were sent to Sir Vernon care of a General Post Office. The address used was 'PO Box Number 500, Parliament Square, London, SW1'. This part of Wynne's activities was carried on without the knowledge of his superiors.

The Japanese obtained most of their local support, however, among those Malays and Indians in the community with nationalistic leanings.

The number of militant nationalists among the Malay intelligentsia was probably never very great; so the number recruited by the Japanese would have been correspondingly small. The most important of them was Ibrahim bin Haji Ya'acob, a journalist who had been trained as

a teacher. In August 1941 he received Straits $40,000 (equivalent to
£160,000 today) from the Japanese Consulate-General's Office to purchase
an anti-government Malay newspaper, called *Warta Malaya*. According to
a secret Singapore Special Branch report dated March 1942, Ya'acob was
a double-agent, who had worked for the British for some time. Before his
arrest under the Defence (Emergency Regulations) at the outbreak of the
Japanese war, Ya'acob was kept in ignorance that he was known to be a
double-agent.

Among those arrested at the same time as Ya'acob was a prominent
actor and leader of a touring theatrical company, called Bachtiar Effendi
an Indonesian with strong nationalist views. He was arrested at Muar, in
Johore State. There he was interrogated by a FMS police officer, H.B.J.
Donaldson, who had been appointed Malayan Security Officer, Johore.
Although Effendi denied any connection with the Japanese, it was known
that he had used his touring company as a cover to spread nationalist and
pro-Japanese propaganda, had collected intelligence, and acted as a link
with other subversives. He was interned in Outram Road jail in Singapore.
After he was released from prison by the victorious Japanese he was seen
in the uniform of a Japanese officer. He was known to have made enquiries
about the whereabouts of Donaldson. Donaldson, who was in the civilian
prisoner of war camp, wrote in 1954, 'Fortunately perhaps, Effendi was
informed that I was amongst the officers who had left Singapore prior to
its capture.'[20]

Ya'acob's pro-Japanese activities involved recruiting candidates for an
anti-British youth organisation called *Kematuan Malaya Muda* (KMM).
The KMM was a front for a Japanese sponsored fifth-column organisation
which went under the code-name '*Kame*', the Japanese word for tortoise.
Kame had links with nationalist organisations in the Dutch territories to
the south, and Bachtiar Effendi was a high official in it.

As well as many teachers (most of them from the Sultan Idris Training
College, a school noted for producing nationalist-minded graduates), the
KMM also recruited a number of minor government officials. Also among
their numbers were Malay princelings and members of Malay military
and volunteer forces – serving with either British-raised units or their
own sultan – and some police officers. The Malay members, or suspected
members, of KMM on the Special Branch list at the outbreak of the war
numbered about one thousand.

The Malays, like most eastern races, had a penchant for secret societies.
Most of these were non-political, but at least one, the Perak River Society,
was very anti-British, and had connections with *Kame*. After the war began
Lieutenant D. Collings, a British Field Security Officer attached to the 11th
Indian Division, reported that members of this secret society were actively
assisting the Japanese as fifth-columnists.

Fifth-column activity in Malaya after the war began, however, did not
extend to sabotage except in a few isolated instances. The principal

fifth-column activity was the spreading of false rumour and propaganda, both of which involved little personal risk for the perpetrator. A more risky activity was that of acting as a guide for the attacking troops. While there were a good number of examples reported, in some cases the 'guides' were acting under compulsion and not from any desire to help the Japanese. Fifth-columnists were frequently engaged in visual signalling in one form or another; arrows made of various materials and laid so as to point to British positions, was a favourite ploy. Fifth-columnists were also reported to have arranged stocks of stores and transport behind the front line. A number of these were 'summarily despatched' when caught. Such summary execution also extended to people caught near the front lines. 'Field Security and other officers reported many cases of natives found within one mile of our front line being shot without further enquiry, the area in question having been declared an "evacuation area" by proclamation and consequently banned to civilians,' says one War Office report.[21] (One wonders how these proclamations were promulgated in a multi-lingual and mainly rural society.)

A young British officer of the 5/14th Punjab Regiment personally shot two natives found near the British front line north of the Slim River. This act horrified his subedar, Tor Khan, and the Indian soldiers in the company, for there was no direct evidence that the two natives were fifth-columnists.[22]

A member of the 2/4th Anti-Tank Regiment, Australian Imperial Force, Sergeant Kenneth Harrison, has written about two Malays he found carrying arms. After inspecting a road block, he wrote, 'On the way back we met two Malays who were carrying blanket-covered parcels. As they were heading for the Japanese lines we stopped and searched them, and found the parcels contained rifles and ammunition.' The Malays were handed over to HQ for questioning. 'That was the last we heard of them', says Harrison, 'but I fear – as fifth-columnists had been a constant problem during the campaign – that we may have been responsible for the loss of two lives.'[23] Most authorities seem to agree, however, that the effect of any fifth-column element in Malaya after the war began was minimal.

A secret 1942 report (only released in London in January 1993) indicates that Singapore Special Branch had strong suspicions about the loyalty of the then Sultan of Johore. [24] The report makes it clear that, to appreciate the nuances of this possibility it was necessary to know something of the Sultan's attitude towards the British. Although the Sultan was generally considered pro-British (see *The Times* obituary of 9th May 1959), the author of the 1942 police report casts doubt on this:

> The Sultan's attitude towards the British regime had never been particularly favourable, and the unfortunate affair of Lydia Hill (when the British authorities intervened to prevent his marriage to her) created in him a very bitter feeling towards us. He followed

her to London in 1938 where he continued his association with her, and there the Nazi Embassy staff took advantage of the situation and kindled in him a pro-Nazi attitude.

The author goes on to report that, after Lydia Hill (about whom a defamatory jingle went the rounds of men's clubs in London at the time, one which even reached India) was killed in a London air raid, the Sultan married a Rumanian woman. He returned to Malaya in January 1941, and was 'reported as still harbouring pro-Nazi sentiments'; but if the Sultan did hold such views it had not prevented him giving £250,000 towards the British war effort in 1940.

The report goes on:

> Under these circumstances soon after his return the Japanese sought to contact him and his entourage. Japanese business-men began to entertain prominent Malay personages of Johore, including personal friends of the Sultan and high-ranking Malay officers of the Johore Military Force [JMF]; and Japanese consular officials often attended these functions. The expense of these entertainments were provided by local Japanese firms, but they were instructed to debit the amounts to 'special account' of their Head Offices in Japan. As a result of this policy, there occurred in May 1941, a series of visits to the Japanese Consulate in Singapore by certain JMF officers who enjoyed the Sultan's confidence, as well by the Sultan's personal ADC.[25]

Singapore Special Branch was so concerned about this affair that, at the end of December 1941, three weeks after the Japanese attacked Malaya, they were recommending the Governor to request the Sultan to declare his position unequivocally. In January 1942 Special Branch received reliable reports that officers of the JMF were saying among themselves and to their men, that they would not have to fight the Japanese as the Sultan would not order them to do so. (The JMF should not be confused with the Malay Regiment which fought bravely against the Japanese.)

> The author of the report stated: 'As far as the writer is aware, the JMF were never in action, but it is not known whether this was due to our policy of withdrawal or to distrust of the JMF by our High Command.'

There were other reports of subversive operations in Johore. General Percival, GOC Malaya Command from 1941, has recorded that a powerful transmitter based in southern Malaya had been sending messages to Japan for some time. Its whereabouts had never been discovered. This may have been the same transmitter from which signals were picked up by the signals section of the 22nd Indian Brigade on 2nd July 1941. The transmitter was using the unknown call-sign 'BCA'. The British operators were given instructions not to contact the station.[26]

Australian signallers, after the war had begun, also picked up transmissions from a powerful radio in the extreme south of Johore. 'For lack of the latest interception equipment,' they were unable to trace its exact location, said Assistant Superintendent H.B.J. Donaldson who was acting as Malayan Security Officer, Johore, at the time. He reported that 'they knew it was somewhere in the vicinity of the Johore Royal *Astana* (or Palace)', but orders were received from High Command that nothing was to be done about this report either.[27]

There was a definite suspicion against the Sultan of Johore's third son, Ahmad, in this respect. Donaldson reported: 'It was known that he had a transmitter licence prior to the Japs attacking Malaya. He was also an officer of the JMF and, as such, was interested in wireless communications for the unit. With the help of an officer of the Australian Royal Corps of Signals attached to the 8th Division [Australian], I spent a long time trying to trace whether Ahmad was transmitting to the enemy but we had no suitable equipment. Ahmad's house was watched to no avail. Various steps were taken to send reliable people to visit the Astana where he lived, and the most we got was that there were lots of wireless parts in the house. The powers that be would not agree to a Police or Military search of the house.'[28]

The Australian Signals Officer Donaldson referred to was in fact Lieutenant R.G. Wells.[29] He, too, wrote a report but it differs in significant respects from Donaldson's. Wells's report was contemporary with the events; Donaldson's was written many years later. It could be that Donaldson's memory had failed him, or, because of the connection with the Johore Royal Family, he only reported an expurgated version of the events. Or could it be that he was deliberately kept in ignorance of some of the facts because it was considered an army matter? The Australian report also shows a dilatory attitude of some, at least, of the senior officers at Malaya Command over matters of suspected espionage, and indicates the care that the authorities took not to offend the Sultan of Johore.[30]

Illegal Wireless Transmitter in Johore Bharu

12 Jan. Lieut. R.G. Wells informed by Security Officer Johore Police that Int. Offr, Malaya Command had advised that an illegal wireless transmitter was operating in Johore Bharu.

(On 18 Dec 41 a permanent interception device had been connected across the telephone line of F.M. Still [Still's initials were in fact H.M.], secretary of the Royal Johore International Club who was suspect, but results to date negative.)

16 Jan 42. In view of lack of activity by Malaya Command, Lieut. Wells obtained permission to endeavour to locate the transmitter.

Two improvised D.F. sets were assembled by Sigs 8 Aust Div, and a tour was made of the suspected area, including the vicinity of the residence of Still, but without result.

17 Jan. Lieut. Wells obtained permission to use D.F. sets of Malaya Command Sigs, located at Kranji, under Capt. McMillan. Three D.F. vehicles were allotted for operation in Johore Bharu.

20 Jan. Twenty-four hour patrol of Johore Bharu and northern sector Singapore Island. Illegal transmitter located to within 2 fairly large areas, but owing to lack of more accurate apparatus, the set's position could not be pin-pointed.

21 Jan. it was decided to cut off power supply in Johore Bharu by sectors, and arrest Still. Permission to arrest refused by Malaya Command on the grounds that the arrest would upset the Sultan of Johore and result in non-cooperation of the Johore Military Forces.

23 Jan. Illegal transmitter opened at 0930 hrs. D.F. set taken to the vicinity of the J.B. power station and the Electrical Engineer ordered to switch off the power sector by sector. The results indicated the sector where Still and the third son of the Sultan of Johore resided – the set going off the air immediately the power in that sector was cut off.

27 Jan. Continued D.F. bearings indicated that the set was in close proximity to the residence of the Sultan's third son, Tungku Ahmad. Further police investigations placed the guilt of Still beyond doubt. Malaya Command authorised the arrest of Still on Singapore Island. On 27 Jan, when on a visit to Singapore, Still was arrested by the Military Police and handed over to Malaya Command.[31]

In his report on the Johore situation, Superintendent Donaldson also recorded that 'there were definite suspicions and a certain amount of accurate information about the loyalty of the Johore Military Force'. He went on: 'The most important information received was that the JMF would go over to the Japanese in toto when they arrived. In view of this information it was decided to disarm the JMF some days before the Japs reached Johore Bharu.'

Additional evidence about the unreliability of the JMF appears in a report made by the Australian Imperial Force (AIF) on 11th December 1941, three days after the Japanese invasion: a signals detachment of the JMF stationed at Mersing on the east coast had destroyed their equipment and abandoned their station. The AIF disarmed the men concerned.[32]

The writer of the secret police report went on to record more about the Sultan of Johore: 'Just prior to to the Japanese occupation of Johore (before our forces withdrew into Singapore) the Sultan made a speech which was on the verge of sedition, if not actually seditious.'

Despite this the police report provides no incontrovertible evidence that the Sultan of Johore was 'disloyal' to the British. As the Ruler of an Unfederated State he had the right to make political decisions for himself, and if he did act in a way to which the British took exception, this may well have been based on a chauvinism born out of 'Johore's well-being first, and anything else second'. This attitude was well-rooted in the ruling class of Johore, but the Sultan was also proud of certain of his connections with Britain. During the Japanese occupation he was invited to a function by senior Japanese Army officers, and came dressed in the uniform of the British Guards Regiment of which he was an Honorary Colonel-in-Chief.

The question of the Sultan's 'loyalty' concerned the authors of both the Australian and British Official Histories. In a letter dated 22nd September 1952, Gavin Long, of the Australian team, wrote the following letter (which is on file at the Public Records Office) to Major-General S.W. Kirby who headed the British side:

> As no doubt you knew, the Sultan of Johore was expansive in his hospitality to General Bennett [the AIF commander], and adopted a generous attitude towards the AIF in Malaya. On the other hand, a Japanese account refers to him as 'very pro-Japanese', and there does indeed seem to be some doubt as to whose interests, other than his own, he really served.
>
> In these circumstances, it is rather important to know as much about him as we can. It appears likely that the British authorities in Malaya kept him under fairly close surveillance. I imagine therefore that our best chance of getting the sort of information we want lies in reference to you.
>
> If you are in a position to help us with this problem, will you please let us know (a) whether any evidence exists to support the Japanese assessment of the Sultan and, if so, what it amounts to, in as specific terms as possible (b) what his standing now is in Malaya.[33]

There is no copy of General Kirby's reply in the official file. This matter was very likely subject to a deal between the political masters of both sets of historians, for no mention of the Sultan in this context is made in either history. This may have been because the evidence is inconclusive, or because the status of the Sultan in Malaya was such that neither the British nor the Australians wanted to raise a matter that might have affected their relations with that country. Perhaps someone concluded that, when it became evident in December 1941 that the British were

about to be defeated by the Japanese, the Sultan owed a duty to his State
and his people to make the best he could of the situation.

The author of the police report was on firmer ground when he accused
another high Malay personage of intriguing with the Japanese. This was
the Prime Minister of Trengganu (another of the Unfederated States), called
Tenku Stia. He links Stia with Ibrahim bin Haji Ya'acob:

> His [Stia's] complicity with [the Japanese] in what was known
> as the 'Rhio Sultanate Plot' was clearly established. This was a
> conspiracy to establish Tenku Stia on the throne of the Dutch
> island of Rhio, with Ya'acob as Premier designate, of course with
> the aid of the Japanese. In addition there appears to have been some
> understanding between Tenku Stia and the Japanese as regards
> Trengganu, and in this the ex-Sultan (who had been deposed by
> the British) was also involved.[34]

Whatever the true extent of Japan's success at subversion amongst the
Malays of all classes, it was not nearly so successful nor as widespread
as their operations among the Indians in Malaya. This extended not only
to Indians in civilian life, but also, and more importantly, to members
of the Indian Army and the Indian States Forces serving there. There
is evidence of the latter as early as 1939. In a Command Intelligence
Summary, numbered 8/39, and dated 30th September 1939, the following
report appeared:

> There are indications that the local Japanese are anxious to effect
> rapprochement with the newly arrived Indian troops. Indian
> Officers have been entertained by Japanese and more prominence
> to Indian matters is evident in the 'Singapore Herald', a Japanese
> newspaper printed in English.[35]

In their subversive endeavours the Japanese were assisted by local cells
of the Indian Independence League (IIL). The Japanese treated the 'Indian
affair' as a matter of considerable importance. Although India, with the
exception of Burma, did not fall directly into their plans for a Greater East
Asia Co-Prosperity Sphere, its situation on the western perimeter of the
area gave it tremendous significance.

A number of top Indian nationalists had based themselves in Japan after
escaping the clutches of the British authorities in India. These included
Rash Behari Ghose, once described by the British Foreign Office as the
'No. 1 enemy of British rule in India', and alternatively described by
Mahatma Gandhi as 'the patriot of patriots'. He had fled to Japan in
1912 after attempting to assassinate the then Viceroy, Baron Hardinge
of Penshurst. Rash Behari had married a Japanese, and their son was in
the Japanese Army.

Another Japan-based nationalist was A.M. Sahay who travelled the country making anti-British speeches. With the aid of these men and their contacts in the eastern countries of the British Empire, Japanese Intelligence seized the opportunity for subversion by providing funds and encouragement. The money spent was to pay huge dividends.

The Indian Independence League had an extensive network of agents in Malaya all busy in subversive operations,[36] and they scored a major success amongst civilians in the Port Swettenham (now Klang) area of Malaya in May 1941. An offshoot of the IIL, calling itself the Central Indian Association and funded by the Japanese, was involved in a serious outbreak of unrest during a strike by Tamil rubber estate workers. Fighting broke out between strikers and estate managers on such a scale that it could not be controlled by the police. Troops from the 1/13th Frontier Force of the Indian Army were sent in to quell the fighting. In retrospect it might have been better to send a British Army unit instead, for setting Indian against Indian could have done nothing for the morale of the Indian Army operating in a foreign land.

But the IIL's greatest successes were with the Indian Army and Indian States Forces based in Malaya. At the outbreak of the Pacific war the Indian Army provided almost fifty per cent of the combined British/Indian/Australian force in Malaya. The Indian States Forces were units raised and paid for by Indian Princes, but they were not part of the Indian Army proper, even though their commanding officers and certain seconded officers were supplied by the Indian Army. Nor were these units generally considered to be of a high standard.

Indian Army battalions based in India were largely insulated from the growing aspirations for independence of Indian nationalists although this insulation was occasionally pierced. The battalions were prideful 'families', and when based in their cantonments and garrison towns were very much self-contained. 'Pride in the regiment' had been fostered over many years, and the continuity of service of British officers who stayed with a particular regiment from subaltern right through to lieutenant-colonel was one of the central features of the system. With the coming of the European War in September 1939, and the consequent huge expansion of the Indian Army (it eventually became the largest non-conscript army the world has seen), this central feature became diluted. Battalions were 'milked' of experienced officers and NCOs who were posted to form the nuclei of new battalions. The officers brought in to fill the gaps were mainly 'war commissioned officers', some direct out from Britain and with little knowledge of India or Indians. Nor could they speak Urdu, the standard language of the Indian Army. Most of these new officers knew little about soldiering, and in many cases did not have time to learn before being thrust into active service.

The insulation of these battalions was severely breached when they were sent abroad to Malaya or the Middle East. There they came into contact with influences scarcely met with in the garrison towns of the sub-continent. Now, thousands of miles away from home, the protective barrier of tradition, usage and family spirit, was less effective.

There was another problem in Malaya, one which may have had a serious effect on some of the Indian units there. Since the 1920s the Indian Army had been going through the process of 'Indianizing' part of its officer corps. Certain Indian officer cadets were sent to Sandhurst and when they passed out they became King's Commissioned Officers (KCO), in exactly the same way as their British counterparts. Others, who passed out through Dehra Dun, the 'Indian Sandhurst', were called Indian Commissioned Officers (ICO), and were also on a par with British officers holding the King's commission. There was a third group of Indian officers, by far the largest, with commissions granted by the Viceroy – VCOs. These were not considered to be on the same level as the others. The most senior of them was subordinate to the most junior KCO or ICO, and VCOs messed separately from the other officers.

Within the confines of an Indian regimental town this influx of Indian officers caused comparatively few problems. There were instances of British commanders and officers farther down the line of command acting with bias towards them, but such instances were rare. Most of the commissioned Indian officers were treated in exactly the same way as their British counterparts, and that included being invited to social events. But there were no garrison towns in Malaya and so conditions were different. Invitations to outside events were often confined to British officers only, and this led to resentment. This attitude on the part of the local European community was not entirely racially inspired. Many of them did not like the army being in the country at all, and Australian officers were often ignored as well. (Apart from certain clubs manned by volunteer European ladies, all 'other ranks' of any colour were virtually ignored by the local European community – except to complain about their behaviour!)

In Malaya (as in Hong Kong) Indian officers became prime targets for the Indian Independence League. The IIL's success rate in creating or nurturing nationalist feelings among this group was high. When resentment of racial bias became mixed with nationalist feelings it created a volatile mixture.

One such event occurred in Singapore exactly a year before the Port Swettenham incident of May 1941. It took place at Tyersall Park Camp. The Indian Army battalion involved was the 4/19th Hyderabad Regiment, one of the battalions undergoing Indianization. Trouble arose when an Indian officer, Lieutenant Mohammed Zahir-ud-Din, wrote a seditious letter to an Anglo-Indian lady called Mrs Grantzer back home in Patna which was intercepted by the censor. The letter expressed the hope that the European War might last for ten years, so that the British Empire would be so exhausted that Indians would be able to turn the British out of the country. Zahir, it appeared, had also been passing on his pro-nationalist views to the Ahir sepoys of his company and to his fellow Indian officers. Another matter held against him was that he was living with a white woman in Singapore. Given the mores of the time this may have been considered by the authorities as being of equal importance to the alleged sedition! This lady was also German. (No explanation is given in the official file as to why a German national was living free in Singapore in May 1940.)[37]

When Zahir was ordered home 'as a result of highly undesirable conduct' and for expressing 'views which are considered to be highly objectionable', his Ahirs mutinied and refused to load their kit on to lorries which were due to take them on exercises. (Ahirs are an ethnic community of Rajasthan, then in northern India, now part of Pakistan.)

No doubt recalling the Indian Mutiny of 1915 in Singapore, the military authorities were taking no risks.[38] They placed on standby two companies of the Argyll & Sutherland Highlanders who were stationed in the same camp. Only the company commanders were told the real reason for the standby order, everyone else being led to believe it was over a strike in the city. The Argylls removed 60,000 rounds of ammunition from the Hyderabad's armoury and placed a guard over their weapons. Another ethnic group of the 4/19th, the Jats, took exception to this 'outside' guard, and trouble started amongst them as well, which lasted well into the next day. The situation was only defused when Zahir was permitted to say farewell to his men at a company parade before being shipped home.

An important matter, which may have had a bearing on this incident, was the fact that the Hyderabads had a new Commanding Officer, Lieutenant-Colonel E.L. Wilson-Haffenden. The sepoys did not know him and had therefore built up no trust in him. It was also reported that the men had no confidence in a British company commander, but the subsequent Court of Inquiry found this to be groundless. The Inquiry was unsatisfactory, however, in that there was a strong reluctance amongst Indian KCOs and ICOs to give evidence. The GOC, Malaya, General Bond, in his report to the Commander-in-Chief, India, stated that he considered the basic cause of the mutiny 'was political education of the Ahirs by Zahir, and that the mutineers were encouraged by the junior officers'. He ended by saying that the regiment was unreliable. Despite his recommendation, the regiment was not removed from Malaya.

Lord Zetland, the Secretary of State for India, was very perturbed about this affair. In a letter to Lord Linlithgow, Viceroy of India, dated 9th May 1940, he said, 'In view of the fact that the regiment in question is I believe an Indianizing unit, this may well prove to be a somewhat serious matter.' Further on in his letter, Zetland mentioned other examples of serious trouble. He commented, 'Following upon the trouble soon after the Indian brigades reached Egypt [as part of Force Heron in 1940] and the serious episode which took place on the [Northwest] Frontier some time ago when a number of English officers were shot, it gives one some cause for anxiety so far as some portions at any rate of the Indian Army are concerned'. He went on, 'I am not of course suggesting for one moment that there is any general disaffection, but one cannot altogether ignore incidents of this kind.'

This letter seems, in fact, to let a cat out of the bag, for although the 'Egyptian incident' receives attention in some books about the Indian Army, the frontier incident does not, although several officers of the Indian Army recall having heard of it.

The troublemakers involved in the 'Egyptian incident' never in fact arrived in Egypt. The Central India Horse (CIH), one of the most famous of the Indian Cavalry Regiments, had arrived in Bombay to be shipped to Egypt as part of Force Heron. It had previously been stationed at Meerut where Sikhs of the 6th Squadron had been in contact with an organization called *Kirti Lehar* which preached independence and a violent brand of communism. One of the classic ingredients of trouble in the Indian Army existed in this case. The previous commanding officer, who had been inefficient, had been relieved by an officer from outside the regiment whom the men had not yet got to know.

The train which brought the Central Indian House to Bombay was shunted into a siding for twenty-four hours, and during that time four of the Sikhs most affected by *Kirti Lehar* propaganda got to work, with the result that the majority of the Sikh *sowars* (cavalry troopers) refused to embark. The rest of the regiment sailed without them. (The ringleaders were court-martialled and deported to the Andaman Islands.)

Lord Zetland left the post of Secretary of State later in 1940. Had he still held the post in 1941 his worries over the morale of parts of the Indian Army would have increased. In March 1941, when Colonel Holt, the Defence Security Officer (MI5) at Hong Kong vacated that position, it was suggested that the post be filled permanently by an officer from the Indian Army or a Punjab Police Officer. In the meantime the post was temporarily filled by an Indian Army officer called Major Kilray who, with a police interrogator, had 'been sent from India to investigate subversive activities amongst Indian troops there'.[39]

The IIL subversion in Hong Kong was considered very serious and Air Chief Marshal Sir Robert Brooke-Popham C-in-C, Far East, based in Singapore, sent the following secret cipher to the C-in-C, India, No. 17299 dated 28th March 1941:

> Following for MI5. Security arrangements to protect Indian troops from enemy agents and local inhabitants in touch with subversive bodies have been under consideration here [Singapore] for some time but particularly since hearing the results of the investigation into trouble in Hong Kong. The situation here is probably less dangerous than in Hong Kong and both police and DSO [Defence Security Officer] are alive to the danger. I consider however that there is need for expert advice, and assistance from India should be sent to Malaya to

examine and report upon conditions in Indian units and put specialized knowledge pertaining to such units at disposal of DSO and civil security authorities. It might be necessary for this officer to remain here permanently. He should in the first instance be prepared to stay for three months and then return to India to report. (This message was endorsed 'MI5 for action'.)[40]

The worries that Brooke-Popham had about subversion amongst his Indian troops were well-founded though the British authorities at that time were only aware of the tip of the iceberg. The IIL was burrowing away at the loyalty of Indian troops, both officers and men. Their success can be measured, first by the lack of morale reported by British officers of several Indian Army battalions after the Japanese war began, and, second, by the number of Indians who, after capture by the Japanese during the campaign, rapidly joined the ranks of *Azad Hind Fauj*, the Japanese sponsored Indian National Army (INA). Lieutenant-Colonel E.L. Sawyer who, as a prisoner of war kept a list of officers who joined the INA, stated, at the end of his document, 'it appears likely from the foregoing and also from subsequent events that the Indian Army, especially among certain units, was subject to Indian independence propaganda prior to the outbreak of war'.[41]

Colonel Sawyer was right. Official British documents only released into the public domain in December 1993 show that there was concern at the highest level over the loyalty of Indian officers to the British Raj, not only in the Far East and Middle East theatres but in Europe too. Lieutenant-Colonel George Wren of the Frontier Force Rifles on secondment to Intelligence reported to Lord Wavell in December 1942 'that we have ... bred a new class of officer who may be loyal to India, and perhaps to [the Indian] Congress, but is not necessarily loyal to us'. Wren's report applied to Indian officers, but there were grave doubts about the loyalty of ordinary troops too. Colonel C.H.T. MacFetridge, of the Mountain Artillery, states that before his unit embarked for Burma from Calcutta in 1942, he received a letter from his GOC holding him personally responsible for any desertions from his unit. MacFetridge lined his men up and had them attest their loyalty in front of the Regimental leaders 'with one hand on a gun barrel'.[42]

For a long time Japanese broadcasting stations had been bombarding Malaya with pro-Indian independence programmes, and in early 1941 these grew in both frequency and aggressiveness. From stations on the island of Formosa they reported unrest among Indian troops based near the Malay-Thai border, stating that the Indians resented their treatment by British officers.

The intensification of propaganda directed at the troops in the north was one of the results of a visit to Thailand by Japan's Chief of Naval

Intelligence, Rear-Admiral Maeda, in April 1941. From that date the tempo of the entire Japanese intelligence and subversion operations in the north was stepped up several gears. As part of this, military officers in civilian guise were placed at the new Japanese Consulate recently opened at Singora. At their Legation in Bangkok, and at their consulates at Singora and Chiengmai, the Japanese now had nearly thirty military and naval attachés of one kind or another. The Japanese Legation spent over £50,000 per month on propaganda matters, according to a British intelligence report, and Colonel Tamura Hiroshi, the official military attaché, had other large sums available to fund espionage.

Thanks largely to the activities of the IIL, some of the Japanese propaganda was based on fact. One of the Indian States Forces battalions, the 1st Bahawalpurs, which had arrived in Malaya in March 1941, was an ideal target for the IIL. Again, the classical ingredient for trouble among Indian troops existed, for it had left India under a newly appointed commanding officer, Lieutenant-Colonel Roger Fletcher. Riddled with dissension even before it sailed from the homeland, and with several of its officers holding latent nationalist views, Fletcher's extraordinary behaviour during the voyage out exacerbated the situation. He found fault with everything, and spoke of the battalion in highly derogatory terms.

On arrival at Penang the battalion was assigned to the menial task – in military terms – of airfield perimeter defence at Sungei Patani as part of the 11th Indian Division. The Indian officers took this as an implied criticism of their professionalism. On top of that, when their tented camp was inundated by torrential rain, Fletcher took this as yet another sign of incompetence and began lashing out with his tongue and his feet. He kicked several officers and men.

Although attempts were made by Brigadier (later Major-General) D.M. Murray-Lyon, commander of the 11th Indian Division, to heal the breach between Fletcher and his Indian officers, they were of no avail. Fletcher was sent back to India leaving behind him a battalion still seething with dissent. The military authorities took this incident very seriously indeed. They summoned Major-General F. Gwatkin, Advisor-in-Chief to the Indian States Forces, from India in an endeavour to calm the situation. He did not have much success.

Several officers of this battalion, who later rose to high positions within the ranks of the Indian National Army, were known to have had contacts with IIL agents during the pre-war months. One of these was Captain A.D. Jahangir, described by one of his fellow Bahawalpur officers as 'a zealous advocate of independence'.[43]

There are many other examples of IIL influences at work on Indian officers in Malaya. Captain Mohan Singh, an ICO of the 1/14th Punjab Regiment, had long held nationalist views. He quickly came under the influence of the IIL, and within hours of his capture by the Japanese in the first few days of the war he was placed in command of the proposed INA with the rank of General.

Some Indian officers with nationalist tendencies were close to the heart of the British defence organisation in northern Malay. One of them, Captain Mohammed Zaman Kiani, again of the 1/14th Punjabis, was a staff officer at General Murray-Lyon's headquarters on Penang Island. Before the war he was closely associated with a Mrs Lakhsami. He joined the INA after capture, and she, as 'Captain Mrs' Lakhsami, commanded the women's regiment of that army.

Not even the Indian units in comparative isolation on the less developed east coast of Malaya, at Kota Bharu and Kuantan, were free from the subversive influences of the IIL. During the pre-war months there were many small incidents each bearing, with the benefit of hindsight, the hallmarks of IIL subversion. Some of these resulted in courts martial, the frequency of which and the scarcity of officers with sufficient service to serve on them, causing a problem.

On the evening of the first day of the Japanese attack on Malaya, 8th December 1941, sepoys of another Indian States Forces battalion, the 1st Hyderabads (not to be confused with the 4/19th Hyderabads of the Indian Army) shot and killed their commanding officer, Lieutenant-Colonel C.A. Hendricks, rather than stand and face the Japanese at Kota Bharu airfield. The proximate cause of this refusal to stand may have been their earlier sight of the groundstaff of the Royal Australian Air Force (RAAF) fleeing the aerodrome in disorder (see below, page 223), but there can be little doubt that the underlying reason was that the Hyderabads did not feel like fighting a war which had nothing to do with them, an argument often used by IIL agents.[44]

The incident with the Hyderabad's was two months into the future when the Japanese took the decision to step up their subversion in Indian Army ranks. In October 1941, they sent Major Fujiwara Iwaichi (who had been trained at *Nakano Gakko*, the Japanese Army Intelligence School), to Bangkok to set up *F-Kikan*. ('F' for Fujiwara, *Kikan* for organisation.) Earlier, at the headquarters of the Japanese 21st Army in Canton, China, he had made contact with three Indian civilians who had escaped from jail in Hong Kong where they had been confined for instigating anti-British activities. They told him that they wished to further the anti-British independence movement in co-operation with some of their comrades who had already been smuggled into Malaya from Berlin and India.

Fujiwara, together with his aide Lieutenant Yamaguchi, arrived in Bangkok on 28th October under an elaborate cover of secrecy and with the assumed names of Yamashita Koichi and Yamada Hajime. One of Fujiwara's first contacts there was a leading Indian nationalist named Pritam Singh. Singh reported the extent of the IIL's efforts to win over to the League many Indian soldiers in northern Malaya.[45] Fujiwara was to become the main Japanese influence behind the formation of the INA.

The British knew of his arrival in Bangkok because they had intercepted a Japanese message, but they did not know exactly what his duties were until secret Japanese documents were captured in January 1942.

Throughout South-East Asia, especially in Thailand and the Dutch East Indies, German and Italian agents were also heavily engaged in espionage and propaganda. Thailand, to the north of Malaya, was a neutral country (until it declared war on Britain and the United States on 25th January 1942). A report of the Far East Combined Bureau (FECB) – the top British Intelligence organisation in the area – dated November 1941, reported that several well-known German 'intriguers' including Baron Leopold von Plessen, and Major Franz Hueber of the Gestapo were operating from the German Legation in Bangkok.

There were even more German agents in the Dutch East Indies (DEI) to the south until the majority of them, along with their Dutch collaborators, were rounded up when Germany attacked Holland on 10th May 1940. According to the British Embassy in Batavia there were in 1940 more than 4,000 German and Austrian residents in the DEI, many of them having risen to high places in the civil administration, police and army.

Close working links at both central and local level were developed between the German, Italian and Japanese intelligence organisations. The best example of the co-operation at central level involved the capture and sinking of the British merchant vessel *Automedon*, in November 1940. A German raider intercepted this vessel in the Indian Ocean after being tipped off by Italian signals intelligence units in East Africa. The *Automedon* was carrying top-secret documents about British plans for the defence of the Far East. The Germans passed these onto the Japanese.[46]

At local level there was considerable contact between German and Japanese agents in Bangkok. The FECB report of November 1941 says, 'It can be taken for granted that if Japanese occupation of Thailand is in Germany's interest, any plans which have been made for this eventuality will receive the active advice and support of the German General Staff through their representatives in the country.'[47]

Some German agents passed as 'Dutchmen' in Malaya and Thailand. A British officer of the Indian Army, who was a spy in the pay of the Japanese in Malaya from his arrival there in late 1940 until he was arrested on 10th December 1941, was known to have been in regular contact with at least one such 'Dutchman'. The actions of this officer traitor, Patrick Heenan, were directly responsible for the virtual destruction of the RAF in northern Malaya during the first two days of the war, which resulted in Japan having air superiority throughout the campaign.[48]

Captain Heenan arrived in Malaya in October 1940 with his battalion, the 3/16th Punjab Regiment. He had been 'recruited' by the Japanese Intelligence Service during a six-months' leave he spent in Japan in 1938–39. Heenan was a highly unpopular officer, and soon after his arrival in Malaya his commanding officer, Lieutenant-Colonel (later Major-General) Frank Moore approached Captain D.J.R. Moore (later Lieutenant-Colonel – no family relationship between them) who was serving as a staff officer with the 11th Indian Division in northern Malaya. Colonel Moore 'was in a fury', and ordered that Heenan be posted away from the battalion immediately, saying Heenan was unsuitable and had made himself thoroughly disliked.

'The next posting away a day or two later was for an officer to go to Singapore for a three-month course in Air Liaison duties. So there I sent him,' reported Captain Moore.[49] 'I saw no more of him until after the Jap War had started about eight months later.'

Heenan was an Air Intelligence Liaison Officer (AILO) at the time of the Japanese onslaught on Malaya. 'The Japs were performing very successful and mysterious bombing of our Air Force on the ground,' Moore said. 'Our Intelligence somehow got on to him and searched his quarters thoroughly and found incriminating papers and evidence (hidden in picture frames etc.).' Moore reported how Heenan was arrested and sent to Singapore. He also said that during his training course in Singapore Heenan had joined a Japanese golf club and became friendly with a number of Japanese. Moore also stated that Heenan was 'in looks and personality very like a previous acquaintance of mine at school [Bedford] and Sandhurst; this was N. Wright who changed his name when leaving Sandhurst to Baillie-Stewart and was involved in a famous spy trial in London in the early 1930s'.[50]

Heenan, as an AILO with a grade of GS03, had access to much secret information and passed this on to the Japanese. He had taken part in pre-war army/air force exercises, had access to the daily changed air force recognition signals, had plane and squadron dispositions in northern Malaya at his fingertips, and would have had access to the British military dispositions in the north. On at least two occasions he gained unauthorised access to the Station Commander's safe at Alor Star airfield.

Heenan's interest in matters which would be of value to his Japanese controllers was wide. Squadron Leader Ronald E. Wardrop, who was Flight Sergeant armourer at Alor Star, reports that Heenan showed considerable interest in weapon loads, and 'asked many questions about the SCI [Smoke Curtain Installation]. Heenan wanted to know everything', says Wardrop. 'The purpose for which SCI could be used, and which planes could carry it. Later, of course, I knew exactly why he had been asking the questions.'[51]

Before the first air attack on Alor Star airfield on 8th December 1941, Heenan was heard to say that he thought the Japanese would use gas during their attacks. This has a direct link with his interest in the SCI installation for, as well as being used for laying smoke screens, the equipment was also designed to deliver mustard gas. Both the RAF and the British Army had the necessary equipment in Malaya to retaliate against any use of gas by the Japanese.

Heenan's superior officer was Major James France, RA. France's memoirs show that he had suspected Heenan of being a spy for some months before the Pacific War began. Further confirmation of these early suspicions has come to light. One of Heenan's fellow AILOs, who was second in command to France, was Captain Harry Landray, on attachment from the Royal Garhwal Rifles who were stationed at Kuantan. Major A.R.E. 'Dick' Clarke was the adjutant of that battalion. He says, 'One day Harry Landray phoned to confide that he was suspicious of a certain brother officer called Captain Heenan with whom he was working. He asked me to report this to our CO, Lieutenant-Colonel Guy Hartigan, which I duly did. Hartigan advised that Landray should rather report the matter to his own CO immediately, especially if Heenan was behaving in a manner likely to be potentially dangerous.' As Harry Landray was killed in a private plane crash some four weeks prior to the start of the Japanese war, these telephone conversations must have taken place in October 1941 or even earlier. Dick Clarke cannot now remember how much earlier it was, only 'that it was sometime before the war'.[52]

These suspicions were not acted upon. This is an extreme example of the kind of blinkered vision that nearly everyone, military and civilian, suffered from in Malaya at that time. Following the Churchill line that there would be no war with Japan, a line often reiterated by the Governor of Singapore and other civilian and military leaders, most people believed them. But even so, it seems extraordinary that an officer who was under suspicion was allowed to carry on in a position within the intelligence community.

Major France was convinced that Heenan attempted to murder him during the night before he was arrested. This has led two Indian Army officers who served in Malaya at the time to postulate that perhaps the airfield death of Harry Landray was not an accident, as he too had suspected Heenan. This is a possibility that cannot be ruled out. Heenan had access to airfields and had flown in planes during training exercises, and had made a point of befriending several RAF groundcrew, including Warrant Officer Swindlehurst, the chief engineer at Alor Star. He could have easily learned how to best sabotage a plane.

Heenan was arrested two days after the Japanese attack on Malaya, having by then been responsible for relaying by radio the aircraft situation at the northern air fields and so enabling the Japanese to catch aircraft on the ground again and again. At the time of his arrest he had in his possession two radio transmitters, one which looked like a typewriter and another fitted into the leather case of a field communion set. He had a code book in the form of a bible. Among the documents found on him were copies of 'situation reports' he was not supposed to have. A contemporary source, written on the very day of Heenan's arrest, says that he was in charge of the entire Japanese spy network between Penang and the Thai border.

An Inquiry into the Heenan affair was held at Taiping on or about the

15th December at which many of his contacts at the aerodromes were interviewed. It can be no coincidence that on that date the following entry appeared in the War Diary of Malaya Command HQ:

2210 hrs. 15/12/41
Lieutenant Butler reported 11 Division cyphers had been compromised and Captain Francom had taken immediate steps to send fresh cyphers to 3rd Indian Corps for 11 Division.

That was followed by:

0025 hrs. 16/12/41
Francom reported that only 11 Division cyphers compromised.[53]

Heenan was court-martialled in Singapore in January 1942. His service in the Indian Army from 1935 onwards had been characterised by his closeness to Indian officer colleagues. In Malaya he was closely associated with officers with IIL leanings. The prosecution at the court martial tried to implicate one of these, Captain A.D. Jahangir, but there was insufficient evidence against him. Heenan was summarily shot on Friday 13th February 1942.

After the fall of France in June 1940 a few Vichy French agents from Indo-China were active in Singapore. One of them, Commandant Maurice Lenormand, was condemned to death by the Free French organisation there, but was rescued by the victorious Japanese before the sentence could be carried out.

The headquarters of the Free French organisation in the Far East was in Singapore, and it had the effect of largely nullifying whatever Vichy French espionage activities existed there. The Free French were headed by a man called C.F. Baron. The territories covered by the organisation and its local leaders were: Singapore (Brizay), Malaya (de Langlade), Thailand (Charleaux) and the Dutch East Indies (Ricard). In Singapore, Malaya and the Dutch East Indies there was a purge of Vichy sympathizers, some of whom were shot. The secretary of Brizay's organisation in Singapore was Gabrielle Lyon, the French wife of Captain Ivan Lyon of the Gordon Highlanders who was on attachment to the security services in Singapore. It was she who helped to interpret for Singapore Special Branch officers when Lenormand was arrested. One of the two liaison officers attached to Baron's HQ was Second-Lieutenant Pierre Boulle who after special training was sent into Indo-China. There he was captured by the Japanese but survived to write *The Bridge on the River Kwai*.

In this account of Axis espionage and subversion in the Malayan area, there is one curious story only fragments of which can at present be told, about a man who arrived in Malaya in January 1942 with elements of the British 18th Division. He had been recruited in India under the surname Ross. When he arrived in Singapore as part of a transport company he held the rank of sergeant.

J.B. Masefield, a senior FMS policeman, both before and after the war, wrote: 'I did tell you of the extraordinary story of Sergeant (Herr) Ross, a German who had some experience as a teacher in the Hitler Leadership School and fetched up pre-war in Karachi as the Assistant German Consul'.[54]

Ross – we will call him that – had spent some time in Czechoslovakia where he had been described as being a dangerous Nazi. In Karachi at the outbreak of the European War he had apparently 'gone over' to the British, explaining that his wife had been treated badly by the Gestapo. He was given funds which were said to have been authorised by the Foreign Office in London. Why he was permitted to join the British Army and sail with the 18th Division from India is not known.

After the capitulation of Singapore he was placed in Changi camp. Described as 'strongly built, not particularly tall, but with a strong voice', he gave a series of lectures in the camp which were pro-German in content. Then one day he was taken away by Japanese guards and was not seen in the camp again. This case is one of the many little mysteries that still surround the fall of Singapore.

By the eve of their attack on Malaya, the Japanese espionage and subversion organisations had paved the way for what was to be a rapid and highly successful campaign. Their intelligence gathering was much more efficient than the British counter-operation, a point acknowledged in a FECB report: 'Japanese espionage and intelligence activities are widespread, efficient and comprehensive. It can be assumed that their reconnaissance of the country has been largely completed; there can be no doubt whatever that their information is much more complete than ours.'

But perhaps of equal importance is the fact that through the agency of the Indian Independence League, the Japanese had nurtured and extended feelings of nationalism in the ranks of some of the Indian Army battalions in Malaya. As the Indian Army formed nearly fifty per cent of the force that was to oppose the Japanese, this factor was not only very important indeed, but it is one the effect of which has been underestimated in most histories of the campaign.

Chapter Five

British Intelligence and Counter-Intelligence

The outstanding characteristic of the pre-war British intelligence and counter-espionage operations in Malaya is their fragmentation. There were over a dozen organisations and committees concerned and, some of these reported directly to ministries in London and not to anyone in authority in Malaya. This led not only to failures and delays in disseminating information and to the duplication of activities, but also to cases where one ministry's operatives were undertaking activities inimical to the expressed policies of others.

Although belated attempts were made to co-ordinate the work of these bodies they were not very successful. On top of that, many parts of the system were amateurishly run and some of the information disseminated was unreliable. Unfortunately, overall effectiveness was also diminished by what can only be described as a deliberate lack of co-operation between certain sections of the intelligence community. Evidence has been uncovered which reveals personal antagonisms and petty jealousies, spoiling tactics by persons out to protect their own little empires, and the actions of others who thought their authority was being undermined.

When one adds to this that most of the constituent organisations within the British intelligence community were hampered by severe cash restraints, it is of little wonder that the efforts of British intelligence in Malaya were poor compared to those of their Japanese counterparts.

No post-war Court of Inquiry armed with all the facts could have failed to reach that conclusion.

On the civil side there were several police authorities in Malaya – the Straits Settlements, the Federated Malay States, and one each in the states constituting the Unfederated Malay States. The SS and FMS each had its own Special Branch, and equivalent organisations existed in some of the Unfederated States. All of these were engaged in gathering information on foreign agents, subversives, and prospective fifth-columnists, although one suspects that the UMS police forces did not have the facilities to work assiduously to this end, even assuming that the desire to uncover such things was there in the first place among the predominantly Malay officers.

The SS and FMS Special Branches were divided into sections with clearly defined responsibilities. Amongst these were the Chinese and the Japanese sections.

Immediately before the Pacific War, Special Branch in Singapore had contingency plans to round up suspected fifth-columnists among the Japanese community. About 500 arrest warrants had been prepared against named individuals who were thought to be potential saboteurs. The warrants were held by the Governor and were only to be used – because of the non-provocation policy – on express instructions from Whitehall. In the event they were never served because within hours of the Japanese attack, every Japanese national in Singapore and Malaya apart from a handful who managed to escape, were rounded up under the so-called Operations 'Collar' and 'Trousers'.

In addition to the Police Special Branches the following intelligence organisations and services operated from headquarters in Singapore:

1. *The Far East Combined Bureau* (FECB). This was staffed by officers of all three Services, but came under the aegis of the Admiral, C-in-C, China Station (latterly C-in-C, Far Eastern Fleet). Its scope extended far beyond the Malayan area, but its interest in Malayan matters was intense due to the existence of the Singapore Naval Base. It had close connections with the Pacific Naval Intelligence Organisation.

2. *Malaya Command.* The military intelligence arm of GOC, Malaya, it operated its own agents in Malaya and in adjacent countries. This was not very efficient prior to mid-1941. In July of that year Major A. Chamier arrived to take charge, and its efficiency improved, although far too late.

   The 8th Australian Division had its own intelligence arm in Malaya. It worked in conjunction with British military intelligence.

3. *Naval Command.* Naval intelligence under the Naval Intelligence Officer. Although largely absorbed into the FECB when that organisation moved to Singapore from Hong Kong in 1938 it still retained some of its duties, including liaison with the Malayan Customs Service and the Master Attendant (the title given to the Harbour Master in Singapore's commercial docks).

4. *Air Command.* The RAF had a small intelligence unit in the area.

These four organisations, while maintaining direct liaison with the various civil police forces, were officially connected with them through the office of:

5. *The Defence Security Officer (DSO).* This was a War Office

MI5 appointment. The DSO was responsible to Sir Vernon Kell, Head of MI5 in London. The DSO's duties covered local security within the armed services. He had direct access to the Governor of Singapore and worked from an office at Police Headquarters. The DSO was appointed Secretary of the Defence Security Committee which, under the chairmanship of the Inspector-General of Police, examined and recommended upon all matters pertaining to security in Malaya.

6. *Secret Intelligence Service (SIS)*. This was MI6, and the local head of it was responsible to the Director, MI6, at the War Office in London. However, MI6 was funded out of the Foreign Office secret vote and on matters dealing with diplomatic intelligence had direct communications with the Foreign Office in London. (A.H. Dickinson, the Inspector-General of Police in Singapore, always referred to the top SIS man in Singapore as the 'Foreign Office Intelligence representative'.)

The Singapore SIS office was set up in 1940, and its function was 'to build up a comprehensive picture of the persons and organisations working against British security in the Far East and to convey this to the various organisations who are in the position to make use of it'. In an early draft of his official dispatch on the Malayan campaign, Air Marshal Brooke-Popham included the following note which was left out of the final version: 'The weakest part of the Intelligence system was the SIS. In the Spring of 1941 the different sections of this were working somewhat independently, and I was not at all satisfied that they were getting the information that was wanted, and that should have been available. Mr. Denham was officially appointed to take control of the SIS and matters improved considerably after this, but there was too much leeway to make up and to have got the Secret Service working satisfactorily improvements should have been started two or three years before.'

The head of SIS in Singapore, G.C. Denham, used the same office as MI5 with the title Assistant Defence Security Officer as his cover. Denham's name does not appear in the Foreign Office Lists of the time.

7. *Ministry of Economic Warfare (MEW)*. In May 1941 the Special Operations Executive (SOE) which came under Dr Hugh Dalton, the Minister of Economic Warfare in London, opened an office in Singapore. It was known as the Oriental Mission (OM). Its remit covered sabotage, subversive activities, and black propaganda in enemy, enemy-controlled, and neutral countries.

8. *Malayan Customs Service*. This service, with its complement

of over 100 European senior officers who were stationed all over the country, was used as a valuable source of intelligence. After the war began, many of the officers joined military units as intelligence liaison officers.

9. *Malayan Security Service* (MSS). As the political layout of Malaya necessitated multiple and separate Police Forces and concomitant Special Branches, the so-called 'Fortress Defence Scheme' set up by MI5 provided for a civilian equivalent of the DSO called the Civil Security Officer (CSO). This position was filled by the Inspector-General of Police, Straits Settlements. In 1939 this officer (A.H. Dickinson) recommended the setting up of the Malayan Security Service. This was designed to co-ordinate the work of the various police organisations, to establish central control of and uniform legislation for aliens, and to provide security control along the Malay-Thai border. Dickinson's committee included the MI6 officer, G.C. Denham. There were a number of local Security Officers (including H.B.J. Donaldson who held this post in Johore). This organisation did not supplant the old civil intelligence services. The Malayan Security Service never really got off the ground, only being operational for a few months before Japan struck.

This summary of British intelligence organisations is based partly on information contained in the papers of A.H. Dickinson,[1] who wrote this overall comment on Military Services Intelligence in Malaya:

It is doubtful whether any Service Intelligence Unit can operate with full efficiency in any Asiatic part of the Empire under normal peace conditions. (In war or disturbances special measures operate.) The Services are handicapped by lack of adequate local knowledge. Few service 'Intelligence' officers remain long enough in Malaya to become familiar with local conditions. They must necessarily obtain their assessments from others; and in some instances they have relied on sources not always known to the local civil authorities as the best judges. In Malaya it is doubtful whether there were even two officers who had an adequate knowledge of the local language and conditions. In certain aspects of intelligence this lack was not of course detrimental, but danger did lie in the use by Intelligence Officers of local agents, on whom control was tenuous. It is doubtful also, whether by reason of the multiplicity of organisations, it was realised how frequently work was duplicated and trails crossed. There was also, it was felt, a failure to appreciate, through inadequate knowledge of local conditions, how frequently the various service organisations could have helped each other.

This last sentence in Dickinson's summation implies that, sometimes at least, the Service organisations did not assist each other. The office of the Defence Security Officer, for example, one of the linchpins of the entire system, should have been held by a young and highly qualified officer with a flair for political assessment. It was no post, Dickinson said, for an elderly or retired officer. He was hinting at a certain lack of dynamism within military intelligence ranks, and not without cause. The FECB itself was staffed with a plethora of officers of colonel, group-captain and naval captain rank, most of whom had been dragged out of retirement.

Dickinson's views on the failure of co-operation between the various intelligence arms are echoed in a secret police report made in 1942.[2] Its authors were police officers who escaped from Singapore, and reported that 'general co-operation between the Special Branch and the military, naval, and RAF intelligence organisations might, we are inclined to feel, have well been considerably closer with advantage to all concerned'.

Some obvious overall conclusions can be drawn from this list of intelligence organisations. In the first place there were too many, and some had overlapping responsibilities. There were also examples of personnel having what seems to be have been dual lines of responsibility: Colonel Gordon E. Grimsdale, Director of Military Intelligence at the FECB, was also part of the structure of the Military Intelligence arm of General Percival's Malaya Command. (This particular example of 'duality' may not have had deleterious results, but others did.) The phlethora of organisations also resulted in too many channels of communication with London.

In a book published in 1992, Sir Andrew Gilchrist made the comment that little had been written about British Intelligence in the Far East. He noted that the area had been almost totally excluded from the five volumes of the official series entitled 'British Intelligence in the Second World War'.[3] He stated that 'when a proper book is written on this subject, I feel sure that the FECB will emerge with credit'. Sir Andrew's views may perhaps have been coloured by his friendship with one of the officers who worked in that organisation – Major 'Porky' Ewing. While certain sections of the FECB, especially the cryptographic section, did carry out excellent work, several authorities in a position to know disagree with Gilchrist on the *overall* expertise of the organisation.

In his post-war dispatch General Percival notes that, 'it must be recorded that HQ Malaya Command was not well supplied with information either as to the intentions of the Japanese or as to the efficiency of their Fighting Services'. He goes on, 'a representative of the FECB painted a very indecisive picture of the Japanese intentions'.[4]

Lieutenant-Colonel B.H. Ashmore, General Staff Officer, Malaya Command (GSOII Operations & Training), who escaped from Singapore, was much more forthright about the standard of both military and civil intelligence authorities, and FECB in particular. 'In my opinion the military and civil intelligence service in Malaya prior to the outbreak of hostilities was extremely incompetent. The FECB used to produce intelligence summaries which were generally noteworthy for their complete lack of intelligence.'[5]

The FECB was not the only intelligence organisation capable of putting out the sort of rubbish of which Colonel Ashmore complained. The following is an example which seems to have emanated from SOE. A M01 Collation File contains a copy of the following cipher message, No. 55023, 5/3/1941, from the War Office to the C-in-C, Far East:

> 1941 is Shintoist year of the serpent. Serpent is closely connected with Japanese Sun-Goddess Amaterasu-O-Mi-Kami and Japanese know anything undertaken in serpent year must be fatal to Japan.[6]

Lieutenant-General Sir Lewis Heath, Commander 3rd Indian Corps in Malaya, made several comments on the standard of British intelligence gathering, none of them complimentary. He was highly critical of British inactivity in the face of the Japanese intelligence activity and complained of the 'crabbed work of our Secret Service and counter-intelligence services'.

An example of an apparent lack of 'fail-safe' follow-up procedures by FECB operatives is shown in the British Official History of the Malayan campaign. In May 1941, it notes, a Japanese Zero fighter was shot down in China. It was reported to have a top speed of 325 miles per hour, considerably in excess of the maximum speed of the RAF Buffaloes in Malaya. This information was forwarded to the Air Ministry in London and to Air Command, Far East, by the British Legation in Chungking. Additional information was passed on by the FECB to Air HQ, Far East, in September, but 'faulty organisation at HQ Far East, whose establishment did not include an intelligence staff, resulted in this valuable report remaining unsifted from the general mass of intelligence information, and no action was taken upon it'.[7] The statement that the RAF establishment in Singapore did not include intelligence staff conflicts with what Dickinson says. The Official History contains many errors, but even if this was not one of them, there were certainly RAF intelligence officers up to the rank of Group-Captain within the FECB organisation and they surely should have noted the importance of this information and seen that it was brought to the attention of the C-in-C, Far East, who was, after all, an airman himself.

Even if this information had reached Brooke-Popham, however, it is unlikely it would have made any difference to the supply of aircraft to Malaya. London was adamant that there were no aircraft to spare and that supplies to Russia must take precedence. Furthermore, even if the top air force brass in Singapore were unaware of the full capabilities of the particular Zero shot down in China, they already knew that the Japanese had superior aircraft to any the British had in the Far East. A booklet issued by the General Staff, Malaya Command, in March 1941, entitled 'Japanese Army Memorandum', listed, among other things, the capabilities of all the then known Japanese aircraft in some detail. It left no doubt that in fighter-planes and torpedo-bombers, the British equivalents were vastly inferior in performance, and that Japanese bombers had at least an equivalent performance to the British Mark IV Blenheim. This General Staff memorandum gives the lie to the oft-mentioned British understimation of the qualities of the Japanese fighting man. Anyone who had read the booklet would have been in no doubt that the prospective foe was a powerful one.[8]

A different view of the FECB has been given by one of its officers, Colonel Grimsdale. He left Singapore in January 1942 to take up the post of Military Attaché at Chungking. On 5th January 1942 the FECB moved, lock, stock and barrel to Colombo aboard *Devonshire*. On 8th March 1942 he wrote from Chungking to his personal friend, General Ismay, Churchill's Chief of Staff blaming officers at the GHQ in Singapore for ignoring much of the intelligence supplied to them:

> Owing to the parsimony of the Treasury in past years, there are so very few officers who know anything about the Far East. I sometimes wonder whether the events of the last three months will bring home to those who refused to allow us to spend more than a few hundred pounds on training language officers (the Colonel, although based in China, could not speak Chinese) and building up a proper 'I' staff out here, the fact that much of the Japanese success has been due to the *very* large sums they have spent on an absolutely first-class intelligence organisation. And it is rather tragic to know that in spite of every kind of warning of what was going on for example in Malaya, none of the local government officials would believe it or take any steps to keep the Japanese under proper control.

Grimsdale was being unfair here, as he made no reference to the non-provocation policy of the British Foreign Office, which had prevented much action being taken about the Japanese in Malaya pre-war. Grimsdale went on:

> I have always felt that one of the worst bits of bad luck was when Dicky Dewing had to be invalided home (Dewing had been Chief of Staff, Malaya). He had an appallingly difficult job and a very patchy staff to help him. Yet he had the whole thing so well

taped that if he had been able to carry on I am perfectly certain his presence would have made an immense difference. We in the FECB perhaps felt his loss as much as anyone. Although, God knows, our sources of information were nothing like as good as they should have been, they were the best available, and Dicky invariably relied on us. Directly he went the rest of GHQ staff never believed us and always called us 'alarmists' when we told them how many divisions or aeroplanes the Japs could use. As it happens, our estimates were more accurate even than we had suggested they were. On the day before the war started one of the GHQ staff said publicly that he couldn't understand why the Governor had got the wind up and mobilised the volunteers! If that was the attitude of GHQ, you can understand why people lower down adopted a complacent attitude.[9]

Air Chief Marshal Brooke-Popham had no high regard for certain sections of the intelligence community. According to him the Secret Intelligence Service, or MI6, organisation in Singapore and the Far East, showed little in the way of expertise. He sent the following cipher message, to the Air Ministry in London on 6th January 1941:

GHFE 138

Recent visit to Hong Kong completes my view of intelligence organisation in Far East. Weakest link undoubtedly is SIS organisation. At present little or no reliance is placed upon SIS information by any authorities here and little valuable information in fact appears to be obtained. I am satisfied that identity of principal officers at Shanghai, Hong Kong and Singapore is known to many. Their chief subordinates are in general local amateurs with no training in Intelligence techniques nor adequate knowledge of military, naval, air, or political affairs.[10]

One of the most flagrant examples of lack of co-operation between sections of the British intelligence-gathering community in Malaya is to be found in the experiences of Colonel Hayley Bell, the Defence Security Officer in Singapore from 1936. Hayley Bell had commanded the 10th Royal Regiment, Queens, in World War One during which he had been awarded the Distinguished Service Order. He spent many years in the Far East although not in Malaya. Both before the 1914–18 war and after it, until he retired in 1931, he served in the Chinese Maritime Customs Service rising to the rank of Commissioner. Born and brought up in Shanghai until he attended school in Britain, he spoke several Chinese dialects fluently.

Hayley Bell's job as Commissioner in the Chinese Maritime Customs was a roving one, and he had been closely associated with British intelligence operations in China. He may have been an undercover MI5 agent there. For his official work he had the use of a small custom's gunboat. His daughter (Mary Hayley Bell, Lady Mills) says he moved his base several times, stationed variously at Shanghai, Peking, Hong Kong, Macao and Tientsin. He was much respected in Chinese circles, and in 1920 was awarded a Chinese decoration. At one point in his career he was Preventive Commissioner and Non-Resident Secretary at the London office of the Chinese Customs Service.[11]

After taking up his MI5 appointment in Singapore Hayley Bell travelled the length of the peninsula sometimes accompanied by his two daughters who assisted him with his office work. Guy Madoc, Officer Commanding Police Department (OCPD) at Kuantan, remembers him, and more particularly, the daughters. 'Hayley Bell turned up at Kuantan sometime between late June and October 1938 with his two striking daughters. He stayed at the Rest House (a government-run hotel) and phoned me one evening. Said he wanted to brief me on something highly confidential. We arranged to meet under a distinctive tree on the golf-course at the back of the Rest House. The meeting was brief. He said he was investigating some conjectural military preparations by the Japanese on the east coast of Siam. He asked if I knew anything, and I answered, "no". He told me that he had an agent currently in Siam and that he might travel south down the east coast and requested that I help him if he arrived in the area. I agreed, and afterwards the colonel invited me to breakfast. I remember meeting the tall and dishy daughters.'[12]

The working and personal relationship between Hayley Bell and the police officer heading the Japanese section of Singapore Special Branch was extremely bad. This man was Major Kenneth S. Morgan, who had taken up the post in 1936.[13] He found Hayley Bell absolute anathema, and the feeling was probably reciprocated. It is possible that some of this antagonism may have stemmed from earlier days in China, where Morgan too, had served. Be that as it may, in 1936 and thereafter Morgan considered that Hayley Bell was trespassing on his own personal patch.

Morgan was an odd man. Most people found him difficult to work with. He suffered from emphysema which brought on bouts of acute breathlessness. He thought he was in perpetual danger of assassination because of his job, so both he and his secretary led a sort of cloak and dagger existence. He had a disconcerting habit of suddenly dropping off to sleep in the middle of a sentence. This happened at Pearl's Hill Jail in late 1937 when he was in the process of interrogating Shohei Goma, one of the most important Japanese agents in Malaya. Morgan and his secretary, Miss Barbara Brown, were locked in an office together with Goma when Morgan dropped off in mid-sentence. Barbara Brown says, 'Goma and I looked at each other – he, I suppose, thinking he might escape, I, thinking of what he could do to me – so I quickly kicked Morgan under the table and the interrogation went on.'[14]

No sooner had Morgan joined the Japanese section of Special Branch than he became something of a law unto himself. It seems that René Onraet, the Inspector-General of Police in Singapore prior to 1939, wielded little control over this particular subordinate.[15] Morgan would never divulge the names of his undercover agents and informants to anyone, not even to his superiors. He insisted for security purposes on having an office of his own. He had his own private secretary, kept his own files and refused to use the Central Office and its clerks. He jealously guarded his voluminous files, which were only partially kept under the official filing arrangements; he built into the system personal idiosyncrasies which ensured that no one could get at them easily without the assistance of himself or his secretary.

So active was Morgan's antagonism towards Hayley Bell that he refused him all access to the files. This made life extremely difficult for Barbara Brown. She says: 'HB used to wander aimlessly into my office and try to get me to show him the files without Morgan knowing, but I couldn't do it, although personally I thought it was very odd and was obstructing HB in his job.'

Barbara Brown's letters are strong evidence that, in counter-intelligence, there was little co-operation in pre-war Malaya between the civilian and military arms. But even stronger evidence of this can be found in reports written by none other than Colonel A.E. Percival, General Dobbie's GS01 and, later, GOC, Malaya Command, at the time of the Japanese victory. Submitted in October 1937 to General Dobbie, Percival's reports indicate that Morgan had information about potential sabotage of military installations in Singapore, information that he had decided, most extraordinarily, to keep from the army.

During a series of security meetings held in the period August–October 1937 between Dobbie, René Onraet, and some of their subordinates including Percival, attempts were made to rectify this lack of co-operation. An office was made available for Hayley Bell at Police Headquarters. Onraet stated that the police 'are always ready to supply the DSO with information on any subject, and that he would be supplied with a monthly précis of the security work undertaken by the police'.

Despite this promise, Morgan continued to hold out. In October, Onraet, under considerable pressure himself, at last leant on the Head of his Japanese section. At a meeting held on 12th October 1937 a statement prepared by Morgan was read out. It detailed information of Japanese activities in Singapore collected by the police over the past five years. It was pointed out, in what seems to have been an attempt to cover up Morgan's intransigence, that under ordinary circumstances none of this information would have been disclosed to anyone outside the police, 'because none of it had been confirmed', though Morgan had expressed the opinion that 'the information concerned can be accepted as being correct'.

A narrative report of this particular meeting kept by Colonel Percival is an indictment of Morgan's attitude which seems to have bordered on mania. Morgan had received information that Japanese agents had buried explosives under defensive works in the Kranji and Changi areas of Singapore, and that explosives had also been placed by Japanese salvage companies on wrecks in the harbour. He had not previously reported this to the military. Morgan's view was that it was not necessary to report the matter of the hiding of a large quantity of explosives in the Kranji area – 'enough to blow up the whole of Singapore', commented Percival – because there was so much explosive legitimately stored by Japanese mining companies in Malaya, 'that the enemy would not need to use this hidden store, and that it was impossible to find by search anyway'. Morgan also commented that the Services were trying to tell him how to run his show, and he was not going to have it.

Percival's summing up of this situation began with a masterpiece of understatement. 'There has,' he wrote, 'been a lack of frankness.' He appreciated the desire to provide only *proven* information but 'considered that the items of information about Kranji and Changi should most certainly have been communicated to the DSO – the latter particularly as the police considered the information sufficient to take action to intercept the explosives'.

His words grew stronger later. 'Readiness to supply the DSO with information is not apparent. It is not possible to feel any confidence in the abilities of Major Morgan. His statements and views ... convey this very strong impression formed by the DSO and Services representatives of an eccentric mentality, ill-balanced judgement, muddled thought, lack of general common knowledge and uncalled for reticence, evident in dealings with this officer over many months.'

In a later memorandum to General Dobbie, Percival went even further: 'Major Morgan is lacking in ability and is not fitted for the appointment which he holds.' Percival had apparently done some checking into Army records – he would have found that Morgan had earlier been a military attaché at the British Embassy in Tokyo – for he goes on, 'this view is supported by information as to his past history and antecedents'. He added, in a statement which seems to sum up much of the attitude that existed in pre-war colonial days, 'On the other hand, he appears to be on a 7- or 10-years contract, so that there may be difficulty in removing him from his appointment.'

Morgan, it must be said, carried out some good counter-espionage work himself. He was still in situ when the Japanese attacked, and became a prisoner of war. He survived the war years, and died at Lavenham, Suffolk in the 1960s.

Despite this lack of police co-operation Hayley Bell set up a small but efficient organization in Singapore and Malaya. According to Brigadier Ivan Simson, in his book *Singapore – Too little, Too late* and in post-war correspondence with A.H. Dickinson[16], Hayley Bell and his team uncovered part of the Japanese espionage network in Malaya, and very early on foretold, with a high degree of accuracy, where the Japanese would land in the event of war coming to Malaya. After the war Simson was given access to a file of intelligence papers in private hands containing copies of correspondence between Hayley Bell, Colonel Sir Vernon Kell of MI5,[17] Sir John Brennan of the Foreign Office, and René Onraet, all dating from the period 1936–39. These documents showed quite clearly that the Hayley Bell organisation did some remarkable work in uncovering Japanese espionage in Malaya. The file also showed that the later reports were not received favourably by either the Singapore civil or military authorities in 1939 in the persons of the Governor and General Bond. The reports touched on sensitive spots, and were deemed to be sensationalist. They rocked the official boat in the still waters which surrounded the 'impregnable' fortress.

It was not only the local boat which Hayley Bell's reports rocked. The intelligence papers seen by Brigadier Simson indicated that the pro-Thai British Minister in Bangkok, Sir Josiah Crosby, also took exception to Hayley Bell's warnings about Thai involvement with the Japanese. The upshot was that the Governor of Singapore, Sir Shenton Thomas, strongly urged General Bond to get rid of Hayley Bell. Sir Shenton also took advantage of a Far Eastern tour made by the deputy chief of MI5, Sir Eric Holt Wilson, in that year, to urge him to replace Hayley Bell. Both he and Bond told Wilson that the DSO was incompetent and did not co-operate with the other intelligence services. Sir Josiah Crosby apparently also weighed in along the same lines when Wilson visited Bangkok.

These criticisms of Hayley Bell were accepted by Wilson in good faith. After he arrived back in London and reported to his chief, Colonel Sir Vernon Kell, the following summary of Wilson's report appeared over the latter's signature: 'It is generally considered that the organisation for defence security [in Malaya] is unsatisfactory at present and that drastic and energetic action is now necessary to remedy the defects.' The major problems identified were lack of funds, and 'poor co-operation between the Services and the DSO and the Services, and a DSO who was incompetent'. The report went on to say that Hayley Bell must be replaced as he was 'ill-qualified for such an important position. He lacks energy and tact and cannot appreciate the Service side of the problem. He considers himself qualified to interfere widely.' The report also noted that Hayley Bell was the recipient of certain Secret Service reports from China, which indicates the range of his intelligence interests, although strictly speaking his MI5 duties should have been restricted to Malayan matters. Anything outside of Malaya was officially the business of MI6.

The end result of the affair was that Hayley Bell was ordered home in May 1939, and his organisation disbanded. Hayley Bell was then sixty-one years of age, only a year older than his main detractor, Sir Shenton Thomas, and he took his dismissal badly. According to his daughter, his death at Chelsea in 1944 was probably hastened by the treatment he had received in Malaya.

Hayley Bell believed his dismissal was engineered by Governor Thomas and General Bond. He said he met Thomas only once, and then the Governor ridiculed the idea of Japan even wanting Malaya. Dickinson's comment on this, when Ivan Simson brought it to his attention, was, 'this could not have been said on the advice of the Inspector-General of Police. For years we had been building up our anti-Japanese section. Who in this case misled him [Thomas] so grievously?'

Simson decided not to publish much of what he had discovered. Because of the way Hayley Bell was dismissed he did not 'want to wash intelligence dirty linen in public'. But he passed some of the information on to Major-General S.W. Kirby who wrote a more extended piece about the Hayley Bell operation in his own book *Singapore – the Chain of Disaster*.[18] But Kirby somehow managed to mix up some of this information. Simson had said that Hayley Bell had obtained much of his intelligence information from an associate who had been born and brought up in Japan and spoke Japanese fluently.[19] Kirby attributed these particular characteristics to Hayley Bell himself; but he was not born in Japan, neither had he been brought up there, and he did not speak Japanese.

One member of Hayley Bell's team for a time was Lieutenant Ivan Lyon of the Gordon Highlanders. He had arrived in Singapore with his battalion in late 1936. A great sailing man, he, together with a colleague, made a voyage up the east coast of Malaya and into Thai waters in a small sloop-rigged sailing craft in 1937, and came back with a comprehensive intelligence report for Hayley Bell. At the time of the Japanese attack in 1941 Lyon, then a captain, was on attachment as a Field Security Officer, and he may even have been the Gordon Highlander captain who escorted the officer traitor Patrick Heenan from northern Malaya to Singapore on 11th December 1941. A little later, as part of the SOE team, he helped set up an escape route for Allied troops through Sumatra.[20]

Something is known about two other men in Hayley Bell's pre-1939 organisation. The more shadowy of the two was a Swiss national, who was half-Swiss half-Japanese by blood, whose name might have been either Bavier of Baviot. He knew Malaya and Thailand well, and gleaned much valuable information. He may have been the Japanese-speaking agent who came up with the Japanese invasion plans for Thailand and Malaya in 1937 on which General Dobbie based his defence appreciation of that year. He may also have been the man whom Hayley Bell enjoined Guy Madoc to help in 1938, 'if he happened to pass through Kuantan'.

The second man was called Becker. According to A.H. Dickinson, he too might have been the Japanese-speaking agent who discovered the Japanese plans. However research has shown that Becker did not speak Japanese although he was a linguist of note. (See Chapter Seven.)

A.H. Dickinson, writing soon after the war, had much to say about the Defence Security Officer who was operating in Singapore at the time of the Japanese landings (two-and-a-half years after Hayley Bell's removal from office). He points out that the creation of the Malayan Security Service had done little to overcome faults in the system, and he criticises MI5 in London for failing in its responsibilities to Malaya:

> The DSO latterly in Malaya was handicapped by the fact that he was not personally equipped, and was consequently not regarded as an expert. There was insufficient appreciation of the importance which should have attached to his appointment, insufficient realization of the wider implications of his work. His office in practice was overwhelmed with elementary and pettifogging detail, insisted upon by the Services, which cluttered up the machinery both of the Services themselves and the Civil police in particular. Nor did his position appear to be defined sufficiently firmly in relation to the Services to give him that authority which war conditions demanded, if there was to be firm control. In effect, this office became largely a post-box which, in the stress of affairs, had to be circumvented as frequently as it was used, both by Services and the Civil police, if wheels were to be kept turning.
>
> It is a matter for regret that MI5 was unable, through the immense pressure of events in Europe, to spare more time for criticism and control of its security responsibilities in Malaya. From its birth, the post of DSO, Malaya, had been an ailing and ill developed child.

The Ministry of Economic Warfare opened its Singapore office of the Special Operations Executive (SOE) in May 1941. It was known as the Oriental Mission, or OM for short. Two months earlier, Lieutenant-Colonel A.G. Warren of the Royal Marines attached to Military Intelligence, Research (MI-R), was sent to Malaya to study the scope for special operations. On Warren's staff, who travelled out with him on the ss *Nestor*, were Captain K. Gerhold, RA and Sergeant Kelly, RE. Gerhold's appointment exemplifies the lack of co-ordination and consultation between government departments in London. Gerhold had previously been an officer in the FMS Police but had been sacked. Unfortunately for Gerhold, a serving officer of the Singapore Police was also on board the *Nestor* and knew the story of the man's banishment from Malaya. Gerhold's feet had barely touched the Singapore quayside before he was shipped back out to Aden. Brooke-Popham pointed out in a cable on 7th May 1941 that, if the War Office wanted details regarding the termination of Gerhold's FMS Police appointment, they had only to contact the Colonial Office.

In retrospect it seems a pity that Warren was not placed in charge of the Oriental Mission, for as a serving officer he would probably have been 'accepted' by the military authorities in Singapore; he certainly would not have made the same mistakes in 'military etiquette' as the civilian who was given the job.

This man, appointed to the post by Dr Hugh Dalton, the Minister in London, was Valentine St J. Killery. He had spent a number of years in the East working for ICI in Shanghai and elsewhere. He was later given the rank Lieutenant-Colonel, though he had no military experience. Although not directly responsible to Air Chief Marshal Brooke-Popham, C-in-C Far East, he could do little without the C-in-C's permission. Killery's remit included the organisation of 'stay-behind' parties to work behind enemy lines if and when an attack came. To train these groups, No. 101 Special Training School (101 STS) was set up near Jurong on Singapore Island.

Killery did not see fit to discuss these plans with General Percival, GOC Malaya Command, who found out about them by accident. There is no doubt that Killery should have approached Percival, although he may have thought the C-in-C had done so. That Brooke-Popham knew about them is evidenced by a minute he wrote to Killery after Percival had protested about Killery's activities. 'I discussed with the GOC the question of left-behind parties in Malaya,' wrote Brooke-Popham. 'As a result of this conversation I have decided not to proceed with this project.'

Killery appealed to the Governor of Singapore in Percival's presence. The GOC stated his objections to the plan which were, he said, threefold. The Europeans to be placed in charge of the groups would not be able to move freely in an occupied Malaya; the scheme absorbed scarce manpower; the formation of the groups implied that an invasion would take place and this would damage morale. Percival did not state another reason which Killery thought was the principal one, that he had not been consulted in the first place.

Further evidence of the lack of co-operation with Killery's organisation appears in the Grimsdale-Ismay letter of 8th March 1942 (see page 83). Grimsdale had said that 'no one at GHQ was really interested' in the SOE plans, and goes on: 'neither the Governor of Malaya [sic] nor Crosby in Bangkok would allow Killery to make the smallest effort to organise anything in their territories!' In November, Percival in fact devised a similar scheme of his own which led to further bad feeling between the Oriental Mission and himself. When it was pointed out that the scheme differed very little from the original one, and that valuable time had been lost, Percival angrily replied that there were several differences, including the fact that his scheme implied military control. Perhaps he gave the game away about the true basis of his orginal objections when he stated, 'had I been consulted at the very start the loss of time in producing a faulty scheme would have been avoided'. Within four weeks the Japanese had landed, and by then it was far too late for OM to accomplish much with stay-behind parties. For this Percival must shoulder some of the blame.

Had a Singapore Inquiry taken place after the war, it could not have failed to note the unfavourable comparison between the British intelligence and counter-espionage efforts on the ground in Malaya, with the success of those of the enemy.

The British intelligence system was fragmented and unco-ordinated. After Sir Eric Holt-Wilson made his survey of Far Eastern intelligence operations in 1938, he reported that 'there was unduly large circulation of security documents', which probably gives a good indication of the rating given to security at the time. It was very often treated as something of a joke.

When Sir Josiah Crosby complained to the Thai Prime Minister in early 1941 about the number of visiting Japanese agents operating in Thailand who were military men disguised as civilians, he was told that nothing could be done about it. But in true eastern fashion the Thai Prime Minister then advised that, should Britain choose to do likewise, his country would turn a blind eye. The idea was taken up, but the thirty or so officers sent into Thailand were almost all amateurs who treated the job as an escapade, an exciting way of getting away from the battalion for a while.

The passports issued to these men described them variously as accountants, lawyers, journalists and traders, but a few were described as comedians, and one as an acrobat. One of the officers concerned in this operation was Major S.P. 'Shep' Fearon formerly of the 5/14th Punjabis, but latterly Officer Commanding Ist Independent Infantry Battalion. His pseudo-profession was journalism, and to him the whole episode was something of a lark. Another officer, sent in only a few days before the Japanese attack, was Captain D.J.R. Moore. He was informed that his recall signal would be the playing of 'Keep the Home Fires Burning' over the radio. But when the signal came it was only the tune and not the words, and Moore was tone deaf. In consequence he only just managed to extricate himself from Thailand in time to avoid capture.

The British intelligence system was also under-financed. In stark contrast to the amount of money the FECB reported the Japanese were spending in Thailand on espionage and subversive activities, the British had few funds to spend in Malaya. In late 1937 a 'special fund' amounting to £2,000 was made available to the Defence Security Officer, Hayley Bell, for intelligence purposes. Even at today's values this does not seem a princely sum to spend on the defence of one of the richest parts of the Empire.

Although some arbitrary action was taken against suspected fifth-columnists by British units in the field after the Pacific War began, post-war reports by Singapore and FMS Police officers indicate that such activity during the campaign was never very high. This is now the generally accepted view but not all authorities agree.

Donald Smith of the Intelligence Corps, who arrived in Singapore with elements of the 18th Division on 13th January 1942, was given field security duties although, as he said, 'ignorance of the native languages was a stumbling block'.[21] He wrote: 'Of the existence of an efficient fifth-column working for the enemy by day and by night, we had ample proof. Our every movement of troops and material was watched and reported. We rushed impotently on motor cycles the length and breadth of the island, investigating the activities of unseen enemy agents. They played a grim game of hide-and-seek with us most effectively.' These agents used to signpost military positions to spotter aircraft by means of lights and even piles of rice.

As part of Singapore Garrison the 2nd Loyals were closely involved in such security matters right from the first day of the war. Lieutenant R.B. Pigott was involved in the round-up of Japanese nationals on 8th December 1941 under Operations 'Collar' and 'Trousers'. A month later, on 2nd January, three companies of Loyals led by the CO, Lieutenant-Colonel M. Shrimpton, searched for an enemy wireless set operating in the vicinity of Tengah airfield on Singapore Island. They raided 'a lair of enemy wireless operators found in a house on Sungei Buloh Estate'. The quarry evaded capture but approximately 1000 rounds of ammunition was found.[22]

For 20th January the Loyal's War Diary notes: '2 Malays shot for behaving in a suspicious manner and carrying lethal weapons – caught by HQ Company lurking by a house in vicinity of lines.' Two days later: 'BAXO personnel brought in one native suspected of being a sniper – he was shot.'

The Singapore Police's view that the incidence of fifth-column activities was relatively small was based on figures of *proven* cases that they themselves were involved in. It would have been inimical to their police training to have included doubtful cases, even when they were made aware that the military had taken stringent action over mere 'suspects'. Since the military were not obliged to report their actions to the police, some cases would not have come to police attention at all.

At least one senior police officer reported cases of the military taking drastic and 'final' action against suspected fifth-columnists – action taken without any proof. Guy Madoc reports that a British Military Policeman 'brought into High Street police station, Kuala Lumpur, a Chinese "suspect" and there shot him dead'. Madoc also reports that, when he was serving as advisor to the British Battalion in Johore, he heard during an air raid a pistol-shot from behind him. '[I] saw a British NCO walking through the lallang [long grass] with a smoking revolver in his hand. As the all-clear sounded there was a commotion, and I saw the same NCO running after an elderly Chinese peasant who was staggering away covered with blood. The NCO went close and shot him dead.' The man had been caught near the forward positions and was a fifth-columnist, Madoc was told, but Madoc was not given any more details of the man's offence and he did not get the chance to ask the Commanding Officer for an explanation. Madoc says that he had been at or near the HQ all that morning, 'and cannot conceive why execution was not stayed until I was consulted. The man was a typical elderly, ignorant, Chinese vegetable gardener, and our front line was dotted with Chinese vegetable gardens. I felt sure there had been a gross miscarriage of justice.'[23]

Unfortunately the incidents reported by Madoc were not the only examples of possible mistakes made by military security units. Field Security Officers made many errors in Singapore according to another senior police officer, J.N.M.A. Nicholls, although those reported by him did not end in shootings.[24] He recalled:

The case of the wealthy Armenian. I well remember this. This was an Army Intelligence and Field Security scare worked up by a young and superficial thinker named Captain Tyrwhitt who haunted Special Branch in Singapore and spread ghost stories around – in this he was abetted by a Captain Golder, an ex-Sergeant of the Shanghai Police who was an army Field Security Officer. The rich 'Armenian' was a well-known Singapore Eurasian. (The man is named in the report.)

The Armenian was suspected of operating a clandestine radio, but no evidence was produced against him. (A.H. Dickinson confirms that the man involved was completely loyal to the British cause.)

Nicholls's report stated that a Military Intelligence Officer, Captain Ivan Lyon, was also involved in this scare, and was behind 'big talk' of a Japanese radio transmitter operating on Singapore Island. Lyon also produced a small-scale map on which he had plotted rumours and information about coloured lights that had been spotted. The plotted points seemed to run in straight lines, and Lyon had deduced direction indicators from these. Police raids were planned on the strength of this information. Nicholls says his own party searched for its objective which turned out to be the kitchen of Mr E.N. Taylor (later Mr Justice Taylor) of the Malayan High Court! The owners or occupiers of other places pinpointed by Lyon turned out to be innocent also. Afterwards, when Lyon's points were plotted on a large scale map it was found that they did not run in straight lines at all.

In the horror and chaos of the war many such errors must have been made. But the Nicholls report is also evidence that strenuous efforts were being made by Field Security Officers to weed out fifth-columnists towards the end of the battle for Singapore, even if some of their efforts were misguided.

In the overall fifth-column situation it is not known what effect the draconian intervention by military security units in the field had on the the incidence of successful fifth-column work. The military action might have had a deterrent effect; and without it the incidence might have been much greater.

Bearing in mind the feeling of horror experienced by that Indian subedar when his British officer shot two Malay suspects out of hand north of the Slim River, and Guy Madoc's belief that he had witnessed a gross miscarriage of justice at the 'execution' of the Chinaman in Johore, one is left with the nagging suspicion that there must have been other deaths of innocents. These dreadful things happen in war when many decisions – literally life and death decisions – have to be taken on the spur of the moment and without due process.

It is not known how many decisions of that kind were taken by the 'death squad' which operated on Singapore Island, the existence of which has gone largely unrecorded. It was made up of officers from Field Security and other security services. At what stage of the campaign its members began their 'weeding-out and disposal' operations against suspected fifth-columnists is unknown. It is not known who issued the orders for the operation. Apart from the names of some of the members of the squad, and the fact that the squad's operations were considered successful, little else is known. Such operations were scarcely the subject for keeping records.

Among the members of this death squad was Colonel A.G. Warren of the Royal Marines who, by rank, may have been its leader. Other members were Captain Ivan Lyon, Captain Tyrwhitt, and Captain Golder. (Ivan Lyon's son, Clive Lyon, confirms the existence of this squad.)[25] Golder was an ex-sergeant of the Shanghai Police and at least three other ex-members of that force on special field security duties in Singapore may have been in the squad too. One Field Security Officer is reported to have detected and himself executed nine Malays between the 9th and 14th February, the day before Singapore fell.[26]

To sum up, the incidence of fifth-column activity throughout the campaign was fairly light, although there might have been spates of heavier activity. Donald Smith's views of a greater incidence on Singapore Island itself may have been based on the reports of men like Tyrwhitt and Golder, whose expertise was not highly regarded by the Singapore Police. How many innocents fell foul of the sometimes extreme action taken by the military, we will never know.

Chapter Six

Thailand, and Operation Matador

Operation Matador, a development of an earlier plan called Operation Etonian, was designed by the British to forestall a Japanese attack on Thailand by invading the country first. Thailand, which lay over the northern border of Malaya, was, as a senior member of the Far Eastern Department of the British Foreign Office described it in August 1941, 'the key to the South'.[1]

Operation Matador suffered from two significant drawbacks: one of them political, the other military. The plan entailed attacking a neutral country and the British were well aware of how that would look to the world and especially to the Americans, who still looked with considerable suspicion at any adventuring on the part of Britain, the arch-imperialist. The British government urgently wanted the United States to come into the war against Germany, and if war with Japan was around the corner, then into that war too. So it was not in Britain's interest to do anything that would offend American public opinion.

On the military side Britain did not have sufficient forces in Malaya to launch such a pre-emptive strike with any great certainty of success against an invading Japanese force. Furthermore, if Matador was to be launched at all, then the timing of it was crucial. British army planners had forecast, correctly as it turned out, that if Japan attacked Thailand her forces would land at Singora and Patani on the east coast. This was what Matador was designed to forestall. British and Indian forces, having attacked across the border, would be dug in behind the landing places and lying in wait for the Japanese. About sixty hours was needed to launch the invasion, mop up any possible Thai resistance, and dig defensive positions. This was approximately the length of time that the Japanese troopships would need to reach the Thai beaches from their bases in Indo-China. So the British had to attack as soon as a Japanese invasion fleet sailed from Indo-China.

The need to obtain the backing of the United States, combined with the need to be certain that any Japanese fleet reported leaving Indo-China was actually making for Thailand (and was not just a Japanese ruse to make Britain become the initial aggressor), resulted in Operation Matador never being implemented. By the time American agreement was gained, and it was clear that Japanese vessels were heading for Thailand, the crucial moment had passed. Hesitancy on the part of the British C-in-C, Air

Chief Marshal Sir Robert Brooke-Popham, perhaps aggravated by an impassioned, not to say hysterical, cipher message from Sir Josiah Crosby, the British Minister in Bangkok, telling him not to attack first, together with some strange and still unexplained lapses in communications, all played their part in this. Crosby's telegram read: 'For God's sake do not allow British forces to occupy one inch of Thai territory unless and until Japan has struck the first blow at Thailand.'

A Royal Commission of Inquiry into the fall of Singapore would have investigated the circumstances surrounding this operation that never was, and the full background to what has been called the Thai problem.

Two events had occurred in the European War in June 1940 which not only had a dire effect on British plans in the Mediterranean but also changed the strategic situation in the Far East. The entry of Italy into the war on Germany's side, coupled with the fall of France, meant that the job of neutralizing the Italian navy now had to be taken on by the Royal Navy. With this extra commitment it became even more unlikely that a large British relieving fleet could ever be sent to the East in the event of a Japanese attack. On top of that, the fall of France laid French Indo-China open to the Japanese; and Singapore and Malaya were within range of aircraft based in the French territory. As one commentator has written, 'Malaya fell when France fell.'

The situation in Europe in mid-1940 wonderfully concentrated the minds of Japanese strategists. The Military Affairs Section of the Army Ministry in Tokyo produced a Grand Plan that took account of all the changes happening in Europe. They called it *Sekai josei no suii ni tomonau jikyoku shori yoko*, which can be freely translated as 'Outline of the Principles for Dealing with the Changing World Situation'. It proclaimed that there had never been such a favourable time for Japan to assert itself and become economically independent of Britain and the United States. The plan became the blueprint for the steps taken by the Japanese over the next fifteen months, steps which were to lead to the Pacific War. A so-called Greater Asia Co-prosperity Sphere would be established, centred on Japan and her conquests in the north and stretching from the islands of Eastern Indonesia to the Indian Ocean and encompassing everything between that line and China. To take advantage of America's indecisiveness in Far Eastern matters, there should be no hesitation on the part of Japan, the authors of the document said, in going to war with Britain and the Netherlands. According to the staff of the War History Institute, Tokyo, in 1966, another consideration reviewed by the Japanese at the time was the possible expansion of German influence in the Far East as a result of their conquest of the Netherlands and France, and what seemed the likely conquest of Britain. The Germans might be their allies, but the Japanese did not want them as substitutes for the existing colonial powers in the Far East.[2]

That Army document was followed in August 1940 by one produced by the Japanese Naval Staff. This advocated the stationing of troops in French Indo-China as a first step to gaining control of Thailand, Malaya and Burma; such a move also serving to tighten the military blockade of China. Indo-China produced minerals, rubber and rice, commodities that would be of inestimable value if, as a result of Japan's move, the United States imposed a total trade embargo; and if that happened Japan would have no option but to seize the oilfields of the Dutch East Indies and British Borneo. The logic had more than an element of circularity in it, but it was a powerful argument and one which admirably suited the purposes of the 'hawks' in the Japanese establishment.

As a first step the Japanese forced the Vichy French in control of Indo-China to agree to the stationing of Japanese military observers at Hanoi. This was followed by the establishment of Japanese army and air bases throughout the northern part of the French colony bordering on China so that, by late September 1940, virtually the entire province of Tonkin was effectively under Japanese control. This all took place peacefully; the French were in no position to resist.

But it was to be the Thais who fired the first shot on French territory, not the Japanese. There had been a long-standing dispute between Thailand and the French over certain areas along the 2,000 kilometres of the Thai/Indo-Chinese border. This dispute, mostly oral, had gone on intermittently ever since 1867 when, under considerable French military threat, Thailand had relinquished her sovereign rights over Cambodia. Later, in 1893, the Thais had been forced to surrender all their vassal states in Laos to the French. The Thais also gave up their somewhat tenuous suzerainty over the States of Perlis, Kedah, Kelantan and Trengganu to the British in Malaya under the Treaty of Bangkok in 1909. In return Britain gave Thailand a loan for the construction of a railway which was to link the existing Thai and Malayan systems (a railway which was to have a high strategic value when the Pacific War came in 1941).

With the change in status of Metropolitan France in 1940, the Thais saw the opportunity to regain some of their 'lost' provinces. Early in the autumn of that year they began making strong demands on Vichy France for retrocession of parts of Laos; demands which were indignantly rejected. This Thai initiative had in fact been instigated by Japan, who saw in the situation a 'legitimate' way to extend her influence in both Thailand and Indo-China. For this purpose they sent in their crack 'advance agent in South-East Asia', Lieutenant-Colonel Jiro Saito, to urge the Thai Prime Minister, Field Marshal Luang Pibul, to make the demands on the French. The Japanese had chosen their agent well. Colonel Saito had been educated in Honolulu and was a linguist of note. He had been a pupil of Colonel Kenjichi Doihara, the so-called 'Lawrence of Manchuria' at the time of the Mukden Incident in September 1931, which paved the way for the conquest of that country by Japan. After that he had spent three years in Bangkok as Military Attaché, and so knew Thailand and its leaders well.

Bangkok and Tokyo now sat back to await the reaction of London and Washington to the Thai demands. It soon became clear that neither Britain nor the United States was prepared to give vigorous support to the integrity of Indo-Chinese territory. So, urged on by Colonel Saito, Thai forces struck in late November 1940. The initial attacks were border skirmishes, but these soon developed into a small-scale war, with aircraft, artillery and tanks taking part. By early December, Thai troops had occupied many of the frontier districts, and their aircraft had bombed Vientiane, the capital of Laos. The French were rather more than astonished at the professionalism shown by the Thai air force, which had not fought in battle since Thailand had offered Britain 500 pilots to fight on the Western Front in 1917.[3] The French complained bitterly that the Thai aircraft 'seem to be flown by men with plenty of war experience'. After the Japanese Foreign Minister, Matsuoka, had summoned the French ambassador in Tokyo and offered to mediate in the dispute, the Governor of Indo-China, Admiral Jean Decroux, made the insinuation even stronger. In the process of firmly rejecting the proposal, he angrily suggested that he would, however, welcome mediation by a *neutral* country.

That the Japanese were pouring military equipment into Thailand is evidenced by a message sent to the War Office in London by the British Military Attaché in Bangkok on 8th January 1941. 'It is becoming increasingly obvious that Japanese arms and equipment are arriving in large quantities in Thailand accompanied by many Japanese officers for purposes of instructing youth classes in their use.'[4] An internal Foreign Office minute in the file containing that message states:

> Our latest information shows that the Japanese are sending aircraft and arms to Thailand in large quantities and Japanese offer to train the Thais in using them.
>
> It is evident that the Thai Prime Minister is becoming more and more committed to the Japanese. Sir J. Crosby has frequently warned him against this but he reports in the present telegram that the situation arising out of the agitation for the lost provinces is getting out of hand and that the Prime Minister does not conceal his belief that we can do nothing to prevent Japan's advance in SE Asia.

Admiral Decroux's defiant attitude was short-lived. The Thai offensive gathered momentum. By January 1941 they had mobilised 80,000 troops, and it seemed to the French that the Thais were equipped with an unlimited supply of modern equipment. Under the land and air onslaught the French defences caved in. (The French had more success at sea. The cruiser *Lamotte Picquet*, together with her escorts, sank several Thai naval vessels.) Once more, Matsuoka summoned the French ambassador in Tokyo to offer mediation. With a strong Japanese fleet now anchored off Saigon, and more Japanese troops pouring into northern Indo-China, the Vichy government in France instructed Decroux to accept the Japanese offer. Thai delegates were then flown into Saigon in a Japanese bomber and an armistice was signed aboard the Japanese cruiser *Natori* there. A little later French and Thai delegates in Tokyo signed an agreement based on Japan's 'disinterested' mediation verdict.

The outcome of the Japanese intervention was not as satisfactory for the Thais as they might have had reason to expect in view of how the Japanese had been wooing them. They received 75,000 square miles of territory around the Upper Mekong in Cambodia (territory which included the ancient city of Angkor) instead of the four times that figure they had asked for. Unbeknownst to the Thais the Japanese had made a secret deal with the French, in which, in return for access to airfields in southern Indo-China, they watered down the Thai demands. This secret deal with the French was to seal the fate of Malaya.

Officially Britain tended to treat the matter of the regaining by Thailand of the 'lost' provinces with kid gloves. (There is a possibility that Sir Josiah Crosby, the British Minister in Bangkok, with or without the cognizance of his superiors in Whitehall, connived over the Thai attacks.) The official British attitude was a matter of expediency and had nothing to do with British views on the rights or wrongs of Thailand's claim to the territories. Britain did not want to annoy General de Gaulle and his Free French, but they had no wish either to do anything which might adversely affect Anglo-Thai relations at this critical juncture. (No doubt the official thinking was that the Thais could always be forced to return the re-acquired provinces to France at a later date.) Thailand was the last land obstacle in the way of Japanese aggression against Singapore to the south and Burma to the west and north, and with the 'appease Japan at almost any price' policy in full swing, Britain had no option but to accept tacitly the new situation. The United States, on the other hand, soundly condemned the Thai actions. However, the American attitude too had little to do with the actual Thai-French situation; the American view was coloured by the new diplomatic closeness of Thailand with Japan, a Japan which had fallen out of American favour ever since its attack on China in 1937.

The possibility that the Free French might try to persuade Britain to harden its attitude with the Thais seems to have worried Josiah Crosby. He sent a message from Bangkok on 27th February 1941 to inform London that a French informant, sympathetic to General de Gaulle, had stated that H.M. Government was bound by an agreement with de Gaulle to maintain the French Empire intact. On 2nd March 1941, the Foreign Office sent the following reply:

H.M. Government have never undertaken to preserve the French Empire intact, but have only expressed determination to 'secure the full restoration of the independence and greatness of France' after the war. This undertaking was confirmed in the P.M.'s [Churchill's] published letter of August 7th to General de Gaulle concerning the memorandum of agreement about the Free French Forces. For your personal information, an accompanying secret letter explained that the undertaking had no precise relation to territorial frontiers.

Thailand was the only independent country in South-East Asia, but had had very close links with the British Empire. Three-quarters of her exports passed through British ports in the area. She relied on Indian gunny for the sacks in which rice, her major export, was shipped. Her foreign debt was held in London. Many of her businesses were in British hands and many of the advisors to Thai ministries were from Britain. It is possible that, had Britain been able to convince Thailand of her power to protect Thai independence, the eastern kingdom would have been wholly inside the Western camp. But Britain had no such power, especially after the war in Europe began in 1939.

Field Marshal Luang Pibul had been Thai prime minister since 1938. (Pibul's surname is sometimes anglicised as Phibun, or Phibul, and even Bipul. The spelling used here is that used in the British Foreign Office files of the time.) Despite a continuous stream of messages to London from Sir Josiah Crosby in the years before the Pacific War began – which indicated that he thought he had considerable influence over the Thai prime minister – there were many indications that Pibul was not wholly to be trusted. Apart from anything else he was not a man of high probity. In 1937, when Minister of Defence, he had been caught up to his ears in a scandal over the sale of certain Royal lands at vastly undervalued prices, and had been forced to resign.[5] However, it was not long before he was back in government, and soon after that he was leading a military dictatorship.

On the surface Pibul was pro-British. The ultra pro-Thai Crosby, definitely thought he leaned in that direction, and Crosby thought he had Pibul at least partly in his pocket. But many British residents in the Far East, and some officials in London, believed that Crosby's views on all things Thai were coloured by the circumstances behind his appointment to his post.

Crosby had spent many years in Thailand. By the time of his retirement in 1943, no less than thirty-five of his thirty-nine years in the Foreign Service had been spent there. He had arrived in 1904 as a twenty-four-year-old cadet, and apart from two brief periods, spent in Batavia and Saigon, and a three-year stint as Minister Plenipotentiary to Panama 1931–34, he had remained there ever since. This must be something of a record in Foreign Service appointments.[6]

His return to Bangkok as British Minister on 22nd May 1934, was made at the behest of the party which had come to power after the 1932 revolution in Thailand, a party then led by Pibul and Luang Pradit who jointly led the revolution which had reduced the powers of the Thai king. This request from a foreign government for a particular official representative may not have been unique but it was highly unusual. Dorothy Crisp, a British political commentator with contacts in high places at the Foreign Office, writing in 1943, considered that this must have effected Crosby's judgement. She wrote of Sir Josiah's situation, 'Now it is not in human nature to believe that those who have asked for one's appointment are they who are the whole time working against one, and the interests one represents.' She accused Crosby of having been blind to the real motives of Pibul. She went on, 'there were Englishmen in Malaya and Singapore who were certain that Luang Pibul, head of the militarist element who eclipsed Pradit, had been in the hands of the Japanese from 1934 onwards and that he had a pact with them'.[7]

Distrust of Pibul was not confined to English residents in the Far East or to British commentators at home. Hugh Grant, the United States Minister in Bangkok, was certain that the Japanese had a firm grip over Pibul and stated this so often that he made himself extremely unpopular with Crosby. Grant's views were reflected in Washington where the Secretary of State, Cordell Hull, told Lord Halifax, the British ambassador, in March 1941, 'I am not at all convinced that the present Thai government is a real friend of this government or any other government except the Japanese. In my opinion Japanese-Thai alliances already exist in the military, political and economic fields.'[8] Hull went even further later when he said the Thais were merely using the British in order better to handle the Japanese.[9]

An American journalist, Mark Gayn, who was Editor of the English Department of the Japanese Domei News Agency in the Far East for five years up to 1940, was a man whose inside position enabled him to learn much about Japanese policy. He, too, recorded that Pibul was in the pocket of the Japanese, and had very early on 'decided to hitch his star to the Rising Sun'. Writing in March 1941, nine months before the Japanese attack on Pearl Harbor, he said that Pibul 'backs collaboration with Japan without any reservations', and that one of the results of Pibul's pro-Japanese attitude had been the relentless suppression of the five million Chinese living and working in Thailand. Under pressure from the Japanese from 1937 onwards, Pibul had introduced harsh restrictions on all Chinese activities in the country. Their schools were closed. Immigration from China was banned, and the number of Chinese employees any business could employ was strictly controlled. All business accounts had to be kept in Thai. Some Chinese language newspapers were closed down. Many of the larger Chinese-owned businesses were in the rice and tobacco industries, and these were taken over by the newly-formed government-owned Thai Rice Company and Thai Tobacco Monopoly.[10]

Early on Pibul had turned his attention to arming his forces by earmarking a quarter of his country's budget for modern weaponry. Military purchasing missions were sent abroad, mostly to Italy and Japan. Pibul was, in fact, an admirer of both Mussolini and Hitler, and established a Thai equivalent of the Hitler Youth Movement in his country. Fourteen warships were ordered from Italy and these were delivered in 1938. (It was some of these which were sunk by the French Navy during the Thai-French hostilities.)

In May 1941 Wing Commander C.F. Cosey, RAF, returned from Thailand with a report on the situation there.[11] He reported it was unlikely that Japan would launch an attack on Burma, Malaya, or the Dutch East Indies without first of all securing control over their lines of communications, with emphasis on Thailand. Cosey said, 'Japanese activities in provoking the Thai-Indo-China dispute and then forcing their mediation upon both parties has provided them with the means of achieving this control with the maximum secrecy and rapidity.' He went on, 'Certain recent actions on the part of the Thai Prime Minister have suggested that he has become pro-Japanese and may even have a pact with them and that his approaches to us are merely attempts to double-cross us for the benefit of his pro-Japanese plans.' Someone in the Foreign Office in London scrawled in pencil against the latter, 'I dispute this view'. The scrawler may have been Anthony Eden, the British Foreign Minister, who often made pencilled and unsigned notes on official documents. The notation would certainly fit in with Eden's views on the Thai situation which tended to follow closely the views held by Josiah Crosby. However, three months *before* that note was scrawled, a secret cipher message, dated 5th February 1941 (and only made public in 1993), was sent from the British Foreign Office to Lord Halifax in Washington, stating that evidence was accumulating that Japan intended to push on south, and that 'there is reason to suppose that some military agreement with Thailand directed against our territories and the Netherlands East Indies is under consideration'.[12]

This apparent contradiction illustrates well the dichotomy of the British position. On the one hand Britain wanted to believe that Pibul was, or could be persuaded to be, in the Western camp. On the other hand, Britain was doing her best to persuade the United States to back her to the hilt over the protection of British territories in the Far East, and was passing on any information received that might move the Americans in that direction. British policy towards Thailand was exceedingly complex.

The Foreign Office was also aware that the document drawn up by the Japanese on 7th February 1941 to end the Thai-French war, and which had been signed by both belligerents, had included a secret protocol that neither of the participants 'would enter into any agreement or understanding with any 3rd Power anticipating political, economic or military co-operation against Japan'. Dorothy Crisp, the British political commentator who seems to have had a source in the Foreign Office, quoted it (without giving the name of her informant) when she wrote in 1943, 'from that moment on Thailand was our enemy unless the government could be changed'.

All the evidence suggests, then, that Pibul was to some extent, and perhaps wholly, in the hands of the Japanese, perhaps from 1934, but certainly from 1940. However, on the surface at least, the British Foreign Minister tended to accept Crosby's assessment of Pibul, even though Crosby's views on Pibul were beginning to change by early 1941. Britain, in no position to fight a war on another front, could not give Thailand any guarantee of protection in the event of a Japanese attack – something Crosby had been pressing for together with a supply of arms and planes for the Thai forces. He had, for example, pressed the British government to supply twelve pursuit aircraft to Thailand as it 'would be useful from a moral more than a purely military point of view. It would encourage the Thai Government greatly as a token of our goodwill in the immediate present and as a forerunner of possible further supplies in the future.' He then quoted the C-in-C, Far East, who had expressed willingness to furnish the planes provided that 'this would really improve the situation substantially'. Crosby ended his message, 'For the reasons stated I believe such a step would be worthwhile if taken immediately.'[13] (In the event the planes were not sent. Had they been, the already inadequate RAF in Malaya would have been in an even worse position compared with the Japanese.)

If Sir Josiah Crosby thought he had much influence over the Thai leader, there was at least a strong likelihood that the reverse was true. Pibul was a clever, hard, calculating man. Like most Thais, he was an irredentist; he wanted the old Thai territories back. With the aid of the Japanese he was able to regain much territory from the French; it is scarcely conceivable that, as an ardent irredentist, he did not also have dreams of getting back the old Thai possessions that were now part of British Malaya and Burma. He was probably neither intrinsically pro-British nor intrinsically pro-Japanese; but he was ardently pro-Thai. If by throwing in his lot with the Japanese, a nation which appeared to be growing in strength as British power diminished, and if the Japanese could help him regain all the lost provinces, then, as a pragmatist, he was ready to bend with the wind. By 1940, with continuing British reverses in the war in the west, it must have become obvious to him that the most favourable wind was blowing from the east. But even then he kept his options open by playing both ends against the middle. (It should also be remembered that Japan and Thailand had two important features in common: both were oriental, and they were both independent.)

Possibly the best example of Pibul's ability to play both ends at once had come about in early 1941 when Crosby complained to him about the number of Japanese agents being allowed into Thailand. Instead of agreeing to curb these Japanese activities, which he had neither the power nor probably the will to do anyway, Pibul suggested that the British put in their agents as well. This suggestion was taken up when, later that year, a number of British military officers were sent into Thailand under various guises (as described in Chapter 5). Another example came in August 1941 when Crosby complained about the appointment of three pro-Japanese Thais as deputy Foreign Ministers. Pibul's reaction was immediately to appoint a Thai with a strong pro-British reputation as Foreign Minister.

There were many indications that Pibul had thrown in his lot with the Japanese. A 'Very Secret' message from the British Consul-General in Saigon to the COIS (Chief of Intelligence Services), Singapore, reported that 'an intercepted letter (just read by me) dated February 1st 1941 from Japanese Legation at Bangkok to Director of Economic Studies, Tokyo [the Japanese collection centre for espionage] proves that the Japanese understanding with Prime Minister Pibul to act as arbitrator [in the Indo-China dispute] was a well-guarded secret since August 1940'.[14] Pibul had also attended a meeting with the Japanese Minister in Bangkok in February 1941 at which a number of Burmese nationalists had been present. The subject discussed was a planned uprising against the British in Burma, where Pibul hoped to regain land along the border.

Pibul's desire was to be on the winning side, and for some time all the pointers had indicated that that side would be the Japanese. In the final analysis, the Thai army put up only a token resistance when the Japanese invasion came, and the Thai air force, the best equipped flying force in the area, put up no resistance at all. Sir George Sansom wrote in an article in 1944, entitled 'The Story of Singapore', that the Japanese 'landed without opposition from the Thais, who indeed appear to have connived at preparations made by the Japanese in the summer and autumn of 1941 for landing in the Kra Isthmus'.[15] Sir George was a diplomat who had spent nearly forty years in Japan, and had worked with the Ministry of Economic Welfare in Singapore prior to the capitulation.

More evidence of Pibul's determination to do nothing to affect his relations with the Japanese came when the question of resistance to possible Japanese aggression was discussed, as urged on the Thais in a message from Winston Churchill, at a Thai Cabinet meeting on 7th December 1941, the day before the Japanese invasion. Pibul was conveniently absent from the capital, but at eight o'clock in the evening of the following day, after the attack, he made a broadcast to the Thai people. In it he said, 'I would like you to know that Japan is our greatest friend in life and death and we have to walk together, shoulder to shoulder, to fight our common enemy. All of you should remember that Britain took a large piece of our land in the south, for which Japan is now fighting. I hope our army will be proud to be in the same front with the Japanese army. Presently we will ally ourselves with Japan.' By 25th January 1942, with Japanese troops already knocking on the back door of Singapore after fighting a brilliant campaign, Pibul knew he had chosen sides correctly. On that date Thailand declared war on Great Britain and the United States. Later that same year, during a banquet held in Bangkok, Pibul stated that his aim was to uproot Anglo-American influence from East Asia with the co-operation of Japan.

Sir Josiah Crosby's degree of trust in Pibul – it would be fairer to describe this as Crosby's trust in his own ability to control the man – was not reflected in British military circles. One MI2 officer in London, Major W. G. Harold, was very concerned about the intelligence operation that led to the influx of British military officers into Thailand. 'Luang Pibul is not in my opinion to be trusted and we cannot exclude the possibility, once our infiltration has been started, that he might go to the Japanese and give them this excuse for themselves stepping into South Thailand.'[16] Indeed, Crosby who had 'negotiated' the deal with Pibul in the first place, was to send a cable on 22nd October 1941 advising that the number of British officers visiting Thailand should be reduced as they were causing trouble for Pibul with the Japanese.

Some British staff officers not only distrusted Pibul, but distrusted some of Crosby's reports. On 23rd November 1941, two weeks before the Japanese attack, Lieutenant-Colonel D. Mackenzie of the British General Staff wrote a letter to the Deputy Director, Military Intelligence. Two passages give a fair summing-up of the military attitude towards Crosby:[17]

> This minister is a bachelor and has long been resident in Thailand with the very natural result that he not only takes a very parochial view, but, as he himself confirms, regards the Thais as wayward children to whom he would wish to stand in the capacity of father confessor ...
>
> I am in entire agreement with Major Chapman's [an officer at the War Office] recommendation that all future telegrams from Sir Josiah Crosby be interpreted with the utmost care.

Although there is no record of what caused Major Chapman to make his recommendation, the fact that he made it against one of His Majesty's longest serving envoys is astonishing. The letter-writer went even further when he suggested the replacement of Sir Josiah at Bangkok. This suggestion got as far as the C-in-C, Far East, Brooke-Popham, who said he could not support the recommendation at that late hour.

Still another British Ministry seemed not to support Crosby's views on Pibul's pro-Britishness. This was the Ministry of Economic Warfare. The Head of its Orient Mission in Singapore, Valentine Killery, and some of his masters in London considered that the need to get America's acquiescence before Operation Matador could be implemented would prove an insurmountable obstacle. The situation became more critical in July 1941 when the Japanese forced the Vichy French to sign a mutual security pact and then marched 40,000 troops into south Indo-China. Not for nothing had Japan's Director of Naval Intelligence, Rear-Admiral Maeda, returned from a reconnaissance of Thailand and Indo-China in June with the report that it was quite safe to make such a move.[18]

Killery and his advisors considered that one way out of the problem of getting American agreement to Matador would be to work for a pro-British *coup d'état* in Thailand (the corollary to that being they must have thought that Pibul was not pro-British). Their aim was to install a Thai government which would invite British forces in and so circumvent the need for getting American 'permission'. Killery's organisation set about this task in the full knowledge that any such coup attempt might result in retaliatory action by the Japanese, a point he made to his superiors in London in a cipher message dated 30th July 1941: 'we realise of course the obvious danger of Japanese military action to protect existing regime during disorder of coup d'etat'.[19] Nevertheless he and his advisors considered the risk worth taking, at least to the extent of seeing the necessary preliminaries in place.

Apparently Killery's superiors in London agreed with him. On 7th August 1941, Gladwyn Jebb, the senior SOE man in London, wrote to Sir Alexander Cadogan, Permanent Secretary of State at the Foreign Office. He stated that Killery had discussed this matter with Crosby in Bangkok, and went on, 'Killery was quite right in raising the subject with Crosby since if anything is ever to be done on such lines, Killery's organisation is the one to do it. Further,' Jebb added, 'if it were ever considered desirable, Killery would not be in a position to do anything unless he had got some machinery established in the country – and this, as you know, he is now attempting to set up.'

Crosby was adamantly opposed to the project. He complained bitterly to the Foreign Office about the 'reckless and irresponsible amateurs serving under Killery' who had, he said, 'little grasp of the political situation in the area'. He sought to impose impossible conditions on Killery's operation. However, unbeknown to him, this did not stop SOE from carrying out some preparatory work.[20]

Certain members of the Thai government were known to be very pro-British. Whether any of these were privy to this British coup plan is not known, though the secret may lie in Foreign Office files on Thailand that remain closed and marked 'retained in department' to this day. In view of his later-known involvement with SOE, it would seem likely that one minister who may have been involved at this time was Luang Pradit who, together with Pibul, had led the 1932 revolution. Since then the two men had fallen out. Pradit was violently anti-Japanese and opposed to most of Pibul's policies. Pradit had Communist tendencies, and was therefore also opposed to any return to the days when the King of Thailand was a power to be reckoned with.

Pradit refused to sign the declaration of war against Britain in January 1942 and, as a result, was kicked upstairs by Pibul to take on the largely figurehead role of Regent, a strange position for an anti-royalist. In that capacity Pradit (also known as Nai Pridi Panomynong), later became head of the secretly-organised and British-sponsored Free Siamese Movement. He was given the code-name 'Ruth' by the British. After the war ended, the Supreme Allied Commander, South-East Asia, Lord Mountbatten, recorded a tribute to Pradit in which he said that there had existed a unique situation wherein 'the Supreme Allied Commander was exchanging vital military plans with the Head of a State technically at war with us'.[21]

If Pradit was privy to SOE plans for a coup, a Briton living and working in Thailand who knew Pradit well, Eric Deane, may have acted as a go-between. It is not certain, but Deane, an employee of Eastern Agencies in Bangkok, may have had connections with either SIS or SOE. (Deane was interned in Thailand during the war, but survived to retire in England.)

In October 1941, leaflets of an extreme anti-Japanese nature were discovered circulating in Bangkok. Pibul blamed the British. This resulted in a violent reaction on Crosby's part, who blamed the SOE, and the British Foreign Minister, Anthony Eden, jumped in on Crosby's side:

> I must know about this organisation that makes our ambassador's life a misery and vitiates my policy, and they must come under direct Foreign Office control. The present situation is intolerable.[22]

Although Killery denied any responsibility in this matter, various members of the Far Eastern Department of the Foreign Office thought he was involved. One of these endorsed the file:

> Sir Josiah Crosby does not adduce any evidence to show that a British agency was responsible for the circulation of this pamphlet. But FEMEW [Far East Ministry of Economic Warfare] are pretty clearly implied. The first step is to find out whether they were really responsible. I have spoken to Mr Jebb who has undertaken to telegraph at once and enquire.

Another FO official, P.N. Loxley, wrote: 'I too had a word with Mr Jebb yesterday. I don't think there is much doubt that FEMEW was responsible.'

This was followed by an endorsement made by another official, Ashley Clarke: 'Sir George Moss brought me the answer to the enquiry made of FEMEW which has just been received. It stated that SOE were not concerned, nor any British official source'. Under this someone had scrawled: 'The important word in Sir G. Moss's message is, I suspect, the word *official*'.

That last writer's suspicion was almost certainly correct. It is likely that those pamphlets were not the work of SOE but the handiwork of another British agent in Thailand. This man, John Becker, was working on a quite separate attempt to create a *coup d'état*. (See Chapter Seven.)

Just how far Killery's *coup d'état* plans had gone is not known. Preliminary secret contacts with pro-British sympathisers may have been the extent of it. It is not known what local support existed for the proposed operation; again, the answer might still lie in other 'retained in department' files.

Amongst the British officers who might have been engaged in preparatory work for Killery's plan was Captain George Laub of the Johore Volunteer Engineers. He was an expert linguist, and was sent into Thailand a few weeks before the war began, where he was murdered by the Japanese in early December 1941. Yet another man who may have been similarly engaged, and one who was definitely on the SOE payroll, was an Australian named George Windred. Killery sent him into Thailand in late November 1941 because 'his own man' – whoever that was – 'appears to have cold feet'. (The man with cold feet, Killery's 'official' man in Thailand, had in fact been recommended by Crosby for the post, but had subsequently decided that the job was too risky.) Windred's main job was to place trained operatives at various key points in southern Thailand to support British troops should Operation Matador be implemented.[23]

A serious British attempt at a *coup d'état* in Thailand was never made despite the fact that several Britons in high places had given Killery's project, or at least the planning of it, their blessing. A second coup attempt also never came to fruition. If either had been successful and had British forces been invited into Thailand this would have obviated the need for Operation Matador as well as the necessity for American agreement to the operation. If such a Thai invitation had caused the Japanese to attack earlier than they did, then at least the British would have had time to consolidate behind defensive positions somewhere in Thailand before the attack came.

It seems much more likely, however, that the Japanese would not have used such a *coup d'état* as an excuse to start the Pacific War a month or two earlier. They would have known that, had they attacked Thailand under those conditions, and thus precipitated a war with Britain, there was a strong chance that the United States would join in. This would have destroyed the Grand Plan for their Pacific conquests. The factor of surprise lay at the very heart of Japan's war strategy. The success of their initial ocean-wide operations depended upon *simultaneous* attacks on Pearl Harbor, Hong Kong, Malaya and Thailand, and give or take an hour or two, that remarkable feat of timing was achieved.

Whether either of the British coup attempts would have been successful will never be known, nor the extent of backing for the plans amongst

Lt-Col. (later Maj.-Gen.) B.W. Key (centre, front) with British and Indian officers of 2nd Royal Battalion, 11th Sikh Regiment, at Bannu, India, December 1937. As a brigadier, on 8 December 1941, Key was in command at Kota Bahru when the Japanese invaded Malaya. (*Courtesy Major Robert Henderson*)

A.H. Dickinson, Inspector-General of Police, Singapore, 1939–46, one of the more impressive figures of the Malayan Establishment. A photograph taken in early 1930s. (*Courtesy Mrs Pauline Asbury*)

Singapore: the Inner Harbour, *c.* 1940, taken from the front of the Fullerton Building. (*Author's collection*)

Below left: Sir Josiah Crosby, Britain's long-serving ambassador to Thailand, until 1942. His views were sympathetically received by the Foreign Secretary, Anthony Eden. (*By courtesy of the National Portrait Gallery*)

Below right: Colonel Francis Hayley Bell, MI5 Defence Security Officer, 1936–39, in Malaya. Photograph taken *c.* 1911. (*Courtesy Lady Mills*)

Above left: Maj.-Gen. W.G.S. Dobbie, GOC, Malaya Command, 1936–39. With his GSO1, Colonel A.E. Percival, he disputed the prevailing view that the jungle was 'impenetrable' and attempted to strengthen the northern defences of Singapore. (*Author's collection*)

Above right: Rear Admiral E.J. Spooner and Mrs Megan Spooner outside Admiral's House at Singapore Naval Base, 1941. Spooner died while escaping from Singapore; Mrs Spooner kept a lively contemporary diary. (*Courtesy Sir James Spooner*)

Below left: Lt-Gen. Sir Lionel V. Bond, GOC, Malaya Command, 1939–41, after Dobbie and before Percival. (*By courtesy of the National Portrait Gallery*)

Below right: Air Vice Marshal John Babington (later Sir John Tremayne), AOC, Malaya, before 1941. Not on speaking terms with Bond. (*By courtesy of the National Portrait Gallery*)

Above left: Sir Shenton Thomas, Governor of the Straits Settlements and High Commissioner for Malaya since 1935 (*right*). With him is Duff Cooper, sent out by Churchill in 1941 as the War Cabinet's representative minister. (*Imperial War Museum—IWM*)

Above right: C.A. Vlieland, Secretary of Defence, Singapore, 1939–41. A portrait taken at Oxford in 1911. (*Courtesy of The Master and Fellows of Balliol College*)

The Defence Committee of the British Cabinet—*front row from left*: Beaverbrook, Attlee, Churchill, Eden, (A.V.) Alexander; *back row*: Portal, Pound, Sinclair, Margesson, Dill, Ismay; and Colonel L.C. Hollis (secretary). (*IWM*)

Brigadier Lewis Heath on the Northwest Frontier, *c.* 1938, with Indian troops in background. As a lieutenant-general he commanded 3rd Indian Corps in the Malayan campaign. (*Courtesy of the Director, National Army Museum*)

Below left: Maj.-Gen. D.M. Murray-Lyon, Commander 11th Indian Division, 1941. (*Courtesy Dr Iain Murray-Lyon*)

Below right: Colonel (later Brigadier) Phillip Parker, OC, 2/10th Baluch Regiment in February 1942, photographed at Bannu, *c.* 1947. He wrote an account of the 'disappearance' of the regiment which has only recently come to light. (*Courtesy Major Campbell Parker*)

Above left: Air Chief Marshal Sir Robert Brooke-Popham, appointed Commander-in-Chief, Far East, in 1940. (*IWM*)

Above right: Admiral Sir Tom Phillips (*right*), who went down with the *Prince of Wales*, 10 December 1941, photographed with his chief of staff, Rear Admiral Palliser. (*IWM*)

Air Vice Marshal C.W.A. Pulford (*right*), AOC, Far East, receives Averell Harriman, President Roosevelt's Special Envoy, as he alights from his Liberator, having flown from Moscow, October 1941. (*IWM*)

The two faces of espionage: (*left*) the British officer traitor, Captain Patrick Heenan, who spied for the Japanese. This snapshot was taken at Cheltenham when he was aged about eighteen (*Courtesy Mark Fletcher*); (*right*) Captain John Neil Becker and his wife, Dorothy Crisp, at their wedding in St George's, Hanover Square, in 1945. Becker worked for Military Intelligence in Malaya and Thailand. Dorothy Crisp, a well-known journalist, wrote one of the first books about the fall of Singapore and published it herself, despite political interference. (*Courtesy Hugh Becker*)

One of the Singapore 15-inch 'big guns', firing out to sea before hostilities began and helping to create, perhaps, one of the myths of Singapore. (*IWM*)

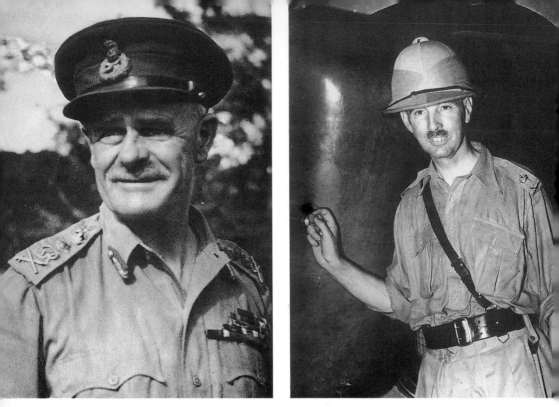

Above left: General Sir Archibald Wavell, appointed Allied Supreme Commander, South-east Asia, in January 1942, and based in Java. (*Courtesy Mrs Pamela Humphrys*)

Above right: Lt-Gen. A.E. Percival stepping off the plane when he arrives to replace General Bond as GOC, Malaya Command, May 1941. (*IWM*)

Vice Admiral Sir Geoffrey Layton, C-in-C China Fleet, confers with his secretary. (*IWM*)

pro-British Thais, both civilian and in the Thai armed services. Without significant army backing neither plan would have had much chance of success.

Even if a coup had been implemented it must remain doubtful whether it would have affected the outcome of the Malayan campaign. The British military forces in Malaya proved not strong enough to withstand the Japanese onslaught at any time during the Malayan campaign. There is no compelling reason to believe that the outcome would have been much different had the initial confrontation occurred on Thai territory. Instead of the retreat starting from the Malay-Thai border, it would merely have begun somewhere farther north.

The only proviso to this argument revolves around what the Thai armed forces might have done when the Japanese attacked, had such a coup previously taken place. If the Thai army and Thailand's well-equipped air force had weighed in against the Japanese forces, this may have made a difference.

Small Thai units did have some success in holding up the Indian Army 'Krohcol' force, a force which was actually sent into Thailand after the war began. Its objective was to capture a valuable strategic position known as The Ledge. The delay caused by these fighting Thais, together with a certain lack of urgency on the part of the Krohcol force commander who, instead of driving forward, kept stopping to ensure that he kept open his line of communication, resulted in the Japanese getting there first.

Had the Thais, on the other hand, fought alongside the British against the Japanese this might have held up the Japanese for a short while. We now know that the Japanese were critically short of some types of shell and stores just before Singapore fell. They were by then at the end of a long and tenuous line of communication. General Yamashita, the Japanese commander, stated after the war that, had not General Percival capitulated when he did, then he would have had to give up his final assault on Singapore. So, a few days gained in Thailand could have affected the final outcome. (The same reasoning applies, of course, to many other factors that had a bearing on the fall of Singapore.)

The role of Sir Josiah Crosby (together with that of Anthony Eden) in the Far East situation in the immediate pre-war years, would have been a subject which a Singapore Inquiry would have had to consider. Crosby's attitude towards the Thais would have needed investigation. So would certain specific matters such as his involvement in the dismissal of Colonel Hayley Bell from Singapore in 1939; his damning of the 'scaremongering stories' emanating from Malaya about the possibility of a war with Japan and Thailand's possible involvement in it; his success in stopping Killery's SOE plans for Thailand; and the circumstances behind his extraordinary, panicky telegram to Brooke-Popham on the eve of the Japanese attack.

Sir Josiah was a fluent Thai speaker. This enabled him to deal with Thai officials directly. Andrew Gilchrist, a member of Crosby's legation staff at the time, has said, 'Crosby was a good ambassador who did his duty, reporting the Thai situation vividly and accurately, and holding courageously to a straight-forward line of policy'.[24] One cannot fault Gilchrist's opinion as to the vividness of Crosby's dispatches. One War Office official endorsed one of Crosby's reports, 'Sir Josiah should write novels – sixpenny stuff to keep kids awake!'[25] And they accurately described the Thai situation as he saw it. However Crosby always disliked any interference in what he considered his own sphere of expertise, and saw little merit in any aspect of British policy towards Thailand that he himself had not initiated. As Charles Cruickshank said in *The Official History of the SOE in the Far East* regarding Crosby's opposition to SOE operations in Thailand, 'the correspondence leaves the impression ... that he [Crosby] was moved as much by a desire to oppose the intruding Killery as a wish to further British policy'.

Even earlier than this Crosby was making difficulties for British intelligence-gathering efforts in the area. In January 1940 the FECB in Singapore circularised all British embassies and consulates in the Far East, and also the Dominions, asking for their aid in gathering information. All replied positively, except Sir Josiah Crosby. In his reply, after pointing out certain difficulties in complying with the request, he said that 'additional functions are not to be lightly assumed' by his staff. He ended by stating what was self-evident. 'I am afraid that I may appear rather grudging in the response given to your request for assistance.'[26]

If Andrew Gilchrist had inserted the word 'rigidly' in his description of Crosby's reporting actions, it might perhaps have more accurately described them. It appears to have been nigh on impossible to make him change his mind once it was made up. Colonel Grimsdale of the FECB says, 'About a week before the war Brookham [one of Brooke-Popham's nicknames] sent me to Bangkok to try and persuade that dreadful old man Crosby to try and do something to help win the war by allowing Killery to start work in Siam. It was quite hopeless.'

The cipher exchanges between Singapore and London, and London and Bangkok, about Killery's Thai efforts were getting out of synchronisation in those final pre-war days. This resulted in some actions being approved in London behind Crosby's back, and when Killery was told to rectify this by informing Crosby direct, he rejoindered, 'you no doubt realise that so long as you insist on his [Crosby's] prior approval a Bangkok organisation is definitely impossible'. A colleague confirmed this, and said it was tantamount to madness to consult Crosby, 'one might as well expect a Chief of Police to sponsor a Guild of Housebreakers'.

On 2nd December, six days before the Japanese invasion, Brooke-Popham received information, probably through the interception of a Japanese message, that certain pro-Japanese members of the Thai government had proposed to Tokyo that in order to make Britain appear the aggressor Japanese forces should land at Kota Bharu in Malaya, and this would almost certainly result in British forces crossing into Thailand, whereupon Thailand would declare war on Britain.

It is not known whether this information was passed on to Crosby. He was certainly never officially told about Operation Matador – so that, according to Brooke-Popham, he could 'state with perfect sincerity that he was ignorant of the plans' in his discussions with the Thais. However, Crosby must have heard some scuttlebutt about the British invasion plans. On 7th December 1941, on the very eve of the Japanese attacks, he sent his panicky telegram to Brooke-Popham, begging him not to attack first. Exactly what effect this had on Brooke-Popham's decision-making processes is uncertain but, as the C-in-C pointed out in his despatch, he could not 'completely ignore the telegram from Sir Josiah Crosby'. The least that can be said is that it could not have helped much.

When Crosby gained his Ministerial post in Bangkok in 1934, was it solely because Sir Josiah had earlier spent a quarter of a century in that country and thus probably knew it better than any other living Englishman? Or was that augmented by Thai knowledge of something about Crosby that might give them a degree of influence over him, an influence that ensured they could rely on his reports to London being biased in their favour?

In certain Singapore and Malayan circles, where he was familiarly known as 'Bing', Sir Josiah Crosby had a reputation for two things. He was known as the man who did not care to hear 'scaremongering stories' emanating from Singapore about a possible war with Japan and Thailand's involvement in it. He took great exception, for example (as did Sir Shenton Thomas) to many editorials on the subject in the *Straits Times*, written by G.W. Seabridge.[27]

The other reference, made far less openly, was to Sir Josiah's homosexuality. The mores of those times made this something that Crosby would have done his utmost to cover up, but, despite this, it was known to some senior government and military officials in Malaya.

Homosexuality was at that time a crime throughout the British Empire. In Malaya, Europeans caught out in the practice were hurriedly shipped home rather than have them face an embarrassing trial. Additionally, apart from the moral aspects, the security services considered homosexuals were open to blackmail. Singapore Special Branch treated suspected homosexuals as potential security risks and their names appeared in that Department's blacklist.

There is no suggestion that Crosby was at any time disloyal to his country. There is no evidence to suggest that he did not report to London all the information that came his way. But the likelihood of the Thais knowing of Crosby's sexual bias could have underlaid their request for Sir Josiah's return to Bangkok as British Minister. Prime Minister Pibul was a devious man. He would have reasoned it would be of benefit to have such a man stationed in Bangkok – a capital where such sexual proclivities could be more easily indulged than in most others – and would likely result in the Thai situation being reported to London biased in his, Pibul's, favour. Richard Aldrich has stated that 'an exceptionally sympathetic prescription for Britain's Thai policy emanated from Bangkok', but he does not cite Crosby's homosexuality as a reason for this.[28]

There would have been no need for overt blackmail by anyone in the Thai government. Aware that Crosby would be keen to stay on in Bangkok, Pibul could safely assume that the British Minister would be inclined to ensure that, wherever possible, he would grant the administration the benefit of any doubt. This would have been particularly valuable to Pibul, if indeed he was pro-Japanese from an early date. Such a pro-Thai attitude would not have been inimical to the interests of the pro-British element in the Thai government either.

If the homosexuality factor be added to the view that it is not in human nature to suspect the motives of those who requested your presence in their country, then, on top of his undoubted regard for the Thais, we have reasons for Crosby's extraordinarily ardent pro-Thai attitude.

This attitude was to put him into conflict with Grant, the American Minister in Bangkok, who, for instance, had reported to his government that he believed Crosby had by wink and by nod acquiesced in Pibul's attack on Indo-China in 1940. This theory of Crosby's involvement may not be at all far-fetched. A number of British Foreign Office files on Thailand were released at the beginning of 1993 having been previously closed for fifty years. Some of these contain information that tends to support Ambassador Grant's thesis.

A 'most secret' communication to the Foreign Office from the British Consul-General in Tangiers, dated 10th February 1941, reported on information supplied by an agent code-named 'André':

> *Franco-Thai Conflict*
> 'André' tells me that there is great pessimism at Vichy over this question and that it is being widely rumoured that HM Minister at Bangkok is responsible for having urged the Thais to take this hostile action. 'André' himself realised that Thailand had been incited by Japan to take action against Indo-China.[29]

The British ambassador in Tokyo, Sir Robert Craigie, reported similar information. In a message to the Chief of Intelligence Services, Singapore, and copied to the Foreign Office, on 15th April 1941, he reported that the Counsellor of the French Embassy in Tokyo had stated that French delegates from Indo-China had brought with them 'certain proof' that Great Britain had supported the Thai claims over French territory. Craigie followed that with another message on the 28th April. He said that the proof had come from Hanoi, that it was considered there was no possibility of it being a Japanese or German forgery, and that the evidence purported 'to prove that Sir J. Crosby, in an effort to counter Japanese influence in Thailand, had secretly but formally supported Thai territorial claims on Indo-China'.[30]

Whatever the truth of those particular allegations, there is no doubt that Crosby held an opinion of Pibul and the Thais that differed appreciably from the opinions of others without his 'vested' interest. Towards the end, even Crosby hedged his bets somewhat. In his dispatch No. 53, of the 25th January 1941, he noted that, 'I have a feeling that the Prime Minister has capitulated to the Japanese to a large degree and that he is working secretly in concert with them.' However, he seemed to edge back to his former convictions two days later in his dispatch No. 59.

> Our only weapon [in the diplomatic struggle with the Japanese over Thailand] is exercise of persuasion with Thais, who are children and it has not been possible to bring these children to reason, with Japan dangling before them the promise of the recovery of their lost provinces. For many reasons it is a wonder to me that Thailand has not gone over to Japanese camp long ago; the fact that she has refrained from doing so up to now indicates her sympathies are not fundamentally pro-Japanese. I still think that by continuing with a policy of tact and friendliness we may keep her from selling herself utterly to Japan.[31]

By February 1941 a tired and worried Crosby may have been becoming concerned by the criticisms of his very pro-Thai stance, including, if he had indeed acquiesced to it, the Thai attack on Indo-China. On 4th February he tendered a resignation letter to Sir Alexander Cadogan, Permanent Secretary at the Foreign Office. However, in it he left the door open for it to be turned down by saying that he did 'not want to abandon a task which is now less easy to perform than it used to be. I shall always be ... at the disposal of the Secretary of State'.[32]

Sir Josiah's resignation was not accepted. An internal Foreign Office minute on the subject read:

> Sir J. Crosby has been our greatest asset in keeping the Thais from going over completely to Japan ...
>
> To take him away now might suggest to the Thais that we are gravely displeased and perhaps unwilling to continue our friendly relationship, but it might also suggest (and would no doubt be interpreted by our enemies as) a disavowal of Sir J. Crosby ...
>
> If we have to take a much stronger line with the Thais, the removal of Sir J. Crosby will be a weapon in our hands.

The fact that the issue of removing Crosby and replacing him by a stronger man was considered a useful weapon to be held in reserve, seems to imply that the Foreign Office knew that Crosby was soft on the Thais. Another hand has endorsed the above quoted file with, 'I don't think we ought to part with such a useful card as Sir J. Crosby until we have to.'

One commentator on Crosby's actions, a man who was in Malaya in those pre-war days, has told this author that he considers that Crosby was so pro-Thai as to be almost anti-British. This is perhaps going too far, although that view is supported by a marginal note made by a Foreign Office official in London on one of Crosby's pre-war messages. It posed the question, 'where [does] allegiance to country come in Crosby's batting order?'

Despite all this, Crosby was never deliberately disloyal to the British cause. He reported many matters to London that the Thais would not have wanted him to report. All that can be said is that his views were certainly slanted by his having being kept in one place for far too long, and probably by the method of his appointment and his homosexuality. By December 1941, the month of the Japanese invasion, another factor has to be taken into account; according to Andrew Gilchrist, the strain under which Crosby had operated for months 'towards the end adversely affected his health'.

Underlying all this is the undeniable fact that Crosby was telling the Foreign Minister, Anthony Eden, more or less exactly what he wanted to hear. It suited Eden to receive reports that the Thai leader was inclined to be pro-British, for it fitted in with the Foreign Office's appeasement and holding policy towards Japan.

After a study of the pre-war Thai situation one is left with several unanswered questions. One of them is, if Crosby did acquiesce in the Thai attacks on French Indo-China, and the evidence seems to point in that direction, did he do this of his own accord, or with the blessing of the British government? If Crosby's stance was taken with the cognizance of those above him, this could be the reason why so many files on the Thai situation are still unavailable to the public and marked 'retained in department'.

Chapter Seven

Captain John Becker, British Military Intelligence

Shortly after midday on 24th August 1948, a British merchant named John Becker was shot and killed in his office in Singapore by a Chinaman. This murder took place in the early months of the long and bloody fight against the Chinese Communist terrorists in Malaya, a conflict that was never termed a war but called the Malayan Emergency.

Within hours of the killing, the Singapore Deputy Commissioner of Police, E.V. Fowler, issued this statement: 'There is no political significance behind this murder. It is purely the case of a man who ran amok without arms in the first place, and who managed to get hold of a weapon.' That a senior policeman found it necessary to make such a statement so soon after the event is perhaps significant. Was Mr Fowler's statement the beginning of an official process designed to obscure John Becker's involvement in undercover counter-espionage activities?

The killing of John Becker on that sweltering day in 1948 brought to an end a career in military intelligence, which had begun well before the start of hostilities in the Pacific in World War Two, of the most fascinating British cloak-and-dagger man to have operated in the Far East. He died still holding the opinion that, had General Percival and others acted upon his pre-war intelligence reports, the fall of Singapore might have been avoided.

This is the first time his story has been told. It has been pieced together from private papers left by John Becker and his wife, Mrs Dorothy Becker who was a professional political journalist during the war years, for which she always used her maiden name, Crisp, under which, for example, she published her book *Why We Lost Singapore* (1943) to which reference was made in the previous chapter. Here she will be called Dorothy Crisp.[1]

The secret British operation planned by Killery of SOE to create a *coup d'état* in pre-war Thailand in 1941 did not get much farther than the preparatory stages. The full facts, probably locked away in British government files on pre-war Thailand, have still not been made public. The little information about Killery's scheme that is available in official files are mainly part of the process of obfuscation and Departmental disclaimers of responsibility made at the time in the face of the violent opposition of Sir Josiah Crosby in

Bangkok, who was backed by the Foreign Secretary, Anthony Eden, in London.

But the SOE scheme was not the only such attempt in 1941 to get the Thais to side with the British rather than with the Japanese. John Becker, at that time a captain in British Military Intelligence, was working along somewhat similar lines, but quite separately from SOE. His direct superior may have been the mysterious G.C. Denham, the MI6 man in Singapore, or it may have been Major Chamier, latterly the Head of Military Intelligence there. If Denham was involved – and there are a few hints in the story that point in this direction – this adds a strange twist to an already confused situation. Although officially MI6 did not exist, the department was funded out of the Foreign Office's secret vote; and the Foreign Secretary, Eden, backed his Minister in Bangkok in opposing anything that would upset the status quo in Thailand. At some stage, too, General Percival, GOC Malaya Command, was party to Becker's plans.

Captain John Becker was a romantic and an idealist, in character miles away from the type of man one associates with espionage. The Becker family can trace themselves back to one Captain Thomas Beck who, in 1745, was beheaded at Carlisle on the orders of William Augustus, Duke of Cumberland, for his part in both the Old and Young Pretender uprisings. Beck's eldest son, another Thomas, was a ship's master who landed troops for Bonnie Prince Charlie. This Thomas and his brothers had prices on their heads and had to make their homes on the Continent. One of the brothers opened a School of Navigation in Russia. Nearer John Becker's own time there was a cousin, Lydia Ernestine Becker (1827–1890), a strong advocate of women's suffrage, and a leader of the movement in the Manchester area. The strange blend of traditionalism and nonconformism in John Becker's character seems to stem from these family influences.

He was tall (six foot), slim and 'extremely good-looking with wonderful blue eyes', according to his niece.[2] The *Straits Times* newspaper once described him as a man 'of great personal charm and sterling character'. He may well have used Lawrence of Arabia as a role model, for his life had many parallels with that of the Arabian adventurer, with something from earlier adventurers thrown in for good measure. He championed Malay nationalism and was strongly opposed to any form of racial injustice. Had he lived in the east of a hundred years before, he might well have fought alongside the first White Rajah of Sarawak, Sir James Brooke, against pirates, headhunters, and moral injustice. In 1942, the third White Rajah, Sir Vyner Brooke, was to say complimentary things about him.

John Neill Herman Becker was born in Sydenham in south-east London on 13th February 1900. The family was well-to-do. He was the eldest son of his father's second marriage. (Of his two elder half-sisters, Enid and Dagmar, Enid married a Malayan rubber planter named John Pickering; and Dagmar married the future Lieutenant-General Sir Arthur Dowler in 1918.) His father, Neill Herman Theodore Becker, who always used the name Herman, had worked for many years in India. In 1890, as the Calcutta-based partner of a German trading organisation, Ernsthausen & Company, he was appointed Imperial German Consul. He formed his own company, Becker & Ross, in 1895, which by 1900 had become Becker & Gray. By that time Herman Becker was based in London and running the company from premises at 24 Fenchurch Street. The company traded very profitably in gunny, shellac, jute, grain, seed and sugar.[3]

Herman Becker was one of those men who appear delightful everywhere except in the home. He could be exceedingly charming on first acquaintance, but it was said he cared for nobody, not even himself. He was forty when he married as his second wife, a very beautiful nineteen-year-old Ethel Scott-Turner, who had connections with some of the oldest families in England. Herman gave young Ethel a hard time. She 'alternated between illnesses and parties, diamond bracelets and tears'. She had three children in under four years, John, Herman Scott, and Ethel Brenda, followed by another, Neill Sydney in 1907. The toll on her health was too much and she died an early death in 1915. (Herman Becker later married as his third wife the mother of General Dowler.)

After attending prep school at Duncombe Park near Ramsgate, John Becker was sent to Haileybury. Perhaps it was there that he developed his gift for languages, for later it was said that he spoke sixteen, including Latin, French, German, Dutch, Malay, Thai and Hindustani.* At eighteen he joined the Irish Guards but by the time he had completed his training the First World War was over. So he left the army and entered Grays Inn. Shortly after that he had a violent row with his father that led to him being sent out East by an uncle. (Something similar seems to have happened with one of his younger brothers, Scott, who ended up in Rhodesia.)

His wife was to write of him in the 1940s:

> His early life had robbed him of certainty, either emotional or spiritual, and turned his brilliant though somewhat academic brain to work in devious ways; as it were, always to provide cover for itself. He had developed an instinctive distrust of those in authority that consorted oddly with his romantic love of royalty, his fondness for uniform and ceremony, and his real devotion to the ideal of aristocracy. This distrust, I think, tended to lead him away from the society of his own people and his elders, and combined with an intense curiosity, to lead him into contacts with the peoples of Asia and even into some outward practising of their religions, because, as he said to me in the

---

*Haileybury, where the East India Company civil servants were trained, specialised in the teaching of oriental languages.

early days of our acquaintance, 'You cannot understand a man unless you understand his faith'.

When he first arrived in the East John Becker was twenty. He spent a short time in Sumatra as a rubber planter, before crossing the Malacca Strait to engage in merchant trading in Malaya. He quickly became an erudite Malay scholar, not only fluent in the spoken language but able also to read and write it in the classic Arabic script, a much rarer attainment.

He quickly developed an interest in all things Malay, and started the process that was later to lead one prominent Malayan politician to call him 'a friend to the Malay race'. He often went among them in local dress, and one of the several aliases he used on these occasions was Abou Hassan. Older than his years he became interested in the Malay nationalism movement which was then in its embryo stage. One of his contacts was Tuan Mohamed Yunus who, in 1926, was to form the Malay Union, a body created to improve the political, economic and social conditions of the Malays in a country dominated politically by Britain and economically by the Chinese domiciled there.

It is not known why but, in 1925, John Becker left Malaya and travelled to Calcutta to became an assistant in his father's firm. He stayed there until early 1928, sharing bachelor 'chummery' lodgings with a group of other young men. (A chummery was a lodging house for unmarried and comparatively junior Europeans in the East.) While there, on 26th November 1926, John joined the Army in India Reserve of Officers as a Second Lieutenant, and did his training with the 18th Royal Garhwal Rifles.[4]

It is from the period of three years he spent in India that we have the first proof of John Becker's strong sense of honour. He had been befriended by a long-standing and well-known resident of Calcutta called Harry Hobbs. In the process of his business dealings Hobbs had somehow stumbled across evidence that certain leaders of the YMCA movement in India, prominent Britons amongst them, had been helping themselves to a considerable slice of the Association's funds. The amount of money involved was very large indeed, and the affair was considered so serious that the Viceroy, Lord Irwin, later Viscount Halifax, aided by his Advocate-General and almost the entire Calcutta Chamber of Commerce, did his utmost to shut Hobbs up for fear that the scandal would affect British prestige in India. But Hobbs would have none of that, although he was put under considerable pressure. One of the men who backed him, though he himself came under pressure too, was John Becker. For this Hobbs was grateful for the remainder of his life.[5]

John Becker was never really happy in India, for his heart lay farther east. When an opportunity came for him to return to Malaya he jumped at it. He went back in 1928 and joined the firm of Frazer Neave Limited which had its head office on Raffles Quay, Singapore. 'F & N', as the company was (and is) universally called throughout the East, engaged in general trade, publishing, and, most famously, the production and distribution of aerated waters. (In that part of the world they are as famous in this field as Schweppes.) Becker worked for them on the mainland of Malaya, in the Netherland East Indies, and in Thailand. By 1933 he was the manager of the firm's office in the federal Malay capital, Kuala Lumpur.

Once again, whenever he had the opportunity, he immersed himself in the life of Malays. He 'took his place among them as of bestowed right, a man who knew the inner workings of their village councils'.[6] He was made an honorary leader of a *kampong* (village) council in the Malacca area. He met and befriended Malays from all walks of life, and became known as the '*Tuan* who visits our homes' (which indicates that such home visits from white men were rare). His interest in Malay nationalism now grew stronger. He had the ambition to see rise from among the Malays a leader or leaders who would carry the country into unity and independent nationhood in place of the existing system of separate sultanates linked politically only by the imposition of British overall direction. He had no wish to see the end of the Malayan royalty, but only to see them combined under the leadership of one man, perhaps one from among them, who would lead a Malay nation to independence. This ambition, wrote his wife, 'sprang from a genuine love of Malays and of Malaya; from a desire to promote English interests; from an almost schoolboy dream of emulation of some of the great figures of the eighteenth century, and from an unacknowledged, unconfirmed desire for power'.

Whether many of his European contemporaries in Malaya agreed with his views, which were far ahead of their time, and not at all in keeping with British policy, is doubtful. In 1933, however, he became friendly with an officer in the Malayan Department of Education named Richard Sidney. The friendship was close despite the fact that Sidney and Becker had divergent views on many matters. In an obituary letter for Becker to the *Straits Times* in 1948, Sidney wrote, 'We always disagreed strongly in our political views – and this made our contacts refreshing and invigorating.'[7]

After about 1934 John Becker's business often took him across the border into Thailand, and he was actually stationed there for lengthy periods. He learned to speak Thai fluently. While there his impulse to encourage nationalism among the Malays became subordinated to a desire also to help the Thais, then living under a military dictatorship. He immersed himself in the local life as well. A Singapore newspaper article in 1948 said of him, 'He entered the life of the country rapidly, became fluent in Siamese and gained considerable influence through his Siamese friends of the Royalist Party,'[8]

The situation of the Thai Royal family in the mid-thirties was a precarious one. After the coup of 1932 which brought Luang Pibul to prominence, King Prajadhipok – a grandson of King Mongkut who had employed Anna Leonowens as governess to his children – changed almost overnight from being an absolute monarch to a constitutional one. Though he continued to reign, and much of the mystique and trappings of majesty was still there, he no longer ruled. The king suffered severely from cataracts and spent much time in the West having treatment for them. He was very pro-British and had a house in England. He was there in 1935 when Pibul asked his assent to the execution of a number of Thai opposition leaders. The king refused the request and then abdicated in favour of his nine-year-old nephew, Ananda Mahidol. (On the eve of the abdication a lone gunman shot and seriously wounded Pibul. For some reason the attacker's name was never revealed.) The new king was allowed to stay in Switzerland where he was attending school, and a Council of Regents acted in his stead. Although some Thai princes continued to hold senior posts in government (for example Prince Viwat was an adviser to the Minister of Finance, and Prince Varnvaidya Varavarn was a member of the Thai delegation that went to Tokyo to negotiate the peace treaty over French Indo-China) any power they now wielded was by grace of Pibul.

There is an unsubstantiated story in the Becker family, stemming from this time, that he had a liaison with a Thai princess and that the liaison produced a child. If the story is true it could account for the strong attachments and undoubted influence he had with some members of the Royalist Party. It was not unknown for Royal Thais to marry foreign commoners. In the first decade of this century the brother of the then king married a Russian named Catherine Desnitsky. Their son, Prince Chakrabongse, a well-known racing driver, married an English girl, Elizabeth Hunter, in 1938, the same year as a cousin, Prince Birabongse, married the first of his two English wives, Ceril Heycock, the daughter of an officer in the Royal Marines. Princess Ubol Ratana, the eldest daughter of the present king, King Bhumibol Adulyadej, married Peter Ladd Jenson in 1972.

In a Singapore newspaper in 1947, Becker is quoted as having said, 'I was in Siam in 1937 and 1938, and I could speak the language well, and through no fault of my own I became deeply involved in Siamese politics, and I can claim to have prevented a revolution.' In that same article Becker stated that he often travelled dressed as a native, further proof of a penchant for disguises.[9]

Becker's journeyings through the byways of Malaya and Thailand, byways in both the geographical sense, and more importantly, in the sense of participating in aspects of Malayan and Thai life not usually traversed by Europeans, gave him access to much inside information. His dual and more than casual interests in the Muslim religion in Malaya and Buddhism in Thailand, probably helped in this. One of the senior Malay personages he came into regular contact with at this time was Dato

Onn bin Jafar, onetime *Mentri Besar* (Prime Minister) of Johore. Perhaps Becker had him in mind for the 'leader among Malays' he was seeking. (At one time Dato Jafar was not popular with the British authorities in Malaya for his nationalist leanings; but they knighted him in 1953.)

But above all else John Becker was an Englishman and when, in 1937, he came to the attention of the MI5 officer in Singapore, Colonel Hayley Bell, he did not hesitate to pass on any intelligence information which might prove of use to his country.

Hayley Bell employed at least two undercover agents. One was a Swiss national of half-Japanese parentage, and the other was John Becker. A.H. Dickinson, Inspector-General of Police in Singapore from 1939, wrote in early January 1970 that he thought Becker might have been the man who discovered in 1938 details of the Japanese invasion plans for Thailand and Malaya. In truth the agent concerned in that particular intelligence coup was almost certainly the Swiss. Dickinson had an extensive file on Becker, and when he wrote the following in 1968, he may have had Becker in mind (although prior to 1939 Becker was not officially a member of any intelligence organisation): 'In [pre-war] Malaya it is doubtful whether there were even two officers amongst all the services organisations operating in Intelligence who had a knowledge of the local languages and conditions.'[10]

There is no record of when and how Becker first came into contact with Hayley Bell, but however it happened Becker, with his linguistic abilities and his many contacts among Malays and especially his contacts with the Royal faction in Thailand, must have soon become an important cog in Hayley Bell's intelligence machine. When that machine was broken up in early 1939 and Hayley Bell sent home, Becker did not stay long either. In fact he may have even preceded Hayley Bell by a month or two, for he left Malaya for home in March 1939. There is no evidence that he was forced to leave.

In England Becker was commissioned into the Royal Army Service Corps on 15th December 1939. He was then thirty-nine years old. During his period of training at an army camp in Wales, the War Office sent around an enquiry into the linguistic abilities of officers. Becker's list was impressive, but as Malay is more properly written in Arabic script rather than the romanised one, he noted that he could write it in 'Arabic characters'. This was picked up by some bright character at the War Office and Becker was promptly recruited into Military Intelligence and shipped out to Cairo. He could not, of course, speak any Arabic apart from the words of that language that have been incorporated into Malay.

On top of his military duties Becker set himself two tasks in Egypt. He set out to learn Arabic, and began pulling every string at his disposal in an attempt to get himself transferred to a military theatre where the accumulated knowledge of years could be more usefully employed.

Throughout 1940 he wrote letter after letter to friends in Malaya and Thailand, trying to enlist their help.

It is not known what his intelligence duties were in Egypt. He was soon promoted to full Lieutenant, and a military pass dating from those days authorised him to operate in civilian clothes. While there he met his brother, Scott, up from Rhodesia and on his way to serve in the Western Desert. He also met his brother-in-law, General Dowler, and possibly persuaded him to use his influence on the authorities to get him reposted.

Becker had earlier befriended an Australian in Singapore named Max Bell, who was a senior partner in the stockbroking firm of Fraser & Company. (Before the days of the present *Straits Times* Share Index, it was Fraser & Co's daily published information which was the main guide to Malayan share prices.) Becker persuaded Bell to write the following letter, dated 19th February 1941, on his behalf to Air Chief Marshal Sir Robert Brooke-Popham in Singapore:

Sir,
    Affairs in Thailand are exercising a number of minds and in the belief that highly specialized knowledge might be of considerable importance I beg to bring to your notice that there is at present serving as a Lieutenant in the RASC in Alexandria one with a very considerable knowledge of persons and places in Thailand. He is Lieut. J.N. Becker. Mr Becker is a Siamese scholar of erudition and up to the time of his return to England in March 1939 was in very close touch with Thai political circles and had access to secret information which was extremely unlikely to become available through ordinary diplomatic channels. Should this information prove useful I shall be glad at any time to amplify the above.[11]

It is not known whether this letter did the trick in getting him transferred to Malaya, but it does show that the C-in-C, Far East, knew of Becker's existence. Anyway, early in the spring of 1941 he found himself flying to Calcutta en route to Malaya. In Calcutta he met an old friend from his earlier days called Stephen Golledge, and told him that he was in 'an Intelligence job but he would not talk (quite rightly!).'[12] From Calcutta Becker took ship and arrived at Penang in April.

His exact movements and contacts thereafter in Malaya and Thailand are not known, but it is known that he moved around a good deal. Dorothy Crisp records that, among his British friends at this time, was 'an Englishman connected with the Foreign Office'. It seems likely that this was G.C. Denham of the Secret Intelligence Service. Another military pass, this time issued in Malaya, shows that Becker was authorised to travel in civilian clothes throughout northern Malaya under 11th Indian

Division Command, and also to certain specified places in Thailand. He was officially attached to 11th Division HQ from June to August 1941, after which he came directly under HQ Malaya Command. In his jungle travels at this time Becker was assisted by a Pathan soldier, probably from the 5/14th Punjab Regiment which was stationed near Penang, the regiment which still prefers to be known by its old title, the 40th Pathans.

During this time he made contact with Mervyn Llewellyn Wynne, Head of Singapore's Special Branch, the man who was writing reports to Sir Vernon Kell, the Head of MI5 in London, without the knowledge of his superiors in Singapore. How far co-operation went between Becker and Wynne is not known.

In Malaya Becker attempted to get the Malays interested in setting up resistance cells and in operating fifth-column units behind enemy lines should this ever be necessary. When the war actually came there was little evidence to show that he had been successful in this, but as there were also few proven cases of Malays operating *with* the Japanese, perhaps his efforts had a beneficial reverse effect.

Perhaps warned by Denham that anything he might do in Thailand was unlikely to meet with the approval of Sir Josiah Crosby, Becker went deep undercover in Thailand whenever he was there. He was virtually cut off from any superior command for days or weeks at a time, and had to operate very much on his own initiative. He began to collect information from his Royalist connections, using a network of 'Buddhist monks who had confidence in him' and who were able to travel throughout the region without any difficulty.

Soon after his return to Malaya, the newly-promoted Captain Becker paid a visit to Singapore. He was then engaged on producing a report on Thai subjects living in Singapore. The paper he produced, of which he kept a carbon copy, listed the activities of the resident Thais including the Thai Consul himself. He ended his report thus: 'At the back of it all is the growing conviction that Thailand is now prevented from co-operation with Great Britain and that she ranks rather as a non-belligerent abettor of Japan than as the benevolent neutral that the newspapers depict.' At about the same time as he produced this report, a Thai Military Mission, arranged with the blessing of Sir Josiah Crosby, was permitted to tour the British defences on the frontier and then view the defences of Singapore Island.

In Singapore Becker went to Military Intelligence HQ to find out what information they had on certain Thais. He was ushered in to the presence of two Regular Army officers senior to himself. Dorothy Crisp reports that, after his request, 'they took a thin, inadequate file from an unlocked drawer'. This lack of security horrified him, and with the thought that any information he supplied to them might be treated in the same cavalier fashion, he determined to teach the two officers a lesson. 'Then and there,' wrote Dorothy Crisp, 'by a completely justified action, John started a train of tremendous trouble for himself, though I believe he never recognised it as the *fons et origo*. He abstracted two of the more important sheets of paper from the file, put them in his pocket unnoticed and soon went away, intending, when the hue and cry was raised, to return them with some strong comment on the unsuitability of touching faith and unlocked drawers in wartime. But complete calm reigned and continued to reign till, at the end of a week, he could bear it no longer.' (Despite Dorothy Crisp's claim of a 'completely justified action', there were surely better ways of achieving it?)

Returning to HQ, Becker asked the same two officers if he could see the sheets of paper that in fact lay in his pocket book. The balloon he had been waiting for at last went up when the still unlocked drawer was opened and the file taken out. After letting things stew for a while, Becker produced the papers and gave a lecture on security. Some months later, one of those men was present 'with no good intent' during an interview Becker had with General Percival.

After that Becker determined never to divulge the name of his associates to anyone for fear that the information might get back to Thailand via an unlocked drawer.

When he buried himself in the north again, Becker had access to £3,000 of his own money, probably banked from his business days in Malaya – equivalent to some £90,000 nowadays – together with another sum which he raised by a 'realisation that deprived him of future income'. He did not hesitate to use these personal funds for intelligence purposes. Although this seems an extraordinary thing to have done, it makes sense only when one considers Becker's character and the parsimony of the British Treasury over intelligence expenditure. Becker, once he had made up his mind on the route to take, a route which in this case was to involve many personal friends, considered himself honour bound to put everything he had into the undertaking.

Becker soon received confirmation from Royalist sources close to Thai government circles that the Prime Minister Luang Pibul was in the pocket of the Japanese, and had been so for a long time. Becker's sources reported that other important Thais, in addition to those who had never bothered to conceal their Japanese sympathies, were also siding with the Japanese, and vast sums of yen were exchanging hands. It was probably Becker's information that helped the British FECB a few months later to estimate that the Japanese had been spending £50,000 per month on propaganda, and other vast sums on intelligence in Thailand.[13] Much of this money was ending up in the bank accounts of top Thais, and early on Becker began listing in an elaborate code (whose key was three Greek lines from Euripides) details of those Thais whose bank balances were being swollen by yen. The main paymaster behind this expenditure was Colonel Jiro

Saito, the man who had masterminded the Thai attack on French Indo-China.

Like Valentine Killery, head of SOE in Singapore, John Becker was convinced that Thailand was the key to the defence of Singapore. So, together with some of his Royalist friends, he began to plot for the restoration of royal power in Thailand. It is not known who Becker's royalist contacts were, for he was always very careful to keep this information to himself. They might have included Prince Varnvaidya Varavarn and Prince Viwat, who were both ardently pro-British. Prince Chirasakti, the adopted son of ex-King Prajadhipok, might have been involved. He was pro-British too, with a house in Virginia Water, Surrey, on the southern edge of Windsor Great Park. Another Thai with close connections to Royalty who may have been concerned in the Becker plot was a man called Asavasena. He was educated in England and after graduating from Cambridge married an English girl named Winifrid who went back to Thailand with him in 1924. During the war years both of them were involved in Royalist-backed anti-Japanese activities, operating from bases in royal palaces that the Japanese never searched. Winifrid risked her life to deliver medical supplies to some of the British prisoners of war as they trekked up-country to work on the infamous Thai-Burma railway. Stories of the legendary 'beautiful blonde European lady' went the rounds of the prison camps. (Winifrid Asavasena was one of the many heroines of the war whose activities have passed without notice. She died in Thailand in 1991.)[14]

Becker's scheme involved an uprising that was planned to produce a change in government. During the uprising it was arranged that damage to European property in Bangkok would occur on such a scale as to justify the arrival in the country of a protective British force, or an invitation for them to intervene. Whether this pre-planning received the blessing of a superior officer in Singapore, is not known for certain. But General Percival knew of the plans very soon afterwards.

In August Becker reported that Japan's admitted 50,000 troops in South Indo-China were in fact 200,000 shock troops.

In late September, just ten weeks away from the beginning of the Japanese onslaught, John Becker arrived in Singapore from Thailand, his plans almost but not quite complete. He set about writing a lengthy memorandum to General Percival. As he was doing this he received information from a source close to the Thai government, by hand of a Buddhist monk newly arrived in Singapore, that the Japanese intended shortly to attack Malaya through Thailand, and that the existing Thai government would not offer any resistance. Hastily finishing his memorandum, Becker dispatched it to General Percival. All that remained, he said, was 'to rush the plot against the Siamese government into effect. It was now – or too late – and there were still some final links to connect.'

When the telephone rang at his civilian lodgings and the man at the other end of the line – one of the officers involved in the open-drawer incident – peremptorily ordered him to hold fire on everything and report forthwith to HQ, Becker had a sudden sinking feeling in his gut. He demanded an explanation, but all he received back was bluster and acrimony.

He knew at once the reason for these orders. The British Minister in Bangkok, Sir Josiah Crosby, was in Singapore at the time, and Becker guessed that Sir Josiah had put a stop to his plan. Crosby certainly was in Singapore on that date. On 29th September 1941 he was at the Far East Defence Conference, and it was at this meeting that the conclusion was reached that no Japanese attack need be expected for several months, something completely at variance with Becker's new information.

Percival, or perhaps Brooke-Popham, probably placed the Becker plan before Crosby where it met with that Minister's opposition. Whatever the exact circumstances, the plan was now off.

Becker was in a terrible quandary. If his Thai associates failed to hear from him he knew they would not delay the uprising for long knowing that the Japanese attack was not too far off. He also knew that if the British did not march into Thailand in support, or as a consequence of the uprising, then it was likely to end in disaster. Torture and death would lie in store for the royalists, and all to no purpose. If he went first to see General Percival to argue for the plan to go ahead and he lost the argument, he might not be given the opportunity to call the whole thing off personally; and he had no intention of divulging the names of his contacts to anyone else.

He came to an agonizing decision, one which was to haunt him for the rest of his life. For the sake of his friends he would do it the other way round; he would call the uprising off, and then go to see Percival. He would leave nothing to chance by making sure that every part of his network knew of the cancellation order. This was no simple task and would take time. Only when he had completed it to his own satisfaction would he report to HQ.

Accordingly Becker absented himself for forty-eight hours during which he sent messages to various places in the north to warn his Thai associates to do nothing. Maybe he was not wholly successful in this. It is likely that the distribution of the anti-Japanese literature, at which Sir Josiah Crosby took so much umbrage in the following month, and which was sent out under the cover of an organisation calling itself the 'Association for the Protection of the Independence of Thailand' was the only part of his plan that did go ahead.

Dorothy Crisp wrote of Becker's decision, 'It was a decision made at a moment of shock and catastrophe, without any time for consideration. To the end of his life he questioned and tormented himself about it. Was it right or wrong?'

When Becker finally reported to HQ he was immediately placed under arrest. He demanded to know why, and was told he was a troublemaker. He demanded to see General Percival and when he eventually got to see him, one of the 'open drawer' officers was in attendance. Becker had his say, and afterwards General Percival was, as Becker reported, 'sitting there with his head in his hands, saying that he could do nothing'.

For three weeks Captain Becker was kept under arrest at Tyersall Barracks, Singapore. There he was questioned about his Thai contacts but refused to give names. All this time he was guarded by two young officers of the Argyll & Sutherland Highlanders. (He was to meet one of them after the war. The officer, who had then just arrived back home after 'enjoying' three-and-a-half years as a guest of the Japanese Emperor, told him, 'Sir, you were right!') Every day he was taken to the nearby Botanical Gardens for recreation, and during one of these visits he managed to get word of his predicament to some Singapore friends. Max Bell was among those who tried to get him released. The story got around certain circles in Singapore but the press was not permitted to publish anything about it, not even G.W. Seabridge, editor of the *Straits Times*, another friend of Becker's, who was no lover of censorship in any form. The Becker affair became a sort of muted, underground *'cause célèbre'*.

General Percival had opposed the plans of Killery, the SOE Head, to set up stay-behind units, mainly it seems because he, Percival, had not been involved in the planning. We also know that, later, he set up very similar plans of his own but, when accused by Killery of doing so, he angrily retorted that the circumstances were different because now they would be under military control. It seems likely that similar circumstances prevailed with the Becker coup plans. All we can say for certain is that Percival knew of the plans and that subsequent to Becker's arrest *he destroyed the memorandum Becker had sent him*. He did this in the presence of one of his staff officers, who in civilian life was a solicitor in Singapore. That officer was still working in the legal profession in Singapore in the 1950s.

Towards the end of October 1941 John Becker was shipped out of Singapore aboard the troopship *Orontes*. The ship was off the Cape of Good Hope when news of the Japanese attacks on Malaya, Thailand and Pearl Harbor came over the radio.

When Becker arrived in England he told no one about his Singapore adventures, but wind of the affair got around anyway. Early in 1942, the Rajah of Sarawak, Sir Vyner Brooke, speaking to the newspapers in Australia, said in reference to John Becker that 'only one British Officer had worked to take the offensive in Malaya, and he had been suppressed'. Lord Addison, at the time serving as an officer in the Territorial Army and a member of Clement Attlee's postwar cabinet, made a public reference to the affair in Britain.

John Becker found himself shunted into the obscurity of the Army Education Corps. He resented any public discussion of the Singapore affair before he knew why he had been treated in this way, and, concerned about his tarnished reputation and the talk which was circulating in London, he persistently demanded to be court-martialled.

Just as persistently his demand was refused. 'Then it was privately conveyed to him that if he would give a full and exact account of all that he had done and intended, with all details of every person concerned, he would be allowed to see the Intelligence All Highest.' To that he gave a prompt and unequivocal 'no'. He pleaded to serve anywhere overseas, but was told he could not leave the country.

Then, out of the blue, in August 1943 he received the following letter from the War Office:

> Sir,
>   I am commanded by the Army Council to convey to you their appreciation of the services which you have rendered to the Army during a period of grave national emergency.
>
> I am,
Sir,
Your obedient servant,
>
> C.W. Lambert

This far from satisfied John Becker. He felt he had been disgraced in Malaya, and in England had endured whisperings and cold-shouldering because, said the whisperers, 'he had done something peculiar'. On top of all that he was still living in a nightmare of uncertainty because he had not heard one shred of news about the fate of his Thai friends. In the end John Becker handed in his resignation to the Army authorities in 1943 and it was accepted, a course of action quite unusual in wartime.

The remainder of Becker's story is not directly concerned with the fall of Singapore. But it needs to be recorded for it gives proof that the British government had no wish for there to be any public discussion on the loss of the fortress from a very early date. Another reason for rounding off the story is the possibility that Becker's death had something to do with his pre-war activities; he himself certainly considered his life was in danger when he went back in 1947, but whether this fear was a legacy from the past or had to do with his new activities, is not known.

About this time Dorothy Crisp had been asked by her editor on the *Sunday Dispatch*, Charles Eade, to write a rebuttal of a book review which had appeared in the *New York Times*. This had talked of 'the weak and bungling British defence of Malaya' (a campaign of three months) and 'the heroic Dutch defence in Java' (an affair of only eight days). Eade thought this was an ideal job for someone who was fast gaining a reputation for being a strong-minded woman who pulled no punches in her writings. The task in fact worried Dorothy Crisp as she felt she did not possess the necessary background knowledge,* this despite the

---

* At this stage she had not met John Becker.

fact that in mid-1943 she had personal discussions and correspondence with General Sir Archibald Wavell, the ex-Supreme Allied Commander, Southwest Pacific.[15] She wrote the article anyway, it was quite well received and from that time on officers and civilians who had escaped from Singapore beat a path to her door, and she built up a stock of information on the Malayan campaign. She also learned something about the political background to it from her sources close to Whitehall. In this she was aided by her friend of long standing, Viscount Bennett, who as plain Richard Bennett had been Prime Minister of Canada from 1930 to 1935, before retiring to England. As an ex-Prime Minister of the senior Dominion, and as a Privy Councillor, Bennett had many powerful and knowledgeable connections.

Dorothy Crisp had firm convictions. In her series of *Sunday Dispatch* articles and her writings elsewhere during the war, she tucked into anything and anybody she thought deserved such treatment. She took an especial delight in turning her sometimes vitriolic pen on Herbert Morrison, then Home Secretary and Minister of Home Security in the War Cabinet. (In the First World War Morrison had been a conscientious objector. He was now, wrote Miss Crisp, 'compelling better people to do defence jobs a good deal more dangerous than picking apples in Kent, which is the position to which he was relegated by the Tribunal before which he appeared in the 1914–18 war.') Winston Churchill did not escape her pen either, but in November 1943 she went too far in that direction. She submitted an article to Charles Eade (very much a Churchill man and who was later to edit two books about his hero) in which she deplored the Prime Minister's undue deference to the United States. She used quotes such as the one from Sir James Grigg, Secretary of State for War, that Churchill 'nearly fell over backwards' in his determination to please the Americans. The offending article did not appear in the *Sunday Dispatch*, and Miss Crisp refused to write for that paper again.

She set to work to write a book about the fall of Singapore, and even set up her own company to publish it. At the same time a bye-election was pending in the London Borough of Acton and she decided to stand as an Independent candidate. She needed a secretary to handle all the work associated with her candidature, and to that end she was put in contact with John Becker who was now a civilian and looking for something to occupy him. She did not win the election, but during the campaign and in spite of, or perhaps because of, their widely different characters, a close friendship developed between them.

Dorothy Crisp learned little about Becker in the first weeks of their relationship. At first he made no mention of his connections with Singapore. That came out almost by accident, and when it did, she had more raw material for her book. It must have been from Becker that she learned of the activities of Colonel Jiro Saito in Thailand, for she mentioned the colonel in her book and it is unlikely that, in 1944, she could have discovered his name from any other source. From Becker she learned of the strategic importance of Thailand. She learned too, of his attempts to bring about a *coup d'état*, but was careful to include only brief references to this in her manuscript, perhaps from fear of the possible consequences.

She entitled her book *Why We Lost Singapore*. In it she criticised various members of the British Government including Churchill, and for good measure she had a tilt at Russia and the United States. She held that Sir Josiah Crosby was the most culpable person for the loss of the fortress, followed closely by General Percival. It was a curious hodgepodge of a book written too soon after the event and without the benefit of close study of all the relevant factors; definitive history is not often produced so close to the events discussed. In a review of it in January 1945, the Malay scholar Sir Richard Winstedt, called it a 'febrile book' which did 'no service to Great Britain', and certainly in it she went too far in some respects, although she also made some valid points.

Dorothy Crisp was wrong in making Sir Josiah Crosby the main culprit, for his attitude towards the Thais was but one of many factors that led to the fall of Singapore. In comparison with some of the other factors it was a minor one. Her treatment of Crosby was possibly the consequence of a remark he made to her at a meeting in London in 1944, added to his earlier treatment of her close friend John Becker's coup plan. (Crosby had been part of an exchange of diplomats in late 1942.)

By coincidence Crosby and John Becker shared the same London club (this was either the Junior Carlton or the Royal Automobile), and Dorothy Crisp wrote to Crosby there. Her letter read, 'I am writing a book dealing with the Far East and I am a little puzzled as to the development of some events in Siam. I wonder if we might have a talk about this in the near future? It would be of great interest to me, if you have time.'

Sir Josiah replied by return of post, saying that he would call at half-past-four the next day. She reports, 'As Sir Josiah entered my sitting-room, he began, "They double-crossed me, Miss Crisp, they double-crossed me," and for the next hour information poured from him like water from a fully-turned tap. It hardly needed my few questions to stimulate the flow, and I got, I think, an accurate idea of the person as well as of his actions.' Sir Josiah's remark about being double-crossed indicates that, at last, he had come to realise that Thai Prime Minister Pibul should not have been trusted. However, that was insufficient justification for attempting to cast him in the role of the arch villain of the eastern debacle.

As soon as Dorothy Crisp began the process of getting her book printed, extraordinary attempts were made to prevent publication of it and to make her subject to the Official Secrets Act. She chose a printing firm in Lewes, Sussex, and sent the manuscript off to them in the early summer of 1944. Unbeknownst to her the printer sent the manuscript to the Ministry of Information for censorship. Never one to accept the thought of censorship lightly, Dorothy Crisp was furious when she learned of this despite the fact that the censor passed the manuscript for publication. (There was nothing in the book that would have aided the enemy, for Singapore had fallen two years before. That must have been the reason why the Ministry passed it.) In the end, the printer's unauthorised action was to help her case.

Now the trouble really began. Despite having been passed by the censor, it soon became apparent that other Government departments were determined to stop the book's publication by one method or another. In July, upon checking progress with the man acting as her agent, she was told 'that the Lewes Police had gone round to the printer and told him that Mr Leo Amery is determined to stop the publication of the book, and so frightened the printer that he refused even to hold the manuscript.' Amery, as Secretary of State for India, was a senior member of the British Cabinet.

Miss Crisp checked this story with the printer, who confirmed that the policeman who had called on and intimidated him was a detective-sergeant, and had stated 'Mr Amery would do anything to prevent publication of the book'. So on 4th July she wrote a letter to Leo Amery, commencing with the pious hope that he was unaware of the crimes being committed in his name. She pointed out that the book had been passed by the censors, and that there was no legal basis for his intervention which she described as 'Gestapo-like, un-English, and altogether indefensible'. She went on to threaten wholesale publicity unless he instructed the Lewes police to apologise to the printers for using his name, and to withdraw all objection to the publication.

While waiting for a reply Dorothy Crisp discovered that the instructions to the Lewes Police had come from someone in Birmingham, where Amery was the Member of Parliament for the Sparsbrook Division. She then received a letter from Amery which said he was unaware of any action being taken about the book, and if it was being taken it was not at his instance, and he was making inquiries. Meanwhile she learned from her agent that the paper supply for the publication (paper was a scarce commodity in wartime and was issued on a quota basis) was in Birmingham and that the supply was 'being tampered with' there.

Determined to get to the bottom of the matter, Dorothy arranged a meeting for the following Monday in Lewes with the Deputy Chief Constable of Sussex. Before she set out on the 'roundabout and tedious' wartime train journey she received a letter from the Ministry of Labour, directing her under the Defence General Regulations 1939, No. 58A, to report to the Admiralty to start work as a £2 per week stenographer.

She realized that this was a new line in the offensive to gag her, for as an Admiralty employee she would come under the Official Secrets Act. Fully aware that there was little chance of getting a directed labour order changed, she nevertheless wrote a note to the Minister of Labour, Ernest Bevin, stating that she could neither type efficiently nor take shorthand. She attached this to the original directive together with a statement of all the present developments, and sent it off.

During her meeting with the Deputy Chief Constable in Lewes he did not contradict her use of Mr Amery's name, and on referring to what she called a 'four-page dossier', he confirmed that the original instructions had come from Birmingham, although he denied 'that the inquiry had been directed' against her.

Back in London Dorothy Crisp donned her formidable war paint. She sent a summary of the entire affair to every Member of Parliament of her acquaintance. One of them, Sir Ernest Graham-Little, drafted a question about the matter to be asked in the House. She wrote to Amery again, pointing out that his name had certainly been used in the affair. She linked in the attempt to direct her into a clerk's job at the Admiralty, stating that 'the whole thing looks remarkably like an attempt to stop my publishing one way or another'.

She had to wait two weeks for a reply to that one. Amery then informed her that he had now been told of the circumstances in which his name came to be mentioned by the Lewes Police. Dorothy wrote, 'It transpired that the enquiries the Lewes police were making were not related to the book but to an individual of whom it was thought the printers might have some knowledge. He finished by saying there was no foundation for the assertion that the printers were intimidated, and that the printers were now ready to print subject to paper being supplied'.

She wrote up this whole affair in her autobiography *A Life For England*, published in 1946.[16] In it she said of that second letter of Amery's, 'apart from the falsehood contained in the first part of the sentence with which the letter ended, the last part of the letter was the sheerest sophistry – paper being the root difficulty'.

Why We Lost Singapore was eventually printed by someone else, but the matter did not end there, for there was still the question of the directed labour order hanging over Miss Crisp's head. She received several registered letters from the Ministry of Labour containing threats of court action. In December 1944, she wrote a letter to the Ministry, which began, 'Mr Amery, operating through the Birmingham and Lewes police seriously interfered with the publication of my book.' She went on to explain why she had not attended a Local Appeal Board. 'I was far too busy dealing with Mr Amery to see the Local Board especially as it seemed clear that Regulation 58A was being used to cripple the freedom of the Press, as a reinforcement of Mr Amery's efforts.' After saying that she would be most happy to produce all the evidence she had to magistrates, she ended, 'I shall not therefore obey your direction'. All this also appeared in her autobiography.

On 25th November 1944 she received the following letter from the Ministry of Labour:

> Dear Madam,
> *Regulation 58A of the Defence General Regulations, 1939.*
> After further consideration of your case, I, the undersigned, hereby withdraw the direction issued to you by post on July 8th, 1944, to perform the services therein specified.

These serious allegations against Leo Amery appeared in print in 1946 and, as Amery made no attempt to sue Dorothy Crisp for libel, it can be taken that there was indeed an attempt by at least one member of the War Cabinet to halt the publication of a book which contained material that some ministers, notably Churchill and Eden, would have found embarrassing. This tends to support the theory that there was never an inquiry into the fall of Singapore because certain high-standing people did not want one.

While all this was going on, Dorothy Crisp and John Becker had found time to fall in love and they were married on the 25th March 1945 at St George's Church, Hanover Square. She continued writing and subsequently became the chairman of the British Housewives' League, while Becker kept himself busy on the lecturing circuit.

After the war, and early in the summer of 1946, John Becker twice had meetings with General Percival who was attending the War Office in the process of writing his Official Dispatch (which was not published until 28th February 1948 as a Supplement to the London Gazette). When Becker asked the General about the pre-war memorandum he had sent to him, he received the reply, 'that one's memory is not as clear as it used to be after four years of internment'. Percival's memory was good enough, however, for him to write the following about Thailand in paragraph 99 of his dispatch:

> [Japan] also increased her political activities in Thailand. The attitude of the Thais was uncertain. On two occasions Thai military officers paid official visits to Singapore, where they protested their friendship for Britain. One of them was actually there when war broke out. On the other hand, there is no doubt that the Japanese were permitted to make preparations in advance for their occupation of South Thailand, for our officers, carrying out reconnaissances in that area, frequently met Japanese there and one of them, though too late, found large petrol dumps on the Patani aerodrome which had been made ready for the occupation.

In July 1946 Becker decided to return to the Far East to pick up the threads of his commercial career and to sort out his financial affairs, so he applied for a passport. By December, the passport not having arrived, it became clear that for some reason officialdom was holding it up. Becker enlisted the formidable powers of his wife and they decided to force the Passport Office to refuse him a passport officially instead of the no-action stance it had adopted, after which Dorothy would start to pull a few strings. They visited the Passport Office and, although the senior official they met did not say so in so many words, they left his presence with his tacit agreement that it was the Foreign Office which was holding the matter up. Perhaps not surprisingly, as Dorothy Crisp's final thrust at the official had been to threaten to write a newspaper article about the subject, three days later the passport arrived. It was, however, endorsed, 'Not Valid for Siam or Burma'.

The Beckers were convinced that a 'foreign power' was involved in the passport affair. Dorothy was to record later that they both thought that Luang Pibul was somehow behind it. But this could not have been so. Quite apart from the fact that the British Foreign Office was unlikely to stop the issue of a passport at the behest of a man who had led his country to declare war on Britain only five years previously, Pibul was not at that time in power in Thailand. He had been replaced as Thai Premier during the war, and after the war had been charged by his countrymen as a war criminal. Those charges had been dropped, but Pibul was now in retirement. (He was to return to power after a bloodless coup on 8th November 1947.) It is much more likely that the passport delay was an internal matter, an attempt by the Foreign Office to keep Becker away from the Far East, and that they finally gave him one to prevent any publicity over the matter. They made sure of keeping him away from the main arena of his original 'troubles' by having it endorsed appropriately.

Becker sailed for Singapore in January 1947 aboard the RMS *Andes*. One of the other passengers on that vessel was Alan Blades, a senior Singapore policeman who had been ordered out of the island before it fell to the Japanese because of his specialised knowledge of subversive activities. Becker and Blades renewed an acquaintance that had begun before the war in the office of Mervyn Llewellyn Wynne, Head of Singapore Special Branch. Wynne had died during the war in a Japanese prisoner of war camp on Sumatra where he had been captured after he too had been sent out of Singapore by the authorities for his own safety. In a letter to his wife Becker described Blades as a 'bearded mysterioso', a description that fitted him well, for several of Blades's colleagues from those days say that he could have been taken for the twin of General Jan Smuts. Becker's later involvement with the security services could have been with either British Military Intelligence, or with Singapore Special

Branch. If it was with the latter, the association may have started with that shipboard meeting.

Becker's first post-war return to Singapore and Malaya lasted only four months, but during that time he travelled the country extensively. Letters to his wife (written in pencil, which makes them difficult to read after nearly fifty years) indicate that he stayed in Kuala Lumpur, Malacca, Ipoh, and at an unnamed place close to the Thai frontier, in addition to Singapore itself. He renewed contacts with many Malay friends including a policeman in Malacca he had known since 1933, Yunus bin Talib, who by now had risen to be an Assistant Superintendent. He met Anthony Brooke, the 'pretender' to the Rajahship of Sarawak, who was seeking to regain his heritage after Sarawak had been ceded to Britain the previous year by his uncle, Sir Vyner Brooke, the third and last 'White Rajah'. In the same letter in which he mentioned Brooke, John Becker wrote, mysteriously, 'I have had strange opportunities offered me of connecting with Indonesia, and also participation once more in the Siamese imbroglio, and were I an unattached bachelor I would seize them, for above all things the Indonesians need an honest broker, and there are wicked men in Siam whom a little puff of honesty would blow away; but neither task is to be undertaken without wholehearted exertion and acceptance of personal danger.' He went on to say that he expected 'to be on the frontier of Siam in a few days'. It is evident that he was once more getting embroiled in South-East Asian politics, or at the very least, flirting with the idea of doing so.

Two weeks later he was writing of having contacts with a trio of journalists and writers, who had already written, or were soon to write, books about the Malayan campaign. They were Ian Morrison, Compton Mackenzie, and Frank Owen.[17]

On 14th March he wrote that the second-hand news he had been able to garner about his pre-war Thai friends was good, but, 'it seems that when any of my friends asked any British official what had happened to me, they were given the stereotyped reply that I was "lost". This reply was given to a high official in the Siamese police only a month ago. That is why I had that interview published in the press here.'

The interview he referred to was the one with the *Singapore Free Press* of 29th March in which he mentioned his pre-war involvement in Thai politics. The newspaper had opened that item with, 'In much the same position as Mr Anthony Brooke, the ex-Rajah Muda of Sarawak, who has been refused permission to enter Sarawak, Mr J. Becker, one-time Army intelligence officer and confident of some of Siam's pre-war political leaders, has been refused permission to return to Thailand.'

In that same letter to his wife Becker recorded that the Russians had increased the staff of their Thai Embassy – Russia's first in South-East Asia – by nearly two hundred. He concluded that 'these will be the pit-face workers for the Communist undermining of all these parts'. Becker's arrival back in South-East Asia in fact coincided with the build-up of Russia's post-war interest in the area.

Becker left Singapore in May 1947 by ship, travelling home via the Pacific and the United States. There is no record of why he chose to travel the long way round, or what he did during his short stay in America. He was reticent about this in his letters home. It may or may not be significant that Luang Pridi, the Thai with strong communist leanings, the man known during the war by the code-name 'Ruth' by both British Intelligence and by the American Office of Strategic Services (OSS), had recently been ousted from the Thai Premiership because of unproven allegations that he had been involved in the assassination of King Ananda Mahidol on 9th June the previous year. The first signs of post-war communist agitation were just beginning to appear in South-East Asia, and perhaps Becker had got wind of some of Pridi's plans to regain power. Indeed Pridi was later allegedly involved in two communist-inspired coup plots, in February 1949 and June 1951 – in the latter one, Pibul, back in power since the end of 1949, was kidnapped and held prisoner aboard a Thai warship – and Pridi's name was often to crop up in police files during the Malayan Emergency.

In view of Pridi's wartime connection with the OSS perhaps Becker travelled to the US to impart any information he had gathered. Pridi's name was in fact to crop up as late as 1967 in what Alec Waugh called 'another instalment in Pridi's communist saga' in connection with the mysterious and still unexplained disappearance of an ex-OSS man called James Thompson who vanished one day while visiting the Cameron Highlands in Malaya.[18] However, all this is conjecture; it is not known what Becker did in the United States.

In January 1948 Becker was back in the Far East again to take up a senior position with the trading firm of Watts & Company. By then the Malayan Emergency had begun, and he joined the police as a Special Constable. Officially his police duties involved him in checking the credentials of Chinese crossing the Causeway between Singapore and Malaya, where the police were on the lookout for known communists.

During 1948 Becker made several trips across the narrow strait that separates Singapore from some of the Indonesian islands. These trips had nothing to do with his work with Watts & Co. It was after one of these trips that he made a gift to one of his Malay friends. The gift was presented in such a way that the friend was left with the impression that it was Becker's way of saying goodbye, that he had a premonition of death.

The last of these trips took place only about a fortnight before Becker was gunned down in Singapore on 24th August. In one of his last letters to his wife he wrote that he had 'meetings with a Russian agent in the Dutch islands', but gave no other details. She, however, learned a little more when she arrived in Singapore the following year, though she did not give the name of her informant. She was told, 'how John had been slipping across to the Dutch islands and that in a certain dress which he could affect extremely well, had met a Russian agent whom he and only two others who knew of him described as dangerous. The other two on hearing of John's death had jumped to the conclusion that the Russian was somehow responsible.'

We do not know for which agency Becker was making these trips, but it may have been Military Intelligence. In a series of letters written to Dorothy Crisp in the two months following Becker's death, Harry Hobbs, Becker's old friend from India, said that 'Colonel Tulloch, now in the hotel [in Calcutta] met John recently. He says the government will miss him as no-one was so well informed about that part of the world. He considers that John was a marked man and did not take as much care of himself as he should considering his prominence.' In one of the later letters Hobbs describes Colonel Tulloch as an Intelligence officer.[19]

A few days before he died Becker talked with Dixon Brown, the Singapore correspondent of the London *News Chronicle*. He talked about Thailand still being the key to the domination of that part of the world, and of the burgeoning Communist interest in the country. From that talk sprang London press stories that 'well-informed sources in Singapore feel that most Far Eastern Communist activities are being directed from Bangkok'.

Becker was shot, allegedly by a Chinese amok who had grabbed a revolver from a policeman, a little after noon on 24th August. Becker's friend Max Bell sent a cable to Dorothy Crisp via her doctor telling her of her husband's death. Four days after that their second child, Hugh, was born.

Despite the immediate denial by the Deputy Commissioner of Police that there was any political significance to the murder, the following appeared on the leader page of the London *Daily Telegraph* of 26th August 1948:

Shot Man Had Enemies

****

Knew Of Malayan Communist Plot

Mr J.N. Becker, murdered husband of Miss Dorothy Crisp, former chairman of the British Housewives' League, who, as reported in the *Daily Telegraph* yesterday, was shot dead in his Singapore office by a Chinese on Tuesday, had political enemies in Malaya. He claimed a special knowledge of the Communist plot to seize power in Malaya.

After commenting on the Foreign Office business over the passport (information obviously supplied by Dorothy Crisp), and his pre-war involvement in Thailand, the article went on;

> In September 1941 three months before the Japanese invaded Malaya from Siam, he told security officers that he had definite information that Siam had already decided to throw in her lot with Japan.
>
> He complained that he was rapped over the knuckles for interfering and that he was recalled to England without any reason. The Japanese invasion began, as he claimed to have forecast, in December.

Dorothy Crisp was not at all happy with the official reports she received from Singapore about her husband's death. Because the alleged murderer was an amok and was incarcerated in an asylum in Singapore immediately after the crime, the Singapore police were saying there would be no inquest. It was reported that the Chinaman, Tan Di Tok, had entered Becker's office and begun to make trouble. Becker had called the police, and an armed Malay constable had arrived. During an attempt to arrest him, by the constable assisted by Becker, the Chinaman had somehow got hold of the policeman's gun and Becker had been shot, dying in the ambulance on the way to hospital.

Dorothy Crisp decided to go to Singapore to get to the bottom of the matter and to see if she could persuade the Singapore Government to grant her a pension on the basis of Becker being a Special Constable, though there was no provision in Singapore law at that time for any such compensation to be paid.

She sailed east aboard the *Corfu*, which stopped at Penang for twenty-four hours on 28th February 1949. She went out there armed with the knowledge that an old friend, the former Malayan policeman René Onraet, had airmailed an introductory letter to the Assistant Commissioner of Police at Singapore, Nigel Morris, in which Onraet had requested that all help be given her.

It was at Penang that the first attempt by the police to intimidate her began. She was met by a senior policeman who had, he said, 'been sent by Gray, the Commissioner of Police in Kuala Lumpur'. The policeman was Superintendent Kenneth Larby. (Larby died in Australia in February 1984.) Larby was embarrassed by what he had been sent to say, and told Dorothy so. He said he was just a messenger and that he had been told to tell her that John Becker had not been working for the police, and that his murder had been an accident, and told her not to press for an inquest. She was appalled at the apparent callousness of all this, and at her first encounter with the police.

Her opinion did not improve on further acquaintance. Although Nigel Morris, the recipient of Onraet's letter, helped all he could and made arrangements for her to meet with E.V. Fowler, the Deputy Commissioner of Police, on 4th March, after that, according to Dorothy, her reception was bad. At her meeting with Fowler he had in front of him 'a very thin file' on the case. She asked if she could see it, but the request was turned down. Fowler then said that no inquest had been held because in England and the Colonies one cannot be held when a capital charge is to be made against a person already in custody until after the trial. He went on to say that 'the murderer is in the loony bin and that there will be no inquest until he is pronounced sane which may not be for four or five years'. Fowler reiterated this as the likely period to elapse, in different contexts on three separate occasions during the interview.

Miss Crisp asked whether there were any witnesses to the murder other than the Malay constable whose gun had been used, and was told 'no'. She was told that the Chinese amok had made a statement and had said, 'I saw a man lying shot'. She asked many other questions, and was left with the distinct impression that in his replies Fowler was expurgating information from the file as he went along.

It was Fowler who first referred to the Larby visit at Penang. Dorothy Crisp had previously asked Nigel Morris for an explanation of this, and he had told her he knew nothing of it. Now Fowler protested equal ignorance, 'and appeared to be highly incensed that anyone should dare to interfere in something that happened in his demesne'. She left that interview, noting in her diary, 'he very unpleasant'.

If the Singapore police ever thought they had a chance of intimidating Dorothy Crisp they were soon to be disillusioned. She was not about to be put off her course by a few mere men, uniformed or not. Through contacts she had arranged to meet the Governor of Singapore, Sir Franklin Gimson, on the following day, and she expected to have a fight on her hands with him over the matter of an inquest. However, she was to get a pleasant surprise. Perhaps Sir Franklin had done his homework on her, for as soon as she raised the subject of an inquest he said, 'If the law does not require one, we must alter the law.' The inquest began on 15th March.

In the meantime Dorothy Crisp went the rounds. She met the Commissioner of Police, Singapore (the top man was no longer called Inspector-General), Robert E. Foulger. He told her in answer to her question that the Malay constable whose gun had been used to kill her husband was an 'Emergency' recruit who had only been on the force for a few months.

She also met Malcolm Macdonald, British Commissioner for South-East Asia, and her husband's old friend, Dato Onn. Curiously, she paid a visit to Phoenix Park, the headquarters of the British Intelligence community in Singapore, although she did not write in her diary any details of who she met there and what was talked about. To get in she must have had special permission from a very senior person. Phoenix Park was a high security area.[20]

A series of strange events began with the start of the inquest. Despite Fowler's statement of only a few days before that there had been no independent witness to the affray, one now appeared in the person of the Watts office messenger. The coroner and jury heard that the Chinaman, Tan Di Tok, had entered Becker's office building without permission or apparent purpose, and on being asked to leave, had refused. The man was said to have been unarmed. John Becker had telephoned the local police station, and an armed Malay constable was sent around. The constable concerned was Ali bin Haji Muslim (No. 3920) who, it transpired, had been on the force for over two years, and not just the few months as Police Commissioner Foulger had told Dorothy Crisp.

The Malay constable now gave a different version of the events from that which he had made in the original police report, even changing his mind about the floor it had all happened on. He stated that in the attempt made by himself and John Becker to arrest the Chinaman, the amok had wrested the revolver from his holster, the lanyard on the gun breaking in the process, and had then fired three shots one of which had hit Becker. The broken lanyard was produced in evidence.

The Indian Inspector, who was conducting the police side of the proceedings, did not impress Miss Crisp either. Several times he was cautioned in attempting to lead witnesses.

Despite all this, on the third day the jury, made up of two Englishmen and three Chinese, returned the verdict that Becker had been killed by a Chinaman of unsound mind, but added riders condemning some general negligence on behalf of the police, and particularly condemning their method of securing the revolvers with which they were armed.

The second rider is an interesting one. The lanyard used was fastened to the gun at one end. The other end was in the form of a noose with a sliding knot, which looped over the shoulder of the man carrying it, the cord passing under the uniform epaulette. The lanyard cord was thick, and unless the cord was faulty to start with, would have required tremendous strength to part it. Despite the jury's rider, no one seems to have queried the point that a lanyard in good condition was virtually unbreakable unless a sharp instrument had been used on it.

It may be that the jury's verdict was correct, and that it was indeed an amok who killed Becker. The constable's conflicting evidence may have been caused by the passage of six months since the murder and by a faulty memory. The production of an hitherto unknown witness may have been the result of a belated additional investigation into the crime caused by Miss Crisp's arrival on the scene. Perhaps the gun lanyard had been a faulty one, or the amok had possessed a madman's strength.

But it cannot be denied that the police attitude throughout indicates a strong possibility that some sort of cover-up was taking place, and if that cover-up was not directly to do with the nature of the crime, nor with the identity of the killer, then it is possible that it was because certain intelligence agencies did not want the matter more thoroughly investigated in case Becker's 'extra-curricular' work came to light.

There is one other matter that might support such a theory. There was no provision in Singapore law for the payment of any kind of award for Special Constables even when killed in the course of their duties, let alone, as in John Becker's case, when he was killed off-duty.

It took Dorothy Crisp a long time and she had to enlist the services of many of her powerful friends back home, but she finally managed to get that law changed. In the Public Records Office there are three substantial files on the subject.[21] This *très formidable* lady involved just about every British politician of note in her claim, including Lady Megan Lloyd George, Alan Lennox-Boyd, Dame Irene Ward, Victor Raikes, D.L. Savory, and George Strauss (later Baron Conesford of Chelsea) who had earlier been a friend of John Becker's. Even the then President of the Board of Trade became involved on the periphery of the matter. He seemed to find something sinister in Dorothy's membership of the British Housewives' League. In a letter about the claim dated 4th December 1950 and addressed to the Minister of State, Colonial Office, he wrote:

> I have discovered that her alias is Miss Dorothy Crisp, who I suspect to have been one of the leading lights in the Housewives' League.
> In the circumstances I certainly do not wish to press you to see her, though it may be that she has a cause.

The letter was signed by J. Harold Wilson, OBE, MP.

One of the letters Dorothy Crisp wrote to the Colonial Secretary in 1950 during her 'battle' points out that a new summary of the events surrounding her husband's death produced by the Colonial Office contradicted information in the Coroner's report. Either mistakes were being committed at official level or attempts were still being made to obfuscate matters.

Dorothy Crisp finally received a pension for life, and her two children also received annual sums up to the time they were eighteen. The pressure she and her friends applied on both the British and Singapore Governments might have done the trick; maybe they caved in under the sustained pressure, a pressure more than hinted at in a note made by an official on one of Dorothy's letters to his Department which had arrived on a Friday. 'This is no doubt in case you or anyone in the office would like a quiet weekend away from trouble!'

The possibility remains, however, that the Singapore authorities finally agreed to pay her to lessen the chance that, in the fallout of her endeavours, information about her late husband's intelligence activities might somehow emerge; that they did not want their underground intelligence system compromised in what was a critical time of the Malayan Emergency.

It is not known what happened to the Chinese amok.

Chapter Eight

The British Leaders in the Malayan Campaign

The professional relationships between some senior officers in Malaya prior to 1941, in both the civil administration and the military, left much to be desired; and even after the personnel changes, which were made between the end of 1940 and December 1941, the situation had not improved. Antipathy still existed between several of the men at the top, the difference being that some of the actors had changed and that there were now more of them on the stage.

The command structure in immediate pre-war Malaya was unusual to say the least. There was not one but three titular Commanders-in-Chief (for a brief period there were four); each had overlapping responsibilities and each reported home to a different British ministry. On top of that there was a 'maverick' Australian general who had direct access to his own superiors in Australia. When one adds that, within the Malaya Command structure, a British General Officer with no up-to-date operational experience had been appointed GOC over the head of a more senior and better experienced general, and that there had been imposed upon the scene a British Minister sent out by the Prime Minister, Churchill, to give some sort of overall guidance and whose arrival was bitterly resented, it can be seen that the seeds of disaster were likely to flower. To change the metaphor, there were too many cooks and enough bad feeling between some of them to make the spoiling of the broth likely; and this was quite apart from the acute shortage of ingredients and trained under-staff they were given to work with. As Brigadier Sir John Smyth later commented, 'there were too many chiefs and not enough Injuns.'[1]

There are many lessons to be drawn from this aspect of the Singapore débâcle, and from the characters of the leaders, their level of experience, their interaction, and how they were regarded generally in Malaya.

Sir Shenton Thomas, KCMG, OBE (1879–1962)

In 1934 Shenton Thomas Whitelegge Thomas was appointed Governor and Commander-in-Chief of the Straits Settlements and High Commissioner for the Malay States. The 'Commander-in-Chief' in his title was an honorific, and indeed he had not had any military experience. But Sir Shenton's position as the representative of the Crown made him the titular head of the senior echelon of leaders in Malaya. His position, especially when the honorific is taken into account, should have ensured that at the very least he be kept well-informed on military matters. This unfortunately was not always the case.

Shenton Thomas had the standard background for someone destined to rise to a high position in the Colonial Service. He attended public school, St. John's at Leatherhead, an establishment which specialized in educating the sons of the clergy. His father was a vicar of the Church of England. In 1901 he graduated from Queens' College, Cambridge. He then joined the teaching profession and for seven years was a master at Aysgarth Preparatory School in the Yorkshire Dales. Following that and a year spent travelling the world, he joined the Colonial Service in 1909. He served in Kenya, Uganda, Nigeria and the Gold Coast, before being made Governor of Nyasaland in 1929. He returned to the Gold Coast in 1932 as Governor and stayed there until 1934. He had married at the age of thirty-three.

Shenton Thomas's biographer, Brian Montgomery (who was distantly related to him by marriage), wrote that during his twenty-five years of service in Africa, Thomas had earned the reputation of being a strong man. However, Montgomery produced little evidence to support that statement.[2] The written evidence of others who knew Sir Shenton well tends to dispute this view, at least in his later years. A.H. Dickinson, the Inspector-General of Police, Singapore, in a letter written in 1967, stated that 'he [Thomas] was not a strong man', and he 'would have made a first-class headmaster of a big prep school.' Again, 'I think he wanted to be liked – a weak trait in anyone's character.'[3]

Montgomery in his book noted that Dickinson was a friend and admirer of Sir Shenton. Dickinson certainly admired some of the Governor's traits, but his strength of character was obviously not one of them. With his many years of police training (he had arrived in Malaya as a police cadet during World War One) Dickinson was a good judge of character. Furthermore, he was very close to the Governor. As an ex-officio member of the Straits Settlements Executive Council he came into almost daily contact with Sir Shenton, and met him at many social functions. There is no doubt that a friendship existed between the two, for when Dickinson was wounded during the battle for Singapore, Sir Shenton somehow managed to visit him at the General Hospital two days after the capitulation to the Japanese. Ex-colleagues report that Dickinson was a man of high probity, loyalty and intelligence. He would not have made those comments about Sir Shenton had he not believed them to be true.

Sir Shenton had on his staff two very strong characters indeed, Charles Vlieland, the Secretary of Defence, and Stanley Jones, the Colonial Secretary. In the same 1967 letter, Dickinson also said of Sir

Shenton, 'nor do I think he was a good picker of men. His one big mistake, from our point of view, was bringing Stanley Jones down [from a more junior position in the FMS] as Colonial Secretary, who *vis-à-vis* the public and the Services created a deplorable image of the Government's ability to take the war seriously.'

This remark tends to support in part at least, the criticisms – decried by Brian Montgomery – levelled at the inactivity of the Singapore civil administration under Sir Shenton during the period before the Japanese war. These criticisms emanated over a number of years from many sources. They came from G.W. Seabridge, editor of the *Straits Times*, writing both before and during the Malayan campaign. They also came from the writings of the British journalist, Ian Morrison, after his escape from Singapore in 1942; and from the authors of the British Official History of the Malayan campaign published in 1957, to name but three.[4]

Important evidence about the character of Sir Shenton Thomas is contained in a Colonial Office file which only came into the public domain in 1992. It is possible that his biographer, Montgomery, did not see references to this matter in the private papers of Sir Shenton to which he had been granted access by the family, for he made no mention of it.

The file material concerns an investigation into the system of justice in the Federated Malay States in 1938, conducted by Sir Roger Hall. The full title of the file is, 'Report of Chief Justice Sir Roger Hall into allegations of incompetency and corruption in the Magistracy of the FMS.'[5]

Sir Roger arrived in Malaya in 1937 as Chief Justice of the Federated Malay States after many years in the African colonies in positions of equal prestige. Sir Shenton Thomas had known Hall since their shared Gold Coast days in 1927. Within a few months of his arrival Hall tendered his resignation to Sir Shenton, who as well as being Governor of Singapore was the High Commissioner for the Malay States. Hall said that he could not serve in a country where the magisterial courts were so bad. Thomas persuaded him not to resign, but instead to set his own work aside and conduct an investigation. This Hall did and delivered a lengthy report on 1st July 1938. During the following month Hall actually did resign 'on personal grounds mainly those of health'.

Soon afterwards rumours of the existence of this report began to reach Sir Grattan Bushe, Legal Adviser to the Colonial Office in London. Bushe wrote in a departmental minute, that he kept 'wondering when it would arrive with the Governor's dispatches'. He goes on, 'A year elapsed and nothing happened so one day when Sir Roger Hall came in to see me about something or another ... I asked him if he had a copy of the report.' Sir Roger did have a copy, and so the cat was out of the bag.

Sir Roger's report catalogued a system of magisterial courts rife with incompetence and riddled with corruption. He reported that 'nearly all the Magisterial work is done by Malay magistrates who (except one) have no legal qualifications.' He was 'soon staggered by cases of apparently gross incompetence' and 'read and heard of allegations as to the honesty of Malay Magistrates which suggested that bribery and corruption were rife.' He was 'horrified to find a consensus of opinion not only as to incompetence but also to venality of these magistrates'. Some of them, he reported, were in debt, in some cases to money lenders.

Hall had looked through the confidential reports on these officers and was struck by their writers' seeming necessity to state such things as, 'no occasion to doubt his honesty', 'so far as I can see trustworthy', and 'as far as I know perfectly honest'. He reported, 'These remarks appear *passim* in the reports. In my long experience I have never before come across the necessity to make such statements in officers' confidential reports, and the fact that they were made appears to me to show clearly how apprehensive the Executive is as to the general honesty of this class of officer.'

After that Sir Roger went on to list a number of actual cases of corruption. An accused man in a case where a Malay child had been run over and killed was discharged after bribing the magistrate with $300. Mr Justice Aitken reported a case where the judgement was offered for sale to the highest bidder. The Chief of Police reported that the ledgers of the owner of a Chinese bus company contained evidence of four payments made to a certain magistrate. One magistrate, who had been given a Government loan in 1934 to pay off his debts 'for the sake of the good name of the service', had been strongly suspected of corruption in giving out land grants in 1936. Although that had not been proven, later that year he was seriously censured over another matter and reduced in salary. The same man was still a magistrate when Hall was conducting his investigation. He gave many other examples.

Perhaps the most serious fact Hall recorded was that the Chief of Police had brought the matter of the state of the magistracy to the Governor's attention as early as 1936. This had been followed by a Resident's Inquiry, but little had been done 'because of the difficulty in proving bribery and corruption, the proof of which always lies deeply buried.'

This, then, was the report that Sir Shenton Thomas, Governor since 1934, had sought to keep from his superiors in London. When the matter blew up Sir Shenton tried to disparage the report by saying of Sir Roger, 'he was not robust', and 'it seems that this country got him down'. Furthermore, he said, 'it was a secret report for the Governor's information, and was strictly confidential', and 'I did not think it necessary to send it home to the Secretary of State'. In his reply to that, Sir Grattan Bushe said, 'when you say it is a strictly confidential document, I hope you do not mean confidential so far as this office was concerned'. Sir Grattan pointed out in an internal Colonial Office memo on the 'very serious allegations' in the report, that, 'they may be wholly true, or partly true, or even not true, but whichever is the case, in my view a Governor, who hides from the Secretary of State such grave events as these, is doing the Colonial Office a gross disservice. The story is quite well-known, and he is simply burying a bomb which, if it explodes, will not harm him (since he will be in retirement) but the unfortunate Colonial Office'.

Sir Shenton received a diplomatically worded but severe blasting from Sir Cosmo Parkinson, the Permanent Under-Secretary of State at the Colonial Office, who pointed out that such a matter could result in acute embarrassment to the Secretary of State if questions were asked in Parliament.

This story indicates that Sir Shenton was not above hiding important matters from his superiors. That may not be an unusual trait, but in this case it shows a singular lack of judgement. Did he seriously think that a matter of this gravity, when both the disease and the doctor's report on it must have been known to many, would not get back to London? It can be argued that Sir Shenton acted in the way he did to protect the good of the service and the reputations of some of his subordinates. In those times the Malayan Civil Service was considered only slightly lower in the British Empire scheme of things than the 'heaven-born' Indian Civil Service, and he may have been persuaded that it was better to keep the matter in-house. Furthermore, as the magistrates concerned were mostly Malays, perhaps he was influenced by a desire not to annoy the Malay sultans. But whatever his motive, the attempt to cover it up indicates certain flaws in his character. By the time he was found out not all of the magistrates suspected of corruption had been replaced, and common sense should have told him that he was sitting on the time bomb mentioned by Sir Grattan Bushe.

This matter of corruption within the Magistracy was not the only field for such crimes in Sir Shenton's fiefdom. Another matter of which no mention was made by his biographer is that during the latter part of 1940 and mid-1941 several senior British officials in the FMS Mines Department were tried and found guilty of accepting bribes over a long period from Chinese, concerning the allocation of tinmining concessions. Vast sums of money, even a pedigree racehorse, were proven to have changed hands. One of the accused, in an attempt to excuse his high style of living, had earlier gone around boasting of his luck at the races. At least one of these officers was deported, escorted to a plane at Kallang airport by the police. Five others were given prison sentences. These men were still in Changi Jail when British civilian prisoners of war were placed in there with them by the victorious Japanese. It is said they advised some of their erstwhile colleagues on which cells were the best from the point of view of shelter from the midday sun!

All this and more – there was a huge homosexual scandal among some senior British Residents about the same time as the Mines

Department case – occurred under Sir Shenton's charge. It makes
the British government's decision in 1940 to ask him to extend his
tour of duty beyond the normal retirement age a rather strange one.
The reasoning behind it was probably a desire for continuity in view
of the critical situation that had been building up in the Far East. Be
that as it may, the opportunity was lost to replace him by a tougher
man, and perhaps to create a Military Governorship, something that was
actually advocated when it was far too late. When Duff Cooper arrived in
Singapore in September 1941 as Churchill's special envoy, he very soon
found the need to advise London that Sir Shenton should be replaced.
(The full details of Duff's recommendation are still not known. Some files
of correspondence on this subject from both Sir Shenton and Duff Cooper
are still officially closed in the Public Records Office.)

If Sir Shenton had been made of sterner stuff, there can be little doubt
that the relationship between the civil administration and the military
authorities over the period of his tenure of office would have been much
closer than it was. This could only have had a beneficial effect on the
overall situation in Malaya. As it was, he had earlier permitted the
situation to develop wherein the Secretary of Defence, Vlieland, and
the GOC of the time, Bond, were barely on speaking terms. Part of
the blame for that lies with the military of course, but Sir Shenton's
position should have enabled him to nip the situation in the bud. As
the then Chairman of the War Committee he should also have used the
weight of his office to prevent the antagonism which developed between
Bond and Air Vice-Marshal Babington.

It was Shenton Thomas who promoted Stanley Jones to the number
two civil post in the colony. It was an exceedingly bad choice. Jones
had an unprepossessing, not to say unpleasant, character, and was an
obstructionist. It was he who became the 'Officer Administering the
Government' during the critical period when Sir Shenton was away on
long leave during 1940.

Many other criticisms have been levelled at Sir Shenton. It has been
said, for instance, that it was his ruling that air raid sirens were not to
be sounded in Singapore without his express permission that resulted in
delay in sounding the alarms and the subsequent deaths of many Chinese
in the first Japanese air raid on Singapore. This may or may not have been
true, for the evidence is conflicting; there may have been other reasons
for the delay.

However it is certainly true that, after seven years in Malaya, the
Governor had not bothered to learn to speak Malay, the lingua franca
among the many non-Europeans who did not speak English. Hugh
Bryson, a senior officer of the Malayan Civil Service (he was Clerk to
both the Executive and Legislative Councils) links this fact with what
he called Sir Shenton's general lack of leadership qualities. 'How could
a Governor who knew not a word of any of the local languages impress

his views on people? You can't really be impressive if you have to pause at the end of every sentence while your words are translated by a bored interpreter who probably hasn't your faith in any case, and paraphrases your appeal.'6

Megan Spooner, the wife of Rear-Admiral E.J. 'Jack' Spooner, who had been stationed at Singapore longer than most other senior service officers, stated in her diary entry for 29th November 1941, 'the Governor seems a poor reed'. (For the same date she recorded that 'the Colonial Secretary [Stanley Jones] reputed to be a bottle-neck and obstructor, absolutely revengeful. Certainly unbalanced. I think he has ophthalmic goitre'.) For 11th January 1942, a month after the Japanese attack, she records a tit-bit she picked up from a War Council meeting: 'War Council presided over by Governor who chatters on small matters all the time. Percival too weak with him.' Two weeks later she wrote, 'Governor is gaga', an expression she recorded again on 4th February, saying that the wife of Lieutenant-General Sir Lewis Heath entirely agreed with her.7

It is undoubtedly true that the military authorities had no great regard for Sir Shenton and never fully trusted him. In consequence they tended to keep him in the dark. Sir Shenton had not aided his cause when he made a very ill-judged, off-the-cuff remark way back in 1935. A visiting Army Staff Officer had been invited to a luncheon party at Government House. During the meal Sir Shenton said to the officer, in a voice loud enough to carry the length of the table, 'I wish you bloody soldiers would go away; your presence here and your attempts to build up defences will only bring war to this country. We should be much better off without you.' This was scarcely a sensible remark to make, and probably from that time on it coloured the relationship between the army and the civilian administration.

A.H. Dickinson has written of the precise circumstances which led the service chiefs to 'isolate', as he put it, Sir Shenton from much information. He reports that:

> The following incident occurred at a small dinner party in Government House in 1940 at which Admiral Sir Percy Noble, C-in-C, Far East was present. The GOC [Bond] was also a guest. During dinner a cipher telegram arrived from the Secretary of State for Sir Shenton Thomas. Sir Shenton sent for a subordinate member of his staff, a Eurasian, Mr G. E. Bogaars in charge of the Governor's office, codes and ciphers, and handed him the telegram to decode.
>
> The following morning Admiral Noble asked me to call on him at the Naval Base. He related to me the above incident, expressing very grave concern indeed about what appeared to him to be a complete absence of any sense of security on the part of Sir Shenton Thomas. He was horrified at the fact of entrusting,

in wartime especially, to a Eurasian subordinate the decoding of secret cipher messages. The C-in-C and the GOC must have reported their fears immediately to the Admiralty and the War Office. Within 24 hours a telegram arrived from the Secretary of State for the Colonies demanding a report. Sir Shenton was deeply disturbed. He asked me to submit a full report on Mr Bogaars. The Special Branch in the ordinary course of its work was in possession of Mr Bogaars' history and connections. A meticulous report was, however, prepared. Satisfactory though this report was it did not wholly eradicate the feeling of suspicion and lack of confidence in the Governor to which the incident gave rise.[8]

Dickinson expanded on this in a letter dated 24th January 1969. He says that the Chief of Military Intelligence at the Far East Combined Bureau (FECB), Colonel Grimsdale, was involved in sending reports home on the Governor's lack of security. He added that the telegram from the Colonial Office which demanded a report on the Bogaars affair, was a 'stinker'.

There is further evidence about this from a source even closer to the Governor than Dickinson was. Muriel 'Molly' Reilly was a volunteer cipher clerk to Sir Shenton as well as being a friend of the family. When Duff Cooper arrived in the colony in September 1941, Molly became his cipher clerk until he left in January 1942, when she reverted once more to her old boss. She says:

> When I returned to Sir Shenton I was horrified to find how little he knew of conditions then prevailing. The reason he was told nothing by Navy, Army, or Air Force, was this. His Chief Clerk, Bogaars, was married to a Japanese and Sir Shenton trusted him implicitly and refused to dismiss him when asked to do so 'as Bogaars was a security risk'. Sir Shenton proved to be right in his faith in Bogaars' integrity, as I saw Bogaars' name appeared in the New Years Honours List after we were back in Singapore'.[9]

Molly Reilly's acceptance of Bogaars's integrity merely because he was later given an honour appears rather naïve from the viewpoint of fifty years on but, as Dickinson confirmed, she was in fact right. George Bogaars was absolutely reliable. However, she was incorrect in one respect; Mrs Bogaars was not Japanese, although this rumour appears to have gained some currency at the time. This unfounded rumour, plus what appears to be a racial bias against Eurasians, on top of the Governor's off-hand method of dealing with official communications, seem to have been the reasons for the Services' distrust of Sir Shenton.[10]

Yet more evidence that the Governor was left very much in the dark is given in a letter written by the Hon. G. Weisberg, the pre-war Colonial Treasurer in Singapore. Weisberg was on leave in Melbourne when the

Japanese attacked Malaya, and immediately managed to persuade the Australian Government to fly him back to Singapore. He records, 'on arrival I was taken to see Shenton and, over a cup of tea, he said he would like me to proceed immediately to Taiping as the Resident had fallen ill. I asked him how the war was going and he replied, "Honestly, Weisie, I don't know. They tell me nothing although I am a member of the War Council"'.*

Weisberg went on, 'I have a clear recollection that Shenton really had no inside information as to what was doing. It was possibly the case of the man in charge (a politician) having no use for the Governor (a Civil Servant).'[11]

Duff Cooper, whom Churchill had sent to Singapore to bring sort of order out of the chaos there, had this to say about Shenton Thomas in a letter carried home in late December 1941 by Captain Tennant of the lost battle-cruiser *Repulse* which had been sunk along with *Prince of Wales* by Japanese aircraft on 10th December. 'The Governor, Sir Shenton Thomas, is one of those people who find it quite impossible to adjust their minds to war conditions. He is also the mouthpiece of the last person he speaks to. When I informed him of my appointment he professed himself delighted, welcomed the idea of a War Council, and was most helpful at the first meeting which we held the same afternoon. That evening he dined with Sir Robert Brooke-Popham and at the meeting next morning he supported the latter's attitude in contesting the need for a War Council and produced stronger arguments against it than Sir Robert Brooke-Popham could produce himself.'

Relations between the Governor and Duff Cooper were to grow steadily worse, and on both sides declined into petty insults behind the other's back. In a secret memorandum to the Secretary of State for the Colonies, Thomas reminded the Secretary of Sir Stafford Cripps's description of Duff Cooper as a 'petulant little pipsqueak'.[12] It was the Governor, or someone close to him, who started the rumour that the Duff Coopers had arrived in Singapore with over a hundred items of luggage, something that Brian Montgomery in his biography of Shenton Thomas, took at face value. In fact this was 'palpable nonsense' says the historian, John Charmley. In his biography of Duff Cooper he quotes Martin Russell, Duff Cooper's private secretary, who says the true figure may have been as high as ten.[13]

The evacuation of Penang gives us further insights into Sir Shenton's character. He had always made it known at meetings of the War Council that he was opposed to any racial discrimination in the event that an evacuation had to take place from any part of the country. This was a

---

* Duff Cooper had taken over the chairmanship of the War Council, up to then known as the War Committee, from Thomas soon after his arrival in Singapore, but it reverted to the Governor when Duff Cooper left in January 1942.

highly laudable viewpoint, but one which left unanswered the question of how it would seem to the British public back home if European women and children were left behind by the British Army to the tender mercy of the Japanese. In the event the military authorities made the decision to evacuate them from Penang, and this operation was carried out on the night of 13th December 1941. There was no practical way to offer the same facility to the substantially greater number of Asian women and children who probably would also have liked to leave. Not surprisingly the decision was to cause consternation and anger among the Chinese, Indian, and to a lesser extent, the Malay population of the entire country, as Sir Shenton had predicted it would. Brian Montgomery quotes Sir Shenton's diary entry for 20th December 1941, a week after the event, in which he wrote, 'Such grave forebodings about Penang that I had to meet representative Asiatics this afternoon. Had to tell them I knew nothing of the evacuation till it had been carried out, that I had instructed there was to be no racial discrimination. It was the most difficult speech I had ever had to make.' This is scarcely surprising since he was not telling the truth.

Instead of supporting the army action which had been backed by Duff Cooper, and whether or not the decision was morally right – given that no British Army commander could ever desert British women and children in that kind of situation, there was really no other practical solution – Sir Shenton took the easy way out by saying that he knew nothing about the evacuation before it happened. If this had been true then the most that Sir Shenton could have been accused of was a desire to save his face with the Asiatics. But it was not true. He had known about the conditions of the evacuation for some hours before it took place. A hitherto unreported cipher telegram, until it was discovered by this author in 1991, gives the game away. It was dated and timed some six hours before the evacuation began, and must have been drafted well before that. Sir Shenton sent the cipher to the Secretary of State for the Colonies.

No. 627 Government House. 1609 hrs 13th Dec.

Not for Publication.

Penang has been raided several times by daylight and damage to Asiatic quarters has been extensive. so far as is known fatal casualties 200 wounded about 1,000 all Asiatic. Owing to destruction of aerodromes in the north air defence has been impossible and the Asiatic morale in consequence bad. Military authorities in collaboration with the Resident Councillor are arranging to control the town. European women and children will be evacuated as soon as practicable.

This episode shows that Sir Shenton was not above bending the truth even when writing up his personal diary, and that he misled that gathering of Asiatics. Although there is no doubt that Sir Shenton would have preferred it had there been no semblance of racial discrimination, looking at the situation in the overall interest of presenting a single military/civilian administration front at a time of terrible crisis, Sir Shenton should have toughed it out at that meeting instead of merely deciding to protect his own reputation.

'Meg' Spooner's description of Sir Shenton as being gaga, was no doubt unkind. On the other hand, if he was responsible for the streamer headline that appeared under the title of the Singapore weekly *Sunday Times*, on the very day of the capitulation to the Japanese, then perhaps gaga is the correct word. The streamer blazoned, '"Singapore Must Stand; It SHALL Stand" – H.E. the Governor'. For some days before that it had been obvious to everyone that Singapore's hours were numbered.

Whatever opinion one may hold about the suitability of Sir Shenton Thomas as the figurehead of the Gibraltar of the east in a wartime situation, it is difficult not to conclude that the lack of confidence shown in him by the military leaders must have had a hugely detrimental effect on him personally, and on the Singapore defence situation generally. Sir Shenton was directly responsible for Civil Defence matters and for the Volunteer Forces; it was he who had to authorise the implementation of many military decisions; and it was he who held the strings of the local privy purse. Had relations between himself and the military been better, and had both he and Duff Cooper tried to co-operate more, the situation in Singapore could only have stood to benefit.

Air Chief Marshal Sir Robert Brooke-Popham,
GCVO, KCB, CMG, DSO, AFC (1878–1953)

Brooke-Popham was educated at Haileybury and Sandhurst and commissioned into the Oxford Light Infantry in 1898. In 1911 he joined the Air Battalion of the Royal Engineers, later to be transformed into the Royal Flying Corps. As a Major in 1914 he was given command of No. 3 Squadron. After the war he had an immense influence on the formative years of the RAF. By 1926 he had risen to be Air Vice-Marshal, and in 1935 he was selected as Inspector-General, RAF with the rank of Air Chief Marshal. He retired in 1937, and was then appointed Governor and C-in-C, Kenya. He rejoined the RAF active list in 1939.

The unlikelihood of a relieving fleet being immediately available in the event of a Japanese attack on Singapore meant that the main responsibility for its defence lay with the RAF. With this in mind the Chiefs of Staff in London decided to appoint an air officer as C-in-C, Far East, the first time that such a post had been filled by someone from the junior service. The appointment went to Brooke-Popham, and he was made responsible for the operational control of the British land and air forces in Malaya and adjacent territories.

Despite his title, however, he was not given control of the navy, which remained under the C-in-C, China Station, but even his control over the army and air force was incomplete, for the GOC and AOC were to remain in charge of their own administrative and financial responsibilities, and reported on those directly to their respective ministries in London.

Last but not least, Brooke-Popham was not the military Governor of Singapore and so had no control over the civil administration; the Governor was still responsible to the Colonial Office. The fact that Brooke-Popham was not a Supreme Commander meant that he was simply an addition to an already cumbersome command structure. Had he been the Brooke-Popham of yesteryear he might have made a better shot at it anyway. But he was already sixty-two years of age, and in December 1941 he had to make extremely difficult decisions.

He arrived in Singapore late in 1940. He had been made aware of most of the difficulties confronting his command before he left England. In a letter he wrote to the Chiefs of Staff on 26th October 1940, he said he fully realised that at that time the requirements of Singapore were relegated to third position behind Britain and the Middle East. He added, in a phrase which might have been the catalyst for his disagreements a year later with Duff Cooper, that he also realised 'that our job in the Far East is not to press for facilities that cannot be given'. By making that point he virtually tied his hands before even getting there.

He went on to record, in words reminiscent of G.A. Henty, the writer of heroic military tales for boys of fifty years earlier, that:

> I hope and believe that the Forces out there ... will not be found wanting and that should an attack on Singapore develop, its defence will be found not unwanting of record in the annals of the British Empire, and may even be quoted to future generations as an example to follow.

Then, perhaps realizing that such remarks might create in the minds of the powers-that-be the notion that Singapore could be relegated even farther down the scale of priorities, he hedged a bit in more Hentyish words:

> But though carrying on even if reduced to a meagre diet of rice and rats and finally after firing one's last round, dying sword in hand in the innermost keep, may be romantic, it would be of little practical value towards the solution of the problem with which we have to deal. For it is not only a question of holding on to an isolated fortress which is only of value in itself, but of ensuring that a naval base can be used by HM ships.

After that he became even more cautious:

> Although the requirements of Singapore are not of immediate
> urgency today, the situation may change at any moment. In view
> of the great importance of the place to the British Empire as a
> whole and in particular to Australia and New Zealand, it would in
> all probability be considered essential, should war break out with
> Japan to make good services deficiencies at the earliest possible
> moment.[14]

In that same letter he pointed out that the only aircraft in Singapore that
could be considered in any way modern were the Blenheim I and the
Hudson, of which there were only a handful. This should be compared
with his later remark in Singapore that, 'We can get on alright with
Buffaloes out here ... Let England have the super-Spitfires and the
hyper-Tornadoes. Buffaloes are quite good enough for Malaya.' Such
crass remarks – and there were many such made by the leaders in pre-war
Singapore – supported the propaganda about Singapore's impregnability;
and it was something so easily disproved by the Japanese in the first days
of the war that it had a disastrous and lasting effect on the morale of the
defending forces.

Brooke-Popham had been primed in London about the divergent views
and antagonisms that existed at the top level in Singapore. His first task
was to get rid of Charles Vlieland, the Secretary of Defence because
General Bond could not work with him. This was soon done with the
quiescent aid of the Governor. Brooke-Popham then turned to disposing
of Bond and the AOC, Babington, who were also utterly incompatible.

Sir Robert noted in a later dispatch that he found 'considerable jealousy
between the Army and the Royal Air Force', and that 'there was a
tendency for one of the Services to work out a plan of its own and
then consult the others, instead of every plan being prepared as for a
combined operation.' He had no problem with Babington, who was due
for a transfer back home anyway, but a problem did arise with Bond. His
successor, General Percival, was late in arriving due to intricate wartime
travelling arrangements, and Brooke-Popham had 'telegraphed over half
Asia' looking for his 'lost General'. Meanwhile he had taken great care to
ensure that Bond knew nothing about the impending change till it was all
settled, when he intended to break the news to him personally. That plan
misfired when an incautious telegram from England arrived and Bond
found out by accident that he was going. Brooke-Popham relates that,
'it was rather a blow for him [Bond], especially the way it was leaked
out'. The C-in-C also noted that the General had taken it admirably, and
hoped that this would be taken into account when his future was being
considered, 'as well as the fact that this climate does affect some people
adversely'.[15]

Babington's convenient transfer from the scene left no aftermath of hostility between him and Brooke-Popham. Indeed, their personal relationship seems to have developed into a friendly one. When, a month or two later, Babington, now promoted to Air Marshal and based at Air HQ Reading, wrote to the C-in-C, he stated that he had just been made aware of the peculiar terms of Brooke-Popham's appointment and he commiserated with him over an impossible task. Babington then sent a note of warning. 'On the authority of Pugg Ismay [Churchill's Chief of Staff], the fundamental governing factor would seem to be the P[rime] M[inister]'s conviction that there will be three months warning of any serious explosion in the Far East. The general effect of that assumption is obvious. In my humble opinion, its lulling effect may be dangerous.' The date of that prescient note was 1st August 1941.

After sorting out these initial personnel problems, one of the major decisions Brooke-Popham had to make was over defensive preparations. There were two schools of thought: to defend the beaches or to hold a line further inland. The decision was not made easier by the earlier siting of several airfields close to the coast. He gave orders for the defence of the beaches, which entailed considerable new construction work. Now a compromise had to be reached between employing troops on the construction of these defence works and teaching them to operate in the jungle.

There is much evidence that the extremely difficult job in Singapore was too much for Brooke-Popham. It was said that he had a habit of falling asleep during conferences. Perhaps the local climate affected him as adversely as he had reported it had with General Bond? He was much affected, too, by the loss of his able and hard-working Chief of Staff, Major-General R.H. Dewing who was sent home after illness. There was a two-month gap before Dewing's replacement, Major-General Playfair, arrived.

By August 1941 the Chiefs of Staff in London began to realise that they had made a wrong appointment, and they initiated plans to relieve Brooke-Popham. When Duff Cooper arrived in Singapore in September 1941, he helped the process along, but even after the decision had been made to send Lieutenant-General Sir Henry Pownall to take over, Duff Cooper did not let up. In a private letter to Churchill dated 18th December 1941, he said that Brooke-Popham 'is a very much older man than his years warrant and sometimes seems on the verge of nervous collapse. I fear also that knowledge of his own failing powers renders him jealous of any encroachment on his sphere of influence. He has looked upon me with suspicion ever since my arrival, disliked my recent appointment and fought hard against the creation of the War Council.'

Duff Cooper was prone to making harsh judgements about people, but in this case his summing-up seems about right. Major-General Kirby in his book *Singapore: the Chain of Disaster* says of Brooke-Popham, 'although he was a man of great charm, he had clearly passed his prime and was not a forceful enough personality to deal with this complicated and difficult situation'.[16] We have, on the other hand, a woman's kindlier summing-up. Meg Spooner's diary entry for 29th November 1941 includes the remark, 'BP is unusual but has a first-class mind.'[17]

Brooke-Popham's lack of decisiveness was shown up most at the time of the initial Japanese attack. The decision to stand down from a pre-emptive strike into Thailand was taken too late; the troops concerned were given little time to change from an offensive to a defensive mode.

It was a bad decision to send out to Singapore an Air Chief Marshal past his prime and with no recent command experience. His appointment tends to add weight to the theory, held by some survivors of the Malayan campaign, that a number of 'expendable' commanders were sent to Singapore.

Lieutenant-General Arthur Ernest Percival
CB, DSO, MC (1897–1966)

A considerable part of the blame for the fall of Singapore has fallen on General Percival. After his return to England from three-and-a-half years as a prisoner of the Japanese he was treated by official circles very much as a non-person. His temporary rank of Lieutenant-General was never confirmed – it merely became an Honorary rank, which resulted in a reduced pension. Nor was he granted the knighthood which was almost automatic for a soldier of that substantive rank.

There is little direct criticism of Percival in the Official History of the campaign. This may well have been caused by the threat he issued in a letter to the historian, Major-General Kirby, mentioned in an internal minute written on 28th April 1953 by A.B. Acheson, the Cabinet Office official who was acting as secretary to the team of official historians. General Percival's letter 'foreshadows that, if the official history is critical of himself or his fellow-Commanders, he will probably wish to publish a reply,' Acheson reported.[18]

Kirby was less kind to Percival in his own (unofficial) book, *Singapore: The Chain of Disaster*, which was published five years after Percival's death. After giving a very brief resumé of Percival's army career, he goes on to say, 'He proved from all accounts to be a brilliant staff officer, but was, however, quite untried as a commander and had neither the drive nor the ruthlessness which was needed by the commander who was to succeed General Bond in Malaya in 1941.'

Although Kirby was probably right in this latter opinion, he should have added that Percival in World War One had commanded everything from a platoon to a brigade, that he had won a MC and a DSO (to which a bar was added while serving in Russia in 1918) and had in the meantime become a protégé of General (later Field-Marshal) Sir John Dill, who was a good judge of character.

Born in 1887, and like Shenton Thomas the son of a clergyman, Percival attended Rugby School. He did not go directly into the army, however. Instead he spent seven years in rather junior positions with a firm of iron-ore merchants in London, before enlisting as a private in 1914. Almost at once he was commissioned into the Bedfordshire Regiment, and had a splendid record in France, earning a brevet majority and then, as a temporary lieutenant-colonel, taking command of a brigade. By 1931 he became a lecturer at the Camberley Staff College, and it was there that Dill's eye settled on him. In 1935 he was sent to the Imperial Staff College, and in 1936 to Singapore as GSO1 to General Dobbie. He stayed there until the end of 1937, and was party to the new appreciations on Malayan defence sent home by Dobbie. In 1940 he went to France as Brigadier, General Staff, to Dill. He was then recalled to England, promoted Major-General, and given command of 43rd Division. Dill then, in early 1941, recommended 'the best officer he had met for some time' for the post of GOC, Malaya. He arrived there in May.

Immediately prior to going to Malaya, Percival was promoted to temporary Lieutenant-General. One of the units under his command there was 3rd Indian Corps, and the Indian Army authorities appointed Lieutenant-General Sir Lewis Heath to take command of it. Heath's was a substantive rank, and prior to Percival's appointment as GOC, Heath was senior to him. As Brigadier Thyer of the Australian 8th Division was to write after the war, 'whoever sanctioned the appointment of Heath subsequent to the appointment of Percival, had much to answer for', for right from the start the two generals did not get on. (Thyer was correct in what he said about the order of appointments. However, Heath arrived in Malaya before Percival.)

Percival was no Montgomery, not even an Auchinleck. What was needed in Malaya was a ruthless, brilliant, no-nonsense, hard-driving, operational general. Percival was a brilliant staff officer; his written reports and appreciations bear witness to that. But his battle experience dated from twenty years earlier, and he was not a tough enough character to exercise firm authority over the other general officers in Malaya. Perhaps he was too much of a gentleman. In her autobiography *Trumpets from the Steep*, Diana Cooper, the wife of Duff Cooper, was to bemoan 'the condition of poor Singapore'. She went on, 'it can't be left ... to the gentleness of GOC Percival'.

Unfortunately Percival's appearance did not help him much either. He was something of an athlete, yet his appearance belied the fact. He was tall and of slight build. He had a soft voice, and his most obvious facial characteristic was a pair of protruding upper teeth, which in juxtaposition to his small moustache made him look rather like a rabbit, according to Stanley L. Falk, the American military historian.[19] Some of Percival's own men were not overly struck by his appearance either: 'He just didn't look the part,' says Artillery Sergeant Harry Blackham. 'And how he could make his appearance even worse by wearing that long obsolete Wolseley helmet, God alone knows.' Blackham goes on, 'I have always felt sorry for him. He was not a known general like the Auk or Alex [Alexander]. Can you possibly think of Percival as "*Perce*"?' That last point of Blackham's is important. Unlike 'The Auk' and 'Alex' and 'Monty', and 'Bill' Slim, for that matter, and even 'Piggy' Heath and 'Billy' Key in Malaya, Percival was never granted a nickname. He might have been respected by his men, but it was not a respect tinged with affection.[20]

Percival made several mistakes during the campaign. Perhaps the most serious one was his belief that the Japanese would attack Singapore across the Johore Strait from the north-east rather than the north-west. This led him to to place his strongest formation, the newly arrived British 18th Division, in the wrong position. In his post-war dispatch of February 1948, and again in his book *The War in Malaya*, published in 1949, he stated that he believed the attack would come where in fact it did, in the north-west. This version of the views held by Percival in February 1942 was disputed by General Wavell and several other competent authorities; and much later, in correspondence with Kirby the official historian, Percival admitted that in this respect his memory had been faulty. (This is not the only known example of Percival's sometimes selective memory.)

An earlier campaign mistake was probably his refusal to allow General Murray-Lyon to withdraw southwards to Gurun from the Jitra Line on 12th December 1941, the fourth day of the war. When forced to withdraw anyway early in the morning of the following day, 13th December, it could not have been more badly timed. It was dark, pouring with rain and the conditions made communications well-high impossible. Some units never received their withdrawal instructions and went straight into the Japanese bag as prisoners, while the losses in equipment were enormous.

Brigadier Ivan Simson, Chief Engineer, Malaya Command, and Head of Civil Defence, records in his book *Singapore – Too Little, Too Late* that in late December 1941, Percival refused to order the construction of defence works along the northern coast of Singapore Island on the basis that 'defences are bad for morale, for both troops and civilians'. The decision horrified Simson.

Meg Spooner, that perceptive observer of the Singapore scene obviously fed with titbits by her admiral husband and others, said in her diary that Percival was too weak with the Governor. Later, towards the end of January 1942, she recorded, 'Jack [Admiral Spooner] feels that Percival has lost his grip – if he ever had it! He is charming and easy but has no drive.'

At a meeting of army commanders a few days before the surrender Percival made a remark which indicated that if he surrendered, his honour would be at stake. Heath replied, 'What honour? You lost that many days ago in the north.' This was a hurtful, cutting and unnecessary remark to make, and one which Percival never forgot.

'To be candid,' he wrote to Heath after the war, 'what upset me ... was the attitude towards me and some of the remarks made at the last two conferences. I have not recorded them [he had] and do not wish to do so, but I felt that they were not quite worthy of a conference of senior officers gathered together at such a time, when I wanted all the help I could get.'

Percival surrendered the city and island to the Japanese on 15th February 1942. Only twenty-four hour's supply of fresh water remained, it had been reported to him. It was this consideration above all others, he said in his report of the Malayan operations, that made him decide at a Senior Commanders' conference on that last morning, to surrender.[21] (There was another inter-related factor that played an equally large part in the deliberations at that last conference, one which Percival never reported on.)

Percival always took umbrage at any suggestion that his decision was influenced in any way by the likelihood of severe civilian casualties if he fought on. After the war he wrote to General Heath:

> I have never accepted, and do not now, that the threat of the enemy breaking through our lines and even if it might result in the death of a large number of Asiatics or Europeans, was a valid reason for the surrender of Singapore. This argument carried little or no weight with me. Whatever you may think yourself, I hope that you will never tell anybody that that was my reason for capitulating.

Whatever other criticisms can be levelled at General Percival, his honour cannot be impugned. He remained with his men in Singapore although his superior, General Wavell, had authorised him to leave. He conducted himself well throughout his captivity. After the war he worked assiduously on behalf of the Far East Prisoners of War Association. Despite the criticisms levelled at him he deserved better treatment in post-war England than he was afforded. His treatment seems especially unfair when compared with that given in the United States to his American counterpart in the Phillipines, General Wainright.

It must, of course, remain doubtful that even if a more dynamic military leader had been appointed as GOC Malaya, given the shortage of trained men, the lack of certain equipment and above all, planes, the end-result would have been any different.

Alfred Duff Cooper (later Viscount Norwich)
(1890–1954)

Duff Cooper arrived at Singapore in September 1941 on what at first appeared to be a visit with rather vague objectives. Earlier, in July of that year, he had been removed by Churchill from an unsuccessful tenure as Minister of Information. He now held the position of Chancellor of the Duchy of Lancaster, a post, as his biographer said, 'reserved for politicians in transit: young men on the way up and failures on the way down are its usual inhabitants'.[22] At the age of fifty-one Duff Cooper could scarcely be numbered among the former.

Duff Cooper soon sent home a report on the Far East and Singapore in particular. He described the inefficiencies he saw caused by overlapping ministerial jurisdictions. He suggested that a Minister for the Far East be appointed, or some similar post with executive powers. He recommended former Australian Prime Minister Sir Robert Menzies for the job. Duff Cooper was involved in another Australian matter in Singapore, and it gives us an interesting insight into his character. In a secret and personal letter he wrote to Churchill on 18th December 1941, Duff disparaged V.G. Bowden. He wrote: 'The Australian who is to serve on the War Council in future is of no account, and therefore better than a better man who might give trouble.'[23] This should be contrasted with the message he sent to the Australian Minister of External Affairs through the British High Commissioner in Canberra, referring to Bowden's appointment. In that he said, 'We are glad to have him with us, and share your confidence in the soundness of his views.'[24]

Churchill gave the recommended job to Duff Cooper himself by appointing him Resident Cabinet Minister for the Far East in December 1941. The concept of placing someone in Singapore with executive authority was a good one, but it was already far too late for the man concerned to be effective. Only a year before, even, something might have been done by a holder of the post. Moreover, Duff Cooper was not given overriding powers; the Colonial Governors in the area, and the Commanders-in-Chief, still reported separately to Whitehall. This was a grave error on Churchill's part, but as Duff Cooper was probably the wrong man for the job anyway, perhaps Churchill was merely hedging his bets. The post needed someone tough; Duff was resolute, but not tough enough. It also needed someone with considerable diplomatic skill and a degree of tact.

Duff Cooper was aware before his arrival in Singapore that Brooke-Popham was going to be replaced, and he did his utmost to speed the process. His reports home on the C-in-C were disparaging. Brooke-Popham did little to help his own cause, and seemed to go out of his way to be obstructive. When, at a meeting of the War Council, Duff asked Brooke-Popham for a list of his military requirements, he received the reply that such a list had already been sent to London and it had been turned down by the Chiefs of Staff. When Duff said he would raise the matter directly with Churchill, Brooke-Popham replied that this would be disloyal to the Chiefs of Staff. At that Duff Cooper lost his temper and said he could not agree that loyalty to the Chiefs of Staff was more important than winning the war. Furthermore, if the C-in-C really believed that certain supplies were essential then no stone should be left unturned to obtain them.

Sir Shenton Thomas was at that meeting and he found Duff Cooper's aggressiveness distasteful. It seems that both Brooke-Popham and Thomas were more interested in preventing Duff from straying on to their preserves, than they were to use a man, however much they might dislike him, who had direct access to the Prime Minister. With such attitudes in the top command, it is hardly surprising that Singapore fell.

Duff did little to hide his views about the abilities of some of the leaders in Singapore. It was said that he sometimes entertained dinner guests by imitating the Governor and the C-in-C. Duff's secretary denied this story, according to Duff Cooper's biographer, John Charmley. However, it is extremely unlikely that the secretary, Martin Russell, attended every dinner party held, while the story fits in with Duff Cooper's known ability as a mimicker and the fact that his tongue tended to loosen when he drank, which he did often.

Duff Cooper was not alone in sending disparaging reports home to Whitehall. In a memorandum marked 'secret' and kept that way until it was made public in 1993, Sir Shenton Thomas wrote:

> The news of DC's appointment to the Far East had been received with little enthusiasm ... We felt we were being landed with a failure. We remembered Sir Stafford Cripps' description of him as a 'petulant little pipsqueak'.
>
> At one of the first meetings there was a heated argument as to the powers of the [War] Council, heated on DC's part. He seemed to think we were to run the war which was not Brooke-Popham's interpretation of the Prime Minister's telegram laying down the terms of reference. I agreed with Brooke-Popham. He had his orders from the Chiefs of Staff and I had mine from the Secretary of State. No man can serve two masters. Eventually DC told Brooke-Popham that he was the worst example of the old school tie he had ever come across. This was to the C-in-C, Far East, in the presence of junior officers and myself. Brooke-Popham behaved splendidly and merely said that the remark was not fair.

Later in the same report Sir Shenton wrote: 'For all I know DC may have urged my recall.'[25]

Duff Cooper left Singapore on 2nd January 1942, recalled by direct order of Churchill. This coincided with the appointment of General Sir Archibald Wavell as Supreme Allied Commander, South-West Pacific. (Wavell had asked for Duff to stay, but this was disallowed by Churchill.)

He had managed to accomplish some positive things during his time in Singapore. Perhaps the most important of these was the appointment of Brigadier Ivan Simson as Chief of Civil Defence. He might have accomplished much more had he been able to get on with the Governor.

Lieutenant-General Sir Lewis Macclefield Heath
KBE, CB, CIE, DSO, MC (1885–1954)

On his arrival in Malaya to take command of 3rd Indian Corps, General Heath must have found it galling to discover that the General Officer Commanding, Malaya Command, was to be Percival. Percival was younger than Heath; nor did he have a record to match Heath's recently earned operational experience. Up to the time of his appointment to Malaya Command Percival had been junior to him.

'Piggy' Heath came to Malaya flushed with the success of having taken part, as one of General Wavell's Divisional Commanders, in conquering the Italians in Eritrea. He was an Indian Army man through and through, having entered that army in 1906. He never attended Staff College but had served as an Instructor at the Senior Officers' School at Begaum in India.

In addition to the gall Heath must have tasted, Percival was known to have a none too high opinion of the Indian Army and little liking for any officer who did not have the letters 'a.s.c.' (attended Staff College) alongside his entry in either the British or Indian Army Lists.

There was little sign of strained relations between the two, however, up to the time of the Japanese attack; but after that friction became evident to several staff officers serving in Malaya.

Perhaps the best source for evidence of the relationship between the two generals is the post-war correspondence between them on the proposed content of the British Official History of the campaign, and in the correspondence of around the same date between General Kirby, the historian, and Percival.

The letter that Percival wrote to Heath about the attitude shown towards him during the last two conferences before the capitulation of Singapore, including the remark about his loss of honour, is quoted on page 162. His rather mild words in that letter to Heath must have covered a deep bitterness, for in his notes to General Kirby on the content of the Official History it looks very much as if he was out to get revenge. He pointed out that Heath had arrived in Malaya in March 1941 when Bond was still GOC, and that he had asked Bond for permission to bring his fiancée from India to Malaya for their marriage. Bond had given permission and the marriage had duly taken place. (Katherine Lonergan, from Auckland, New Zealand, was Heath's second wife. She had been a nursing sister in India. Heath, already over fifty, and despite having only one eye and a withered arm, seemed to have a way with the ladies.) After commenting on Heath's attitude during the campaign, Percival wrote that having a 'pregnant wife in Malaya might have had a profound effect'.

He went on to say a great deal more:

> As soon as the operations started, General Heath gave one the impression of developing 'withdrawal complex'. He always seemed to me to be thinking how soon he could disengage his troops from the enemy and how far he could take them back. Think he never agreed with the official strategy laid down in London and endorsed in Malaya of imposing the maximum of delay on the Japanese at every stage and so gain time for the arrival and deployment of reinforcements. Heath convinced, as I understand it, we should have withdrawn all our forces to Johore and fought out the battle there.

Elsewhere in his correspondence with Kirby Percival laid into Heath even more, saying that he had an Indian Army complex, and 'had not been to any of the Staff Colleges, and had seldom come into contact with British troops. The Indian Army was everything. Disintegration of many Indian formations had a material effect on him.'

Apparently in an attempt to sound more fair-minded, he went on, 'Speculation Heath being senior by date of rank might have resented being placed under me. Showed no signs of this.' But then he brought up matters that were in no way germane to the conduct of the campaign. He reported that, in the Japanese senior officers' prisoner of war camp on Formosa, two factions developed. One, led by Percival himself, fought for its rights and did its utmost to embarrass the Japanese. The other faction in which he included 'Sir Shenton Thomas, Heath, Sir Henry Trusted [Chief Justice, FMS], and all the Americans', strove 'for appeasement and the least line of resistance'.

All these comments he passed to Kirby, and even if they were meant to be treated as confidential they tend to conflict with his threat that, if the Official History contained anything detrimental to him or his senior commanders, he reserved the right to reply.

Heath was not alone in thinking that an early withdrawal south to Johore would have been militarily the best option after the failure to hold the Japanese in the extreme north of Malaya. Colonel Thyer, on the staff of Australian Major-General Gordon Bennett, thought so too, and there were others of like mind. In Johore the British and Indian forces from the north could have linked up with the 8th Australian Division already stationed there, and there would have been time to prepare efficient tank defences. Had that strategy been adopted the Japanese might have been delayed far longer than was the case, or even stopped altogether. According to Colonel (later General) I. Sugita, General Yamashita's chief intelligence officer, the Japanese were surprised that there were not stronger defences in Johore, and they had expected their advance to be stopped long before they reached the vicinity of Singapore.[26] The principal argument against the adoption of that strategy is that the airfields in central Malaya, from which Singapore and convoys approaching it could be bombed, would have been handed to the Japanese on a plate; but since they captured the airfields quickly anyway, it would have made little difference to the actuality of Japanese air supremacy.

Percival also made little allowance for Heath's intimate knowledge of the fighting capabilities of his Indian battalions, many members of whom had never seen a tank until they were confronted with a Japanese one. A concentration of all Percival's forces in depth along a single line of defence, might have stiffened the fighting resolve of the Indian battalions. To use Percival's own phrase, the 'disintegration of many Indian formations' might not then have happened.

Meg Spooner in her diary entry for 4th February 1942 on which date she had had the Heaths to dinner, wrote: 'General Heath has a strong, honest and not unclever face. His left arm is withered. He thinks there are too many generals here.' This latter remark links with something else General Percival told Kirby. 'After withdrawal to Singapore, Heath suggested that, as his Corps HQ was no longer required, he should be evacuated to India.' Percival turned the idea down on the basis that it would have made a bad impression on the Indian Army. (On the subject of there being too many generals in the area, the list in Appendix 1 includes fifty officers of the rank of brigadier and above who at one time or another served during the Malayan campaign.)

It is impossible to say how the campaign might have ended had Heath and not Percival been in overall command. The end-result would probably have been the same. Of one thing we can be certain, though. The campaign would have been fought differently.

Admiral Sir Tom Spencer Vaughan Phillips
KCB (1888–1941)

Admiral Phillips had limited sea-going war experience when he was given the double step promotion from Rear-Admiral to Acting Admiral to take command of the Eastern Fleet in October 1941. Like Percival on the army side, Phillips was considered the naval staff officer *par excellence*. He had been Vice Chief of Naval Staff from 1939 up to the date of his new appointment. He was a man of small stature; and he had a temper which was prone to surface if he thought he was not getting his way.

The sending of a small force of capital ships (originally one battleship, one battle-cruiser, and one aircraft carrier), to be known as Force Z, to Singapore to act as a deterrent to the Japanese was one of Churchill's pet schemes. 'The deterrent concept dominated his thinking on Far East strategy almost to the eleventh hour,' wrote the naval historian Stephen Roskill.[27] Churchill insisted that the force 'should consist of the smallest number of the best ships', and he wanted *Prince of Wales* to be one of them. The First Sea Lord, Admiral Sir Dudley Pound, proposed to send instead four old 'R' Class battleships into the Indian Ocean, and not to Singapore; but Churchill argued strongly against sending obsolescent ships to an area where they would in no way be a deterrent. When this matter was discussed at a Defence Committee meeting in London on 17th October 1941, one of the officers who argued the navy case against sending *Prince of Wales* to Singapore was the then Rear-Admiral Phillips.

All this verbiage about deterrents, and what did or did not constitute one, should be compared with the internal memorandum which Admiral Layton circulated around his China Station command only a month before that Defence Committee meeting in London. In it he reiterated that it was the intention to send a powerful fleet – which Force Z was not – to Singapore in the event of war with Japan. Roskill wrote that this 'was the background to the shocking disaster which was to destroy British prestige throughout the East and, in the long run, must surely have contributed to our loss of empire.'

Phillips's new appointment was not highly regarded by some senior admirals. Admiral Somerville wrote, 'I shudder to think of the Pocket Napoleon and his party ... no solid experience to fall back on. They ought to have someone who knows the stuff and can train that party properly on the way out.'

Churchill had thought highly of Phillips in the early stages of the war in Europe, right up to the time, in fact, when Phillips had blotted his copybook in the Prime Minister's eyes by opposing retaliatory bombing of German cities, and the diversion, in March 1941, of forces from North Africa to Greece. After that relations had cooled between them. Churchill always insisted on being consulted over Flag Officer appointments, and sometimes he initiated them; but in Phillips's case the initial recommendation probably came from Admiral Pound.

Despite the lessons to be learnt from the Taranto episode in November 1940, when British carrier-based torpedo-planes had carried out a highly successful attack on the Italian Fleet in the harbour, Phillips was convinced that planes were no match for battleships at sea. He would listen to no one who tried to convince him otherwise. The authority for this statement is General Hastings Ismay, Churchill's Chief of Staff, who wrote in his Memoirs:

Admiral Tom Phillips refused to admit that properly armed and well-fought ships had anything to fear from air power. Nor was he alone in that opinion. Even WC [Churchill] whose forecasts were not often at fault, was one of the many who did not believe that well-built modern warships properly defended by armour and AA guns were likely to fall a prey to hostile aircraft. The battles royal which raged between Tom Phillips and Arthur Harris [Air Marshal 'Bomber' Harris] when they were Directors of Planning in their respective Departments were never-ending and always inconclusive.

One of their arguments ended in this way:

> Bert Harris exploded, 'One day, Tom, you will be standing on a box on your bridge, and your ship will be smashed to pieces by bombers and torpedo-aircraft. As she sinks, your last words will be, "That was a ******* great mine!".'[28]

The Force Z which arrived in Singapore on 1st December 1941, was significantly different to the one originally planned, for it lacked the aircraft-carrier HMS *Indomitable* which was supposed to be part of it because it had gone aground in the West Indies. Force Z now consisted of the battleship *Prince of Wales*, the battle-cruiser *Repulse*, and five elderly destroyers.

Late in the afternoon of 8th December 1941, the day Japan attacked Thailand and the northern Malayan port of Kota Bharu, Admiral Phillips sailed Force Z north with the intention of destroying the Japanese landing fleet. With no air reconnaissance available – the airfields in north-east Malaya and the one at Kuantan were abandoned on the first day of fighting – Phillips was relying on the element of surprise. So when, on 9th December, he found that his fleet had been spotted by the Japanese, he turned about. That night he received a message from Singapore stating (incorrectly as it turned out) that the Japanese were also making a landing at Kuantan, halfway down the east coast of Malaya. Phillips diverted to investigate Kuantan on 10th December but, finding nothing, headed south once more. Within hours the fleet were located by Japanese planes based in Indo-China and both capital ships were sunk. Phillips went down with his flagship.

The loss of the two capital ships shocked the world. It shook Churchill to the core. He wrote, 'In all the war, I never received a more direct shock. As I turned over and twisted in bed, the full horror of the news sank into me. There were no British or American capital ships in the Indian Ocean or the Pacific except the American survivors of Pearl Harbor who were hastening back to California. Over all this vast expanse of waters Japan was supreme and we everywhere were weak and naked.'[29]

Churchill tended to blame Phillips for the disaster. He said that his own idea had been from the start that, after Force Z had made its deterrent effect felt in Singapore, it 'should then disappear into the immense archipelago'. This idea of the plan being for the fleet to do a disappearing act is not borne out by the records; this seems to have been something Churchill dreamed up after the event in an attempt to absolve himself from blame in the matter. In what may have been another attempt to place the onus on Phillips, in March 1942, Churchill enquired of Admiral Pound whether Phillips could have used a smokescreen to shield his ships from the Japanese planes. Pound answered in the affirmative, but said that he presumed Phillips had preferred to keep a clear field of fire. This would fit in with Phillips' theory of the effectiveness of anti-aircraft fire.

To have disappeared with his ships into the vastness of the Eastern Archipelago the moment the Japanese attacked as suggested by Churchill would not have been in keeping with the traditions of the Royal Navy. It is doubtful whether any admiral would have done anything other than what Phillips did; sail north against the enemy.

But a more experienced admiral might have used smoke screens and certainly would have called for air cover from Singapore as soon as he knew he had been sighted by Japanese aircraft that morning. Instead, Phillips maintained absolute radio silence. A squadron of Buffaloes was eventually scrambled from Singapore after Captain Tennant of the *Repulse* radioed for them. But by then it was too late. When they arrived over the scene all they saw were the destroyers of Force Z picking up survivors from the capital ships.

Vice-Admiral (later Admiral) Sir Geoffrey Layton,
GBE, KCB, KCMG, DSO (1884–1964)

Admiral Layton succeeded Admiral Sir Percy Noble as C-in-C, China Station, in 1940. This command was gobbled up in December 1941 by the arrival of Admiral Sir Tom Phillips as C-in-C, Eastern Fleet. But as the official date for Layton to strike his flag was 10th December, and Phillips arrived in Singapore on 1st December, for nine days there were four Commanders-in-Chief in Singapore, not merely three.

Layton was one of the few top people in Singapore who got on well with Duff Cooper. Duff Cooper described Layton to Churchill 'as most co-operative. He is not brilliant but he is a thoroughly sensible, experienced and trustworthy sailor. He is receptive to new ideas, wastes no time talking and knows his job. I feel that I can completely rely on him and I should be very sorry to lose him.'[30]

Before taking up the China Station appointment Layton had been Second in Command, Mediterranean Fleet; before that he had held other operational appointments. In view of that experience and his year in

Singapore he might have thought the command of the Eastern Fleet was to be his until it went to Phillips. It is to Layton's credit that he never mentioned his feelings over this matter, nor did he comment on the fact that Phillips, who was considerably junior to himself in substantive rank, had been given a double-step promotion to enable him to take the job. The irony was that, after Phillips went down with *Prince of Wales*, Layton became C-in-C, Eastern Fleet, for the ship on which he had embarked for home was hastily summoned back to Singapore for that purpose.

Meg Spooner's views on Layton contrast sharply with Duff Cooper's. There are a number of entries about him in her diary, none of them complimentary. On 31st December 1941, she wrote that her husband, Rear-Admiral E.J. 'Jack' Spooner 'was very nervy and jumpy. C-in-C [Layton] like an octopus and seizes everything to himself. Jack doesn't know half that is going on and the C-in-C interferes in everything.' An entry for two days later reads, 'Jack said to C-in-C that he would like to attend War Council – C-in-C replied, "Waste of your time, dear boy".' On 3rd January, 'Jack went to War Council for first time. C-in-C dismissed him after he had made a statement on convoys by saying, "I don't think we need to keep the RA any further, Mr Duff Cooper". Layton is now showing his true feelings. I always felt he resented Jack in some way. I think he would have liked somebody efficient but less independent and less clever. I know he was jealous of this house and yet he and she refused to take it when they arrived here in September 1940.' (The Spooners lived in the splendiferous 'Admiral's House' on the Naval Base. The Laytons resided in the city in a lesser residence.)

Admiral Layton was to lose much of his reputation with his men over his treatment of the survivors from *Prince of Wales* and *Repulse*. This still rankles with some of them. Some of the survivors from the capital ships were posted to other ships, whilst selected ones, about 900 in all, were shipped out for Colombo aboard an old transport. The morale amongst those left behind was low, and became lower as they were organised into units and sent to various destinations in Malaya. Some were sent to man railway locomotives, and others to man the ferry boats in Penang Harbour. One party engaged in the latter assignment aboard the *Violet* was not impressed with the panic and disorganisation caused by the bombing they saw in Penang, so the ratings left their posts, jumped a lorry, and made their way back to Singapore, complaining that they were dead beat. The young sub-lieutenant in charge tried to stop them but failed. The affair ended in a court martial for all concerned. Everyone, including the officer, was found guilty but all were given the minimum sentence.

After this Layton sent a message to Rear-Admiral Spooner as the officer directly responsible for the Navy in Malaya:

This is not at all inspiring. Officers and men do not seem to realize that war is not always a very pleasant game and setbacks and dangerous experiences must be met with fortitude. Officers and men at Hong Kong had a very unpleasant and nerve-shaking experience which lasted for fourteen days but it did not impair their fighting spirit. I wish to hear no more sentimental rubbish about survivors not being fit for the next job that comes along – they should be only too ready to get their own back.[31]

There was a serious shortage of manpower in Singapore and the survivors had to be used. But Layton should surely have allowed them at least a brief respite after their ships had been sunk under them. And the comparison with Hong Kong was unfair; the naval men there had not survived a major sea battle defeat.

Nor did Layton improve his reputation when he left Singapore well before it fell. He left on the 5th January aboard HMS *Dragon* (in convoy with *Devonshire* which was taking the staff and equipment of FECB out of danger's way.) His last message to the naval people left behind could have been better phrased: 'I have gone to collect the Eastern Fleet. Keep your heads high and your hearts firm until I return.' The statement smacked, some of his men still maintain, of the 'f∗∗∗ you, I'm alright, Jack' sort.

Layton went on to better things. He became C-in-C, Ceylon, and was a success in the job. It seems that the British government had taken on board at least one lesson from Singapore, for they subordinated some of the Governor of Ceylon's powers to him. (The Governor concerned was Sir Andrew Caldecott.)

A heavy attack by Japanese carrier-borne aircraft on Colombo and Trincomalee was successfully beaten off on 5th April 1942, during which the Japanese lost twenty-seven planes. Layton remained in Ceylon until 1945.

Major-General (later Lieutenant-General) Henry Gordon Bennett, CB, CMG, DSO, VD (1887–1962)

General Gordon Bennett, commander of the Australian 8th Division in Malaya, is the most controversial figure to feature in the Malayan campaign, and more has been written about him than perhaps anyone else involved. He was a controversial figure even before the unusual circumstances of his escape from Singapore.

Born in Victoria, he trained as an accountant before joining the Australian militia in 1912. In World War One he served at Gallipoli and in France, and was promoted to brigadier-general before he was twenty-nine. Between the World Wars he returned to business life and served in the Australian Militia, the equivalent to the Territorial Army in Britain. Australia had only a small standing army at that time which was built around a Staff Corps. In the 1930s Bennett published a number of articles impugning the professionalism and efficiency of this Staff Corps, until he was ordered to desist, but he continued to air his views orally to anyone who would listen. There was some truth in his criticisms, but his tactless method of promulgating them made him few friends. He had no time for staff officers, and they in turn marked him down as an ill-balanced man. It is from this time that his rivalry with a fellow officer, General Blamey (later Field Marshal Sir Thomas), stemmed.

Early in World War Two Bennett had hoped to get command of the AIF in the Middle East, but this went instead to Thomas Blamey, who was his junior. However in 1941 Gordon Bennett was given command of the smaller AIF in Malaya.

Gordon Bennett lived up to the reputation that many red-haired men have. His nickname was 'Ginger'. He had a fiery and impatient temperament. He was bellicose and inclined to be bombastic. He did not suffer anyone he considered a fool at all, let alone gladly. He seemed to delight in treading on people's toes, especially if the toes belonged to staff officers.

In Malaya he liked to sing the praises of his men and there is nothing wrong with that. In an interview with Tom Fairhill of the Australian newspaper *Argus* on 19th December, he said, 'Every Australian here is more than itching to get on with the fighting.' Again, he was reported to have said before his men came into contact with the Japanese, 'The yellow Huns of the East will get the same reception that their brother Huns in Europe got from the old AIF in the last war.' This was all good stuff, but in the process of praising his own men he often went out of the way to make unfair comparisons with the British troops stationed there, and this did nothing for good relations.

He hogged the limelight and was always prepared to give newsmen direct interviews even after hostilities with Japan began. Strict censorship was then in force but somehow he got away with it. This, of course, endeared him to a few of his particular cronies in the media, but not to some of the others. Giles Playfair, a broadcaster in Singapore, had this to say on 25th January 1942:

> There is a good deal of resentment at the moment (justified I think) at the disproportionate amount of publicity given to the Australian troops. But the streamer headlines which greeted the news they'd gone into action, when compared with the consistent official silence about the doings of British troops, have hardly been justified by events, for in fact the Australians seem to be staging the fastest retreat of the entire campaign. Maybe the odds have been weighted too heavily against them. Maybe they have fought with great gallantry. But so, too, have our own men, and their ordeal has been measurably longer.[32]

A.B. Lodge, an Australian, has written, 'Bennett's insistence on press coverage for his troops was divisive and tended to highlight the differences between the Australians and the other troops in Malaya'. Elsewhere he said, 'In many ways he [Bennett] seemed to regard the British as much adversaries as allies.'[33] Writing six months after the fall of Singapore, the Australian newspaper tycoon, Sir Keith Murdoch, said in a newspaper article, 'Our own part was marred by a constant jarring and belittlement of our British and Indian comrades.'[34]

General Percival attempted to eliminate at least one of the differences between the Australian and British troops. He requested Bennett to reduce the Australian meat ration to the British scale. Bennett refused, despite the fact that his own Chief Medical Officer, Colonel A.P. Derham, was in agreement with a reduced meat scale on purely health grounds.

If the British found Bennett difficult, then so did many members of his own staff. Apart from the meat scale episode, Bennett clashed with Colonel Derham on anti-malaria measures. Colonel (later Brigadier) J.R. Broadbent later reported that he was disillusioned with his job on Bennett's staff, 'as the General would not listen to advice'.

Very early on in Malaya, Bennett clashed over training policy with one of his Brigade Commanders, Brigadier H.B. Taylor, who was one of the pre-war staff officers Bennett so actively disliked. Colonel J.H. Thyer stated that he attempted to mediate between the two and that 'it was possible to bring the two together but, at the last, it was merely an armed truce'.[35]

Colonel Thyer had this to say about his own relations with General Bennett:

> I was initially CO 8th Div. Signals until departure of Col. Rourke. It is understood that I was then selected personally by General Bennett as his GS01. Throughout the period of training and during the operations, the co-operation between GOC [Bennett] and GS01 was excellent. This was due to the fact that I considered it imperative that I should subordinate myself completely to the GOC in order to achieve smooth working. It in no way indicated that I agreed with the tactical and strategical decisions of the Commander. On the contrary, I disagreed in a major way.

Colonel Thyer was fair-minded enough, however, to add:

> General Bennett left after the surrender and I was very displeased with the manner of his departure. Then for 3½ years I was forced into the company of men who shared my views. It is very probable that these circumstances may have given me a bias against General Bennett which is reflected in the criticisms and opinions [recorded in the report].

Under the heading 'Conflict in Command' in the same Australian report, the authors say:

> It was well-known in Malaya before the operations and it was amply borne out during the operations, that the Australian GOC was incapable of subordinating himself to Malaya Command or of co-operating wholeheartedly with other commanders. From discussions in captivity with Generals Percival, Heath, Key, and Keith Simmons, it appears that the relations between them and the Australian GOC were more strained than the above statement would indicate.
>
> In fairness to General Bennett it must be stated that his attitude may have been entirely impersonal and that he was at all times battling for the rights and entity of the AIF. That may be perfectly true, but the result was the same, a decline of unity of command and integration of effort.

Colonel Thyer reports that Bennett successfully pleaded with General Percival to have the AIF allotted a separate role in the defence of Malaya, that of defending Johore in the south instead of being used as a reserve for General Murray-Lyon's 11th Division in the north. This had the effect of 'separating Percival's forces into two separate compartments, 3rd Indian Corps in the north and the AIF in the south'.

Bennett's independent views were helped by the fact that he had the right of direct reference to his superiors in Canberra. Percival had to take this into account in all his dealings with him.

General Kirby in his *Singapore, the Chain of Disaster* criticises Bennett for invariably placing his HQ too far back from the front line. He states that Bennett 'believed in control from the rear, assisted by liaison officers, and never went forward in action to see for himself'. This criticism is borne out by the Thyer report.

The contents of a letter from an Australian soldier who was ordered out of Singapore before it fell, gives further interesting insights into General Bennett's character, if the contents are true. (The letter also indicates that one can get out of the stickiest of situations providing one knows the right people!) It was written by Tom Carey (Serial No.785105) on the 27th July 1942, who was then training to be a pilot in Salisbury, Rhodesia. It was intercepted by the censor, and marked 'correspondence suspected to require special attention'. The letter was addressed to the Hon. W.J. Scully, Minister of Commerce, Canberra. The file it was in was only made public in the British Public Records Office in 1993.

Dear Mr Scully
Just a note to let you know that I am well and am getting along exceptionally well with my course here I am making the grade

easily, my previous flying knowledge is a big help. Please thank
Mr. Forde for me, (Author's note: Frank Forde was Deputy Leader
of the Australian Labour Party) if it had not been for Forde and
yourself I would now have been a prisoner of Japan, please God I
will soon be in action against our enemies. You mentioned in your
letter to me to Malaya that you did not receive my first letter I
wrote to you, well I am now able to tell you that my first letter
was confiscated by General Gordon Bennett. It seemed so strange
to me that Major-General Bennett never visited our battalion the
whole time we were in Malaya, his job as leader of the AIF was
to visit the troops under his command and see how their training
progressed, we of the 2/26 Bn AIF never ever saw our leader *once*,
of course I realize that he was a very busy man, entertaining
society, posing for films etc. etc. Major-General Bennett also said
that he was in Singapore as late as 16th February, well I have my
own opinion on this matter. I left in the last hours of Singapore
and I know all about his escape.[36]

If Tom Carey was implying that General Gordon Bennett left Singapore
before the capitulation (and would have therefore been technically a
deserter), he was in error. This opinion of an earlier escape is held strongly
by some men who fought in the campaign, but can be easily disproved.
Bennett was in attendance at a conference with General Percival on the
morning of 15th February; he was with Colonel Thyer, someone who held
no brief for his General, late in the afternoon of 15th February. And two
British soldiers who escaped on a boat with him have reported precisely
on the details of the escape. It is quite clear that Bennett escaped *after*
the capitulation.

It is a fact that Bennett had made provisional plans to escape well in
advance. As early as 3rd February Colonel Thyer had been invited to
join the escape party – he had even been given an escape kit – but he
turned down the opportunity.

Bennett's version of his escape, given after his arrival in Java was a
highly romanticised version of what actually took place. (The versions
of two members of the Singapore Volunteers who joined up with him on
the Singapore waterfront are given in Appendix 2.) The two Australian
officers who accompanied him were his aide, Lieutenant Gordon Walker,
and Major C.J.A. Moses. It has been suggested, perhaps unfairly, that
Bennett chose that particular duo in order to maximise the publicity of
his escape in Australia; Walker being a scion of one of the top families
in New South Wales, while Moses' peacetime job was General Manager,
Australian Broadcasting Corporation.

Gordon Bennett was no coward, so fear was not the reason he fled
Singapore. But the reason he gave for not staying with his men does not
stand up to investigation. He said that he escaped in order to bring out

with him his knowledge of Japanese jungle fighting methods. There were others in Malaya with a much more intimate knowledge of that than he had; his troops had only been fighting the Japanese for a month, whereas some British and Indian units had been fighting them for well in excess of that. Furthermore, Colonel Stewart of the Argylls was ordered out of Malaya for that precise purpose, as were other more junior officers. It is much more likely, as one of Gordon Bennett's biographers has noted, that he felt the war could not be fought successfully without him. He also knew that the top position in the Australian Army had become vacant, and he very much wanted to get the appointment ahead of his rival Blamey.

After Bennett's arrival in Java had been flashed to Australia and prior to his arrival in Sydney on 1st March 1942, Mrs. Gordon Bennett gave interviews to newspapermen. This was unfortunate to say the least, for what she said must have somewhat marred his 'heroic' arrival home.

The following appeared on the front page of the *Melbourne Argus* on 27th February 1942:

> Mrs Gordon Bennett said she felt sure that General Sir Archibald Wavell had ordered her husband to get out of Singapore. She said, 'In the last letters I received from my husband he indicated to me that he would never leave his men. Because of this I feel certain that, without such an order from General Wavell, he would never have tried to escape.' Those letters were dated January 14th.

One wonders what Bennett had to say to his wife when he learned what she had said, for he had not received any such order from Wavell or anyone else.

In April 1942 Bennett produced a report on the Malayan campaign in which he said the prime cause of failure was the low morale of Indian troops.[37] In this report and in the book he wrote later, he made little mention of an important factor in the actual fall of Singapore itself, the failure of some Australian units to put up much resistance to the Japanese between 8th and 15th February 1942. His failure to say much on this subject is perhaps scarcely surprising in view of his fighting words throughout 1941.[38]

There was a subsequent enquiry in Australia into Bennett's behaviour and although this largely exonerated him from any blame except for an error in judgement in leaving his men, he was never given another active command. He was later promoted to Lieutenant-General, but he resigned from the Army before the end of the war, never having achieved his ambition to lead the Australian Army. He died of a heart attack while sitting in his car in 1962.

The men he left behind in Singapore did not think his action was a mere error of judgement. They christened their plimsolls 'Gordon Bennetts' and the term 'doing a Gordon Bennett' came to be synonymous with 'doing a bunk'. In army circles in Australia itself, he was known as 'Fleet of Foot Bennett'. It was a big come down for a proud man.

General Sir Archibald (later Field Marshal Earl) Wavell
GCB, GCSI, GCIE, CMG, MC (1883–1950)

General Wavell arrived on the scene when it was already far too late to save Singapore.

General Sir Henry Pownall's appointment as C-in-C, Far East, in succession to Brooke-Popham was overtaken by events. On 30th December 1941 Wavell learned that he was to be appointed Supreme Allied Commander, South-West Pacific. He was to command all American, British, Dutch, and Australian (hence ABDA command) forces in what was defined as the strategic area comprising Burma, Malaya, the Philippines, the Netherlands East Indies and all waters in between. He received his final orders on 4th January and reached Singapore on the 7th, the very day the British fought and lost the crucial battle at Slim River.

It was the Americans who recommended Wavell for this first Supreme Allied Command. It was the only one (apart from the special case of Generalissimo Chiang Kai-shek, who as Supreme Commander in China operated only on Chinese territory) in the entire war that did not go to an American. (Admiral Mountbatten's later Supreme Command in South-East Asia was the natural successor of Wavell's command, although the areas covered were not exactly the same.) One suspects that the Americans knew there was little chance of glory for the incumbent of this position in 1942, and so preferred it to go to a Briton, even though it included the Philippines.

Wavell flew to Java on 10th December and decided to set up his ABDA Command at Lembang, a few miles away from the Dutch HQ at Bandung. General Pownall became his Chief of Staff. This decision to set up headquarters on Java rather than on Singapore Island has sometimes been criticised, especially by ex-Far East prisoners of war who thought that Wavell should have been on the island with them. But it was the logical decision. Personnel of four countries had to be brought in to man the HQ, some of them flown in from halfway round the world. An effective communications network had to be set up covering the entire area of the command. This could not have been done in Singapore which was already under daily air attack and where the communications system was already severely overloaded.

Another criticism has recently arisen over Wavell's appointment. When in early 1993, Wavell's report on the behaviour of Australian troops during the battle for Singapore was made public for the first time, several Australian sources described Wavell in less than flattering terms. The President of the Australian Returned Services League was reported in the *The Times* newspaper as having said, in reference to Wavell's sacking by Churchill as C-in-C, Middle East, 'Everyone should remember that Wavell was a disgraced commander.'[39] Wavell, however, had been far from disgraced in the Middle East; his sacking came about over of a policy disagreement with Churchill, something which happened to several other distinguished commanders in the course of the war.

Wavell's first task was to order a complete regrouping of forces in Malaya after the Slim River defeat, for Singapore was the linchpin of the strategy to hold on to whatever was possible in the area of his command. (Burma, because of its geographical position and with Japan holding Thailand and most of Malaya and so making it extremely difficult to get there from Java, though Wavell managed it twice – should more sensibly have been placed under the C-in-C, India.)

Wavell had few resources, and those he did have had to be put in order. There was no chance of giving support to the Americans in the Philippines. The British and Dutch naval units he had available were busy providing escorts for convoys to Singapore where all the troop reinforcements he could muster must for the present be concentrated. American naval units provided him with a small and weak strike force; he badly needed more cruisers. But above all he needed aircraft, and only a fraction of those originally planned for ABDA, mainly from America, arrived in time. Many were lost on the way, and some were to be diverted for the home defence of Australia. As Robert Woollcombe wrote in his book *The Campaigns of Wavell*, 'the first Supreme Allied Commander had no chance'.[40]

On his first visit to Singapore, Wavell made the discovery that there were no landward defences on the island. He ordered them to be constructed at once, but not enough could be done in the time now available. He made several tours of the battle areas in Malaya, and some of the decisions he made were criticised by the authors of the British official history. He acquiesced in Percival's deployment of troops on Singapore Island even though he believed Percival to be wrong. Some of the criticism is therefore valid. However, it must be remembered that on top of everything else he lacked in Malaya, Wavell lacked time.

Wavell was himself unhappy about his lack of achievement in Malaya. He was in the habit of writing to Joan Bright Astley who had once been his secretary in London. She was now employed in the Special Information Centre in the War Cabinet Offices in London. In a letter on 20th February 1942, a week after the fall of Singapore, he said:

We have lost the battle here by a month or six weeks I think – the additional time that we should have gained at least in Malaya and Singapore and the time by which we should have built up in these islands an air force capable of holding and hitting back. I have a hunch the Jap is stretched to the utmost in the air but he is using his forces boldly and well and has been too quick for us ... I went four times to Singapore and Malaya in a month but could never stop the rot, the front always seemed to be crumbling under my hand. I am still wondering if I might have found the answer somehow. I won't tell you more of the sad story here. You will have seen something of it in the official records and cables and can judge for yourself how my failure came about. I feel I ought to have pulled it off but the dice were rather heavily loaded and the little yellow man threw them with considerable cunning. I hate making excuses. I was given a job and have fallen down on it, whether it was 'on' or not others can decide, I feel myself that it might have been but I think it wanted a bigger man than I have ever pretended to be. So that's that. We shall win the war all right in the end.[41]

As the American military historian, Stanley L. Falk, has noted, Wavell really played a limited role in Malaya.[42] He had not the time to play anything other than that. So he was probably being a little hard on himself in this letter; but it takes a big man to admit failure, whatever the circumstances surrounding it.

The relationships between the top leaders in Singapore were bad. During the whole of World War Two there was never another military theatre where so many wrong leaders, were in the wrong place, at the wrong time. Singapore was a disaster waiting to happen, and it did not need the extra difficulties brought about by the inability of some of these leaders to get on with each other.

Some of the men who fought under General Percival in Malaya – and despite the input of the others, he was the leader in the hottest seat – have intimated that Churchill and his advisors might have deliberately sent an expendable general out there knowing the task to be impossible. Percival, of course, was recommended for the post by his mentor, General Dill, and Dill well knew the difficulties involved in Malaya. He obviously thought that Percival, with his pre-war experience of Singapore, was the man most likely to succeed if anyone could. There is no evidence in his case, or in any of the others, to support the theory of expendability.

Chapter Nine

The Commonwealth Fighting Forces: Training, Equipment and Weapons

The total number of troops involved in the battle for Malaya and Singapore on both sides is difficult to compute. An attempt to come to a reliable figure for those on the British side, based on information in official British documents, is made below (see page 185). What is not in doubt is that the aggregate of the Commonwealth forces, after all the late reinforcements had arrived, was larger than the force used by the Japanese during the campaign.

After the fall of France in 1940 French Indo-China lay open to the Japanese. At the same period the advent of Italy into the war, together with the loss of the French Fleet to the Allied cause, ensured that no large British relieving fleet could be transferred from the Mediterranean to the Far East. Almost exactly a year later Hitler's invasion of Russia, on 22nd June 1941, relieved Japan of fears of a possible Russian attack on their western flank. The Japanese were now able to concentrate on their push to the south without having to worry unduly about their traditional enemy. The only flank attack that now seemed possible was one from the east, from the American fleet based on Pearl Harbor.

Hitler's attack on Russia had an important side-effect. As the Australian historian, David Day, has written, 'Putting his anti-Bolshevism to one side for the duration of the war, Churchill immediately undertook to supply Stalin with the wherewithal of war.'[1] Overnight the Far East slid from the number three position on Churchill's scale of defence priorities to number four; it was now behind Great Britain itself, the Middle East, and Russia. By implication, the defence of Australia and New Zealand, to which Singapore was considered the key, was also relegated to a lower position.

During the six months from June to December 1941, Britain dispatched to Russia a total of 676 aircraft and 446 tanks.[2] These totals well exceeded the highest estimate for the requirements of Malaya Command. In addition, many more aircraft and tanks were sent to the Middle East, together with most of the newly-raised battalions of the British and Indian Armies.

The questions must be asked, would it have been possible to divert some of the aircraft and tanks that went to Russia and the Middle East to Malaya, and should this have been done? Could a division of troops have been spared earlier than the 18th British Division which arrived in Malaya when it was already too late? Most historians have agreed with Churchill's world strategy, and it should be remembered that one factor behind his mid-1941 decision to relegate Singapore was that, whereas wars were actually being fought in Russia and the Middle East, the Far East, except for the war in China in which Britain was not engaged, was still at peace. Churchill's decision to downgrade the importance of the Far East, however, did not meet with unanimous approval in Whitehall, and certainly the Australians accepted it only with the greatest reluctance. The Chief of the Imperial General Staff, General Dill to whom Churchill used to refer disparagingly as 'Dilly Dally', always regarded the Middle East as less vital than Singapore.[3] The Director of Military Operations at the War Office in London, Major-General (later Sir) John Kennedy, said of some of the decisions made in 1941, 'Mr Churchill was, of course, responsible as Prime Minister for deciding the allocation of manpower and of industrial production to the three Services. We in the general staff were quite sure that the decisions he gave at this time were dangerously wrong.'[4]

The 2nd Earl Wavell, son of the field marshal (who died in 1950), wrote during the mid-1950s of an incident in November 1941 which illustrates the strong feelings that General Dill held over the importance of the defence of Singapore:

> One of his [Dill's] Military Assistants told me, and General Pownall confirmed it, that there was a severe disagreement in the War Cabinet or Defence Committee, sometime about November 1941, when Dill wished to reinforce the Far East with aircraft at the expense of the Middle East, but the P.M. over-ruled it. Among Dill's papers, which I have been through, there is a pencilled note which he wrote to the Secretary of State for War [Henry David Margesson, later Viscount Margesson] – presumably while the meeting was going on – indicating he would resign at once, and the Secretary of State scribbled that he would do the same. I am told that Dill took the advice of Trenchard and in the end didn't resign at once, but agreed to the announcement that he would retire on reaching the age of sixty. [Margesson left his Ministry early in 1942.][5]

In that same letter Earl Wavell said:

> Reading through Winston's account of events in Malaya I detect a much more charitable note both towards the commanders and the troops over the failures in this campaign than, for example, some of his severe strictures of Auchinleck's battles in the Desert,

whereas I suppose far more serious tactical errors were made and less resolution was shown by the troops in Malaya than in the battles in the Desert. My feeling is that Winston himself had it rather on his conscience that he had not taken Dill's advice over Malaya and, consequently, treats the mistakes in Malaya much more generously.

When the crunch came in December 1941, the 18th British Division, orginally intended for the Middle East and trained for the desert, was 'found' and diverted to Singapore, but the main part of it arrived only ten days before the surrender. Fifty-one Hurricane fighters in crates which reached Durban on 18th December were also diverted and transshipped to Singapore together with pilots and ground staff, again to arrive too late. This leaves one with the impression that extra forces, aircraft and tanks, could have been obtained earlier from somewhere had Churchill not consistently underestimated the Japanese threat, as he did in his Most Secret directive dated 28th April 1941:

DIRECTIVE BY PRIME MINISTER AND MINISTER OF DEFENCE

Japan is unlikely to enter the war unless the Germans make a successful invasion of Great Britain, and even a major disaster like the loss of the Middle East would not necessarily make her come in, because the liberation of the British Mediterranean Fleet which might be expected, and also any troops evacuated from the Middle East to Singapore would not weaken the British war-making strength in Malaya. It is very unlikely, moreover, that Japan will enter the war either if the United States have come in, or if Japan thinks that they would come in consequent upon a declaration of war. Finally, it may be taken as almost certain that the entry of Japan into the war would be followed by the immediate entry of the United States on our side.

These conditions are to be accepted by the Service Departments as a guide for all plans and actions. Should they cease to hold good, it will be the responsibility of Ministers to notify the Service Staffs in good time ...

There is no need at the present time to make any further dispositions for the defence of Malaya and Singapore, beyond those modest arrangements which are in progress, until or unless the conditions set out [above] are modified.[6]

That directive clearly shows that Japan was Churchill's blind spot. He just did not appreciate her expansionist aims or needs or capabilities. Either that, or his refusal to countenance further reinforcements for Singapore was part of a Machiavellian scheme to draw America into a war with Japan if it came: Japan might attack a weak Malaya, but was less likely to attack a strong one; and any attack on Thailand and Malaya might well have brought the United States in even without a Pearl Harbor. But there is no evidence that Churchill was working to any such hidden agenda.[6a]

In 1941 there were no less than sixteen divisions under Middle East Command – six in the Desert, two engaged in mopping-up operations in the Italian North African territories, four in Iraq and Persia, and two in Palestine and Syria. Surely one of these could have been spared early enough if the will to do so had been there?

On the major equipment side, if, say, even twenty per cent of the planes and tanks sent to Russia during the six months which preceded the attack on Malaya – which would amount to 130 planes and 90 tanks – together with similar numbers from the Middle East, had been diverted to Malaya, they would have made a significant difference providing they had arrived early enough. It is doubtful if such a comparatively modest diminution in supplies to Russia and the Middle East would have affected the final outcome in either of those theatres of war. Many of the crated aircraft that were sent to Russia were never taken out of their boxes and were allowed to rot, as was witnessed by some of the RAF pilots Britain sent to Russia. That could not have been foreseen by Churchill, of course. In July 1942, five months after the fall of Singapore, one of the Arctic convoys was so heavily attacked that 'ships carrying 500 tanks and 260 aircraft' went to the bottom.[7] Others must have been lost prior to the fall of Singapore, though not on that vast scale. Had any of the planes and tanks sent to Russia between June and December 1941 been sent to Singapore instead, they almost certainly would have got through. It was a longer supply route, but far less hazardous.

British, Indian and Australian forces in Malaya were soundly defeated by a smaller force of Japanese. Colonel Tsuji, Chief of Planning Staff to General Yamashita, the commander of the attacking Japanese 25th Army, reported in the book he wrote about the campaign that 60,000 Japanese troops were involved.[8] Tsuji, a clever and cunning man, with a penchant for blowing his own trumpet, probably deliberately understated the numbers involved to enhance his own role in the campaign. By the time he wrote his book in 1960 few of Tsuji's senior officers in the Malayan Campaign were left alive to gainsay him. Tsuji was also an evil man. If the British had managed to catch him he would have been a major figure in the dock after the war in the War Crimes trials.[9]

In his post-war dispatch General Percival put the size of the Japanese force at 150,000 but this was a gross overestimate. Lionel Wigmore, the author of the Australian Official History, gives a figure of 125,400, without stating his source.[10] Stanley Falk, the American military historian, gives figures of 80,000 combat and combat support troops, plus 30,000 line-of-communication troops.[11] As these line-of-communication troops were spread over Thailand and Malaya, Falk did not consider that they took part in the combat. Falk had access to copies of Japanese documents, so his estimate of 80,000 Japanese combat troops seems to be the most reliable of the published figures.

The Malaya Command Forces

There has always been doubt over the aggregate number of men who served under Malaya Command up to the time of the capitulation. Books and articles published since the war have variously estimated the figures as between 86,000 and 138,000. The British and Australian Official Histories are not much help because the evidence in British official documents (some of which may not have been available to the official historians in the 1950s) suggests that the authors overestimated the number involved when they recorded it as 138,708.

Any attempt to produce a reliable estimate must start with the totals given in an encoded message from Malaya Command on 23rd December 1941, sent in answer to a query from the Australian government about the troop strengths in Malaya. The message recorded the number of troops on 5th December, three days before the Japanese invasion. The figures have the appearance of being precise.

Regular Forces:	British		19,391
	Australian		15,279
	Indians		37,191
	Asiatics		4,482
Volunteer Forces:	British		2,430
	Indian		727
	Asiatics		7,395
		Total	86,895
Stationed in Borneo:	British		56
	Indian		994

At this stage the Indians made up 49 per cent of the total; the British, 25 per cent; the Australians 20 per cent; and Asiatics 6 per cent.[12]

Army reinforcements began arriving on 3rd January 1942, and continued to arrive up to 5th February, ten days before the capitulation. It is in these reinforcement figures that the main difficulty lies in coming to a reliable final total. An Admiralty document in the Public Records Office (reproduced in Appendix 3) gives details of the reinforcement convoys, and in some cases, but not all, an estimate in round figures of the number of men involved.[13] Other documents in official files fill in some of the missing information, but in two cases give conflicting figures.[14] In the case of the Australian reinforcements there are also two figures to choose from, the 3550 shown in the Admiralty document or the higher figure of 4000 given in the History of the 8th Australian Division.[15] Another difficulty lies in the fact that the British 18th Division arrived in three separate convoys between 13th January and 5th February. To add to the problem of analysing the figures, some of the reinforcing ships carried replacement Royal Air Force and Royal Navy personnel in addition to troops, and some Royal Artillery units after arriving in Singapore were immediately re-embarked for Java.

The best possible estimates of the number of reinforcements from an examination of all the figures seems to be as follows:

1.	45th Indian Infantry Brigade	Arrived 3.1.42	6,000
2.	53rd Infantry Brigade (Part 18th Div.)	Arrived 13.1.42	See 5. below.
3.	44th Indian Infantry Brigade	Arrived 25.1.42	6,000
4.	2/4 M.G. Battalion, plus other reinforcements for the Australian 8th Div.	Arrived 24.1.42	3,550
5.	British 18th Division, (figure inclusive of 2. above, and part 6. below)	Arrived 29.1.42	17,000
6.	Remainder of 18th Div. (see 5. above) plus reinforcements for 9th and 11th Indian Divs.	Arrived 5.2.42	3,800

Reinforcement Total   36,350

A document in file WO106/2536 gives a figure of 4,850 for 44th Indian Infantry Brigade. The difference between this and the 6,000 mentioned in the Admiralty document is probably accounted for by the inclusion in the latter of replacements for other units. The War Office document mentioned above breaks down the troops of 44th Indian Infantry Brigade into various grades of personnel, and the overall figure includes 431 so-called 'followers'. It is likely that all the other figures for the Indian Army include a proportion of these non-combatant camp-followers, but there is now no reliable way of separating these out for all units. Most of these non-combatants would have become prisoners of war along with the soldiers, apart from any who might have managed to fade into the resident Indian community in Malaya. Anyway, as the Indian Army could not operate without these men, they were a necessary part of the whole. Like Kipling's Gunga Din, they also served.

The reinforcement figure, when added to the 5th December troop total, gives a final count of 123,245. This figure takes no account of various subsidiary units such as the Dalforce Chinese Irregulars (about 4,000 strong) raised early in the campaign, and the Royal Marines, survivors from the *Prince of Wales* and *Repulse*, who amalgamated with the Argyll & Sutherland Highlanders to become the 'Plymouth Argylls'.

The figure of 123,245 is not too far away from General Percival's estimate of 125,000.[16] Neither is it far away from the Japanese round figure estimate of enemy killed and captured of 120,000.

To compare the British total with the 80,000 Japanese combat troops it is necessary to reduce it by the size of the administrative 'tail', that is, the British non-combatants. (There were few non-combatants in the last days when many men from administrative units were armed and thrust into the front line.) According to the British Secretary of State for War, in answer to a question asked in the House of Commons in 1945, the administrative tail in all British armies of World War Two, varied between 11 per cent and 30 per cent of the total. It is likely that in Malaya the percentage was nearer the lower than the higher figure, for example, the number on the staff of the Deputy Adjutant-General in Malaya was tiny compared with other theatres of war, and there were continuous complaints about the shortage of military policeman. Also, as all reinforcements for Malaya were 'begrudged' right up to the end, this 'shortage' probably applied to all non-combatant units. Furthermore, as the Commonwealth troops were pressed into an ever diminishing perimeter, most of the line-of-communication troops became full-time combatants.

It seems reasonable, therefore, to reduce the figure in Malaya by, say, 18 per cent. This gives a combat and combat support troop total of 101,060. This figure exceeds the estimated Japanese strength by 25 per cent.

At the time of the Japanese assault on Singapore Island the Commonwealth forces were probably down to 100,000. Japanese and Indian National Army sources indicate that by then 10,000 Indians had joined the INA. (This was probably the roughly correct figure for Indians captured on the mainland, although some remained 'true to their salt' and did not join the INA ranks.) The number of Commonwealth killed at that time was about 8,000, with another 3,000 British and Australians taken prisoner.

The Commonwealth Battalions

One feature which stands out in any examination of the combined Commonwealth force in Malaya is the unevenness of quality and training throughout it. This applies especially to the Indian Army battalions which made up half of the total.

Many famous Indian regiments featured in the Malayan campaign, but the general quality of officers, non-commissioned officers, and troops in them had been lowered by the process of 'milking'. This transfer from established battalions of a large proportion of their experienced personnel to cater for the needs of the new battalions being raised in India, led to a diminution of standards. The Indian Army was to become the largest non-conscript army the world has ever seen, but a price had to be paid for that rapid expansion. Veteran officers, NCOs, and men were taken away from units in which they had spent most of their professional lives, and transferred to form the nucleii of new battalions. Experienced officers were replaced by emergency commissioned officers, some freshly out from England with no experience of India or Indians, let alone able to speak Urdu. The Regimental History of the 18th Garhwal Regiment comments that the loss of even one officer who could converse freely with the men in their language was a serious and irreparable loss during the campaign.

None of the better trained new units of the Indian Army ended up in Malaya, so it is hardly surprising, taking all this together, that the proud traditions of that Army were dealt a blow in Malaya. Many of the Indian reinforcements which arrived after the campaign had begun were virtually raw recruits. They were thrown into battle at once – there was no alternative – with catastrophic results.

Some Indian and British battalions, as part of the permanent garrison, had been in Malaya for many months prior to hostilities, but even among these training was uneven in quality. All these units spent a high proportion of their time constructing fixed defences. Defence construction had been neglected by General Bond, General Percival's predecessor as GOC. In June 1941, however, the C-in-C, Brooke-Popham, ordered the construction of defences covering the main roads into Thailand and all defended beaches. (No special instruction was included about construction of defences on the northern shores of Singapore Island.) Some of this work was carried out by civilian labour, but most was done by the troops themselves. The 2/18th Royal Garhwal Rifles arrived in Malaya in November 1940 and almost immediately were sent to Kuantan. The Regimental History reports, 'some jungle training had been carried out early in 1941, but thereafter all available men had to be employed continuously on the construction and improvement of beach defences, which included a double-apron barbed wire fence and various types of anti-landing-craft obstacles'.

One factor, often overlooked, is that barbed wire fences, and any other defence constructions with metal components, did not last long in the Malayan climate. Wire fences erected one year had, as likely as not, to be renewed in the following year.

A short time before hostilities began authorization was received from the War Office for six civilian labour companies to be formed, but in their wisdom the authorities only agreed to pay a fixed rate of 45 cents per day for the coolies. As the going rate for labour was about twice that amount, it proved impossible to raise all six companies.

Even with the long-stay battalions in Malaya a balance had to be struck between defence construction and field training. Percival, who only arrived in Malaya in May 1941, decided 'that the proper course was to build up a foundation of good individual and sub-unit training, which could be done concurrently with the construction of defences'.[17] In the circumstances this was a correct decision. Percival also planned to carry out higher training in the monsoon months of December–February, but the Japanese put paid to that. In the event even unit training had to be curtailed as political tension in the Far East built up from August onwards and units were as often as not placed on a war standby footing.

Field training was also affected by other factors. Some battalions spent much time training in 'embussing' themselves and their equipment for the proposed attack into Thailand which never came off. Planters complained about damage whenever manoeuvres took troops into rubber plantations. Night operations were curtailed by order of medical officers because of mosquitoes and the malaria they brought with them. On top of all this the section of Malaya Command in charge of training did not act professionally. According to Lieutenant-Colonel I.M. Stewart of the Argyll & Sutherland Highlanders, 'the training side of the General Staff scarcely functioned'.[18]

Few units were well-trained in jungle operations. The decision to undertake this kind of training seems to have been largely left to individual battalion commanders. There was no jungle-training school for officers as Brigadier W.St.J. Carpendale of the 28th Indian Brigade discovered when he asked whether one existed when he arrived in Malaya in August 1941.[19] The best jungle-trained battalion was the 2nd Argyll & Sutherland Highlanders. So keen was their Commanding Officer, Lieutenant-Colonel Stewart, on this type of training that some of his fellow commanders considered him a maverick. The Argylls fought magnificently throughout the campaign and it has generally been accepted that this was due to Stewart's insistence on this specialised form of training. The Australian General, Bennett, was also a keen proponent, and most of the Australians to arrive early in Malaya from February 1941 onwards carried out considerable training in the jungle.

Much has been made of the lack of jungle training of the Commonwealth forces compared with the Japanese, but this factor may have been overrated. The Japanese troops used in Malaya had been well-trained in all military operations, and many were veterans from the war in China. Some Japanese units had received specialist jungle training together with training in amphibious landings. In comparison, there were few veterans among the Commonwealth forces, and a substantial proportion of those who arrived later had received little training of any sort, let alone in jungle warfare. But the Malayan campaign was not a jungle war in the sense that the post-war Malayan Emergency was, or the later 'Confrontation' with the Indonesians in Borneo, or, indeed, the Vietnam War. *The Malayan campaign was fought mainly along the line of the finest network of roads in South-East Asia.* There was some jungle fighting to be sure, and the Japanese often made use of the terrain in bypassing and then encircling the retreating Commonwealth troops, but the majority of the fighting, and certainly all of the major battles, took place within spitting distance of well-surfaced roads and in comparatively open country. Japanese tanks were, several times, the key to winning battles, and tanks could not have operated in dense jungle. It can be argued therefore, that more jungle training for the Commonwealth forces *per se*, would not much have affected the outcome.

Some of the jungle-trained Australian battalions did magnificently well in the initial ambushes they set in northern Johore, but the military technique of laying ambushes is scarcely confined to thick jungle. In fact, the Australian ambushes took place along the edges of first-class roads; the first of them, at Gemas, close to an important bridge.

The fact that the jungle-trained Argylls fought well in Malaya does not of itself defeat the argument that perhaps the importance of this type of training, or rather the lack of it in the Malayan campaign, has been somewhat exaggerated. The Argylls, the 'thin Red Line', with their long and proud fighting tradition, would certainly have distinguished themselves anyway.

Major Dick Clarke, who was the young adjutant of the 2/18th Royal Garhwal Rifles stationed at Kuantan, confirms that little of the fighting he was concerned in went on in thick jungle, and his battalion did most of their early fighting on or near the east coast of Malaya. That side of the country was far more jungly and less developed, with far fewer roads, than the west side down which came the main Japanese thrust. Clarke says that he would not be alive now if the Japanese had pursued his escaping battalion through the jungle.[20] In general it seems that the jungle often afforded the retreating Commonwealth forces cover to escape, but it was not often used to fight in.

What was lacking with the later Indian and Australian reinforcements to arrive in Malaya was military training of any kind. Colonel J.H. Thyer, Chief of Staff to Major-General Gordon Bennett of the AIF, had this to say about the last batch of Australian reinforcements to arrive:

> They had not become acclimatized and were in poor physical shape after some weeks at sea. Some had sailed within a fortnight of their enlistment. A large proportion had not qualified at a small arms course, nor been taught bayonet fighting ... It is regretted to state that some ... had never seen a Bren gun and none had handled a sub-machine gun or an anti-tank rifle. Worse still was the fact that some had never handled a rifle.[21]

When the bulk of the British 18th Division arrived in Malaya less than a fortnight before the capitulation, they were 'soft' from having been cooped up in troopships for weeks, and had no time for acclimatisation. They had been trained for the desert rather than the jungle, but this latter factor was relatively unimportant. Apart from its 53rd Brigade, which arrived earlier, the 18th Division was deployed only on Singapore Island. There is jungle on the island but even if the 18th had been trained to fight in it, it would have made little difference to the outcome for, by that time the Japanese had already won.

An interesting story surrounds the convoy that brought the British 18th Division to Singapore. When Winston Churchill met President Roosevelt aboard the *Prince of Wales* on 10th August 1941 off Newfoundland to agree the Atlantic Charter, that historic meeting sowed the seed for later American naval assistance with the convoy code-named 'William Sail 12X', which carried the British 18th Division from Halifax, Nova Scotia, across the Atlantic to Cape Town *before* the Americans were officially in the war. Roosevelt, who was having to contend with a hard core of isolationists in his country, found his pre-war task of assisting the British made easier after the U-boat attack on the USS *Greer* on 4th September. In answer to an urgent and 'most secret' message from Churchill he agreed to furnish US troopships and escorts to transport the 18th Division to the Middle East, which was its original destination.

The 18th Division sailed from several British west coast ports and arrived at Halifax during the first week in November, a month before the Japanese attack on Pearl Harbor. There they were transferred into waiting American transports: *Mount Vernon* (ex-ss *Washington*), *Leonard Wood, Joseph T. Dickman, Orizaba, Wakefield* (ex-ss *Manhattan*), and *West Point* (ex-ss *America*). One of the divisional units, the 9th Royal Northumberland Fusiliers, had voyaged to Halifax with other units aboard the *Warwick Castle*, a ship of 20,000 tons, and the men were not very pleased when attempts were made to cram them into some of the comparatively less luxurious American ships. Something of a revolt took place – armed American seamen were involved in helping put it down – but finally the matter was resolved by spreading the troops more evenly over the fleet. The 9th were made to suffer for this 'mutiny'. When they got to India, they had to undergo forced route marches with full packs.[22]

The convoy sailed from Halifax on 10th November escorted by an aircraft carrier (*Ranger*), two cruisers and eight destroyers of the US Navy. It zigzagged its way down to the Caribbean and then across the South Atlantic to Cape Town. Several supposed U-boat sightings were made during the voyage but not one of them was factual. Unbeknown to the Americans, the British had been reading German naval signals since the capture earlier in the year of an Enigma decoding machine. The British knew the location of every U-boat and advised Captain D.B. Beary, USN, the convoy commodore, on the safe courses to take throughout the voyage. However, as the British had not told the Americans the source of their information the Americans considered zigzagging a necessary protective device. (Churchill did not inform Roosevelt of Enigma and the 'Ultra' decrypts until January 1942.) Had the Americans been told, a day or two of voyaging time might have been saved.

While the convoy was in South African waters news came of the attack on Pearl Harbor, so the United States was now officially in the war. After rounding the Cape of Good Hope the American escorts were relieved by ships of the Royal Navy.

Urgent appeals from Singapore to Whitehall for more troops resulted in the destination of 18th Division being changed. The 53rd Brigade Group was to sail direct to Singapore, while the rest of the Division was to sail for India to await further orders. Some of the ships called in at Durban. The 53rd Brigade and its equipment were now loaded on *Mount Vernon* and two British and two Dutch ships, one of which was *Oranje*, which were to make up the Singapore convoy designated DM1.

One of the units aboard *Oranje* was the 6th Heavy Anti-Aircraft Regiment. The 6th was a complete regiment in that it had its own sapper and signals units attached. Before leaving England the regiment had been supplied with the new Mark II Radar sets. These were under the charge of a Royal Corps of Signals radar officer with the rank of captain. In Durban he disappeared, taking with him full information of the radar equipment, including operating and service manuals. Captain Peter Kenward writes: 'Our captain radar officer skipped ship in Durban and took with him every detail about our latest sets. The incident was hushed up very quickly, but there is no doubt that he had made prior arrangements to defect.'[23]

Convoy DM1 arrived safely in Singapore on 13th January.

On 23rd January General Wavell ordered the remainder of the 18th Division to embark at Bombay for Singapore. One of the ships in the convoy was *Empress of Asia*, a 17,000-ton vessel built for the Canadian Pacific Railway Company in 1913, and which had seen better days. She carried a Merchant Navy crew of nearly 400, a high proportion of them stokers because she was a coal-burning vessel. Many of the stokers, or 'black gang' as they were called, were Liverpool-Irish. One of the units she carried was the 125th Anti-Tank Regiment, RA. The author of their official history says, 'what memories the mere mention of that old hulk brings back'.[24]

Lieutenant-Colonel Dean of the 125th was detailed as OC troops on 23rd December 1941 when his men embarked at Bombay. Initially he refused to take over the ship because of its filthy condition – amongst other things it was crawling with cockroaches – but the Principal Sea Transport Officer overruled him as the orders were that the ship must sail that day. This was not the first trouble that the ship's master, Captain J. Bisset Smith, a Scot from Banffshire, had experienced on that voyage, nor was it to be the last. The crew was a scratch crew, not up to the shipping company's usual high standards. The vessel was not a happy ship, and this is partly attributable to the make-up of the crew, and partly to the bad conditions on board. In the particular case of the stokehold gang there was another consideration. In wartime good quality stoking coal was difficult to come by, and the use of an inferior quality made an already strenuous job doubly difficult.

Before the start of the voyage seven seamen deserted in Liverpool. At Freetown one man was arrested by the police and imprisoned. Five more men deserted at Durban. Captain Smith tried to change a number of troublemakers in the crew in South Africa but no replacements were available, and, anyway, the South African authorities refused permission for the men to be discharged. One more seaman was to flee the ship at Bombay.

The ship now formed part of convoy BM12 which sailed from Bombay on 23rd January. The other transports were *Felix Roussel*, *Devonshire*, and *Plancius*. The escorts varied during the voyage, but included the cruisers *Exeter* (of Battle of the River Plate fame), and *Danae*. The men of 125th Anti-Tank Regiment did not know their destination until after the ship sailed, so very likely the ship's crew did not know either. But soon they did find out, and the Liverpool-Irish amongst them, most of whom were officially neutrals because they were citizens of Ireland, did not much fancy being taken into the Singapore war zone.

The convoy sailed via the Sunda and Banka Straits, and it was on 4th February, the day before the scheduled arrival in Singapore, when it first came under attack by Japanese planes. Only slight damage was sustained by the *Empress of Asia* during that first attack, but it was enough for the black gang to down shovels and crowd up on to the 'fiddley-deck'. That mutinous incident – it was nothing less notwithstanding the extenuating circumstances – is indelibly imprinted on the minds of some of the troops on board. Tom Brown recalls that the stokers 'were ordered back down at the point of a revolver, and it was either the captain or the first mate who said, "you either stoke or die"'.[25]

E. Pearlman was another soldier on board. He writes, 'When the stokers refused to work the captain asked for volunteers from amongst us. We had quite a few ex-miners with us and they manned the fires until the stokers were persuaded to go back to work.'[26]

The disruption of the stoking caused the steam-pressure to drop and the ship fell behind the rest of the convoy. Captain Smith was not being completely honest when he later recorded, 'We had been allotted this position on account of our steaming difficulties, the ship almost invariably dropping astern of station when fires were being cleaned.'[27] She never did regain her position, either because of the amateur efforts of the soldier-firemen or because the professionals did not put their backs into it when they resumed their duties.

On the morning of 5th February a black smudge was seen ahead 'which everyone thought was a cloud – we later found it was Singapore with a pall of black smoke hanging over it'. Then a formation of Japanese aircraft came over. The *Felix Roussel* was hit twice and, according to Bill Bowden of the 9th Royal Northumberland Fusiliers, there was some loss of life on board.[28] Then the planes singled out the sternmost laggard as the easiest target and came into attack. Soldiers aboard *Empress of Asia* put up a curtain of fire but eventually a bomb hit the ship 'with a sickening thud. The bomb had passed over the bridge, through the roof [*sic* – the proper terminology is deck-head] of the Officer's Lounge, and exploded somewhere below.' This was followed by more hits, and fire soon took hold. The author of the History of the 125th says that a fire-party made up of black gang members tried to put out one of the fires but because of the low steam pressure only a trickle came from the water-hoses. He remarked, 'had the circumstances not been so serious we could have appreciated the humour of the situation'.

With great seamanship Captain Smith sailed his blazing ship as close to Singapore as he could and then ran her ashore near Sultan Shoal. (He was subsequently awarded the MBE.) Boats from other ships in the convoy and some small vessels sent out from Singapore, including the harbour tug *Varuna*, rescued many men. HMAS *Yarra* gallantly went alongside the stricken vessel and took off over a thousand troops and crew. Only sixteen men, all soldiers except for one crew member, were lost.

None of the military equipment aboard the ship was salvaged. The lost equipment included a large quantity of small arms meant for Dalforce, the Chinese Irregulars. The loss of all the stores and equipment on board was a serious blow. The *Empress of Asia* was the only ship carrying reinforcements to Singapore to be lost.

Many of the deck and engine-room crew of the *Empress of Asia*, including most of the mutinous stokers were posted to other ships and escaped from Singapore. Some lost their lives during the escapes. The catering staff, almost to a man, volunteered for duty in the Singapore hospitals, and ended up as prisoners of the Japanese.[29]

One Liverpool-Irish crew member who did not escape used his Irish nationality to avoid internment by the Japanese. Under the alias 'Stephen Early' he wrote several anti-British pieces for *Shonan Shimbun*, the Japanese successor to the *Straits Times*.

Morale and Equipment

In any theatre of war acclimatisation of troops is an important factor, and perhaps especially so in a climate like Malaya's. Even Indian troops found the extreme humidity of Malaya debilitating, not a bit like the conditions they were used to back home. In those days when air-conditioning was only just beginning to appear in Malaya, it was known what a debilitating effect the climate had on foreigners. It was one of the factors which caused European officers of the Malayan Civil Service to take an unconscionably long time over even the smallest of matters; even urgent decisions could not be made quickly. The Physiology Department of King Edward VII College of Medicine in Singapore had been making a special study of the deleterious effect of the climate on foreigners, and on on 23rd May 1940 the *Straits Times* carried an item on the subject, reporting that the College was conducting an investigation into 'the effects of air-conditioning and the effect of the tropics on Europeans'.

Morale, or rather the quick loss of it, was an important factor too on the British side during the campaign. Proper training would have prevented much of this. Field-Marshal Montgomery has written:

> New and untried troops must be introduced to battle carefully and gradually with no failures in the initial ventures ... Great and lasting harm can be done to morale by launching new units into operations for which they are not ready trained ...'

Monty's dictum was not followed in Malaya. Many poorly trained units were launched into battle almost as soon as they stepped off the ships. In his dispatch Percival said of the 45th Indian Infantry Brigade: 'This brigade had never been fit for employment in a theatre of war. It was not that there was anything wrong with the raw material but simply that it was raw.'

It has often been stated that the British underestimated both the fighting qualities of the Japanese and the standard of their equipment. Japanese pilots were supposed not to be able to see well in the dark, or fly above 15,000 feet! The quality of their planes was reported as suspect. When on 14th February 1941 Brooke-Popham flew to Australia to meet the War Cabinet there, he blithely reported that British pilots and their Brewster Buffalo aircraft were considerably superior to the Japanese who 'were not air-minded'. Later in the year he repeated the sentiment when he said that the Brewster Buffalo fighter, the centre-piece of his air force, was quite good enough for Malaya.

Brooke-Popham may have been too old for his job but he was not a fool. Even apart from the matter of the 'lost' intelligence report on the Japanese Zero fighter from China which was somehow never passed to Air HQ in Singapore, and which contained full performance details of the plane which had a superior speed to the Hurricane MkII except at heights over 20,000 feet,[30] he had ample if less specific information of Japanese capabilities in the form of a memorandum produced by the General Staff in Singapore. So Brooke-Popham was making those statements for propaganda purposes – or perhaps to obscure the true state of matters from the Australians. Perhaps he deliberately chose to ignore the information contained in the memorandum in his public utterances knowing that, in view of Churchill's attitude over Singapore, he would have to make do with what he had. That form of propaganda backfired. The Japanese certainly did not believe it, but many of the local people in Malaya did. Such remarks might have raised the spirits of the local populace in those months before the war, but it did nothing to increase their awareness of forthcoming danger. The civil population, and some of the military, took the optimistic public statements of Governor and commanders at face value. When it became obvious that there was a gulf between those statements and reality, they were shattered.

In March 1941 the General Staff based at HM Naval Base in Singapore issued a pamphlet entitled 'Japanese Army Memorandum'.[31] It went into some detail about the expertise and morale of the Japanese Army and Army Air Force and of the equipment they had available. With this at hand neither the commanders in Malaya nor their masters in Whitehall had any reason to be complacent.

The report forewarned of a tactic the Japanese were to use extensively during the Malayan campaign: 'Envelopment is normally used in all operations.' It also pointed out that Japanese Army engineers were expert at constructing and repairing bridges, their expertise being of a 'high order', which they proved over and over again during the campaign. Japanese landing craft were described in some detail. (The pamphlet contained photographs of landing ships.) The report went on to state that the Japanese Army was well trained in night landings from the sea and in other night operations. The small Japanese tank, described as a 'tankette', and similar to the ones actually used in Malaya, was also described in detail.

The memorandum contained a whole section on pursuit, defined as 'the following up of hostile withdrawals' which became the main feature of the Japanese campaign against the British. 'They press ... with considerable vigour ... Tanks ... often employed with great effect to maintain the momentum of pursuit'. That section was a blueprint for the coming Japanese operation.

According to Colonel Tsuji[32] the Japanese used only 80 tanks in Malaya but it seems that he was again attempting to make the Japanese victory appear even better than it was. Wigmore, the Australian official historian, and the American, Falk, both use the significantly higher figure of 180.[33] (Percival gives 300 in his dispatch.) In contrast the British had none at all during the mainland fighting, and the 16 tanks which did arrive aboard the *Empire Star* on 29th January with a detachment of men from the 100th Light Tank Squadron, were not only obsolescent, but most were unserviceable and so were not used at all except as static gun platforms. Perhaps they had been sent in belated response to the rather plaintive request from the C-in-C, Far East to the War Office of 24th July 1941: 'Would it be possible to supply old British or American tanks which are unsuitable for service in the Field to protect aerodromes here.'[34]

Troops were also short of mortars and anti-tank rifles. Some companies had so few of the latter that, when during the fighting one was lost, it became a major disaster. The 2/18th Garhwalis apparently thought that they were unusually well provided with anti-tank rifles when they were supplied with sixteen in early 1941. Most units got far fewer, and even sixteen does not seem a generous provision for a battalion.

Throughout the build-up to the campaign many Commonwealth units arrived in Malaya separated from their equipment which sometimes took days and even weeks to catch up with them. This obviously affected unit training. Guns even arrived without the associated ammunition. In an official minute dated August 1941 a senior Ordnance officer at HQ wrote:

> Guns were arriving in Malaya without ammunition. 26×75mm guns had arrived. (36,000 rounds not with guns.) The operational consequences of the arrival of these guns without ammunition, especially in view of the present artillery deficiencies in Malaya, are too obvious and too serious to need explaining.[35]

Even when they received the equipment they wanted it seems that Malaya Command often had difficulty in moving it around the country. Major G.E.P. Cable of the Indian Army Ordnance Corps, reported that both pre-war and during the war itself, the military got little in the way of priority on the Malayan railways: 'private interests set higher than the military'. The army's own administration processes did not help either. Roper says that railway staff were often unable to identify the consignee owing to the use of codes for addresses. These codes were frequently changed for security reasons. 'The question of the use of the code from the security point of view as balanced against confusion and non-delivery of urgent and essential stores, appears to require careful weighing up.'[36]

The authors of the Official History after the war were trying to discover what authorisation for military expenditure had been granted to General Percival, and when. In answer to a query about this from A.B. Acheson, the Cabinet Office official directing the team of historians, the War Office replied on 7th April 1952 as follows:

Query over expenditure powers of GOC.

> On the outbreak of war with Japan full powers with Vote 10W accounting were extended to those commands. Under Vote 10W powers a C-in-C was authorised to carry out services and to purchase stores at his discretion without prior reference to War Office subject to accounts being reported monthly to WO. C-in-C had in effect a free hand.

The free hand, coming 'on the outbreak of war with Japan', arrived a little too late in the day.

Aircraft

The 3rd Army Air Group available to General Yamashita, together with the 2nd Navy Air Flotilla, provided him with a total of 534 first-line aircraft.[37] Without exception they were all modern aircraft.

There was no excuse for the British authorities' denigration of the quality of the Japanese air fleet, for the Japanese Army Memorandum issued by the General Staff in Singapore had gone into detail about the characteristics of their planes. Under the general statement that the Japanese Air Services were efficient from a flying point of view, the report listed the maximum speeds and flying endurances of six types of Japanese aircraft. It was clear from this that their fighters, bombers and torpedo-bombers were in every case better than the British equivalents, and with fighters and torpedo-bombers, significantly better.

Instead of Malaya Command's own estimate of their needs of around 600 aircraft, and instead of even the Chiefs of Staff lower estimate of 336 to be supplied 'by the end of 1941', the British had a total of only 246 when hostilities began. In view of the RAF's performance against high odds during the Battle of Britain this number might have served the purpose had they all been first-class aircraft. But they were not. 158 were so-called operationally serviceable first-line aircraft, the other 88 being in reserve. The operationally serviceable planes included 24 obsolete Vildebeeste torpedo-bombers with a maximum speed of only 100 mph, and 60 obsolescent Brewster Buffaloes, a plane already discarded by the Americans. Only 47 Blenheim and 24 Hudson MkII bombers came anywhere near their Japanese equivalents in quality. (The other three aircraft which made up the total of 158 were Catalina flying-boats.)

Most of the British planes based on the three north-western Malayan airfields were destroyed by the Japanese in the first two days of the campaign, helped by radio signals sent out by the traitor, Captain Patrick Heenan of the Indian Army. After that, with the overwhelming numbers and quality of their aircraft, the Japanese had complete mastery of the skies.

Chemical Warfare

In 1937 Japan began making extensive use of gas weapons in their war with China. In October of that year the Chinese government made a formal protest about this to the League of Nations, and a year later they accused Japan of using mustard gas on the Yangtze front. The Chinese produced witnesses, including a European doctor who stated that he had treated gas casualties. A Russian source estimated that in some Sino-Japanese battles, up to ten per cent of the Chinese casualties were caused by gas weapons.

The War Office in London treated the possibility of gas warfare very seriously indeed. Eleven days prior to the Japanese attack on Malaya, the War Office sent out a 'Most Secret' cipher signal to the Commanders-in-Chief in all theatres of war.[38] The message was dated 27 November 1941:

IN THE EVENT OF GAS BEING USED ON ANY FRONT DECISION TO RETALIATE WITH GAS WARFARE MUST BE TAKEN BY WAR CABINET. SUBSEQUENT TO THIS DECISION CONTROL OF THE USE OF GAS WEAPONS WILL BE RESPONSIBILITY OF C-IN-C's.

The British were so concerned over the possibility of gas attacks that they took the defensive measure of supplying Malaya Command with the means to retaliate in kind. They also sent out a gas warfare specialist to conduct a series of anti-gas training sessions. He was Captain C.P.G.S. de Winton of the South Wales Borderers. All the Commonwealth troops in Malaya were supplied with gas masks. However most of those who served in the campaign knew nothing of the gas deterrent's existence as it was kept a closely guarded secret.[39]

Although Japan had signed the Geneva Protocol against the use of gas in 1925, they, along with the USA and several others among the thirty-eight signatories, never ratified it. In 1933 the Japanese established an Army Chemical Warfare School at Narashino, near Tokyo. There, with the efficiency and application which has become their hallmark, the Japanese set about upgrading their study of this type of warfare. For five years before that they had been manufacturing mustard gas and the improved variety of it, known as Lewisite. On Formosa they conducted trials in its use under tropical conditions, and they developed bombs, rockets, sprays, anti-tank weapons, and other devices for delivering it.

After they had tried it out in China in 1937 the Japanese were so impressed with the success of this kind of warfare that the Narashino School produced a pamphlet for distribution amongst its students entitled 'Lessons From the China Incident'.

Both the RAF and the army in Malaya were supplied with the means to retaliate. The air force received its supply of mustard gas, under the codename 'Flannelfoot', in mid-1941. To deliver the gas all that was needed was the fitting of a special nozzle to the tanks designed to spread smokescreens from the air – an operation known as 'SCI', short for Smoke Curtain Installations. The RAF had 300×500lb 'refills' of mustard gas for the SCI tanks in Malaya. They also had 500×250lb and 4,000×30lb mustard gas bombs.

The army's gas ammunition arrived in Malaya later than the RAF's. It came in the form of a stock of 25-pounder mustard gas shells. The first consignment arrived at Singapore aboard SS *Medon* on 4th September 1941, followed by a second consignment on SS *Silver Beech* which docked two days later. The shells were listed on the ships' manifests under 'Chem Y', the 'Y' standing for Yperite (from Ypres, where the Germans first used this type of warfare in 1915). By 13th December, five days after the Japanese attacked Malaya, the ordnance authorities in Singapore were able to note on their Ammunition Status Report that, of their total requirement for 22,080 mustard shells, they had received 11,800.[40]

Only the most senior army and RAF officers, plus a handful of technicians, were aware that Malaya Command had these gas stocks. Not even the Chief Medical Officer was informed, though if there had been an accident his staff would have been required to treat any casualties. It was not until early 1944, and as a direct result of an horrific accident at Bari, Italy, when an Allied ship carrying mustard gas blew up and at least 3,000 service personnel and civilians died as a result, that orders were given that Chief Medical Officers must be informed whenever gas supplies were moved into their areas.

It is not known if the army's supply of gas shells was distributed around Malaya before the start of the war, but some of the RAF's 'Flannelfoot' was held at Alor Star aerodrome in the north. Soon after hostilities began this was moved south to Kuala Lumpur aerodrome, which already had a supply of gas bombs. Later on it was all transported to Singapore.

It was at Alor Star some weeks prior to the start of the war that Flight Sergeant (later Squadron Leader) Ronald Wardrop, the station armourer to 62 Squadron's Flight 'A', was approached by Captain Patrick Heenan, the Air Intelligence Liaison Officer who was spying for the Japanese. He questioned Wardrop closely about the SCI installations.[41] It is interesting to speculate, in view of the earlier Japanese liking for the use of gas in China, that it may have been Heenan's information about the British retaliatory capability that prevented the Japanese from using chemical warfare on any great scale in Malaya.

There were several reports during the campaign that the Japanese in fact did use a mild form of gas or some other form of chemical weapon on occasions. The first of these reports occurred during the Japanese landings at Kota Bharu. Lieutenant-Colonel O.B.M. North, MC, a major with the 3/17th Dogra Regiment on those beaches, was always convinced that the Japanese used some form of gas during those landings. Captain R.B. Monteath was a young officer there too, and he says, 'The shells [from naval ships] were throwing up sand which the monsoon blew through the slits in the pillboxes, and they also filled with the smoke from our own Bren guns as the fighting became more intense. It may have been the sand and fumes that stung our eyes and faces or it may have been a kind of tear-gas. Whatever it was, the men had to fight in their gas masks.'[42]

The War Diary of General HQ, Far East, recorded for 12th December: 'A prisoner captured by 8th Brigade Kelantan stated that he belonged to infantry unit 16th Division from Canton. This unit supported by Naval Landing Party. Japanese helped in landing by 5th Column. British POW's have been tortured. Toxic gas used in small quantities. No confirmation of use of gas – this and statement about POW's should not be given publicity because of undesirable effect on Indian troops.'[43]

A gas report was made on 13th December 1941 when Australians stationed at Kota Tinggi, Johore, reported that after Japanese planes had been seen over the vicinity, two Gas Spray Detectors located near HQ 2/9th Field Ambulance Unit appeared to have become contaminated. An investigation into the claim was inconclusive.[44]

The Deputy Director, Military Intelligence, Far East, sent a message to the War Office on 6th January 1942 in which he described a gas grenade, as taken from the information given in a captive Japanese soldier's notebook. He remarked 'specimens now obtained. Contain prussic acid. Intended for use against AFV's [Armoured Fighting Vehicles]. Also suitable for use against enclosed spaces such as pillboxes.' A later message from General Percival to the War Office stated that these grenades were definitely being carried by the enemy although he had not received confirmation of their actual use in battle.[45]

All the most serious gas incident reports were made by the Australians. One of these was passed on by General Percival to the War Office on 7th January:

> No.29508.
> AIF 3 Platoon bayonet charge which forced Japs back squealing in confusion discarding their rifles. This stage, Japs used gas forcing our troops to cease advance ... Gas appeared whitish blue smoke spread from forward areas to 1000 yards rearward.
> Air cleared 25 minutes.
> Casualties. 3 only 1 of which is in hospital with inflamed trachea. He believes weapon primarily smoke candle. Several men vomiting next day. Comment by G (CW) Malaya Command [probably Captain de Winton], smoke candle impregnated toxic agent.[46]

On 16th January some bombs dropped four days earlier 'had contained small marble-sized bags. On exploding these caused blisters and burns.' This was followed on the 30th January by a message from Percival to General Wavell: 'enemy using tear-gas bombs'.[47]

Three more gas incidents on the Australian front were reported on 28th, 29th and 30th January, the latter involving the AIF 27th Brigade, where again the Japanese repelled a bayonet charge with the use of gas.

All this evidence seems to indicate that the Japanese did use some form of chemical warfare in Malaya but only in isolated incidents, and whatever substances were used caused comparatively mild symptoms.

In February 1942, as it became clear that Singapore would fall, urgent and pragmatically-worded internal minutes began circulating around the staff at War Office in London. A Lieutenant-Colonel, General Staff, wrote on the 8th:

1. There is a considerable stock of CW shell and also RAF CW weapons in Malaya. From a propaganda as well as an operational point of view it would be most undesirable that this should fall into Japanese hands in the event of an evacuation of Singapore. To blow up CW shell at the last minute might result in CW casualties being caused among civilian population or the Japanese which would be even more unfortunate.
2. We think that a telegram should be sent to GOC Malaya asking him what plans he has made to deal with this problem: if stocks are not too large it might be possible to dump them in the sea.

On 9th February another Staff officer confirmed that the stock of mustard gas shells held in Singapore was 11,800. He stressed that those stocks were the only army CW weapons in the Far East, and that they would be very difficult to replace quickly. Because of that he advised that they be evacuated if at all possible. He ended by saying that if evacuation was not possible, 'we think that dumping in the sea, or in a deep swamp, is the next best solution'.[48]

Lieutenant-Colonel A.W.G. Dobbie joined in the exchange of minutes that same day:

1. It is assumed that CW ammo. will be held available for retaliation as long as possible.
2. We agree . . . we are short of CW weapons in the East and would like these preserved if possible.
3. If this is not possible, 25-pdr shell should be dumped in deep water, whence it could not be salvaged. Probably our design of BE shell is unknown to the enemy: its secrecy should be preserved.
4. Presumably the same treatment should be applied to RAF weapons. Probably the designs of certain parts of SCI, notably the nozzle, are especially secret and, if the whole cannot be removed, these should not fall into enemy hands.
5. We know of no method of destruction on land which would prevent the enemy knowing CW weapons had been stored if they occupied a site soon afterwards. Neither blowing up nor burning can be guaranteed to cause no casualties. Hence evacuation or dumping in deep water would alone achieve the result described in Minute 1.

Following on this exchange, a 'Most Secret' cipher was sent to GOC Malaya by the War Office on 10th February:

MOST IMMEDIATE

1. ESSENTIAL NO REPEAT NO CW ARTILLERY AMMU-
   NITION OR RAF EQUIPMENT SHOULD FALL INTO
   JAPANESE HANDS (a) TO MAINTAIN SECRECY OF
   DESIGN (b) TO AVOID GIVING AXIS EXCUSE TO
   INITIATE CHEMICAL WARFARE.
2. CONSIDERED HERE THAT EVACUATION PREFER-
   ABLE TO DUMPING IN DEEP SEA OWING TO SHORT-
   AGE OF STOCKS THROUGHOUT FAR EAST THEA-
   TRE. SUGGEST EXPLODING OR BURNING UNDESIR-
   ABLE OWING TO CERTAINTY OF CONTAMINATION.
3. PLEASE REPORT PLANS FOR DENIAL IN LAST
   RESORT.
4. PLEASE PASS TO AOC AS FROM AIR MINISTRY.

On that same day a cipher was sent to Durban ordering that the 2,000 chemical shells stowed in No.5 'tween deck on the Blue Funnel vessel *Autolycus*, originally destined for Singapore, be unloaded there and held pending further instructions.

Almost a month previously, on 15th December, at a conference held in Air Vice-Marshal Pulford's office in Singapore, it was decided that the RAF gas weapons then being held at Kuala Lumpur be returned to Singapore. Two days later, at another meeting, it was decided that 'charged gas containers to be removed from Kuala Lumpur to Batak Quarry'. The removal began that day.[49]

On 19th December it was decided that the 'caves considered suitable for storage now too near firing line. To be stored in lighters in creek at Pasir Panjang under guards'. (The caves of Batak Quarry lay to the north-east of Singapore City, and were probably considered to be in danger of bombing by Japanese aircraft.)

During the next three weeks there was much discussion over what was to be done with 'Flannelfoot'. Finally, it was moved to St John's Island off the south coast of Singapore on 11th January, and then loaded aboard ss *Silver Larch* on 2nd February which sailed for Java. So the RAF had successfully evacuated their CW weapons almost two weeks before the fall of Singapore. By then they no longer had any reason for keeping it on the island for there were no planes left to arm with the weapons even if it had been needed.

The army's problem was not quite so simple. With the possible threat of Japanese use of gas still hanging over his head, General Percival had to do a balancing act between giving himself enough time to dispose of his 11,800 mustard shells, and keeping them available for possible retaliatory purposes. It was obviously desirable to keep them up to the last possible moment, but this meant that evacuation by ship was out of the question.

The only option left to Percival in the circumstances was to hang on to them until he knew that all was lost, and then to dump them.

This dumping operation began on 11th February. Captain Thomas Pickard of 31/7th Coast Regiment, RA, was an interested spectator from his command position on Blakang Mati Island (now called Sentosa). He noted in his 'Narrative of the Western Anti-Torpedo Boat Defences', that 'on Wednesday 11th February, the Berlayer area was subject to a lot of [enemy] shelling. A working party of 100 men (RAOC) were dumping 25-pdr mustard gas shells (11,800 in number) on Berlayer Pier, from whence they were being ferried into the Examination Anchorage for disposal. This was obviously the Jap target and their spotter aircraft was observed overhead.'[50]

The men engaged on that highly dangerous operation were living on luck. Captain Pickard records that several enemy shells fell extremely close to the pier and that some fell on the War Accommodation Area close to it. He drily relates, 'no material damage was done and the work proceeded'.

Major (later Lieutenant-Colonel) Noel James of the Indian Army Ordnance Corps was in charge of some of the men engaged in the handling of the gas shells on the second day of the dumping operation. He wrote that he volunteered his unit's help (he did not record the reaction of his men when he told them what he had let them in for).[51] Having volunteered, he collected together British and Indian Other Ranks from the ordnance depots under his charge, crammed them into lorries and made for Berlayer Pier. The gas magazines were situated in the cliffs overlooking the pier, 'which were in turn overlooked by a battery of 6-inch coastal defence guns'. The rest of Colonel James's gas story is best told in his own words. He must have dined out on it on numerous occasions after the war.

'We got our positions organised and carried the heavy boxes of 25lb shells down the side of the hill, along the jetty and dumped them in the barges that were waiting. All this time the Japs were shelling the coastal defence guns very hard, although unfortunately not very accurately. I say unfortunately because every shell which did not register a hit on the guns registered one near us, all the 'overs' or pluses fell within twenty yards of us and very unpleasant it was. It was extremely hard to keep the men working, the tendency being to drop everything every time a raid happened (which was once every five minutes) or a salvo dropped near us. As the process was continuous not a great deal was accomplished until I detailed two officers to work with the men and myself stood at the end of the jetty and endeavoured to appear cool, calm and collected, a state very foreign to my real feelings. The Brigadier [Eveleigh] joined me there and the sight of the red band on his hat helped to steady the chaps. We shifted the bulk of the stuff that day and I was told that the RAOC, having had a decent break, could finish it off the following day. The Brigadier was most grateful to me or to us rather for the assistance as the stuff would never have been moved without our help. The Staff were warned about what the Nips' reactions would be to discovering gas shell. As this was two days before the surrender, it did nothing to raise my morale and it made me think that surrender was somehow inevitable.'

Further confirmation of this hair-raising operation comes from Lieutenant-Colonel H.M.J. Jensen, who was then a major in the RASC and in charge of the actual barging operation.[52] He says of the James report, 'the only thing Major James seems to have forgotten was the arrival of the friendly (??) bullets from the machine-guns of the Malay Regiment on the other side of Berlayer Creek which were unpleasant and unnecessary additions to the Jap shells and bombs'.

Captain Pickard's position on the north-western tip of Blakang Mati would have given him an excellent view over the 'Examination Anchorage' where the shells were supposed to be dumped. His report included a map which shows this anchorage as being very close to the north-western point of the island. However Colonel Jensen, who was in charge of the barges, disputes that part of the Pickard report. He writes, 'that may well have been the Staff idea, but let me assure you that there were not sufficient crews or boats available for such an operation. In fact the main objective was to dump the mustard gas out of sight as fast as humanly possible and so it was dumped in the nearest deep water in Keppel Harbour as quickly as possible so that we could all get out of a very unhealthy situation.'

Keppel Harbour is the site of the main port of Singapore. It is a very narrow stretch of water between the main island and smaller islands to the south, and the Port of Singapore's commercial wharves line its northern shore. The water there is not very deep. Colonel Jensen reports that the British salvaged the gas shells after the war, but the hazardous and difficult underwater search for 11,800 shells, even assuming that the boxes they were in remained intact after four years, could not have been one hundred per cent successful. Apparently over the years the occasional shell has been washed up on surrounding beaches. According to ordnance experts at the National Army Museum in London shells could still to this day be surviving intact even in those warm and salty tropical seas.

It has long been the practice for old and unwanted ammunition to be dumped at sea. The regular 'Dumping Ground' for ammunition from Singapore is marked on Admiralty charts of the area and lies about twenty-five miles east of Horseburgh Lighthouse which itself lies about the same distance east of Singapore. The depth of water there is 24 fathoms (50m), over twice the depth of water in the deepest part of Keppel Harbour. But as Colonel Jensen has pointed out, there was no time to dump those mustard gas shells anywhere except in Keppel Harbour itself.

Let Colonel Jensen have the final word on this subject. 'I would never go swimming from any of the beaches in that part of Singapore.'

The Singapore guns

The saying, 'they were facing the wrong way like the guns of Singapore', expresses the best-known of the various Singapore myths, but it is based on uninformed criticism.

The guns of Singapore were designed and positioned in the south of the island as a deterrent against an amphibious attack, and in that respect the military planners were eminently successful. The Japanese did not even consider trying to seize the island by a direct maritime assault. They were well aware that, throughout history, port citadels have been taken from the rear, hardly ever from the front.

The famous 'myth' is even wrong in a narrower sense. While a few of the big guns were incapable of firing into Johore, some of them could do so, and several of those that originally could not, because of nearby constructions and overhead canopies, were soon converted, as the Japanese advanced down the peninsula. Brigadier W.J. 'Bill' Birkle of the RAOC, who had much to do with the initial siting of the guns, was fond of pointing out that some had a 240-degree angle of traverse from the start, which he compared favourably with the 120-degree angle of the German guns overlooking the Pas de Calais. By clever manhandling some of the Singapore guns were given a 360-degree traverse.[53]

Some of the big guns fired extensively at the advancing Japanese in Johore and later on the north of the island. This is evidenced by a table of ammunition expenditure which appears in the Official War Diary of the Royal Artillery Fixed Defences, Singapore. It serves to illustrate one of the two 'real' problems involving the big guns.

Approximate expenditure of coast artillery ammunition

		Changi	Faber
15"	APC	194	–
9.2"	HE	75	75
9.2"	APC	200	217
6"	HE	600	240
6"	CPBC	50	540

Notes: 1. Changi and Faber were the two Artillery Fire Commands in Singapore.
        2. APC = Armour-piercing shell; HE = High Explosive.[54]

The problems over using the heavy fire-power of most of the five 15-inch, six 9.2-inch, and eighteen 6-inch guns, against land targets lay not in their siting, but in certain technical matters. Nevertheless three of the largest guns, all six of the 9.2-inch, and six of the 6-inch, were used against the Japanese.

The first of the technical problems was that, as the guns had been intended for use against ships, the ammunition for the 15-inch and 9.2-inch guns was mainly armour-piercing shell (APC). What was required against land targets was high explosive shell (HE), which has completely different characteristics. APC shell has a relatively thin casing, a nose-fuse, and a heavy high-explosive charge. HE, on the other hand, has a thicker casing, a relatively light high-explosive charge and a base-fuse. Lieutenant-Colonel C.C.M. Macleod-Carey, has written of using APC against land targets: 'I expect the shells with a high angle of descent drilled a hole about 20 feet deep and there was none of the fragmentation which is essential for anti-personnel requirements.'[55]

It is known from Japanese sources that the shells made a terrifying noise when they came over and shook the earth when they landed, but in the main they did little damage.

Colonel Macleod-Carey has also reported a ship-engagement by the Singapore guns which has never been mentioned in any official account, probably because many of the records were lost. Around midnight on 14th February, only eighteen hours before the capitulation, Mount Faber Command received a signal that an unidentified ship was approaching the entrance to Keppel Harbour. Searchlights from Silosa and Labrador batteries picked up an 8,000-ton vessel at a range of 7,000 yards. The vessel was challenged and gave an incorrect reply. Six 6-inch guns opened fire and the ship was hit and disappeared. Assuming that the ship was not a friendly one, this was the only direct success of the Singapore guns against shipping.

One of the subsidiary reasons for not supplying HE shell for the 15-inch guns was that their 'barrel-life' was limited to 200 rounds, after which the gun barrels (which weighed about 100 tons each) had to be changed.

There was only one HE shell for the 15-inch guns on the whole of the island. This was found at the Naval Base and was transferred to Johore Fort.[56] No special mention was made of the firing of this lone HE shell among the total of 194 shells fired by the three 15-inch guns which could bear on Johore.

Frantic cables went out from Malaya Command in January for more HE shell to be sent. A reply was received on 28th that a supply for the 9.2-inch was being dispatched from Ceylon and the UK and that some for the 15-inch guns would be dispatched from the Middle East at the 'first opportunity'. None of it ever arrived.[57]

The second 'real' problem with the Singapore guns, was the fact that no fire-control or range tables had been prepared for landward firing. It is difficult to see how it would have been possible to prepare these in pre-war days. It is one thing to fire practice shells out to sea, but quite another to lob them into an inland area. Sea-firing practice was a regular occurrence off Singapore, and shipping was always warned well in advance. Even so it caused problems with the Dutch authorities on the islands to the south. Masters of Dutch ships and the *nakhodas* of native craft took exception to the sudden appearance of a man-made waterspout off the starboard bow, and complained.

When the guns were used on the advancing Japanese, use had to be made of Observation Posts but, as one War Diary pointed out, 'OP's from which the effect of long-range fire from coast guns could be reported were hard to find and communications were non-existent. The whole solution of this problem obviously depended on the probable dispositions of the troops of the Field Army.'[58]

To sum up, the Singapore guns did not point the wrong way, and they eminently served the military concept that put them there in the first place. Had more HE shell been available they would have been used to better account.

Communications

One of the most serious problems British troops suffered from in Malaya is one which has received scant attention in the published histories. Poor communications was a problem which affected everyone from Commander-in-Chief down to platoon commanders in the field.

There were communications problems between Kota Bharu and Singapore during the first hours of the attack, and later that day one of the factors which may have caused Brooke-Popham's delayed order to 3rd Indian Corps HQ to stand down from Operation Matador was that he did not receive confirmation of the Japanese landings over the border in Thailand until about eight hours after the event. The reason for this delay is unknown. The matter did not end there, however, for poor communications meant it was a further four hours before the change of plan order reached 11th Division who then had to move to only partly-finished defensive positions around Jitra.

When the change of orders arrived at 11th Division it caused a fresh set of problems; the problems seemed to be feeding off each other. In accordance with earlier instructions some wireless links had switched over to Matador frequencies, and to changes in codenames. It took some time to change back again and there was a lot of confusion. Lieutenant-Colonel A.S. Milner, in charge of 3rd Corps Signals, reported, 'the following two days were to show how seriously a last-minute change of plan can affect Corps commands especially when the latter are largely dependant on civil lines over which the military has no control'.[59]

The British Official History reported that the troops defending the north had no proper signal organisation and had to rely almost entirely on civilian communications. The telecommunications cable followed the main trunk road up the peninsula, and the reason it had not been duplicated by a military system was that no cable had been available for the purpose. Only a small part of the system had been duplicated in South Johore by Australian Army Signals staff. So, apart from southern Johore, all service and civilian communications had to pass over this single system. Many of the civilian telephone exchanges were taken over in part by military operators when hostilities began. These operators had their own system of priorities, but even these were not foolproof. General Percival's calls to his divisional commanders were scrambled, and on one occasion at least this led to difficulties. In the process of a shift handover, the new man pulled the plug on Percival thinking that the garbled conversation was going on in Chinese! All the civilian lines were capable of being tapped into, and although most of the civilian staff of the Malayan telecommunications system are reported to have stayed at their posts to the end, there could be no guarantee of the loyalty of all of them to the British cause.

As Far East tension increased in the weeks before the war so the civilian telephone system throughout Malaya and the military system on the island of Singapore became impossibly overloaded. Re-routeing became impracticable as HQ and RAF demands for additional circuits increased. Perhaps it was this situation that accounted for the notation that a duty Royal Signals officer wrote in his log for 1st December 1941. 'Owing to pressure of work, pigeons are being overloaded. This has resulted in false launchings in which bird has failed to take off and damaged crown of head.'[60] There is no way of knowing whether he was being facetious or not.

Signal traffic blockages were often caused by the failure of the originator of a message to use what were called the 'Deferred' and 'All Informed' methods, and by the abuse of priority prefixes and by sending unnecessary messages. This was mostly caused by lack of training.

Out in the field, once the war began, the situation was worse. In general, wireless communications in Malaya were useless. In the first place many units were short of sets. For example, the 2nd Battalion of the East Surrey Regiment stationed at the heart of the Jitra Line defences had only one No. 19 wireless set. This linked them with Brigade HQ, but all other communcations had to be carried out over signal line or by runner. In the second place, wireless communication in the geographical and meteorological conditions of Malaya with the types of sets available, was virtually impossible. Sergeant Harry Blackham, who was in charge of a Battery signals section of 5th Field Regiment RA, says that he had been supplied with Australian 101 sets, and that 'except for freak transmissions they were completely useless. I can recall no more than three or four occasions when fire orders were successfully transmitted by them. This must have been due to the terrain, rubber, jungle, etc. as they were fairly new and had functioned perfectly in India before we left. I [once] suggested to my CO, Major Don, that dropping all the sets over the nearest bridge would at least give me another twenty odd signallers to use. He lost his rag when he saw I meant it. Wireless really was as useless as that.'[61]

Later, on Singapore Island, the 54th Indian Brigade reported that, with their No. 18 wireless sets, communications were only possible between 1000 and 1800 hours.

The troops were therefore thrown back on using line, runners, and dispatch riders. The main difficulty with the first of these was the shortage of wire. This was a general shortage but particularly acute with the special variety needed for underwater installations. During November 1941, the month before hostilities began, the signals section of the 22nd Indian Infantry Brigade was saying that 'the lines East of the ferry [at Kuantan] and the lines West of the ferry have not yet been joined because of lack of submarine cable, which is essential for a safe crossing'.[62] So serious was the shortage of all types of wire that a special order was sent to Australia with a personal message to the Australian Prime Minister to hasten it up.

The 18th Division brought its own stock of wire, but most of it was never offloaded from the ships. The War Diary of its Artillery HQ says:

A certain amount of technical equipment and stores was never landed at all, as directly the heavy equipment was offloaded many ships were ordered to sail forthwith to clear the harbour. One result of this was a great shortage of telephone cable. Later this shortage was to become very serious as few wireless sets worked and these were most unreliable.[63]

Laying wire in a terrain of jungle, plantations and swamps had its own difficulties, of course. Harry Blackham recalls:

Wireless having proved so useless, we were thrown back on to good, old-fashioned line telegraphy and telephony. That of course meant that wire and plenty of it was a priority, and shortage of it caused problems as we were not always – hardly ever – in a position to pick it back up. I overcame this by methods that did not find favour with authority. Until our last year in India the line equipment we used was the D111 phone and wire which utilised a single wire laid from one terminal on one phone to a similar terminal on the other phone. The circuit was completed by a metal rod wired to the second terminal on each phone and rammed into the ground. In India the ground being so hard it was necessary sometimes to water the ground into which the earth pin was rammed, sometimes by unconventional means! However, in about 1939/40 we were issued with new line instruments called Don V. This 'improvement' entailed the use of double-twisted wire, each wire at each phone being attached to one of each of the two terminals. This system, known as the Metallic Return, was no more effective than the old Earth Return, but I suppose some boffin back home got a CBE for it. Unfortunately in practice and particularly in action, it had a tremendous drawback. It needed TWICE as much wire for obvious reasons. It needed TWICE as many reels from which the wire was to be laid, and hopefully, eventually collected. It also of course, meant TWICE as many changes of reel-laying drums. Eventually, short of wire, I got the 'tiffy' to make me as many earth pins as he could and then spent every spare minute untwisting every drum I had. It was a time-consuming job which did not find favour with the CO. Happily it always worked well, otherwise I might have been in real trouble. The damp climate of Malaya was a great help, the earth pin needing no artificial watering.

The communications system throughout the Malayan campaign was not up to the job. The main telephone system was overloaded, and the security arrangements on it could not be relied on. It seems there had been no testing of wireless equipment pre-war to find sets that were capable of giving a good performance in the special Malayan conditions; perhaps such an operation was considered not worthwhile with the overall equipment priorities being what they were. There was a shortage of wire, a shortage made worse by the Don V 'improvement', and the authorities seem to have taken no proper cognisance of the difficulties of laying wire in jungle and swamp.

Radar Installations

One type of equipment the British did have in Malaya which the Japanese did not, was radar. So secret were the radar installations, 'that it was a court martial offence even to mention RDF [Radio Direction Finding]', says Wing-Commander Toby Carter.[64]

The first two installations arrived at Singapore in March 1941. One was erected close to Changi, and the other at Mersing about one hundred miles up the east coast of Malaya. Carter comments on the extreme slowness of the erection works, 'work which took a few weeks in the UK took six months in the Far East'.

The equipment for three more installations arrived later, and these were sited in Johore, the third one at Kota Tinggi lying between Singapore and Mersing. The perennial problem of communications in Malaya caused delays in setting up the installations. But by August 1941, 'the RDF plan for Malaya was fairly well crystallised', though no installations were available for the north of the country.

The first Japanese aircraft to attack Singapore early on the morning of 8th December 1941 were successfully picked up at a range of 75 miles. Although this information was passed on to the appropriate authority, no air raid sirens were sounded, and the several bombs that fell on the city caused casualties. According to Wing-Commander Cave, who was on duty that night, the sirens were not sounded as the Governor of Singapore had issued instructions that they were not to be sounded except on his personal authorisation for fear of alarming the civilian population. When he did finally give permission, the official responsible could not be found. Parts of this story have been disputed. What is not in dispute is that the sirens were not sounded.

So secret was radar (the pictures taken of the much heralded arrival of HMS *Prince of Wales* at Singapore, were retouched to remove all traces of the radar antennae before they appeared in the press all round the world) that extraordinary measures were taken to destroy every installation before the Singapore capitulation. Some RAF teams took huge risks during the process, but they were successful.

The 6th Heavy Anti-Aircraft Regiment arrived in Singapore on the 13th January 1942 without their guns (which seemed to have ended up in the Middle East). Two batteries were immediately transshipped to Java, while the other took over some of the guns already on the island (and already in short supply). But they did have radar sets with them. It was Captain Peter Kenward's job to see them destroyed before the capitulation.

The Japanese did not discover any of the secrets of radar at Singapore.

The Chinese Irregulars and other 'native' troops

Why was greater use not made in Malaya of locally raised forces?

Two Malay Regiments had been raised, and General Percival reported that both fought well during the campaign. It may have been possible to raise extra regiments of Malays before the war but this would have cost money that neither the British government nor the Singapore administration were willing to spend. Such extra regiments would have needed to be armed, of course, and armaments in general were in short supply.

Most of the Chinese in Malaya were anti-Japanese and regiments could easily have been raised. But quite apart from the expense involved in training and arming them, there were other political considerations to take into account. Many of the Chinese were 'overseas Chinese', that is, they were not Malayan citizens, had not been born there, and their allegiances lay outside Malaya. Also the Malay Sultans would probably have objected if the Chinese had been recruited wholesale. Many of the more militant Chinese had communist sympathies, and the Singapore government had been waging a campaign against them for a number of years, and some had been imprisoned. To have used them in Chinese regiments would have required a volte-face by the administration, and this did not take place until it was too late. The Governor, Sir Shenton Thomas, held a meeting with Chinese leaders, some of them let out of jail specially for the occasion, on Christmas Day 1941, and out of that meeting came the formation of the Dalforce Irregulars. This belatedly-formed force, a high proportion of whose members had communist sympathies, put on an impressive show towards the end despite being poorly-armed. (Most of the arms destined for these Irregulars were destroyed in the *Empress of Asia* fire.)

Perhaps Shenton Thomas and his administration should have shelved its anti-communist attitude earlier, like Churchill had with the Russians (and Mountbatten was to do later with the Thai leader, Luang Pradit). On the other hand the Singapore government had good reason to fear the Communist build-up in Malaya. Some of those members of Dalforce who managed to survive the fall of Singapore and the subsequent Japanese purge of their numbers, disappeared into the jungle and caused the Japanese much trouble during the occupation. After the war these same men formed the nucleus of the pro-communist anti-British force in the Malayan Emergency.

Altogether it is not surprising, even though it would have been beneficial at the time, that the Malayan Chinese were never recruited on a large scale to fight the Japanese.

Chapter Ten

The Loss of Northern Malaya

Major Angus Rose, an officer of the Argyll & Sutherland Highlanders now serving as GSO2 at HQ Malaya Command, went on duty in Singapore's War Room at midnight on 7th/8th December 1941. In view of sighting reports of Japanese convoys (see below, page 219) made by Hudsons of the Royal Australian Air Force on 6th December, he and his fellow staff officers were more than half expecting the 'balloon to go up' that night.

Nevertheless the telephone call from Kota Bharu which came through shortly after one o'clock in the morning and told of the first Japanese landings, still caused deep shock. But it was not only the news itself that Rose found shocking. He wrote of the telephone call in his book *Who Dies Fighting*.[1] After reporting the landings, Kota Bharu operations staff asked whether they should bomb the troop transports or the escorting cruisers. 'Go for the transports, you bloody fools', shouted the Chief Operations Officer down the mouthpiece. Rose said that his uppermost thought at that moment was, 'Dear God, didn't they even know that!' That one thought, coming at the very beginning is somehow illustrative of the conduct of the entire Malayan campaign on the British side.

The landings at Kota Bharu, which began at 0025 on 8th December local time, were the first moves in the Pacific War.[2] The attack on Pearl Harbor from aircraft carriers on the other side of the ocean began one hour and ten minutes later, although, because of the intervention of the International Date Line and the difference in time zones, the history books record the attack on Pearl Harbor as occurring on 7th December 1941.

Within the space of a little over an hour, in a magnificent piece of logistical timing, in a plan of truly imposing breadth and daring, the Japanese had launched attacks against Malaya and Pearl Harbor and had invaded Thailand. They followed this up by invading Hong Kong at dawn, and made air assaults on Clark Air Base in the Philippines, on Guam, and on Wake Island. In the space of twelve hours the Japanese military machine had made itself felt all over the North Pacific Ocean.

The main Japanese landings on 8th December 1941 were at Singora and Patani in Thailand, while the landing at Kota Bharu was a secondary attack made to capture the north-eastern airfields. From the Thai ports the Japanese thrust southwards down the two roads to the Malayan frontier near the west coast, their first troops crossing the border on

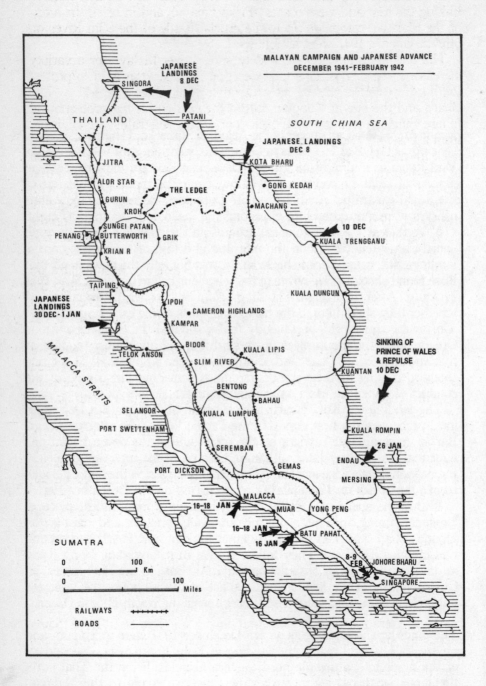

MALAYAN CAMPAIGN AND JAPANESE ADVANCE
DECEMBER 1941–FEBRUARY 1942

JAPANESE
LANDINGS
8 DEC

SINGORA

PATANI

THAILAND

SOUTH CHINA SEA

JAPANESE LANDINGS
DEC 8

JITRA

ALOR STAR

GURUN

KROH

THE LEDGE

KOTA BHARU

GONG KEDAH

MACHANG

10 DEC

KUALA TRENGGANU

SUNGEI PATANI
BUTTERWORTH

PENANG

KRIAN R

GRIK

KUALA DUNGUN

TAIPING

JAPANESE
LANDINGS
30 DEC–1 JAN

IPOH

CAMERON HIGHLANDS

KAMPAR

BIDOR

TELOK ANSON

SLIM RIVER

KUALA LIPIS

MALACCA STRAITS

BENTONG

BAHAU

SELANGOR

PORT SWETTENHAM

KUALA LUMPUR

SEREMBAN

KUANTAN

SINKING OF
PRINCE OF WALES
& REPULSE
10 DEC

KUALA ROMPIN

26 JAN

ENDAU

MERSING

PORT DICKSON

GEMAS

16–18 JAN

MALACCA

MUAR

YONG PENG

16–18 JAN

16 JAN

BATU PAHAT

SUMATRA

8–9
FEB

JOHORE BHARU

SINGAPORE

0   100
            Km

0   100
            Miles

RAILWAYS   +++++++

ROADS

10th December. (At that time there was no road in northern Malaya linking the east and west coasts.) From then on, and in brief, the story of the Malayan campaign up to the crucial Battle of the Slim River on 6th/7th January 1942 went as follows.

The defending forces were widely spread over Malaya for a variety of reasons: the dispositions for Operation Matador; the need to protect the north-western airfields; the protection of the three airfields at Kota Bharu and the one at Kuantan, all on the east coast; the protection of Johore, Singapore's immediate back door, by the Australian 8th Division, from a possible landing; and the necessity to garrison Singapore Island itself in case the Japanese launched an amphibious assault. The problem of this dispersion is more easily understood when it is remembered that Malaya approximates in size to the area of England and Wales, with Singapore Island about the size and position of the Isle of Wight to the south. The irony of the British dispositions was that one of the main reasons for the wide dispersion was to guard airfields that had no adequate air force.

The Japanese overran the British northern defences around Jitra on 12th/13th December, causing heavy losses of men and equipment to the 11th Indian Division under Major-General Murray-Lyon. The British began to retreat. Only occasionally leavened by a short stand, the retreat became almost continuous.

Major Phillip Parker, an officer on Murray-Lyon's staff, wrote a contemporary memoir of the campaign which has previously been unknown outside his family.[3] He records more than a few failures to blow bridges successfully, or of bridges blown prematurely with British forces still on the wrong side of them. 'Many demolitions failed: others went up when they should not have done so', he wrote. (The difficulty of storing explosives in good condition under Malayan climatic conditions was probably a contributory cause.) Parker also reports several instances of casualties caused by 'friendly' fire, and of chaotic conditions on the roads as men and equipment moved south.

After Jitra, the British soon vacated their next position at Gurun, and on 18th December Penang, Britain's oldest possession in the Far East, was evacuated.

The Japanese, equipped with tanks and enjoying total air supremacy, surged on, with the townships of Taiping, Kuala Kangsar, Ipoh, and Kampar falling to successive Japanese onslaughts; the British positions at the latter place being turned by an amphibious landing on the flank. Here and there the British made stands, but all were short-lived. Some successful ambushes were laid, including one by armoured cars of the Volunteer Corps south of Ipoh. But they 'overdid the ambush with result they themselves got caught and badly shot up'.

The last chance of holding the Japanese north of Johore was at Slim River. 'For some unexplained reason, anti-tank defence was not properly developed,' Major Parker wrote. 'Warning received of presence of enemy tanks, but mines not laid and anti-tank guns not in position.' On 6th January the tank blitz came, 'blazing merry hell. 4/19th [Hyderabads] caught on move scattered. 5/2nd Punjab scattered. Argylls melted away.'

After Slim River, the federal capital Kuala Lumpur lay open to the Japanese onslaught.

The main convoy of nineteen Japanese transports carrying General Yamashita's 25th Army had left the port of Samah on Hainan Island with their escorts at 0600 hours on 4th December. They were to link up with seven transports and their escorts which sailed from Saigon on the following day. The rendezvous was a point in the middle of the Gulf of Siam at 0900 hours on 7th December.

As the British were able to read the Japanese naval code, JN-25, and British signal stations on Stonecutter's Island, Hong Kong, and at Singapore were intercepting Japanese naval signal traffic, it is likely that this information was quickly available at the highest level in London. James Rusbridger and Eric Nave (it was Nave who broke the code) state in their *Betrayal at Pearl Harbor* that Churchill and the Chiefs of Staff in London knew in advance of the attack on Pearl Harbor. If James Rusbridger's thesis is correct then it follows that Churchill must also have known of the fleet movements from Hainan and Saigon on 4th December, although he might not have known the fleet's destination. As not a single JN-25 decrypt has ever been made public by the British government there is nothing in open files at the Public Records Office to prove that Churchill had this prior knowledge, but the fact that none has been released indicates that something is still being covered up. Proof that the British could read the JN-25 code is given by copies of a few fairly innocuous transcripts of intelligence material that have popped up in archives in Australia and New Zealand. It was not until 1980 that the United States finally acknowledged that they, too, had had the ability to read the Japanese codes from well before Pearl Harbor. (Some heavily censored transcripts have been made available in that country.)

During the writing of their Official History of the Malayan campaign, the Australian historians came across information which led them to suspect that the British C-in-C in Malaya had been slow in advising all concerned of the attack on Kota Bharu which preceded the attack on Pearl Harbor by well over an hour. The implication is that if the C-in-C had acted more quickly, the Americans might have been placed on their guard.

Gavin Long, the Chief Australian historian, wrote to Brigadier H.B. Latham, of the British Official History team on 15th October 1951. The original letter is missing from the relevant file at the Public Record Office, but it is referred to in Latham's reply.[4] The particular matter under discussion was the timing of Brooke-Popham's message to the

British authorities that the Japanese had attacked and hence that war with Japan had commenced. The 'in clear', that is, the uncoded signal, used for that purpose was the code-word CANNAMORE.

Brooke-Popham's Cannamore message went out at 0500 hours on 8th December local Singapore time, and Latham's letter and the attachments to it endeavoured to show that the C-in-C had not been at fault in 'waiting a bit before he declared war on Japan'. They included a breakdown of all the timings involved, in GMT, Singapore, and Hawaiian time. Latham's letter and the documents attached to it are given in Appendix 4. That seems to have satisfied the Australians, for they did not mention this matter at all in their Official History. It is not mentioned in the British one either. So, whatever information it was the Australians had discovered earlier, it did not lead them in the direction of anything resembling Rusbridger and Nave's main thesis.

On 5th December, the day after the Japanese fleet sailed south from Hainan, Brooke-Popham was authorised to implement Operation Matador on his own initiative, providing it was obvious that the Japanese were going to attack British or Dutch territory or were to violate Thailand. According to the British Official History, the C-in-C could launch Matador 'if there were good information that a Japanese expedition was advancing with the apparent intention of landing on the Isthmus of Kra [Thailand]'. The timing of Matador was crucial to any chance of its success, yet there is no evidence that Brooke-Popham was given information based on JN-25 decrypts about the Japanese fleet sailings. Had he received such information he might well have decided to make an early strike. As events turned out – and given the British estimate that to launch Matador successfully and to be able to consolidate on the beaches, sixty hours warning of Japanese intentions was necessary – the ideal time for Matador to have been launched was at midday on 5th December.

At 1030 hours on 6th December a break came in almost forty-eight hours of continuous heavy monsoon rains at Kota Bharu. It was long enough for three Hudsons of No. 1 Squadron, RAAF, to take off from the airfield. Before their aircraft trundled down the still soaked runways, the pilots had received instructions to search for signs of Japanese shipping, and it was shortly after midday that Flight-Lieutenant Jack Ramshaw sighted three Japanese ships about 185 miles north of Kota Bharu. Fifteen minutes later he sighted a much larger fleet of twenty-two transports with a dozen escorts. At that time the fleet was steering west, and not southwards towards Malaya or Southern Thailand. Ramshaw had been spotted by the Japanese, and when he saw a plane being catapulted from one of the warships he headed for cloud cover and signalled his news to base. He was then at the edge of his aircraft's range and he was ordered to head for home. (He was killed in a sortie the following day.) Soon after another Hudson sighted a second large fleet; but this too was not heading for Kota Bharu at the time. After the Hudsons got back the weather closed in again, and although some other reconnaissance flights were made the following day, low cloud and rain prevented any further sightings.

A more dynamic commander than Air Chief Marshal Brooke-Popham might have gone for broke upon receiving the Hudson's reports; he might have taken upon his shoulders the entire responsibility for attacking a neutral country. Brooke-Popham was not like that. The panicky telegram from Sir Josiah Crosby in Bangkok, urging him not to attack into Thailand, no doubt also affected his state of mind. Admiral Geoffrey Layton seems to confirm that Crosby's telegram had a significant effect. 'Telegraphic discussion with HM Minister in Bangkok and the Foreign Office as to the tone to be taken with regard to the possible violation of Thai neutrality culminated in an impassioned appeal from Sir Josiah Crosby that we should take no steps to attack or occupy any Thai territory before the Japanese did so.'[5] If Brooke-Popham had implemented Matador when he received those first sighting reports there might just have been enough time for the British troops to get to Singora and Patani to confront the Japanese on the beaches, though they would not have had any time to dig defences. They might just have made it, providing the Japanese fleet had not immediately headed south on hearing of the British invasion. But this was an unlikely eventuality. Any such positive move would have put the Americans at Pearl Harbor on active war alert, and on 6th December, the day of the sightings, the Japanese carrier fleet was not yet in an attacking position off the Hawaiian Islands.

Brooke-Popham ordered 11th Indian Division on the west coast of Malaya to the first-degree readiness for Matador. This was carried out in driving rain. The troops remained on standby until they received the cancelling order for Matador during the afternoon of 8th December, twelve hours after the Japanese landings at Kota Bharu. Then they had to take up defensive positions along the half-completed 'Jitra Line', again in driving monsoon conditions.

The following notes were recorded by the British official historians in 1949, based upon what Lieutenant-General Sir Lewis Heath had told them about Matador and its cancellation:

The only chance of Matador was on 6th December when Jap convoy was first sighted. Even then, judging by the Japanese-bolstered Thai operation later encountered on the Kroh Road, success was doubtful, as delay on the Singora Road would have been fatal.

After the 6th the opportunity was lost. Brooke-Popham's conclusion (rather wishful thinking) that the Japanese were threatening Bangkok settled the matter. Once in the Gulf the Japs had the initiative. Percival should have ordered occupation of the Jitra Line much earlier. He should have made Brooke-Popham cancel Matador instead of which he attended a Legislative Council meeting in the morning of the 8th and couldn't be got at. Heath did not get the cancel order until 1pm. Occupation of the Jitra Line was made in a hurry. Conditions were bad. Torrential rains made a 6-mile march the equivalent of 12 miles. Troops depressed. Heath at that time thought that delay was due to reference to Whitehall. He did not then know that the responsibility for launching Matador had been delegated on 5th December.[6]

In these same notes Heath said that 'Brooke-Popham had no command and no adequate Staff. Couldn't make up his mind.' Of General Percival he said, he 'was no commander'.

The delay in standing down from Matador had a serious effect on morale. The effect of a change from an offensive stance to a defensive one is in itself bad enough on troops keyed up for battle, but when the change comes after many hours on standby, when the troops are tired and wet through from the rains, and when they were beginning to wonder about the decisiveness of their commanders, it is much, much worse. Furthermore, they then had hastily to attempt to complete half-finished defences along the Jitra Line, in atrocious weather conditions in positions already waterlogged. And it was during that time that the great confusion was caused in communications as units had to change from Matador wireless frequencies and codes. The British and Indian forces in the north-west began the campaign with their morale at a very low pitch.

The landings at Kota Bharu in the north-east were made by the Japanese 56th Infantry Regiment supported by artillerymen, engineers and signallers, totalling about 5,500 men. They landed from three transports using a fleet of small landing barges. The operation was made in such heavy seas that about one-fifth of the force was drowned during the process; but that did not stop the remainder from pouring ashore.

The first landing craft were guided in by lights exhibited by a Chinese fifth-columnist. The British had known of him for sometime, but it had been decided there was insufficient evidence to arrest him.[7]

Australian aircraft operating from the nearby airfield scored some early successes. They made ten direct hits on one of the transports which caught fire and sank. Another transport was damaged. Initially there was some confusion among the Australian pilots because the enemy escort ships were flashing the correct British recognition signal for the day, the letter 'K'.[8] The Japanese may have learned the signals from their officer spy, Captain Patrick Heenan, who, as an Air Liaison Intelligence Officer, had access to such information.

The Japanese lost fifteen landing craft both to aircraft attacks and gunfire from the beach, and a further eleven were damaged. In the battle for the beaches and the town they lost some 700 men in addition to those who never made it ashore. Overall it was by far the single greatest loss of men sustained by the Japanese throughout the campaign.

The Kota Bharu area was defended by 8th Indian Brigade under Brigadier (later Major-General) B.W. Key.[9] 'Billy' Key, one of the few British commanders to enhance his reputation during the campaign, has been described as having the look of a British bulldog. He was shortish, thickset and robust, with a tough determined chin. Some of his character had obviously rubbed off on his men, for they put up a stout resistance on the beaches until they were overrun. Key had had to spread the force available to him very thinly, and they could not hold off an attack from a determined foe who apparently was prepared to accept substantial losses. Two of Key's battalions, the 3/17th Dogra and the 2/10th Baluch, were stationed in pillboxes and dug in along the beach. The Dogras had ten miles of beach to cover, and the Baluchis, twenty-five; their task made more difficult by the fact that the beaches were intersected by creeks and backed by swamps. The Dogras felt the full brunt of the initial attack and fought magnificently, says artillery Sergeant Harry Blackham who saw them at it. But by 0400 hours, after heavy fighting and severe losses on both sides, the Japanese had captured two strong points. Despite several desperate attempts at counter-attacks, from then on it was mainly a matter of the Indian survivors withdrawing in the best possible order for the remainder of that day.

On 10th December the Japanese landed more troops at Besut, about thirty miles south of Kota Bharu, and close to the Gong Kedah airfield. Realising that he was in danger of losing his entire brigade – which was at the end of a long and tenuous line of communication – Key asked for and got permission to withdraw. Then for twelve days his force retreated down the single-line mountain railway to the central Malayan town of Kuala Lipis, blowing up the bridges behind them as they went.

Meanwhile, on 8th December the remainder of the Japanese 25th Army had landed at Singora and Patani in Thailand, and met with only desultory and shortlived opposition from a few Thai army units. Then they began to move south down both the Singora-Jitra and Patani-Kroh roads towards the Malayan frontier.

Over on the west coast of Malaya the Blenheims of 62 Squadron at Alor Star airfield, and of 27 Squadron at Sungei Patani airfield, the latter with a flight of Buffaloes as escort, were ordered up at dawn to join in the attack on the Japanese transports off Kota Bharu. When 62 Squadron arrived over the target area they found that the RAAF Hudsons had left nothing to attack, so they diverted north to Patani. A hit-and-run attack there in the face of Japanese fighters and heavy ack-ack fire was unsuccessful, and they returned to base. By the time the Blenheims of 27 Squadron reached Kota Bharu, the weather had closed in, so they returned to Sungei Patani without having dropped their bombs.

Throughout the remainder of that day and the one following, the British stationed at the north-western airfields were astonished at the success the Japanese had at finding British planes when they were at their most vulnerable. Time and time again aircraft were destroyed, either on the ground after returning from a sortie and in the process of refuelling, or when about to land. This was put down, said the report on 'Operations in Malaya and Singapore' signed by General Wavell in June 1942, 'to information sent from the vicinity of the Northern aerodromes. At least one European was detected using a secret transmitter for this purpose.'

Although the Wavell report did not name Captain Patrick Heenan of the Indian Army, it shows that General Wavell knew of the existence of a traitor.[10]

Over on the east coast, all through that first day, Kota Bharu airfield came under heavy Japanese air attack. Several British aircraft were destroyed and damaged in addition to two which were shot down during sorties. In mid-afternoon a rumour spread like wildfire around the airfield that the Japanese had broken through the defensive perimeter. That started a chain of events which led to the precipitate and disorderly evacuation of the airfield, and to the murder of a British officer of the Indian Army in charge of the unit guarding it. Someone, it is not known who, informed Air Vice-Marshal Pulford in Singapore by telephone that the airfield was under infantry attack although it was not at the time. Pulford immediately ordered the surviving aircraft to fly south to Kuantan. It was unfortunate that, for some unexplained reason, the Station Commander, Wing Commander 'Beery' Noble, RAF, was absent from the operations room while this was taking place. The surviving planes flew south filled with stores and carrying some of the Australian ground crew. An unauthorised person then ordered the denial scheme to be put into effect, and ground staff fired the Operations Block and the Equipment Stores.

The mystery deepens. Apparently without the knowledge of Wing Commander 'Curly' Davis, the RAAF Squadron Commander, orders were then issued that all the remaining ground staff were to assemble at the main gate. Up to this point most of the accounts of the evacuation are in broad agreement.

The Australian writer, E.R. Hall, says in *Glory In Chaos*,[11] that the firing of the Operation Block had a most demoralizing effect; Beery Noble, in a desperate attempt to defend the aerodrome (which was still not under attack) assembled 'about 200 ground staff who did not appear to be particularly enthusiastic at the prospect of acting as infantry'. After discussions with the army the idea was abandoned and, says Hall, 'Curly Davis ordered No. 1 Squadron personnel to board trucks and half-an-hour later at 1845 the trucks left for Kuala Krai.' At that rail terminal they boarded a train for the south. 'The evacuation was well-organised,' Hall sums up, 'and there was no panic.' One's immediate reaction to that, in view of his earlier mention of the demoralizing effect of the firing of the buildings, is to ask why, if the evacuation was as orderly and as well-organised as he said it was, did the word panic come to be mentioned?

Other reports differ from Hall's. Several indicate that the evacuation of the airfield was indeed precipitate and not at all orderly, and this seems to be borne out even by the glossed-over version given in the British Official History: 'A joint reconnaissance by the brigadier [Key] and the wing commander [Noble] proved that the rumour [of the infantry attack] was false, but the damage was done, and by 6.15 pm the station and squadron maintenance staff had left in local transport for the railhead at Kuala Krai. Although they had set fire to the operations room and to most of the stores, they had failed to destroy the stocks of bombs and petrol or to make the runways unfit for use.' This failure fully to implement the airfield denial programme surely indicates a degree of precipitousness about the evacuation.

Vice-Admiral Sir Geoffrey Layton, whose 1942 War Diary was never published and of which a full copy was only made public in Britain in January 1993,[12] reported in it that he had heard authentic reports of a panic evacuation of the Kota Bharu airfield.

Sergeant Harry Blackham of 5th Regiment, RA, was stationed at Kota Bharu. At the time the evacuation from the airfield was taking place he was in attendance on his CO, Major Don, at a battle conference held by General Key some three miles down the road from the airfield, at a place from where the fighting on the beaches could be observed. The whole party then returned to the airfield. 'When we drove through the gate at the corner of the airfield we were shattered by the disorder and near panic,' writes Harry Blackham. 'There were simply dozens of air force blokes running around climbing into lorries. Major Don and some of the brigadier's party dived among them, trying to find the reasons for their actions. They could get no sense out of anyone. There were yells that the "Japs were over there". What was certain was that no one was going to get any sensible answers and although there were several people with stripes up, there was no sign of any officers.'[13]

Whatever the exact circumstances of the evacuation of Kota Bharu airfield, one thing seems certain. The spectacle of the air force people leaving was too much for the Indian States Force battalion, the 1st Hyderabads, on airfield defence duties there. They did not want to stay either and, when their commanding officer, Lieutenant-Colonel C.A. Hendricks, on attachment from the Indian Army, tried to stop them fleeing, some of his men shot and killed him.[14]

At a top-level Air Force conference held in Singapore on 31st December it was decided that there was need for a Court of Inquiry to be held into the evacuation of the northern airfields.[15] Air Command must have considered the matter very serious indeed to have arranged to hold an inquiry at such a time, but Kota Bharu was not the only station that was precipitately evacuated. The conference minutes stated that 'all possible information is to be sent to the court and those officers who have been concerned in the evacuations will all be called to give evidence'. The inquiry was presided over by Group-Captain J.P.J. McCauley, RAAF, and other members of the Court were Group-Captain Coggle, RAF, and Flight-Lieutenant Macotta, RAAF. In regard to Kota Bharu the Court found that No. 1 RAAF Squadron had pressed home attacks against the enemy landing force with determination and good results. (There can be no argument with that, and had the RAAF and the RAF been in a position to repeat that kind of performance later in the campaign, Singapore might perhaps never have fallen.) The Court also held that an orderly and timely evacuation took place. Quite apart from the reports to the contrary, it is difficult to see how the Court came to that conclusion when the denial scheme had not been fully implemented.

Over on the west coast, Sungei Patani airfield, which had been on the receiving end of an air hammering since early morning of 8th December, was considered untenable for aircraft, so later that day the surviving planes of 27 Squadron and 21 Squadron were moved south to Butterworth. This was meant initially to be a temporary measure, but the aircraft never did return because on 9th December the ground staff left after, it was subsequently reported, being told by Indian troops that the Japanese were on the doorstep. The Japanese were nowhere near at the time, for the battle at Jitra well to the north was still two days off. Nor was the denial scheme at this airfield initiated, and stores, bombs, fuel and runways were left intact.

On 9th December Alor Star airfield, the most northerly one on the west coast, was also abandoned, the seven surviving Blenheims of 62 Squadron flying to Butterworth fifty miles to the south. (On that date the freshwater pipeline feeding Alor Star aerodrome was blown up by saboteurs. These might have been members of Captain Heenan's spy organisation, for a contemporary record stated that he 'controlled all the subversive elements in the northern area from the Prai river to Penang and the Thailand border'.)

From Butterworth that afternoon one of the 62 Squadron Blenheim pilots now stationed there made the flight that won him what was chronologically the first of the four VCs awarded during the campaign. (It was not promulgated until 1946.) The Blenheims of 62 Squadron and 34 Squadron were about to take off for a raid on Singora when they were attacked by Japanese planes. Only one of the British planes, piloted by Squadron-Leader A.S.K. 'Pongo' Scarf, managed to get into the air. He and his navigator, Flight-Sergeant (later Squadron-Leader) G. 'Paddy' Calder, DFC, DFM, pressed home a lone sortie against Singora in the teeth of heavy flak and attacks by enemy fighters. The plane was badly damaged and Scarf was mortally wounded. He managed to get his plane back behind British lines to crash-land it at the now-evacuated Alor Star airfield. Scarf, aged twenty-eight, died in hospital the following day.

From that event sprang one of the Singapore myths. The story went that Scarf's wife Elizabeth, known as 'Sally', was a nurse at Alor Star hospital and that he died in her arms after she had volunteered two pints of blood for a transfusion. It made a romantic, if very sad tale. Unfortunately it is not true.

It is not known who invented the story but it appeared in several books.[16] Sally Scarf (later Sally Gunn) did nothing to discredit the story, and why should she have? – it made such a tellable tale. Sally was indeed a nurse at Alor Star, but she, along with all the other 'military' wives in the north had been sent south the day before her husband's death. It was especially necessary to get her away from the front line as she was well into a pregnancy (which in itself is evidence that part of the story is false, for no doctor would have taken blood from a pregnant woman).

Two unmarried nursing sisters at the General Hospital were left behind. One of these was Miss Phyllis Briggs (later Mrs P.M. Thom). Let her diary tell the true story:

> Suddenly an ambulance arrived. In it was Pongo Scarf, a young RAF officer we knew well. His plane had crash-landed in a field nearby. Pongo was badly wounded. He was given a blood transfusion but his condition was hopeless. His wife Sally was one of our nursing sisters, but during the previous day she had left Alor Star with the rest of the Service wives, so poor Pongo died without seeing her again. I was determined that he would be properly buried. We managed to get a coffin from the jail. Another sister came along with me in my Morris 8 and we followed the ambulance bearing the coffin to the local cemetery where a grave had been dug. On our way we met two army padres driving towards us. I stopped the car and asked them if they would come with us to say a prayer, so later when I saw Sally I could tell her that we had done all we could.[17]

The true story of Pongo Scarf's death and burial is in a way even more touching than the myth. Unfortunately Phyllis Briggs never did see Sally again. Pongo Scarf now lies buried in the military cemetery at Taiping.

Later that same day, Butterworth, the last of the north-western airfields, was abandoned. The RAF now had very few planes left north of Kuantan. Air Vice-Marshal Sir Paul Maltby in his dispatch on air operations, wrote: 'Some of the personnel of No. 21 Squadron, RAAF, and No. 27 Squadron, RAF, both of which had already been driven out of Sungei Patani, did not behave at all steadily.'[18]

It is not surprising that when the retreating British troops, suffering badly from lack of air cover, passed through these abandoned airfields several days later and found signs of early and precipitate departure, they were not too pleased with the RAF.

On the day following the evacuation of Butterworth airfield, on 10th December, the officer-traitor Captain Heenan was arrested there. After issuing the order for the arrest Major-General Murray-Lyon said to the arresting officer, 'we were sure someone was passing information on our every move'. Heenan had done his spy work well, for by then due to his efforts almost the entire strength of the RAF in the north had been destroyed. For the remainder of the campaign the Commonwealth forces had to fight an enemy who controlled the air.

There is one more important story to be told concerning the airfields in Malaya. If the comparative closeness of the Japanese invaders was an excuse for the precipitate air force evacuations of the other northern aerodromes, it was not so at Kuantan, for there the Japanese Army was still three weeks away.

Kuantan is a small port halfway up the east coast of Malaya. Apart from the airfield itself, which was still under construction when the 2/18th Royal Garhwal Rifles arrived to protect it in November 1940, the town was important as the outlet for the mines at Sungei Lembing, the largest lode tinmine in the world, and also because a road connected it to the central Malayan town of Jerantut, strategically situated on the rail spur to Kota Bharu.[19] Once the war began it was important that the airfield be held to prevent the Japanese using it, for it was within fighter-flying range of Singapore.

The Hudsons of the Australian No. 1 Squadron which evacuated Kota Bharu on 8th December, landed at Kuantan that night, joining other Hudsons of the Australian No. 8 Squadron. Also at Kuantan were twelve Vildebeestes and six Blenheims of RAF Squadrons 100 and 60 respectively. On the morning of 9th the Blenheims were ordered south as the airfield was considered congested.

On the previous day planes based at Kuantan had joined in the attack on the Japanese at Kota Bharu. These had been refuelled and rearmed by the Australian ground staff when they arrived back, as had the Hudsons from the north. Throughout the early morning of 9th December the ground staff were kept busy. An underground fuel tank had not been completed and so fuel had to be hand-pumped from drums into tankers. The Australian E.R. Hall reports the conditions in general at the airfield as being deplorable and that the ground crews were exhausted. Perhaps these were the reasons for what was to happen later.

A report came in that a small convoy had been sighted, and Australian bombers made ready to take off and attack it. Meanwhile the acting CO of No. 8 Squadron, Squadron-Leader P. Henderson, RAAF, had asked Air HQ if he could move his reconnaissance Hudsons to a better defended base because Kuantan had neither fighters nor anti-aircraft guns. He was told to stay where he was. This was almost certainly because it was the intention to use the Hudsons for reconnaissance for the Royal Navy Force Z which had sailed from Singapore the previous evening and was steaming northwards to attack the Japanese landing fleets.

Then, dead on 1000 hours, the air raid sirens went off as nine Japanese aircraft were sighted. In bombing and machine-gun attacks the Japanese destroyed three aircraft on the ground and set fire to several buildings. There were no casualties. Although defending troops of the 5/11th Sikh Regiment put up a barrage of machine-gun and Bren gun fire, they did not hit any of the planes, although one was later reported shot down by an Australian Hudson returning from a sortie.

The officer in charge of the operations room at Kuantan during the attack was Flight-Lieutenant C.C. Williams, RAAF, and he used the Green Line (secret) telephone to Air HQ, Singapore to report the attack. E.R. Hall says, 'What he was told in reply was either confused or confusing.' Williams maintained that he was told the airfield was to be evacuated. On the other hand the officer he spoke to at Air HQ maintained that he only passed the message that all flyable aircraft were to be flown to Singapore. Anyway, it was Williams's version that was passed to Squadron-Leader Henderson according to Hall's version of events.

Hall goes on to say that Henderson attended to the dispatch of his aircraft and crews but did not instruct any officer to look after the ground staff and, as rumours of a general evacuation abounded, 'they took matters into their own hands'. They began leaving in buses and other transport obtained from a nearby village. There was no problem in this because, 'the Malays were most co-operative'. In this transport they made their way to the railway at Jerantut, a hundred miles inland and eventually ended up in Singapore.

Mr Hall was writing many years after the event, and although his book contains the names of many Australian airmen, he does not mention one man who was there at Kuantan, Pilot Officer Roy Bulcock, RAAF.

Bulcock was the officer-in-charge of the ground crew employed in plane refuelling, and he wrote his own book about the Malayan campaign *Of Death But Once*, which was published within six years of the events it described.[20] Bulcock's account is thus a near contemporary one based on personal experience. He gives a different version of events to that of Hall, who did not list Bulcock's book among his references.

Bulcock says that there was bedlam after the air raid. The CO (the Station Commander, Wing-Commander Councell, RAF) was on the telephone talking to Singapore.[21] He was saying, 'It's absolutely ridiculous, I tell you. Nothing like that has happened at all. The damage is immaterial.' Bulcock commented, 'someone had telephoned them before the CO turned up and told a very panicky story, greatly exaggerating the facts. One man alone had started something, the result of which would have tremendous effects.'

Councell instructed Bulcock to arrange to refuel some aircraft that were due to return that afternoon, and it took him half-an-hour to sort out the octane of the fuel required. 'In that half-hour that little flame of panic had spread like wildfire. I looked out on a deserted Station. No. 8 Squadron* had rushed to their aircraft, dumped all the bombs and spare equipment ... loaded up sixteen or seventeen men and taken off for Singapore ... The balance of the ground staff ... seeing their officers depart, commandeered the Station transport and drove madly for the railway station at Jerantut.'

When the CO returned from an inspection trip around the airfield, Bulcock goes on, he was absolutely stunned by the rapidity of the events. He told Bulcock to leave with the last truck of Australians that was just pulling out, but Bulcock refused. There were then only four ground staff officers left on the base, Councell himself, the Adjutant, the Armament Officer, all British, and Bulcock. The four later went to the adjacent army mess for a meal, where a captain was holding forth, 'I saw a bloody Flight-Lieutenant soon after the raid started. He ran down to the side road with two friends, blew the door-lock off a private car with his pistol, drove the car on to the main road so fast that he skidded into a deep drain and couldn't get out. Then he held up the Post Office bus with his gun, made all the passengers and driver get out and drove off at full speed.' Other army officers were telling similar stories.

Bulcock ended his account of the Kuantan airfield incident with the sentence, 'For the first and last time in my life I felt ashamed of being an Australian.'

Pilot Officer Basil Gotto, RAFVR, was a Vildebeeste pilot of 100 Squadron which was at Kuantan during that raid. After it was over his squadron received orders to take off for Seletar (Singapore). They were instructed to look for an enemy ship that had been reported offshore and to attack it *en route*. When Gotto and his air-gunner, Flight-Sergeant Hardy, got to their plane they found a bullet had punctured the starboard petrol tank and so the squadron flew off without them and without another of the Vildebeestes which also could not take off for an unspecified reason.

Gotto's War Diary is another contemporary document. It was written within a few months of the event when the facts must have still been crystal clear in his mind.[22] He wrote:

> It was not till then that we had time to see what the rest of the Station was up to, and we were dismayed to see signs of panic on all sides. This was quite unwarranted. The attack had done remarkably little damage to the Station, and there was not a single casualty.
>
> All the fires had burnt themselves out, and the rain and low cloud precluded the chance of another air attack. There were

---

* Bulcock deliberately omitted the squadron number in his book, but it has been inserted here by this author.

rumours of Japs having landed at Kuantan, but they were quite without foundation. The Station Commander, Wing Commander Councell, I think, made a great mistake in not appearing on the Station after the raid. He remained shut up in the Operations Room, and, except for individual squadrons like our own, there was no leadership or clear orders. The other Squadron still there was an Australian Hudson Squadron, and there is no use denying that they panicked badly; they just jettisoned everything out of their aircraft, crammed in as many men as possible into them and dashed off to Singapore leaving numbers of their ground crew to look after themselves. Later, up at the Mess, we found they had not even collected their kits and had left everything, including valuable cameras and suchlike lying around.

Later, Gotto's air-gunner, Flight-Sergeant Hardy, reported it had been rumoured that 'it was every man for himself', and that two of their own squadron's ground crew sergeants had fled with the Australians.

Gotto thought the panic may have been started by fifth-columnists. He wrote, 'I do not know quite what to make of the panic at Kuantan, but I think that, even if it had been started on purpose, it could have been averted by the Commanding Officer being seen about and giving orders.'

So there we have two contemporary eyewitness versions of the events from air force officers, one Australian and one British, which are broadly in agreement. Major Dick Clarke, at that time a lieutenant and adjutant of 2/18th Royal Garhwal Rifles at Kuantan, confirms that there was indeed a panic evacuation; during the raid, he says,

some aircraft on the ground were damaged. Also a hanger and other structures but there were few if any casualties among the RAAF ground staff who manned the aerodrome. I happened to be visiting the posts in the Kuantan area and diverted with my driver to the aerodrome after the raid had ended. I was surprised to find the area more or less deserted and found a soldier of 5/11th Sikh Regiment who were located in the vicinity. He told me that there had been complete panic and everything with wheels had been commandeered by the RAAF personnel who didn't even attempt to collect their belongings before departing at high speed ... to Jerantut. At this point my driver butted in and said 'how is this possible? They are all sahibs'. I replied without thinking 'they are not sahibs, they are Australians'. It did not occur to me at the time that I probably have more Australian relatives than 'pommy' ones![23]

Conductor A.F.J. North, of the Indian Army Ordnance Corps, confirmed the panicky evacuation of Kuantan airfield in his diary, adding a note about its effect on the Indian troops in the area. 'Evacuation of the RAAF personnel followed this raid, and it is considered that this somewhat hurried departure rather shook the morale of the Indian troops.'[24]

The hurried and unnecessary evacuation of Kuantan airfield was also reported in an official naval document dated 26th December 1941, by Lieutenant-Commander H. Austin. Austin was sent to Kuantan ten days after the events outlined above – the Japanese did not take Kuantan until the New Year – to lay a minefield off the port. He was told the story by several officers of the 22nd Indian Brigade. His report, although based on hearsay, is important in that it was presented as evidence to the later Court of Inquiry held in Singapore. Firsthand reports from army witnesses were of course not available, as by then the army was too busy fighting. Neither was Pilot Officer Gotto's report.

Austin wrote:

A stick of bombs was dropped, one of which demolished the cook house. Immediately the RAAF decided to evacuate the aerodrome, every available bomber being heavily overloaded with personnel and taking off. The RAAF ground staff stampeded in panic, seizing lorries and private cars and went away to Jerantut ... as fast as they could. Within a short time there was nobody left except the Military guarding the airfield. No action whatever was taken by the RAAF to render the airfield useless to the enemy.

This defection of the RAAF on the East Coast of Malaya is surely one of the most shameful episodes in the history of the British Empire.[25]

A few of the ground staff at Kuantan were in fact British, and they disappeared along the road to Jerantut as well. But by far the great majority were Australian.

At the Inquiry held at Singapore in January 1942 Austin's Kuantan report was entered in evidence, but then quickly withdrawn. It seems that some kind of cover-up process was already going on. According to E.R. Hall, the Court, with its Australian President Group-Captain McCauley, concluded with regard to Kuantan, that 'there was an order which caused the evacuation ... the flyable aircraft flew to Sembawang [Singapore] and the ground staff were evacuated without control by road'. No copy of the Inquiry records now exists, so Hall presumably obtained this information direct from Australian participants in it. He also reports that the Court held, 'that Wing Commander Councell, RAF, was deficient in his duties as Station Commander as he had not prepared any plan for the defence of or emergency movement from his station, and that at the time of the enemy attack he was apparently absent from his post without excuse. The Court recommended that he be court-martialled.'

This all seems somewhat unfair. According to the Australian, Bulcock, who had no reason to protect Councell's hide at the expense of his own countrymen, Councell was asleep at the time of the attack after having been on his feet for the previous thirty-six hours. Although Gotto criticised Councell for not being around, it is possible that he did not know as much about the situation as Bulcock who was a member of the Station staff. And, surely, the main responsibility for the defence of the airfield was the army's. The airfield defences put up a good defence despite the fact they had no anti-aircraft guns of any sort. Furthermore, Hall mentions the word 'panic' several times in his account of Kuantan, which was garnered many years after the event from surviving RAAF personnel, although denying that any such thing took place. Like the lady in *Hamlet*, it seems that Mr Hall's informants did protest too much.

From the Kuantan area come the two earliest reports in the campaign of desertion by British officers of the Indian Army. Captain Keith F. Comyn had been sent to the 2/18th Garhwalis under 'special report' from the 2/10th Baluch Regiment. (The device of sending an officer to another battalion on special report was used when someone had done something reprehensible, but which was not bad enough to earn a court martial and possibly being cashiered out of the army.) In the early days of the war Comyn was sent up the coast to Dungun with a patrol. One *naik* from that patrol returned, reporting that the rest of the patrol had been killed but that, prior to that, Comyn had disappeared into the jungle. Weeks later Comyn fetched up in the same POW camp as his fellow officers and found himself ostracised. No court-martial action was taken against Comyn after the war but he was removed from the Indian Army on medical grounds. He was later mixed up in black market transactions with a well-known nude model of the times called 'Yolanda' – her photographs often featured in the magazine *Men Only*. Then he went to Australia, where he was drowned in a swimming-pool accident.

The other man to desert from the Garhwalis was an ICO of half-Indian extraction. He absconded with the Australian ground crew from the airfield. He eventually fetched up in a POW camp too. He told stories, not to his fellow Garhwali officers who knew better, of having been involved in hand-to-hand fighting with the Japanese. He was ostracised as well, and he too escaped a court martial after the war.

Meanwhile, over on the west coast, as the bulk of the British and Indian troops around Jitra were frantically attempting to complete their defences before the arrival of the Japanese spearhead forces pushing down the road from Singora, a small column of Indian infantry supported by sappers, and code-named Laycol, was sent over the border into Thailand in an attempt to hold up the Japanese advance. A larger force, code-named Krohcol, crossed the border on the Kroh-Patani road in order to capture a strategic point known as The Ledge. These constituted the only parts of Operation Matador to be implemented.

Laycol had some success against Japanese troops and tanks before retiring 'in accordance with enemy pressure'. The sappers blew up several bridges during the retreat. This column was led by Brigadier W.O. Lay.

Krohcol's advance was slowed by determined resistance put up by Thai border guards, and the Japanese reached The Ledge first. On 10th December the column fought a ferocious battle with crack troops of the Japanese 5th Division well supported by tanks. Outnumbered, and after having lost many men, Krohcol began falling back. Lieutenant-Colonel C.E.N. Hopkins-Husson of 5/14th Punjab was a young lieutenant at the time and took part in Krohcol. He and his company were cut off during the retreat and almost did not make it back because 'some nervy person had given instructions to blow a bridge' when he and his men were still on the wrong side of it.[26] This was the first incident of this kind in the campaign; but it was far from being the last.

A few hours before dawn on 10th December the Japanese crossed the Malayan border north of Jitra. They were met first by forward troops of the 1/14th Punjab Regiment at Asun, two miles north of the main Jitra positions. According to the Official History, Japanese tanks caused utter consternation among the Punjabis, many of whom had never seen one before. They fell back on positions held by 2/1st Gurkha Rifles, who were still engaged on laying wire and digging defences.

The Gurkhas came under fire that evening and with one of the only two anti-tank rifles issued to them, they disabled three tanks.[27] The action was fought in monsoonal rain, so that Molotov cocktails could not be lit to supplement the fire of the two anti-tank weapons. As more tanks came up, the Gurkhas retired, but some were cut off by infiltrating Japanese and had to make their way back to British lines by many and devious routes. Some were even captured by the Japanese but then managed to escape. One such party afterwards captured seven Japanese themselves, 'whom they shot at their own request'.

This much vaunted Samurai attitude, of death rather than capture, was not universal among the Japanese. On 22nd December a section of 5th Regiment, RA, under Captain McEwan captured the pilot of a downed Zero. Sergeant Harry Blackham reports, 'we levelled our guns at him. He appeared demented, and speaking fair but disjointed English entreated us to kill him. He grabbed the muzzle of one of the rifles and put it against his chest, saying, "Shoot, shoot". He apparently wished to die for his Emperor, but McEwan felt he was too valuable a prize to be given that pleasure and ordered us to take him to our truck. We found his automatic pistol was under his thigh, cocked and with the safety off. It seemed his desire to die for his Emperor was not so strong as we had thought.'[28]

One party of Gurkhas finding themselves cut off behind enemy lines, found a boat on the beach and sailed in it across the Malacca Straits to Sumatra. They were almost shot there by Dutch beach guards who thought they were Japanese, but were eventually flown back to Singapore where they insisted on being transported north to rejoin their regiment.

The British and Indian forces should have learned lessons at Jitra on how to deal with Japanese tanks, yet there is evidence from later in the campaign that they had not, or that what had been learned had not been generally promulgated. General Heath recorded:[29] 'Murray-Lyon when he realised the Japs had tanks should have seen that his troops fought behind tank obstacles.' Yet at Slim River a month later the tank barriers the British erected proved inadequate.

During those first days of the campaign the pre-war efforts of the Indian Independence League, latterly supported by Major Fujiwara's F-Kikan organisation, to subvert the Indian forces, began to bear fruit. One of the first Indian officers to be captured was Captain Mohan Singh of 1/14th Punjab Regiment. Already a disgruntled man from real or imagined racial prejudice in the Indian Army, and an ardent, though up to that time mainly a closet, supporter of nationalism, he quickly co-operated with the Japanese. He was given the task of converting Indian prisoners of war into members of the Indian National Army (INA). Most Indian officers and men, true to their salt, stood firm, but a large number went over. In a very short time Mohan Singh, in what must have been one of the fastest promotions in military history, was made a general by the Japanese. Militarily the INA was never a success, but as many members of it were later to achieve prominence in post-war India, politically it had some importance.

A little after noon on 10th December, the battleship *Prince of Wales* and the battle-cruiser *Repulse* of Admiral Sir Tom Phillips's Force Z, were sunk off the east coast of Malaya by air torpedo and bombing attacks. The two ships and their escorting destroyers, returning south after an aborted mission to strike at the Japanese landing ships at Singora, were diverted to Kuantan from where a report had come that the Japanese were making a landing. The ships had no air cover, due to the loss of Kota Bharu airfield and the others in the north-east, and the evacuation of Kuantan airfield itself on the previous day. The news not only caused consternation and deep dismay to the Allies around the world; it caused a further sharp drop in the morale of the Commonwealth troops in Malaya.

There are many questions surrounding the circumstances that led to messages being sent to Singapore that Kuantan was under attack from the sea. The Kuantan incident, or enigma as it has sometimes been called, has never been fully explained. The messages from Kuantan caused Rear-Admiral Palliser, Admiral Phillips's Chief of Staff in Singapore, to relay the information to *Prince of Wales*, after which Phillips altered course to investigate. There have been questions raised over whether a landing ever took place at all, and if it did, who the infiltrators were;

and why was it that the infantry and artillery units in the area opened up with everything they had; and who was it who sent the first message that the beaches were under attack? In other words, what started the chain of events that led to the two capital ships being diverted to Kuantan and, only hours later, to their destruction?[30]

Lieutenant Dick Clarke was the adjutant of 2/18th Royal Garhwal Rifles, the regiment defending the beaches north of Kuantan. The beaches to the south, and the airfield, were defended by 5/11th Sikh Regiment, Artillery support was supplied by 63/81st Battery, 5th Field Regiment RA, under Colonel Jephson, and a section of the 21st Mountain Battery, Indian Army, under Captain Coleman. Dick Clarke recalls that, during the week before the Japanese invasion at Kota Bharu on 8th December, most of his regiment's officers had gone down with dengue fever. He himself was the last one to get it, and still had a temperature of 103° when news of the landings at Kota Bharu came through. 'I forced myself out of bed,' he says, 'and maybe it was the shock of that news that brought my temperature down rapidly.'

The Regimental History of the Garhwalis, the Malayan section of which was based on what Dick Clarke and other officers wrote up during their prisoner of war captivity, makes only brief mention of the events of the 9th and 10th December at Kuantan. Dick Clarke says that, because it was written in Changi and at other places where there were Australian prisoners, it was considered politic to omit details of the evacuation of the airfield. It was also deemed politic to touch only briefly upon the events of that same night, which drew the ships of Force Z into the coast.[31] The Garhwali History briefly reports:

> On the same night [of the day of the airfield evacuation] an attempted landing was reported from the northern part of the beach defences by, among others, the artillery forward observation officer at Tanjong Api. Defensive fire was opened and spread southwards along the whole front. On the morning of 10th December HMS *Prince of Wales* and *Repulse* were seen off Kuantan from the high ground; both were sunk by air attack shortly afterwards.

The Regimental War Diaries of the 2/18th Garhwalis, the unit manning the defences where the purported landing was made, were destroyed by burning during the retreat to Singapore, so no amplification of that brief passage is available from that source. But as adjutant, and therefore the man responsible to his CO for writing up the War Diaries, Dick Clarke is an important source of information about what exactly went on that night. He writes:

> Until after the war I was never asked what really happened

during the night 9/10 Dec 41 on the beaches north of Kuantan. We always regarded it as a minor probe to which we over-reacted.

The front was divided into three sectors: 'D' Company Northern, 'A' Company Centre, and 'B' Company Southern. The northern boundary was the mouth of the small Balok river and the southern was the Tanjong Api light.* Battalion HQ was in a bungalow just east of the Besarah Road about half way up the regimental front. The defences consisted of concrete pillboxes at about 1000-metre interval with a double row of dannert wire linking them. The companies, less those manning the pillboxes, were deployed in platoon stand-to positions to the rear. Purpose-built hutted camps to accommodate each company were tied into the defensive system. Communications were line telephones from Battalion HQ to Companies, also from Battalion HQ to pillboxes. There were additional line telephones on a separate Company-Platoon-pillbox network. Battalion HQ was connected to Brigade HQ (at the aerodrome) by the civilian postal telecommunications system and also by line telephone for security.

After dark on the night of 9th Dec I was at Bn HQ writing a letter home having dined well in the bungalow which doubled as the Officers' Mess when we were alerted by the sound of continuous gunfire. It must have been about 2200 hours because one of our young officers had turned ashen and I told the orderly to bring him a glass of whisky. He replied that, in accordance with Malaya Command orders, the bar was closed at 2200 hrs. Lt ... was however given his whisky and quickly recovered!

My first reaction was that the beaches were being shelled from the sea and I immediately phoned 'A' Company, the centre sector, for information. Capt. K.G. Douglas said that machine-gun fire had broken out in the northern sector followed by a barrage in front of the wire from our guns. I then contacted the northernmost pillbox on the field telephone and was told by the NCO that *kishti* – open boats – were coming ashore and he had fired on them. There were casualties and these had been lifted back on to the boats which were pulling out to sea again. He said that 2" mortar fire from 'D' Company was also brought down and that the boats were dispersing, but that heavy shelling had commenced and was continuing along the line of defensive wire. Whilst I was receiving this report other messages were coming in, including one that a gas attack had developed – this was later discounted. As the CO [Lieutenant-Colonel G.E.R.S. Hartigan,

* Tanjong Api is the jutting headland that protects the northern side of the Kuantan River entrance.

MC], was not present at the time, I, using the line telephone to Brigade HQ reported that there had been an attempted landing from small boats which had been repulsed, and a possible gas attack. The latter was corrected later when it transpired that the acrid smoke from shell bursts had been mistaken for gas.

It quickly became apparent that the landing was only a probe to see whether the beach defences were effective. Unfortunately for our battalion, when the guns started firing our pillboxes all opened fire on their fixed lines and thereby the enemy were given all the information they needed.

It was only after the sinking of the *Prince of Wales* and *Repulse* that we learned that our overreaction had caused the ships to change course. We were also told that an intercepted message in clear from the Kuantan wireless station had been picked up by Force Z. It was later discovered that such a message had been sent to Singapore by a civilian named 'Fitch' who was employed in local government at Kuantan who apparently had authority to use the wireless station. He was never under suspicion but must have somehow tapped our telephone line or maybe assumed from the sound of gunfire that a landing was taking place. I would like to point out however, in support of my own battalion, that 5 Fd Regt RA were not requested to bring down fire on our front and also that it was not understood what prompted the Forward Observation Officer at the extreme south of the defences at Tanjong Api, to report a landing eleven miles away which he could not possibly have seen.

This seems to indicate that the first report of landings made to Brigade HQ might have come from the 5th Field Regiment RA officer manning the artillery observation post (OP) at Tanjong Api, who was some eleven miles away from the scene of the boat landings. Dick Clarke claims that the landings could not have been seen from the OP, which must be true considering the distance involved and the fact that it was night. The artillery were not shelling some 'mother ship' out at sea which might have been in view of the men at Tanjong Api OP, but *along the line of the beach defences*. This suggests that the OP must have received information about landings over their own line communications, as artillery guns were already firing before Clarke spoke to his northernmost pillbox. The Garhwali pill-boxes were not connected directly to any of the artillery OPs.

The History of 5th Regiment RA gives a different version. It states that 'the OP of 21st Mountain Battery reported that Japanese were landing near Pelingdong in five boats, and immediately opened fire on them with the result that they got back into their boats and started to go north. Infantry corroborated this report. At this, all the remaining artillery sprang to life and opened up on previously arranged targets in the area. It was the first occasion the enemy had been definitely located, and there was great excitement, not only at the guns, but also at Regimental HQ. One immediate result was that everyone spoke far too fast on the telephone.'

This indicates that the first landing report emanated from the 21st Mountain Battery's OP at Bukit Pelingdong. This was under the command of Captain Coleman, but whether he was actually at the OP at the time is not known. Brigadier Painter, commanding 22nd Brigade, gave the same version after the war, stating that, 'a mountain battery OP reported an attempted landing from five boats and claimed to have foiled it by fire'. Painter also confirmed that the massive artillery barrage put up had been authorised. He says, 'craft were reported to be laying close in. These reports moved progressively from north to south. Artillery support ... was called for and considerable artillery action ensued. The deductions drawn from these reports was that the enemy was feeling the defences systematically from north to south and the order was given for artillery fire to be opened on the undefended beaches south of Kuantan River mouth, up to the limit of range, to create the impression that these were also held.'[32]

During conversations with this author, Dick Clarke has expanded upon the Kuantan events. He said there was no 'landing' as such, but heavy defensive fire laid down by the artillery along the entire front plus machine-gun and supporting rifle fire did take place. The Japanese were merely making an investigative probe to test and learn about our defences, with, at the most, *three* boats.

This account of the number of boats ties in with the reports from further down the coast a few days later when three 'ship's lifeboats' were washed ashore. Lifeboats are open boats, like the ones described by the Garhwali NCO. They had been holed by bullets and contained some items of Japanese equipment.

A new 'odd piece' to the puzzle comes with the mention of the 'in clear' wireless report made by the man 'Fitch'. F.H. 'Fred' Fitch, of the Malayan Forestry Department, was at that time serving as an officer with the FMS Volunteers at Kuantan. He ended up a POW of the Japanese and confirmed to Dick Clarke in the camp that he had indeed sent an 'in clear' radio message to Singapore about the landings. The content of the message is not known. Neither is it known to whom the message was sent, or indeed if it ever got through to Singapore. Fred Fitch died at Croydon in Surrey on 23rd October 1993 (five days after this author tried to contact him). He has not left any papers that might have helped to throw light on this matter.

Dick Clarke says that as a prisoner of war he attended a lecture given by a naval officer in Changi camp, and the officer stated that an 'in clear' radio message regarding the attack on Kuantan had been picked up by the *Repulse*. Clarke says that a marine officer from the *Repulse*, Lieutenant G.A. Hulton, had later confirmed this too. Lieutenant Hulton (Sir Geoffrey Hulton, 4th Baronet) died in November 1993, so no confirmation is now available from that source either. It is now unlikely that this new twist to the enigma will ever be unravelled. Patrick Mahoney, one of the authors of what is arguably the best book about the loss of Force Z, says he never heard any mention of such a message.[33]

The signal that Rear-Admiral Palliser sent to Admiral Phillips regarding the 'landings' at Kuantan was received by *Prince of Wales* just before midnight. It was brief and to the point.

IMMEDIATE.
ENEMY REPORTED LANDING KUANTAN. LATITUDE
03.30 NORTH.

It was probably enough in itself to cause Phillips to decide to divert to Kuantan, but we are left with the intriguing possibility that the content of an 'in clear' message emanating directly from Kuantan may have helped him to make that decision. All the earlier messages sent from Kuantan that night greatly exaggerated the situation, and some of the senders were surely affected by the excitement of the occasion, as shown by the extract from the 5th Regiment, RA History. It is likely that a message sent by a part-time volunteer officer who was not close to the action (the radio station was not near the beaches) and who may have based his report solely on the noise of the firing coming from the beach, would have exaggerated it most.

Very soon after the catastrophic loss of the capital ships the authorities began looking for a scapegoat. Lieutenant C.J. Windsor, RMNVR, a well-known local trader in civilian life, and who was something like a character from a Joseph Conrad novel, fell into that category. He was arrested and taken to Singapore aboard HMS *Hungjao* because it was believed he was somehow implicated. Windsor was later released as there was no evidence at all to connect him with the débâcle. The main thing against him seems to have been the fact that he was descended from Germans and had changed his name from Winckle to Windsor during the First World War. He managed to leave Singapore before it fell and spent the rest of the war in South Africa. He returned to Malaya after the war and made several attempts to clear his reputation. He was not wholly successful in this, as rumours about his involvement still went the rounds. But one senior Singapore police officer, Guy Madoc, investigated the matter post-war and concluded that Windsor was indeed innocent.[34,35]

The so-called Jitra line was not a good defensive position. General Heath commanding 3rd Indian Corps, stated that there was no reason for occupying the Jitra position except that it was less bad than any other position. The reasons for having any sort of defensive line there at all were twofold: the north-west was Malaya's largest rice-producing area, and, it contained the three north-western airfields which, it needs to be remembered, had been sited by the RAF without consultation with the army, whose job it was to protect them. By the time the Jitra battle began, all the northern airfields had been abandoned by the RAF, and the only reason to hold them now was to prevent them falling into enemy hands. The Jitra front was about fourteen miles wide, stretching from jungle-clad hills inland to a tidal mangrove swamp near the coast. It crossed two major roads and the railway, and traversed rubber plantations and flooded paddy fields.

Major-General Murray-Lyon's troop dispositions at Jitra have come in for considerable criticism. By covering every possible approach across this front his force had no depth at all. It might have been better had he concentrated in depth along the two main roads south, but it must be said that his planned dispositions were known in advance by both his immediate superior, General Heath of 3rd Corps, and by the GOC Malaya Command, General Percival, neither of whom countermanded them.

As the forward units fell back on the main defences another of the many tragic errors between 'friendly' units occured. A sapper officer blew a bridge before an artillery unit had crossed it; the men got over, but their guns did not. Such things happen in any war, but it seems that more of them happened in Malaya than in other theatre; or perhaps more of them are remembered because Malaya was a defeat and not a victory.

On 11th December, in the knowledge that his line of communications was in danger because of the enforced retreat of Krohcol over on his right flank, Murray-Lyon sought permission to withdraw thirty miles south to Gurun, which was thought to be a natural stronghold. General Percival refused the request on the basis that such an immediate retreat would have been bad for morale. No doubt he was right, but what followed was to have a far worse effect on the already low morale of the 11th Indian Division. General Heath commented, 'Percival should have given Murray-Lyon permission to withdraw to Gurun. When permission was given it was far too late. What could have been an orderly withdrawal by day became a night scramble.'

All day long, as the Jitra battle raged, signs of demoralisation became manifest. Brigadier Carpendale reported something he had seen with his own eyes: 'One company of 2/8th Punjab looked very bad and I saw at once that it had no intention of advancing.' But such incidents were not confined to Indian troops. Colonel Swinton of the East Surreys reported that 'a company of Leicesters have just gone through my HQ like a dose of salts – I'm trying to stop them and get them back to the front'.

The Japanese assault forces were again supported by tanks. Night brought no respite from the onslaught. Most of the British and Indian reserves were brought up. Although several attempts were made to counter-attack, by 0600 hours on 12th December a wedge had been driven into the centre of the British right flank where the 15th Indian Brigade was situated. To restore the integrity of the front, Carpendale, the brigade commander (he had taken over from Brigadier Garrett who was missing at the time) called up his remaining reserve, the 1/8th Punjab. Murray-Lyon saw them and commented to his GS01, Colonel Harrison, that he had not seen looks on men's faces like that since March 1918. It was to get worse. The Punjabis came under 'friendly' fire from the 2/19th Jats causing some of them to bolt. Rallied by their commander the Punjabis pushed forward under heavy fire, but many were killed before that counter-attack petered out.

In private correspondence with General Percival after the war, General Heath wrote of the Jitra battle, 'the enemy showed an almost uncanny sense of directing his attacks against the most profitable targets. It was the common belief, which I feel must be accepted, that the enemy profited tremendously from the aid of locals whose knowledge was not merely confined to the terrain but included detailed knowledge of our dispositions.' Heenan, the officer traitor, had been arrested the day before with current situation reports in his possession which he was not supposed to have. Almost certainly this information had been passed to the Japanese.

The part-destruction by the RAF of the airfield at Alor Star behind the front line did nothing to help the morale of the troops. Brigadier Carpendale reported the RAF had even destroyed a quantity of Bren and Tommy-guns and ammunition which his troops could have used. 'It made a very bad impression on the troops,' he said. Incidentally, Carpendale wrote that units of his former command, 28th Indian Brigade, had been delayed in moving into position on 9th December by 'Police and Customs barriers being closed over all bridges and State borders. These authorities attempted to take the numbers of our vehicles, and let them through one by one.' There were still examples of lack of co-operation between civilian arms and the military even after the war had started.

Murray-Lyon reported his position as untenable and he finally received Percival's permission to withdraw to Gurun, the 'better' position he had wanted to occupy two days before. Disengagement and withdrawal took place during the night of 12th/13th December. The withdrawal instructions did not get through to some units due to bad communications. In most cases they had to be relayed by liaison officers who often had no idea where some of the outlying units were situated. 2/1st Gurkhas was one unit which never received the message. The battalion only learned of the withdrawal at first light when they discovered that the positions around them had been vacated. By then the battalion 'had had no food for 52 hours and only a few hours sleep in 58 hours. In this period they had dug two positions, fought one action and marched some 20 miles off the roads.' Even so, most of the Gurkhas still managed to get through to Gurun. Some other withdrawing units were ambushed by infiltrating parties of Japanese, and some fought to the last man and the last round. All in all, Jitra was a major disaster, with the 11th Division suffering severe casualties and losing much equipment, not least in the scramble to retreat.

The War Diary of General HQ, Singapore, commented ominously on a memo which General Heath had sent to General Percival on 14th December:

> General Murray-Lyon painted a gloomy picture of his ability to hold the Gurun position due to fatigue of troops and losses of infantry. General Heath's opinion was that if it was required to have 11th Division reconstructed for use later on, it would be wrong to make them fight at Gurun. He thought we should go right back to the Perak River without contesting the advance, except on the Muda by use of 3 Cavalry [with their armoured trucks] and by demolition.[36]

This opinion of Heath's was probably one of the reasons that prompted Percival to say after the war that Heath was too defeatist.

General Murray-Lyon's description of the state of his men was accurate. If he needed any confirmation of the low morale of some of his troops, he got it firsthand. In a 'Most Secret' summary of events concerning the 11th Division, dated 13th December, he reported:

> Now a most regrettable incident took place, but one which illustrates the state of morale of some of the units of the Division at this stage. When the bridge went up (Alor Star road bridge), although there had been no firing except for a few revolver shots against the motor cyclists and one burst of LMG fire, 1/8 Punjab which was sitting down in a palm grove about 600 yards from the bridge rose as one man and started to run down the road in a panic. Two companies of 2/16 Punjab did the same. It was only by getting into my car and getting ahead of them that I managed to stop them and turn them back.
> In the case of the 2/16 Punjab companies I actually had to threaten some men with my pistol before they would stop.[37]

It was now obvious to all that the Indian Army units in Malaya, for the reasons that have already been discussed, were not just low in morale, but were suffering from 'the jitters'. Not for nothing did the authors of the Frontier Force Regimental History record that: 'The expressions "to jitter" and "jitter parties" etc. were used in the Japanese campaigns of the Second World War to describe the Jap method of simulating an attack by a demonstration with noise, shouting and fire.'[38] Signs of the jitters were everywhere apparent.

Throughout the campaign, whether an Indian unit would stand and fight or turn and flee, often seemed to depend on the character and fighting attributes of its immediate commander. A sister company of the two 2/16th companies Murray-Lyon had to deal so strongly with, fought bravely to the last round under their Captain Holden. There were many such examples of unit bravery, but it was the jittery episodes which had such a decisive effect on the battles.

In his book *The War In Malaya*, General Percival remarked that Gurun was 'one of the strongest natural positions in North Malaya'. It is a defile that lies between Kedah Peak to the east and the thick jungle around Bukit Kuang in the west. The main arterial road and the railway from the north converge in it. The trouble was that the natural defences had not been augmented, and by the time they reached it, the troops of 11th Division were dog-tired and largely demoralised. The relentless Japanese gave them no time to develop defences, or even to rest.

Once again, led by tanks, the Japanese infantry attacked and managed to push back the British left flank held by 6th Indian Brigade. A counter-attack was led personally by Brigadier Selby, and some lost ground was recaptured. But as the Japanese gradually built up their numbers it became obvious to General Heath when he visited the front that the position could not be held for long. He obtained permission from Percival to fall back to the Muda River. During the fighting at Gurun and the subsequent withdrawal further heavy losses of men and equipment were sustained.

Almost from the start of the campaign reports came in that Europeans were operating with frontline Japanese troops. From the Muda area came one such report which Major Cyril Wild, an officer serving on General Heath's staff, recorded in his personal War Diary: '1400 hrs on 16 Dec, party of enemy in Malay dress headed by German try to cross Pekaka bridge, reported by 5/2nd Punjabs.'[39]

In a separate incident an Indian Army jemadar reported that a white man clad in a 'strange khaki uniform' had tried to cross a bridge shortly before it was to be blown. The man called out to the jemadar that he was British but, as he was acting suspiciously, he was refused permission to cross. The man ignored the order and in the ensuing hand-to-hand fight with the jemadar he was shot. Japanese troops hidden in the jungle on the far bank immediately opened fire on the jemadar, who was subsequently decorated for his courage. Later, when the Indians tried to recover the white man's body for intelligence purposes, they found it had been removed.

A War Correspondent, Ian Morrison, recorded other instances.[40] A jemadar and a havildar-major of a Sikh regiment, out on reconnaissance fourteen miles north of Ipoh, came across a tall blond man in khaki uniform. The white man killed the havildar but was killed in his turn by the jemadar, who then attempted to carry the body back to British lines. He had to leave the body when he was almost caught by a Japanese patrol, but he did bring back with him the weapons the white man had been carrying which, rather strangely, included a Japanese sword.

A soldier of the Argylls claimed to have shot a white officer in enemy uniform with an armour-piercing rifle. This incident on top of the others reported by Indian units caused Major-General Murray-Lyon, commanding 11th Division, to tell correspondents that there were white officers with the enemy, and that they were not just observing operations but were taking an active part in directing them.

One of the later sightings of Europeans was made by an officer. Lieutenant Fuller of 2nd Loyals spotted one and thought he was German. 'On the far side in due course the enemy put in an appearance to inspect the damage [to a bridge], among them being a German officer who was spotted by Lt. Fuller's platoon. Unfortunately it is not quite certain that he was one of the casualties inflicted.'[41]

The Australians spotted one of these Europeans on 6th January south of Muar. Two gunners saw a white man in uniform clambering out of a tank they had just disabled. The man grabbed a bicycle that was on the back of the tank and pedalled madly northwards.

Captain W. Tennant of HMS *Repulse*, the most senior survivor from the capital ships of Force Z, in the collection of notes about the Malayan campaign which he dictated after being repatriated home (he left Singapore at the end of December 1941) and which were based on his conversations with men who had taken part in the fighting, stated:

> The Japanese used riot drill tactics, sending over successive waves, the first waves being led by officers who looked like Germans because of their big build, dressed in slacks, shirt and helmet. The leaders were not prominent except in the first waves.[42]

In a cipher message to General Wavell on 4th February 1942 and repeated to the War Office in London, General Percival stated:

> Independent reports from various units of Germans operating with Japanese in Malaya strongly indicate that they are in fact present but impossible estimate scale or precise nature of their assistance since no mention in captured documents or by prisoners of war.

Percival went on to say that prisoners would be further examined on this subject.[43]

It is beyond doubt that there were white military men operating with the Japanese forces in Malaya. Furthermore, they were experienced enough in warfare to have been placed in the van of attacking units.

The Japanese, a very prideful and militant Asian race, would not have stuck white men in the van of their forces unless their presence was considered to be of value. No theory has previously been advanced as to the origin of these men. However, some British War Office files lodged at the Public Records Office contain some clues as to where they might have come from.

The four-months war between Thailand and the French in Indo-China over Thai claims to some of the French territory ended in February 1941 after the Japanese had intervened as arbiter. One of the French army units involved in that short-lived war was the 5,000-strong 5th Regiment, French Foreign Legion. Then, as in more recent times, a large proportion of the Legion were German nationals. The theory advanced here is that it was some of the Germans from the Legion's 5th Regiment who assisted the Japanese forces in Malaya. In 1945–46, when the French returned to Indo-China, it was found that this unit had largely 'disappeared during the Japanese occupation'.[44]

The French Foreign Legion had divided loyalties in the Second World War. The notion that a legionnaire's allegiance was to the Legion above all else was suspended during that conflict. The Legion in Algeria and Morocco remained in Africa and gave its allegiance to the Vichy authorities. So did the Legion's 6th Regiment in Syria under General Dentz, where they actually met in battle the Legion's 13th Demi-Brigade under the Free Frenchman, General Montclar.

The circumstantial evidence in British War Office files, which tends to support this new theory, is contained in messages sent to London from the British Military Attaché in Bangkok. He reported on 10th August 1941 that a German Jew deserter from the Legion in Indo-China, identified only as Adolph S., had arrived at the British Legation there. Adolph S. had stated that 'several German legionnaires had been advised to pretend to join the Free French forces and become spies'. This suggests that the Germans were at the very least attempting to make their presence felt in the area.[45]

After further interrogation of Adolph S. (who must have been given asylum in the Legation buildings) the British Military Attaché sent the following cipher message to the General Staff, Far East, on 11th December:

> To GS01 Far East. Message No. 163. Adolph S. German Jew deserter Foreign Legion Indo-China came British Legation Aug 10th and stated that there are 28 German deserters Foreign Legion now at Bangkok. They have all been found employment through the aid of [Thai] General Pratainak Montri. They have all been interviewed by German Legation and by German Military Attaché who has instructed various of them to get in touch with British Legation with a view to

joining Free French forces and becoming agents for Germans. German Military Attaché told remainder that Vichy Government has been approached with a view to release of all Germans from service with Legion in Indo-China. It is intended to form a German Corps in Far East. The nucleus of this Corps already exists in Japan and German Military attaché warned all deserters in Thailand that they will have to join this and stated that arms and equipment were ready for them. Adolph S. further stated that number of Germans in Legion was between 500 and 800 and that when he left 80% of these were Nazi.

If Adolph S.'s estimate of the numbers of Nazi sympathisers in the Legion's ranks in Indo-China is correct – and who might have known better than a Jew? – then there were between 400 and 600 of them. Picked men from among this number, especially any who spoke English, would have been extremely valuable to the Japanese as aides and advisors. The legionnaires had served for a long time in Indo-China, and had seen active service in the Thai war and in many local skirmishes with Cambodian and Laotian nationalists. They were thoroughly acclimatised, and were used to operations in an environment similar to that of Malaya.

This could account for the 'strange khaki uniform' noted by the Indian Army jemadar. It might also account for there apparently not being a record anywhere of these men. Many legionnaires served under names which were not their own, and the Legion publishes no records.

In addition to the white men serving with the Japanese army, there were two reports of white officers piloting Japanese planes. Both had been shot down. One of them died in his plane but the other was captured. Two German-speaking RAF officers, named Powell and Lofton-Paten, were sent north from Singapore to interrogate this man, but no record of this interrogation has been found.

During this part of the withdrawal Captain Wylie of 2/1st Gurkhas reported that his men – who had by then fought, dug three positions, marched 64 miles, had not had a single regular ration meal for over four days, and had only a few hours spasmodic sleep – were 'marching asleep, automatically. After a halt it was the greatest difficulty to wake everybody up and get on the move again.'

The decision to make what was to be a short-lived stand at the Muda had been largely dictated by the need to protect the nearby island of Penang, or at least to cover its final evacuation. Penang was the oldest British possession in the Far East, and the loss of it entailed the forfeit of considerable prestige. Of equal importance, the island was a junction for undersea communication cables and was a moderate-sized port.

Georgetown, on Penang Island, had been under air attack since 11th

December, and heavy casualties and damage had been sustained. On the night of the 13th the controversial evacuation of 'European women and children only' had taken place. Percival now advised the War Council in Singapore that there was no point in trying to hold on to Penang unless the mainland could be held; that the Muda River position was in danger of being outflanked by Japanese forces pouring down the Patani-Kroh road chasing the remnants of the Krohcol column. The decision was taken to evacuate the small remaining garrison on 17th/18th December.

Penang was another example, like the airfields, of the denial system not being implemented properly. The powerful radio station was not destroyed, so that soon after they occupied the island the Japanese were broadcasting propaganda from it all over South-East Asia. Many small craft were left intact, later to be put to good use by the Japanese in their landings further south.

General Heath now ordered a withdrawal to the Krian River where it was hoped that the swamps in the area would provide an effective anti-tank barrier and allow the severely mauled 11th Division time to rest and refit.

Over on the right flank on the Kroh road, 5/2nd Punjab Regiment met their first action under fire. Their commanding officer, Lieutenant-Colonel Cecil Deakin, reported that 'there were distinct signs of jitters'.[46] The 5/2nd Punjab was one of the 'Indianized' regiments of the Indian Army. All but a few of the most senior officers were ICOs, Indian Commissioned Officers, who had passed through the Dehra Dun Military Academy. Deakin reported that several of them showed 'a lack of calmness'. One NCO was placed under arrest for cowardice in withdrawing without orders. At one time 'rearward movement was stopped at the point of a revolver'. Again, 'the withdrawal of two companies had, it must be admitted, been solely due to unwarrantable panic'. Another officer 'was asked at the point of a revolver why he had withdrawn without orders'. The officer answered that the order to withdraw had been given by a more senior Indian officer, one who at the time was missing – rather conveniently one cannot help thinking. Later on summaries of evidence were sent to Brigade HQ on three sepoys suspected of inflicting wounds upon themselves.

The Argyll & Sutherland Highlanders were sent in to protect the flank of the main retreating force. They were soon engaged in heavy fighting, but broke contact on 18th December to join the remainder of the 11th Division behind the Krian.

By now the pattern of Japanese tactics was taking shape. General Yamashita's men moved fast down roads and tracks, using bicycles and motor cycles. Forward troops travelled very lightly, carrying with them only what was strictly necessary. They infiltrated behind British forces whenever they were held up. Tank-led thrusts were made against strong points. The infantry was ably supported by engineers who either erected temporary bridges or repaired demolished ones with remarkable speed. They used captured military vehicles and stores, and rounded up civilian transport and bicycles and turned them to their own use. There were several reports that the Japanese were using stockpiles of bicycles and other equipment that had been secreted during the pre-war months. In the air they had complete mastery.

The larger of the surviving British naval units in the Far East were now mainly occupied in escorting reinforcing convoys into Singapore. Only naval auxiliary units of doubtful quality were available to operate around the Malayan coast. Some Dutch submarines, which were under the strategic control of the C-in-C, Far Eastern Fleet, had some successes against Japanese shipping, their captains earning British decorations in the process. But like the RAF, the Royal Navy was to play only a minor supporting role in the battle for Malaya.

General Percival's aim was to delay the Japanese in the north as long as possible to give time for reinforcements, including vital air reinforcements, to arrive at Singapore. He had to achieve this delaying action without losing too large a part of his existing force, for they too would be needed to defend the Naval Base and 'fortress'. It turned out to be an impossible task.

The Japanese were now advancing down the Kroh-Grik road, causing more danger to Heath's right flank. He obtained permission to withdraw once more, this time behind the Perak River. Unfortunately this line of defence was not a good one as, for most of its course, the river runs parallel to the line of Japanese advance. While the main force retreated, the task of delaying the Japanese fell to the Argylls of 12th Indian Brigade on the Kroh road, and over to the west, to 28th Indian Brigade. These two forces took it in turn to withdraw, each covering the flank of the other.

Near Lake Chenderoh Power Station on 21st December, panic again set in among 5/2nd Punjab. An Indian captain reported that the enemy in his vicinity were letting off squibs. Colonel Deakin drily remarked, 'he was told that there was no known case of squibs causing loss of life, and to go out and stall the Japanese parties'.

Throughout the campaign the morale of the Indian troops was often detrimentally affected by the content of leaflets dropped by Japanese planes. During the fourth week of December a leaflet in anglicized Hindustani and English was distributed widely:

> The cruel English without tanks and planes are keeping the Indians here for sacrifice. You may have heard that their whole fleet has been sunk. Think and save yourselves. For your protection a large army has joined us. Escape to us.
> Free India Council.[47]

Percival made extensive command changes on 23rd December. In cables sent to the C-in-C, India, and the War Office he reported that he had promoted 'Paris, Stewart, Selby and Moorehead.' He proposed dispatching Major-General Murray-Lyon to India 'at the first opportunity' and Brigadier A.C.M. Paris was to take over command of 11th Division. (As Commander, 12th Brigade, Paris had been in Malaya longer than any other senior officer. His brigade – consisting of 2nd Argyll & Sutherland Highlanders, 5/14th Punjab, and 4/19th Hyderabad – had formed 'Force Emu', which had arrived in Malaya in August 1939.) Percival went on to report that he was 'granting sick leave to Brigadiers Lay, Carpendale, and Garrett, but do not propose re-employing them as Brigade Commanders'.[48] There is little doubt that British generalship up to this time, with but rare exceptions, had been lacking even given all the extenuating circumstances. As a result it seems that a search for likely scapegoats was already going on. But Percival must have changed his mind about Brigadier Lay for he merely transferred him from 6th Indian Infantry Brigade to the 8th. This proved to be a mistake.

By Christmas Day the bulk of the retreating forces had crossed the Perak. Few of them had had any chance to rest, and morale was sinking ever lower. On 27th December Colonel Deakin reported that 4/19th Hyderabad of 12th Brigade had been given the task of carrying out an outflanking counter-attack. He remarks, 'this seemed suicidal without the barrage and in view of our withdrawal. However, we had enough in hand in breaking off a hand fighting action and getting away, to be very concerned about the action of another battalion.' He went on, 'it was heard later that this attack was allowed to stand at the personal request of the CO, 4/19th Hyderabad, as he wished to blood his battalion; it had not yet been in action with the enemy. It seemed a strange way to go about it!'

On the following day the Hyderabads passed through Deakin's position going the wrong way, in what he described as 'rather a disorganised and demoralised condition, which did not do much to raise the morale of the men of the battalion, to say the least of it'. Worse was to follow. Deakin reported:

> At about 1430 hours Lieutenant Webber, Signals Officer Argylls, came into Battalion HQ and stated that the two forward companies of Argylls had broken and that the enemy were using tanks. This was cheering news!

Now came the only report in the entire campaign which is critical of the Argylls:

> It was found that Major Gairdner (acting CO, Argylls) and the remainder of the Argylls were coming back in confusion and

some panic amongst the troops was discernible; but what was
of even graver import was that they had carried with them A
and B companies of the battalion. Panic was spreading and the
CO, second-in-command, and Captain Luck had to hold up any
further withdrawal of the men of the battalion at the point of their
revolvers. The Argylls withdrew, and some order was evolved
out of chaos. Ruthless measures were taken.

Deakin did not elaborate on that last statement, but later that day he
recorded:

The battalion had again proved disappointing. It was heartbreak-
ing after it had seemed that the battalion had found its battle
legs again. The only excuse is the weariness of the men and
the bad example set by the other two battalions including the
British one.

On the same day, the 27th, the town of Ipoh was abandoned to the
Japanese, with the British now retreating towards Kampar. The now
reformed Argylls were once again fighting desperately. Then for two
days Japanese pressure eased against stiff British opposition, especially
that put up by the so-called British Battalion, an amalgamation of what
was left of the East Surreys and Leicesters. The easement did not last
long, for the British now found their left flank threatened by men of
the Japanese 11th Infantry Regiment under Colonel Watanabe who had
landed at several places south of the Perak River entrance using a flotilla
of small craft including some of those captured at Penang.

A fierce battle took place on 2nd January at Kampar, but now with
the British line of communication threatened by Watanabe's force, the
newly-promoted Major-General Paris had no recourse but to order another
retreat, this time to the last natural defence line north of the Johore border,
the Slim River.

Also on 2nd January the Japanese attempted another landing on the
west coast, this time in the vicinity of Kuala Selangor Lighthouse. It was
beaten off with heavy losses by artillery fire. Harry Bläckham was there
with the 73rd Field Battery. He writes:

I have not seen this action written up in any official or unofficial
literature. Accepting that it was of a comparatively minor nature,
I would have thought that, our successes being very thin on the
ground, it would have been worthy of some notice. We had been
joined by a Malay Volunteer section with their 18-pounders. On
the 2nd we saw craft out at sea, and we readied for action. There
was one larger ship of about 1500 tons, and she was trying to
protect six motor launches, each towing four or five others. All

were packed with Jap troops. About 600 yards from shore the small boats came on alone apparently expecting an unopposed landing. They really were a dream target and it was easy to shoot over open sights against slow moving small boats. We opened fire when they were 300–400 yards off and two of the motor launches and several of the towed boats were hit in the first salvo, and some were capsized by near misses. The rest turned back towards the parent ship. One section switched to the larger target, and two hits were scored which started a fire near the stern which burned until she was out of effective range. It was estimated that the enemy lost about 1000 men.

Whether or not that estimate of Japanese casualties was correct, the incident deserves to be recorded, for as Harry Blackham says, British successes were few and far between.

One of the many small mysteries of General Percival's conduct of the campaign is why he never used the 1st Independent Infantry Company for the purpose it had spent several months training for. This company was never included in any Corps or Divisional Order of Battle, a fact deplored after the war by its commanding officer, Major (later Lieutenant-Colonel) S.P. 'Shep' Fearon, of the 5/14th Punjab, who wrote in 1981 that his proposal that the company's name be included on the Indian Army Divisions Memorial at Sandhurst had received the blessing of General Billy Key. Fearon's company, 301 strong, had been formed on 1st April 1941 from 'volunteers' from all the British units serving in Malaya and from most Indian Army units.[49]

Seventy five per cent of the force was Indian and the rest British. It was self-contained with its own signals and motor transport sections, and was divided into five platoons.

In the early days of its formation 'much unnecessary trouble was caused by the poor quality of the British troops sent to the company. It was a heaven-sent opportunity for Commanding Officers to get rid of the worst elements in their own units. This was slowly put right.' (During a training session at Kuantan, eight of the company's British other ranks went on a drunken rampage in the town. They were returned to their regiments.) The company had been specially trained for operations behind enemy lines. They had trained in guerrilla warfare, in harassing lines of communications and derailing trains. Fearon said they were a 'highly trained band of experts', yet he also had to admit that 'the role of the company was never clearly defined, and several conferences at Singapore on this question left it nebulous in the extreme. The impression gained was that the Company was more an embarrassment to Malaya Command than a help.' At one stage he was told his men were to be used on the northern flank of Operation Matador.

As hastily formed commando-style units were used to raid in the enemy rear on occasion, the failure to make use of this specially trained unit for such operations seems strange. Fearon says that the Brigadier, General Staff (Brigadier Torrance) showed no interest in the unit. Perhaps this had something to do with the preponderance of Indians in it. Percival never had a very high opinion of the Indian Army, and possibly some of this rubbed off on his staff.

An incident occurred on 5th January close to two bridges that crossed the Slim River in the Batang Berjuntai area. The British Official History glosses over it largely, one suspects, because it showed extraordinary incompetence on the part of one of Brigadier R.G. Moir's Staff Officers who had been sent to take charge of the troops in the vicinity. (Moir was the Commander, Line-of-Communications Troops in Malaya, and had temporarily been given command of a scratch force in the area.) Major Fearon reported on the affair and other associated matters because the Staff Officer later made a report on the behaviour of a detachment of sixty Australian troops under Major D.T. Lloyd who had been attached to Fearon's command, a report which Fearon considered unjustified.

The Staff Officer (whom Fearon did not name, but who was a Major Heywood) first of all tried to get rid of Fearon's second in command, Captain Hofman, unbeknownst to Fearon and for no good reason. Later in the morning, with the unit under mortar fire from the far bank, Heywood attempted to change one of Fearon's platoon dispositions, ordering the platoon commander to take his men and 'swim the river and twist their tails'. The platoon commander refused, saying that he was under orders from Fearon to hold his position until ordered to withdraw. Later, strong words were exchanged between Fearon and Heywood over this matter.

About midday Heywood ordered Fearon's two spare platoons and the Australian detachment to advance over the bridge 'up to the T-junction and then, turning east, to drive the enemy into an estate where they were to be annihilated'. That order was bad enough, said Fearon, but worse was to follow. 'If our troops after meeting the enemy were to attempt to withdraw back over the bridge, said Heywood, he would order the blowing of the bridge to prevent the move.' Major Lloyd, commanding the Australian detachment, refused to undertake these extraordinary orders if his line of retreat was to be cut off. Fearon also protested strongly against the orders, and asked for them to be put in writing and the threat to blow the bridge categorically withdrawn. Later the whole plan was changed, and the responsibility for blowing the bridge was given to Fearon, who reported 'the AIF detachment under Major Lloyd then carried out a brilliant little operation north of the river, recapturing a hill dominating the road leading to the T-junction'. Fearon adds drily, 'Shortly after this the Staff officer was persuaded to leave for Jeran to have a look at other areas in his command. The CO, 3rd Cavalry, at Jeran never forgave me for persuading him to go there.'

The 3rd Cavalry Regiment of the Indian Army, to which Fearon was referring, had arrived at Penang on 28th November 1941, a little over a week before the Japanese attack. It had only five regular officers with it under Lieutenant-Colonel J.G.B. de Wilton. The average age of the cavalrymen, called *sowers*, was just seventeen. They had arrived in Malaya without their armoured cars, which did not catch up with them until after the campaign had begun. 'Thus the men were unable to gain experience in driving or maintaining them.'

The armoured cars, when they did arrive, were Marmon-Harringtons fitted with Vickers machine-guns. There was a fitting on the vehicles for a Boyes anti-tank rifle, but not the rifle itself. The officers were dismayed as the men had been trained with the Boyes and on the Bren gun but not the Vickers! On top of that the Marmon-Harrington had a poor cross-country performance, and so was 'more or less tied to the roads'.[50] General Heath, who had been expecting a well-equipped and fully trained armoured reconnaissance regiment, was horrified.

From 3rd Cavalry comes further confirmation of one of the ubiquitous problems of the campaign, poor communications. It is not much use having a reconnaissance unit, even a poorly trained one, if it cannot communicate properly with HQ. 3rd Cavalry reported an almost complete breakdown of wireless communications:

> The wet weather and the enclosed nature of the country may have been contributory factors, but the fact remains that the sets had not functioned properly from the beginning. Lieutenant Nicholls was a first-class signals officer and had spent a great deal of time trying to get the sets to function so this breakdown was all the more disappointing. Control, therefore, had to depend to a large extent on verbal and written messages delivered by despatch riders. All other units suffered equally during the campaign.

Under all but incessant air attacks at Slim River, the British had only forty-eight hours to dig themselves in. Exhausted and demoralised men were forced to work at night. Colonel Deakin wrote, 'the battalion was dead tired ... had withdrawn 176 miles in three weeks and had only three day's rest. It had suffered 250 casualties ... the spirit of the men was low and the battalion had lost fifty per cent of its fighting efficiency. During 5th January, I found a most lethargic lot of men who seemed to want to do nothing but sit in slit trenches. The deadly ground silence emphasised by the blanketing effect of the jungle was getting on men's nerves ... the jungle gave men a blind feeling.'

On 6th January General Percival sent the following message on tactics to all units:

> Operations have tended to develop more and more on guerrilla lines.

I believe that our young and inexperienced troops are now getting their second wind.

It is developing into a guerrilla war so let us also adopt guerrilla tactics. Formations should reduce their transport by sending all vehicles which are not immediately wanted well to the rear. Every platoon and section should be taught to become both tank hunters and Japanese hunters.

The object must be to destroy as many Japanese as possible and also to destroy his morale by constantly attacking him.

The doctrine to be inculcated into every officer and man is that they must always be looking for a way of getting at the enemy. If they are cut off, they are well placed for attacking the enemy from behind and should make every effort to do this before seeking to rejoin their own unit.

The tactics suggested were good, but Percival's statement that his inexperienced troops were getting their second wind, was over-optimistic. There is no evidence to show he was right. Perhaps it was a device to raise morale. One can also conjecture, in view of what had gone on before, that part of the reason for his advocating the sending of transport well to the rear was to stop it being used by troops fleeing southwards.

In the matter of transport Major Fearon commented:

Perhaps one of the most exhausting features of the campaign was the almost continual movement by night without proper lighting. Drivers fell asleep driving. Ditched vehicles were a common sight. It was necessary to have three drivers for every vehicle, one for day running and two for night.

He added:

Two 3-ton lorries of the Australian GP Transport Company joined us at Telok Anson and remained with us to Singapore. These two lorries with only one driver apiece did excellent work. The finest drivers of the lot were those of the AIF Transport Companies who appeared absolutely imperturbable right up to the end.

When the Slim River battle began early in the morning of 7th January, General Paris had only two brigades, the 12th and 28th, to protect the roads leading to the several bridges across the river. The balance of his force, made up of the combined rumps of the badly mauled 6th and 15th Brigades, had been sent over towards the west coast to protect his flank.

The Japanese attack came shortly after midnight. The British had laid a series of anti-tank barriers, but they were were quickly overrun by

Japanese infantry followed by the tanks themselves. They broke through the 4/19th Hyderabad position, virtually destroying that battalion. Then came the turn of the 5/2nd Punjab, and a heavy encounter began. 'The din,' reported Colonel Deakin, 'defies description. The tanks were nose to tail with their engines running, their crews yelling, their machine-guns spitting tracer, and their mortars and cannon firing all out.' The noise of exploding mines and Molotov cocktails, and of anti-tank rifle fire, added to the din. 'By 0700 hours it was apparent that organised resistance by the Battalion was nearly at an end.' Deakin's force fell back, only about thirty of them following their commander back to British lines.

Deakin wrote:

> How many men of the Battalion were killed and wounded and how many took to the jungle was not known and perhaps will never be known. Be what it may, the Battalion had disintegrated and had failed to stand and fight to the last man. Whether or not an Indian Battalion can be expected to stand against an overwhelming number of tanks with practically no anti-tank defence is not a question for decision in the War Diary.
>
> It must at once be admitted that the Battalion had been disappointing and had failed to come up to expectations as a fighting unit and at times had showed a great lack of collective and individual courage. The Indian Commissioned Officers except Lieutenant Chadda had failed to show leadership and that spirit of self-sacrifice and courage which is essential to Indian troops. Whether British Officers would have done so under similar conditions cannot be said, but the two in the Battalion who had the opportunity, did so.

Deakin went on to list some of the extenuating circumstances: a high proportion killed even before Slim River; no replacements; it had fought day-in and day-out for nearly a month with only three days of actual rest; when there had been no fighting at night, the troops had been on the move; they had been confronted by an enemy in overwhelming numbers and 'who pushed on relentlessly and with little regard to casualties'; incessant 'horror' from the air.

Deakin finished, 'Finally, if the condition of the troops of the 12th Brigade had been recognized and faced up to, the Slim River disaster might never have occurred.'

For disaster was exactly what it was. It was the Argylls turn to be hit next. Due to bad communications and lack of intelligence they were caught off-balance as Japanese tanks roared towards the Trolak bridge where demolition charges failed to go off. The Argyll area became the scene of innumerable and disconnected small fights. One Argyll company was practically annihilated, and only about a hundred men of the entire battalion managed to escape. Many were captured, soon to end up as prisoners in Pudu Gaol, Kuala Lumpur.

Having virtually destroyed the 12th Indian Brigade, the Japanese ploughed into Brigadier Selby's 28th Brigade positions. Under heavy pressure the Gurkhas were forced to withdraw, and many were lost while trying to ford the fast moving river. The Japanese had won a decisive and brilliant victory, created mainly by aggressive use of tanks.

On 30th December, a week before the Slim River battle, the Japanese on the east coast had attacked Kuantan with its important but long-evacuated airfield. As the British forces over in the west kept falling back, Brigadier Painter was concerned that his 22nd Brigade around Kuantan could be trapped in central Malaya. He was ordered to evacuate on 3rd January, and in a fighting rearguard action most of his force managed to escape westward. During the withdrawal from Kuantan, Lieutenant-Colonel A.E. Cumming, commanding 2/12th Frontier Force Regiment, earned the campaign's second Victoria Cross for leading his men in several fierce and close-range fights, although severely wounded.

On the day of the Slim River battle, General Sir Archibald Wavell arrived in Singapore on his way to set up his ABDA HQ in Java. The war had been going on for exactly a month, and now the whole of northern Malaya was in Japanese hands, and the door to Kuala Lumpur, the federal capital, was open to the enemy.

However, over the Johore border, the as yet untested Diggers of the 8th Australian Division were waiting to get to grips with them.

Chapter Eleven

The Battle for Johore

With the exception of a few supporting units such as the 2/3rd Reserve Motor Transport Company, the two Australian Brigades which constituted the 'short' 8th Division (a division usually consists of three or more brigades), had yet to see any fighting. The 2/3rd had performed brilliantly in support of some of the Indian battalions in the north, especially the 5/14th Punjab. Colonel Stokes, the Punjabis commanding officer, had served with the Australian veterans of the unit in Mesopotamia during World War One. A personal relationship had developed and there was no way those diggers were going to let down their old cobber. Several times the drivers under Major Kiernan extricated Stokes and his men from dangerous situations. Colonel Stewart of the Argylls was also to write a glowing tribute to these Australian drivers, as had Major Fearon of the 1st Independent Infantry Company. These Australian veterans were a credit to their country.

Well before the war began Major-General Gordon Bennett embarked upon a propaganda programme designed to build up his troops' confidence, and, it must be added, his own self-esteem. He made statements such as, 'one AIF man is equal to ten Japs', and, 'if there's any annihilating to be done around here, we are the ones who will be doing it'.[1] This was excellent morale-boosting stuff; but when he made remarks that disparaged the quality of British and Indian troops in the area compared with his own men, he was not just exaggerating for morale's sale. He made himself extremely unpopular with his British counterparts.

Although some of Bennett's units were among the best trained in Malaya, overall AIF training was patchy. 'Compared with the battle-trained veterans [of the 5th Japanese Division] we were babies,' wrote A. H. Harrison, an Australian gunner of 2/4th Anti-Tank Regiment.[2] His regiment was armed partly with 2-pounder guns, partly with 75mm guns, and partly with some odd guns captured from the Italians in North Africa. 'Apart from firing six shots out at sea from a few old French 75s, none of us had ever handled an artillery gun since we enlisted. We were going into action with a 2-pounder gun we had never fired, except in theory.' He went on, 'it was strictly amateurs v. professionals. Fortunately we were not aware of it.'

Harrison went on to describe the strange reluctance of some Australian infantry commanders to use anti-tank support. He singled out two commanders for special criticism in this regard, Lieutenant-Colonel Galleghan, 2/30th at Gemas, and Lieutenant-Colonel Robertson, 2/29th at Muar. He put forward two main reasons for this attitude. He said first that the commanders could not have received intelligence reports about the previous exploits of Japanese tanks at Slim River, and put this down to lack of efficiency on the part of Intelligence, pointing out 'that no sane commander who knew about the rout at Slim River could have been anything but eager for anti-tank support'. The second reason he gave was infantry commanders' reluctance 'to accept semi-independent groups into the Infantry orbit'. In the nature of things, anti-tank unit commanders, who were often mere second-lieutenants, were more expert at siting and control of their guns than infantrymen. 'The crux of the matter,' says Harrison, 'lay in an exaggerated regard for rank.' (In military terms, artillery units 'were in support but not under command'.)

It was over training matters that Major-General Bennett and one of his brigade commanders, Brigadier H.B. Taylor, fell out, a pre-war breach in relations which had serious effects during the campaign.

After the Slim River débâcle General Wavell was aware that it would now be impossible to halt the Japanese north of Johore. What was left of 11th Indian Division was a spent force and time was needed for it to rest and regroup. Twenty-five miles south of the Slim River (and about the same distance north of Kuala Lumpur) the Malayan road system became a complex of excellent roads, difficult to defend against Yamashita's tanks. A retreat to north Johore was therefore Wavell's only course. A strong line of defence could be established there using 9th Indian Division which was withdrawing from central Malaya, and General Gordon Bennett's 8th Division which would move up from Mersing although, since one brigade was left behind to guard that area, this entailed the Australian force being split into two. The defence line would run east to west across Malaya on the general line Mersing-Segamat-Muar. The 9th Indian Division would come under Bennett's command together with the newly arrived 45th Indian Brigade, commanded by Brigadier H.C. Duncan. This was to be called Westforce; the Australian Brigade left on the east coast constituting Eastforce.

The balance of 3rd Indian Corps would defend southern Johore while it rested and regrouped. The plan was for the vanguard of the British 18th Division – the 53rd Brigade expected to arrive at Singapore on 13th January – to relieve the Australian brigade left behind at Mersing which would then allow Bennett's Division to be reunited. The 53rd would, it was hoped, have time to carry out some training and become acclimatised.

This all looked good on paper, but it had several drawbacks apart from any spanners the Japanese might throw into the works. The main one was the splitting up of the Australian Division, about which Gordon Bennett was not at all happy; and the defence of eastern Johore had been severely weakened. Also Bennett's staff, with no war experience, were now to control Indian Army units they had not previously worked with. On top of all that, the envisaged defence line was only 120 miles north of Singapore.

The authors of the British Official History criticised this plan, not without justification. They considered that Heath, with his now experienced 3rd Corps Staff, should have retained control with different troop dispositions, but maybe Wavell was swayed in his decision by the initially favourable impression the outspoken and aggressive General Bennett had on him. Nor did General Percival care much for the plan. It was imposed on him, so it was said by General Kirby in his book *Singapore – The Chain of Disaster*, without discussion after Wavell had kept Percival waiting for sometime in an ante-room. Wavell was obviously not impressed with Percival's performance to date. Having issued his instructions Wavell then left for Java on 10th January, though he was to be back three days later.

Indian troops fighting rearguard actions vacated Kuala Lumpur on the 11th, whilst over to the east 9th Division was able to withdraw successfully from central Malaya. The Japanese air force could have badly mauled both withdrawals, but chose instead to concentrate on attacking the Singapore airfields.

At a conference held on 12th January at Segamat with Generals Bennett and Barstow (Major-General A.E. Barstow, commander 9th Indian Division) Percival received information about his Indian troops that disturbed him considerably. Following the conference he sent the following personal message to Wavell in Java:

Am NOT repeat NOT happy about state of morale of some Indian units. Believe Garhwalis and Dogras will continue to fight but some others doubtful. On 10 January two coys 2/9th Jats surrendered without fighting. Believe trouble due to enemy propaganda working on fertile ground resulting from excessive fatigue and enemy complete command of air.[3]

By daylight on 14th January all of Heath's units had passed through General Bennett's forward outposts. At General Heath's request there was now another change in command of 11th Division. Major-General Key took over, vice Major-General Paris. Key had orders to restore its morale as quickly as possible. The relieving of Paris, who reverted to his substantive rank of brigadier, looks much like another attempt to find a scapegoat, for the defeats at Kampar and Slim River could scarcely be laid at his door as the 11th Division was tired and dispirited well before he took command.

The loss of Kuala Lumpur was yet another blow to British prestige while conversely its capture boosted Japanese morale to a new high. To the delight of the Japanese commanders they captured with the city vast quantities of what they had come to call 'Churchill supplies' which the retreating British forces had failed to destroy. Among the many railway wagons captured was one containing newly-printed military maps of Singapore Island. Furthermore, the Japanese had to carry out only minimal repair work on the Kuala Lumpur airfield before they were able to use it.

The British denial system did not work well throughout the campaign. Although the civilian authorities did not seem to give the policy their wholehearted support, the blame for this must rest largely on the shoulders of the military. A strict scorched earth policy, like that carried out by the Soviets in their own country, would have been impossible; Malaya was populated by Asians who, largely, were not retreating southwards, and the land had to be left liveable for them. But even the less harsh British denial system was often left unfinished.

The main reason for the general failure of the denial plans, however, probably lies in the fact that they were designed to be carried out at the last possible moment and with morale generally low, the men left behind to do the job were not prepared to hang around for long.

Despite the impression that Colonel Masanobu Tsuji, General Yamashita's Chief of Staff, tried to give in his book about the campaign[4] that everything on the Japanese side went entirely in accordance with the plans he had drawn up, there is evidence, much more reliable than Tsuji's, that Yamashita expected to be stopped in his tracks in northern Johore. After the war General Douglas MacArthur's G2 section in Tokyo, led by General Willoughby, had Yamashita's reports to the Nippon government translated. Yamashita had reported that he was surprised at the lack of real opposition in Johore, and could not believe he would reach the Johore Causeway without savage fighting. This view is supported by Colonel (later General, Japanese Defence Force) I. Sugita who was Yamashita's Senior Intelligence Officer. He said, in 1966, that the absence of major defence works in Johore surprised the Japanese, and that, had strong defences been vigorously defended here, the Japanese might never have captured Singapore.[5]

The key to the defence of north-west Johore was the area between the small port of Muar on the west coast and the main road which, curving to the east from Tampin, passed through Segamat forty-odd miles inland. To defend this area Bennett had only four brigades, and one of these was the newly-arrived 45th Indian Infantry made up largely of raw recruits. The Japanese under Colonel Watanabe had already demonstrated their expertise in mounting outflanking landings from the sea, yet Bennett chose to use the inexperienced 45th to guard his coastal left flank, although it has to be added that both Wavell and Percival must have acquiesced in the decision. In a letter to Major-General Kirby, the Official British Historian, dated 13th October 1953, Wavell's son, the second Earl Wavell, and himself a soldier, said of his father, 'I still don't quite know how he did not come to have realised the unsoundness of Gordon Bennett's dispositions on the Muar Line during his visit on 13th January.' On top of everything else, 45th's commander, Brigadier Duncan, apparently did not much care for Australians and made no secret of the fact. One of Bennett's staff officers, Captain (later Lieutenant-Colonel) C.J.A. Moses, described Duncan as a very arrogant man with a caustic tongue who would not discuss things with him, and spoke about 'bloody Australians'. General Bennett deployed the remainder of Westforce along the main road.

On 15th January Bennett, who had come out of the command shake-up best of all, cabled his Minister for the Army in Melbourne (Bennett having recently returned from a quick visit to the AIF in the Middle East):

> Personal Army Minister. Am alive and fit am commanding forces covering Western Sector with British Indian Australian troops under my command. Now in action and in contact enemy. Our troops eager for fight. Trust enemy will soon realise I am alive.[6]

This showed his bellicose attitude, and at first it seemed he was living up to it.

Bennett was a great proponent of ambushes, and on 14th January his 2/30th Battalion set one up on the main road at Gemas just east of the bridge there. The ambush had been well practised. The twenty-minute action was a brilliant success, the Japanese losing many men. They would have lost many more had not one of their patrols cut the signal line to hidden Australian artillery batteries. It had been planned for them to open fire on the enemy bunching up west of the bridge after it had been blown, but although the gunners could hear the action they were unable to fire without direction.

Over on the west coast the rawness of the 45th Brigade showed almost as soon as the Japanese Imperial Guards hove into sight on 15th January. The Guards destroyed two companies of 7/6th Rajputana Rifles north of the Muar River and, after some fierce fighting, took the town of Muar the following day. Bennett's decision to deploy the Rajputanas north of the river instead of south of it, is one of many decisions he has been criticised for. Colonel J.H. Thyer, Bennett's Chief of Staff, said during a post-war conversation with Major-General Kirby:

> The orders for the 45th Brigade for the occupation of this line were by Bennett. Bennett had an ambush complex. If you could set ambushes right along your front it would fix everything, and that is why he ordered [Brigadier] Duncan to have two companies of each battalion across the Muar River.[7]

During the same conversation Colonel Thyer stated that, when Percival and Heath went forward to Segamat to meet with Bennett, 'he cruised around, dodging them, and then came back to Johore Bharu'. This suggests that Bennett was avoiding any possible interference with his plans.

The 4/9th Jat and 5/18th Garhwal Regiments of the 45th Brigade also came in for heavy punishment and, by the evening, the left flank of Westforce had crumpled. In addition to these frontal attacks the Japanese had also landed troops at Batu Pahat, in the rear of the 45th Brigade positions where there were many Japanese-owned rubber plantations. The Japanese army therefore had excellent intelligence of the area.

Captain F.E. Mileham of the Jats has left an account of his battalion's part in the campaign.[8] Most of it does not make inspiring reading. Such was the low morale of his men, who had only been in Malaya for two weeks, that, after learning that the CO, Lieutenant-Colonel J. Williams, and the Adjutant had been killed, he was advised by one Indian officer not to let the troopers learn of this for fear of driving morale still lower. Later a subedar tried to take some men down the road to Singapore without orders. He became abusive when stopped. Mileham reports, 'I put him in charge of Jemadar Ram Sarup and another VCO and I didn't see him again and think he was probably disposed of quietly.'

Brigadier Duncan, commander of the Brigade, later led a bayonet charge in which he was killed. (General Bennett once said of Duncan that he would have made a better junior officer than a brigade commander.) Mileham reports how, in that engagement, Second Lieutenant Frank Cope of the Jats 'dashed out from the cover of a ditch and endeavoured to carry the Brigadier to safety but was killed in the process'. Officer witnesses thought it was a deed worthy of a Victoria Cross, but like many other brave actions during the campaign it went unrewarded. Most such deeds were not, of course, reported until 1945. On top of this time-delay, authority is more inclined to reward bravery in victory than in defeat. However one Victoria Cross was awarded for this part of the battle.

With the collapse of his left flank General Bennett ordered his Australian 2/29th Battalion to Muar to restore the situation. By then he knew that his Division was not to be reunited; instead of getting his entire brigade from Mersing he only received one of its three battalions, the 2/19th under Lieutenant-Colonel C.G.W. Anderson. The events around Muar had developed so fast that General Percival gave the newly-arrived 53rd Brigade to General Heath to guard Bennett's line of communications instead of sending it to Mersing as originally planned. This was a mistake which probably could have been avoided. Bennett's Division had trained together and would have fought better as a unit.

Gunners attached to the Australian 2/29th put up a good performance against Japanese tanks early on the morning of 18th January, but at other points on the left flank the battle was not going at all well. The 45th Brigade, or what was left of it, was falling back on Bakri in some disorder. 'The Indians gave way in panic,' reported one Australian, 'piling into their trucks, and made a desperate bid to get away ... racing their engines in low gear, blowing horns furiously, and shouting at each other, impeding the 2/29th who were trying to push through to the front line.' The Australians took pot shots at the tyres, and the Indians, thinking they were under fire from Japanese, fired back. Bennett now sent in Anderson's 2/19th to support the 45th.

Bennett's main inland position around Batu Anam was now itself under severe pressure. That pressure and the situation over on his flank made the position untenable, and so he ordered a withdrawal to Segamat. Bennett and his officers were beginning to experience the despair and frustration their British counterparts had been experiencing for the past six weeks. Was there no way to stop the Japanese? It may have been reaction to this frustration that caused harsh words to be exchanged between Bennett and Heath at a conference called by Percival at Yong Peng on 19th January. The Australian Brigadier Galleghan was to say of the campaign generally, 'Heath and Bennett were antagonistic to each other; yet both believed in quickly concentrating the forces in Johore rather than prolonging the resistance in the north. Had they pulled together they might have persuaded Percival.'

On the death of Brigadier Duncan the command of the force on the left flank had fallen to Lieutenant-Colonel Anderson of the Australian 2/19th. He was to lead a combined force of Indian and Australian survivors in an epic fighting retreat to get back to British lines. His conduct was brilliant. Wireless contact with his force was at best intermittent and towards the end he was completely out of contact with Westforce HQ. On 22nd January two planes from Singapore managed a drop of food and medicine. Anderson kept his wounded with him as long as he could, but finally had to leave them behind. Most of them were to be massacred by the Japanese Guards Regiment, a war crime for which General Nishimura, the Guards commander, was to pay for with his life after the war. Eventually Anderson led to safety about 900 men out of the original 4,000, split about equally between Indians and Australians. For his gallantry and bold leadership he was awarded the Victoria Cross.

Meanwhile, on 20th January a disastrous 'friendly fire' incident took place. A defile close to a strategically important road junction ran between two hills, Bukit Belah and Bukit Pelandok, on the road to Yong Peng from the coast. The Japanese had taken Pelandok and so commanded the defile. As the defile was on Lieutenant-Colonel Anderson's line of retreat, Brigadier Duke of 53rd Brigade decided an attempt had to be made to retake it. The plan was for 3/16th Punjab to occupy Bukit Belah by dawn on 20th January whereupon 6th Norfolk would attack the other hill assisted by fire from the 3/16th. It seems that not only did one section of Norfolks start out early, but they also went up the wrong hill.

The only officer of the 3/16th Punjab Regiment who served in Malaya who is still living is Alan 'Kim' Butterworth, an acting captain at the time.[9] The incident is still stamped very clearly on his mind:

> Our CO Colonel Moorehead decided to send up 'D' Company under Second-Lieutenant Gerry Palmer, and also decided to go along himself to 'boost morale'. Nearing the top of the hill they came under heavy fire [from the Norfolks]. They shouted to the Norfolks with no result. They also heard taunting remarks from obviously Jap troops [who joined in the fire]. Colonel Moorehead was killed and Gerry Palmer was badly wounded by a grenade; the second in command, a VCO, gave the order to withdraw having suffered a loss of 22 killed and wounded; they carried down Gerry Palmer and he was sent to hospital.

Kim Butterworth concludes:

> The action was a disaster; the Japs were already up there and the company came under fire from both the Norfolks and the Japs.

It is not known what proportion of the twenty-two casualties came about from friendly fire. But Gerry Palmer's wounds (he survived them and three-and-a-half years' internment) were caused by a Japanese bakelite grenade. The loss of Lieutenant-Colonel H.D. Moorehead was a grievous blow to the battalion and to the campaign. He had commanded the Krohcol column, so had been in the thick of action from the beginning. Throughout he had been a great inspiration to his men. One of his havildars on hearing of his death, said, 'My heart is broken. There will never be a man more brave than he.' His adjutant, Captain C. Charlton, was to write, 'His death was a tragedy that should never have been allowed to happen, but to have served under him is the one compensation that the survivors of the battalion have left.' Praise indeed.

In the end, it had been all for nothing, for the British did not gain control of the defile. Apart from its obvious effect on the morale of the Punjabis, the incident had not improved that of the 6th Norfolks either.

While Colonel Anderson was conducting his retreat, the worsening military situation was not made easier by certain recriminations and threats emanating from the Australian camp. General Bennett, according to an official British file[10] complained bitterly on 20th January that he should have been permitted to withdraw earlier:

> He stated that his G staff had telephoned [Malaya Command] at

about 1300 hours stating that they were in touch [with the 2/19th and 2/29th Battalions] and asked permission to give the order. No decision was given. Enquiries made later in the afternoon were met with a denial that the original request had ever been made. He maintained that the two battalions might be lost through indolence or inefficiency of staff, and that he intended to make a full report. He added that if the two battalions were lost 'All Australia would know the reason'.

On 21st January a small specially trained Dutch unit was sent behind enemy lines from Labis to harass communications. The force was led by Captain Supheert and Lieutenants Kroon and Schultz, and consisted of eight engineers, eighty native jungle fighting troops and forty native porters (who were convicts). Captain Ivan Lyon, now of the SOE, was involved in the preparations for the expedition, and was at Labis to see them off.

In the remaining days on the mainland some units of the Commonwealth forces were to experience occasional minor successes, but such events were few and far between. However Artillery Sergeant Harry Blackham did experience one of these:

On January 23rd we were stationed near Kluang when we were told we were to go on an independent mission in support of 5/11th Sikhs in an advance on Niyor 10 miles to the north on the railway. We were exultant. At last we were to go the other way! Everyone's spirits rose.

Local planters told us that with care sufficient paths through secondary jungle were negotiable. We made very good progress, until 5/11th Sikh patrols spotted the main Jap body. The probing Sikhs reported back, and Colonel Parkin, one of the very best type of Indian Army officers, opted for an immediate attack. (The result made many of us wonder whether there would have been a different end to the Malayan campaign had similar tactics been generally employed.) Though the surrounding rubber trees were far removed from such, slight undulations in the land must have made the Sikhs think they were back on their beloved frontier. The Japs were routed so easily it made many of us wonder why we were so far down country!

What is more, when the the Sikhs went in with the bayonet, the Japs not only fled, they fled yelling, many of them dropping their weapons as they did so. One can understand to some extent. The sight of a horde of six-foot bearded, ugly Sikhs with turbans askew and yelling their heads off, frightened the life out of me – and I was behind 'em!

The Sikhs were brought to a halt only by a road block. They

immediately put up a perimeter style defence *à la* Khyber, around the whole force and Brigade HQ were contacted to request support, emphasising our limited success and suggesting the possibility of a further advance. We were advised to sit tight.

This story, and several similar incidents during the later stages of the campaign mainly involving Australian troops, show that the Japanese did not stand against cold steel. As Harry Blackham said, it is perhaps tragic that such tactics had not been employed widely from the start. The story also shows that even when limited success was achieved there was a strange reluctance on the part of commanders to take advantage of them.

It was probably General Gordon Bennett's lack of active military experience since World War One that left him open to the severest criticism of his generalship. It was not cowardice that led him always to set up his headquarters too far back from the front line. Major-General Kirby, the author of the British Official History, wrote in his own later book on the Malayan campaign, that 'Bennett was a man who believed in control from the rear, assisted by liaison officers, and never went forward in action to see for himself and to discuss matters with his brigadiers.'[11]

One of Bennett's brigade commanders, Brigadier D.S. Maxwell, a militia man and a doctor by profession, tended to rely heavily on Bennett. In consequence he always located his own HQ as close as he could to his Divisional HQ, so he too, was frequently out of touch with events. Lieutenant-Colonel (later Brigadier) F.G. Galleghan who commanded the Australian 2/30th Battalion at the Gemas ambush, said:

> He [Maxwell] had had no experience of issuing orders. He had never been told that a commander should go forward. At Gemas there was a perfect position for headquarters half a mile behind the rear battalion. Instead, Maxwell's HQ were 15 miles back at Segamat.

Galleghan added later that 'Maxwell never saw a forward post at any stage of the war.'[12]

Brigadier Maxwell's own explanation for his HQ always being an average of fifteen miles back from his forward troops, which during post-war interviews he agreed was too far, was that General Bennett 'was in agreement that he should be in close touch with the Division'. As Bennett had promoted Maxwell to command of the brigade presumably because he was impressed with Maxwell's military abilities, one cannot help wondering why he now thought his disciple needed this kind of cosseting. This placement of HQs too far in the rear was to play its part later on Singapore Island.

The subject of HQ placement was a long way from being the only criticism of Brigadier Maxwell, however. One of Bennett's staff captains, H.E.Jessup, said, 'Bennett had an attack complex, and Maxwell a withdrawal complex.'[13] Even Bennett seemed to have had second thoughts about his protégé. He told General Kirby after the war that he had to remind Maxwell when he complained about the fatigue of his men, that they had then only been in the war for two weeks compared with the seven of 3rd Corps. Maxwell was essentially a doctor and his men to some extent his patients.

When the battle for Johore began, Air Vice-Marshal Pulford's air force, even including the fifty-one hastily assembled Hurricanes that arrived crated on 12th January, was outnumbered by well over four to one. Pulford used his meagre force to the best purpose, but he had to concentrate on protecting the four airfields on Singapore Island and in giving as much cover as possible to the reinforcing convoys as they came within range. As the army withdrew southwards and the bombing attacks on Singapore grew in intensity, he had little option but to withdraw his bombers and reconnaissance aircraft to Sumatra. The Dutch aircraft which had operated gallantly from Singapore island also withdrew to guard the Netherlands East Indies.

On the night of 26th/27th January the two old destroyers, HMS *Thanet* and HMAS *Vampire*, made a valiant attempt to intercept a Japanese supply convoy protected by a cruiser and modern destroyers off Endau on the east coast. *Thanet* was lost, but *Vampire* managed to escape. On the previous day the convoy had been attacked twice by the RAF. Among the many British aircraft lost were ten Vildebeeste planes with most of their crews. No wonder the obsolete Vildebeeste, with its top speed of around 100mph, was known as the 'flying coffin'. Few Vildebeeste crew members were to survive the war. After that, Pulford had still fewer aircraft with which to defend Singapore.

At a meeting Percival had with his senior officers on the 25th one of the matters discussed was the possible withdrawal to Singapore Island. The exact circumstances are not clear, but apparently Generals Heath, Bennett and Key left that meeting with the impression that Johore would definitely be evacuated, though Percival had at that time made no final decision. However, he had given General Heath permission to issue a map with the phased withdrawal plan marked on it. Acting on his impression of that meeting General Bennett issued instructions for the withdrawal to take place at midnight 26th/27th. As Stanley Falk says, perhaps the heavy pressure his Westforce was experiencing from the Japanese 5th Division 'encouraged Bennett in this belief'.[14]

Be that as it may, on 27th January Percival was given authorisation by General Wavell to make such a withdrawal at his own discretion. By now Japanese pressure was so great that it was no longer a question of whether or not to withdraw, but of how it could be done with the least possible loss.

Over to the east Brigadier H.B. Taylor, and his Australian 22nd Brigade at Mersing, received Bennett's order to withdraw and began doing so on the night of 26th/27th. He fell back on Jemaluang. He set up an ambush on the way and inflicted heavy losses on the Japanese 55th Regiment. In the process of falling back Taylor, 'reluctantly' according to the Australian Official Historian, had to abandon Captain J.L. Edgley's company of the 2/18th, which was cut off. In a statement about Taylor's withdrawal, Colonel Thyer, the Australian Chief of Staff, was less kind than the historian about this incident. He said, 'Taylor withdrew to Jemaluang and abandoned a Company in the Nithesdale area on the plea that his first duty was to comply with Heath's [withdrawal] order.'

Of much more significance, during the first phase of the withdrawal Brigadier Painter's entire 22nd Indian Brigade was cut off. The main fault for this lies with Brigadier Lay of the 8th Indian Brigade. Lay was the man Percival had reported he was granting 'permanent' sick leave to a month before but then reprieved and transferred him from the 6th Indian Brigade to the 8th in place of Key, promoted to command 11th Division. It is likely that Lay was already a broken man.[15]

Lay's 8th Brigade was placed to the south of Painter's brigade, and one of his Indian sappers wrongly blew a railway bridge between the two positions. The bridge was Painter's only direct route to the south. Along with the bridge went the telegraph line, then the only means to communicate with Painter because he had sent his radio equipment south earlier with his transport. Lay also failed to occupy a position selected by the commander of 11th Division, General Barstow, but instead moved further south down the railway towards Sedenak, thus leaving a considerable gap between the two brigades. Lay made no attempt either to repair the telegraph line or to inform Painter that the bridge in his rear was down.

The man who soon took over command of 8th Brigade from Lay, Colonel (later Brigadier) W.A. Trott, was in attendance at the dramatic meeting between General Barstow and Brigadier Lay which followed this incident. He presumably kept a diary of events, because this is how he described it:

On the morning of the 28th January as was General Barstow's habit, we set out from Sedenak to go up and see his commanders. We had not gone very far when we met Lay. Barstow said, 'Where are your battalions?' Lay said, 'They're all about here.' Barstow said, 'Good gracious me, you've sold the show, there must be a very big gap between you and 22nd Brigade.' 'Oh well,' said Lay, 'we blew the bridge accidently last night.' 'Well,' said Barstow, 'what is the position?' [Lay] 'There is a good deal of fire coming from the right flank.' Barstow said, 'Hell take you man, get a battalion on to that high ground.' He was very cross indeed. I was very nearly put in command myself. He considered that a very serious tactical error had been made a) in blowing the bridge and b) in not covering the bridge. 'Now,' he said, 'get the battalion on the move straightaway. I am going up to see Painter.'[16]

Trott went on to record that:

Lay was useless as a brigadier. He was washed up. If you think Lay's reaction would have been to draw his sword and rush in, you're quite wrong. I would never have left the railway, and would have fought through there against all odds.

Strong words from one army officer about another.

Australian Staff Captain Moses was also at that meeting. He recorded in his diary that General Barstow said he would have to replace Brigadier Lay.

It was during General Barstow's attempt to reach Brigadier Painter that he was killed. Colonel Trott and Captain Moses were in attendance at the time, but both managed to escape. Barstow's loss was a major catastrophe, for not only was he one of the better British generals, he was just about the only one amongst them who could get on well with Gordon Bennett.[17]

Brigadier Painter and his 22nd Brigade attempted a wide trek through the jungle to get back to British lines but eventually he and 350 survivors had to surrender. Less than a hundred men of 22nd Brigade eventually managed to reach the Johore Strait and cross into Singapore after the causeway had been blown. During the trek Painter records that on 1st February, when they met up with a Japanese patrol, men of 5/11th Sikhs, tired out after days of jungle marching, refused to fight: 'Officers of the regiment and of Brigade HQ tried to rally them but without success. A similar condition prevailed amongst the few remaining troops of 2nd Frontier Force Regiment.'

Painter went on to say that some of the Sikhs, together with the men of Frontier Force, discarded their equipment and went over to the enemy. He added, 'OC 2nd Royal Garhwal Rifles reported that his men were in hand.'

Thus the main blame for the loss of Painter's Brigade (and indirectly the death of General Barstow) must lie with Brigadier Lay. However the Australian Colonel Thyer casts the blame a little wider. He said, after the war, that Colonel J.B. Coates, on General Heath's staff, should have requested that the 27th Australian Brigade, some six miles north-east of Lay's position and thus guarding one of his flanks, be asked to stand firm until Painter's force had closed back on 8th Brigade and made contact. He went on:

> On the contrary the withdrawal order given late on the 28th after Bennett's return [from a meeting with Heath] did not make any allowance for the predicament of the 22nd Brigade. This might horrify you. It is contrary to the accepted demands of military virtue. But in looking at it you must try to recognise a gradual build-up of a psychology which vitiated the principle of co-operation and the full sense of responsibilities to subordinate commands. Of this there is ample evidence. Duke [Brigadier Duke commanding 53rd British Infantry Brigade] mucked about with his brigade in front of Yong Peng and left an attack stillborn.

Then Colonel Thyer mentioned Brigadier Taylor's abandonment of a company of the 2/18th because of Heath's order to withdraw. 'He [Taylor] had no thought of protest.' Thyer added:

> Key would not delay his withdrawal on to the Island. I asked him to hold up for two hours to protect our rear at the Senair road junction. These are incidents within my knowledge. There are numerous others. The thought prevailed 'just another unit lost'.

The first withdrawals were carried out under extremely difficult conditions. Westforce suffered most from Japanese attempts to wreck the plan. Japanese fighters and bombers made attack after attack. A flanking troop movement was beaten off by a bayonet charge from Australians of 27th Brigade. The yellow smoke flares used by the Japanese to repel the charging Australians caused another gas alarm.

In just two short weeks the Australians had caught the withdrawal bug. By that time the British and Indian troops had had plenty of practice at it, but even so, Brigadier Lay did not properly conduct his brigade's part in the final one on the mainland. It is scarcely surprising therefore that some of the Australian units did not withdraw to Singapore Island well either. In their case the situation was made worse by their lack of training in withdrawal exercises. Withdrawal was a dirty word with General Bennett to the extent that, as Colonel Galleghan says, 'one of the mistakes he made in our training was that he never let us do withdrawal exercises'. Germane to this, O.D. Gallagher, the Singapore correspondent for the London *Daily Express*, wrote:

> Major-General Bennett often told war reporters in interviews that his men would never retreat because they did not know how to retreat – they had not been trained to retreat. The spirit was admirable, but the wisdom of the decision doubtful. How

could the Australians be expected to make an orderly, fighting withdrawal if such a manoeuvre had not been included in their training?'[18]

The final stage of the withdrawal plan to Singapore island was for the Australian 22nd Brigade, reinforced by Gordon Highlanders, to cover a four-mile perimeter centred around the Johore Causeway. They would hold the perimeter allowing 3rd Indian Corps to pass through. Then they in turn would fall back through an inner perimeter manned by a unit who would be prepared to fight to the death if necessary to allow time for the causeway to be blown. In all of Malaya Command there was only one unit with that kind of fighting reputation. The 2nd Battalion Argyll & Sutherland Highlanders, now consisting, with replacements, of less than 250 men, took up positions there.

Early on New Year's Eve the Australians, and the Gordon Highlanders manning the outer perimeter, withdrew and crossed the causeway. They were piped on their way by the two remaining Argyll pipers. Unaccountably the Japanese did not put in an appearance. Then the Argylls themselves marched over led by their pipers. Their commander, Colonel Stewart, accompanied by his batman, was the last to cross. It was a heart-stirring and glorious finish to an inglorious campaign.

Then sappers blew the charges they had laid, and parts of the causeway disappeared in a cloud of smoke. The charges also destroyed the pipeline which brought fresh water to the island's reservoirs.

After a retreat lasting fifty-five days, far longer than both the retreat from Mons in World War One and the retreat to Dunkirk in the Second, the men of Malaya Command were back in the 'impregnable fortress' which for most of them had been their first stop in the Far East. But far from being 'impregnable' it was, in fact, unquestionably pregnable.

Chapter Twelve

Retreat in the West

The first air attack on Singapore had come in the early hours of the morning of the first day of the campaign. Lieutenant (later Lieutenant-Colonel) Charles Verdon of the Royal Marines was aboard *Prince of Wales* during that raid on 8th December 1941: 'We were moored alongside the Naval Base. The place was ablaze with lights. We heard the Jap planes go over, and heard them coming back again after they had dropped their bombs on the city. As the sound of their engines died away the dockyard lights were at last switched off!'[1] That delayed reaction on the part of the authorities seems to encapsulate the performance of officialdom in the ten weeks before the fall of Singapore. The raid caused 193 casualties, mostly among the Chinese population, including 60 fatalities.

Since the end of December Japanese planes had come over every day creating havoc in the streets and causing many more casualties. How many people died in these air raids was never fully documented.[2] Brigadier Ivan Simson, who combined the job of Director-General of Civil Defence with his military one of Chief Engineer, said the number of killed and wounded could have been as high as 2,000 each day towards the end. Burials went on at the rate of about 150 daily, but many bodies lay undiscovered on rubble-covered bomb-sites and stayed there until they rotted.

There were many other signs of war. Trains from the north brought down an ever-growing stream of military casualties; and the city was overflowing with refugees from the mainland. Many civilians had been evacuated from the island, but as evacuation was carried out on a voluntary basis many of the earlier ships that came in with supplies and reinforcements, ships of substantial size which could have carried away many of the people known as *bouches inutiles* (literally, useless mouths), left either empty or half-empty.

For example, *Orion* and the Dutch *Marnix Van Sint Aldegonde*, sailed on 31st December for Australia and Cape Town respectively, with European women and children and wounded soldiers on board, but they could have carried many more.[3] Right up to the last two weeks before capitulation the civil administration made little attempt to organise a proper evacuation and by that time the number of available ships was severely limited. But even when *Devonshire* and the Free French *Felix Roussel* sailed for Bombay on 6th February in Convoy Emu, the two

vessels carried only 2,400 people between them, and many more could
have been crammed aboard. Almost to the end officialdom caused delays
by insisting on passport checks. Most people were required to pay
their own passage money and when signs of profiteering appeared the
Governor, Sir Shenton Thomas, issued an order controlling ticket prices.
The P&O company was given the job of organising passages and when
the bombing caused them to move out of their city centre offices this
made the task of obtaining passages even more difficult.

Some civilians organised their own evacuation near the end, even going
to the length of commandeering the ship they used. One escapee who
reached India, P.E.M. Holmes, reported:

> No thanks are due to the Government for evacuation. Every
> person I met got out on his own initiative with no assistance
> and, in one case, Owler of Thorneycrofts and his men together
> with the Hulme Pipe people, commandeered a 2,000-ton steamer
> which was lying unused, loaded 200 tons of coal into it, and
> took off together with 810 passengers, the ship being designed
> for about 40 ... There was no Government attempt to evacuate
> women, and a good many must have been left behind.[4]

Another successful escapee was Mrs C.M. Battenberg. She later wrote:

> You will wonder how it was possible for everything to be left so
> late, but must remember that we were told by the Governor that
> there would be no organised evacuation and that Singapore 'must
> and will not fall'. No one ever dreamed for a minute that Singapore
> would go and practically everyone was taken unawares. There
> was no warning given to the civilian population which would
> have enabled them to dispose of valuables and make financial
> arrangements in time.[5]

The matter of race was the root cause of the Governor's lack of
enthusiasm for a compulsory evacuation policy. Few Malays and Indians
wanted to leave, but a number of Chinese did so wish for they had more
to fear from the Japanese. But where were they to go? The Netherlands
East Indies was prepared to take some, and even Australia eased her
'whites only' policy to an extent, but would not have been prepared to
take an unlimited number of Asians. So, in the main, the evacuations
which did take place were for Europeans only, but even these were not
compulsory. Brigadier Simson was highly critical of the official failure
to compel evacuation, calling it 'a sort of perverted kindness, which in
fact is really being far more cruel both to those who have to stop behind
and to those who should have left under orders'. One can sympathise
with the Governor's lack of enthusiasm for any policy which smacked

of racialism. He thought that any order compelling Europeans to evacuate – they would have had little difficulty in finding a haven somewhere – would have looked extremely bad in the eyes of the local populace, which is undoubtedly true. But his attitude contrasts strongly with the policy adopted by the Governor of Hong Kong who ordered out most of the white women and children in that colony well before the war began. If a Military Governor had been in charge of Singapore there is little doubt what his decision would have been. An early evacuation would have saved the lives of many of the women and children who died trying to escape in the fleet of small ships that fled the island during the last few days, or in Japanese prison camps over subsequent years.

The Singapore censors kept a tight grip on everything published. Very few of the ordinary populace of the island were aware of just how badly the military situation on the mainland was going. The news that was released was usually well out of date and full of false optimism. Right up to the end the authorities were reluctant to tell the truth. Had they been more open the number of voluntary evacuees among the European women and children would have been larger and they would have left earlier and almost certainly reached safety.

Officialdom came in for severe criticism in other matters too. The Air Raid Precaution organisation did its best in the face of much reported official apathy. Said a business man, C.E. Hudson:

> The ARP organisation consisted of a band of keen businessmen backed by a sterling body of Asiatics. What was done by these men, in spite of official obstruction and complete lack of understanding, assistance and sympathy, was astonishing. That it functioned at all was due entirely to these men, not to any efforts of the Government. It is right and proper that this should be made known.[6]

There was much criticism about the way employees of the Malay Civil Service (MCS) conducted themselves in those last weeks. George Seabridge, Editor-in-Chief of the *Straits Times*, writing in India in March 1942 within weeks of his escape from Singapore, said:

> Singapore itself was in a state of almost complete chaos from the end of December. Civil Servants who had evacuated from the Malay States sought to set up temporary departments in Singapore for no other apparent reason than the preservation of their jobs. Even the FMS Income Tax Department set itself up in Singapore after the last of the Federated States had fallen into Japanese hands.[7]

Other critics had similar stories to tell. As well as trying to maintain their own little empires there is evidence that civil servants and other people in Government employment just could not adjust to wartime conditions. Everything still had to be carried out by the book. As Brigadier Ivan Simson wrote:

> Officialdom was generally chairbound and lacked the drive and urgency needed to get things done quickly. Quick decision and action proved impossible for those whose working lives had been spent on committees and deliberations when it seldom mattered if action was taken next week, next month, or next year. They were incapable of acclimatizing themselves to the speed essential in war.[8]

Simson went on to cite examples of official delays, and of urgent matters that were 'lost' in government machinery. Even when the Governor himself got involved matters were still often passed from department to department, exactly as they had been in pre-war days.

What was the reason for this official apathy? Like most civil services and government agencies the Malayan Civil Service (MCS) was not a meritocracy. Promotion was invariably based on seniority. It used to be said that providing you made only minimal provable mistakes, kept your nose reasonably clean, were prepared to cover your superior's errors and omissions (without making it obvious just how often one was having to do so?), got drunk only in private, and providing you were not an obvious faggot; and providing the climate either retired off or killed off all the other members of the class of '28 before it did you, then you would rise to the most senior post in the Department. Methods and procedures were passed down and were deviated from only at one's peril. It was a lay form of apostolic succession.

Although the system could and did produce some senior men of distinction – A.H. Dickinson, Inspector-General of Police was one, although strictly speaking the police were not part of the MCS – it often led to mediocrity and lethargy at the top, the latter accentuated by the exigencies of the climate, the effect of which rose in remorseless progression as retirement age crept ever closer.

Criticism of the European residents of Singapore was not confined to Government employees. There were various reports about the amount of drinking and desperate revelry to which residents were prone in the ten weeks between the attack on Kota Bharu and the capitulation. These stories seem to have been started by certain British newspaper correspondents out to make good copy, and many writers in Britain and Australia have since embroidered the tales.

Europeans stationed in the tropics have always indulged a little more heavily than they might have done back home; the need for liquid intake is higher, and the comparatively high salaries combined with low prices meant that more could be spent on entertainment. 'The good life' was one of the perks of living in a hostile environment. But there is little in the way of firm evidence to show that much more drinking went on among the white civilian population in those last days than had gone on before. Certainly there was a tendency for people to enjoy themselves whenever they could in those last tense weeks; there were nightly dances at Raffles and other city hotels and, at the other end of the scale, the New World and Great World dance halls with their taxi-dancers did a roaring trade. But one can hardly blame the participants for that. These tension-relieving practices of a populace under air attack were not confined to Singapore. As anyone who lived through the London 'blitz' will recall, life tended to be lived to the hilt then, for tomorrow you might be dead.

Certain preparations had been made in Singapore for the coming siege. (Newspapermen were forbidden to use that word by the censors; they had to use 'investment' instead.) The Pavilion and Capital cinemas had been taken over as food dumps. A form of rationing had been introduced, far more generous than that in Great Britain. Many cattle had been brought in from the Dutch Indies and mainland Malaya. N.R. Jarrett, the British Resident in Selangor, later reported that a MCS Veterinary Officer was faced with the job of denying to the enemy 2500 head of Government-owned Bali cattle. These cattle were grazing peacefully in coconut estates in the Banting area a little south of Kuala Lumpur as the Japanese neared. The Vet (his name is not known) tried unsuccessfully to arrange rail transportation; he could not obtain road transport either. He toyed with the idea of slaughtering the stock but apart from the mammoth size of the task, the very thought of it appalled him. Instead he recruited relay teams of Tamil 'cowboys' to make a 200-mile cattle drive down the east coast road to Singapore. He lost only three of his charges on the way even though he had often to get them off the road to allow military transport through. The herd crossed the causeway only a few days before the last Commonwealth troops.

January brought with it outbreaks of looting on the island. Some of this was the work of Asiatics, but by the end of the month most of it was being laid at the door of small marauding bands of British, Australian and Indian troops coming in from the mainland. Desertions had begun. The duty officer at Fortress HQ reported on 29th January:

> Patrol sent out has found five deserters, four from Navy, one from RAF, all European. They apparently took a boat from Seletar. Patrol caught the RAF man but not the Navy. The RAF man is now at Calder Harbour boom. The boat has been destroyed.

No indication is given about the fate of the RAF man, but one suspects that the action taken was drastic.

At the end of January, too, some Chinese youths took advantage of the situation as many full warehouses were put to the torch as part of the denial process. A seventeen-year-old lad, Lee Tian Soo, was one of many who decided to rescue an item or two for his family rather than see them go up in smoke. He made off with some bundles of cloth only to be thwarted by a gang of Indian soldiers who snatched his loot from him.[9]

Much of the looting by soldiers was of alcohol. When this situation showed signs of getting out of hand, the Governor issued a proclamation on 29th January imposing a curfew from 9pm to 5am. That helped the fight against looters and it also put paid to most of the night-time rollicking in the hotels. This was followed on 30th January by a proclamation of martial law. From now on anyone found acting against the public security, or looting, committing treason or helping the enemy, would be shot.[10]

The withdrawal from the mainland, completed on 31st January, had been a closely-guarded secret. It was not generally known until twenty-four hours later when the Sunday newspapers for 1st February informed their readers that the island was invested. Noel Barber probably best summed up the feelings of the Singapore citizenry at that time in his book *Sinister Twilight*:

> To the people of Singapore, this was the classic beleaguered citadel of military history – stoutly defended, well prepared for siege warfare, and above all surrounded by Churchill's 'splendid moat' across which, given a determined defence, no enemy could hope to force a passage. At first Europeans compared their role in history yet to be written with the embattled defenders of Malta and Moscow, not realising that the circumstances were completely different – that Malta was an impregnable fortress honeycombed with rocky shelters, whereas Singapore was a shelterless, swampy island; that Moscow was the heart of a country whose citizens preferred death to dishonour, whereas Singapore was a hotchpotch of many races with hundreds of thousands of people who hardly knew what the struggle was about.[11]

During the second week of February another step was taken to stop looting and drunkenness among the troops, for by then the deserter situation was clearly getting out of hand. An order was issued that all stocks of alcohol were to be destroyed and an absolute ban was imposed on the sale of it. A report from Hong Kong, which had fallen on Christmas Day 1941, that drink-crazed Japanese soldiery had gone on a rampage of murder and rape, played its part in this decision of the Governor's and was the official reason given for it but, despite the destruction order, deserters and stragglers were somehow able to ferret out supplies of some sort or another up to the end. An ex-Senior Officer of the Singapore Police took part in this operation:

> Early in February I was sent to John Littles, one of the department stores in Raffles Place, to supervise the destruction of their stocks. We decided that the best way to supervise was to give a hand. We started smashing the bottles against a wall. How long this orgy took I can't remember, but I do remember thinking that this was the craziest few hours I was ever likely to see. We must have destroyed a fortune.[12]

Similar operations but on an even larger scale went on at bonded godowns in the docks and at the one run by Caldbeck McGregor in the city. One-and-a-half million bottles of whisky alone were destroyed, which gives an indication of the scale of the operation. Chinese *samshu* stills which produced a potent liquor from fermented rice did not escape the net either; 60,000 gallons of it was run to waste. All this liquor ran away into storm drains or directly into the sea with the fumes pervading the immediate areas for days afterwards.

Private liquor stocks had to be destroyed as well, or unofficially and hastily disposed off in a more congenial way. Edwin Glover, Managing Editor of the *Malayan Tribune*, tells how he disposed of his private cellar which he had collected and stored for years for his retirement at Cameron Highlands:

> The previous day I had already handed over twenty cases for distribution among the [nearby] troops ... but there remained some very special bottles to be broken rather than leave them behind to rouse the licentious fury of possibly already victory-drunk invaders. We spent the next hour smashing bottles of precious liquid from some of the finest vineyards of France. We were not the only people engaged in the same occupation that night.[13]

Glover also reported how he knew Singapore was to fall when the Chinese shopkeepers and bar owners began demanding cash in place of the established practice of chit signing. 'It was then I knew that Singapore's number was up.'

As on the mainland, parts of the denial system on Singapore Island did not work well. The army personnel who were guarding the northern shore in the vicinity of the Naval Base after the Base was vacated by the Royal Navy, were surprised to find many facilities there virtually intact, and they were able to help themselves from stocks of supplies the Navy had left untouched. This was despite the fact that many of the Dockyard personnel, who escaped from Singapore, produced reports in India that indicated they had left the Base in ruins. This may not have been entirely the fault of the people engaged in the denial process. When M.E. Adams, the Superintendent Civil Engineer at the Singapore Naval Base, made his report in Colombo on 28th February 1942, he said:

> It was exceedingly difficult to get definite decisions concerning denial. Both RAMY [Admiral Spooner] and myself were seriously concerned after the fall of Batu Pahat and pressed the War Council for definite decisions ... but they were always reluctant to assume the worst, and neither then nor very much later was the impression given that the Island would fall.

The monsoon weather, which had played a significant role at times during the battles on the mainland, was kinder on Singapore Island during those first few days of February 1942. The monsoon had affected the operations of the Australian reconnaissance Hudsons during the forty-eight hours preceding the outbreak of war, and detrimentally affected both sides during the initial landings at Kota Bharu. Later, heavy monsoonal rains had inundated many of the defensive positions at Jitra. Now, as if to compensate for all that, the days and nights were fine and clear in Singapore. It was close to the end of the north-east monsoon season and, although it was still very hot, the energy and mind-sapping humidity had dropped.

As the defending forces took up their allotted positions, Japanese air attacks increased in intensity. The sight of a friendly aircraft overhead was now a rare treat, and the gunners of the anti-aircraft defences with their paltry 150 guns – most of them light Bofors and mainly disposed around the island's airfields and Keppel Harbour – had their work cut out. Now shells from Japanese artillery positioned on the mainland added a new dimension to the general horror.

The denial programme was speeded up. Banks fed Straits $5 million in notes into a furnace. The police took their records out to sea and dropped them overboard in weighted sacks. The machinery and slipways at the small shipyards on Tanjong Rhu were destroyed, although many Chinese-owned engineering businesses received official exemption from destruction by order of the Governor.

During the ten days before the end, the sky over Singapore was black from the smoke of burning oil installations, from those in the north around the deserted naval base, down to those on the islands to the south of Singapore. The air was so full of oil smuts that they sometimes fell like black snow. Said Muriel ('Molly') Reilly, 'I would awaken up at night almost choking on the smoke and oil-laden atmosphere. At times the whole blue sky was obscured by this pall and on one occasion, when some rain fell, our house was covered with a black oil film.'[14] When the stocks of rubber in the godowns of Keppel Harbour were put to the torch, this added to the pall of smoke and brought with it such a distinctive and acrid stench that some people who were there are still able to 'smell' it.

One of the ships of Convoy BM11, bringing in the British 18th Division and its equipment which arrived on 29th January, was the *Empire Star*. As she was sunk in the Atlantic later in 1942, possibly the only survivor from that Singapore voyage still living is Edward Green, who was then eighteen and an assistant steward. He wrote a short memoir of events which is a unique shipboard record of what went on in the dock area in the two weeks which ended with the ship sailing on the night of 11th/12th February.[15] Unlike the other ships in her convoy, which were all troop-carriers, *Empire Star* was a cargo vessel carrying guns, army vehicles and ammunition which had been transshipped into her at Ellesmere Port three months previously and in India.

Empire Star spent the first part of her stay in the port anchored in the Dangerous Goods Area from where her crew had a grandstand view of the ever-increasing aerial bombardment of the city and docks. There was a great need for the 2,000 tons of ammunition and sixteen tanks she had on board, but it made her a time-bomb. This was the reason for her long wait at anchor; none of the regular stevedores or barge operators would go near her, and if she had been moored alongside the wharves and been hit, the resulting explosion would have demolished the entire port. Japanese bombers made no attempt to attack the ship while she was at anchor; she did not even suffer a near-miss although other craft in the anchorage were attacked. The ship finally berthed on the 6th February – the day after the crew were long-distance witnesses to the burning of the only Singapore reinforcement ship to be lost, the *Empress of Asia*.

Empire Star was berthed under cover of darkness and, because no stevedore was prepared to work such a cargo under such dangerous conditions, 'every member of the crew went down the hatches', reports Eddie Green. The discharging operation had barely begun when Japanese bombers came in to attack. 'Panic stations, ropes cast off, and back to the anchorage. We all got the feeling our cargo was known to the Japanese.' Eddie's surmise was almost certainly true. Information supplied by fifth-columnists would have made the Japanese aware that one well-aimed bomb whilst she was alongside could have done the work of many squadrons of aircraft.

General Percival stated in his post-war dispatch and in his book *The War in Malaya*[16] that in his opinion the Japanese would launch their invasion against the island in the north-west, where in fact they did land. But after the war he acknowledged in a letter to General Kirby, the Official Historian, that this was incorrect and had been based on hindsight; that he really expected them to attack in the north-east. (Percival was almost alone among the senior British Generals to think this. It is known that both Wavell and Gordon Bennett thought that the

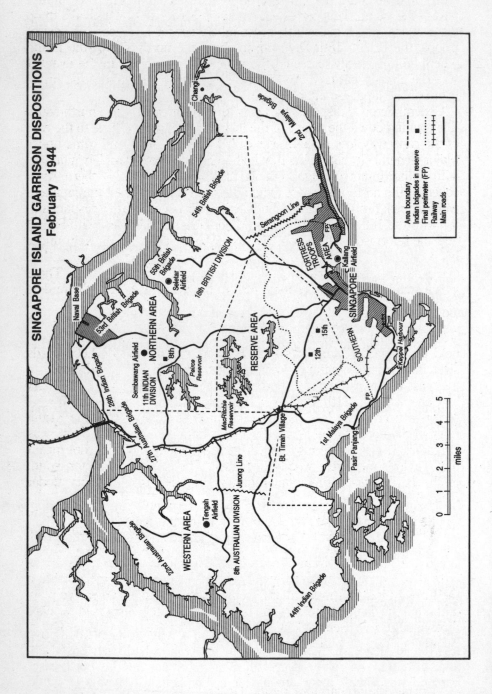

SINGAPORE ISLAND GARRISON DISPOSITIONS
February 1944

Japanese attack would come where it did.) Percival added in his letter to Kirby that he could not, however, afford to neglect the defence of any part of the island. This corrected version is borne out by Percival's troop dispositions, which make little sense otherwise, for he placed his newest troops, the British 18th Division, to cover the north-east of the island where he mistakenly expected the attack to come from. In the event it was the already battered Australian 8th Division which bore the initial brunt of the Japanese attack.

General Percival disposed his army thus: the area west of a north-south line running down the centre of the Island from a point a little to the east of the causeway (see map 4), was called Western Area and came under Major-General Gordon Bennett, who had his 8th Australian Division and 44th Indian Infantry Brigade under his command. The Northern Area, covering the north-east coast (where Percival had assumed the Japanese would attack first) was Lieutenant-General Sir Lewis Heath's responsibility with the 18th British Division (Major-General M.B. Beckwith-Smith) and the reformed 11th Indian Division (Major-General B.W. Key) under his command. The Southern Area took in the remainder of the coastline and was the responsibility of Major-General F. Keith Simmons. There was a small central reserve force held in the Reserve Area in the middle of the island.

The battle for Singapore was fought and lost in the north-west where General Bennett divided his area into three sectors. The Causeway Sector, held by Brigadier Maxwell's 27th Brigade, had a front of 4,000 yards stretching from the natural boundary of the Kranji River in the west to just east of the causeway, where his right flank leant on the left flank of General Key's 11th Division. The responsibility for the north-west sector, a front of no less than 16,000 yards stretching from the Kranji river in the north to the Berih River halfway down the west coast, was Brigadier Taylor's with his 22nd Brigade. The length of his front meant that Taylor's men were widely dispersed. The south-west sector, south of the Berih, was 44th Indian Infantry Brigade's responsibility under Brigadier Ballentine.

The southernmost tributary of the Kranji River is separated by only three miles from the head of the Jurong River which has its mouth on the south of the island. This narrow stretch of land between the rivers was called the Jurong or Kranji-Jurong Line. The British Official History is critical of Bennett for apparently not giving consideration to incorporating the Jurong Line, four miles inland from the coast, into his defensive plan, 'although the danger of infiltration between the widely dispersed forward units should have been evident'. This view is supported by Colonel Thyer, Bennett's Chief of Staff. The Report on Operations of 8th Australian Division says:

During the preparatory period General Bennett would give no

consideration whatsoever to the preparation of the Kranji-Jurong Line, nor its incorporation in any plan.

Colonel Thyer authorised and took full responsibility for a defensive plan and recce of the area without the knowledge of the Divisional Commander.

Later happenings were to prove him correct. Had a more wholehearted attempt been made regarding this position some of the disasters which were to befall may have been averted. What is certain is that the battalions would have been given the opportunity to prove their mettle instead of being disintegrated and defeated in small pockets. Instead of 40,000 yards [the report was including the length of 44th Brigade's south-west sector] of coastline to hold, there would have been only 4,000 yards of good defensive country plus the necessary protection against the actual crossings of the river.[17]

As the Jurong Line, or rather the failure to hold it, was crucial to the battle for the island, it is worthwhile following up Colonel Thyer's indictment of Bennett over this matter. In an interview with the official Australian and British historians in 1953 Thyer said that, after he had taken the responsibility to get the line reconnoitred on his own shoulders and without Bennett's knowledge, 'I gave it [the map of the now reconnoitred area] to Bennett first; he told me it was a defensive line, and went into a tantrum about the withdrawal complex'. Thyer added later on, 'I think another aspect of this Kranji line stems from my original introduction of it to Bennett. He would have nothing to do with it. When forced upon him he does not like to admit it to me, so he works independently of me. I give orders to 44 Brigade and he gives orders to 15, which gives them the same job. [The reserve 15th Indian Infantry Brigade was to come up in support.] He didn't want to make a fool of himself in front of me. He would never admit he was wrong.' This is a strong indictment coming from Bennett's trusted Chief of Staff[18]

During the first week of February the Commonwealth forces hastily prepared whatever extra defences they could in the time left available. Captain Tufton Beamish (a Member of Parliament after the war and later Baron Chelwood), who was then an 18th Division Staff Officer, reported on the defences they found when they took up position on the north-east coast of the Island:

The only defence works I saw were blockhouses every 400 or 500 yards. They were made of tree trunks. None were sited on the water's edge and therefore none were suitable for our purposes.

No attempt had been made to camouflage them. No field of fire had been cleared.

Apart from this the only other defence works that were there were either three or four gun emplacements. They were made of sand bags and loose earth and were poorly camouflaged.

Apart from the above there was not so much as a shallow trench or a strand of wire to be seen. ... As regards material available ... we could certainly get extremely little wire.

The supply of anti-tank mines was totally inadequate.

Cutting instruments for clearing a field of fire were unobtainable – the men had to use bayonets and the few machetes they had got.[19]

Here we can rebut another of the Singapore myths. Ever since Brigadier Ivan Simson published his *Singapore: Too Little Too Late* in 1970,[20] General Percival has been blamed for the philosophy that, to have constructed a range of defences along the northern shore of the island, would have been bad for the morale of civilians and troops who would then believe the worst was about to happen. Writers since 1970, as Simson did himself, have taken Percival's statement about this, made at a meeting Simson had with the General on 27th December, as evidence that Percival was the man responsible for this view. Not so. It seems that Percival's superior, the C-in-C, Sir Robert Brooke-Popham, had a hand in it, and as the man in charge he must accept full responsibility. His papers contain the following passage: 'Not having more defences on West side of Malaya and North side of island was a problem of morale and man-hours. I was always on my guard against the fortress complex.'[21]

General Percival can thus be relieved of at least part of the weight of that particular responsibility. Even if the idea was his, Brooke-Popham was in a position to overrule him.

In the Australian sector similar conditions and shortages of equipment applied as Beamish had found on Heath's front. The Australian Official History records that, 'In many instances the swampy nature of the ground made it impossible to dig trenches, and breastworks had to be thrown up.' During brief respites the men engaged in this work could gaze across the Johore Strait at Japanese soldiers busy on the other side, for in places it was less than a mile wide. Sometimes, even when it was possible to dig trenches, Australian troops refused to do so. Charles March, of the Royal Australian Engineers stationed on the extreme north-west tip of the island, recalled that the Japanese

were supposed to be landing on the other side of the island, but we could see thousands of the buggers.

Our job was to prepare slit trenches but our blokes wouldn't dig. They said it was too bloody hot. Stuff the trench. Then a shell would come over and there'd be four of us in a one-foot deep slit trench.[22]

Throughout this period the Japanese kept up an intermittent barrage, and by 4th February this shelling, together with bomb attacks, had so damaged Tengah airfield at the centre of Bennett's area that the RAF abandoned it. By that time there were few aircraft left to use it anyway.

During the early days of the siege Australian gunners could not understand why they were not given permission to fire on Johore Bharu where some of the taller buildings, including the Sultan's palace, were being used by Japanese artillery spotters. This may have partly been due to a desire by the military authorities to keep to a minimum damage to the Sultan of Johore's property. Captain H.E. Jessup, Bennett's G3 Intelligence officer, said, 'Bennett refused permission to fire on it [the palace]'. (Bennett was a personal friend of the Sultan's.)[23]

But the principal reason was probably to conserve ammunition for a siege expected to last three months. The rules for this rationing of ammunition were strict and comprehensive: a certain number of rounds per day per type of gun, allocations not transferable from gun to gun, nor accumulative from day to day. In the 18th Division area there was another reason for not permitting heavy artillery fire. It was still hoped that Brigadier Painter's lost 22nd Indian Brigade would make it to the Strait. (Only about 100 men finally did.) These rules persisted until 8th February, although on 5th February belated permission had been granted to fire on the Japanese spotters in Johore Bharu.

By 6th February British Intelligence had formed the view that the Japanese would definitely attack in the north-west, but by then, of course, it was too late to make major changes to the general troop dispositions. Percival urged Bennett to send patrols out across the Strait from Taylor's sector. For some unexplained reason Percival had to exert considerable pressure on Bennett before patrols were eventually sent on the night of 7th/8th February. They reported large concentrations of the enemy, whereas patrols sent across from the 18th Division area reported none. The report from Taylor's patrols was available at his HQ by dawn on the 8th, but when Percival visited Bennett's HQ at noon the report had not yet reached there. It did not arrive at HQ Malaya Command until the middle of the afternoon, by which time the Japanese had begun an intensive artillery bombardment and it was too late for much to be done. Bennett had set his HQ close to Bukit Timah village on the very edge of his command area, as usual too far back from the front, although whether this had anything to do with the delay in receipt of the patrols' reports is not known.

In an earlier chapter the considered views were recorded of the Australians, Colonel Thyer and Colonel Kappe, on the quality of the Australian reinforcements that arrived in Singapore in late January. The military attributes of the 942 men of the 2/4th Machine-Gun Battalion, and the 1,907 raw and untrained replacements for other units, were to play a significant part in the events that now followed.

The 2/4th had been formed in Western Australia in late 1940. It was commanded by Lieutenant-Colonel M.J. Anketell, a militia officer with World War One experience. The battalion had been trained in South Australia and at Darwin. It was from the latter port in the north that it embarked aboard the *Marella* on the final day of 1941. The ship carried the battalion to Port Moresby where it was transshipped into the troopship *Aquitania* (which had brought in reinforcements for the Australian garrison on New Guinea). *Aquitania* next sailed for Sydney to pick up the raw replacements, and then on to Fremantle off which she anchored on 15th January.

The 2/4th by that time had received fourteen months home training, far more than most AIF men before they were sent overseas; they were veterans compared to most others. Colonel Anketell (who was to die of wounds the day before Singapore capitulated) or perhaps a more senior officer ashore, made the decision that no shore leave was to be granted even though this was the battalion's home port. Probably this decision was made because of concern that the raw replacements would not return, for one group could hardly have been given shore leave without the other. If that was the reason for the no shore leave policy, it was to backfire. In a display of ingenuity that in other circumstances might have been considered praiseworthy, many of the 2/4th went absent without leave by shinning down mooring ropes and rope ladders into water-boats, tenders and other craft ferrying out stores, and taking the craft over, made for the shore. An interested witness was J.M. Roualle, an officer of the Malayan Customs Service who was one of 76 civilians who had joined the ship in Sydney. (After the war began in Europe many people from Malaya took their leaves in Australia. Those on leave in the Sydney area after the Japanese war started used to meet regularly in a Sydney theatre to hear the latest news from Malaya and to receive their recall orders.)[24]

When the troopship sailed from Fremantle 94 soldiers had still not been rounded up by the provosts and local police. This lapse of discipline among trained troops could not have passed unnoticed by the untrained replacements, nor did it augur well for the future. With the benefit of hindsight it seems a mistake that the 2/4th were made to make the wide detour around the entire Australian continent; it would have been better had they have been taken directly to Singapore from Darwin in the *Marella*.

Convoy 'MS2' consisted only of *Aquitania* and the cruiser HMAS *Canberra*. The ships experienced some bad weather *en route* and during it the liner was able to outsail her senior consort.[25] Because Admiral Sir Geoffrey Layton in Singapore did not want the famous troopship to come within range of Japanese aircraft, the Australians were transferred into smaller vessels when the convoy reached Ratai Bay on the Java side of the Sunda Strait on 20th January. These arrived in Singapore on 24th January.[26] More than likely the Australians did not relish the transfer from the comparative luxury of the 45,000-ton liner to the cramped conditions aboard the smaller vessels which averaged only 2,500 tons. The officers and civilians were in reasonable comfort in whatever cabin accommodation was available – J.M. Roualle recalls passing the time during the three-day voyage playing bridge – but the soldiers, about 500 to each ship, would not have been so comfortably ensconced. Their introduction to the Far East war zone could not have been much worse.

The untrained raw replacements were poor military material. Some had never handled a rifle. An ugly rumour abounded that some of them were the sweepings of the Sydney dock area and that others were convicts who had been paroled providing they 'volunteered'. Although this rumour went the rounds of Singapore – and is remembered by several people who were there – no evidence has been found to substantiate it. Whatever the truth may be, the men were definitely not professionally fit for combat and, what is more, they had already witnessed a major breakdown of discipline among their better trained comrades in Fremantle. It was these men, from both sections of the reinforcements, who were to be spread around the various Australian battalions in Singapore, thus diluting the combat efficiency, discipline and morale of all.

Why were such untrained men sent to Singapore when there were about 87,000 trained militia men in Australia? The militia were, in fact, debarred by law from volunteering for overseas service except in the mandated territories. All AIF battalions, in both the Middle and Far East, had to be specifically raised for overseas duty, and only a small percentage of the militia, officers and men, were ever permitted to transfer over. Furthermore, it had become the policy to carry out the greater part of the training of AIF battalions 'on the job'; in other words most left Australia's shores with not much more than basic training. This policy might have been satisfactory for the Middle East and for the original AIF units in the Far East, for they had time for training, but it was not correct for these later reinforcements, especially as 2,000 of them had received no training at all. The author of the Australian Official History was highly critical of the decision: he wrote of the 'blunder of sending untrained men forward to a division then going into battle ... the needs of the 8th Division should have been foreseen ... if necessary a shipload of reinforcements could have been sent from the Middle East where, in mid-December, after all units had been filled there were 16,000 in the reinforcement pool'. The inclusion of the untrained men in the Australian battalions in Singapore was a major factor in the events to come, and for this the politicians and military authorities in Australia who sent them must take a full share of the blame. It cannot be expected that raw and untrained men will fight well, or at all, against an experienced and deadly enemy.

According to Colonel Thyer, the 2/18th received 90 men to replace previous casualties, the 2/19th, 370, and the 2/29th, 500. Lieutenant-Colonel

Thomas Hamilton of the RAAMC says that the 2/19th, commanded by Lieutenant-Colonel Anderson, VC, received a total of 620 replacements, not 370. Anderson told Hamilton that 'scores of them did not know how to load a rifle; while hand-grenades and mortars were absolute mysteries'.[27] The other three battalions were virtually intact, and so needed few replacements. However, the balance of the raw reinforcements permitted 'the raising of an additional platoon in each rifle company'. This point is important for it means that all six Australian battalions received a share of these untrained reinforcements, not just the three that had sustained most casualties on the mainland.

The other brigade under Bennett's command, Brigadier Ballentine's 44th Indian, was 'largely composed of recruits who had either less than three months service with the Battalion or who joined shortly before embarkation'.[28] Ballentine described the milking of his battalions in India which left him with many untrained sepoys under eighteen years of age as 'appalling'. Like the Australian reinforcements, they had arrived at Singapore only in late January and had had no chance to acclimatize. It was this raw battalion that was guarding Brigadier Taylor's left flank and it could not have added anything to that officer's peace of mind.

Two days before the Japanese landings Ballentine reported that 'the forward posts of the left wing of their left battalion [the Australian 2/19th under Colonel Anderson] were not on the beaches but several hundred yards in rear of the beaches'. Possibly this was necessitated by the nature of the ground in the vicinity of the shore, or, as Beamish had reported on the north-east coast, this was where engineers had constructed the defences earlier. Ballentine made no note of the reason for this off-the-beach positioning of the defences, which of course, made the Japanese landings when they came that much easier.

The fifteen-hour artillery bombardment which preceded the Japanese assault reminded some of the veteran Australian officers of the trench warfare in France. Lieutenant-Colonel A.L. Varley (to be promoted to brigadier on 12th February and placed in command of 22nd Australian Brigade vice Brigadier Taylor) wrote in his diary that, during his four years service between 1914–18, he had never experienced such concentrated shellfire over such a period. He reported that eighty Japanese shells were counted as having landed in his 'D' Company area in one minute, although it appears that the typical figure over his whole area was six or seven per minute. The bombardment was sustained and intensive, but it caused comparatively few casualties, probably because of the softness of the ground. Even so, the scale of the bombardment must have had a devastating effect on the nerves of the new Australian soldiers. It also had an extremely detrimental effect on communications. Communications on the west coast of the island were no better than they had been on the mainland, and the problem was made considerably worse because the shelling cut many field telephone cables.

The Japanese struck across the strait two hours after nightfall on 8th February. It was a clear night and the moon was not to rise until the early hours of the following morning. The enemy hit at that part of the front covered by Taylor's over-extended brigade and defence was patchy. In places artillery and forward defence posts took some toll of the enemy but, as the authors of the Report on Operations of 8th Australian Division said, 'the Japs crossed the Straits and landed in the AIF sector practically unopposed'. In this context it is interesting to note what Brigadier A.S. Blackburn, VC, the commander of the Australian Forces on Java, had to say during an interview in 1953 with the Australian and British Official Historians. Even though it is hearsay, it comes from a distinguished source:

> Blackburn said as a prisoner he had met a brigadier of the 8th Division and talked to him about the crossing of the straits to Singapore Island. Blackburn said that he couldn't understand how the Japs had made the crossing, and questioned the brigadier closely. After some time the brigadier said, 'Look here, Arthur, I'll tell you what happened. I knew it was hopeless so I withdrew my men back from the beaches and let the Japs through.'[29]

Blackburn did not name the brigadier, but it would seem that it must have been Taylor rather than Maxwell as the initial attacks were made on Taylor's front.

The Japanese were able to land in several places and made swift progress, though in some instances the landings were only successful on the second or third attempt. (The artillery units attached to Ballentine's Brigade in the south did not engage until 0500 hours because of a failure in communications.) Colonel Thyer reported that the 'tidal mangrove swamps were a disadvantage to the defence and actually conferred an advantage on the Japs who were well trained in such landings.' Some isolated Australian units fought gallantly in the way 'diggers' are renowned for, but others did not, *and yet others were not there to fight at all* (as will be shown in the next chapter). As with British and Indian troops during the campaign, it seems that much depended upon the character of the unit commander and the relationship he had built up with his men; his personal bravery and commitment often being the difference between whether his men stood or scuttled off. With the new men, of course, there had been no time for any such relationship to be built up.

The authors of the Australian report on the operations of 8th Division described the first hours of fighting after saying the landings were practically unopposed:

> There is considerable evidence to show that Brigadier Taylor

disobeyed Divisional orders in not searching the Straits with
B.E.L's [searchlights]. There are claims in the narrative that the
Japanese suffered in crossing but such casualties to the enemy
were very local and not general over the AIF sector. Brigadier
Taylor had given an order to his battalions that in the event of
being pressed they were to withdraw into defensive battalion
perimeters. The result was that on the Japanese effecting a
landing the Brigade automatically commenced a withdrawal
movement which could not be checked.

Many of the unit withdrawals were disorganized and some were panic-
stricken, with men staggering back weaponless and almost naked.[30]
Parties became separated, and some ended up back in Singapore. By
dawn on 9th February the 22nd Australian Brigade was, at least for the
time being, no longer an effective fighting force. At midnight General
Bennett had placed the reserve 2/29th Battalion of 27th Brigade under
Brigadier Taylor's command but it took so long to collect this widely
dispersed battalion together and find transport for it, that it did not arrive
in the area until dawn. Bennett also sent in a Special Reserve Battalion
made up of service unit troops with a few infantry replacements.

At 0830 on 9th February General Percival ordered his only central
reserve, the weak 12th Indian Brigade, to move into the area. Percival
has been criticised in the Official British History for not moving the 18th
Division over from the still quiet north-east coast at this stage, which he
might well have done providing he had reinforced the Serangoon Line,
the Jurong Line's equivalent over on the east side of the Island.

Bennett ordered Taylor, who was then based near Tengah airfield,
to counter-attack even though the 12th Indian Brigade was not yet in
position. But Taylor, upon learning that the Japanese were working
around both flanks, and as communications with Bennett were by
then impossible, took the decision to fall back to the Jurong Line.
Bennett, still thinking in terms of attack, was appalled when he heard
of Taylor's action.

Guy Hutchinson of the Johore Volunteer Engineers (JVE) which was
operating with Taylor's brigade, reported incidents which illustrate the
unevenness of discipline in the AIF. On the morning of 9th February 'a
mob of the AIF came through, in a hurry too, most of them without arms
... they were a rabble and quite out of control'. Then, a couple of hours
later, 'another lot of the AIF came into view through our positions. But
this time it was different, they were our pals, the 2/10 Royal Australian
Engineers, two officers, a CSM, and about thirty men, all armed and
properly dressed (our previous visitors had for the most part nothing
but their shorts and tin hats). These at once joined us.' He goes on to
say that, a little later, the commander of the JVE, 'disgusted with the
AIF and not being able to get any orders, put us temporarily under the

command of Stewart of the Argylls, who were coming up on our left. On our right we were supposed to have the [Australian] 2/19th. We never saw them.'

Brigadier Ballentine, whose brigade was on Taylor's left flank, wrote of the night of 8th/9th February:

> No information was passed to HQ 44 Ind. Inf. Bde., and the Field Regiment [Royal Artillery] was powerless to intervene against the hostile landing until about 0500 hours on 9th February when information was given that the Australians had been driven back at least 2,000 yards from their western beaches. Fire was then opened on beaches. No information came in from from 22 AIF Brigade. Their left company in close reach of our right withdrew without warning and without attack from the enemy.
>
> At first light Australian stragglers without arms or equipment passed Bde HQ ... About 100 such passed. They were collected and put into lorries to keep out of sight of troops and sent back.
>
> Patrols sent out from 6/14 and 7/8 Punjab Regiments. One advanced 1000 yards North of [Bulim] road and to the West of the aerodrome and reported seeing neither Japanese nor Australians. A patrol North of Chao Chu Kang made no contact. At about 0900 hours a composite Battalion of Australians formed from 1st Reinforcements and odds and ends arrived at Brigade HQ. They were given guides and sent to join two companies 7/8 Punjab at 660178 with a view to reconnaissance from there by OC 7/8 and possible counter-attack. They never arrived, disintegrated and departed whence they came.
>
> At about 1400 hours the Brigade Major 22nd Australian Infantry Brigade visited [us]. He stated they had been completely overrun during the night and by daylight were no longer able to put up an organised resistance.

Brigadier Ballentine's brigade was reliant upon the Australian Division for supplies. The supply arrangements broke down on 8th February, and from then on his brigade had to rely on their own 'skill in scrounging'. His men were near starvation by the time of the capitulation, 'A more complete breakdown and chaos of supply could not be imagined'.

Because their line of withdrawal was threatened by what had gone on to the north of them, during the evening of 9th February Ballentine was ordered to withdraw his brigade to the Jurong Line. Percival now placed the Northern Area Reserve, the 6/15th Brigade under Bennett.

Meanwhile, on the afternoon of 9th February, something occurred which was to have a far-reaching effect on future operations. General Percival produced an anticipatory plan to concentrate his forces around the perimeter of Singapore town *should* the enemy break through and advance down the Bukit Timah Road, the main route to the city from the west. He sent this out in a secret and personal instruction for the information of his senior commanders. On receipt of this General Bennett issued an operation order to the brigades under his command allotting them positions on this inner perimeter. Both generals were at fault in this matter. Percival should have ensured, by adding a rider to his order, that it was not to be passed down the line; Bennett should have ensured, when passing it on to his brigadiers, that it was quite clear that it was only an anticipatory order.

Back in the dock area *Empire Star* was brought alongside again. The Japanese attack had placed the ammunition dumps around Kranji in jeopardy (something else General Percival should have forestalled by having the ammunition transported farther inland) and the ship's cargo was now of the utmost importance. The gravest risks were to be taken to get it unloaded. 'Now,' says Eddie Green, 'it was unload at all cost. How we managed not to get hit was a miracle.' Still no stevedores would come aboard, and once again every member of the merchantman's crew became a docker. 'Bombs were falling,' says Eddie Green, 'and shells were whistling overhead. All around us the sheds on the quayside were blazing. The ship was unloaded in record time, I can tell you.'

That same evening the Japanese attacked across the Strait at a new point just east of the Kranji River in Brigadier Maxwell's sector. Australian artillery, mortar and machine-gun fire was at first effective. As the Japanese gained a foothold hand-to-hand fighting began, and slowly Maxwell's men were pressed back. Again, as was his wont, Maxwell's Brigade HQ was situated only a mile from Bennett's HQ, and six miles south of his frontline troops.

Maxwell always maintained that he was given permission to withdraw from the Causeway area by somebody on Bennett's staff, though there is much doubt about this. He ordered Colonel Oakes of 2/26th Battalion to withdraw about a mile southwards if and when he thought it necessary. Oakes was also ordered to co-ordinate the movements of the 2/30th Battalion, which was guarding the Causeway, with his own, and in the event Oakes ordered that battalion to withdraw also, thus abandoning the Causeway which, despite the British demolitions, was still crossable at low water. In the process Oakes exposed the left flank of General Key's 11th Division. None of this was known to Bennett until 0500 hours on 10th February, and he then relayed the information to Malaya Command.

When this news reached General Key at 0630 hours on the 10th he telephoned Bennett and asked for the immediate reoccupation of the Causeway area but, according to the British Official History, 'was told there were insufficient Australian troops to do this'. The History makes no mention of why this was so. If Maxwell's two battalions (the third one had been sent to reinforce Taylor) had been considered enough to hold the Causeway area in the first place, then they should have been enough at least to attempt a counter-attack. The likely reason is that Bennett was aware that some of Maxwell's new rifle platoons were already breaking away from the main units and were making rearwards towards Singapore City. In the process they took with them some of the veteran troops. Low morale is the most contagious of battlefield diseases. The Malayan businessman, Raymond Thomas, who escaped from Singapore on the night of 15th February, made a statement to the authorities when he reached India on which the interviewer based the following report. Thomas was a personal friend of Major-General Keith Simmons.[31]

> He could not say that the Australians, morale was good. From what he saw of the Australians he considered their discipline was too lax. On the 9th the Australian Brigade (27AIF) which was stationed west of Singapore Causeway chucked in its hand and came down into Singapore. He used to see them lying about in the streets outside his offices which faced the waterfront. They were badly behaved and appeared to have abandoned their guns.
>
> He could not understand why they behaved so badly. He had fought with Aussies in the last war and considered that their behaviour then was far superior to the behaviour of the Australians in Singapore.

The Australian battalion stationed west of the Causeway to which Mr Thomas referred was the 2/26th, commanded by Lieutenant-Colonel A.H. Boyes. Boyes's failure to hold his men may well have been the reason for his replacement on the 9th by Lieutenant-Colonel R.F. Oakes.

General Key had no option but to order his own reserve, the 8th Indian Brigade, forward to secure his flank, and they succeeded in taking back some of the lost ground. The 8th had been newly-constituted and now only partly resembled the brigade which had confronted the Japanese first on the beaches of Kota Bharu, which to the veterans in the brigade must by now have seemed a lifetime ago.

Captain L.S. Young of the Gurkha Rifles reported of this incident:

> The Australians, without orders, left their area. The unit occupying the area next to the Causeway handed a scrawled pencil note to a 2/2 GR Havildar which merely said, 'Position so and so Bde. now 13 milestone (3 miles back).'
>
> On 10th morning an effort was made to drive the enemy back into the sea. [Before] zero hour two Indian Bns. were in position, but there was a Bn. missing in the middle ... the Japs walked through the gap. The missing Bn. was an Australian Bn. It reappeared in Singapore town preferring drink and rape to that of doing its duty.'[32]

It was Bennett's intention to hold the Jurong Line and he ordered his dispositions accordingly. But at about 0900 hours on 10th February Brigadier Taylor had received a copy of Bennett's orders based on Percival's secret anticipatory plan of the day before. Taylor took this to be an order for an immediate withdrawal to the inner perimeter line. Confusion now began piling on top of confusion. He ordered all his units to withdraw but for some reason forgot to relay the withdrawal instructions to 2/29th and the Special Reserve Battalion under his command. When questioned about this in 1953, Taylor said 'he thought that for a period he forgot them, but there were no orders he could have given them'. Taylor then reported to Bennett's HQ where he 'received no direction from Bennett, but only abuse for misreading the order'.[33]

The overall defence plan was now dissolving into chaos, with neither Bennett nor Percival having up-to-the-minute information about the situation, which was fluid in the extreme; those in command at the centre had little knowledge of or control over the flow. Here and there courageous and isolated stands were made but, overall, confusion reigned, and disaster was staring everyone in the face. Unit withdrawals, both forced and unforced, authorised and unauthorised, were continually exposing the flanks of adjacent units. When Brigadier Paris, commanding 12th Brigade, sent patrols northward to make contact with Maxwell's 27th Brigade, they reported back that they had reached the enemy-held Kranji road junction without sighting an Australian. Realising that his northern flank was unprotected, Paris withdrew to Bukit Panjang village thus abandoning the northern end of the Jurong Line. In doing so he completely uncovered the right flank of the Special Reserve Battalion to his south.

In the middle of the morning of 10th February a copy of Bennett's order based on Percival's anticipatory plan reached Brigadier Ballentine at his HQ at the southern end of the Jurong Line, and he passed it on to his battalion commanders. So did Brigadier Coates of the 15th Brigade immediately to his north. Early in the afternoon a company of Ballentine's raw 6/1st Punjab Battalion came under fire and broke, and began to stream back towards Pasir Panjang on the south coast. This caused confusion amongst other troops in the area, including, according to Ballentine, 'several officers and 60 men (numbers afterwards verified at Pasir Panjang) of the British Battalion'. (The British Battalion, the combined remnants of the Leicesters and East Surreys, was part of 15th Brigade.) Ballentine obtained permission to readjust his line, but the rearward movement got out of control. The western front now went down like a row of dominoes. The withdrawal of the 44th exposed the left flank of 15th so they retired; their retirement exposed the left flank of the Australian Special Reserve Battalion whose other flank had been exposed earlier by Paris' withdrawal, and they had no option but to withdraw. It did not end there. All these withdrawals exposed the right flank of the

1st Malay Brigade on the coast in the Southern Area, so they too pulled back, in their case to Pasir Panjang.

So by the evening of 10th February General Yamashita had gained control of the Causeway, the Jurong Line, and the western half of the island with comparatively small effort on the part of his troops. Though the capitulation was still five days off the fate of Singapore was sealed.

During these last two weeks General Percival had other concerns apart from the conduct of the campaign. On 28th January he sent the following message to the War Office in London:

> GOC Malaya to War Office. Message 29079. Ammunition in main magazine Singapore Island cannot be destroyed without an explosion which would wreck everything for considerable radius. This would include hospitals. Quite impractical to clear areas. Believe ammo of no use for enemy armaments. In these conditions see no alternative to its exception from scorched earth policy. Do you agree.[34]

(This message seems to indicate that some eighteen days before the actual capitulation, Percival was foreseeing the likelihood that Singapore would fall.)

The answer Percival received appears singularly unhelpful, especially as it arrived over a week after he sent his own message.

From War Office to ABDACOM repeated GOC Malaya.
No. 69071 6.2.42.

1). [Quoted above message in full. Then:–]
2). The over-riding consideration is that the Fortress must be held to the last. If, however, the worst appears imminent and inevitable, policy should be to fire off ammo, if possible, at the enemy. Balance of ammo and magazines themselves should be destroyed or otherwise denied the enemy.
3. We cannot, of course, contemplate blowing up sick and wounded men in hospitals. Surely some arrangements could be made to evacuate these from the danger zone.

There is no need to describe the next few days fighting in detail. There were several reasons for the resistance of Singapore being shortened. Amongst them were General Percival's failure to utilize the 18th Division on the west coast, and the effect of his issuance of that anticipatory order on 9th February; General Gordon Bennett's follow-up order which apparently confused Brigadier Taylor (and probably Brigadiers Ballentine and Coates as well) as well as Bennett's earlier failure to incorporate the Jurong

Line into his defence plans, and the fact that his HQ was set too far back; Brigadier Taylor's failure to send patrols over to Johore until it was too late; Brigadier Maxwell's decision, probably unauthorised, to withdraw from the Causeway and the fact that his HQ was much too far from his front; Brigadier Paris' uncovering of the right flank of the Australian Special Battalion; the 'breaking' of the 6/1st Punjabis and some of the men of the British Battalion.

There were also reports of unmilitary behaviour and a breakdown of discipline of some army units on the island. This factor and its significant effect on what turned out to be a short-lived seige of the 'fortress', has not previously been given sufficient weight by historians. This is mainly because the relevant British files were kept under official wraps for fifty years until 1993 (see the next chapter).

The previously closed British files deal mainly with the behaviour of troops of the Australian Imperial Force. However, the breaches in military virtue on Singapore Island cannot be exclusively laid at the door of the Australians. An authoritative, contemporary, and previously unrecorded source will show how one seasoned Indian Army regiment was also involved in a very serious breach of discipline. The canker of low morale and its extreme consequence, desertion, spread far and wide, and was the final link in the chain of disasters which led inexorably to the raising of the white flag of surrender and the biggest defeat in British military history.

Chapter Thirteen

'This Inglorious Business'

General Sir Archibald Wavell flew into Singapore for the last time on the morning of 10th February. The first visit he made was to General Bennett's Western Area HQ where he, Percival and Bennett narrowly escaped death in a Japanese bombing raid. The building they were in received a direct hit but the bomb failed to explode. The Australian Military Intelligence Officer, Captain D.H. James, was convinced that the local fifth-column was responsible for this attack through a wireless transmission.[1]

It was quickly clear to Wavell that the battle was not going well and, furthermore, that Bennett had little knowledge of the course of events in the Causeway sector. Wavell went next to see General Heath, and then on to General Key's 11th Division HQ where he learned of the extent of the danger to that division's left flank due to the withdrawal of the 27th Australian Brigade.

Wavell and Percival laid down a plan to create a force from three battalions of the 18th Division to bolster the defence of the Western Area. After that the two generals paid a second visit to Bennett's HQ where they were informed that the Jurong Line had been lost. Wavell ordered a three-phased counter-attack, the first part to commence that very evening, and the final part to culminate in the recapture of the Jurong Line the following afternoon. The plan never really got off the ground, however. As with most British plans throughout the campaign, events were to overtake the planners who were playing a game with many of their counters missing. In this case some of the missing counters were Australian units. In the report he made after his escape from Singapore General Bennett said, 'After conference with General Wavell, line to be pushed forward easy stages ... This impossible.'[2] Before that, in Part 8 of the same report, he had said, without giving an indication of what troops he was talking about, 'Some units suffered heavy casualties by desertion. At first deserters were collected and returned to units, towards the end this impracticable as morale low.'

General Wavell left for Java early on the morning of 11th February on the seaplane which had flown him in. He slipped and fell on the quay on the way and damaged some bones in his back. Then his aircraft was delayed because the sea in the vicinity of the take-off path was littered with small craft containing soldiers attempting to escape from Singapore.

With all he had seen and heard and experienced during his visit it is not surprising that the cable he sent to Winston Churchill from Java later that day was less than optimistic. These are some relevant parts of the message:

> Battle for Singapore is not going well ... I ordered Percival to stage counter-attack with all troops possible ... Morale of some troops is not good and none is as high as I should like to see ... The chief troubles are lack of sufficient training in some reinforcing troops and an inferiority complex which bold Japanese tactics and their command of the air have caused. Everything possible is being done to produce more offensive spirit and optimistic outlook. But I cannot pretend that these efforts have been entirely successful up to date. I have given the most categorical orders that there is to be no thought of surrender and that all troops are to continue fighting to the end ...

General Wavell must have been aware that the morale situation was very much worse than this cable to Churchill indicated, and that it had already resulted in some desertions. From early in the morning of his visit a series of entries in the War Diary of GHQ Malaya Command[3] made reference to this situation. They referred to 'stragglers' and to men trying to board boats to escape from the island. Most, though by no means all, of the references were to Australians:

> *0720 hours, 10th February*
> Commander Southern Area rang up with info that there were a number of troops in lorries in Orchard Road having apparently spent the night there. (Deputy Provost Marshal informed.)
> *1600 hours 10th*
> Reference large numbers of Australian troops in Singapore. General Bennett reports that approx. 600 have been picked up in the last 3 days and have returned to their units and will be used in the attack. Casualties are not by any means heavy and General Gordon Bennett does not require reinforcements as yet.
> *1835 hours 10th*
> Captain Bell to BGS [Brigadier, General Staff]. Have just had a telephone message from *Laburnum* [naval depot ship] saying that AIF troops were all around *Laburnum* getting into boats and sampans. Could a strong guard be put on Harbour Board gates to stop this and could these people be cleared out of Harbour Board area?
> Phoned above to Brigadier Newbigging 1851 hours. He stated he would report what steps he had taken.*

1920 hours 10th

Duty Officer Southern Area to GIII(Service). Report received from OC 'M' sector Town Beach. '30 AIF have abandoned two carriers near Cenotaph unloaded kit into launch nearby and are casting off.' AIF informed.

1943 hours 10th

Stragglers from Leicester/Surrey battalion contacted on Bukit Timah Road stated enemy to be in some strength about 9 MS [milestone] Jurong Road. No sign of enemy on investigation by Liaison Officer.

1235 hours 11th

Brigadier Moir has established stragglers posts on right Newton Circus, centre crossroads Orchard Road-Grange Road, left crossroads River Valley Road-Tiong Bharu Road.

1240 hours 11th

Brigadier Newbigging reports further stragglers posts have been established under BORs. Stragglers of AIF will be returned to Tanglin.

1925 hours 11th

Heavy AA Regt. report from Telok Ayer. About 200 AIF unarmed attempting to evacuate in any available craft. AIF Duty Officer informed, who stated that the Provost Section were checking.

2140 hours 11th

Report from Brigade Major Heavy AA, re another 200 AIF stragglers in Yacht Club area forcing their way through and are taking available craft, setting about in them and generally breaking the place up. They attempted to break into Frazer & Neaves using money to bribe the watchman and also money no object for boats if obtainable. They are rolling about the Indian AA positions and causing a disturbing influence in that area.

1230 hours 12th

Commander Packard with a naval party is boarding *Mata Hari* and is going to try to persuade the party of AIF and Recce Battalion to leave.

Lt-Col Scrimmance has arranged a party under a field officer to be at *Laburnum* to disarm these men under arrest, if they do land it will be about 1230 hours at *Laburnum*.

1615 hours 12th

GII (Waller) spoke to Commander Frampton ref. U61A. Party came ashore and were handed over to military authorities without giving any trouble. [Appendix U61A referred to the *Mata Hari*,

---

* If the deserters involved in this incident had boarded *Laburnum* with the intent of sailing her away, they were unlucky. The ship was a hulk without engines.

which was one of the small ships being used to evacuate civilian women and children.]

Several of these GHQ War Diary entries are supported by corresponding entries in the War Diaries of the units which initiated the reports, wherever these have survived. Perhaps the most illuminating of the entries above is the one for 1600 hours on 10th February. The reference to 600 Australians being 'picked up over the last three days' indicates that some desertions from the front had begun on 7th February, the day *before* the Japanese landed on the island. This particular entry is also important for other reasons.

The word 'deserter' was not being used in these official entries. The omission of the word was almost certainly a matter of deliberate policy and the result of an order from someone very senior; no commander likes to admit that he has any such creature under his command. There is no need for similar reticence here, but it is necessary to define what is meant by a deserter in the Singapore context.

Before doing so it must be pointed out that by no means all the men who escaped from Singapore were deserters. Some men, mainly British and Indian from early fighting in the campaign on the mainland, found themselves cut off behind enemy lines and had made their way to the sea and managed to reach Sumatra across the Malacca Strait. They were not deserters. One such man was Sergeant Walter Gibson of the Argylls who told part of his escape story in his book, *The Boat*.[4]

Other men and sometimes complete units were officially ordered to leave after the siege of Singapore began. Amongst the latter was the entire Australian 2/3rd Motor Transport Company which had done such magnificent work from the very start of the campaign. There being no further use for them on the island they were shipped out on 9th February aboard the *Darvil* (Captain W. Lukin) and *Kinta*. Some volunteers from the 2/3rd helped to crew these two vessels because their native crews had left them. The 2/3rd ended up in Java and were finally captured when that island fell. (At least one of those gallant veterans had the opportunity to escape from Java but did not take it. Frank Coombes was involved in transporting equipment down to a ship at one of the Javanese ports. The ship was about to sail for Australia and the ship's captain urged Coombes to get aboard and escape with them. He declined as to do this would have been desertion.[5]

In the Singapore context deserters can be divided into two categories. The first includes any person who escaped from the island prior to the capitulation on the evening of 15th February, unless he escaped from behind enemy lines or unless he was among the selected groups who were given official permission to leave and who were issued a chit to that effect. The fact that many deserters who had boarded ships and sampans before the capitulation, and then only made it as far

Maj.-Gen. Gordon Bennett, GOC 8th Australian Division in Malaya. A controversial figure. (*IWM*)

Troops of the Australian Imperial Force marching to barracks after disembarking in Singapore. (*IWM*)

An Indian battalion advancing in column through characteristic Malayan countryside. (*IWM*)

British and Indian officers of the Royal Ludhiana Sikhs, March 1939 at Nowshera. In the centre, and on the left of Sir George Cunningham (Governor of North-west Frontier Province) is Brigadier (later Major-General) A.E. Barstow. Barstow, one of the British forces' most vigorous commanders in Malaya, was killed in the campaign. (*Courtesy Major Robert Henderson*)

The four VCs of the Malayan campaign: (*above left*) Sqn Ldr A.S.K. 'Pongo' Scarf, awarded posthumously for actions against the Japanese in Thailand, December 1941; (*above right*) Lt-Col. A.E. Cumming, 2/12 Frontier Force Regiment, East coast of Malaya (January 1942); (*below left*) Lt-Col. C.G.W. Anderson, MC, AIF, Malaya peninsula, January 1942; (*below right*) Lt Thomas Wilkinson, RNR, awarded posthumously for HMS *Li Wo's* action south of Singapore against a heavily guarded Japanese convoy. (All *IWM*)

Following an attack by Australian troops, two Japanese tanks lie destroyed, and a crew member dead. (*IWM*)

The coalburning troopship *Empress of Asia* (16,909 gross registered tonnage) leaving New York in 1941, a few months before she was lost off Singapore. This photo reveals she was already something of a 'rustbucket'. (*Courtesy Canadian Pacific Ltd*)

The *Empire Star* (12,656 gross registered tonnage) off Lyttelton, New Zealand, 1938. She was sunk at sea eight months after the fall of Singapore. (*Courtesy Mrs Lettice Nichols*)

Captain Selwyn N. Capon of the *Empire Star*, a photo taken aboard SS *Doric Star* in 1934. Capon was promoted CBE for his inventive and courageous handling of *Empire Star* under Japanese air attack. (*Courtesy Mrs Lettice Nichols*)

Singapore's Empire Dock ablaze, 15 January 1942, one of the last pictures to leave the city. The clouds of smoke arose from burning oil dumps. (*IWM*)

The northern skyline of Singapore Island during the week-long siege of February 1942. (*Reproduced from* MALAYAN POSTSCRIPT *by Ian Morrison*)

February 1942. Smoke from fires on the Naval Base, Singapore Island, form a black cloud over the whole city. In the centre is the Town Hall; to the right the spire of St Andrew's Cathedral. (*Australian War Memorial*)

A stick of Japanese bombs bursts on Kalang aerodrome. (*Australian War Memorial*)

British soldiers being made prisoner at Singapore, February 1942. (*Popperfoto*)

The famous picture of the surrender of Singapore as, accompanied by a Japanese officer, General Percival (*right*) makes his way to a meeting with General Yamashita, 15 February 1942. On the left is Colonel Wild, carrying the white flag. (*Popperfoto*)

as Sumatra and Java where they were eventually captured by the Japanese and became mixed up in the general mass of prisoners of war, does not alter the basic premiss that such men were deserters from Singapore.

The second category of deserters was certainly much larger than the first, and includes anyone who left the Singapore front line with the intention of not returning to it. It also includes those men who may have started out as battlefield stragglers but who later refused to return to the front line.

One other relevant matter needs clarifying. It has been said that other troops who had been kitted out with the Australian-type slouch hat were mistaken for Australians; the Loyal Regiment has been singled out in this context. It is of course possible that some Loyals were taken for Australians, but this is not likely to have amounted to many. The Australians on the island outnumbered the Loyals by about 20 to 1, and most men from downunder can be easily identified by means other than their choice of headgear. Anyway, the most normal headgear for all soldiers in those last dark days would have been the tin helmet; the front line, the town and the docks were under continual bombardment from 8th February onwards, and it would have been a very foolish soldier indeed who walked around in any form of soft hat when a hard alternative was available.

There is little doubt that by 10th February the morale of most troops engaged in the fighting had reached rock bottom. Eyewitness reports show that there were many Australian stragglers, some of them leaving the front panic-stricken, and of Indian and British troops breaking from their units in the Western Area in disorder. These reports were to grow ever more frequent as the end neared, and in the main the finger was pointed at the Australians.

Most books written about the campaign have referred to there being deserters in Singapore, and most authors have agreed that the majority of them were from the AIF. The British War Correspondent, O.D. Gallagher, was one of the first to touch on this subject. Writing in 1942, and therefore still subject to censorship regulations, he only hinted at the problem when he said, 'The end came quickly. The behaviour of a large number of Australian troops was peculiar.' Gallagher, who was in Singapore but escaped before the end, was an eyewitness to much that went on.[6] Major Colin Ingles, a Malayan Public Works Department officer serving with the Indian Engineers, wrote much more openly in his diary which was privately published in 1945. For Friday 13th February 1942 he wrote, after commenting that no one could understand why the Japanese were being so successful on the island, '... The Australians may have something to do with it, as more and more of them seem to be roaming about town, armed with loaded Tommy-guns and rifles, very drunk for the most part, and with neither officers nor discipline.'[7] A Chinese Singapore resident writing in 1946 went even further. His account was based on interviews with local citizens, and included reports of rape:

> It was alleged that even before the entry of the Japanese troops, rape had already been committed by stray patrols of retreating Australian and Indian soldiers. They were somehow separated from from the main bodies, being temporarily isolated by the sudden forced retreats ... Bewildered, confused, and without proper leadership, discipline among them went to pieces. Unfortunate women here and there fell victims to these disorganised troops, who at the time of the outrages were soaked with strong drink.[8]

Dr Cecily Williams, a much-loved and respected long-time resident of Singapore who worked at the Tan Tock Seng Hospital, has been quoted in many accounts. She had this to say:

> During the last week everything became more and more harassing and disintegrated. When I drove about, the town was full of evacuating and deserting soldiers, most of them Australians looking utterly disorganised and defeated. They had mostly thrown off their equipment, they were looting the shops or sitting in rows with their boots off down near the quays; they were pushing women and children out of the way to get behind buildings when bombs were falling nearby; they were crowding females and children off the boats that were getting away. Many of them must have been killed by the Japanese on the islands off Singapore. It was a terrible show.

All the above references are from non-Australian sources, but there are also several Australian witnesses. After commenting that the Australians had too few men guarding too much frontage, Captain David James of Australian Military Intelligence recorded:

> By 0800 hours 9th February, hundreds of bedraggled Aussies were streaming down Bukit Timah Road on the way to the city. The Military Police (UK and AIF) attempted to check them but they were in no mood for homilies from 'Red Caps'. Some paused long enough to accept a cigarette, light it and say, 'Chum, to hell with Malaya and Singapore. Navy let us down, airforce let us down. If the *bungs* (natives) won't fight for their bloody country, why pick on me?'[9]

David James went on:

There was more truth than discipline in the retort; we have no kodoism, no kempetai and no bullet in the back for a straggler. But sometimes our 'dangerous thoughts' are allowed too much expression for the good of a common cause when we have our backs to the wall ... Still – even in England during war – there were strikes for higher pay for making munitions or loading them aboard ships. No civilian was shot for that withdrawal of service from the State – the right to strike (official or unofficial) is part of our democracy. Those who were trotting down Bukit Timah Road that morning were on unofficial strike, not for hard cash but for a few more years on earth.

James, who omitted to mention the word 'duty' in that passage from his book (even though the concept of duty was more fashionable then than perhaps it is today), went on to comment that the Australian stragglers were but a small proportion of the whole 'stragglers movement': unfortunately, most of the other evidence shows that he was wrong in drawing that conclusion.

John Robertson published his book *Australians At War, 1939–1945* in 1981.[10] He wrote of the Causeway sector, 'the defenders possibly misjudged the situation and retreated. By sunset on the 10th the western third of the island was in Japanese hands. Next day Singapore waterfront was crowded with a mass of demoralised troops looking for any means of leaving the island. Some were Australian, though it cannot be said how many. Some of the blame for the panic-stricken flight by some Australians rest with incompetent officers at Army HQ, Melbourne, who, though better trained soldiers were available, selected for the last reinforcements to go to Singapore, 1,900 raw recruits, some with defective rifles.' Further on he said, 'Bennett's leadership was not faultless. His Australian troops put in an uneven performance and did little to delay disaster.'

Another Australian, T. Hall, writing in 1985, quotes an officer of the Royal Australian Navy who was in Singapore on special duty.[11] The officer recalled the lack of discipline, the looting, and the defeatism that was everywhere apparent:

And the Australians were always the worst. The best when they were good, the worst when they were bad. There was one group of Australians that had been getting a terrible pasting and the Japanese were coming across everyday and machine-gunning them from the air. One day they just threw down their weapons and said they were not going to fight any more ... [their] senior officer ... almost pleading with them ... but to no avail. I reported what had happened, but I think the whole thing was hushed up afterwards.

That episode was indeed hushed up; and for over fifty years so was the much wider situation of which that episode was but a small part.

Hank Nelson, also writing in 1985, had this to say in a book published by the Australian Broadcasting Commission:[12]

> A minority of the troops decided that flight and the chance of a charge of desertion were preferable to staying in Singapore. At Keppel Harbour, Patrick Levy [Warrant Officer P.R. Levy, AIF] says, 'we were chasing men who were running into the water and throwing their weapons away. They were panicking, trying to commandeer boats. Dr Albert Coates [Lieutenant-Colonel Sir Albert Coates of Ballarat, Victoria] [saw] a group of Australians, displaying the independence and aggression which in other circumstances made them great soldiers, [who] forced their way at gunpoint on to one of the last boats taking out civilians.

Another Australian reference comes directly from someone who was there. Captain H.E. Jessup, in civilian life a pearler and planter from Brisbane, was an Intelligence officer on General Bennett's staff. In Sydney in January 1953, he said that, after Wavell's last visit, 'We had the feeling Singapore was doomed . . . There was a feeling that we, surely, would not be left in the lurch – probably ships would be available in Singapore to get us away. There was a large number of stragglers on this account.'[13]

Another man who was there was V.G. Bowden, the Australian government's representative in Singapore. He sent the following cable to Canberra on 12th February 1942: 'Groups of Australians and others had boarded a vessel without authority and in it had sailed to the Netherlands East Indies.'*

Bowden's message probably referred to the escape of about 140 deserters who boarded the *Empire Star* on the night of 11th/12th February. This is the most 'famous' of the deserter incidents, but although it has featured in a score of books, only scraps of the full story have previously been told. The story, researched fully for the first time, is told here not only because it features deserters, but because it is a record of courage and skill on the part of merchant seamen, and of the bravery of a group of Australian nurses, and because taken as a whole it is a microcosm of the horrors of war, showing both the heights to which man's spirit can reach, and the depths to which it can plunge.

The *Empire Star* was alongside Keppel Harbour wharf on 11th February when her master, Captain Selwyn Capon, OBE, received orders from Naval HQ to evacuate women, children, air force personnel, and

---

*Bowden made a bid to escape at General Percival's suggestion on 14th February. His small craft, the *Osprey*, was threatened by a group of deserters, including Australians, armed with Tommy-guns and grenades. Bowden and his party transferred to another ship. He was later brutally murdered by the Japanese on one of the islands south of Singapore.

certain other officially-designated escapees as part of the last 'big ship' evacuation convoy. The embarkation programme went on all day and well into the evening, the latter stages of it illuminated by the flames from nearby burning sheds, and all of it happening against a frightening background of noise made by shells whining overhead. Steward Eddie Green says:

> The next moment we were invaded by hundreds of women and children. At noon they were flooding aboard a cargo ship with room for only twelve passengers. The captain ordered us all ashore to try to find anything edible; we had been in every shed that was left standing so we knew where to go.
> Later on sixty Australian nurses joined us from the military hospital – they had drawn straws with the other sixty left behind for a chance to escape. These were followed by a group of 20–25 New Zealand air force pilots.

The air force group was, in fact, made up of Australian, New Zealand, and British officers and there was also a large group of non-officer air force technicians. Before this influx, Eddie Green says that a group of Scottish soldiers left to guard the harbour had come aboard 'for a fag and a cuppa, nothing stronger for these lads. I borrowed writing paper and envelopes for them to write home. I finished up with forty letters and all these lads were worried about was the money for the postage. Who said the Scots are mean?' (The letters, eventually mailed from Australia, could have been the 'last post' to come out of beleaguered Singapore.)

One of the RAF technicians on board was Flight-Sergeant (later Squadron-Leader) Steve Stephen. He says:

> When we arrived at Keppel Harbour to board the *Empire Star* there were armed guards – British – every few yards. Drunken looting Australians were swarming up the mooring ropes trying to get on board. They had looted the dockland warehouses and were intent on getting away come hell or high water.[14]

Another of the RAF technicians was Sergeant (later Wing-Commander) Eric Bott:

> I came out of that hell-hole on the *Empire Star*. I remember quite a tussle to get on board. I and a number of other RAF personnel had been left behind at Seletar airfield after the main body of airmen had been evacuated to Java and Sumatra. Our task was to repair and fly out a number of bomb-damaged Hurricane aircraft. We then inhibited further use of the airfield by placing unrepairable aircraft across the remaining take-off area, all this under shell

fire. We were then ordered to make our way to the docks. This meant crossing the island not knowing where the Japs were. We had a fairly powerful American Ford mini-bus, we were well armed and had orders to fight our way through if we met with any opposition. [The men with Bott were Sergeants McKay and McDermott.]

We arrived at the docks to be faced with the most God-awful mêlée of people you could imagine. There were nationalities of all kinds trying to get on board this one remaining ship, abandoned cars were everywhere, with harassed officials at the gangplank and a mob of Australian soldiers clubbing their way on board. British military police were just as vigorously attempting to club them back but with only partial success.

As things were my two colleagues and I had little chance of getting on board without assistance but luckily for us a ship's officer seeing our plight threw down a rope ladder and helped us scramble on board.[15]

Flight-Lieutenant A.D. Elson-Smith was one of the Australian air force officers on board. In 1945 he published anonymously a book about his Malayan experiences called *Great Was The Fall*.[16] The original manuscript contained references to the Australian deserters aboard *Empire Star* but these were struck out by Australian censors. In the book Elson-Smith also named Captain Heenan of the Indian Army as a traitor; that was not removed by the censors. This piece of selective censorship resulted in the book being the only published reference to the traitor's name prior to 1993.[17]

Eddie Green recalls the Australian deserters as being well-armed. So does a Straits Settlements policeman, N.G. Morris, who was an Assistant Superintendent at the time and who witnessed the scene from the quayside with Captain W.A. English of the Military Police. He says that the police were prepared to rush the ship to get the deserters off, but finally did not do so for fear of a blood bath; some of the deserters had Tommy-guns and there were many women on the ship and the quay.[18]

Any attempt to rush the ship would certainly have led to bloodshed in view of the mood the deserters were in. Men who had clubbed their way aboard were hardly likely to leave meekly. Furthermore, the ship's decks and the adjacent quay were covered in a huge jostling mass of people. One wrong move could have ignited the scene. John Dodd, another airman on board, had been among the first and now found himself pressed hard up against the rail of the ship and looking down at the crowd of women, children, and military personnel on the quay who were hoping that the already crammed ship could take a few more. He saw an angry and frightened young European woman clutching the hand of a boy, aged about three, and two suitcases. She was arguing with two officials on the gangway who were ordering her to leave the luggage behind. Then out of the crowd behind her surged a group of about twenty desperate and armed Australian soldiers. The officials who tried to stop them were knocked out of the way with rifle butts and the group marched up the gangway.

It may have been from that incident that the story grew of a British officer who tried to stop some of the Australian deserters boarding the ship and was shot and killed. The officer concerned was named in the story as Captain Kenneth Atkinson, RN. It is quite possible that Atkinson was on the quayside that night, but he certainly was not shot. He escaped aboard one of the fleet of small craft, the *Yin Ping*, which left Singapore on 13th February. (Captain Atkinson lost his life during the escape in the vicinity of the Banka Strait.) The story of Atkinson's 'shooting' seems to have been first published by Richard Gough in 1987 in his book *Escape From Singapore*[19], and has been used in several books and articles since then including one by the present author. Gough says he obtained the story from Colonel Alan Warren of the Royal Marines who was in charge of the official escape route from Singapore. The naval historian, Stephen Roskill, had heard of the story too, making a note of it in his memoirs. It is not known when Roskill learned of it, but as he died in 1982 it must have been sometime before then. Perhaps he also got it from Warren who died in 1975.[20] Warren himself must have got the story at second hand for he had already left Singapore by the time of the alleged incident. The fact that Captain Atkinson was not murdered does not prove, unfortunately, that no one was shot on the quay that night by deserters. The present author's research has revealed that several other persons, who had never met Warren, had heard the same or a similar story over the years since 1942, so the possibility remains that someone was shot. If something like that did happen, then it was not reported to Assistant Superintendent Nigel Morris who was on the quay; but with the chaotic conditions that obtained that night some such incident could well have taken place without his knowledge. One thing is certain; if a killing did take place, then the victim was not a Royal Navy captain. In his efforts to get to the truth of this matter, this author has been able to eliminate from the enquiry all the naval captains who were in Singapore at the time.

In order to prevent any more gangway incidents like the one reported by John Dodd – who incidentally went on to say that the lady and the boy who were pushed aside by that last group of Australians, did *not* make it on board – and with his ship already crammed with well over 2,000 souls, Captain Capon ordered the gangway to be raised. Such was the haste to get *Empire Star* away before any more unauthorised personnel could board her, that British soldiers on the quay almost caused a catastrophe. Eddie Green reports, 'in the haste to help us escape they let go our mooring ropes a little too soon. Apart from the blazing buildings it was very dark, and as we floated away there was panic until the engineers got the engines going.' He goes on, 'In the darkness we looked back and wondered about the fate of all we had left behind. Exhausted we flopped down where we could, our accommodation having been taken over, even if we could have managed to reach it through the crowds.'

A New Zealander of No. 488 Squadron, R.B. Johnston, was also aboard the ship. He says that some of the deserters left on the quay showed their disappointment by machine-gunning the ship as it pulled away.[21]

Throughout that day another merchant ship and two naval ships, which were also to be in that last convoy, were loading up with evacuees in other parts of the port. The Blue Funnel Liner *Gorgon* was anchored out in the Roads, and loaded nearly 400 people from boats. A party of deserters managed to board her too. Major J.C Westall, RM, was one of the official escapees on board, and he later reported that there were forty-five deserters, sixteen of them British and the remainder Australian. Unlike the other ships in the convoy the *Gorgon* was to bypass Batavia and make directly for Fremantle, where she arrived on 20th February. All the deserters were there taken off under armed guard. Another witness to this incident was Peter Melliar-Smith of the Malayan Geological Survey.[22] It is not known what happened to these men after they were taken ashore at Fremantle. The *Gorgon's* complement of evacuees included two American Military Liaison officers, Colonel Tormey and Colonel Craig.

HMS *Kedah* was late arriving alongside one of the smaller berths in the port complex. One of her 750 passengers was Molly Reilly, cipher clerk to Sir Shenton Thomas and Duff Cooper. As she waited anxiously on the quay with her husband (who was to stay behind) for the ship to arrive she reports that 'Singapore was a glowing inferno – the sky was one huge black pall of smoke from the oil fires. As night came on, it looked even worse, with the sky ablaze from the huge fires that were everywhere. To add to the nightmare the big 15-inch gun from Blakang Mati kept firing over our heads.'

HMS *Durban* lay in the man-of-war anchorage. Her logbook states that, before she arrived in the port, the glare from burning oil tanks and the huge pall of smoke over the island were sighted fifty miles away while she was still south of the Durian Strait. Amongst her share of the evacuees was a group of Army Japanese-speaking interpreters who were being evacuated for their own safety. Lieutenant Michael Ringer of the Indian Army was among them. Also on board was Major Angus Rose of the Argylls who was later to write, apropos the Australians:

At a conference before the war the subject of discipline (or lack of it) of the Australians was raised. Gordon Bennett said that the 'Australian standard of discipline suited the Australian troops and it would prove its worth on the day of battle.' I did not doubt the truth of the first statement but had grave misgivings about the second.

Empire Star left Singapore during the early hours of the 12th, threading her way through the protective minefields in convoy with the other ships; their track marked by temporary lights exhibited from boats manned by a few of the Royal Navy personnel left on the island because some marker buoys were out of position. By daybreak the convoy was well clear of Singapore and making top speed in an attempt to clear the Durian Strait by dawn. At about nine o'clock, when south of that Strait, they were found by Japanese aircraft. First dive-bombers screamed in to attack, followed by waves of high-level bombers. Over a period of fours hours *Empire Star* sustained three direct hits; the enemy's fury seemingly concentrated mainly on the cruiser and on the merchant ship which they would have loved to have destroyed when she was alongside Keppel Harbour and carrying that cargo of ammunition.

Those four hours seemed a lifetime to those on board as Captain Capon skilfully managed to dodge most of the bombs. 'We had a great captain,' says RAF Corporal Norman Clarke, 'he got us to Java.'[23] The ship used her own weaponry and the guns brought aboard by some of the RAF men to good effect. A Hotchkiss gun manned by the RAF shot down one Japanese dive bomber for certain, and Captain Capon recorded another 'probable'.

According to the entry in the ship's official logbook[24] fifteen men were killed during the attacks, but in Captain Capon's later private report to Blue Star Line he mentioned the figure fourteen. The true figure was probably well in excess of this.

Many people were injured during the attacks, but if the deserters had lowered the image of Australians in John Dodd's eyes, then the Aussie nurses who stayed on deck throughout the attack to tend the wounded lifted it right back again. Dodd's was not the only tribute to the courage and devotion to duty of that group of Australian nurses. During one attack a nurse was seen to throw herself across the wounded man she was tending to protect him from further harm. Eddie Green wrote, 'the sixty Australian nurses were invaluable with the wounded, and some individual cases of gallantry covering and shielding the wounded on the open deck whilst being machine-gunned deserved the highest praise'.

Squadron-Leader Steve Stephen, for one, is convinced that there were far more than fifteen fatalities on board; he saw at least that number himself. John Dodd reported that a 'Leading Aircraftman' McDermott, who may or may not have been the 'Sergeant' McDermott companion of Eric Bott, was killed on board, and the name McDermott does not appear on the captain's list of the dead. Eddie Green definitely witnessed one unrecorded death. He saw a very badly wounded airman crawl to the ship's rail 'and pull himself overboard off the boat-deck into the sea below. He must have been in terrible agony and I was too far from him to be of any help – maybe he did not want any.'

Captain Capon listed the number of persons on board as 2,161 but added that no proper muster was possible and that he was convinced that the actual figure was appreciably in excess of this. (One report even sets the figure at 3,500.) The ship was so crowded that proper sea burials were not possible and some bodies were slipped overboard with only a few words said over them by a minister who was on board. Some bodies, says Steve Stephens, were committed to the sea and all the minister could say was, 'name unknown, no identification'. Some of the unknown dead were Australian deserters who had thrown away their identification tags. Among the dead who were listed by name and serial number by Captain Capon were six of the Australians. There is no need to mention the names of these dead men here, but two of them appear to have been brothers from New South Wales who had consecutive serial numbers.

The names of two of the Australian deserters will be given here, one of them being the senior officer amongst them. Throughout the initial stages of the voyage tannoy messages were frequently transmitted asking for Captain Blackwood of the Australian Armed Forces to report to the bridge. Steve Stephen says 'as far as I know he never did'. Another Australian aboard *Empire Star*, a deserter by his own admission, was Roy Cornford. He and a group of his mates had commandeered a small boat in Singapore and boarded the ship from it. Cornford told the authors of the book *Return from the River Kwai*[25] that when the ship reached Batavia the ship's captain reported that Cornford and his party had shot and forced their way on to the ship. He said they were taken off in Batavia and jailed, but eventually the group escaped into the hills, hiding out for two months before surrendering to the Japanese.

Apart from listing the number of AIF on board (he said there were 139 but with the unrecorded dead it was probably higher, and as the count was almost certainly made after the air attacks it probably did not include the recorded dead either) Captain Capon made no mention in the Official Logbook or in his report to the shipping company about Australian deserters. Almost certainly he was instructed to handle the matter in this way by the convoy commander, Captain (later Vice-Admiral Sir) Peter Cazalet of HMS *Durban*. High Command would not have wanted the deserter business made public. Captain Cazalet's own official report reads as follows:

> Whilst on passage *Empire Star* had informed me that he had on board 100 deserters from the AIF who had forced their way on to the ship at Singapore and might cause trouble. I was told that they were armed with Tommy-guns and revolvers and refused to leave the ship until it reached Australia. The Captain of *Empire Star* asked that a strong guard should be made available when

the ship berthed. This was asked for in my 'arrival' signal, and it is understood that a guard from units of the AIF then stationed in Java, was detached. It was at that time expected that the *Empire Star* would berth on the evening of the 13th February.

While this strong Australian guard of 100 men was waiting for the ship to berth it apparently became obvious that they were unreliable and unlikely to be able to deal efficiently with determined deserters. I was accordingly asked to deal with the situation.

I at once warned off the marine detachment (40 men) and in addition collected a party of 30 seamen volunteers in charge of my First Lt. (Lieutenant-Commander H.P. Brister). My intention was that the actual rounding up of the deserters should be carried out by the sailors, the marines remaining discreetly in the background in case of trouble.

This plan was adopted in order to disconcert and surprise the deserters who would probably be expecting a large posse of soldiers with whom they were prepared to be truculent.

The seamen party went on board immediately the ship docked at 0700/14th, dressed, I regret to say, in a variety of rigs and looking as far removed from the normal army guard as it is possible to imagine. The plan was completely successful.

The deserters were nonplussed and almost before they realised what they were doing they had obeyed Lt. Commander Brister's peremptory orders to give up their arms, fall in properly and stop smoking. They were at once marched off the ship where my marine detachment took charge of them and finally turned them over to an army guard. I am informed that the deserters (actually 135 in number) were led by an officer – a captain – who had removed his 'pips'.

What happened to these deserters at Batavia is uncertain. At least some of them, according to Roy Cornford, were imprisoned before finally being captured by the Japanese. Eric Bott reported that, several weeks after the ship's arrival at Batavia, he was stationed at a Dutch airfield on the outskirts of the city. 'I became aware of groups of Australian soldiers, ostensibly on guard duty. I recognized amongst them faces from the ship and realised they were the deserters from Singapore.'

Sergeant (later Squadron Leader) R.D. Phillips, adds, 'In Batavia I was detached to take over the prison which was full of Aussie deserters, nine to a cell.' He states that there were about a dozen cells.[26]

In addition to the Captain Atkinson myth another story grew up around the *Empire Star* episode. An old 'China-hand', popular and loquacious in his cups, Captain Percy Bulbrook of the Straits Steamship Company, used to 'drink out' in the Singapore Captain's Club in post-war years on the

story that he had been shown a bullet-pocked wall and dark stains in
Batavia port where it was said that one in five of the deserters had been
shot. Val Kobouky, a Czech employee of Borneo Motors, and an escapee
aboard *Empire Star*, heard later that one in ten of these deserters had
been executed, a modern example of Roman-style decimation.[27] These
two stories may in fact have had a small basis in truth. The Australians
had no death penalty for desertion, so it is extremely unlikely that any of
them were shot. But Molly Reilly, who escaped on HMS *Kedah* in the same
convoy, witnessed what happened when that vessel docked in Batavia:

> We were told the women were to be got off the wharf as quickly
> as possible as there were 169 (or 196, I have forgotten which)
> Australian deserters on the *Empire Star*, who had barricaded
> themselves in below decks and were armed ... We saw, drawn
> up on the wharf, a party of 100 British Tommies ... However, we
> heard afterwards that someone had persuaded the Aussies to go
> quietly. There is no death penalty for desertion in Australia, but
> there were two British Tommies with the Aussie deserters and
> these two men were shot. What happened to the Australians I
> never heard ...

Molly Reilly was a highly intelligent woman with friends among the top
British officers in Java at that time. Her version of events is probably
true and the shooting of the two British soldiers, *pour encourager les
autres*, was the genesis of the later stories. If these executions did take
place they were probably illegal, which could be one of the reasons for
there being no record of them. Although the 1881 Army Act was still in
force, it seems that some legislative process, perhaps an order in council,
had to be promulgated before deserters could be shot under the terms of
the Act.

There were many other reports of Australian deserters boarding or
attempting to board ships in Singapore. Commander C.R. St.G. Tucker,
who was the Boom Defence Officer there, later reported that:

> One of my officers who sailed with me to Batavia, after I left that
> port, had the unpleasant duty of meeting a ship which had been
> forced to sail from Singapore at the point of a pistol. Apparently
> about 200 Australians rushed the ship. On arrival at Batavia,
> where they found themselves covered by the machine-guns of
> the Dutch and the marines, they laid down their arms.

It was incidents like these that led Dr Rittmer, the Minister of Propaganda
in the Dutch East Indies, to say that the spectacle of a large number of
Australians being taken through Batavia under an armed guard had so
disgusted the Dutch that he thought it better for the British to keep out of

Java. There are other stories of desertions which come from both unofficial and official sources.

One is from the papers of Thomas Kitching, Chief Surveyor of Singapore, who was to die on 14th April 1944 while a prisoner of the Japanese. He has been described by someone who knew him as 'a well set-up man, not given to exaggeration'.[28] On 11th February 1942 he wrote of troops, without specifying their nationality, being 'everywhere in Town; it seems peculiar there should be so many doing absolutely nothing, when you'd expect every sound man to be on the front line, resisting this [Japanese] advance. There's nothing visibly wrong with them. What is the explanation? If it is the obvious one – desertion – we are finished. I cannot understand it all.'

Kitching was more specific the following day when he was in the process of destroying his liquor stocks:

> It may be a precaution in case we have to capitulate, we don't want drink-inflamed Japanese soldiery about the place, but a contributory cause is certainly some heavy drinking by our own men – the Navy rifled the drink stocks when they took over the Royal Singapore Golf Club, and the Aussies put the lid on it yesterday – they had broken and behaved very badly. The town was full of them last night, many were tight and many were demanding to know when they are going to be evacuated! And these are the men, who when we entertained them in our house before the war reached Malaya, used to have one stock remark: 'all we want is a chance to get at them bloody little Jappos before we are sent back to Australia! D'you think I can get two on one bayonet?'
>
> The Aussie troops seem in many cases to be completely out of hand ...

Kitching and a friend, David Nelson, went into the city to get their cars but they had to beat a hurried retreat because some Australians began taking pot-shots at them. After trying to get some up-to-date news, he records, 'the one certain fact seems to be that the Aussies have been incredibly lacking in morale, discipline and guts'.

H.R. Oppenheim was a chartered accountant and a member of the Volunteer Artillery. He also kept a diary.[29] He and another man called Ackhurst were in a unit sent out to round up Australian deserters. On 11th February he wrote that he and Ackhurst had:

> captured some in Raffles Place and I was left in charge of them ... while the Military Police was sent for. A subaltern came up and said to them, 'I always knew the Aussies were born without guts but I hope the next generation are also born without tongues'.

Ran into Gunner Scott who is trying to regain his battery. His job has been to go out and shoot Australian deserters of whom there are so many. Went up Tanglin Road and saw streams of deserters pouring into the town, mostly Indians and Aussies.
12th February. Moved to ... East Coast Road ... those on the guns told me that the RAF ground staff had all bolted from Seletar and ... now say 'he bolts like an RAF grounder' when anyone bolts. Saw numerous Australian officers running away.

One of the most damning of the reports about the Australians, because of its source, comes from the Senior Chaplain to the Forces in Singapore, Padre (Major) Edward Rowles. In his post-war memoir he wrote for Tuesday 10th February 1942, '. . . even then Australian troops were snooping around with rifles and looting from the surrounding houses. Two small parties thus inclined decided otherwise when they saw that I, too, was similarly armed.' Strong words indeed from a non-combatant Roman Catholic priest.

One of Singapore's most prominent residents, Sir Roland Braddell, was a solicitor and for many years a member of the Legislative Council. In a letter to his wife dated 17th May 1942, he said, 'here I must tell you that the greater part of the Australian Infantry who are completely undisciplined had been leaving the fighting lines – indeed they had twice left important positions – and bands of men had been going around boarding or trying to board ships.'[30]

Toby Carter, then a Flight-Lieutenant (later Wing-Commander) wrote that 'the instances of breakdown of morale or discipline that I saw or heard of were almost exclusively among soldiers of the AIF.' He went on to give several examples he had seen for himself. Then he says, 'after ... Kallang aerodrome had been evacuated and the personnel should have been embarked, Group-Captain Rice arrived ... and said he had been detailed to embark but had been unable to do so as the ship had been rushed by armed Australian deserters.[31] Toby Carter was among the many official escapees who were to make reports about the sometimes atrocious behaviour of men who must have been deserters, and who were again, mainly Australians, along the Sumatran escape routes.

V.L.F. Davin (later Major) was a young officer of the 5/14th Punjab Regiment. He had been injured in a motor accident on 14th December at Baling after 'a footslogging withdrawal from Kroh'. The accident paralysed his left leg but he was fit enough to become a Staff Officer at Singapore HQ before the end. He was sent out to investigate the incidence of desertion and writes, 'I did meet various groups of Australian soldiers who were wandering around NOT under command and being generally bolshie. I can quote one group of three tall and very fit looking men whom I asked why they were not with their units. Their response was that they hadn't come to fight without air cover and that they were leaving.

To which I replied by asking them about the Indian and British troops that had already been fighting without air cover for two months. Their response was and I quote (I have always remembered the exact words) "More fool them". They went one way and I limped away another. At least one of them had a Tommy-gun and I was in no position to do anything more.'[32]

H.R. Oppenheim also told of a Gunner Scott whose job it had been to go out and shoot Australian deserters. There is no evidence that any such shootings took place, but there is evidence that an order of that kind was given. Alan Butterworth writes that his 3/16th Punjab Regiment 'finished up as a reserve behind the Australian positions on the West Coast. When they broke we were ordered to shoot them running through our lines! Eventually we were ordered to the south coast opposite the Raffles Hotel, again to shoot Aussies escaping in small boats. Also ordered to destroy all alcohol stocks in Raffles Hotel. We did so with the alcohol but told the Indian troops to shoot high (*uncha maro*) with the Aussies. We also could not destroy some genuine Napoleon Brandy so buried it in slit trenches along with the odd body.' (Alan Butterworth learned after the war that the brandy had been discovered during a road building programme.)

Molly Reilly had this to say after travelling from her home into the city with her Australian husband:

Rather disturbed to see the hundreds and hundreds of Aussies straggling along the Johore-Singapore main road – others sitting on the side walks – most of them clad only in shorts – no arms – no equipment! Seemed all wrong when the Japs were only a few miles away.

After arriving at her office in the Governor's residence, Sir Shenton Thomas told Molly, 'The Australians have certainly let us down.'

George Wort was an officer of the 1st Battalion, Malay Regiment. He wrote up his memoir of the war as a prisoner in Changi.[33] For 10th February he entered, 'West Coast Road was now pretty full of Indian troops of low morale, and not a few Australians. Many of these troops were falling back without arms.' He also said that eleven badly shaken soldiers from the British Battalion had arrived at his position and that one of them was in such a condition 'that he had to be got away so that our Malay troops would not see a white troop in this state'.

Lieutenant-Colonel M. Elrington, commanding 2nd Battalion Loyal Regiment reported for 13th February, 'the position of my forward companies became very unsatisfactory as their security depended entirely on the successful denial to the enemy of the northern slopes of the Pasir Panjang Ridge. These were covered by Australian machine-gunners attached to the 1st Malay regiment who were well positioned for the job, having a perfect field of fire. A minor adjustment of my front line had to be made to protect my left flank and, while this was in progress, the Japanese attacked strongly along the slopes of the ridge which had been accurately shelled and bombed for two hours previously. They gained a lightning success; the machine-gunners disappeared and were next reported to be in Singapore town.'

Colonel John Dalley, the policeman in command of the Chinese guerrillas known as Dalforce, was stationed with his men on the West coast. He reported:

> The Australian Machine-Gun Battalion did not stand. They moved back. They were frightened and make no mistake. When I walked back to the road where I'd left my car I went up to Colonel Assheton AIF – a fine chap – and said, 'I don't think your chaps are very happy. They aren't liking this very much.' I walked round with him for half-an-hour – he could hold those men when he was around. Their spirits went up at once. I heard afterwards that he was killed very early in the piece. I felt the battalion wouldn't be so good without that particular CO, and that's what happened. They were all newcomers, hardly trained. It was very sad.*

Many Australians of 22nd Brigade streamed through Tengah airfield on 9th February 1942 and were seen throwing their arms away, in some cases dumping them down wells. Wing Commander Gregson, a RAF administrative officer based on the aerodrome, immediately called for volunteers from the ground staff to form a squad 'to help plug the gap'. The squad, which included officers and other ranks, became known as 'Gregson's Grenadiers', and it is reported that they did 'a terrific job' in the retreat to the final British perimeter.

Another feature of the Singapore fighting was the incidence of self-inflicted wounds, a matter mentioned in several books. Alf Johnson of the Royal Northumberland Fusiliers reports that there were many such cases during the attack on the island. He mentions two. 'Our platoon sergeant 'accidently' shot himself in the foot, and a full corporal shot out his middle finger whilst cleaning his revolver. But their hopes of a boat to Blighty were hopeless, because the last ships taking evacuees had gone.' Alf Johnson also wrote that his platoon officer, Second-Lieutenant Willis, stopped some British and Australian deserters at the point of his revolver. 'He said he'd shoot the first man who tried to pass – he rounded them all up and we escorted them back to our positions.' Over the next few hours they disappeared again. 'They obviously had no stomach to fight a lost cause.'[34] To balance this Alf saw several acts of heroism, one of which he

---

* Lieutenant-Colonel C.F. Assheton, a militia officer from New South Wales, was the CO of 2/20th Battalion with attached platoons of the 2/4th Machine-Gun Battalion – the unit which had given the trouble at Fremantle. Colonel Assheton was killed on 9th February, aged 41.

still vividly recalls. The battery officer of a Royal Artillery unit nearby was calling out his fire orders while leaning against a low wall and at the same time holding his intestines in with his hands. There was a gaping hole in the officer's stomach.

Until January 1993 it was evident from the many reports, official and unofficial, first-hand and second-hand, and from entries in the War Diaries, that there had been a deserter problem and that most of the deserters were Australians. But the reports gave an uncertain indication of the overall *size* of the problem. Nor has any historian or writer postulated that the deserter issue played a significant part in the fall of Singapore Island. It was not until certain British files, which had remained secret and unopened for fifty years, until 1993, were permitted to be read by the public that a clearer picture of the extent of the problem began to emerge.

In fact there has long been one readily available report – one which showed that at least one senior commander considered the deserter situation had been crucial to the fall of Singapore. By the time of the Japanese attack on the island Rear-Admiral E.J. Spooner was the senior naval officer there. He was in no doubt on 10th February that Singapore was lost. Neither was he in any doubt about one of the principal reasons for what was to be a short-lived siege. On that date he sent a handwritten letter to Captain Peter Cazalet of HMS *Durban*. In it he said he thought Singapore would be lost during the next two days. He went on, 'the present state of affairs was started by the AIF who just turned tail, became a rabble and let the Japs walk in unopposed'.[35]

Spooner had latterly been privy to all the information available to the innermost councils in Singapore. His statement was a generalization which took no cognisance of the gallant resistance put up by some Australian units. Nevertheless, it is unlikely that a senior officer would have penned such strong words had there not been considerable evidence to support them. He had no reason to make such a statement had his premiss not been true. Later, in perhaps the last letter he wrote to his wife (who had left Singapore earlier) he said, 'the Australians are rushing the sampans'.

Amongst the documents that came into the public domain at the beginning of 1993 was Vice-Admiral Sir Geoffrey Layton's complete War Diary, only portions of which had been available before.[36] Sir Geoffrey made many criticisms, implied and categorical, of official and military policies regarding Singapore. He also made special mention of the Australians:

I must mention the Australian troops particularly, because they are bound to be subject of much controversy. I have spoken to many officers and others on this subject, and I have read many reports. There is no doubt that the net result of these is this: The Australian troops in Malaya were, before the Japanese attack, fit and of magnificent physique, but they were idle, undisciplined and unprincipled, and, in spite of their sensitive arrogance, had not the self-respect that enables men to appreciate the worth of others. It was the worst possible thing for them that they spent ten months in idle waiting and that they were not flung into the battle as soon as it started. They have very good material among them, but the only possible school for it is battle, and battle alongside well-trained and disciplined troops. Given that experience, they can be magnificent troops, and some were magnificent in Malaya. But the evidence is too overwhelming that many, and I am afraid the majority, threw their hands in as soon as things looked black, and spread the canker of their panic the further by the previous reputation of their country's fighting men.

Sir Geoffrey did not confine his criticisms to the Australians:

As regards the Navy, morale was high in the ships of the China squadron, in spite of the realisation of the antiquity and inferiority of their ships. But among Naval personnel on shore, and in particular among the survivors of the *Prince of Wales* and *Repulse*, who had to be ruthlessly re-employed on shore as soon as they were fit, morale was patchy. The survivors had, of course, had a severe shock, and by the time bombing of their accommodation at Singapore had become frequent many were at the end of their tether.

Admiral Layton's remarks about the Australians had been available for public scrutiny well before 1993. They featured in an intelligence file at the British Public Record Office that had come into the public domain some years previously. But, like Admiral Spooner's letter to Captain Cazalet, it took on greater significance in company with the new evidence which had now emerged. Taken as a whole it put a new complexion on the deserter problem. If Admiral Layton's view that the majority of the Australians had thrown in their hands was correct, then this must have had a considerably greater effect on the brief siege of Singapore than had previously been even remotely envisaged.

As soon as the official escapees began arriving in Ceylon and India – they included officers, other ranks and civilians – they were interviewed by Intelligence officers who produced reports. The Chief Censor in India also began compiling a summary of extracts from letters which some escapees wrote home. These reports were sent to London, and some of the escapees eventually arrived there too.

On 1st June 1942 Brigadier J.K. Coffey, the Australian Military Liaison Officer to the Imperial General Staff, approached Colonel Spurling at the British War Office saying that he and the High Commissioner, Stanley M. Bruce (a former Australian Prime Minister), had heard several stories about the behaviour of Australian troops in Singapore which had been going the rounds of London. He had been asked to find out whether these stories could be substantiated.

A process of official obfuscation and disinformation was put in hand. Anglo-Australian relations were already under strain because of Canberra's belief that they had been misled by Britain over the defence of Singapore. (The Australians had already withdrawn their 7th Division from the Middle East. Originally intended to be landed in Java, it ended up back in Australia.) A series of internal memos on this subject began the rounds of Whitehall. One said:

> It is most important that no impression should be given that there is any form of War Office report on the behaviour of the Australian troops in Singapore. The fact that we have collected a few stories, most of which cannot possibly be substantiated, does not enable us even to start compiling a report. There is grave danger of most undesirable political repercussions if anyone should think we are doing so.[37]

The collection of a 'few' stories was by then about sixty, and although the collecting together of them may not have been a result of a government directive, they were in circulation around the innermost sanctums of Whitehall.

Brigadier Coffey followed up his oral request with a letter dated 4th June. (See Appendix 6.) The draft reply basically said that much of the material which was at hand was hearsay evidence, and that it did not help in arriving at any firm conclusions, and that anyway it was just possible that General Wavell's expected report might either substantiate or refute the stories, so let us wait. Brigadier Coffey, or perhaps Mr Bruce himself, must have become more persistent, for the extraordinary suggestion was made that perhaps Mr Bruce should be allowed to see the material providing he undertook not to tell his government! It is not known if Mr Bruce availed himself of this offer. If he did it must be doubtful whether he kept to the enforced undertaking. Surely his first duty would have been to remit any such knowledge home to his political superiors? Stanley Bruce was down-to-earth and practical, with a reputation for having little truck with either theory or rhetoric. Sir Robert Menzies wrote of Bruce's tenure as High Commissioner, 'In London, he had one country to serve, his own. He never permitted himself to forget it.'[38]

The British Prime Minister, Churchill, received the following internal memo on 5th June 1942 from the War Minister, P.J. Grigg:

Prime Minister

I think you should be aware that Auchinleck [now C-in-C, Middle East] has recently asked for the reintroduction of the death penalty for desertion in the field and cowardice in the face of the enemy. I enclose a copy of his letter for your information together with a note on the political history of the question.

Directly we introduce legislation we are at once in the following dilemma. If legislation is necessary, the facts and figures must be very serious. But, if they are serious, we can't afford to tell them either to our friends or to our enemies. So far as Libya is concerned, I must very much doubt whether the facts would justify the request. On the other hand the behaviour of the Australian troops in Malaya (see reports attached) make a much more powerful justification. But we daren't disclose these facts and anyhow we can't legislate for the Australians.

Init'd. PJG. 5.6.42.

General Wavell's report on Operations in Malaya and Singapore was dated 1st June 1942.[39] It did not refute the stories about the Australians, but confirmed them. After commenting on the refreshingly offensive spirit shown by the Australians at first, the report said:

Thereafter a rapid decline must have set in, because signs of a break in morale were noticeable even before the Japanese landing in their sector. Large numbers of AIF stragglers were seen in the town: many undoubtedly took the opportunity to desert in boats to Sumatra. Finally, the events of the night 8th/9th February seem to have destroyed almost completely their discipline and morale ...

Beyond any doubt morale and discipline had by this time [11th February] gone to pieces. The news of the landing and the failure of counter measures had been the final blow. The AIF according to incontrovertible evidence were affected more seriously at this crisis than some of the other units. The Commander Westforce [Bennett], issued his orders for a counter-attack to be carried out on the morning 11th February. One formation, at least, carried out their part; the AIF did *not* and in his report the Commander says that the counter-attack was impossible. There can only be one deduction ...

For the fall of Singapore itself, the Australians are held responsible.

Wavell's report must have arrived in Britain by the end of June, but Brigadier Coffey was not informed of the fact. It seems that he or Stanley

Bruce kept on pressing, for on 28th August Churchill sent the following personal memo to his immediate colleagues.

No. 335/2
No one should see these reports except the War Cabinet. It would be a mistake to stir these matters in any way. We have quite enough coming towards us in the future without adding to work and controversy. Anyhow the longer these matters are left alone the better, and the more chance there is of their resurrection being postponed till after the war is won.

[Initialled] WSC.

Churchill followed this up with another memo dated 6th September:

No. M 353/2
To Secretary of State for the Dominions. I do not see why Mr Bruce should get to hear of the existence of these documents. They deal with the past and not current business. I particularly do not wish it to be known outside our own war cabinet circle that there are such despatches in existence, because this will lead to questions about them and a demand for their publication. The whole of this inglorious business is being effaced by other events, and there are more to come.

Mr Bruce would, I think, feel bound to report to his Government, and this would open up another train of annoyances. I am therefore against showing them to him. Should he, however, find out through some inadvertent remark, I do not see that great harm would be done. I should say we had withheld the documents from him out of delicacy, as they reflected upon the Australian troops, and that I had no intention of a controversy breaking out on such a point which would be injurious to Imperial sentiment.

WSC.

Wavell's report was based on what he had seen for himself, on War Diaries that had been got out of Singapore (including, one suspects, certain important Appendices to these War Diaries that are now missing from the consecutive sequences in them), and on reports made by official escapees.

The sixty or so reports in the latter category were a mixed bag. A few were angry in tone, even bordering on the hysterical; but most were couched in measured terms. Most were by military personnel, but a number were by civilians, including a long one by the influential editor of the *Straits Times*, George Seabridge, who had a lot to say about the bad discipline of the Australians pre-war. But the most important of them was the one made by one of the senior officers of HQ, Malaya Command, who was ordered out of Singapore just before the capitulation. He was Lieutenant-Colonel (later Brigadier) H.C. Phillips. He made his report in India. He had been Percival's GSO1 (Operations).[40] In it he stated that when the Japanese attacked across the strait on the evening of the 8th February

> there was practically no opposition or firing by the Australians. *By the morning of 8th February* (Author's italics) Australian Battalions were reported to be down to 200 other ranks. The remainder had deserted to Singapore Town, where as fast as they were rounded up by Australian patrols and sent up to personnel collection centres they again deserted.

As the nominal size of a battalion was around 1,200 men, this indicates that in excess of 80 per cent of some units at least were missing from the front line on the morning of 8th February. The Japanese invaded the island that evening.

Colonel Phillips went on to report an extraordinary incident which took place on that same morning during the softening up process by Japanese artillery. Brigadier Maxwell, commanding the Australian 27th Brigade, visited GHQ, Malaya Command, and saw General Percival. According to Phillips, Maxwell said:

> In civil life I am a doctor. If the patient's arm is bad I cut it off, but if the whole body goes bad then no operation can save the patient – he must die. So it is with Singapore – there is no use fighting to try to prolong its life.

Phillips added that Maxwell was shown the door.

That Maxwell intended to make such a visit is confirmed by the Australian, Colonel Thyer, although he indicates that he spoke to Maxwell on this matter after the initial Japanese landings, but before the landings in Maxwell's own sector, which would have made it on 9th February. He reported, in 1953, that 'Maxwell considered that what was going on on Singapore Island after the Japanese landings was senseless slaughter. Maxwell was going back to Percival to urge him to surrender.' Thyer went on to say that he urged Maxwell not to do this but to go to Bennett.[41]

Although Maxwell was a doctor in civilian life and used medical metaphors in his approach to Percival, in Malaya he was a brigade commander. One can call him, because of his views, either a defeatist or a pragmatist. The very least he can be accused of, if he did not take Thyer's advice and go to see Bennett first, is a serious breach of military etiquette by going over his immediate superior's head.

Was his caring attitude towards his men the sole reason for making this astonishing approach, an approach made *before* his own brigade at least, had fired a single shot at invaders on the island? Or was it because he was aware that many of his men were not prepared to fight and had vacated the front line? This theory is supported by that War Diary entry for 10th February which stated that some Australians were missing from the front before the Japanese attack, and by Colonel Phillips's statement that Australians were already absent from the front in great numbers on 8th February.

Did Maxwell take Thyer's advice and go to see Bennett first? If he did, did he afterwards see Percival with his superior officer's blessing? He was close to General Bennett who had promoted him to command of 27th Brigade in the first place. It is known that Bennett thought little of the chances of holding Singapore (he started planning his own escape about the 3rd February according to Colonel Thyer who was invited to accompany him but did not go) and Bennett stated in an interview with General Kirby and the Official Australian Historian on 30th January 1953, that:

the fact that when the troops got back to the island the Naval Base had been destroyed was a blow to their psychology, adding, 'We said, what are we defending?' There was a feeling that all was lost and from now on we were achieving nothing. To say that one was depressed was to put it very mildly.'[42]

In view of Bennett's nature and the aura of pugnacity and fighting spirit which he had gone to great lengths to build up about himself, he could not have made such an approach to Percival. But to avail himself of someone else, someone who had thought the idea up and volunteered to make it, and one who in another life was a caring medical man to boot, may have been an opportunity not to be missed.

In a letter to General Sir Lewis Heath after the war, General Percival said:

From what I have since heard I believe that Gordon Bennett painted a very false picture, both to you and to me, of the situation on his front and the state of his troops. He was a very vain and self-centred man and I believe now, though I admit I did not fully realise it at the time, that from the time he left Segamat he had but one object in mind. You can guess what I mean. I believe that, if the Australians had been properly led, they would have risen to the occasion even at the eleventh hour.

General Heath had previously written these words to General Percival:

'I didn't realise to the full extent to which the AIF had been blowing own trumpets till they were seen at close quarters on the Island.'

Colonel Phillips gave it as his opinion, 'That Australians did not fight because, a) they had no discipline, and b) they all considered it a waste of time trying to defend the island. In his opinion this idea percolated down through the division from the Divisional Commander who is thought to have held strong personal views on this question.'

Another of Percival's Staff Officers to escape with permission was Lieutenant-Colonel (later Colonel) B.H. Ashmore of the Scots Guards. He was GSO1 (Staff Duties).[43] He made his report when he reached India:

> Heavy fighting took place in the Western Area all day of the 10th and 11th February. The AIF had by this time definitely cracked and the roads leading from the West were littered with Australian soldiers in all degrees of demoralisation. Considerable looting of private houses, including my own, took place by these men in search of liquor. The docks were full of them and quite a large number managed to get away. The reason for this 'crack' is difficult to understand as the AIF had fought extremely well in Johore and at the battle of Gemas but there is no doubt whatsoever that something failed. I am of the opinion that it was largely due to lack of discipline. Where discipline is weak it takes very little for a panic to set in.

Here is a selection of other reactions and opinions taken from the previously secret files:

Major J.C. Westall, Royal Marines (a Staff Officer in Naval Intelligence) – who had escaped aboard the *Gorgon* – said, 'with regard to the much discussed Australians, I can only say that on 11th February the waterfront was a mass of demoralised troops looking for any means of leaving the island. I should say that at least 80 per cent of them were Australians, the remainder British and Indian, the latter appearing more lost than broken. I personally saw cases of Australian officers endeavouring to persuade their men to return to their units, but who flatly refused to do so.'

In charge of operating No. 4 Water Transport Company in Keppel Harbour was Major A. Hart-Davies, RASC. He reported: 'Deserters from the Australian Army were looting the Singapore Harbour Board godowns all the time during the last three days before the capitulation and as my unit was stationed on an island in the harbour these men kept up a running rifle fire at my men and boats, the Australians being unable to get to them for further desertions. I am pleased to report that only one warrant officer was creased in the back of the neck.'

Part of one of the statements in the files caused something of a sensation when it was made public in January 1993. It caused a furore in Australia. A British major in the Malayan Volunteer Force J.C.K. Marshall said: 'The Australians were known as daffodils – beautiful to look at but yellow all through.'

This is the type of sweeping generalization that would be made unthinkingly by soldiers in such circumstances. Many Australians in Malaya fought bravely. Men of the 8th Division earned a Victoria Cross, one Distinguished Service Order, four Military Crosses, a Distinguished Conduct Medal, and four Military Medals, during the campaign. Although no doubt some of the deserters were cowards, cowardice is not the only motive for desertion.

A copy of Captain Tufton Beamish's long letter from India to his Member of Parliament father, which had been passed on to Churchill, was included in one of the files. Beamish was on the Staff of 18th Division. Here are relevant extracts from his letter:

> Everything I know of General Gordon Bennett inclines me to think him a most ordinary soldier and perhaps an even more ordinary man ...
>
> The general behaviour and attitude of the AIF on Singapore island certainly reflects nothing but discredit on its Commander ...
>
> As for the battle itself ... The AIF did not comply with their orders and many forward posts withdrew or were withdrawn. Their resistance as a whole can but have been feeble and half-hearted. Their casualties in the early stages were not heavy. Some localities may have fought gallantly. I know that several posts withdrew without firing a shot and before they had come under fire ...
>
> In actual fact the AIF was in need of a rest and their morale was extremely low. I am not exaggerating when I say that many of them had no intention of doing any more fighting. Several hundred Australians were in the docks days before the capitulation looking for a boat home.[44]

There are many other reports of this nature in the files. Lieutenant (later Vice Admiral Sir) John Hayes, said, after reporting that Admiral Spooner had ordered armed guards to be placed on the boats lying off *Laburnum* because Australians were storming them, '... in the neighbourhood of the Oranje Hotel the streets were full of obvious deserters. They loitered in twos and threes, armed and shouting the news that "they won't be long now". A number of them were drunk and the large majority were certainly Australians ... There were NCOs among them but all shred of discipline had gone ... It was hard to believe that such utter demoralisation among trained, disciplined men could exist'.

One of the interviewing officers in Colombo, Lieutenant-Colonel Pearse, wrote how he had 'received numerous reports from evacuees from Malaya regarding the bad behaviour of Australian troops in the battle for Malaya. Many of my informants appear to be reliable people, the last two of whom I have spoken to being members of the Press Censorship Department, Singapore, Messrs Pierson and Cameron, both of many years experience in Malaya.'

One Volunteer Force man was interviewed at Colombo on 28th July 1942. The interviewing officer reported: 'The informant's opinion of the Australian troops at Singapore is not high. The secretary of the Union Jack Club was shot by them because he would not supply liquor, the Rex Hotel was smashed up for the same reason, and Australians were looting while the Japanese were invading the island.'

The report of the interview of Major W.H. Aucutt of the FMSVF, goes, 'On the island he saw no fighting at all but he did see a great many Australians in Singapore town and many of them were drunk. The 2/19th and 2/20th Australian battalions used to draw their rations from his supply section. He noticed that the ration indent numbers were going down every day. He asked one of the Australian NCOs whom he knew, why this was so. The NCO replied, "If you're thinking what I guess you're thinking, you're right". Parties of Australians used to come to the section stating that they had been sent to draw seven days' rations. They never got them. It was felt by a number of people that the lack of fighting qualities of the Australians affected the morale of the other troops on the island.'

Lieutenant N. Bell, MRNVR, saw many Australian deserters on 12th February. They were rushing the boats. Val Kobouky, a Czech civilian, described Australians as 'roving brigands'. He reported that a group of young Australian officers went berserk after a dinner party in their honour, and smashed up their host's house.

A Lieutenant-Colonel of the Durham Light Infantry on secondment, reported that while discipline throughout was not good, the AIF were the worst offenders. 'They pride themselves,' he said, 'in their free and easy ways, and such ways may not have serious consequences when things are going well, but their effects are very different in a losing battle.' He went on to say that when he remonstrated with one of the deserters who were straggling all over the town, the man threatened to blow him to hell with two Mills grenades.

An Inspector of Mines in the Malayan Civil Service named M.C. Hay, then serving as a Lance-Bombadier with the FMSVF, reported, 'There were many stories of the cause of the fall and I hope some day there will be a proper enquiry. I think the chief causes were – the Australian troops were insufficiently trained and this was the cause of their desertion.' He added another cause that applied to British and Indian Army officers: 'Methods of war suitable for Salisbury Plain or the Indian Frontier were used instead of those for jungle warfare.' He confirmed that an order had been issued that deserters be shot. '[During escape] we marched in single file and answered all challenges with "Patrol" or "looking for our unit" as troops had been told to fire on anyone escaping. Later on we found out that this order had been given a week previously when the Australians were running for it and it had not been countermanded, although several regular units had been told on this afternoon to try and escape individually.' (Hay escaped on the night of the capitulation. It was his party which linked up with General Gordon Bennett's escape party.)

The only report in the files that mentioned the Australians favourably was that of Lieutenant-Colonel Stewart of the Argylls. He said, 'The AIF to my knowledge fought very well indeed ... It is true that a number straggled down into the town and did make an early getaway, but that equally applies to British troops.'

Lieutenant-Colonel J.M Spurling, in his covering letter with the reports sent to the Deputy Director Military Operations at the War Office, wrote: 'In fairness to the Australian troops it must be remembered that they fought well in Johore. It appears that from General Gordon Bennett downwards, the majority of the Australian Division were of the opinion that it was useless to try to defend Singapore Island. Thus, being intensely individualistic, and lacking discipline, they just never tried. I do not think they necessarily funked it.'

Taken as a whole the reports represent a substantial body of evidence, much of it based on personal observation, and the whole underpinned by the two reports from senior staff officers which show that the scale of desertions was very high indeed. Unless one is prepared to believe that the reports were a tissue of lies, or all a gross exaggeration, or that, because the sources were all British, they were biased, it meant that the deserter factor must have been an important consideration when the decision was made to capitulate.

As the sources of these reports were all British, this did lead to accusations of bias when excerpts from them were published in the press in early 1993; and there is no doubt they were deficient in that respect.

In the process of research into published Australian material for confirmation, or otherwise, of the scale of desertions, something very interesting soon came to light. When General Gordon Bennett arrived in Australia after his escape he produced a report which mainly attributed the blame for the fall of Malaya and Singapore to the low morale, inexperience and lack of training of Indian Army troops. But he also reported that, on 11th February, the AIF casualties were approximately 7,000 killed or missing with approximately 2,000 wounded in hospital. So, according to Bennett, on 11th February – note the date – the Australian losses were about half of his total force of 18,500 men. (He did not define what he meant by 'missing' in this context, or if he did, it did not appear in the summary of the report that the Australian government remitted to London.)

The Official History of the Australian Medical Services[45] however, gives the following figures for AIF casualties up to 15th February:

Killed in action		405
Died of Wounds		111
Missing		1919
Wounded in action	approx.	1364

Leaving aside the wounded this gives a total of killed and missing of 2,435. There is a discrepancy therefore of 4,575 between Bennett's figures for the 11th and the official ones for the 15th. There are only two possible explanations for this: either the 'missing' men had been captured by the 11th, or they were somewhere else other than at the front line, or, of course, a mixture of the two. Incidentally, the British Official History puts the total of all Commonwealth dead and wounded in the Malayan campaign at 8,700. The Japanese killed and missing total for the campaign was 9,824.

Neither the Australian nor the British Official Histories, nor any of the surviving War Diaries, give any indication that by the 11th, three days after the attack, anything like 4,500 men of any nationality had been captured by the Japanese on the island of Singapore. Colonel Tsuji, Chief of Staff to General Yamashita, also makes no mention of captives on this scale in his book about the campaign.[46] Surely if they had been taken he would have mentioned it, as the capture of that number of prisoners after less than three days on the island would have caused the Japanese no end of a logistical problem – not to mention that it would have been a feather in their caps they, and Tsuji would have wanted to vaunt. No other account of the campaign, including those by Britons and Australians who were there, has ever mentioned this either. That HQ, Malaya Command, War Diary entry for 1600 hours on the 10th, says, *'Casualties are not by any means heavy and General Gordon Bennett does not require reinforcements as yet.'* (Author's italics.) Other reports indicate the same: that casualties, which would have included an estimate of missing men, missing in the sense that they were behind enemy lines, were not at all heavy; so it cannot be that between 1600 hours on 10th February and sometime on the following day, 4,500 of Bennett's men were taken prisoner. So, they must have been otherwise absent from the front.

There are copies of certain Australian archival material in the British Public Records Office. One of them is called the Report on Operations of 8th Australian Division in Malaya, from which quotations have already been used elsewhere in this book.[47] The existence of this report in Britain has apparently escaped the notice of historians, for although it was made open to the public in 1977, none of the books written about the Malayan campaign since that date have referred to this source. The report had been brought back to England from Australia in 1953 by the Official Historian, Kirby, but it seems that he was not permitted to make use of the material in it relating to the deserter situation. The Australian Official Historian did not use it either. In fact, while both official histories tend to gloss over the deserter situation, there is more on the subject in the Australian than in the British one.

This Australian report was compiled by Colonel J.H. Thyer and Colonel C.H. Kappe of the AIF, from extensive notes made by them when they were prisoners of war. It contains material from most captured Australian officers. It is thus a contemporary source of great reliability, and, most importantly, it is an Australian document. It also contains evidence that gives the lie to General Gordon Bennett's later professed admiration for General Percival and the excellent relations he said he had with Malaya Command.[48] In Bennett's official report he said: 'AIF found nothing but full co-operation when staff Malaya Command was approached. Relations most friendly throughout.'

The 8th Division Report paints a completely different picture:

> It was well-known in Malaya before the operations and it was amply borne out during the operations that the Australian GOC was incapable of subordinating himself to Malaya Command or of co-operating wholeheartedly with other commands. From discussions in captivity with Generals Percival, Heath, Key, and Keith Simmons, it appears that the relations between them were more strained than the above statement would indicate.

The report noted that 'the Japanese crossed the Strait and landed in the AIF sector practically unopposed'. (A 'practically unopposed' landing certainly does not lead one to think that many men could have been taken prisoner during the process.) Then, speaking first about the mainland battles, then the retreat to Singapore Island, and finally about the stand at the final perimeter, comes the following:

> The conduct of the AIF in Malaya has been subject to some criticism. A close inspection of the narrative will show that in the main the units in Malaya fought reasonably well; and any gratuitous charges, as may have appeared in the Press from time to time are both ill-informed and unfair. The fact must be faced, however, that the AIF did not measure up to the task required of it in a heartbreaking withdrawal. Ultimately the morale deteriorated, and in the last stages only two-thirds *at most* of those fit to fight were manning the final perimeters.
>
> It is known that the units in Libya and Greece behaved in a similar manner in parallel circumstances. There can be only one

explanation for this and it is submitted that the Australian, in
the early stages of a war, lacks military virtue.

This quote from an incontrovertible and authoritative Australian source
shows that, towards the end, less than two-thirds of those Australians
'fit to fight' were available to do so. Unfortunately it is too vague to give
much guidance on the actual numbers involved. All that can be said is
that it proves beyond any doubt that there were Australian deserters
and that the number of them was very substantial indeed.

The authors of the report then went on to talk about the necessity
of providing proper training in peace, and said that unless the national
attitude towards this was changed, then due allowance must be made for
the lack of military virtue in the Australian soldier. They then said that
this applied equally to British troops.

As also happened in India and London, evidence about the fall of
Singapore began accumulating in Australia within a short time of the
event. This evidence would have come from many sources, quite apart
from General Bennett's report.

The *Gorgon*, with up to 400 evacuees on board, arrived in Fremantle
on 20th February and others were to arrive at various Australian ports
during the succeeding weeks. Many of these evacuees, especially the
military ones, would have been interviewed by Intelligence officers in
exactly the same way as were those evacuees who arrived in India and
Ceylon. The two American officers aboard *Gorgon*, Colonel Tormey and
Colonel Craig, would have made excellent witnesses, not only because
of their rank, but because, being Americans, their reports could be
considered unbiased. One British intelligence officer, Major Westall of
the Royal Marines, was also on that vessel.

In Singapore on 13th February an official band of 100 Australian
military evacuees was organised. On that date General Percival issued
instructions for any remaining air force and naval personnel to leave the
island along with selected army officers and other ranks with specialised
knowledge. Admiral Spooner had found spaces in the fleet of small craft
he had got together for about 3,000 last-minute evacuees. Altogether 1,800
of these spaces were allotted to the military, including the hundred to
the AIF. In fact, of the Australian official party, only 39 who were led
by Colonel J.R. Broadbent managed to get aboard a ship. The rest were
held up at the dock gates – which deserters, mainly Australians, were
attempting to rush – and so never got away.

Colonel Broadbent and most of his party eventually arrived back in
Australia. Broadbent himself arrived on 6th March. Leaving aside the one
by General Bennett, Broadbent's report on Singapore must have been the
most important one received. He had been Bennett's Assistant Adjutant
and Quartermaster General. He was an experienced soldier having served
with the AIF in France in World War One.[49]

It must have been Colonel Broadbent who was the unnamed Australian colonel mentioned by Molly Reilly in the following section of her memoir, for he was the only one of that rank to escape. They were on the same ship to Australia. Broadbent, if it was indeed he, had strong views about the behaviour of the Australians in Singapore, and would have reported so to the authorities. Molly Reilly said:

> One morning at breakfast my cabin companion and I were joined by a grey-haired Colonel and four young officers. The one topic was Singapore – and the possible reasons for its fall. We sat dumb. We were much too embittered to say anything and in addition we felt it was not politic on the boat to say what we thought about the fall of Singapore as we were both firmly convinced that, had the Aussies put up any sort of resistance, we would not be destitute and homeless as we were! But we had been shown such kindness on the boat we decided to say nothing, as we could see that the lads were very upset and ashamed and guessed there was a 'nigger in the woodpile' somewhere. This particular morning one of the officers said, 'I just can't understand how the Japs ever got on to the island – it couldn't have had any proper defences – who on earth let the first lot through', and then the Colonel burst out with, 'I'll tell you how the Japs got on the island – my men let them through – and the Japs landed with scarcely any opposition. When the Japs dropped bombs the troops just threw away their arms and equipment and ran like rabbits. I tried to rally them and pointed out that the Jap bombing was nothing to what I had gone through in France in the last war from the German shells – I grant that we had no air support at all, but neither had we in France – but the troops were completely demoralized long before the Japs got near them – and so the first 300 Japs landed – and there were thousands of our men to stop them *and* guns – and so it was the beginning of the end. I'm an Australian – but I'm going back to get out of this uniform because I'm ashamed of it. These ladies have us to thank for having lost home and everything they possess.' With that he got up, leaving a stunned silence on the part of the officers at the table.

Molly Reilly's memoir was dated March 1942 and was written in Melbourne where she obtained a cipher job with Australian Military Command. A friend urged her to get the memoir published, but by the time the censors had finished with it she decided against that course. (The censors were insisting that all the references to Australians in it must be deleted.)

Several Australian pressmen escaped from Singapore and got back to

Australia. One whole party of them got away, and one of their number, Athole Stewart, the Press Conducting Officer to the AIF, wrote a book about the party's escape.[50] He and his fellows would have reported to the authorities what they knew of the last days of Singapore even though censorship regulations prevented them publishing much on the subject. But despite the efforts of the censors there can be little doubt that what the pressmen knew would have percolated through the press grapevine.

Other home-based reporters would have picked up quite a lot of information from crew members of ships, especially those arriving in Australian ports with extensive, and therefore newsworthy, bomb damage like the *Empire Star* which underwent repairs in Sydney in early March 1942.

A number of RAAF, RNZAF, and RAF officers (Flight Lieutenant Elson-Smith was among the former) got back too. All would have had their stories to tell. On a different level, the High Commissioner in London, Stanley Bruce, would have remitted messages about what he had heard (and perhaps been shown) in London. So would the Australian Government representatives in India and Ceylon.

Rumours about the behaviour of their troops in Singapore went buzzing around the island continent until August 1942, though few knew what exactly had happened. The rumours were no doubt fuelled by the stories told by civilian evacuees and the crews of merchant ships, by hints dropped by pressmen and, perhaps most of all, by the stories about soldiers being taken off a ship under armed guard at Fremantle.

Unable to refer to the matter directly because of the censorship regulations, many articles began appearing in Australian newspapers on the benefits of discipline in troops and how that affected morale. Although at first no specific mention was made of Singapore in this context, it was clear that the substance of the articles concerned the fall of that fortress.

The articles set a high moral tone. In one, which appeared in the *Melbourne Argus* on 1st July 1942, four months after Singapore had fallen, George H. Johnston wrote:

> In the past few weeks much has been spoken and written about morale and discipline in war. And always the thought has occurred to me that morale is a creation of the spirit of men and women that flourishes with training and guidance, that discipline, though often foreign to the Australian character, comes from training and from knowledge of the values of discipline ...
>
> Trainees – most of them mere youngsters who found when bombs began to fall that the swaggering, disorderly truculence (which some youngsters seem to think always goes with an Australian uniform) was not much use when sticks of bombs were falling. Some of the loudest talkers were the

swiftest runners, and some of them would have won marathon competitions.

In the same edition of that newspaper there appeared a report copied from the 30th June edition of the London *Times*:

> Various papers received from General Sir Archibald Wavell regarding loss of Malaya and Singapore were unsuitable for publication in wartime, said Mr Churchill in the House of Commons today. Their publication would clearly cause much ill will in parts of the Empire.

On 2nd July 1942 the *Melbourne Argus* started to run a series of articles about morale by a Professor Chisholm. Under the heading 'Training for Victory' the following appeared:

> Observers who have seen Australian soldiers in action have given some illuminating instances of the advantages of real discipline and training and the dangers attendant on the neglect of these – a difference sometimes between life and death.

In August the Australian government must have decided that the only way to end the rumours and perhaps at the same time instil in their soldiers the need for strong discipline, was to make an official comment based on all the reports they had received. On 17th August the Director-General of the Australian Department of Information wrote an article entitled 'New Light On The Fall Of Singapore'. He chose as the medium for publishing it one of his own newspapers, the *Adelaide Advertizer*. It was quickly taken up by most other newspapers in the land, and transmitted abroad by Reuters. It was published in India, but never in Britain. The author of it was the newspaper tycoon, Sir Keith Murdoch. (Rupert Keith Murdoch who has set his horizons rather wider than his father, is his son.)[51] The article is very long, so it is précised here:

NEW LIGHT ON THE LAST DAYS OF SINGAPORE

So ended the greatest surrender in British history, and the most bitter tragedy that has come into the life of Australia.

Few men have escaped who saw the last moments of the catastrophe, but many specialists in various arms were hurried away during the final days, and a trickle of men escaped from the front to the Dutch islands. From these most of the essential facts have now been gathered about that last great battle – the battle that should never have been fought, but having been entered upon, should have been a very different kind of fight ...

Why the island passed so quickly into Japanese hands is explicable only by researches into the intricate subjects of morale, tactics and leadership.

There were fully 90,000 British troops to give battle; stores and munitions were ample; yet from the first the garrison had few chances, and except for some sections of officers who maintain to this day that if the Australians had held on the north-western beaches we would still have the island, the feeling of hopelessness seems to have been general. In a percentage of the troops it was so close to the crust of morale that it soon broke through into demoralization ...

It has been claimed that by the time the Japanese soldiers set out for the island beaches ... every Australian beach position had been blown out. This cannot be so, but it is true that our men had been hammered by shell and by bomb, and that the reply from our guns had been feeble ...

But we had not had heavy casualties, nor did we have them in subsequent fighting ...

We were overwhelmed in our forward positions, particularly where the 19th battalion with its sixty per cent new reinforcements stood; our reserves failed to make effective counter-attacks, or even effective stands; and a good many of our men appeared far behind our lines, unnerved and not knowing where to go.

The Japanese came straight through the middle of the Australian positions ... The only landing for the first two days was against the Australians. Singapore was lost in the first day's fighting ...

There were, of course, many heroic incidents, much brave fighting and counter-charging worthy of the best tradition. We had sad defections, and it was notable that the men who did not stand were the boozy 'tough' men, who had always had the wrong ideas of discipline and were noisy and boastful ...

On the 10th, the Australians formed a perimeter between the reservoirs and the city. Only about 2,000 of the original six infantry battalions and machine-gun battalions were mustered there. Other personnel brought the AIF numbers up to something like 5,000, and here they held their own until the end ...

Our own part [in the pre-war preparations] was marred by a constant jarring and belittlement of our British and Indian comrades, by inadequate discipline, and finally by the percentage of weak and undisciplined soldiers breaking down under the strain of battle ...

The worst trouble we were under was the indiscipline of small elements that were never thoroughly digested by the better men. Too long has it been a distorted tradition of the last war that discipline is not necessary to attain high fighting value, indeed that indiscipline marked the first AIF. All who knew the stern battle-discipline of the earlier soldiers know how mistaken is this view.*

The main part of the Australian force was magnificent. They were imbued with deep patriotic devotions, and had prepared themselves for their soldier tasks until they were like steel ...

Today in Singapore, renamed Shonan, 'the City of Light and Peace in the South' ... our own men are in prison camps, and we know little about them. We do not know even who are dead, although we do know the number is not great ...

Could they [the prisoners] get a message freely to us, what would they say?

They would have us ... know from their own harsh experience, that weak indiscipline must be eradicated from the Army wherever it shows up ...

So there it was, straight from the horse's mouth; from a man who, as Director-General of the Department of Information was a member of the enlarged Australian War Cabinet, and accordingly would have had access to all the available reports on Singapore.

The total of Australian troops in Singapore was about 18,500. Of these the fighting men, made up of six battalions of infantry, two machine-gun battalions, and various front line support troops, probably amounted to a minimum of 12,500. (The other 6,000 – it may have been fewer – would have been administrative and logistical troops.) If we reduce the front line figure by the number of dead, missing, and wounded – later officially recorded as about 3,800 – this gives a balance of 8,700 men. (Some of the casualties must have been administrative troops, but this calculation is in round figures.) Sir Keith Murdoch reported that the number of front line troops on the final perimeter was only 2,000, which means there was a shortfall of 6,700 in this category who were not there manning the front line. No doubt a few were already prisoners by that time, but their number would not have been great, for as Sir Keith said 'but we had no heavy casualties nor did we in subsequent fighting'. This is confirmed by British sources. Furthermore, not all the deserters would have been front-line troops. Administrative troops based well behind the front line, would have been witnesses to the exodus towards the city and

---

*Keith Murdoch was a war correspondent in the Great War serving with the AIF. Amongst other places, he served at Gallipoli.

the docks. So who can doubt that many of them would have joined in the rush? According to Sir Keith, 3,000 'other troops' were brought into the perimeter (the Australian Official History confirms the use of a number of administrative troops on the front line) so that accounts for all but 3,000 of the non-front-liners. If only half of this rump deserted (in line with the half of the front line troops that were missing) that would bring the total number of Australian deserters up to a figure in excess of 8,000.

That is close to one half of the total and the figure is in keeping with Admiral Layton's comment on the Australian troops, 'that many, and I am afraid the majority, threw their hands in'. It is in line with the information in Colonel Phillips' report. It is not out of keeping with the general statement made in the Report of Operations of the Australian 8th Division that 'two-thirds *at most* of those fit to fight were manning the final perimeter'. Finally, it is in keeping with the tenor of the body of reports made public in Britain in 1993.

Lionel Wigmore, the Australian Official Historian, wrote, without specifying the nationalities involved, that:

> The extent of the movement from the island is indicated by the fact that although many who took part in it died and others were captured, about 3,000 reached Java, Ceylon, and India through Sumatra.

He was referring to the deserters who escaped from the island. But the greater proportion of the deserters probably made little attempt to leave. Boats were in short supply, and anyway, without a knowledge of the local waters and of seamanship, escaping in open boats was a hazardous undertaking, not to mention the attention such craft would get from the Japanese air force.

An important and largely unknown event, which is not mentioned in any of the histories of the campaign, proves both that the deserters at Singapore were not exclusively Australians, but also indicates that the overall scale of desertions was very high indeed. The event concerned involved the disappearance from the final front line perimeter of almost an entire regiment of the Indian Army on the penultimate day of the campaign. The evidence for this statement is in the campaign memoir of the Commanding Officer of the battalion, the 2/10th Baluch Regiment, a memoir which until now has only been seen by that officer's immediate family.[52] It is confirmed in the official history of the Baluch Regiment.[53]

On or about 4th February 1942 the newly-promoted Lieutenant-Colonel Phillip Parker took command of 2/10th Baluch. As a major he had previously served as GS02 with 11th Indian Division and some passages from his memoirs dealing with his experiences in that capacity have appeared earlier in this book. He was a soldier of considerable experience, having joined the Indian Army in 1919.

The 2/10th was not one of the new and untrained units to arrive late at Singapore. As part of 8th Brigade it had confronted the Japanese when they first landed at Kota Bharu. On Singapore Island the battalion received replacements, both officers and men, for some of the casualties sustained on the mainland, but most of the battalion consisted of by now battle-seasoned men. However, the classic ingredients for trouble in the Indian Army existed within its ranks. The men did not know their new CO (Colonel Parker's parent regiment was 12th Frontier Force Rifles), and there was no time for this to be even partially rectified. Like all the battalions in Malaya it suffered from a dearth of experienced officers. Furthermore, as Colonel Parker's report shows, Indian independence influences had taken root amongst the troops.

Colonel Parker's recorded criticism of the conduct of his new command began on 12th February when the battalion was operating in the Nee Soon area in the north of Singapore Island. On that date he picked out for special criticism his 'B' Company under Captain Barhan-ud-din. He wrote:

> 'B' Company reported later that enemy had advanced in columns down main road preceded by civilians – LMG [light machine-gun] post overwhelmed. As main road was in full view up [to] 500 yards, this section appears not to have been on alert – should have done great execution.

He went on to note:

> Men of Baluch Regiment were very shaky for lack of leaders. On two occasions foremost platoons came out of action without orders but were stopped and went back into positions nearby. But they were in poor fighting form.

On that same date 8th Brigade, of which 2/10th Baluch was still part, was ordered to withdraw southwards, and on the following day, the 13th, they took up positions south of Paya Lebar. The 2/10th's task was to cover a major road junction on the north-east side of the final British perimeter around Singapore City. At about 1500 hours on 13th February, while he was attending a CO's conference, Colonel Parker received a message that the enemy was approaching his position from the north. The remainder of the story is best told in his own words:

> 'B' Company Baluch were out of touch for some time but were in position by latter part of afternoon. Troops dug in but practically

no wire available. Dispositions: right forward 'B' Company; left forward 'A' Company. In rear 'A' Company – 'C' Company. Echeloned back on right and in touch with 14 Punjab. Reserve 'D' Company. HQ at Braddell Rd/Paya Lebar Rd crossroads. Some Jap mortar fire onto forward positions on main road about 1600 hours. Enemy made no attempt to come on and companies had the afternoon to dig in and get to know their positions. Two platoons of 'D' Company were used to bring up food and the wire for forward companies. This continued through the greater part of the night. Companies were linked to Bn. HQ by phone but that to 'B' Company was faulty.

As soon as dark fell 14 Punjab opened an increasing wild fire – largely tracer and the disease spread to some extent to Baluch area. Very disturbing and upsetting in view of normal Japanese tactics which were similar when they penetrated our areas. MMG fire could be seen and heard to our rear and was, I believe, Manchesters who fired across our rearward line of communications. An attack or at least infiltration was anticipated in the early hours of 14th and in the hope of disorganising any such move, periodic concentrations of artillery fire were called for from supporting battery of 135th Field Regt. Target, south edge of Paya Lebar. 'A' Company reported many 'shorts' and stated one platoon had been wiped out. I certainly noticed one shell at this period which on passing over me sounded very low and likely to be a 'short'. Later 'A' Company reported platoon had suffered casualties from own artillery fire but still in position. Wild fire continued all night but in decreasing strength.

'A' and 'C' Companys reported suspected infiltration about 0400 hours. About 0500 hours orders issued by phone to all companies to start clearing up infiltration at 0545 hours. 'A' Company also to patrol to and ensure contact with 'B' Company to whom phone had been very poor most of the night. By about 0700 hours all companies reported areas clear of any enemy (I don't believe there was any infiltration) and touch established with 'B' Company. Adjutant visited companies and was with OC 'A' Company [Leigh] and OC 'B' Company [Barhan-ud-din] about 0700 hours.

About 0720 'A' Company reported enemy had entered their left forward platoon area. Ordered to hold on at all costs. About 0730 hours 2 i/c, 'C' Company [Hilder], reported one platoon of 'A' had fallen back onto 'C' Company and shortly afterwards that enemy had entered 'C' company position but that Sanghal [OC, 'C' Company] was alright and could be heard shouting. Then [Hilder said] 'Here they come, I'll report again in a few minutes.' There was no further report and no reply to my calls. Adjutant came back wounded and reported Japanese in 'C' Company area, all men standing up and apparently a lot of talk going on. He estimated only 25 Japanese in the position and offered to lead a counter-attack with the one platoon of 'D' Company which was on hand. [One platoon 'D' Company had been ordered to occupy high ground between 'B' and Reinforcements during the night; one platoon had not reported back from carrying up wire.]

Adjutant sent back for treatment: VCO ordered to launch immediate counter-attack and secure 'C' Company position. Coke's Rifles [the old designation of 13th Frontier Force Rifles] asked to place a platoon in Baluch area to secure main road vice reserve platoon of 'D' Company. 'B' Company also reported 'gone'. There had been no sound of heavy fighting anywhere.

Situation reported to Brigade who said Garhwal Rifles on way up and would come under command OC Baluch. Runner for platoon 'D' Company reported 'C' Company position retaken and no Japs in sight. Found Leigh and some IRO's dead on position, all others gone and all rifles and equipment abandoned on position. Same situation on 'C' Company position but no sign of Sanghal or Hilder [latter must be presumed dead] *and* platoon of 'D' Company also gone!! Line adjusted to exclude 'A' Company position – otherwise remained same throughout 14th and 15th. Further wild fire on night of 14/15 but not so bad as previous night. No attack launched against 8 Brigade front.

The disappearance of A, B, and C companies Baluch must be attributed to desertion and in view of their later activities with INA, Capt. Barhan-ud-din and Capt. Sanghal must be suspected of being the persons primarily responsible for the defection of their companies, though not perhaps entirely responsible as, in view of the short time Barhan-ud-din had been with 2 Baluch [i.e. from 6 Feb] it seems that disaffection must have been fairly general. Furthermore, the Subedar Major's denial of any knowledge of disaffection was, to me, unconvincing and I felt that though he might not be affected, he was at least aware of some seditious movement.

Colonel Parker's evidence shows that A, B, and C Companies of 2/10th Baluch deserted on the day prior to the capitulation. Parker's report is, in fact, confirmed in the regiment's official history, the relevant section of which was written by Lieutenant-Colonel J.G. Frith, Colonel Parker's immediate predecessor in command of the battalion. Frith had left the regiment early in February 1942 after being ordered to India to raise a new battalion. He did not, however, get away from the island and became a prisoner of war.

Colonel Frith's version of the events on 14th February differs from

Colonel Parker's only in detail. His report also supplies an idea of the number of men involved. He says that after the fighting on the mainland the regiment's strength was down to 400 officers and men, but that there were sufficient Baluch reinforcements in the Rest Camps to bring the regiment up to strength. If we take this to be 800, then the deserters must have numbered 600.

In his recently published history of *The Indian Army: Fidelity and Honour*, Lieutenant-General S.L. Menezes says that in January 1942, over 200 volunteers of the Indian National Army, 'as part of F-Kikan, commenced training for the assault on Singapore'. They were divided into sections led by VCOs with one Japanese attached to each section. 'The sections successfully infiltrated, and planted the Japanese flag on the island on 14th February, mingling with units still fighting, and thus affecting large scale surrenders.'[54] This seems to indicate that there were other incidents like the Baluch one – though perhaps on a smaller scale.

Major Fujiwara Iwaichi in his book *F-Kikan*, also confirms one mass surrender of Indian troops, probably the Baluch although he says it took place on 13th February and not the 14th. He says, 'Captain Allah Ditta of the INA shouted in a loud voice urging the Indian soldiers on the other side to join the INA ... his action produced a visible impact upon the Indian officers and men. They stopped shooting and listened to his speech in silence. They were carried away by his appeal and replied with a cheer. At that moment the resistance of the Indian regiment crumbled and its soldiers discarded their arms and joined the INA. The incident spread like lightning to Indian soldiers in the rear ... The surrendered Indian soldiers formed into companies and marched away from the front'.

The Garhwal Rifles mentioned in Colonel Parker's text which was sent to fill the gap in the line was the 5/18th under the command of an Indian officer, Lieutenant-Colonel Bonsle (who himself became a senior member of the INA). Second in command was Major (later the Reverend) Robert Nesham. He confirms that the Baluchis had disappeared just as Parker described. He says the incident was well-known throughout the ranks of the captured Indian Army in Malaya.[55]

Colonel Parker mentioned 'wild fire' as having started on his flank with the 14th Punjab on the night of 13th/14th February. That was indeed the case, and is confirmed by Lieutenant-Colonel Cecil Hopkins-Husson of 5/14th Punjab. He says the unit concerned was a Dogra company of his battalion which was positioned close to Bidadari Cemetery. He reports that it was discovered at dawn that, instead of killing Japanese, they had slaughtered a herd of cows which had been grazing the cemetery. Hopkins-Husson also confirms Parker's statement that there was no heavy fighting on that section of the front on night of 13th/14th.

One other point in Colonel Parker's report is of particular interest. He noted that Lieutenant Hilder, second in command of C Company 'must be presumed dead'. The War Graves Commission records show Hilder as being killed in action on 15th February 1942. Like Colonel Parker, Gerald Hall Hilder was an Australian by birth. He was an emergency commissioned officer and thirty-one years of age. Information has come to light that Hilder was in fact beheaded by the Japanese. This must have taken place very soon after the events recorded above. Did he try to escape and was he beheaded for that? Or was he beheaded because he was the only British witness left alive after the Baluch incident?

The Baluch incident was the largest incidence of desertion from the Indian Army. But it was not the only one. On 12th February a patrol of 'B' Company, 1st Cambridgeshires, under Captain W.V. Gurteen, came across some Japanese near to the MacRitchie Reservoir. 'He was astonished to see between four and five hundred of the enemy relaxing by the water's edge. He noted that many Indian troops were with the Japanese.'[56]

All these desertions can be attributed to the successful operations of the Indian Independence League.

Chapter Fourteen

The Fall of Singapore

Friday 13th February 1942, 'Black Friday' as it came to be called, was considered by most troops and white civilians left on the island, and by many of the local population, as the worst, the most miserable day of the siege; worse even than the day of capitulation itself.

It was the day when the last dim flicker of hope died for most of them. The final convoy of large ships had sailed early the previous morning, and most of the people left behind realised now that they were there to stay. The Chinese, by far the largest national group, knew that their worst fears were to be realized; they would soon be under the thumb of the enemy who had been raping their motherland for years. The troops knew that there was to be no repeat miracle of Dunkirk; no fleet of naval ships and merchantmen accompanied by a vast flotilla of 'little ships' would come sailing to the rescue from across the water under a protective umbrella of Spitfires and Hurricanes.

During the previous night General Percival had ordered withdrawal to the final perimeter, which was a rough semicircle around the city, its two termini resting on the waterfront east and west of the town. The line was mainly unfortified.

Like the other days of the siege, Black Friday dawned fine though it is unlikely that many people had the mind to note such things even if they lived outside the areas covered by the canopy of smoke from countless fires, the flames from which were leaping skyward unchecked because there was now no adequate water-pressure to fight them. Some city dwellers, Chinese, Malay and Indian, had boarded up their homes and shops and trekked towards the largely battle-free eastern end of the island. But the influx of refugees from the mainland and other parts of the island had, it was estimated by Sir Shenton Thomas, brought the civilian population within a three-mile radius of the waterfront up to around the million mark. The contraction of the perimeter had brought with it such a concentration of military equipment within the city limits that there was scarcely a part of the city that could not now be regarded as a legitimate military target. Streets, pockmarked with craters, were blocked by rubble and abandoned cars. As Japanese bombs and shells continued to rain down in Yamashita's desperate bid to get the campaign over with before his ammunition ran out, there was everywhere a sickening stench of burned and decaying bodies, of burning rubber and oil, mixed with the smell of cordite.

An eyewitness to the onslaught and devastation gave this graphic description of his own trip up Orchard Road:

> A petrol station on our left blazed up – two cars ahead of us were punted into the air, they bounced a few times before bursting into flames. Buildings on both sides of the road went up in smoke ... Soldiers and civilians suddenly appeared staggering through clouds of debris; some got on the road, others stumbled and dropped in their tracks, others shrieked as they ran for safety ... We pulled up near a building which had collapsed onto the road – it looked like a caved-in slaughterhouse. Blood splashed what was left of the lower rooms; chunks of human beings – men, women and children – littered the place. Everywhere bits of steaming flesh, smouldering rags, clouds of dust – and the shriek and groan of those who still survived.

Few people apart from those immediately concerned, knew of the plan to issue 3,000 passes for places on the fleet of about forty small craft which Admiral Spooner had managed to assemble and which was to sail during the dark hours of the coming night. The plan was kept as secret as possible for fear of a mad rush to the docks developing on top of the deserter situation, now at its height and almost completely out of control. But secret or not, it is hardly surprising, in view of the prevailing situation, that the business of selecting which 3,000 people were to go led to not a few disgraceful incidents and to later criticisms of individuals involved.

1200 of the boat passes were to go to civilians. They were meant to be issued to those whose talents and experience would be useful to the war effort elsewhere, but a few were reserved for some of the remaining European women and children. The passes were supposed to be issued under guidelines set out by the Governor who was aware that some officers of the Malayan Civil Service and the Police had already absconded without permission. On that Black Friday the Governor cabled London, posting seventeen named senior police officers as deserters.*

Some of these non-military absconders left under very dubious circumstances. A party of eight senior police officers commandeered two marine police launches. The ringleader of the group was an Assistant Superintendent of Special Branch called F.I. Tremlett. When the boats reached Batavia Tremlett's 'explanation' of his behaviour was that he had

---

* In fact there were eighteen: another officer had also absconded but this was unknown at the time. These men had apparently not taken kindly to the Governor's general instruction that the majority of government officers were to stay at their posts, as he himself intended to do.

been under orders from the Inspector-General of Police (IGP) to remove to a place of safety two counter-espionage Chinese Agents (Wong Ching Yuk and Francis Huang). The IGP – Dickinson – stated after the war that his orders that the Chinese be gotten away did not mean that Tremlett had to go with them. Be that as it may, it is difficult to see that it required the services of seven other senior police officers to manage the escape of two Chinese, however important they were.

In charge of one of these launches was Assistant Superintendent A.J.A. Blake, known as 'Bugler'. Whatever justification there might have been for this group of officers leaving, there was no justification at all for what happened after they had navigated the minefields and reached the Straits. A fellow officer has called it 'a disgusting show'. Bugler Blake ordered the Malay members of the crew over the side; they were lucky to swim back to tell the story for there are many sharks in Singapore waters. Perhaps Bugler Blake's conscience pricked him in later life, for after the war he took to the cloth.

Signed 'explanations', as they were called, of these officers' conduct were recorded by the British Consul-General in Batavia. Two other senior police officers who made individual escapes to Java, also supplied explanations. A further group of eight led by C.H. (later Sir Claude) Fenner, reached Colombo, where their explanations were reviewed by the Governor of Ceylon, Sir Andrew Caldecott. His covering letter which accompanied the explanations to the Colonial Office in London, included the phrase, 'though technically deserters, I sympathise with their actions and recommend that it be condoned'. The Colonial Office accepted Sir Andrew's recommendation. He was an old Malaya hand himself, had spent twenty years in the Malayan Civil Service, and risen to be High Commissioner to the Malay States in 1933.

In the end, the explanations of all eighteen police deserters were accepted, and their actions condoned by the Colonial Office, but the episode was to have important repercussions on the efficiency of the police on the Malay Peninsula and in Singapore after the war.

Some police officers with specialized knowledge, and others considered at special risk from Japanese retribution (Mervyn Llewellyn Wynn and Alan Blades were just two names in this category), and a few of those who had been seconded to military units, left Singapore honourably and with permission.

During the 1950s, ex-IGP A.H. Dickinson wrote extensively about these police desertions. He was never permitted to see the 'explanations' which were kept in a closed Colonial Office file until 1994. In one letter he said:

Preceding the capitulation certain officers of the Straits and FMS Police deserted. I am not concerned with cases in other departments. Happily such cases in proportion to the total personnel of

Government, were rare. Police officers of an armed, disciplined and semi-military Force must be considered apart. Sir Shenton Thomas immediately cabled the Colonial Office reporting these officers as deserters.

Dickinson had issued the following internal memorandum on 11th February 1942:

> H[is] E[xcellency]'s instructions are that the Straits Settlement's Police do not:
> resist the enemy by force of arms;
> our sole duty is the maintenance of internal order;
> instructions already issued as regards looting continue in force and are endorsed by H.E.;
> in the event of the fall of the Fortress, H.E. instructs that the civil population could best be served by placing our organisation at the disposal of the Japanese Commander should he wish to make use of it.[1]

This was followed by a notice dated 13th February, the day after the first police desertions.

> To remove any doubt remaining in officers' minds the following is the position:
> 1. After the fall of Singapore they are free agents and owe loyalty only to the Empire. The Malayan Government will have no claim on their allegiance.
> 2. They are free to go whenever opportunity offers, the moment the final surrender of this Fortress has been announced.
> 3. Any officer who leaves the Service before is treated as a deserter and will forfeit absolutely all claims to pension and gratuity which he may have earned. The Government have issued an order to this effect.
> 4. HE's proposal to offer the services of the Officers remaining is in no way binding on the individual.
>
> [Signed] A.H. DICKINSON
>
> P.S. The above does not hold good if Armistice terms include a clause imposing on the British Government responsibility for the temporary maintenance of law and order. In this event every officer is bound to obey.

This clarification of the official view had not prevented the second batch of police officers from deserting.

Much to the disgust of Dickinson, and of all the other policemen who had stayed at their posts and who became prisoners of the Japanese, several of the deserters were reinstated in their old jobs after the war.[2] The Colonial Office in the form of Mr Edward Gent – soon to be Sir Edward and a by no means highly regarded or efficient High Commissioner for Malaya – having followed on from Caldecott's recommendation and condoned the desertions, could see no reason for not sending these men back. At a meeting with Gent at the Colonial Office in 1945, Dickinson, just back from a dreadful three-and-a-half years as an enforced guest of the Japanese, 'was shocked, indeed horrified, to be told that we should not have stayed at our posts'.

A number of the civilian exit passes were handed to Brigadier Ivan Simson, Director-General of Civil Defence. Simson distributed some himself, gave a batch to his assistant, F.D. Bisseker, for distribution and another batch to Group-Captain R.L. Nunn, the Head of the Public Works Department.[3] Simson signed one pass for Bisseker's personal use. Unfortunately some of those who did not get away never learned of this and thought that Bisseker had issued one to himself. This led them to naming one of the *pissoirs* in their prison camp after him, which was grossly unfair.

The Nunn story is of a different ilk. Although he had been expressly forbidden by the Governor to leave, he issued passes to himself and his wife. (Apparently she would not leave the island without him.) In what might have been an attempt to obscure the facts of his departure, he also offered passes to his immediate subordinates, eighty-one of whom accepted. Others did not, however, because they were aware that the Governor considered that the experience and knowledge of Public Works officials was needed in Singapore in those last days.

The Nunns got away on a ship called the *Kuala* which was soon sunk. The Group-Captain then commandeered another vessel under the pretence that he was carrying despatches to General Wavell from the Governor. After reaching Sumatra, and probably using the same bluff again, he got his wife and himself placed at the head of the evacuation queue at Padang. There they boarded the Dutch *Rooseboom*. Two days out the ship was sunk by Japanese bombers. In what was a brave end to a rather ignoble episode, Nunn pushed his wife to safety through a porthole before going down with the ship. Unfortunately Mrs Nunn did not survive the subsequent lifeboat voyage. Neither did Brigadier Archie Paris, an official escapee, who was in the same lifeboat.

Some non-Government civilians did not leave well either. One prominent member of the Singapore trading community and a member of the Legislative Council, Sir John Bagnall, left Singapore because it was considered that his knowledge of the tin industry would be of benefit to the war effort. There was nothing wrong with that; it was the manner of his going that enraged so many people. This pillar of the establishment barged his way along the quayside towards a boat, 'wielding a suitcase so effectively' to knock aside other prospective passengers, including women and children. This hurried exit was witnessed by several people, and earned him the local soubriquet of *lari kwat*, a mellifluous sounding but poor Malay rendering of, 'strong (meaning fast) runner'.

The civilian doctors of the Malayan Medical Service, including those who were in the Volunteer Services, elected to stay behind to a man; well, almost to a man. One of their number who was serving with the Malayan Royal Navy Volunteer Reserve deserted about a week before the capitulation. He reached Java and eventually was placed on a ship as Supernumerary Surgeon for her voyage from Batavia to Australia. He got away with his naval desertion, and after the war returned to Singapore to take up private practice there. He was not popular with those of his erstwhile colleagues who had survived the Japanese camps.

Another naval officer deserter was Commander G.E.W.W. Bayly, also of the Malayan Royal Navy Volunteer Reserve. In civilian life he had been Superintendent of the Singapore Convict Prison, the number two man in the Prison Service in Malaya. He was in charge of auxiliary vessels under Rear-Admiral Spooner, but sailed from Singapore on one of them on 11th February without permission. The ship he used was the *Bulan*, one of the vessels Admiral Spooner had earmarked for the later evacuation. Spooner sent a message ordering Bayly to be held at Batavia pending his own arrival there. It was perhaps fortunate for Bayly that the admiral died *en route*. Apart from a punch in the face from an officer who knew the story, and who came across him later in the war in Colombo, Bayly got off scot-free. His report on sailing away with the *Bulan*, which was accepted by the Naval authorities in Colombo, reads like an apologia; in it Bayly went to much length to explain why he left Singapore without his admiral's permission without exactly saying that he had.[4]

The bad example set by the few in these small ship escapes was more than balanced by many acts of heroism. A retired Australian merchant navy captain, W.R. Reynolds, who was running a mining operation in Malaya, repaired an abandoned Japanese fishing vessel and escaped in it. He picked up and towed a motor vessel carrying 262 women and children to Sumatra. When he heard that there was a large party of evacuees stranded on an outlying island, he went back twice into the danger zone to pick them up. In all he helped 2,000 souls to Sumatra. In the end he reached India himself.

The tiny HMS *Li Wo*, a 700-ton auxiliary patrol vessel under the command of Lieutenant T. Wilkinson, RNR, sailed from Singapore on 13th February, and on the following day sighted a Japanese invasion fleet, including a cruiser and destroyer, making for the Dutch Islands. With no chance of escape, Wilkinson hoisted battle ensigns and engaged the enemy with the one ancient 4-inch gun on board. Little *Li Wo* was hard hit. The captain decided to sell his ship as dearly as he could, and ringing for maximum revolutions, steamed for the nearest transport. He rammed her amidships. A few minutes later gunfire from the cruiser sent *Li Wo* and her captain to the bottom. There were some survivors who were able to bear witness to this gallant action, and after the war Lieutenant Wilkinson was posthumously awarded the Victoria Cross, the fourth and last of the Malayan campaign.

One or two stories from those last days manage to illustrate at one and the same time, selfless courage together with baser human characteristics. One hitherto unrecorded act of bravery was that of an Australian able seaman. He was probably a crew member of HMAS *Vampire*. He had contracted gonorrhoea during that vessel's last visit to Singapore and was left ashore for treatment. The doctor who treated him was Captain A.W. Frankland, RAMC. As the Japanese advanced across the island, this Australian who, of course, was not bedridden, used to borrow an ambulance and drive it up to the Australian sector of the front. He brought back the occasional wounded man but, more often, men who were the worse for drink. At the hospital the latter were 'dried out', after which the Aussie sailor drove them back again. He did this over several days, his journeys getting progressively shorter as the Japanese got nearer. After the war he wrote to Dr Frankland. *Vampire* having been sunk in 1942, and all her records lost, the sailor was in danger of being accused of desertion. He wrote asking for an affidavit about the circumstances of his discharge from the ship. Dr Frankland was more than happy to oblige.[5]

In view of the chaos and confusion of those last days of Singapore, it is not surprising there were several unproven and unprovable accusations of desertion made against specified people. One such was made by Captain T.E. Pickard, Royal Artillery. He was stationed on one of the islands to the south of Singapore. He reported that on the morning of 15th February, some hours before the capitulation, he obtained permission in the form of a signed chit from his Commanding Officer for a group of Royal Engineer sappers on the island to make a break for freedom as there was no longer any use for their services. While the men, who were led by a corporal, were making ready the *tonkang* for the escape, Pickard reported that a small boat arrived from Singapore with two officers on board. One was wearing major's epaulettes but the other, who introduced himself as a major of the Indian Army, was not in uniform. They explained, said Pickard, that they had been officially ordered to escape and that they were looking for water transport for themselves and for between 130–160 men, a lot of them wounded. They had left the remainder of their party at Jardine Steps on the Singapore waterfront, where some of them were already in small boats which could be towed. If they could get a motor launch they were going back to bring these men away. As the story seemed quite genuine, the senior officer on the spot, Captain Ritchie, said they could use the *tonkang* which the corporal was making ready.

Soon afterwards the *tonkang* shoved off, and Captains Ritchie and Pickard followed its progress until it was out of sight beyond Peak Island. It went straight through the boom gate at the eastern end of Singapore Harbour and 'at *no* time did it go near Jardine Steps or for that matter any other place in the harbour', reported Pickard. He wanted to know what happened aboard the boat. Did the corporal refuse to make for Jardine Steps, or was the story of the wounded men a myth? Pickard and Ritchie escaped after the capitulation and in Sumatra were able to confirm that the Indian Army major had reached there. Pickard ended his report, 'the solution to this rather nasty little mystery should be found'. The Indian Army major was named by Pickard. Research has shown that he was an officer of 22nd Indian Brigade, and that he was drowned whilst attempting to escape aboard a ship from Padang. By the 15th it was probably too late for this officer to have been one of those officially selected for evacuation on the 13th. Although from late in the afternoon of that last day, the dividing line between a deserter and an escapee was somewhat blurred – due to a report which gained wide circulation that a cease-fire would take effect some four hours before it actually did – this would not have covered this officer's escape attempt which was made in the morning.

At a senior commanders' conference held on 13th February it was agreed, according to the British Official History, that there was no prospect of a successful counter-attack due to 'the exhaustion of the troops'. No official record exists of the deliberations of that conference or of the subsequent ones held. But one thing is certain; among the many important matters discussed must have been the incidence of deserters and the effect this was having on other troops. The problem must have been high on the agenda, for the evidence was lying all over the town. Many deserters had left the island, but many more were still in or around the city centre and dock areas. If Major Westall's estimate of the percentage of deserters who were Australian is taken as a guide – he said 80% – then based on the computation made in the previous chapter the number of deserters would have been in excess of 10,000. If, say, 4,000 had got off the island (the 3,000 plus those lost in the attempt, as mentioned in the Australian Official History), then another 6,000 were still around the town. This estimate does *not* include the men of 2/10th Baluch who disappeared on 14th February, or any other Indian troops who deserted and went behind enemy lines. In total, the number of desertions could have exceeded 12,000.

Tension ran high at that commanders' meeting on the 13th, at which recriminatory brickbats began to fly. We know from Percival's post-war private correspondence with General Heath and with the Official Historian, that it was at that meeting on 13th that Heath told Percival 'that he had lost his honour some time ago in the north'. There must have been other things said at that conference and the subsequent ones that the generals concerned preferred subsequently not to make public.

During General Wavell's last visit to Singapore he had issued instructions to Percival that he must hold out at all costs. This order was based on the one Wavell had himself received from Churchill on 10th February which included the following phrases:

> There must at this stage be no thought of saving the troops or sparing the population. The battle must be fought to the bitter end at all costs ... Commanders and senior officers should die with their troops. The honour of the British Empire and of the British Army is at stake.

By 13th February the water supply was causing concern. Bombs had damaged the water mains in many places, and much water was running to ground. Nevertheless Percival made the decision to carry on fighting, but ordered that he be kept updated on the water situation.

On that evening of the 13th, as dusk began to fall, an event occurred that provided a fitting climax for a dreadful day. Captain Patrick Heenan, the traitor whose actions had been a principal cause for there having been no air cover for the retreating forces, was taken down to the waterfront. He had been sentenced to death by court-martial in early January but the sentence had not been carried out.* At the quayside he was told to look at the setting sun for it would be the last one he would see. It is doubtful whether much of the sky was visible under the pall of smoke that hung over the dying city even had Heenan been inclined to look for it under those circumstances. If he did look, it would not have been for long. A sergeant of the Military Police shot him in the back of the head and then pushed the body into the sea.

Early the following morning Brigadier Simson told Percival that a complete failure of the water supply was imminent. At a commanders' conference a few hours later it was reported that up to half the supply was now running away. Although Percival considered the shortage serious, he decided that it did not yet make the defence of Singapore impossible. Although the morale of his men was at breaking-point, he once again decided to carry on the fight.

During that day's fighting a group of Indian soldiers, falling back before the enemy and still firing their weapons, entered the grounds of Alexandra Military Hospital. The Japanese took this for an excuse to commit one of their worst atrocities. Attacking the hospital they bayoneted to death a number of staff and patients, including one lying on an operating table. They then herded 150 staff and patients into an

---

* For the possible reasons, see Elphick & Smith *Odd Man Out*.

adjoining building, and massacred them the following morning. A few
lucky ones survived to tell the tale.

General Bennett made two extraordinary moves that day. He placed
his troops in a circle centred on the Tanglin Barracks, and in a message
to Canberra, the one in which he confirmed that his non-fighting troops
except hospital staff were manning the perimeter, he said: 'Wavell has
ordered all troops to fight to the last. If enemy enter city behind us will
take suitable action to avoid unnecessary sacrifices.'

He did not inform Percival of this. When Percival heard about it
after the war he made the comment that Bennett had the right to
communicate with his own Prime Minister, 'but surely not to inform
him of an intention to surrender in certain circumstances when he had
not even communicated that intention to his own superior officer'.

The Johore Volunteer Engineers were under Bennett's command
and received orders to join this circular perimeter. Guy Hutchinson
says:

> We got word from the AIF to move ... and go along Napier or
> Nassim Road and take up position facing Singapore to guard their
> rear in case the Japs broke through. This was the last straw, and
> Jack Crosse [the JVE commander] told the officer bringing the
> message to tell the AIF to do their own work; that they had run
> and left us ever since we had come on the island; and that they
> could defend their own rear; we were not going to retire one more
> inch; they could do what they liked about it; we were taking no
> more orders from them. We didn't get any.

Bennett, concerned about the availability of artillery ammunition, issued
an order that AIF guns should fire only in the defence of the Australian
part of the perimeter. He did not tell his superior officer of that decision
either. Later, the Australian gunners could see the Japanese mounting
an attack on the 1st Malaya Brigade to the south of their position, but
because of Bennett's order, did not open fire in support of the Malays.

At another commander's meeting held late in the afternoon of the 14th
the water situation was reported to have improved slightly. Curiously,
although the reservoirs were now in enemy hands, water was continuing
to reach the city pumping stations. This was due to the gallant action
of a Government Water Engineer at the main pumping station at the
reservoir, who, together with his wife, kept the pumps going despite the
fact that they were behind enemy lines. The names of this gallant pair
seem to have gone unrecorded.

The question of what might happen to civilians in the town if the
Japanese were to smash their way through was one of the matters now
considered by the commanders, although in his private correspondence
with General Heath after the war, Percival maintained that he did

not allow such considerations to affect his military judgement of the situation.

At a meeting in the Fort Canning bunker at 0930 hours on 15th, with the Japanese continuing to push forward on some sectors, Percival summarised the latest position. Although military food stocks were low, fairly large civil stocks were available. There was an adequate stock of small arms ammunition, but shell of all kinds was in short supply. He told his fellow generals that there were two alternatives. They had either to counter-attack immediately in an attempt to regain control of the reservoirs and certain food and ammunition depots, or to capitulate. The commanders, according to the Official History 'were still unanimously of the opinion that, in the circumstances, a counter-attack was impracticable', although the circumstances referred to were not specified. The Official History goes on, 'Confronted with this, and with no immediate solution for the critical water problem, Percival decided to negotiate a capitulation.'

From this it appears that the water problem played a crucial part in the final decision to surrender. But what were the circumstances which made the mounting of one last effort impracticable? It was obviously not the water situation, and anyway, one of the expressed purposes of mounting an attack was to regain the reservoirs. There was an adequate supply of small arms ammunition, and probably enough shell left to back a counterstroke. The basic reason that no counter-attack was made, and capitulation was decided upon instead, was surely the deserter situation. By that time the disappearance of the 2/10th Baluch would have been known to the senior commanders, for Colonel Parker stated that he had informed his Brigade Commander who would have passed the report upwards. Even though in the post-war Percival-Heath correspondence, Percival intimated that Gordon Bennett had not been open with him about the state of his troops, which means that the exact state of AIF was not known to Percival then, he must have known enough.

Major Cyril Wild, a Japanese-speaking staff officer, was in attendance at that last meeting. He recalled that after it had been agreed to surrender, General Bennett remarked, 'How about a combined counter-attack to recapture Bukit Timah?' Wild went on, 'This remark came so late, and was by then so irrelevant, that I formed the impression at the time that it was made not as a serious contribution to the discussion but as something to quote afterwards. It was received in silence and the discussion proceeded.'

Percival had by now received permission from Wavell to surrender as soon as he concluded that it was no longer possible to cause the enemy casualties. Percival decided to seek a cease-fire at 1630 hours, but the time finally agreed on with the Japanese was 2030 hours.

Because of this change of timing, and because the original time somehow got widely circulated, it can be argued, as the Australian

Official Historian did, that 'the dividing line between desertions and escapes was in some instances indefinite'. Any men who left during those last four hours deserve the benefit of the doubt, but they must have been a small percentage of the total who left Singapore. By that time there were few boats left, anyway.

Subsequent to the decision to capitulate, General Gordon Bennett issued an order to his men that included the sentences: 'All ranks stand fast within unit areas and will concentrate at first light to be completed by 0830 hours. All precautions must be taken to ensure that the spirit of the cease-fire is not destroyed by foolish action.' He denied afterwards that this meant that no one should attempt to escape. He himself left that same night.

At 2030 hours on Sunday 15th February 1942, all the radio transmitters in Singapore went off the air. 'The end – an inglorious end – had come. No last desperate struggle; no Dunkirk or Crete. Just the pathetic fizzle and splutter of a damp squib.'

These were the words with which Colonel Phillip Parker ended his memoir of the campaign.

Chapter Fifteen

Summary and Conclusion

The factors which led to the loss of Malaya and the fall of Singapore were manifold, in the full dictionary sense of that word – various in kind and/or quality, and many in number.

Winston Churchill at best misjudged the Japanese situation. At worst he may have deliberately turned a blind eye to the East, prepared to risk the loss of the Far East possessions, sacrificing them for the duration of the war in his ardent desire to get America to come into it. In a minute he wrote to General Ismay on 10th September 1940, he said:

> The prime defence of Singapore is the Fleet. The protective effect of the Fleet is exercised to a large extent whether it is on the spot or not ... the present Middle Eastern Fleet ... could in a very short time, if ordered, reach Singapore ...
>
> The danger of a rupture with Japan is no worse than it was. The probabilities of the Japanese undertaking an attack upon Singapore ... are remote ... They are not likely to gamble.

That was written a little over two months after the fall of France had laid Indo-China open to Japanese occupation, an event which drastically changed the strategic situation in the South China Sea.

Seven months later he was writing that 'Japan is unlikely to enter the war unless the Germans make a successful invasion of Great Britain.' This sort of thinking led him to order no 'further dispositions for the defence of Malaya and Singapore'. He made that decision in the teeth of threatened resignations from the CIGS and the Secretary of State for War.

Churchill, and Anthony Eden who was Foreign Secretary from 1940–45, apparently discounted the dangers posed by the ever closer relationship between the Thais and the Japanese. In this they were led by reports of the roseate kind emanating from the British Legation in Bangkok.

In July 1941, four months before the Japanese attack on Malaya, the committee conducting the Inquiry into the fall of Crete, which had been set up on Churchill's instructions, reported that the main factor in the loss of the island and many British, Australian and New Zealand soldiers with it, had been the overwhelming superiority of the German air force. Even this object lesson did not persuade Churchill to authorise air reinforcements for Singapore. Although strategically he was right to give preference to

Russia and the Middle East, surely some air reinforcements should and could have been spared for Singapore?

If any one man can be blamed for the fall of the fortress then the prime candidate must be Winston Churchill, who was involved in the Singapore Fortress concept right from the beginning, and who, in 1941, was responsible for relegating its defence to the second division. It was probably the realisation of his major part in this that caused him never to press for the Singapore Inquiry he once promised, and why he never gave a satisfactory explanation for not holding one.

This summation of his role in the affair is based on the information that is presently available in the public domain. There might be other, hidden, reasons which cemented his resolve. If Rusbridger and Nave in their book *Betrayal at Pearl Harbor* are correct, then he had prior knowledge of the attack on the American Fleet, but did not pass it on. If they are right – and the fact that not a single JN-25 decrypt has ever been released by Britain indicates that there is still much being covered up in the so-called national interest – then there may be something directly concerning the attack on Malaya also hidden away. Many files on the Far Eastern situation dating from that time have come into the public domain since early 1993, but a number still have not. One of those in the latter category is a Cabinet Office file with the title 'Implications of a Public Inquiry into the fall of Singapore'. Perhaps the secret, or part of it, is hidden there?

But just as no single factor can be blamed for the fall of Singapore, no one man can really be blamed for it either. The situation might have been saved. If there been more dynamic leadership in pre-war Malaya, and consequently more co-operation between the various arms, both military and civil, then some of the glaring omissions and mistakes, such as the siting of the airfields without consultation with the army, could have been avoided. Perhaps efficient defences in Johore and on the north coast of Singapore Island would have been constructed. They might have delayed General Yamashita who, towards the end, was suffering from being at the end of a tenuous supply line.

Later on, tougher men than Brooke-Popham and Percival should have been found to take charge. Wavell might have been such a man but he arrived when it was already too late.

Nor did Duff Cooper's advent on the scene help much. The idea of some form of co-ordinator was good, but he was not the man for the job and his terms of reference were too vague. For that Churchill, the man who sent him out there, was to blame.

The situation where the two top British generals on the ground, Percival and Heath, seemed to have had diametrically opposed views on how the campaign should be run, could and should have been avoided. It was a stupid, unthinking error to appoint as Percival's number two a general of more seniority and more up-to-date war experience than his chief. It caused friction between the two senior army leaders. Such friction on the comparatively small Singapore stage was of much greater significance than if it had taken place in one of the larger theatres of war.

The following is the surviving fragment of a letter General Heath wrote in 1949, preserved in the Heath papers at the Imperial War Museum, London. It indicates Heath's feelings about Percival's generalship, and his views on how the early stages of the campaign should have been conducted:

Dear Percival,
I have been long, for one reason or another, in thanking you for your complimentary copy of your *The War in Malaya*.

At first, I thought it was senseless of you to add to the library but perhaps it was not so silly.

You have, helped by the writings of others, presented a very readable account and I am very glad you have, long after the event, altered your opinion of the worth of the troops.

The discerning reader only will appreciate that you yourself or you and Brookham were so greatly responsible for the hole in which the poor 11th Indian Division was to find itself enmeshed in the first days of hostilities. Hitherto, loyalty to you and the decision to avoid unpleasant disclosures has constrained me from ventilating the errors which led up to the serious and unnecessary mauling which the 11th Division received in the opening days of the campaign.

I refer in particular to the appalling failure to come to a timely decision as to the cancellation of Matador and secondly your failure to place reliance upon Murray-Lyon when he sent his first request to be permitted to withdraw upon Gurun. The battle of Jitra and the operation at the Ledge would have been a very different story had your orders to cancel Matador been received early on the 8th December.

As you are well aware I was not an advocate of a hasty advance to seize Singora and I consider only advantage could have been reaped from an early decision that Matador would be of no avail.

As you now appreciate, and as I advocated at frequent intervals throughout the 7th, the time had passed when any useful purpose would be served by Operation Matador and great complications would arise from keeping the troops standing by in readiness for the operation. The story of the Battle of Jitra must make you feel very conscious of the havoc caused by that 12-hour delay in giving Murray-Lyon permission to withdraw from the Jitra position.

I know from your very false conception of the course of the operations written by you in Manchuria that you reposed no great faith in the manner in which I had served you and it seems obvious that you still are not satisfied that I did the best under the circumstances. However, I can rest satisfied that the great majority of commanders felt that I had fought the losing battle as well as could be done under the circumstances, circumstances which during the progress of the campaign you never began to appreciate.

The tragedy of Slim [River] would never have been had you not turned a deaf ear to my remonstrances about the unsuitability of Stewart's proposed dispositions. After the battle had been fought and lost, General Wavell appeared and listened to Stewart's account of how his troops broke. Wavell listened attentively to what Stewart had to say and afterwards remarked to me, 'Well, I have never listened to a more garbled account of operations.' I excused Stewart's failure to be coherent by saying that he was much below form through strain and weariness. I did not absolve myself from responsibility or lay it on your shoulders as I might have done and moreover when . . .

Unfortunately, General Heath's letter ends in mid-sentence and at the end of its third page. The remainder of the letter must have been of equal interest. The letter is in Heath's own handwriting. It is either a copy of a letter actually sent or the draft of a letter which Heath subsequently decided not to send. Towards the end of his life he was a sick man, and perhaps he decided not to send it as he did not wish to renew controversy with Percival.

There was a general lack of understanding and appreciation of the military capabilities of the Japanese, and the British leaders both at home and in Malaya, did not seem to take much note of the information on the subject they did have in the Japanese Army Memorandum issued by the General Staff in Singapore in 1941. There was a failure also to appreciate until it was too late that the Japanese had all the military virtues. Joseph C. Grew, the American ambassador in Tokyo for the ten years preceding the attack on Pearl Harbor had this to say in 1943:

Probably no other factor has contributed more heavily to the preliminary victories achieved by the Japanese in this war than the offensive spirit which permeates all of the armed forces of the Empire. This spirit, recognized by competent military men as the most vital intangible factor in achieving victory, has been nourished and perpetuated since the foundation of the modern Japanese Army. The Japanese High Command has counted heavily upon the advantages this would give them over less aggressive enemies. When they struck, they made no provision for failure; they left no road open for retreat. They struck with all the force and power at their command.

The Japanese, whom Ambassador Grew described, do not seem to be much like the ones the British or the Australians talked about in Malaya; the ones who could not see in the dark, or fly above 15,000 feet, or two of whom might fit on the point of one bayonet.

The British were woefully short of aircraft, and lost a good part of the planes they did have in the first two days. They had not a single tank on the mainland, and found no answer to the excellent use the Japanese made of theirs. Much British equipment arrived considerably later than the men who were to use it, and in some instances guns arrived without the associated ammunition. The quality of the military communications equipment in Malaya was abysmal.

The aspects of the British Intelligence operation in the area which stood out, were its fragmentation, lack of co-operation, lack of funds, and lack of expertise. Not only did the intelligence left hand not know what the right hand was doing, but all the digits were unco-ordinated. This was in stark contrast to the intelligence system the Japanese had built up.

The Indian Independence League did its work well before the war and after it started. It took advantage of the nationalistic tendencies of some Indian officers and troops, and of grievances, both real and imagined, they had against their British officers. So when some of the Indian units in north-west Malaya were stood down from an offensive to a defensive mode, and had to take up positions in waterlogged and half-built defences, and when soon afterwards they were suddenly confronted with the first tanks they had ever seen, all this coalesced into lower morale. General Heath said the men at Jitra were depressed. We have evidence from General Murray-Lyon, Brigadier Carpendale, Colonel Deakin, and Captain Mileham, amongst others, that the initial low morale became progressively lower. The only Indian Army units to escape this in the first instance, were those over on the east coast of the country, but that was to change, as with the 2/10th Baluch. The advent of later raw and untrained troops made the situation worse.[1]

Although most British troops fought well on occasion, they did not escape the general malaise.

Pre-war training had in many instances been subordinated to the construction of defences. This was made worse by a parsimonious government back home refusing permission for the correct rate-for-the-job to be paid for civilian construction gangs.

Lack of morale and fighting spirit was soon to surface in some Australian and British air force squadrons. This led to the precipitate evacuation of some of the aerodromes. The most important of these was that of Kuantan on the eve of the loss of *Prince of Wales* and *Repulse*. Had aircraft, even the relatively poor ones the British had available, been stationed at Kuantan on 10th December 1941, maybe, just maybe, the ships would have survived. Their loss brought about another lowering of morale, this time not least among Brigadier Painter's men around

Kuantan who thought they had been responsible for the catastrophe. About Force Z itself, it certainly was not the strong deterrent fleet that Churchill thought it was.

British generalship throughout the campaign was not at all what it should have been, with only Generals Key and Barstow gaining some credit; and Barstow was to die as an indirect result of a lack of military virtue on the part of Brigadier Lay, which also led directly to the loss of Brigadier Painter's 22nd Indian Brigade.

When the Australians entered the fray, they had some resounding early successes, but it did not last. Soon they too, caught the withdrawal bug, and in their case it was made worse by their lack of exercises in this important part of the Military Training Manual. Someone tougher than General Percival was required to control and earn the respect of General Gordon Bennett. Perhaps then, as Wavell said, the Australians might have come good even at the eleventh hour.

On the island of Singapore the already battered Australians were placed where the fresh British 18th Division should have been. That error was Percival's, although Wavell did not overrule him. As was his wont, General Gordon Bennett set his own HQ too far back, so that when the Japanese onslaught began he was in no position to know what was going on on the beaches. Earlier Bennett had failed to include the Jurong Line in his defence plans. Brigadier Maxwell, as was *his* wont, placed his HQ too close to Bennett's. Maxwell himself admitted during an interview on 26th January 1953, 'that he did not think he was military-minded enough to realise the real danger on the Causeway front', quite an admission for someone of his rank.

The dilution of the Australian battalions by raw replacements and the indisciplined 2/4th machine-gun battalion, had a knock-on effect. It seems that the Australians in general were especially affected by the absence of an effective British air force, probably because, after Crete, they had been promised by their government that they would never again have to fight without adequate air cover. Their morale plummeted more quickly than anyone else's, perhaps due to the fact that they were only briefly able to live up to their commander's pre-war billing of them. Such boasts have a habit of backfiring. Their tough image disintegrated before the Japanese juggernaut, and except for those veterans from World War One, they did not have the moral fibre or the training to act well in retreat. Even the fact that their own government saw Singapore as the northernmost bastion of the Commonwealth's defence, did not prevent many of them throwing in the towel.

Finally, towards the very end, almost an entire Indian Army regiment deserted.

Throughout the campaign the denial system was rarely implemented properly. Airfields were not blown effectively, and neither were bridges. On Singapore Island itself many installations at the mighty Naval Base were left virtually intact. This may not always have been the fault of the people engaged in the denial process. When M.E. Adams, Superintendent Civil Engineer at the Base, made his report at Colombo on 28th February 1942, he said:

> It was exceedingly difficult to get definite decisions concerning denial. Both RAMY [Admiral Spooner] and myself were seriously concerned after the fall of Batu Pahat and pressed the War Council for definite decisions ... but they were always reluctant to assume the worst, and neither then nor very much later was the impression given that the island would fall.

Conclusion

An appendix in General Wavell's 'Report on Operations in Malaya and Singapore' of 1st June 1942 contained the phrase, 'for the fall of Singapore itself, the Australians are held responsible'. That is unacceptable as it stands, even though the Australians were responsible for allowing the Japanese to land on the island of Singapore with such ease. The fall of the citadel was not an isolated event. Many factors led to the situation the Australians found themselves in when they first confronted the Japanese in Johore, and the effect of those factors was to continue for the remainder of the campaign.

However, the deserter situation, of which the Australians were a substantial part, did shorten the siege of Singapore. British planners considered that the 'fortress' could hold out for three months; that had been one of the reasons for 'rationing' shell expenditure immediately before the attack on the island. General Wavell reckoned that if the Singapore defenders could have held out for six weeks he *might* have been able to turn the tide with reinforcements, especially air reinforcements, which were due to arrive in Java.

The shortness of the siege of Singapore was caused by desertion, desertion on a scale never before known in the annals of the British Army. Excepting the special circumstances of 1917 when Czarist forces on the German front deserted to the Bolshevik cause, the Singapore experience is probably the highest incidence of desertion from any army, anywhere at any time.

Churchill's secret session speech of April 1942 on the fall of Singapore was published in February 1946. Writing in the *Illustrated London News* of 9th February that year, Cyril Falls, Chichele Professor of War History at All Souls, Oxford, and the man who had succeeded Basil Liddell Hart as military correspondent to the London *Times*, commented that the speech still left unexplained the mystery of the sudden collapse of the island fortress. He said there should be a Singapore Inquiry, covering all the

political and military ground, and that everything connected with the
meteoric successes of the Japanese demanded study. He went on, 'It may
be said that this can be given without the necessity of a public enquiry.
That may be so, but there is such a thing as national responsibility, and in
a democracy this must be based upon public knowledge. Understanding
of these problems should be part of the national education.'

The actual fall of Singapore had little to do with the water shortage
situation. If the decision had been made to hold out longer, it is unlikely
that many would have died of thirst, though many would undoubtedly
have died in continued air attacks. The water table on the island is high
and one has only to dig down a few feet to find it: indeed that was
the reason given for no underground air raid shelters being constructed
pre-war. The water would have been brackish but drinkable at a pinch.
(Dick Clarke of the Garhwalis says that during his battalion's escape from
Kuantan they often drank from pits dug in the jungle. The water did not
taste good, but it was better than none at all.)

Be all that as it may, if the defenders had made a counter-attack on
that last day, Singapore may not have fallen. General Yamashita's Chief
of Intelligence, Colonel Sugita, said in September 1966 that the Japanese
were so short of ammunition – some units had none at all – that Yamashita
had himself visited the front line early that day and apologised to the
troops for the shortages, and encouraged the use of the bayonet. This is
confirmed in Major (later Lieutenant-General) Fujikawa's book, *F-Kikan*.
He says for 15th February, 'The Japanese were facing an acute shortage
of ammunition.' Commenting on the capitulation negotiations held later
that day, he said, 'Yamashita was concerned with a dwindling supply
of munitions and increasing casualties, and he could not afford to let the
negotiations drag on much longer if he was to avert the crisis that his
armies were facing.' A few pages later he noted, 'If the British had come to
know about our shortage of manpower and munitions and if they had held
out for a few more days, they could have defeated the Japanese forces'.

A British counter-attack, therefore, might have been successful despite
Japanese air supremacy. Such overwhelming supremacy does not of itself
bring swift victory against ground forces as the Allies were to discover
in June 1944, on D-Day and the days following.

However, by 15th February it was obvious to the British commanders
in Singapore that the morale of the troops still at their posts was low;
and many men had fled, and other deserters were all over the city.

The incidence of deserters certainly shortened the length of the siege,
but it cannot be said that they caused the fall of Singapore without adding
a portfolio of provisos. The deserter situation was the terrible end-result
of many other factors which together did cause it.

Appendixes

1. Senior Army officers in the Malayan campaign

2. Reports concerning General Gordon Bennett's escape from Singapore

3. Reinforcement convoys – Singapore

4. The 'Cannamore' Warning

5. HMT *Empire Star*

6. Imperial General Staff (Australian Section)

   Notes

   Bibliography

   Abbreviations used

   Outline Chronology of Events, May 1940 to February 1942

   Index

Appendix 1

Senior Army officers in the Malayan Campaign and their Commands

Notes: a) Some of the ranks were temporary, the holder later reverting to a lower rank. The various changes in command of Divisions and Brigades means that some units appear several times in the list.
   b) The list is not definitive. There were probably a few other officers of Brigadier rank in Malaya Command.
   c) Major-Generals and Brigadiers are listed alphabetically.

The list shows that the British forces in Malaya were not exactly short of senior officers.

  1. General Sir Archibald Wavell, Supreme Cmdr. ABDA.
  2. Lieutenant-General Sir Henry Pownall. COS, ABDA.
  3. Lieutenant-General A.E. Percival. GOC Malaya Cmd.
  4. Lieutenant-General Sir Lewis Heath. GOC 3rd Ind.Corps
 *5. Major-General A.E. Barstow. 9th Indian Division.
  6. Major-General M.G. Beckwith-Smith. 18th British Div.
  7. Major-General–Gordon Bennett. 8th Australian Div.
  8. Major-General B.W. Key. 11th Indian Division.
  9. Major-General D.M. Murray-Lyon. 11th Indian Division.
@10. Major-General A.C.M. Paris. 11th Indian Division.
 11. Major-General I.S.O. Playfair. Chief of Staff Malaya Cmd.
 12. Major-General F. Keith Simmons. Singapore Fortress.
 14. Brigadier W. Aird-Smith. DAAG 11th Ind. Division.
 15. Brigadier E.H.W. Backhouse. 54th British Inf. Brigade.
 16. Brigadier G.C. Ballentine. 44th Indian Infantry Brigade.
 17. Brigadier W. St.J. Carpendale. 28th Indian Inf. Brigade.
 18. Brigadier B.S. Challen. 15th Indian Infantry Brigade.
 19. Brigadier C.A. Calleghan. CRA, Australian 8th Div.
 20. Brigadier J.B. Coates. 15th Indian Infantry Brigade.
 21. Brigadier A.C. Curtis. CRA Fixed Defences.
 22. Brigadier C.L.B. Duke. 53rd British Infantry Brigade.
*23. Brigadier H.C. Duncan. 45th Indian Infantry Brigade.
 24. Brigadier G.C. Eveleigh. DDOS, Malaya Command.
 25. Brigadier W.L. Fawcett. BGS, 3rd Indian Corps.
 26. Brigadier F.H. Frazer. 2nd Malay Infantry Brigade.
 27. Brigadier K.A. Garrett. 15th Indian Infantry Brigade.
 28. Brigadier E.W. Goodman. CRA 9th Indian Division.
 29. Brigadier W.O. Lay. 8th Indian Infantry Brigade.
 30. Brigadier H.F. Lucas. (R.E. No further details.)
 31. Brigadier C.A. Lyon. Penang Fortress.

32. Brigadier T.H. Massey-Beresford. 55th British Inf. Bde.
33. Brigadier D.S. Maxwell. 27th Australian Brigade.
34. Brigadier R.G. Moir. Line of Communication Troops.
*35. Brigadier H.D. Moorehead. 15th Indian Infantry Brigade.
#36. Brigadier T.K. Newbigging. Chief Administration Officer.
37. Brigadier C.W.E. Painter. 22nd Indian Infantry Brigade.
38. Brigadier A.E. Rusher. CRA 11th Indian Division,
39. Brigadier C.D.K. Seaver. DDMS, 3rd Indian Corps.
40. Brigadier W.R. Selby. 28th Indian Infantry Brigade.
41. Brigadier H.C. Servaes. HQ RA 18th Division.
42. Brigadier I. Simson. CRE, Malaya Command.
43. Brigadier I. McA. Stewart. 12th Indian Infantry Brigade.
44. Brigadier C.H. Stringer. DDMS, Malaya Command.
45. Brigadier H.B. Taylor. 22nd Australian Brigade.
46. Brigadier K.S. Torrance. BGS, Malaya Command.
47. Brigadier W.A. Trott. 8th Indian Infantry Brigade.
<48. Brigadier A.L. Varley. 22nd Australian Brigade.
49. Brigadier A.W.G. Wildey. RA Anti-Aircraft Defences.
50. Brigadier G.G.R. Williams. 1st Malay Infantry Brigade.

* Indicates killed in action.
@ Died in escape attempt.
# Brigadier Newbigging (this is the correct way to spell his name, with a final 'g')
was the officer who carried the Union Flag at the British surrender. The officer who
carried the white flag in the same picture was Major Cyril Wild, Staff Officer 3rd
Indian Corps.
< Brigadier Varley was promoted and took command of 22nd Brigade after Brigadier
Taylor was removed from the command by General Gordon Bennett in the last few
days of the campaign.

Appendix 2

Reports concerning General Gordon Bennett's escape from Singapore

WO 106/2579C. PRO.

Lance. Bdr M.C. Hay FMSVF
Inspector of Mines, Malayan Civil Service.

[During escape] we marched in single file and answered all challenges with 'Patrol' or 'Looking for our unit' as troops had been told to fire on anyone escaping. Later on we found out that this order had been given a week previously when the Australians were running for it and it had not been countermanded, although several regular units had been told on this afternoon to try and escape individually.

Luckily we found our way through the barb wire entanglements fairly easily and reached the sea. We there found a sampan with 3 men in it, one stark naked, and they said in a conspiratorial tone, 'I suppose you will want to know who we are.' To which we replied, 'No, but row us out to another sampan.' Then the stark naked man said, 'This is Major General Gordon Bennett. I am his ADC and this is *the* Major Moses.' (We found out afterwards he was the chief war correspondent for the Australian papers and head of the Australian Broadcasting Company.)

He had an idea of running to Malacca – poor fish. Eventually they got a larger sampan and we all rowed out to the *Twacow* making a hell of a noise. The General in a complete flap and frightened out of his wits yelling one thing, the ADC shouting another, Moses trying to row and hitting Charles Wood on the head with the handle of his oar, which was too long, and in the midst of this my haversack and all my belongings went overboard.

Came across many other boats with escapees in them. Luckily we got rid of the General and his party during the morning as he jumped a motor launch. He promised to send us help – but of course he didn't – and the next thing we heard of him was on the wireless telling a fabulous yarn about his escape. He is a poor worm. I cannot write all the despicable things he said and did.

Captain J.B. Colley, RASC. **Officer-in-Charge Water Company at Changi. Escaped with party of Volunteers.**

General Gordon Bennett was very keen to get away. When the question of payment for hire of the junk was brought up he said – 'Pay him 5,000 dollars if necessary. The Australian Government will pay us back.' When he was taken off subsequently they had the greatest difficulty in persuading him to contribute 50 dollars towards the cost of the hire of the junk. General Gordon Bennett's plan was to make for Malacca where he said he had friends who would help him escape to Burma. (Author's note: Malacca was occupied by the Japanese.) The rest of the party paid no attention to this suggestion but set course for the Sumatran Coast. Captain Colley lived with General Bennett for four days and thought that although he was easy to get on with he was a bit of a windbag. On the 19th February the party hailed a motor launch in charge of an RASC officer and General Bennett asked to be taken off the junk. At first the officer i/c launch was not keen to do so but after repeated requests on the part of General Bennett took him off and that was the last the party saw of him.

Captain Colley said that General Bennett reached Padang several days before his own party did and caused considerable resentment there by a broadcast in which he partially gave away the escape route being used.

****

The information in the above two reports from official British files is augmented by extracts from a diary of another of the escapers with General Gordon Bennett. It was kept by Gunner H.R. Oppenheim of the Volunteer Artillery.

Extract from Diary of H.R. Oppenheim, Royal Commonwealth Library. In civilian life Oppenheim was a Chartered Accountant with the firm of McAuliffe, Daws and Hose, Ipoh.

Sunday, 15th February ... decided to make a dash for Sumatra. We reach the sea just on midnight. There we find a sampan in which are Major-General Gordon Bennett, his ADC Gordon Walker, and the head of the Australian Broadcasting Company, Major Moses. They intended rowing to Malacca but decided to come with us. We eventually reach the *tunkow*. I lose my haversack and all my worldly goods in getting on board from the sampan.

Monday, 16th February. There was complete chaos on the sampan [on the way out to the larger craft]. Charlesworth announced we were rowing the wrong way, meaning the sampan was being rowed backwards, but we thinking he means being rowed in the wrong direction argue and shout at him. The General screams like a young girl and curses Gordon Walker who is standing up in the nude, for being so, saying it would be scandalous if the Japs saw him like that. He was like that because he had swum out to collect the sampan. Charlesworth tried rowing with a small oar while Moses tries with a large one and the rest of us with bits of wood. Consequently the sampan spun round in circles and Moses' oar kept hitting Charles on the head. Eventually we get underway and Gordon Bennett again suggests rowing to Malacca and Gordon Walker suggests making for an island ... Luckily we strike the *tunkow* and manage to board her. On board we find some escapees who, not being able to persuade the *taikong* to sail, had gone below. Two of them decided to return to the shore and so dove overboard but being tired are drowned or taken by sharks. This stops the others from following suit. Finally we persuade the *taikong* to sail. Then two soldiers jump on board and threaten to shoot us if we resist them. We don't. We have on board umpteen cases of AA shells which the *taikong* had been chartered to ship from Seletar to Singapore. We had to sleep on these cases. We calculated the value to be about £7,000 and have dreams of salvage payments.

(Author's note: There were a total of 21 service personnel on board. Oppenheim listed them by name and rank. The list includes Hay and Colley, see above.)

Everyone argued about the route to be taken. First Hay is put in command and then Wray takes over forcibly. It was he and Smeaton who jumped our boat, and he turned out to be a deserter who had been hiding in the islands. He was a Canadian. It was touch and go whether there would be a general shooting match on board as everyone was in a vile temper and on edge. The Chinaman wanted to go to Tanjong Penang but we believed the Japs were there. Bennett completely useless, first crying then imploring Moses or Walker to do something. Eventually we crash into some fishing stakes and anchor for the night.

Tuesday, 17th February. Most of the day we were becalmed. Several Jap planes fly over us throughout the day (we dumped some of the ammo overboard to lighten the boat and sacrificed £2,000) and we have to lay low under the tarpaulin covering the ammo. Very hot and uncomfortable. A slight breeze came in the afternoon and a little rain which we collected in our mackintoshes but it turned out to be brackish. Our supplies consist of water, seven bottles plus a 2 gallon kerosine tin half a jar belonging to the *taikong*. Food, 12 tins of bully, 1 of orange juice, 1 of shrimps, 2 emergency rations and 1 tin of Irish stew, plus a little rice of the *taikong's*. At 2.00 we anchor and collect more water from a spring.

Wednesday, 18th February. We reach Sumatra at 7.30. Only have a small school map. Cannot make out where we have hit Sumatra. See large junk full of soldiers, also motorcraft full of troops. Several Jap planes too.

Thursday, 19th February. Set sail in the early hours. Very slow progress. At 10.30 a motor boat comes alongside and the General and his party jump on board to leave us without a word of thanks, but they do leave $100 towards the expenses of the *tunkow*. Everyone cheers up after their departure. Stop about midday at Kuala Pedada for water. Wray also leaves us which is quite a relief. After a lot of arguing with Hay, I persuade them to take on board a Malay pilot ... This was lucky otherwise we would never have found the Indragiri which flows for several miles at right angles to the sea, hence its mouth is hard to see.

Author's note:

The Indragiri river was the start of the official escape route across Sumatra.

These contemporary reports show that the circumstances surrounding General Gordon Bennett's escape were rather less than the heroic tale which appeared in the Australian press of the time.

Appendix 3

Reinforcement Convoys – Singapore

From File ADM 199/1185. PRO, Kew.

Secret.

Title Convoy.	Ships	Escort	From	To	Contents
BM9A	Devonshire Lancashire Ethiopia Varsova Rajula	Dragon Durban Vampire Jupiter Encounter Hobart	Bombay 1.12.41	Singapore 3.1.42	45th Indian Infantry Brigade.
BM9B	El Medina Risaldar Rajput Jalarajan Madura	Danae Electra Express Stronghold Goulburn Burnie Tromp De Ruyter Hobart	Bombay 22.12.41	Singapore 6.1.42	M.T. and Stores for 45th Indian Infantry Brigade.
DM1 (Ex-WS 12ZM)	Narkunda Oranje Sussex Abbekerk Mount Vernon	Emerald Exeter Durban Hobart Jumna Jupiter Encounter Vampire	Durban 24.12.41	Singapore 13.1.42	53rd Infantry Bde. Group, 232 Squadron RAF, 6th Hvy & 35th Light Regts., 85th A/T Regt.
BM10	Cap St.Jacques Talthybius Islami Rohna Ekina Takliwa Jalakrishna Subadar Jalavisar Brittany Loch Ranza Jalaratna	Exeter Enterprise Danae Electra Stronghold Sutlej Yarra	Bombay 8.1.42	Singapore 25.1.42	44th Indian Infantry Bde. Group (6000 troops). M.T. and stores for 18th Div. Carriers for Recce. Regt.

S2	*Aquitania* (to Ratai Bay Java.) Transshipped into smaller Dutch steamers for on carriage to Singapore.	*Canberra* *Express* *Thanet* *Tenedos* *Vampire* *Dragon* *Java*	Sydney 10.1.42	Ratai Bay Java 20.1.42 Singapore (after transshipment to smaller vessels), 24.1.42.	2/4th M.G. Bn. A.I.F. reinforcements for 8th Div. (3,500)
BM11	*Empire Star* *Duchess of Bedford* *Empress of Japan* *Wakefield* *West Point*	*Exeter* *Dragon* *Durban* *Glasgow* *Thanet* *Tenedos* *Express* *Electra* *Caledon*	Bombay 19.1.42	Singapore 29.1.42	5 Light AA Batteries. 1 Lt. Tank Squadron. Railway Coy. 18th Div. (less 53rd Brigade Grp. 17,000 troops). Stores.
BM12	*Empress of Asia* *Felix Roussel* *Devonshire* *Plancius*	)*Encounter*)*Exeter*)*Danae*)*Sutlej*)*Yarra*)))****	Bombay 23.1.42	Singapore 5.2.42	Drafts for 9th and 11th Divisions (3800 troops) Stores. Div. troops for 18th Div.
DM2 (Ex-WS 14D)	*Warwick Castle* *Empress of Australia* *City of Pretoria* *Triolus* *Malancha* *Dunera* *City of Canterbury*	))))))))	Durban 14.1.42	Batavia 3.2.42 5.2.42	Wing HQ and Ground Staff Singapore for 3 fighter sqdns. 77th Heavy and 21st Light AA Regts. (4000 troops.) AA Guns, M.T. and Stores. 48th Lt AA Regt.

****Note: Convoys combined at 0501Z/28 in 0105 North, 9128 East, but DM2 afterwards diverted to Batavia, except *City of Canterbury* which went to Singapore. (It is not known which units were on board this ship.)

(Author's note. The last sentence in the note above illustrates the difficulties involved in coming to a precise figure for the number of troops who took part in the campaign. Even the authorities on the spot were unsure of what units were on what ships.)

Appendix 4

The 'Cannamore' Warning

From File CAB106/126. PRO, Kew.

Letter from   Brigadier H.B. Latham
Queen Anne's Chambers
41 Tothill Street
London SW1   15th October 1951

To Gavin Long
Official War Historian
War Histories Branch
Commonwealth of Australia
Acton
Canberra, ACT

Dear Gavin Long

I am now able to reply in full to your letter of 19th September 1951 and I attach:

1. Copy of appendix contained in GHQ Far East War Diary for October 1941 giving the details as to how all concerned were to be informed of any aggression in the part of Japan.

    This makes it clear that in such an event the single word telegram 'Cannamore' was to be sent in clear followed by a further telegram in cypher with details.

    In view of the uncertainty which prevailed at Kota Bharu, I do not think one can blame Brooke-Popham for waiting a bit before he 'declared war on Japan'.

2. List of events which occurred at Pearl Harbour to show that the Americans had ample warning of the approach of the Japanese forces and that the receipt of the 'Cannamore' telegram would scarcely have increased their state of readiness.

3. List of events which took place in Malaya and we must remember that the time of the Japanese landing as 0025 hours was not established till long afterwards.

I hope this clears up the points raised by Wigmore. It is of interest to note that the news of the attack on Pearl Harbour was received in Washington at 1830 hours GMT 7th December. This was 20 minutes after the time given in Malaya Command War diary for the dispatch of the first 'Cannamore' telegram.

Yours ever
Harry Latham

MOST SECRET   IMMEDIATE   COPY

TO : EASFAR

RPTD : ARMINDIA

FROM : TROOPERS

Cable No. 94731   Dated 9/10/41

Following from CHIEFS OF STAFF.
M.O.10. COS.F.E. No.36 Ref. COS.F.E. 8, dated 17/5 para 6.

Necessity for collective action. We cannot lay down in advance what action by Japanese should be regarded as constituting an act of war and therefore automatically bringing appropriate counter measures into force (see para 3(b) of COS telegram to C-in-C Far East 56253 (M.O.10 13/3).

Two. The procedure at para 3 below designed to reduce to a minimum the time involved by the necessity of inter-Governmental consultation will be brought into force forthwith.

Three. Any authority in the Far East mentioned in para 4 below who receives information from any of the territories with which he is concerned that action on the part of the Japanese is either impending or has taken place which is in his view such as to necessitate immediate military counter measures will send to his own higher authority in LONDON and to the other authorities mentioned in para 4 an on clair telegram marked 'MOST IMMEDIATE' (consisting of the first code word contained in my No. 94732 9/10) this warning message (receipt of which will be at once acknowledged by the LONDON authority telegraphing the second word in my 94732 9/10) means that the sender considers that the facts reported in a succeeding message in cypher prefixed by the first code word call for immediate consideration by the Governments concerned of the nature of the military counter measures to be taken. This cypher telegram will also be repeated to the authorities mentioned in para 4.

Four. The authorities concerned in these arrangements are the four Commanders-in-Chief to whom this telegram is addressed ... the British Ambassadors at Washington Tokyo Chungking and Shanghai the British Minister at Bangkok and the Governors of Burma Hong Kong and Fiji.

Five. You should repeat to the Governments of Canada the Commonwealth of Australia New Zealand and the Union of South Africa any telegrams which you may send under the instructions in para 3 above. These Governments are being invited to consider the introduction of similar arrangements to ensure that information of the kind described in para 3 would be communicated to them without delay and would be furnished by them to us and to our various authorities as in that para. The Netherlands and United States Governments also are being asked to arrange that their respective superior authorities in the Far East will ensure that information received by them would be sent to London and repeated to the Commander-in-Chief Far East through the most appropriate channel.

Six. (a) C-in-C Far East pass to C-in-C China as from Chiefs of Staff (b) C-in-C Far East pass to Governor Straits Settlements as from Colonial Office for information (c) This telegram also sent to C-in-C East Indies and repeated Military Mission Washington.

MALAYA

Receipt and Transmission of News of Landings

During the afternoon 7th December news began to reach GHQ Far East of the movements of ships of the Japanese convoy which had been sighted the previous day and afterwards lost. At 1750 hours a cruiser and a merchant ship were seen 112 miles North of Kota Bharu steaming almost straight for Singora (Kra Isthmus – Siam). At 1848 hours under conditions of very bad visibility four Japanese vessels were seen 60 miles North of Patani (Siam) steaming South. This last information reached C-in-C Far East between 2000 and 2100 hours. He immediately proceeded with GOC Malaya (Percival) to Air Headquarters. He was not convinced that the Japanese intended to attack Malaya or even to land in Siam, and for these and other reasons informed the Chiefs of Staff that he did not intend to launch 'Matador'.

Subsequent news of events is given in detail below.

Serial.	Authority.	Extract.
1.	W.D.GHQ	At 2320 hours 7 December, Kota Bharu

	Far East	(probably RAF) reported three small ships off the coast at 2300 hours.
2.	W.D. 9 Ind Div.	Message from 8 Ind Inf Bde (Kota Bharu) sent 2324 hours 7 December and received 0108 hours 8 December:
		'Three small ships unidentifiable in dark reported moving South of Sabak. All informed.' (Note. HQ 9 Ind Div was at Kuala Lumpur where was also HQ III Ind Corps (Heath). There is nothing of interest on this subject in the War Diary of III Corps of which the appendices are incomplete, but it is clear from what follows that Heath was in close touch with both 9 Ind Div and Malaya Command.)
3.	Despatch of Air Vice-Marshal Maltby, for AOC Malaya (Pulford who died in NEI.)	'At about 0030 hours 8th December OC Kota Bharu (RAF) rang up Air HQ and stated three ships had been seen by the beach defences. This message was followed by another at 0100 hours confirming the presence of these ships, stating that shelling was taking place, and that brigade HQ (8 Ind Inf – Key) were being asked to clarify the situation. On this Air HQ ordered the dispatch of a single Hudson with flares to see what was happening. Before this could be done, at 0115 hours definite information came through from Kota Bharu that landing on the beaches by the Japanese had started from three to five ships lying 3 miles offshore. OC Kota Bharu was immediately ordered to take offensive action with all available Hudsons ...' (Note. Previous to this the RAF were not permitted to attack the convoy.)
4.	W.D. GHQ Far East	Entry recorded at 0120 hours 8 December:
		'Japanese attempted a landing at Kota Bharu. Brigadier Key asked for bombing attack.'

5.	W.D. 9 Ind Div	Received by phone from 8 Ind Inf Bde at 0130 hours 8 December, Bde Comd.(Key) speaking:

'Although I previously reported ships off this coast on evening 7 December, RAF report has been "No hostile ships in the neighbourhood". At 0101 hours landing craft were lowered from the ships and are now being shelled by our guns in the neighbourhood Badang-Sabak-Pa'amat. Aeroplanes can also be heard overhead. Enemy does not appear to have shelled the beaches or dropped bombs. Our RAF (Kota Bharu) has been informed and are in touch with Singapore in connection with action to be taken'.

III Corps informed at 0145 hours and 22 Bde at 0215 hours.

6.	W.D. Malaya Command	At 0135 hours 8 December GS02 spoke to III Corps and found that Lt-General Heath already knew of the Japanese landing and Key's request for bombing attack. GSO1 informed Singapore Fortress.

7.	W.D. Malaya Command	Entry recorded at 0159 hours 8 December:

'GHQ (Far East) informed us that "Cannamore" telegram was dispatched at 0140 hours, followed by cypher telegram to Troopers etc.'
(Note. This entry had been previously overlooked. 'Cannamore' was the code prefix to a telegram which C-in-C Far East (as well as certain other commanders) was authorised to send if Japanese action or impending action were such as in his view to necessitate immediate military countermeasures).

8.	W.D. Malaya Command	Entry recorded at 0215 hours 8 December:

'Air Officer Commanding spoke to GS01. First attack at Kota Bharu apparently repelled. Ships moving down South.'

9.   W.D. GHQ   Entry recorded at 0217 hours 8 December:
        Far East
                            'Report that first landing at Kota Bharu
                            had been repelled. Ships moving South to
                            Kemafin beach. Five Hudsons bombing
                            them.'

10.   W.D. GHQ   Entry recorded at 0217 hours 8 December:
        Far East
                            'Cannamore' telegrams dispatched to all
                            addresses as laid down.'
                            (Note. Serials No. 7 and 10 refer to the
                            single word 'Cannamore' telegrams sent *in
                            clear*. The 'Cannamore' telegram sent in
                            cypher was not dispatched till 0500 hours
                            8 December and a copy is attached. But
                            please do not publish this in full
                            without the consent of your Government
                            Cypher Security Branch).

11.   W.D. 9   Message from 8 Ind Inf Bde received 0215
        Ind Div   hours 8 December:

                            'Consider landing probably a mistake or
                            feint. No actual landing known to have
                            taken place. RAF have engaged ships
                            which are believed to be sailing South.
                            2 FFR moving to areas Badang – Sabak.'

   Subsequent messages told of heavy fighting on or around the beaches at
Kota Bharu.

(This author's note. Everything in brackets in the above summary was added
by Brigadier Latham.)

MOST SECRET   CIPHER TELEGRAM

This message will not be distributed outside British Government Departments or Headquarters or re-transmitted, even in cipher, without being
paraphrased.
            (Messages marked OTP need not be paraphrased).

17455

From:– C-in-C Far East

Desp. 0500 8/12/41
Recd. 0015 8/12/41

To:– The War Office
C-in-C India
C-in-C East Indies
Washington. MA Tokio. MA Chungking.
Consul General Shanghai. MA Bangkok. GOC Burma.
GOC Hong Kong. Fiji. CGS Ottawa.
CGS Melbourne. CGS Wellington.
CGS Pretoria. CZM Manila.

MOST IMMEDIATE.

G.R. 58 412/6 cipher 8/12

Cannamore. Following for Chiefs of Staff.
Landing is being attempted at Kota Bharu.

C.4 (Telegrams)   To:– M.O. 10 (for action)

Table of Events at Pearl Harbour

Times.

G.M.T.	Singapore Local	Pearl Harbour Local	
1412 7 Dec	2142 7 Dec	0342 7 Dec	Submarine sighted in restricted area off Pearl Harbour. Report not verified.
1715 7 Dec	0045 8 Dec	0645 7 Dec	Submarine sunk inside the harbour by gunfire and depth charges. Verification awaited.
1730 7 Dec	0100 8 Dec	0700 7 Dec	Army mobile radar unit detected aircraft raiders at distance of 132 miles. No notice taken of report.
1810 7 Dec	0140 8 Dec	0740 7 Dec	Arrival of Japanese aircraft over Oahu Island.
1825 7 Dec	0155 8 Dec	0755 7 Dec	Attack began.

(Note. The events quoted above and the GMT and Pearl Harbour timings were obtained from the Admiralty. The Singapore timings are calculated on a difference of 7½ hours from GMT, which is also the basis of calculation by Churchill in his Vol.III. It is noted that the Commonwealth Astronomer in his letter of 15th November 1950 to Mr Wigmore gives the difference as 7 hours 20 minutes. This small disparity does not really affect the answer to Mr Wigmore's questions.)

(This author's note. All spellings in the above documents, including the two ways of spelling the word 'cypher' and the place-names Tokyo and Pearl Harbor, are as given in the original documents.)

Appendix 5

HMT *Empire Star*

Official No. 163219; Port of Registry Belfast; 12,656 tons. Sailed from Singapore with a crew of 88 including four members of the burnt out *Empress of Asia*.

Captain Selwyn Norman Capon 1890–1942. Born in Norfolk. Awarded OBE for services during First World War. Awarded CBE for war services at Singapore. Captain Capon was lost after *Empire Star* was torpedoed and sunk by a German submarine in the North Atlantic on 23rd October 1942. Four men were killed on board, the rest took to the boats in bad weather. The captain's boat was never seen again. Captain Capon's name along with the names of the other 29 crew members lost, are inscribed on the Merchant Navy War Memorial, Tower Hill, London.

Copy of the 'lost' Report to Blue Star Line. (It is typical of the often understated official wartime reports by Merchant Navy captains about attacks on their ships.)

Report of Attack by Enemy Aircraft upon HMT Empire Star in N.E.I. Waters on 12th February 1942.

On this day, 12th February 1942, *Empire Star* proceeding in convoy with m.v. *Gorgon* and under escort of HM Ships *Durban* and *Kedah* from Singapore to Batavia, carrying evacuated military personnel and civilian refugees, and at the same time a considerable amount of RAF equipment and stores, was, for a period of over four hours, subjected to intermittent attacks by enemy (Japanese) aircraft.

The presence of enemy aircraft was first reported at 8.50 a.m. when the convoy was about to clear the southern end of Durian Strait. The first attack on *Empire Star* was made by six dive-bombers at 9.10 a.m. During same the ship sustained three direct hits: 1st, the after end of No.5 Hatch, starboard side; 2nd, on the poop Deck, starboard side, abreast No.6 Hatch, in which case bomb pierced steel deck and exploded in Poop Space blasting off beams and wooden hatch covers; and 3rd, the after end of the Boat Deck, port side, piercing the steel deck and exploding in the Engineer Officers' Accommodation causing considerable damage to same, also seriously damaging No.4 Lifeboat. Fires were caused in each instance, these being quickly brought under control and extinguished. As a result of this initial attack 12 military personnel were killed and 17 military and ship's personnel severely injured. Two of the severely injured (military) subsequently died of wounds. The ship's personnel consisted of the 2nd officer, Mr James D. Golightly, Art.No.3, who sustained severe injury to left arm, and Charles P. Barber, A.B., Art. No.24, who received a shrapnel wound in the right thigh. The wounded were immediately attended to by RAF medical officers and nurses of the 10th and 13th Australian General Hospitals who were among the military personnel carried. In repelling the dive-bombing attack A.A. fire resulted in one dive-bomber being definitely brought down, being seen to crash into the sea some distance away, whilst another was also seen to be hit, breaking off with smoke pouring from its tail.

The subsequent intermittent attacks which followed were made by formations of aircraft totalling at least some 57 or more planes – according to the numbers actually seen and counted – all of twin-engine heavy bomber type. Each of these later attacks was carried out from high-level, the heights estimated varying from 7,000 to 10,000 feet. A very considerable number of bombs were dropped in each instance but the evasive action resorted to succeeded in reducing these efforts at the ship's destruction to near misses, any damage sustained by the ship's hull through which, remaining to be ascertained whenever the opportunity should present itself. In the course of these whole salvoes of bombs dropped very close to on both sides, often not more than 10 to 20 feet away and it was during one of these that a bomb struck and completely carried away No.4 lifeboat which had already, as previously mentioned, been badly damaged by bomb blast in the initial dive-bombing attacks. The final attack upon the ship was made by a formation of nine aircraft at about 1.10 p.m. when again the vessel miraculously escaped with a series of extremely near misses on both sides. This terminated the series of attacks upon the convoy, mainly directed it seemed against HMS *Durban* and *Empire Star* presumably in view of these two ships providing the largest and therefore the most attractive targets.

The evasive action resorted to in the course of the afore-mentioned attacks was that most strongly advocated and recommended by Captain Sir Philip W. Bowyer Smyth, Bart, RN, formerly in command of HMAS *Perth*, who was a passenger in this ship from Australia to the U.K., Sept.-Oct. last year, and who had had to contend with innumerable such attacks in said cruiser during that vessel's Mediterranean service in recent operations. I would also add that invaluable assistance was rendered me in the taking of this evasive action by Captain George Wright of the Singapore Pilot Service who had remained in the ship on clearing from Singapore and by the 3rd Officer, Mr James P. Smith, both of whom all through coolly kept the attacking aircraft under close observation, keeping me at the same time advised of their manoeuvrers and their probable and eventual angle of attack.

Throughout this long and sustained attack the ship's company, one and all, behaved magnificently, each going about his allotted duty with a coolness and spirit of courage unquestionably deserving of the highest praise. It was fortunate that the damage caused by the three direct hits mentioned did not seriously affect the ship's fire service and prompt action and yeoman service by the fire parties under the direction of the Chief Officer, Mr. J.L. Dawson, prevented any serious fire developing in the initial critical stage of the attack.

The RAF contingent carried provided additional machine-guns and machine-gunners for supplementing the ship's A.A. defence and it was the Hotchkiss in the starboard wing of the Navigating Bridge, manned by RAF personnel, which accounted for the dive-bomber definitely brought down.

Under the existing circumstances, being those of emergency, it was not possible to obtain positive and accurate figures of the military personnel and evacuees on board. Such general muster, however, as could be made, and this under extreme difficulty, gave the following figures which must be regarded as purely approximate:–

RAF)		
BEF)	1573)	
RN)	)	
	)	
AIF)	139)	1845
	)	
Nursing Services & Signal Section	133)	
Civilian Evacuees:–		
Women	128)	
Children	35)	199
Men	36)	
Civilian passengers authorized by		
S.T.O. Singapore for Australia,	29	29
the majority being women.		
Crew and D.B.S's	88	88
	Grand Total	2161

I am convinced that these figures are an underestimation of the numbers actually carried at the time and that a really accurate muster, had it been possible, would have provided figures appreciably in excess of those given above.

(Signed.)   Selwyn N. Capon
OBE

7.3.42.   Commander

(Author's notes:
   1. *Empire Star* was fitted with the following guns.
      1×6inch long-range surface gun
      1×3inch high-angle AA gun
      4×Twin Lewis guns
      2×Strip Lewis guns.
   2. D.B.S. is the abbreviation for Distressed British Seaman, and would have covered the four survivors from the *Empress of Asia* on board.
   3. As well as Captain Capon's CBE the following awards were received by crew members:

Chief Engineer R.F. Francis	OBE	*
Chief Officer J.L. Dawson	OBE	
Snr. Second Engineer H.C. Weller	MBE	
Second Officer J.D. Golightly	MBE	
Third Officer J.P. Smith	MBE	
Bosun W. Power	BEM	*
Carpenter S. Milne	BEM	

Officially commended:
Jnr. Second Engineer J.J. Johnson
Snr. Third Engineer J. Middleton
Jnr. Third Engineer J.R. Mitchell
Chief Steward C.E. Ribbons   *
Cadet R. Foulkner
Cadet R. Perry   *
Able Seaman C.P. Barber
Donkeyman H.E. Heaver

(The asterisks mark those men who were lost with their captain on 23rd October 1942.)

This number of awards was collectively among the highest awarded to the crew of a single merchant ship during World War Two.
The awards were promulgated in the London Gazette on 15th September 1942 only five weeks before the ship was lost. The

first part of the official eulogy read, 'The Master's coolness, leadership and skill were outstanding, and it was mainly due to his handling of the ship that the vessel reached safety.'

Captain Capon received the following letters of commendation for his actions:

1.

NCS. 42/198

> Royal Australian Navy
> Naval Control Service
> 44 Bridge Street
> Sydney
>
> 9th March 1942

The Master
S.S. Empire Star
c/o Blue Star Line
19 Bridge Street
Sydney NSW

Dear Sir
   I have pleasure in informing you that the Naval Board have instructed me to pass the following message on to you:

'The Naval Board have received information of the intense and sustained air attacks against Empire Star on the twelfth of February 1942 off Singapore, and wish to congratulate you on bringing your ship, although damaged, through the ordeal. The Naval Board have pleasure in transmitting this report to the Admiralty.'

> Yours faithfully,
>
> G. Rawson
> Lieutenant-Commander R.A.N.
> Acting Naval Control Officer.

(Author's note. Geoffrey Rawson was a noted Australian maritime historian. Among his works are several on matters dealing with the mutiny on the *Bounty*.)

2.

Blue Star Line
40 St. Mary Axe
London EC3

1st June 1942

Captain S.N. Capon
m.v. Empire Star
422 Unthank Road
Norwich
Norfolk

Dear Captain Capon

Confirming our interview today, I now have pleasure in enclosing a cheque for £100 as a small token of our appreciation for your services in the recent evacuation from Singapore.

We again place on record our high appreciation of those services.

Yours truly
Blue Star Line Limited
General Manager

Appendix 6

From WO106/2591. PRO, Kew.

IMPERIAL GENERAL STAFF

(Australia Section)

Australia House
Strand
London W.C.2.

4th June 1942

Lieut.-Colonel J.M.K.Spurling
War Office (M.O.2)
Whitehall
S.W.1.

Dear

I have heard recently some rather alarming stories about the behaviour of the A.I.F. in Malaya in general, and Singapore Island in particular. Several Australians have come to me with these stories asking me whether I am in a position to deny them or otherwise. They have also come to the High Commissioner's notice and he, too, is most anxious to know whether there is any truth in them or not.

The stories are circulating around London in Clubs and so forth, and are briefly as follows:

1. a) The A.I.F. did not fight too well in Johore, and their discipline during the retreat left a lot to be desired.
   b) There were some bad cases of interference with the native population, including rape.
   c) Numbers of men deserted back to the Island. This story is not so well supported as those which follow.

2. The collapse of Singapore was in great part due to the fact that the Australian Division in the Western Sector did not fight at all, being convinced that there was no point in it.

3. Singapore city was full of Australian deserters who were rioting all over the town, and drunkenness was rife.
   In one case, a large party of Australians attempted to rush

a ship taking away refugees. This involved firing between the Australians and the guard on the ship.

4. The story of Major-General Gordon Bennett's escape as given by him and as published in the Press, is a pack of lies from start to finish. He was, in fact, got away by a party of F.M.S. Volunteers whom he beseeched to take him with them. It is also suggested that he actually left before the surrender.

The War Office will, no doubt, have collected all available evidence from both Service and civilian personnel who have returned from Malaya, not particularly on this subject, but so that a comprehensive picture can be formed of the reasons for our defeat. In the course of this investigation, no doubt you will have got some evidence which will tend either to disprove or to prove the stories mentioned above.

So that we in this office may know what line to take, I should be very grateful indeed for any information you are able to let me have.

Yours sincerely
J.K. Coffey.

Draft reply dated 14th June 1942.   SECRET.

Dear
Spurling has shown me your letter of the 4th June saying that you have heard stories about the behaviour of the A.I.F. at Singapore, and asking whether we could let you know if there was any truth in them.

As you will know from the various statements which have been made on the subject of the Malayan campaign, we have so far had only one report, which is that of General Gordon Bennett.

We know that General Wavell also has been busy on a report which will probably arrive in the course of the next few weeks.

We have also seen and heard from various individuals, officers and others, who have arrived in this country, about some of the aspects of the campaign, but most of what they had to tell us, whatever the subject, was in the form of hearsay evidence. It does not help us, therefore, to arrive at any firm conclusions on what actually did take place.

It is just possible that General Wavell's expected report, or his official Despatch when that comes in later, may give us some help, either by substantiating the stories to which you refer, or by refuting them as we sincerely hope will be the case. My personal opinion, however, is that General Wavell is unlikely to be of much help to us in this connection. The real evidence on this subject, as well as on all the others on which we need information, will come from those officers and others who are now prisoners of war in Japanese hands; and we will have to wait for it until after the war.

You have already been given a copy of the report sent in by General Gordon Bennett. As I have said, his is the only really first-hand account we have had so far. I suggest that it is quite possible that he may be in a position to answer your questions with fairly definite statements. You may care to consider referring to him the various stories you have heard.

                    Yours
                    Initials (indecipherable)

Notes

INTRODUCTION (pages 1–6)

1. Quoted in Richard Holmes and Anthony Kemp, *The Bitter End*, Antony Bird, Chichester, 1982.
2. Reginald Burton, *The Road to Three Pagodas*, Macdonald, London, 1963.
3. H.G. Blackham, correspondence with the author, 1993.
4. The poem, entitled 'J'y suis, J'y reste' (Here I am, Here I stay) is signed with the *nom de plume* 'Kempas', which is Malay for a type of timber. A copy of the poem has been kindly supplied to me by Guy Madoc, who was a senior police officer in Malaya. The original is to be lodged at the Imperial War Museum, London.
5. Charles Eade (compiler), *Secret Session Speeches*, Cassell, London, 1946. (In accordance with Parliamentary custom, secret session speeches were not recorded even for official or historical purposes. Churchill prepared full texts before delivering them, and from these Eade compiled his book.)
6. W.S. Churchill, Vol. 4, *The Second World War – The Hinge of Fate*, Cassell, London, 1951.
7. Paul Freyberg, *Bernard Freyberg, VC – Soldier of Two Nations*, Hodder & Stoughton, London, 1991.
8. Raymond Callahan, *The Worst Disaster – The Fall of Singapore*, Newark, 1977.
9. John Keegan, foreword to Penguin one-volume edition of Churchill's *The Second World War*, London, 1989.
10. Callahan, op.cit.

CHAPTER 1: THE RISE OF MODERN JAPAN AND ITS EFFECT ON BRITISH POLICY (pages 7–13)

1. See P.G. Rogers, *The First Englishman In Japan*, Harvill, London, 1956; and article, Peter Elphick, *Will Adams, the Shogun's Englishman*, Seascape, October 1987. Will Adams was the inspiration for James Clavell's hero, John Blackthorne, in his novel *Shogun*.
2. On 15th February 1915 – twenty-seven years to the day before the fall of Singapore in World War Two – part of the 5th Light Infantry, Indian Army, in Singapore as part of the garrison, mutinied. Many British officers and local civilians of several nationalities were killed. The mutineers set free some of

the captured crew of the German armed raider *Emden*, in the hope that by doing so they might get German aid. At one stage the mutineers came close to taking over Singapore. After the mutiny was put down with the help of Japanese, Russian and French marines, 47 mutineers were executed, 22 of them being shot at the same time in front of 15,000 spectators.

3. Richard Storry, *A History of Modern Japan*, Penguin edition, London, 1982.

CHAPTER 2: THE SINGAPORE NAVAL BASE (pages 15–26)

1. War Cabinet 'A' Minutes, 616A, PRO, Kew.
2. N.H. Gibbs, *History of the Second World War, Vol. I, 'Grand Strategy'*, HMSO, London, 1976.
3. WO106/2430. PRO. Appreciation of Japanese Attack on Singapore, November 1937, by Colonel (later Lieutenant-General) A.E. Percival, GSO1, Singapore.
4. Cab. Cons. 64 (1924). PRO.
5. CID 322-C. CID 193rd,198th,199th, meetings. PRO.
6. Stephen Roskill, *Churchill and the Admirals*, Collins, London, 1977.
7. Roskill, ibid.
8. BTY/17/9/88–93, BTY/17/43/2–3, BTY/17/48/4–5, Beatty Papers, National Maritime Museum, Greenwich. As quoted in *The Beatty Papers*, edited by B. McL. Ranft, Scolar Press for the Navy Records Society, London, 1989.
9. Roskill, op.cit.
10. CID 199th meeting; Cab. Cons. 24(1925)3. PRO.
11. CID 215th meeting, 1926. PRO.
12. CP169 (1928), PRO.
13. Letter to the Editor, *The Times*, 11th November 1948.
14. Russell Grenfell, *Main Fleet To Singapore*, Faber, London, 1951.
15. N.H. Gibbs, op.cit.
16. Sir Laurence Guillimard was Governor of the Straits Settlements until 1928. He was followed by Sir Hugh Clifford (1866–1941) who had a two-year tenure. Then came Sir Cecil Clementi (1875–1947) who held the post until Sir Shenton Thomas took over in 1936.
17. CO273/635/1. RNVR in Malaya. PRO.

CHAPTER 3: PRE-WAR PLANS FOR THE DEFENCE OF MALAYA, SINGAPORE AND AUSTRALIA (pages 27–44)

1. An example of the naïve views on Singapore defences held by many in Britain has been given by Squadron Leader S. Stephen. In 1938 he chose the subject 'Naval Defence of the British Empire' for the set task of his final RAF passing-out examination. In his thesis he wrote, 'The southern part of the Malay Peninsula is a British possession and has no cause for expecting a land attack from the north.' After quoting that extract to this author in 1993, Squadron Leader Stephen remarked, 'And I passed!'

2. wo106/2542, 'Extract from lecture given by General Sir Lewis Heath'. PRO, Kew.

3. Later Lieutenant-General Sir William Dobbie, GCMG, KCB, DSO. Born 1879. Commissioned into Royal Engineers, 1899. Retired from the army under the 'age rule' in 1939. Was appointed Governor of Malta in 1940, and for the next two years he was to epitomise the gallant defence of that island. Died 1964.

4. wo106/5399. Far East Appreciation In The Event Of War With Japan, July 1936. PRO.

5. wo106/2430. PRO.

6. wo106/2431. New Proposals for the Defence of Malaya, Oct/Nov.1938. PRO.

7. Later Lieutenant-General Sir Lionel Bond. After his relief by General Percival in May 1941, Bond was permanently retired. He died in 1961.

8. C.A. Vlieland (1890–1974). Exeter College and Balliol College, Oxford. Joined the Malayan Civil Service as a Cadet in 1914.

9. C.A. Vlieland, *Disaster in the Far East*, a memoir in the Liddell Hart Centre for Military Archives, King's College, London.

10. Later Air Marshal Sir John Tremayne (b.1891). He renounced the name Babington in 1945.

11. wo106/2437. Mobilization of Volunteer Forces, Jan/Feb 1940. PRO.

12. Edwin Maurice Glover, *In 70 Days*, Muller, London, 1946.

13. A.H. Dickinson, papers and correspondence in Bryson Collection, Royal Commonweath Library.

14. Sir Robert Brooke-Popham (1878–1953) had retired from the RAF in 1937 after a distinguished career. Later he was appointed Governor of Kenya. In 1939 he was reinstated to the active list.

15. See *Their Secret Wartime Correspondence*, a selection of Roosevelt-Churchill letters, edited by F.L. Loewenheim, Barrie & Jackson, London, 1976.

16. David Day, *The Great Betrayal*, Angus & Robertson, Sydney and London, 1988.

17. CAB65/1. War Cabinet Conclusions, 19th October 1939. PRO.

18. CAB65/2. War Cabinet Conclusions, 2nd November 1939. PRO.

19. Sir Robert Menzies, *Afternoon Light*, Cassell, London, 1967.

CHAPTER 4: ESPIONAGE, SUBVERSION, AND THE INDIAN INDEPENDENCE LEAGUE (pages 45–76)

1. Papers of A.H. Dickinson, Bryson Collection, Royal Commonwealth Library, London.

2. *Lessons of the Russo-Japanese War*, an article by Lieutenant-Colonel Picard, 1905. Translated from the French by Lieutenant-Colonel W. Malleson, of the British Military Intelligence Department, and published in both Britain and India. Copy in the India Records Office, London. File No. L/Mil/17/20/22.

3. René Onraet, Inspector-General of Police, 1936–39, in *Singapore – A Police Background*, D. Crisp, London, c.1945. *Ronin* is Japanese for 'wave men', namely masterless warriors. However, throughout Japanese history and

legend, the *ronin* appears in several guises: as a mercenary warrior owning little more than his weapons but extremely jealous of his honour; as a swashbuckler ready for any form of excitement; and as a social misfit.

4. FO371/22173/532. PRO, Kew.
5. Onraet, op.cit.
6. WO208/1530 No. 089275. PRO. The full text of this intercepted message will be found in *Odd Man Out – the Story of the Singapore Traitor*, Peter Elphick and Michael Smith, Hodder & Stoughton, London, 1993.
7. The rate of exchange was 8 Straits dollars to £1 sterling. The pre-WWII pound is considered to have been worth 32 times what it is in 1993. So, to convert pre-war Straits dollars to present-day sterling values, one should multiply the dollar by four.
8. René Onraet, op.cit.
9. WO193/913. CX37963/553, PRO.
10. WO193/913, PRO.
11. FO/22173/532. 'Japanese Espionage in Malaya', PRO.
12. CO273/644/9, PRO.
13. A full discussion of this case will be found in an article by Brian Bridges, 'Britain and Japanese Espionage in Pre-War Malaya; The Shinozaki Case', Journal of Contemporary History, SAGE, London, Vol.21, 1986.
14. WO193/913. Collation File No. 27, Far East Espionage, PRO.
15. WO193/913, PRO.
16. C.E. Collinge correspondence, Bryson Collection, Royal Commonwealth Library. Collinge worked for Travers & Co. in Singapore.
17. The Wyatt and Wylie reports can be found in the Bryson Collection, Royal Commonwealth Library.
18. H.P. Bryson, Malayan Civil Service. Letter to A.H. Dickinson, BEAM Collection, Royal Commonwealth Library.
19. M. Ll. Wynne, *Triad and Tabut: A Survey of the Origin and Diffusion of Chinese and Mohammedan Secret Societies in the Malay Peninsular, 1800–1935*. Singapore Government Printer, 1941. The copy in the India Records Office is missing chapters 26–36 and the appendixes.
20. Report by H.B.J. Donaldson. Bryson Collection, Royal Commonwealth Library.
21. WO106/2579C, PRO.
22. Subedar Tor Khan survived three-and-a-half years as a prisoner of war. After the war he was made an Honorary Captain and became an ADC to Field Marshal Sir Claude Auchinleck.
23. Kenneth Harrison, *The Brave Japanese*, Rigby Limited, Adelaide, 1966.
24. HRH Major-General Sir Ibrahim, Sultan of Johore, GCMG, GBE. (1873–1959).
25. WO106/2579C, PRO.
26. WO172/125. War Diary, 22nd Indian Infantry Brigade, Signals Section, PRO.
27. H.B.J. Donaldson report in Bryson Collection, Royal Commonwealth Library.
28. H.B.J. Donaldson, ibid.
29. Later Major R.G. Wells, No. VX14024. Secretary and accountant of Castlemaine, Victoria. Born 1st January 1920. Captured at fall of Singapore. Transferred by s.s. *Ubi Maru* to Sandakan POW Camp, North Borneo,

July 1942.

30. Copy in CAB106/153, PRO. The Wells report was included as an appendix to the Signals War Diary, 8th Australian Division.

31. H.M. Still had been on the Special Branch Black List for some time. Although he was married with two children, he was a notorious homosexual, and that was enough to get him on the list. Nothing much seems to have been done to him after his arrest, perhaps because of his connection with the Sultan through the Royal Johore International Club, or perhaps because of official worries of repercussions if Tungku Ahmad was also involved. Still was alive in mid-1957. At that time he was sighted at the Malacca Rest-House by an officer of Singapore Special Branch.

32. WO106/2528. Item XVa 67, PRO.

33. CAB103/340, PRO.

34. WO106/2579C. PRO. (The writer of the police report referred to other reports on the Stia affair which had appeared in the *Straits Settlements Police Journal* dated 31.12.1941, and reproduced in DIB Survey No.9 of 28.2.1942.)

35. WO208/1522, PRO.

36. See, Joyce C. Lebra, *Japanese Trained Armies in Southeast Asia*, Columbia University Press, 1977.

37. 'Discipline of Indian Troops in Singapore', India Records Office, London. L/WS/1/391. WS4367.

38. See Chapter 1, Note 2. For the full story of the 1915 mutiny see, R.W.E. Harper & Harry Miller, *Singapore Mutiny*, Oxford, 1984.

39. File L/WS/1/391. India Records Office, London.

40. L/WS/1/391, ibid.

41. Papers of Lieutenant-Colonel E.L. Sawyer MBE. Imperial War Museum, London. 88/33/1. Colonel Sawyer's MBE was awarded for this work which he carried out at great risk to his life.

42. Colonel C.H.T. MacFetridge, correspondence and telephone conversations with the author, 1993.

43. Mahmood Khan Durrani, *The 6th Column*, London, 1955.

44. Further details of Hendrick's murder can be found in Elphick and Smith, op. cit.

45. Fujiwara Iwaichi, *F-Kikan – Japanese Army Intelligence Operations in SE Asia During World War II*, Hong Kong, 1983.

46. Full details of the *Automedon* incident are given in James Rusbridger & Eric Nave, *Betrayal at Pearl Harbor*, O'Mara, London, 1992.

47. WO208/1925. FECB Report No. 5401, November 1941, PRO.

48. Heenan's full story is given in Elphick & Smith. op.cit. Some additional information has come to light since *Odd Man Out* was published in 1993.

49. Memoirs of Lieutenant-Colonel D.J.R. Moore. EUR 226, IOLR/E/1/311, India Records Office, London.

50. Neville Baillie-Stewart (b.1911) was the famous 'officer in the Tower'. He was arrested, held in the Tower of London, and, in 1933, found guilty of passing military information to the Germans. He was sentenced to five years imprisonment and cashiered from the army. After his release he went to live in Germany. He was arrested there in 1945 and sentenced to five years for broadcasting for the Germans. Released in 1949, he went to live in Ireland using the names 'James Scott' and 'Patrick Stewart'. He

died there in 1966.

51. Squadron Leader R.E. Wardrop in conversations with the author during 1993.
52. The telephone conversation was written up in the Garhwali War Diary, but this document was destroyed during the retreat from Kuantan.
53. wo172/17, PRO.
54. J.B. Masefield, correspondence and conversations with Peter Elphick, 1992.

CHAPTER 5: BRITISH INTELLIGENCE AND COUNTER-INTELLIGENCE (pages 77–95)

1. A.H. Dickinson papers, Bryson Collection, Royal Commonwealth Library.
2. wo106/2579C. PRO. Only released in to the public domain in 1993.
3. Sir Andrew Gilchrist, *Malaya 1941*. Hale, London, 1992.
4. Operations of Malaya Command, From 8th December 1941 to 15th February 1942. Lieutenant-General A.E. Percival, London Gazette, 26th February 1948. Section 64.
5. Papers of Lieutenant-Colonel B.H. Ashmore, OBE. Scots Guards. Imperial War Museum, London.
6. wo193/603. SOE/FE/2. PRO.
7. S. Woodburn Kirby, *The War Against Japan*. Official History of the Second World War, HMSO, London, 1957.
8. Japanese Army Memorandum issued by General Staff, H.M. Naval Base, Singapore, March 1941. Copy in India Records Office, London. L/Mil/17/20/24.
9. Letter from Colonel Grimsdale to General Ismay, 8th March 1942. Ismay Archive IV/Gri, la-7/2d. Liddell Hart Centre, King's College, London.
10. wo193/913. Collation No. 27 Far East Espionage, 23/10/40 – 18/12/41. PRO.
11. Some of this information was kindly supplied by Lady (Mary) Mills, Colonel Hayley Bell's daughter, in correspondence with the author during 1993.
12. Letter from G.C. Madoc, CBE, KPM, to the author 16 June 1993.
13. Major Kenneth Stayce Morgan. Assistant Superintendent SB, Singapore from 23rd February 1936. Served earlier in Shanghai Police, and prior to that was a Military Attaché at the British Embassy in Tokyo.
14. Information about K.S. Morgan in a) Letters from Mrs Barbara Herdman, née Brown, to H.P. Bryson, dated April 1972. Bryson Collection, XII 26, Royal Commonwealth Library; (b) and from a senior ex-policeman of the Singapore Police Force who wishes to remain anonymous.
15. René H. de S. Onraet, Inspector-General Strait Settlements Police, 1936–39. Born in Mauritius in 1887, he had arrived in Malaya as a Police Cadet in 1907. He returned to Malaya after the Second World War as Police Advisor to the British Military Authority.
16. (a) Ivan Simson, *Singapore – Too Little Too Late*, Leo Cooper, London, 1970, (b) Correspondence between Ivan Simson and A.H. Dickinson, Bryson Collection. Royal Commonwealth Library.

17. Major-General Sir Vernon Kell, KBE, CB, Director of MI5 from 1909 to 1940. Born Yarmouth 1873, died 1942. Linguist, spoke French, German, Russian and Chinese. Acted as correspondent for the *Daily Telegraph* in China during Boxer Rebellion. He has been described as Britain's first spy-catcher, and probably ranks as one of the most successful.
18. S.W. Kirby, *Singapore – the Chain of Disaster*, Cassell, London, 1971.
19. See Simson correspondence in Bryson Collection, op.cit.
20. Later Lieutenant-Colonel Ivan Lyon, DSO. Colonel Lyon commanded the successful Operation Jaywick attack on Japanese shipping in Singapore Harbour in 1943. He was killed during an attempt to emulate that feat a year later.
21. Donald Smith, *And All The Trumpets*, Geoffrey Bles, London, 1954.
22. wo172/147. War Diary, 2nd Loyals. PRO.
23. Guy Madoc. Report on police officers who served as Army Liaison Officers. Not dated. Royal Commonwealth Library.
24. Report by J.N.M.A. Nicholls in Royal Commonwealth Library. Nicholls was one of the most senior of the establishment of 77 Assistant Superintendents of Police in pre-war Malaya/Singapore. He was appointed temporary Commissioner of Police, Singapore, for a period after the war.
25. Clive Lyon, interview and correspondence with the author, 1993.
26. PREM3/168/3. Operations in Malaya Report endorsed by General Sir Archibald Wavell. PRO.

CHAPTER 6: THAILAND, AND OPERATION MATADOR
(pages 97–116)

1. FO371/28124. Ashley Clarke minute dated 12th August 1941. PRO.
2. CAB106/180. PRO. Report on discussions at the War History Institute, Tokyo, September 1966, by Colonel Wards of Historical Section, Cabinet Office, Whitehall. (Originally closed to 1997, this file came into the public domain in 1994.)
3. D.J.M. Tate, *The Making of Modern South-East Asia*, Vol. 2., OUP, 1979.
4. FO371/28108. '1941 Siam'. (File marked closed to 1992.) PRO.
5. wo106/5701. Command Intelligence Notes, MCIS No.7/1937. PRO.
6. Sir Josiah Crosby, 1880–1958. OBE, 1918; CIE, 1919; KBE, 1928. Interned by Japanese December 1941. Was part of exchange of diplomatic personnel at Lourenço Marques, August 1942. Author of *Siam: The Crossroads*, 1945; *Siam*, 1945, Oxford Pamphlets, No.26. See *Times* obituary, 5th December 1958.
7. Dorothy Crisp, *Why We Lost Singapore*, Crisp & Co., London, 1943.
8. Cordell Hull, *Memoirs* Vol. 2. Hodder & Stoughton, London, 1948.
9. Probably the best short study of Anglo-American relations with Thailand in the years leading up to the war is *A Question of Expediency: Britain, the United States and Thailand, 1941–42*, Richard Aldrich, Journal of South-East Asian Studies, Vol.XIX, No. 2 September 1988.
10. Mark Gayn, *The Fight for the Pacific*, The Bodley Head, London, 1941.
11. FO371/28122. F4259. PRO.

12. FO371/27962. Japan File 523. Cipher No.693, 5th February 1941, Foreign Office to Lord Halifax. (File marked closed to 1992). PRO.
13. FO371/28123. F7248G. 4th August 1941. PRO.
14. FO371/28111. PRO.
15. Sir George Sansom, *The Story of Singapore*, Foreign Affairs Vol. 22, New York, 1944.
16. WO193/915. Infiltration in Thailand, 13th May 1941–30th August 1941. PRO.
17. WO193/917. PRO.
18. Asada Sadao, *The Japanese Navy and the United States*, in D. Borg and Shumpei Okamoto, editors, *Pearl Harbor as History: Japanese-American Relations 1931–1941*, Columbia University Press, 1973.
19. FO371/28134. F7487/246/40. Cable No.472, 30th July 1941. PRO.
20. FO371/28121. PRO.
21. Pradit was a French-trained lawyer. Sir Andrew Gilchrist describes him as 'a stocky, self-reliant Siamese of middle height, with great natural dignity'. He had personal magnetism and had much influence over young Thais. He was in a very powerful position after the war until a 'palace coup' in November 1947 put Pibul back into the driving seat. Pradit's strong leftist leanings caused him to end up an embittered political exile in China in the 1950s. Like the Malayan People's Anti-Japanese Army, and the organisation set up in Burma by U Aung San, the Free Siamese Movement was very strongly Communist. These movements were supplied with arms and advisors by SOE. The arms were not surrendered after the war and became the arsenal for Communist-inspired insurrection in all three countries. Lying between Burma and Malaya, Thailand was still the key to the region after World War Two and the Chinese Communists and the Russians understood this well. In 1948 the Russians opened an embassy in Bangkok, at that time their only one in that part of South-East Asia.
22. FO371/28126. PRO.
23. Charles Cruikshank, *The Official History of the SOE in the Far East*, Oxford, 1983.
24. Sir Andrew Gilchrist, *Malaya 1941: The Fall of a Fighting Empire*, Robert Hale, London, 1992.
25. WO193/917. PRO.
26. FO371/24715. PRO.
27. These editorials are referred to in a letter from H.P. Bryson to Mrs Barbara Herdman, 8th April 1972. Bryson Collection, Royal Commonwealth Library.
28. Aldrich, op. cit.
29. FO371/28110. '1941 Siam'. (Closed until 1992.) PRO.
30. FO371/28153. 'Far East, Siam, 1941'. (File marked closed until 1992.) PRO.
31. FO371/28109. (File marked closed to 1992.) PRO.
32. FO371/28153. (File marked closed to 1992.) PRO.

CHAPTER 7: CAPTAIN JOHN BECKER, BRITISH MILITARY INTELLIGENCE (pages 117–144)

1. Family papers of Mrs Dorothy Becker, also known as Dorothy Crisp (1906–87), kindly made accessible to the author by her and John Becker's children, Rev. Dr Liz Carmichael and Hugh Becker. The Becker story is also based on information in files at the PRO in Kew; from the papers of A.H. Dickinson; and from information contained in the transcripts of intelligence material that many years ago ended up in private hands, and some of which was seen by Brigadier Ivan Simson, the author of *Singapore – Too Little, Too Late*.
2. Information from Mrs Hilary Morton.
3. Information from Thacker Indian Directory, various annual editions.
4. Indian Army Lists 1927.
5. Harry Hobbs, Managing Director, H. Hobbs & Co. Ltd., Calcutta, musical instrument dealers. Information from Thacker Indian Directory, 1929 edition. The upshot of the YMCA affair was that the head man in London was fired, and four men in India – Messrs Spratt, Bradley. Hutchinson and M.N. Roy – were each sentenced to twelve years penal sertitude.
6. Becker family papers.
7. Letter from R. Sidney to the Editor, *Straits Times*, Singapore, 31st August 1948, and copied to Dorothy Crisp.
8. *Straits Times*, 25th August 1948, front page.
9. *Singapore Free Press*, 29th March 1947, front page.
10. Dickinson letters in Bryson Collection, Royal Commonwealth Library.
11. Copy of letter from M.B. Bell to C-in-C, Far East, in Becker family papers.
12. Letter dated 10th September 1948 from S.E. Golledge to Dorothy Crisp.
13. wo208/1915. Thailand, Japanese penetration of. FECB Report No. 5401, November 1941. PRO.
14. Information kindly supplied to the author in 1993 by Winifrid Asavasena's niece, Mrs Doreen Riley, and by Alfred Johnson who heard many of the stories of this eastern 'Florence Nightingale' in the Japanese camps.
15. This meeting is referred to in a letter from Wavell to Miss Dorothy Crisp, dated 18th June 1943. Becker family papers.
16. Dorothy Crisp, *A Life For England*, Crisp & Co., London, 1946.
17. Ian Morrison, *Malayan Postscript*, Faber, London, 1942; Compton Mackenzie, *Eastern Epic*, Chatto & Windus, London, 1951; Frank Owen, *The Fall Of Singapore*, Michael Joseph, London, 1960.
18. William Warren, *The Legendary American*, Houghton Mifflin, Boston, 1970; Alec Waugh, *Bangkok*, W.H. Allen, London, 1970.
19. Letters in Becker family papers.
20. It was still a high security area ten years later in 1959. This author visited Naval Intelligence there in 1959–60 with intelligence material he had unofficially collected when master of a British ship sailing out of Singapore. Subsequently the author was shown, but not allowed to retain, a letter of thanks for his efforts, signed by the Admiral in charge of the station.
21. co953/9/3, co953/9/4, and co953/3/7. PRO. The latter file was originally closed to the year 2000. After Hugh Becker and the author wrote to the

Foreign & Commonwealth Office the file was placed in the public domain in January 1994.

CHAPTER 8: THE BRITISH LEADERS IN THE MALAYAN CAMPAIGN (pages 145–180)

1. Sir John Smyth, *Percival and the Tragedy of Singapore*, Macdonald, London, 1971.
2. Brian Montgomery, *Shenton of Singapore*, Leo Cooper, London, 1984.
3. A.H. Dickinson, Inspector-General of Police, Singapore, in a letter dated 8th June 1967 to Harold Fairburn, one of his predecessors in that post. Royal Commonwealth Library.
4. (a) G.W. Seabridge in a range of articles and leaders in the *Straits Times* throughout 1939–41. (b) Ian Morrison, *Malayan Postscript*, Faber, London, 1942; (c) Official History, *The War Against Japan*, HMSO, London, 1957.
5. CO967/73. PRO.
6. H.P. Bryson correspondence with A.H. Dickinson, 1960–70. Bryson Collection, Royal Commonwealth Library.
7. Diary of Megan Spooner, King's College, London.
8. A.H. Dickinson. Report, prepared in 1969. Bryson Collection, Royal Commonwealth Library.
9. Letter from Mrs M. Reilly to H.P. Bryson. Bryson Collection, Royal Commonwealth Library.
10. Post-1945 George E. Bogaars became Confidential Assistant Secretary to the Colonial Secretariat in Singapore. His first wife died some time after 1950. After retirement from the Colonial Service he was appointed Warden of a Malayan Student Hostel in Melbourne. He later returned to Singapore, but ended up in Formosa where he married a lady of 'good standing'. He was still there in 1968.
11. Letter from G.Weisberg to H.P. Bryson, 1968. Bryson Collection, Royal Commonwealth Library.
12. CO967/78. (Closed to 1993.) PRO.
13. John Charmley, *Duff Cooper*, Weidenfeld & Nicolson, London, 1986.
14. Letter Brooke-Popham to Cs-of-S subcommittee, 26th October 1940. Brooke-Popham papers, V/4/5, Liddell Hart Centre for Military Studies, King's College, London.
15. Letter Brooke-Popham to General Ismay, 16th May 1941. Brooke-Popham papers, V/1/12.
16. S. Woodburn Kirby, *Singapore: The Chain of Disaster*, Cassell, London, 1971.
17. Megan Spooner, Diary. op.cit.
18. CAB103/340. PRO.
19. Stanley L. Falk, *Seventy Days to Singapore*, Robert Hale, London, 1975.
20. H. Blackham, letters to the author, 1993.
21. Lieutenant-General A.E. Percival, Operations of Malaya Command, from 8th December 1941 to 15th February 1942. Supplement to *London Gazette*, 20th February 1948.
22. John Charmley, op.cit.

23. co967/77. PRO.
24. Quoted by Frank Legg, in *The Gordon Bennett Story*, Angus & Robertson, Sydney, 1965.
25. co967/78. PRO.
26. CAB106/180. PRO. Report on discussions held in Tokyo in 1966 between Colonel Wards and officers of the War History Institute, Tokyo.
27. Stephen Roskill, *Churchill and the Admirals*, Collins, London, 1977.
28. Memoirs of General (later Baron) Hastings Ismay. (1887–1965.) 'Pug' Ismay was Chief of Staff to Churchill at the Ministry of Defence, 1940–46. He had previously been Secretary to the Committee of Imperial Defence, 1936–38. An intensely loyal man, especially where Churchill was concerned, his memoirs were written with much discretion; so much discretion in fact, that they do not contribute greatly to the history of the war.
29. W.S. Churchill, *The Second World War* (omnibus volume) Penguin, London, 1989.
30. co967/77. PRO.
31. ADM199/357. PRO.
32. Giles Playfair, *Singapore Goes Off the Air*, Jarrolds, London, 1944.
33. A.B. Lodge, *The Fall Of General Gordon Bennett*, Allen & Unwin, London, 1986.
34. Sir Keith Murdoch, in *The Advertiser*, Adelaide, 17th August 1942.
35. CAB106/162. Report on Operations of 8th Australian Division in Malaya, compiled by Colonel J.H. Thyer and Colonel C.H. Kappe. PRO.
36. wo106/2550B. PRO.
37. wo208/1529. Major-General Bennett's Report. PRO.
38. H. Gordon Bennett, *Why Singapore Fell*, Angus & Robertson, Sydney, 1944.
39. The Times, 12th January 1993.
40. Robert Woollcombe, *The Campaigns of Wavell 1939–1943*, Cassell, London, 1959.
41. Wavell letters to Joan Bright Astley. Imperial War Museum, London.
42. Stanley L. Falk, op.cit.

CHAPTER 9: THE COMMONWEALTH FIGHTING FORCES; TRAINING, EQUIPMENT AND WEAPONS (Pages 181–213)

1. David Day, *The Great Betrayal*, Angus & Robertson, Sydney, 1988.
2. Lionel Wigmore, *The Japanese Thrust*, Australian War Memorial, 1957.
3. Diary of General Sir Henry Pownall; edited by Brian Bond under the title, *Chief of Staff*, Lee Cooper, London, 1974.
4. Major-General Sir John Kennedy was Director of Military Operations from 1940–43.
5. CAB106/340. PRO. Letter from 2nd Earl Wavell to Major-General S.W. Kirby. The letter is dated 13th October, but no year is given. As the letter was written as a comment on the manuscript of the Official War History which was published in 1957, the year was probably 1955 or 1956.
6. wo106/2620. PRO. Churchill's directive is marked 'MOST SECRET', 'WAR

CABINET', 'TO BE KEPT UNDER LOCK AND KEY', and endorsed, 'It is requested that special care may be taken to ensure the secrecy of this document.'

6a. Churchill's blind spot, and his belief in 'fortress' Singapore, are illustrated in his 'Memorandum on Sea Power, 1939' (see text in *Winston S. Churchill* by Martin Gilbert, Companion Volume V, Part 3. Churchill's keenness to involve the Americans is revealed in his first telegram to Roosevelt after becoming Prime Minister: 'I am looking to you to keep that Japanese dog quiet in the Pacific, using Singapore in any way convenient'.

7. David Day, op.cit.

8. Masanobu Tsuji, *Singapore 1941–1942*. OUP, 1988.

9. See Ian Ward, *The Killer They Called God*, Media Masters, Singapore, 1992.

10. Lionel Wigmore, op.cit.

11. Stanley L. Falk, *In Seventy Days*, Robert Hale, London, 1975.

12. The total did not include a New Zealand contingent, the No. 24 Construction Unit consisting of 15 officers, 15 NCOs, and 130 other ranks. This unit was evacuated aboard *Talthybius* in January 1942. It is mentioned in AIR23/4637 at the PRO, Kew. For some reason this unit does not appear in any of the published lists of units. (The *Talthybius* probably took the New Zealanders only as far as Batavia, for she arrived back in Singapore shortly afterwards and was bombed in Empire Dock. She sank there in early February. She was salvaged by the Japanese and renamed *Taruyasu Maru*.)

13. ADM199/1185. PRO.

14. wo106/2536, PRO.

15. Copy in CAB106/162. PRO.

16. Percival Dispatch. Supplement to London Gazette, 20th February 1948.

17. Percival Dispatch. ibid.

18. wo106/2613A. Extracts from Notes, Lieutenant-Colonel I.M. Stewart. PRO.

19. Brigadier W. St.J. Carpendale, 'Report on operations of 11th Indian Division in Kedah and Perak, 1941.'

20. Correspondence and telephone conversations between Major A.R.E. Clarke and the author, 1993.

21. Colonel J.H. Thyer & Colonel C.H. Kappe, Report on Operations, 8th Australian Division. Copy in File CAB106/162. PRO.

22. Information from A. Johnson, 9th Royal Northumberland Fusiliers.

23. Correspondence between Peter Kenward and the author 1993–94.

24. 125th Anti-Tank Regiment RA, 1939–1945. Foreword by Lieutenant-Colonel J. Dean, RA. December 1946.

25. T.D. Brown, 125th Anti-Tank Regiment. Correspondence with author, 1993.

26. E. Pearlman, 125th Anti-Tank Regiment, who now lives in Israel. Correspondence with author, 1993.

27. Quoted by George Musk, in the Canadian Pacific Railway's *Histories of Individual Ships*. Mr Musk makes no mention in his book of the bad condition the ship was in.

28. Correspondence between William Bowden and the author, 1993.

29. Information from the Official Crew Lists, *Empress of Asia*. Registrar-General of Shipping and Seamen, Cardiff. Details of the loss of *Empress of Asia* have appeared in several books, but the account given here is the full

story, and includes hitherto unpublished details about the main reason for the loss.

30. Dennis Richards & Hilary St. G. Saunders, *The Fight Awaits – Royal Air Force 1942*, HMSO, London, 1962.
31. Japanese Army Memorandum. Issued by GS, HM Naval Base, Singapore. Reprinted with additions and modifications March 1941 by GS India. Copy in File L/Mil/17/20/24, India Records Office.
32. Tsuji, ibid.
33. Wigmore, ibid. Falk, ibid.
34. wo193/509. PRO.
35. wo193/512. PRO.
36. From microfilm copies of papers of Colonel R.L. Roper, National Army Musuem, London, 7912.3. App. II, History of 9th Indian Div., O.S.
37. Figures from 1) Douglas Gillison, *'Royal Australian Air Force, 1939–1942'*, Australian War Memorial, Canberra, 1962; 2) Richards & Saunders, op.cit. 3) Phillip Rivers, *'Clipped Wings – The Collapse of British Air Defence Malaya, 1941–42'*, unpublished manuscript, 1990.
38. wo193/711. PRO.
39. For a general account of gas in warfare, see Robert Harris and Jeremy Paxman, *A Higher Form Of Killing*, Chatto & Windus, London, 1982.
40. wo193/945. PRO.
41. Letter from Squadron Leader R.E. Wardrop to the author, 1993.
42. Letters from Captain R.B. Monteath to the author, 1992.
43. wo172/15, PRO.
44. wo172/18. 'GS Operations, Appendix'. PRO.
45. wo193/723. No. 50A. PRO.
46. wo193/723. No. 50A. PRO.
47. wo106/2557 & wo172/20. PRO.
48. wo193/711. PRO.
49. AIR23/4637, Personal War Diary, Chief Equipment Officer, AHQ, Far East, Group Captain Herbert E. Tansley. PRO.
50. wo106/2550A. PRO.
51. Papers of Lieutenant-Colonel Noel James (1910–1985). Liddell Hart Centre, King's College, London.
52. Letters from Lieutenant-Colonel H.M.J. Jensen, OBE, to Captain P.R. Rivers and to the author, 1993.
53. Brigadier W.J. Birkle (1900–1990). See obituary in *Daily Telegraph*, 26th April 1990.
54. wo172/176. War Diary, RA Fixed Defences, PRO.
55. Lieutenant-Colonel C.C.M. Macleod-Carey, article in 'War Monthly' No.34, 1976.
56. wo172/176. Fixed Defences, Singapore Report, February 1942. PRO.
57. wo106/2522 & wo172/176. PRO.
58. wo172/176. PRO.
59. CAB106/89. PRO. 3rd Indian Corps Signals History, Malaya, by Lieutenant-Colonel A.S. Milner.
60. wo/172/221. War Diary Chief Signals Officer, Malaya Command. PRO.
61. Letters from Sergeant H.G. Blackham to the author, 1993.
62. wo172/125. PRO.

63. WO172/91. PRO. War Diary 18th Division HQ RA.
64. Dr Toby Carter, was a Flight-Lieutenant in Singapore engaged in radar duties. The information on the Singapore radar installations has kindly been supplied by him.

CHAPTER 10: THE LOSS OF NORTHERN MALAYA (pages 215–256)

1. Angus Rose, *Who Dies Fighting*, Jonathan Cape, London 1944.
2. a) CAB106/126, PRO; b) Dato H.L. Wrigglesworth, *The Japanese Invasion of Kelantan in 1941*, Privately published, Singapore, 1991.
3. Memoir of Major (later Brigadier) Phillip Parker, Indian Army.
4. CAB106/126. PRO.
5. ADM199/1185. C-in-C Eastern Fleet's War Diary, 1941–1942. PRO.
6. CAB106/190. PRO. This file was closed until 1983.
7. From the text of a lecture given as a prisoner of war by Lieutenant-General Sir Lewis Heath.
8. Wrigglesworth, op.cit.
9. Major-General Berthold Wells Key, CB, DSO, MC, (1895–1986).
10. Peter Elphick & Michael Smith, *Odd Man Out – The Story of the Singapore Traitor*, Hodder & Stoughton, London, 1993. The fact that Wavell knew about a traitor was not included in *Odd Man Out* because the Wavell report did not come into the public domain until early 1993.
11. E.R. (Bon) Hall, *Glory In Chaos*, Sembawang Association, West Coburg, Victoria.
12. PREM3/168/4. PRO.
13. Correspondence between H.G. Blackham and the author, 1993.
14. Elphick & Smith, op.cit.
15. AIR23/4637. PRO.
16. One of the earliest writers to mention the story was N. Shorrick, *Lion In The Sky*, Federal Publications, Singapore, 1968.
17. 1) Diary of Miss P.M. Briggs. 82/24/1. Imperial War Museum, London; 2) Correspondence between Mrs P.M. Thom and the author, 1993. This author had the pleasure recently of putting Pongo's sister, Mrs Kit Hair, in touch with Mrs Thom, and for the first time Mrs Hair heard the true story. She writes, 'I never accepted Sally's account of giving blood and that they hadn't time to bury him. How I wish Mother could have known.'
    One last point about the Pongo Scarf affair. The surviving members of 62 Squadron have always been convinced that two VCs and not just one should have been awarded for the sortie made by that solitary Blenheim. Paddy Calder assisted Pongo to fly the plane back although he was not a pilot. What has not been recorded before is that Calder also helped in crash-landing the plane. Members of 62 Squadron always suspected this, but Paddy Calder is a very modest and unassuming man, and one who had no wish to detract in the slightest way from the honour of the award made to his old comrade. The author met Paddy at the Squadron reunion at Stratford-Upon-Avon in April 1993, and for the first time and in the

presence of several witnesses, Paddy agreed that Pongo would not have been able to land the plane without his help. This is recorded here as a tribute to two very brave men.

18. Dispatch by Air Vice-Marshal Sir Paul Maltby on Air Operations in Malaya and the Netherlands East Indies. *London Gazette*, 20th February 1948.

19. The proper name for Kuantan airfield was Batu Sembilan, Malay for 'Ninth Milestone'. The local natives had another name for it, *Larang Garuda*. The garuda (after which the present Indonesian National Airline is named) is a large mythical bird that was supposed to pick up huge rocks in its talons then fly out to sea and drop them on unsuspecting villagers in their fishing craft. Whether this says anything about the type of bomb practice conducted by the RAF and RAAF is not known!

20. Roy Bulcock, *Of Death But Once*, Cheshire, Melbourne, 1947.

21. Wing-Commander Richard Basil Councell (Personal No.26049). Councell had been in Malaya since 1938 when, as a Squadron Leader, he had been attached to No. 205 Reconnaissance Squadron, Seletar, Singapore. He was promoted Wing-Commander 1st September 1940, and became Station Commander Kuantan, 1st April 1941.

22. Basil A. Gotto, *100 Squadron versus Imperial Japan*. Unpublished diary which he wrote in early 1942 at Palembang, Sumatra, whilst a prisoner of the Japanese. He and others were held in a school-house initially, and he wrote his diary in some exercise books he found there. Before being moved on he hid the books in the loft of the building. After the war a friend recovered them from the local police station, where the finder had taken them.

23. Correspondence between Major A.R.E. Clarke and the author, 1993.

24. From microfilm copy of papers of Colonel R.L. Roper, National Army Museum, London, 7912.3. Notes by BOWO, 22nd Ind. Inf. Bde.

25. ADM199/1473, PRO.

26. Correspondence and interviews with Lieutenant-Colonel C.E.N. Hopkins-Husson, 1992–93.

27. Unpublished War Diary of Captain (later Lieutenant-Colonel) C.G. Wylie of 2/1st Gurkha Rifles.

28. Harry Blackham, op. cit.

29. CAB106/190. PRO.

30. Elphick & Smith, op.cit.
    Some information not previously published about the incident was researched by this author for the book *Odd Man Out*. It filled in a few gaps, but also raised a few more questions. Additional research, together with previously unpublished information from an officer involved in the chain of events, now enables more of the pieces of the jigsaw to be placed in position, and for a few wrong pieces to be discarded. Unfortunately, the process leaves another odd piece that was not there before!

31. This attitude (understandable, but a curious way to treat the recording of history) was far from unique. It was still being adopted in 1965 when Lieutenant-Colonel Denis Russell-Roberts of 5/11th Sikh Regiment wrote his book *Spotlight on Singapore*. Russell-Roberts was also at Kuantan and he glossed over those events as well.

32. CAB106/192, PRO.

33. Martin Middlebrook and Patrick Mahoney, *Battleship*, Allen Lane, London, 1977.
34. Guy Madoc knew Windsor well. Madoc was to become General (later Field-Marshal) Templar's right-hand policeman during the post-war Malayan Emergency and is a much respected figure in Colonial Police circles.
35. Elphick & Smith, op.cit. A fuller description of the Windsor incident has been told in *Odd Man Out*. It will suffice to record here only some new titbits of information that have come to light since that book was written. The information is circumstantial, and some of it is hearsay, but it bears out the contention that Windsor was not guilty of any treasonable act.

   Lieutenant Dick Clarke had met Windsor, who was always called 'Ceejay' after his initials, at Kuantan. He says that Windsor was not a sociable man and so spent little time in the local club. As in all towns in Malaya at the time, the local club, usually named after the town it was in, was the main rendezvous and watering-hole for Europeans, and it was an unusual man indeed who did not make regular use of its facilities. But being unsociable does not make a man a spy.

   Clarke says, 'We were surprised when he was arrested. It was said he was no traitor. After the war I met Lieutenant Francis Maynard RNRV who was on the ship sent to arrest Windsor. He said that he thought it unlikely that he was implicated because he would have been much more effective had he been. I myself think that he would have gone out of his way to get to know us soldiers had he been a spy.'

   C.J. Windsor's widow, Mrs Edna Windsor, died at the Merlin Hotel, Kuantan, where she had lived for many years, in early 1993. She was a very much respected member of the local community, as indeed her husband had been. He died in the 1960s.
36. wo172/15. PRO.
37. Major-General D.M. Murray-Lyon, Report on 11th Indian Division, Short Summary of Events 7th-24th December 1941. IOR L/WS/1/952, India Records Office, London.
38. *The Frontier Force Regiment*, Gale & Polden, Aldershot, 1962.
39. Unpublished papers of Colonel Cyril Wild. Imperial War Museum, London.
40. Ian Morrison, *Malayan Postscript*, Faber, London, 1942.
41. Lieutenant-Colonel M. Elrington, 'The Story of the 2nd Battalion The Loyal regiment in Malaya'. CAB106/174, PRO.
42. CAB106/144. PRO.
43. wo106/2528. Ops XVb/116, Message No.031001. PRO.
44. James Wellard, *The French Foreign Legion*, André Deutsch, 1974.
45. wo193/865. PRO.
46. Lieutenant-Colonel C.C. Deakin and Major G.M.S. Webb, War Diaries of 5/2nd Punjab Regiment, 6509–14, National Army Museum, London. Colonel Deakin was one of the few commanding officers in the Malayan campaign who made no attempt to cover up in his reports the deficiencies he found in his men. Although one can appreciate the reasons why other officers tended to gloss over such matters, cover-ups of this nature do not help the correction of similar shortcomings in the future. They also affect the correct historical interpretation of military events.

47. The Hindustani version was:
Zalam angrez bagair kisi taink ya hawai jahaz ke Hindustani bekason ko muft me halal karwa rahe hain ap sun chuke hoge ke un ka bahari ebra sabh dub chuka hai. Socko aur jan bachao. Ap ki rakhwali ke lie bahut fauji hamare pas pahunch gae hain. Ap bhi bach kar a jao.

Azide Hindustani Sabha.

48. wo193/875. PRO.
49. CAB106/36. No. 1 Independent Infantry Company, by Major S.P. Fearon. See also the unit's War Diary wo172/208. PRO. In addition to Fearon, the officers of the unit were, Captain R.A. Hofman, Northamptonshire Regiment (killed 15th February 1942); Lieutenants J.H. Proctor and J. Surgeon, both of the Loyals; D.C.W. Nunnely, 2nd Gordons; R.G. Daniel, East Surreys; J. Branston, Leicestershires; L.H.A. Maclaren, 5/14th Punjab; Second Lieutenants S. Martin, 5/11th Sikhs; R.D. Newton, 1/14th Punjabis; A.E. Holland, 18th Garhwalis. Lieutenant Smith of the RIASC was in charge of the General Purpose Transport section.
50. Brigadier H.W. Picken, *Nobody's Own*, History of 3rd Cavalry.

CHAPTER 11: THE BATTLE FOR JOHORE (pages 257–271)

1. A.H. Harrison, *The Brave Japanese*, Rigby, Adelaide, 1966.
2. Harrison, ibid.
3. wo172/20. PRO.
4. Masanobu Tsuji, *Singapore 1941–1942 – The Japanese Version*, Ure Smith, Sydney, 1960.
5. CAB106/180. PRO. Report on discussions held at the War History Institute, Tokyo, September 1966, between Colonel Wards and Japanese Official Historians.
6. CAB106/153. Miscellaneous Australian Papers concerning War against Japan. PRO.
7. From transcript of a conversation between Colonel Thyer and Major-General S.W. Kirby, Adelaide, 19th January 1953. CAB106/151. PRO.
8. Report of Captain F.E. Mileham. 9102–302–1–5. National Army Museum, London.
9. Captain Alan Kimball Butterworth, 3/16th Punjab Regiment, who presently lives in India. Correspondence with the author, 1993.
10. wo172/20. General Staff, Appendix. PRO.
11. S.W. Kirby, *Singapore: The Chain of Disaster*, Cassell, London, 1971.
12. Transcript of interview with Brigadier Galleghan. Major-General S.W. Kirby and Lionel Wigmore, 22nd January 1953.
13. Transcript of conversation between Captain H.E. Jessup and Major-General Kirby and Lionel Wigmore, Sydney, 23rd January 1953.
14. Stanley L. Falk. *Seventy Days To Singapore*, Robert Hale, London, 1975.
15. Brigadier William Oswald Lay (1892–1952). Lay had earlier spent five years in Malaya, where he was on the General Staff in 1929–31. Then he had been appointed Staff Officer, Local Forces Malaya, 1932–34. In his *Who's Who* entry for 1952 he made no mention of his command of 8th Brigade.

The entry records, '6th Indian Infantry Brigade 1939–42. POW 1942–1945.' The first part of that entry is incorrect. (Entries in *Who's Who* are based on information obtained from the person concerned.)

16. Transcript of conversation between Brigadier W.A Trott and Major-General S.W. Kirby, Adelaide, 19th January 1953. CAB106/151. PRO. (Trott, an Australian serving in the Indian Army, returned to Australia after the war.)

17. Major-General A.E. Barstow, CIE, MC, (1888–1942), as a cadet at Sandhurst, 'won the sword' in his final year. His parent regiment in the Indian Army was the Sikh Regiment. (General Heath and General Key were also 'Sikhs'.) Barstow was very proud of his regiment and was known as 'Whiz-bang Sikh'. It may have been his attachment to the regiment that caused him to go forward to contact Brigadier Painter's 22nd Brigade, of which the 5/11th Sikhs were part. This is the belief of Lieutenant-General Harbakhsh Singh (Indian Army, retired) who was a junior officer with the Sikhs in Malaya. He obtained details of Barstow's death from Dewa Singh, Barstow's batman, who was with the general when he was killed.

    Dewa Singh became a prisoner of war at the fall of Singapore. It is indicative of the 'family' relationship which existed in the Indian Army, that Nancy Barstow, the general's widow, provided a private pension to Dewa Singh until her death. One of General Barstow's nephews was Group Captain Leonard Cheshire, VC.

18. O.D. Gallagher, *Retreat in the East*, Harrap, London, 1942.

CHAPTER 12: RETREAT IN THE WEST (pages 273–297)

1. Lieutenant-Colonel C.J. Verdon, RM, telephone conversations with the author, 1993.

2. Lee Geok Boi, *Syonan, Singapore Under The Japanese*, Singapore Heritage Society, Singapore, 1992.

3. *Orion*, 24,000 tons, had accommodation for nearly 3,000 troops. She had been in drydock at Singapore for repairs to her bows damaged in a collision with HMS *Revenge* in the South Atlantic in September. *Marnix Van Sint Aldegonde* was not much smaller at 20,000 tons. She also had accommodation for 3,000. She was later badly damaged by German torpedo planes off the Algerian coast on 6th November 1943. The 3,000 troops she was carrying were safely got ashore before she sank.

4. Report by P.E.M. Holmes, 3rd March 1942. wo106/2579C. PRO. Holmes did not record the name of the vessel taken over by the Thornycroft people.

5. Report by Mrs C.M. Battenberg, 10th March 1942. wo106/2579C. PRO.

6. C.E. Hudson, 'Changi Guardian' (a POW publication), 13th April 1942. Hudson had been the Divisional Warden, Tanjong Pagar, Singapore, down by Keppel Harbour.

7. George Seabridge. Report dated March 1942 in wo106/2573B, PRO. (British officialdom has a penchant for secrecy way beyond the acceptable 'thirty-year rule'. The official file containing this report was closed until 1993. Yet a copy of the Seabridge report had been lying in an open file

at the India Records Office for many years. Perhaps there is a moral in this somewhere.)

8. Ivan Simson, *Singapore: Too Little, Too Late*, Leo Cooper, London, 1970.
9. H. Sidhu, *The Bamboo Fortress*, Native Publications, Singapore, 1991.
10. *Our 70 Years*, Chinese Newspapers Division, Singapore Press Holdings, 1993.
11. Noel Barber, *Sinister Twilight*, Collins, London, 1968.
12. From the memoirs of a senior ex-policeman of the Straits Settlements police, who wishes to remain anonymous.
13. E.M. Glover, *In 70 Days*, Frederick Muller, London, 1946.
14. Memoir of Muriel Reilly, Bryson Collection, XII.24, Royal Commonwealth Library.
15. Edward Green (b. 1923). Memoir of events in Singapore, January/February 1942. Copy kindly supplied by him to this author, 1993.
16. a) Lieutenant-General A.E. Percival, Operations of Malaya Command, London Gazette, 26th February 1948; b) *The War in Malaya*, Eyre & Spottiswoode, London, 1949.
17. Copy in CAB106/162. PRO.
18. CAB106/151. PRO. Colonel J.H. Thyer interview with Official Australian and British historians, Adelaide, 19th January 1953.
19. Letter from Captain T. Beamish to his father, Rear-Admiral T. Beamish MP, 1942. Extracts handed to Mr Churchill. PREM3/16817B, PRO. (Closed to 1993.)
20. Ivan Simson, op.cit.
21. Brooke-Popham Papers, V/8/10/2, Liddell Hart Centre, King's College, London.
22. Quoted by Richard Holmes & Anthony Kemp, *The Bitter End*, Antony Bird, Chichester, 1982.
23. Captain H.E. Jessup, interview with Major-General S.W. Kirby and Lionel Wigmore, Sydney, 23rd January 1953.
24. Information received from J.M. Roualle, 1993. Mr Roualle was a member of the Volunteer Force in Malaya. He became a prisoner of war of the Japanese. He stayed with the Malayan Customs Service post-war until 1958.
25. RMS *Aquitania* (45,000 tons), one of the best known of all passenger ships, was the last liner constructed with four funnels. Built in 1914, she was capable of 23 knots. In 1915 she was used as a troopship to the Dardanelles. By the time she was broken up at Gairloch, Scotland, in 1950 she had steamed over 3,000,000 miles and carried 1,200,000 passengers, having crossed the Atlantic no less than 475 times.
26. At Ratai Bay the convoy was redesignated 'MS2A'. The on-carrying ships were six Dutch KPM vessels, *Both* (2,601 tons), *Reael* (2,561), *Reijnst* (2,462), *Sloet van de Beele* (2,977), *Van der Lijn* (2,464) and *Van Swoll* (2,147), together with the British merchantman *Taishan* (3,174 tons).
27. Thomas Hamilton, *Soldier Surgeon in Malaya*, Angus & Robertson, Sydney, 1958. Hamilton commanded the Australian 2/4th Casualty Clearing Station.
28. Account of Brigadier G.C. Ballentine, Cmdr. 44 Indian Infantry Brigade. File 7309–2. National Army Museum, London.

29. CAB106/151. PRO.
30. J. Bowyer Bell, *Besieged: Seven Cities Under Siege*, Chilton, Philadelphia, 1966. Mr Bell was quoting an eyewitness.
31. Raymond Thomas interview, 3rd June 1942. WO106/2550A.PRO. (closed to 1993.)
32. WO106/2550B. PRO.
33. Transcript of interview with Brigadier H.B. Taylor, held on 27th January 1953. CAB106/151. PRO.
34. WO193/878. Operational Messages 7/12/41–14/3/42. PRO.

CHAPTER 13: 'THIS INGLORIOUS BUSINESS' (pages 299–343)

1. David H. James, *The Rise and Fall of the Japanese Empire*, Allen & Unwin, 1951.
2. Summary of General Gordon Bennett's Report in WO106/1529. PRO.
3. WO172/21. PRO.
4. Walter Gibson, *The Boat*, W.H. Allen, London, 1952.
5. Frank Coombes, as quoted by J. & C. Blair, *Return from the River Kwai*, Simon & Schuster, New York, 1979.
6. O.D. Gallagher, *Retreat in the East*, Harrap, London, 1942.
7. Colin W.A. Ingles, *Singapore to Colombo*, Privately published, London, 1945. (Copy in National Army Museum, London.)
8. Chin Kee On, *Malaya Upside Down*, Singapore, 1946.
9. David H. James, op. cit.
10. John Robertson, *Australians At War, 1939–1945*, Heinemann, 1981.
11. T. Hall, *The Fall Of Singapore, 1942*, Methuen, Sydney, 1985.
12. Hank Nelson, *Prisoners of War – Australians Under Nippon*, ABC, Sydney, 1985.
13. Record of interview between Captain H.E. Jessup and the Australian and British Official Historians, Sydney, 23rd January 1953. CAB106/151. PRO, London.
14. Letter from Squadron-Leader S. Stephen to the author, 12th January 1993.
15. Letter from Wing-Commander E. Bott to the author dated 27th January 1993. Sadly, Eric Bott died in November 1993.
16. *Great Was The Fall*, by 'An RAAF Officer', Perth, 1945. The present author was able to trace the anonymous officer through certain clues in the narrative.
17. See Peter Elphick & Michael Smith, *Odd Man Out*, Hodder & Stoughton, London, 1993.
18. Nigel G. Morris in conversations with the author in 1993.
19. Richard Gough, *Escape From Singapore*, London, 1987.
20. Information with copy of relevant portion of the Roskill memoirs kindly supplied by Nicholas Roskill.
21. Letter dated 2nd February 1993 from R.B. Johnston.
22. Telephone conversation between Peter Melliar-Smith and the author, 1993.
23. Letters from J.N. Clarke to the author in 1993.
24. Official Logbook, *Empire Star*, No. 163219, at Registrar-General Ships and Seamen, Cardiff. Blue Star Line now has no copy of Captain Capon's report;

it was lost or destroyed in one of that company's moves to new premises. A copy has been kindly supplied, however, by his daughter, Mrs Lettice Nichols, and is reproduced in Appendix 5 along with copies of other *Empire Star* documentation.

25. J. & C. Blair, op.cit.
26. Correspondence between Squadron Leader R.D. Phillips and the author, 1994.
27. Report in wo106/2550B. PRO.
28. Papers of Thomas Kitching, Bryson Collection XII/I, Royal Commonwealth Library.
29. In Bryson Collection, Royal Commonwealth Library.
30. ADM199/622B. PRO. (File marked closed to 1993.)
31. a) T. Carter Papers, Imperial War Museum, London. b) Letters from Dr Toby Carter to the author, 1993.
32. V.L.F. Davin. Letters to, and telephone conversations with, the author, 1993.
33. Memoir of George Wort, later Brigadier (1912–1984). King's College Library, London.
34. Alf Johnson, correspondence with the author, 1993.
35. Rear-Admiral E.J. Spooner to Captain Cazalet of HMS *Durban*. Cazalet Papers, Imperial War Museum, London.
36. PREM3/168/4. PRO.
37. wo106/2591. PRO.
38. Sir Robert Menzies, *Afternoon Light*, Cassell, London, 1967.
39. PREM3/168/3. PRO.
40. wo106/2573C. PRO. (Closed to 1993.)
41. CAB106/151. Colonel J.H. Thyer, February 1953, during interview with British and Australian Official Historians.
42. CAB106/151. PRO.
43. Both Phillips and Ashmore escaped on 13th February 1942 aboard the auxiliary HMS *Malacca*. They carried some official papers with them. Although *Malacca* was scuttled after bomb damage in the Tjemako River, Sumatra, on the 14th, both men eventually reached India with most of their precious paper baggage.
44. PREM3/168/7. PRO.
45. Allen S. Walker, *Australians at War. Medical Services*, Australian War Memorial, Canberra, 1953.
46. Masonobu Tsuji, *Singapore, The Japanese Version*, Ure Smith, Sydney, 1960.
47. CAB106/162. PRO.
48. See Gordon Bennett's book, *Why Singapore Fell*, Angus & Robertson, Sydney, 1944.
49. Colonel (later Brigadier) J.R. Broadbent, in private life a grazier from Mount Fairey, New South Wales, was born at Ballarat in 1893, and was a graduate of the Duntroon Military Academy.
50. Athole Stewart, *Let's Get Cracking*, Sydney, 1943.
51. Sir Keith Murdoch (1886–1952). Managing Director and Managing Editor of Herald (Melbourne) Group. He had been appointed to his government post in June 1940.

52. Malayan Campaign memoir of Major (later Brigadier) P.W. Parker. Phillip White Parker was born in Claremont, Perth, Western Australia on 15th April 1900 and died at Warminster, England, on 9th January 1988. (See obituary in the *Daily Telegraph*.) He was first commissioned on his birthday, age nineteen. His memoir was written in Changi Camp within weeks of his capture by the Japanese. It has been kindly loaned to this author by his son, Major Campbell Parker, who writes that, when his father was sent to work on the Burma–Siam railway, 'he had been running a radio and news service within his camp and, being suspicious that he was about to be rumbled by the Kempetai, he buried all his private papers in a grave marked 'PRIVATE RECORDS' in the hope that one day the right side would win and his papers be sent to a forwarding address buried with them. After the war they duly found their way to him which is a minor miracle in itself.

'Father was, in fact, arrested, tried by court martial and sentenced to five years solitary confinement in Changi Jail as convict No. 572! Shortly before the Japs capitulated he was released to an Army Hospital.'

53. W.S. Thatcher (compiler), *The 10th Baluch Regiment in the Second World War*, The Baluch Regimental Centre, Abbottabad (Pakistan), 1980.

54. Lieutenant-General S.L. Menezes, *The Indian Army: Fidelity and Honour*, Vikram, New Delhi, 1993.

55. (a) Telephone conversation between Rev. Robert Nesham and Major Dick Clarke, April 1994; (b) Telephone conversation between Rev. Nesham and the author, May 1994.

56. From accounts written by officers of 1st Cambridgeshires, and edited by Dennis Hutt.

CHAPTER 14: THE FALL OF SINGAPORE (pages 345–356)

1. MSS IND. OCN. s123. Dickinson Papers, Rhodes Library, Oxford.

2. The names of all eighteen police officer deserters, some of the 'explanations', notes by the British Consul-General in Batavia and by Sir Andrew Caldecott in Colombo, and other associated documents including Sir Shenton Thomas's message posting them as deserters, are in File CO273/669/7 at the PRO.

The post-war reinstatement of these officers was to have a serious effect on the efficiency of both the Singapore and FMS police forces. Two factions developed, 'those who stayed' and 'those who did a bunk', the former often refusing to have anything at all to do with the latter. The loss of efficiency engendered by this was one of the reasons why the Colonial Office drafted in some policemen from Palestine, who took over several of the more senior police appointments despite the fact that they knew nothing at all about Malayan conditions. Now there were three factions; neither of the first two wanting much to do with the third! As this was the period building up to the Malayan Emergency, the 'war' against Chinese Communist terrorists, this bad feeling and lack of co-operation undoubtedly had a detrimental effect on the police-run anti-Communist operations.

3. In the MCS Lists of the times, Nunn is designated 'Major' Nunn. The RAF title

evidently stems from him having been at some time the Officer Commanding, Malayan Volunteer Air Force, according to information in file AIR24/504, at the British Public Records Office.

4. ADM199/1473. PRO.

5. Information received from Dr. A.W. Frankland, 1993.

CHAPTER 15: SUMMARY AND CONCLUSION (pages 357–364)

1. A little-known fact is that the fall of Singapore made recruitment into the Indian Army from among the Indian martial races extremely difficult for a number of months during 1942. Recruiting officers were confronted with lamenting and irate mothers and wives who wanted to know why, instead of a pension, they had received notification that their menfolk in Malaya were *ghoum* – 'missing' (or lost) – and *shayad quaidi* – 'perhaps prisoner'. At a critical time in the war, recruitment to the largest volunteer army the world has known was brought almost to a standstill. (The author's thanks to Major Robert Henderson for this information.)

Bibliography

Primary Sources

Original documents which have been consulted at the Public Records Office, Kew, are listed in the chapter notes.

First-hand accounts of the many people interviewed, both face-to-face and over the telephone, and those who have written to the author with information, are also listed in the chapter notes.

In addition, the following unpublished sources have been consulted:

Lieutenant-Colonel B.H. Ashmore, papers. Imperial War Museum, London. (IWM)

Becker family papers, courtesy of Hugh Becker and the Rev. Dr. Liz Carmichael.

Miss P.M. Briggs, diary. (IWM)

Brigadier G.C. Ballentine, papers, (7309–2). National Army Museum, London. (NAM)

Air Chief Marshal Sir Robert Brooke-Popham, papers. Liddell Hart Centre for Military Studies, King's College, London. (LHC).

Bryson Collection, Royal Commonwealth Library. This collection includes correspondence and papers of many individuals. The following were particularly useful:
H.P. Bryson; C.E. Collinge; John Dalley; A.H. Dickinson; H.B.J. Donaldson; Barbara Herdman; Thomas Kitching; Guy Madoc; J.N.M.A. Nicholls; H.R. Oppenheim; Muriel Reilly; Brigadier Ivan Simson; Colonel J.D.Wyatt; I.S. Wyllie.

Captain Selwyn Capon, papers. Courtesy of Lettice Nichols.

Brigadier W. Carpendale, Report on Operations of 11th Indian Division in Kedah and Perak.

Dr Toby Carter, papers. (IWM)

Vice-Admiral Sir Peter Cazalet, papers. (IWM)

Lieutenant-Colonel C.C. Deakin and Major G.M.S. Webb, War Diaries 5/2nd Punjab Regiment, (6509–14). (NAM)

A.H. Dickinson, papers, (MSS IND OCN s123). Rhodes Library, Oxford.

Edward Green, *Empire Star* memoir.

Basil Gotto, '100 Squadron versus the Imperial Japanese'.

Lieutenant-General Sir Lewis Heath, papers. (IWM)

Lieutenant-Colonel C.E.N. Hopkins-Husson. War experiences dictated to and transcribed by Peter Elphick. (NAM)

General Hastings Ismay, 1st Baron Ismay, papers. (LHC)

Lieutenant-Colonel Noel James, papers. (LHC)

Captain F.E. Mileham, papers, (9102–302–1–5). (NAM)

Lieutenant-Colonel D.J.R. Moore, papers (EUR226, IOLR/E/1/311). Oriental and India Office Collections, London. (OIO)

Major-General D.M. Murray-Lyon, report. (IOR/L/WS/1/952). (OIO)
Brigadier Phillip Parker, private war diary and papers. Courtesy of Major Campbell Parker.
Lieutenant-General A.E. Percival, papers. (IWM)
Registrar-General of Ships and Seamen, Cardiff. Extracts from Crew Lists and Official Log Books of *Empire Star* and *Empress of Asia*.
Colonel Robert L. Roper, papers. (NAM)
Padre (Major) E. Rowles, SCF, Singapore memoir (unpublished)
Lieutenant-Colonel E.L. Sawyer, report on membership of Indian National Army. (IWM)
Megan Spooner, diary. (LHC) Courtesy of Sir James Spooner.
C.A. Vlieland, papers. (LHC)
Colonel Cyril Wild, papers. (IWM)
Brigadier George Wort, papers. (LHC)
Lieutenant-Colonel C.G. Wylie, personal War Diary of an officer of the 2/1st Gurkha Rifles.

Other manuscript sources

Patrick Mahoney. Research notes for book *Battleship*.
Phillip Rivers. Manuscript entitled 'Clipped Wings – the Collapse Of British Air Defence, Malaya 1941–42'.

Published books – partly annotated select bibliography

Allbury, Alfred, *Bamboo and Bushido*, Robert Hale, London, 1955.
Anon, *British Vessels Lost At Sea, 1939–1945*, HMSO, London, 1947.
Anon, *The Frontier Force Regiment*, Gale & Polden, Aldershot, 1962.
Anon, *Malaya 1941–42*, Queen's Royal Surrey Regiment Museum, 1985.
Anon, *Our 70 Years*, Chinese Newspaper Division, Singapore Press Holdings, 1993.
'An RAAF Officer'. *Great Was The Fall*, Perth, Australia, 1945. This obscure book, which named Captain Patrick Heenan as the Singapore traitor, is epistolary in style, consisting of letters sent home from Malaya to the author's wife in Australia. The present author's research, later confirmed by Mrs May Elson-Smith, the recipient of the letters, has shown that the book was written by the late Flight-Lieutenant A.D. Elson-Smith, RAAF.
Barber, Noel, *Sinister Twilight: The Fall of Singapore, 1942*, Collins, London, 1968.
Bell, J. Bowyer, *Besieged: Seven Cities Under Siege*, Chilton, Philadelphia, 1966.
Bennett, Henry Gordon, *Why Singapore Fell*, Angus & Robertson, Sydney, 1944. Written by the Australian General who fled Singapore without orders on 15th February 1942.
Bond, Brian, ed., *Chief-of-Staff*, Leo Cooper, London, 1974. The diary of General Sir Henry Pownall.
Braddon, Russell, *The Naked Island*, Werner Laurie, London, 1952.
Bradley, James, *Cyril Wild: The Tall Man Who Never Slept*, Woodfield, Fontwell, 1991. Biography of the Japanese-speaking staff officer who was given the

unenviable task of carrying the white flag at the capitulation of Singapore. He was killed in an air crash after the war whilst investigating Japanese war crimes.

Brooke, Geoffrey, *Singapore's Dunkirk*, Leo Cooper, London, 1989.

Blair, Joan & Clay, *Return From The River Kwai*, Simon & Schuster, New York, 1979.

Borg, D. and Shumpei, Okamoto, eds., *Pearl Harbor as History: Japanese-American Relations 1931–1941*, Columbia University Press, 1973.

Bryant, Arthur, *The Turn of the Tide*, Collins, London, 1957. Based on autobiographical notes of Field-Marshal Viscount Alanbrooke.

Bulcock, Roy, *Of Death But Once*, Cheshire, Melbourne, 1947. By an officer of the RAAF. He was stationed at Kuantan during the precipitate evacuation of that airfield on 9th December 1941.

Bulloch, John, *MI5*, Arthur Barker, London, 1963.

Caffrey, Kate, *Out In The Midday Sun*, Deutsch, London, 1974.

Callahan, Raymond, *The Worst Disaster – The Fall Of Singapore*, Newark, 1977.

Calvocoressi, Peter, and Wint, Guy, and Pritchard, John, *Total War*, Volume 2, Penguin edition, London, 1989.

Charmley, John. *Duff Cooper*, Weidenfeld & Nicolson, London, 1986.

Chin Kee On. *Malaya Upside Down*, Singapore, 1946.

Chippington, George, *Singapore – The Inexcusable Betrayal*, Hanley Swan, 1992. One of the many books written to coincide with the fiftieth anniversary of the fall of Singapore. Written by an officer of the 1st Leicesters, a regiment which eventually combined with the 2nd East Surreys in Malaya to become the 'British Battalion'.

Churchill, Winston S., *The Second World War*, 6 volumes, Cassell, London, 1948–1954.

Churchill, Winston S., ed. Charles Eade, *Secret Session Speeches*, Cassell, London, 1946.

Cooper, Duff. *Old Men Forget*, Hart-Davis, London, 1954. Contains a chapter about the author's period in Singapore.

Craig, William, *The Fall of Japan*, Weidenfeld and Nicolson, 1967.

Crisp, Dorothy, *Why We Lost Singapore*, Crisp, London, 1943.

Crisp, Dorothy, *A Life For England*, Crisp, London, 1946.

Cruickshank, Charles, *The Official History of the soe in the Far East*, Oxford, 1985.

Dartford, G.P., *A Short History Of Malaya*, Longmans, London, 1956.

Day, David, *The Great Betrayal*, Angus & Robertson, London, 1988. A work of special significance. Gives an Australian viewpoint of Anglo-Australian relations regarding the defence of Malaya and Singapore.

Donahue, A.G., *Last Flight From Singapore*, Macmillan, London, 1944.

Dull, P.A., *A Battle History of the Imperial Japanese Navy, 1941–1945*, Annapolis, 1970.

Durrani, Mahmood Khan, *The 6th Column*, London, 1956. The formation of the Indian National Army.

Edwards, Bernard, *Blood and Bushido*, SFA, Upton-Upon-Severn, 1991.

Edwards, Jack, *Banzai You Bastards!*, Souvenir Press, London, 1991.

Elphick, Peter, and Smith, Michael. *Odd Man Out – The Story of the Singapore*

Traitor, Hodder & Stoughton, London, 1993. The life and spying activities of Captain Patrick Heenan. Gives an account of espionage and counter-espionage activities in Malaya.

Falk, Stanley L., *Seventy Days To Singapore*, Robert Hale, London, 1975. A work of particular significance, by an American military historian. Excellent and perceptive account of the entire Malayan Campaign and some of the events leading up to it. Comments on strategy, tactics, logistics, and on the commanders of both sides.

Fergusson, Bernard, *Wavell Portrait of a Soldier*, Collins, London, 1961.

Foot, M.R.D., *SOE*, 1940–1946, BBC, London, 1984.

Frei, Henry P., *Japan's Southward Advance and Australia*, Melbourne University Press, 1991. By a Swiss scholar with a deep knowledge of the Japanese. Whilst teaching at Wako University in Tokyo he had access to many original Japanese documents.

Freyberg, Paul, *Bernard Freyberg, VC, Soldier of Two Nations* Hodder & Stoughton, London, 1991. Contains an account of the loss of Crete, and the ensuing Inquiry ordered by Churchill.

Fujiwara Iwaichi, *F-Kikan – Japanese Army Intelligence Operations in Southeast Asia During World War II, Hong Kong, 1983. (First published in Japan in 1948.)*

Gallagher, O.D., *Retreat in the East*, Harrap, London, 1942. A contemporary account by a newspaper correspondent who escaped from Singapore.

Gayn, Mark, *The Fight For The Pacific*, Bodley Head, London, 1941.

Glover, Edwin M., *In 70 days*, Muller, London, 1946. Contemporary account of life in Singapore immediately prior to its fall. By a Singapore newspaper editor.

Gibbs, N.H., *History of the Second World War Vol. 1, Grand Strategy*, HMSO, London, 1976.

Gibson, Walter, *The Boat*, W.H. Allen, London, 1952.

Gilbert, Martin *Winston S. Churchill*, Volume V, Companion Volume 3, Heinemann, London, 1991

Gilchrist, Andrew, *Bangkok Top Secret*, London, 1970.

Gilchrist, Andrew, *Malaya, 1941: The Fall of a Fighting Empire*, Robert Hale, London, 1992. Contains an account of the intense diplomatic activity in Bangkok in 1940 and 1941. By a diplomat who was there, albeit in a junior capacity.

Gillison, Douglas, *Royal Australian Air Force, 1939–1942*, Australian War Memorial, Canberra, 1962.

Gough, Richard, *Escape From Singapore*, London, 1987.

Grenfell, Russell, *Main Fleet To Singapore*, Faber, London, 1951.

Hall, E.R. (Bon), *Glory in Chaos*, Sembawang Association, West Coburg, Victoria.

Hall, T. *The Fall Of Singapore*, Methuen, Sydney, 1985.

Hamilton, Thomas. *Soldier Surgeon in Malaya*, Angus & Robertson, Sydney, 1958. The author commanded the Australian 2/4th Casualty Clearance Station in Malaya.

Harper, R.W.E., and Miller, Harry, *Singapore Mutiny*, Oxford, 1984.

Harris, Robert, and Paxman, Jeremy, *A Higher Form Of Killing*, Chatto & Windus, London, 1982.

Harrison, A.H., *The Brave Japanese*, Rigby, Adelaide, 1966.

Hocking, Charles, *Dictionary of Disasters at Sea*, Lloyds, London. 1969.

Holmes, Richard, and Kemp, Anthony, *The Bitter End*, Antony Bird, Chichester, 1982.

Howorth, D. *Morning Glory: The Story of the Imperial Japanese Navy*, Hamish Hamilton, London, 1983.

Hull, Cordell, *Memoirs*, two volumes, Hodder & Stoughton, London, 1948.

Hulugalle, H.A.J., *British Governors of Ceylon*, Associated Newspapers, Colombo, 1963.

Ike, Nobutka, *Japan's Decision For War*, Stanford University Press, USA, 1967.

Ingles, Colin W.A., *Singapore To Colombo*, Privately Published, London, 1945.

James, David H., *The Rise and Fall of the Japanese Empire*, Allen & Unwin, London, 1951.

Kennedy, Major-General Sir John, *The Business of War*, Hutchinson, London, 1957. Major-General Kennedy (1893–1970) served as Director of Military Operations (DMO) under two CIGS, Sir John Dill and Lord Alanbrooke. He was thus in the inner circle of Churchill's advisors. He has been described as being the right man in the right place at the right time. His book, based on notes he kept rather than a diary, was disparaging of some of Churchill's decisions and 'flights of fancy'. It chipped away somewhat (as did Bryant's *Turn of the Tide*, based on the Alanbrooke diaries) at the popular conception of Churchill's achievements. Later research has proved Kennedy's assessment to be largely correct.

Kennedy, Joseph, *British Civilians and the Japanese War in Malaya & Singapore, 1941–1945*, London, 1987.

Kennedy, Joseph, *When Singapore Fell, Evacuations & Escapes*, London, 1989.

Kirby, Major-General S.W. and others. *The War Against Japan*, HMSO, London, 1957. This is the Official British History of the war against Japan. It was written under terms of reference which forbad much attribution of blame to individuals. Much important information the historians had at hand about the Malayan campaign was excluded for political reasons.

Kirby, Major-General S.W. *Singapore, The Chain of Disaster*, Cassell, London, 1971. In his own book (published after his death) Kirby included some material that was omitted from the Official History, and it was far more critical of the British commanders. However, Kirby still left much unsaid.

La Forte, Robert S., and Marcello, Ronald E., (eds), *Remember Pearl Harbor*, SR Books, Delaware, 1991. Eye-witness accounts of America's own 'worst disaster'.

Leasor, James, *Singapore, The Battle That Changed The World*, Doubleday, New York, 1968.

Lebra, Joyce C., *Japanese Trained Armies in Southeast Asia*, Colombia University Press, 1977.

Lee, Geok Boi, *Syonan: Singapore Under The Japanese*, Singapore Heritage Society, 1992.

Loewenheim F.L., *The Secret Wartime Correspondence*, Barrie & Jenkins London, 1976. A selection of the correspondence between Churchill and Roosevelt.

Mackenzie, Compton, *Eastern Epic*, Chatto & Windus, London, 1951. This book is marked Volume 1. No further volumes were written.

Mason, Philip, *A Matter Of Honour*, London, 1974. A history of the Indian Army.

Menezes, Lieutenant-General S.L., *Fidelity and Honour: The Indian Army*, Viking, New Delhi, 1993. A recent history of the Indian Army by a retired general of that army.

Menzies, Sir Robert, *Afternoon Light*, Cassell, London, 1967.

Middlebrook, Martin, and Mahoney, Patrick, *Battleship*, London, 1977. The best and fullest account of the loss of *Prince of Wales* and *Repulse*. Based on many personal accounts of survivors.

Montgomery, Brian, *Shenton of Singapore, Governor and Prisoner of War*, Leo Cooper, London, 1984. Biography of Sir Shenton Thomas. Based on selective research.

Morris, John, *Traveller From Tokyo*, Cresset Press, London, 1943.

Morrison, Ian, *Malayan Postscript*, Faber, London, 1942. Contemporary account of the fall of Singapore by a newspaper correspondent. (Morrison was killed during the Korean War.)

Musk, George, CPR *History of Individual Ships*, London.

Nelson, Hank, *Prisoners of War – Australians Under Nippon*, ABC, Sydney, 1985.

Norman, Diana, *Road From Singapore*, Hodder & Stoughton, London, 1970. The story of John Dodd. Part of the book covers his escape from Singapore aboard *Empire Star*.

Onraet, René, *Singapore – A Police Background*, Crisp, London, c1945.

Owen, Frank, *The Fall Of Singapore*, London, 1960.

Percival, Lieutenant-General A.E., *The War In Malaya*, Eyre & Spottiswoode, London, 1949.

Pool, Richard, *Course For Disaster*, London, 1987. Contains an account of the voyage of Launch ML310 and the deaths of Rear-Admiral E.J. Spooner and Air Vice-Marshal C.W. Pulford. By a naval officer who was aboard the launch.

Prasad, Bisheshwar (ed.), *Official History of the Indian Armed Forces in the 2nd World War, 1939–1945*, Orient Longmans, Kanpur U.P., 1960.

Ranft, B. McL. (ed.), *The Beatty Papers*, Scolar Press for the Navy Records Society, London, 1989.

Reith, G.W., *1907 Handbook To Singapore*, Oxford, 1985.

Richards, Denis, and Saunders, Hilary St. G., *The Fight Avails – Royal Air Force 1939–1942*, Vol. 2, HMSO, London, 1975.

Rogers, P.G., *The First Englishman In Japan*, Harvill, London, 1956.

Robertson, John, *Australians in the War 1939–1945*, Heinemann, 1981.

Rose, Angus, *Who Dies Fighting*, Jonathan Cape, London, 1944.

Roskill, Stephen W., *Churchill and the Admirals*, Collins, London, 1977.

Rusbridger, J., and Nave, E., *Betrayal at Pearl Harbor*, Michael O'Mara Books, London, 1991.

Russell-Roberts, Denis, *Spotlight on Singapore*, Times Press, London, 1965. One of the best-written of the earlier books about the Malayan campaign by an officer of the Indian Army who took part in it. The author, quite properly, highlights the events in which the Indian Army did well, and records several courageous feats. However, parts of the book are misleading, and were either based on imperfect information, or were part of a process intended to gloss over certain matters. For example, on page 265, he wrote, with reference to men who joined the Indian National Army: 'It should be recorded here that one Regiment, the 2/10th Baluch Regiment, remained loyal to a man.' This is not true. Two officers of 2/10 Baluch, Lieutenant Burhan Ud Din and Captain P.K. Sehgal joined the INA (Indian National Army) early on and were promoted to Lieutenant-Colonel by the Japanese. (Their 'promotion' placed them among the seven most senior of the Japanese appointees.) Later, two other Baluch officers, Lieutenant K.P Thimaya (October 1942) and Lieutenant S.C. Ghosh (28th October 1943) also joined the INA ranks.

Shinozaki, Mamoru, *Syonan, My Story*, Singapore, 1975.

Shorrock, N., *Lion in the Sky*, Federal Publications, Singapore, 1968.

Sidhu, H., *The Bamboo Fortress*, Native Publications, Singapore, 1991.

Smith, Donald, *And All The Trumpets*, Geoffrey Bles, London, 1954.

Silver, Lynette Ramsey, *The Heroes of Rimau*, Leo Cooper, London, 1991.

Simson, Ivan, *Singapore – Too Little Too Late*, Leo Cooper, London, 1970.

Skidmore, Ian, *Marines Don't Hold Their Horses*, W.H. Allen, London, 1981. Short life of Colonel A.G. Warren, Royal Marines.

Smyth, Sir John, VC., *Percival and the Tragedy of Singapore*, Macdonald, London, 1971.

Stewart, Athole, *Let's Get Cracking*, Sydney, 1943.

Storey, Neil, *To Singapore and Beyond*, Holyboy, Norwich, 1992. Brief history of the 4th, 5th, and 6th Battalions of the Royal Norfolk Regiment.

Storry, Richard, *A History of Modern Japan*, Penguin edition, London, 1982.

Tate, D.J.M., *The Making of Modern Southeast Asia*, Vol. 2, Oxford, 1979.

Tomlinson, H.M., *Malay Waters*, Hodder & Stoughton, London, 1950.

Thorne, Christopher, *Allies of a Kind*, London, 1978. Explores the often strained relationship between the United States and Britain during the war against Japan.

Tsuji, Colonel Masanobu, *Singapore: The Japanese Version*, London, 1962.

Van der Vat, Dan, *The Pacific Campaign: World War II – the US/Japanese Naval War 1941–1945*, Hodder & Stoughton, London, 1992. The emergence of Japan as a world power. Descriptions of Pearl Harbor attack and other sea battles.

Walker, Allan S., *Australians at War, Medical Services*, Australian War Memorial, Canberra, 1953.

Ward, Ian, *The Killer They Called God*, Media Masters, Singapore, 1992. The story of Colonel Tsuji Masanobu, General Yamashita's Chief of Staff. Tsuji would have been tried as a war criminal had the British managed to get their hands on him. He was responsible for the massacre of many Chinese in Singapore, and for other atrocities.

Ward, Ian, and Modder, Ralph, *Battlefield Guide – The Japanese Conquest of Malaya and Singapore*, Singapore, 1989. An illustrated and briefly documented guide map to the campaign.

Warren, William, *The Legendary American*, Houghton Mifflin, Boston, 1970.

Waugh, Alec, *Bangkok*, W.H. Allen, London. 1970.

Wellard, James, *The French Foreign Legion*, Deutsch, London, 1974.

Wigmore, Lionel, *The Japanese Thrust*, Australian War Memorial, Canberra, 1957. The Australian Official History. A far more professional job than its British counterpart. However, like the British Official Historians, the author left much unsaid.

Winstedt, Sir Richard, *Malaya and its History*, Hutchinson, London, 1948.

Woollcombe, Robert, *The Campaigns of Wavell – 1939–1943*, Cassell, London, 1959.

Wrigglesworth, Datu Michael, *The Japanese Invasion of Kelantan in 1941*, Kuala Lumpur, 1991.

Wynne, M. Ll., *Triad and Tabut: A Survey of the Origin and Diffusion of Chinese and Mohammedan Secret Societies in the Malay Peninsular, 1800–1940*, Singapore Government Printer, 1941.

Articles

Aldrich, R., 'A Question of Expediency: Britain, the United States and Thailand, 1941–1942', Journal of Southeast Asian Studies, Vol.XIX. No.2.

Bridges, Brian, 'Britain and Japanese Espionage in Pre-war Malaya; The Shinozaki Case'. Journal of Contemporary History (JCH), Vol.XXI.

Callahan, Raymond, 'The Illusion of Security: Singapore 1919–1942', JCH, Vol. IX, No.2.

Kasza, Gregory, 'Fascism from Below. A Comparative Perspective on the Japanese Right, 1931–1936', JCH, Vol. XIX, No.4.

McKale, Donald, 'The Nazi Party in the Far East, 1931–1945', JCH, Vol. XII, No.1.

Smith, Malcolm, 'A Matter of Faith: British Strategic Air Doctrine before 1939', JCH, Vol. XV. No.3.

Abbreviations used

AA	Anti-Aircraft (defences)
ABDA	American/British/Dutch/Australian (Command)
ADC	Aide-de-Camp
AIF	Australian Imperial Force
AILO	Air Intelligence Liaison Officer
AOC	Air Officer Commanding
Bde	Brigade
BEAM	British European Association, Malaya
BGS	Brigadier, General Staff
Bn	Battalion
BORs	British Other Ranks
CID	Committee of Imperial Defence
CO	Commanding Officer
Coy	Company
CSO	Civil Security Officer
CW	Chemical Warfare
DDOS	Deputy Director Ordnance Supplies
DEI	Dutch East Indies (See NEI)
DSO	Defence Security Officer
FECB	Far Eastern Combined Bureau
FMS	Federated Malay States
FMSVF	Federated Malay States Volunteer Force
GHQ	General Headquarters
GOC	General Officer Commanding
GSO	General Staff Officer (Various grades, GSO1, GII, etc.)
HQ	Headquarters
IASC	Indian Army Service Corps
ICO	Indian Commissioned Officer
IGP	Inspector-General Police
IIL	Indian Independence League
INA	Indian National Army
JMF	Johore Military Force
KCO	King's Commissioned Officer
MA	Military Attaché
MCS	Malayan Civil Service
MSS	Malayan Security Service
NEI	Netherlands East Indies (See DEI)
OC	Officer Commanding
OM	Oriental Mission (SOE)

OP   Observation Post
POW   Prisoner of War
RA   Royal Artillery
RAAF   Royal Australian Air Force
RAAMC   Royal Australian Army Medical Corps
RAOC   Royal Army Ordnance Corps
RASC   Royal Army Service Corps
RCS   Royal Corps of Signals
RE   Royal Engineers
RNZAF   Royal New Zealand Air Force
SB   Special Branch
SOE   Special Operations Executive
SS   Straits Settlements
SSVF   Straits Settlements Volunteer Force
UMS   Unfederated Malay States
VCO   Viceroy's Commissioned Officer

Outline Chronology of Events
May 1940 to February 1942

1940

10th May	Germany invades Netherlands. Japanese demand oil supplies from Netherlands East Indies.
25th June	France signs armistice with Germany.
27th September	Japan signs Tripartite Pact with Germany and Italy.
16th October	US export embargo on strategic materials to Japan.
	Singapore commanders, in tactical appreciation to British Chiefs of Staff, request 566 planes for Malaya.
Late October	Far East Defence Conference in Singapore. Dutch and American representatives attend.
17th October	Sir Robert Brooke-Popham appointed C-in-C, Far East.
Nov. to Jan.	Thai-French Indo-China 'dispute'.

1941

8th January	Chiefs of Staff agree to target figure of 336 aircraft for Malaya 'by end of 1941'.
Mid-May	Lt-Gen. percival takes up post as GOC, Malaya Command. Formation of 3rd Indian Army Corps in Malaya under Lt-Gen. Sir Lewis Heath.
13th April	Japan signs neutrality pact with Soviet Union.
22nd–26th April	Inter-service conference at Singapore between Britain, US and Holland. Australia, New Zealand and India represented.
22nd June	Germany invades Soviet Union. (Japan now considers her western flank secure.)
21st July	Vichy-French government submits to Japanese demands for bases in southern Indo-China.
26th July	US freezes Japanese assets in America.

9th August	Churchill and Roosevelt meet off Newfoundland. Atlantic Charter born.
29th September	Duff Cooper calls conference in Singapore. Decision reached that only a British fleet can deter Japanese aggression.
October	Negotiations in Washington between US and Japan reach deadlock.
16th October	Militant leaders take over Japanese government.
November	Two Canadian battalions arrive Hong Kong to bolster its defence despite British view that the colony was indefensible. Canadians sent after request from London to Ottawa on recommendation of recent GOC, Hong Kong, Maj-Gen. A.E. Grasett, a Canadian.
1st December	*Prince of Wales* and *Repulse* arrive Singapore.
8th December	Japan attacks Malaya, Thailand, Pearl Harbor and Hong Kong. First air raid on Singapore. Planned British pre-emptitve strike into Thailand abandoned, but two small probes made, one codenamed Krohcol, designed to capture the strategic height 'The Ledge'.
9th December	Kuantan airfield abandoned.
10th December	*Prince of Wales* and *Repulse* sunk south of Kuantan.
11th December	Krohcol column fails to reach 'The Ledge' and retreats.
12th December	British forces from Kota Bharu commence retreat down rail line to Kuala Lipis.
13th December	British forces in retreat south of Jitra.
14th-15th Dec.	Action at Gurun, followed by another withdrawal.
16th–17th Dec.	Penang evacuated.
23rd December	British withdraw across Perak River.
25th December	Hong Kong capitulates.
30th December	First Japanese land attack on Kuantan.
30th Dec. to 2nd Jan.	Action at Kampar, followed by further British withdrawal.

1942

3rd January	45th Indian Brigade Group arrives Singapore.
4th January	British troops take up positions at Slim River.
7th January	Decisive Slim River battle fought. Japanese forces spearheaded by tanks. British forces rolled back with heavy losses. Central Malaya now open to Japanese.

7th January	General Sir Archibald Wavell, new Supreme Allied Commander, Southwest Pacific, visits Malaya.
11th January	Japanese enter Kuala Lumpur.
13th January	British 53rd Brigade Group (part 18th Division) arrives Singapore. Fifty crated Hurricane fighters also arrive.
14th January	Australian 8th Division deployed in Johore enters fray. Highly successful ambush at Gemas, heavy Japanese losses.
15th January	Fighting at Muar. Two battalions 45th Indian Brigade routed.
19th–23rd Jan.	Epic escape of cut-off Australian and Indian troops from Bakri/Yong Peng area.
24th January	Australian reinforcements arrive Singapore.
27th January	22nd Indian Brigade cut-off at Layang Layang, and lost.
30th–31st Jan.	British forces retreat across Causeway to Singapore Island. Singapore now under continuous air attack.
5th Feburary	Remainder British 18th Division arrives Singapore. Reinforcement ship *Empress of Asia* sunk.
7th February	Japanese softening-up shellfire intensifies.
8th Feburary	1900 hours. Japanese launch amphibious attack against Australian positions on north-west coast.
10th Feb.	Jurong defence line lost to Japanese.
12th Feb.	British retreat to final perimeter around Singapore city.
15th Feb.	General Percival surrenders the 'fortress' unconditionally.

Index

Acheson, A.B.: 197

Adams, Geoffrey: 2

Adams, M.E.: on 'denial' system, 363

'Adolph S.': German deserter from French Foreign Legion, 24–6

'Advertizer' The (Adelaide): 335–7

Air Forces: British and Japanese compared, 157, 198

Alexander, A.V., First Lord of Admiralty, 39

Alexandra Hospital: atrocity at, 353–4

Amery, Leo: 133–5

Anderson, Lt-Col. C.C.W., VC: 262, 263, 264

Anglo-Japanese Treaty of Alliance: 9, 12

Anketell, Lt-Col. M.J., AIF: 287

Anti-Comintern Pact: Japan signs, 13

'Argus', The (Melbourne): 334, 335

Argyll & Sutherland Highlanders: training, 189, 244, 255–6, 271

Army Act, 1881: 314

Air Raid Precautions (ARP) in Singapore: 275

Ashmore, Lt-Col. B.H.: 326

Assheton, Lt-Col. C.F., AIF: 318

Atkinson, Capt. K., RN: 287

Austin, Lt-Cmdr H.: report on evacuation of Kuantan airfield, 231

Australia: Singapore as her first line of defence, 33, 40; defence and Imperial relationship, 40 et seq; Menzies' declaration of war on Germany, 41

Australian Imperial Force (AIF): strength of 8th Div, 185 et seq; gas reports by, 201–2; training policy, 257; split into two, 258; dispositions on island, 283, quality of reinforcements, 286–9; casualties in campaign, 330

Australian Imperial Force, Malaya, units: 2/3rd M.T. Company, 257, 302; 2/4th Anti-Tank Regt., 257; 2/30th, 258; 293; 2/19th Bn, 262, 263, 289, 292; 2/29th Bn, 262, 265, 288, 291; 2/4th M.G. Bn, 286–9; 2/18th, 288; 2/26th, 293–4; 2/10th Royal Aust. Engs., 291; 22nd Bde, 318

Australian medals in campaign: summary of, 327

Australian Official History: 5; 338; Col. Thyer on, 5

Babington, Air Vice Marshal J.T. (AOC, Far East): as Vlieland's ally, Defence Committee, 32; relations with GOC, 34; report on defence, 35; views on Malayan defence, 37–8; see note 10, Chap. 3

Bagnall, Sir John: 349–50

Ballentine, Brig. G.C.: 283; on quality of 44th Ind. Bde, 289; on Singapore defences, 289, 292, 295

Barhun-ud-Din, Capt.: 339, 341

Barstow, Maj.-Gen. A.E.: 259; loss of 22nd Ind. Inf. Bde, 268 et seq., killed, 269; see note 17, Chap. 11

Battenberg, Mrs C.M.: 274

'Bavier' or 'Baviot': Swiss/Japanese agent of Hayley Bell, 89

Bayly, G.E.W.W.: 350

Beamish, Capt. Tufton: 284–5; on Gordon Bennett, 327

Beatty, Admiral of the Fleet, Lord: as Chief of Naval